S0-DVC-464

MICROSOFT

WORKS 4
COMPLETE CONCEPTS AND TECHNIQUES

Gary B. Shelly
Thomas J. Cashman
Kathleen Shelly

boyd & fraser

A DIVISION OF COURSE TECHNOLOGY
ONE MAIN STREET
CAMBRIDGE MA 02142

an International Thomson Publishing company I(T)P®

CAMBRIDGE • ALBANY • BONN • CINCINNATI • LONDON • MADRID • MELBOURNE
MEXICO CITY • NEW YORK • PARIS • SAN FRANCISCO • TOKYO • TORONTO • WASHINGTON

COURSE
TECHNOLOGY

SHELLY
CASHMAN
SERIES®

© 1997 boyd & fraser publishing company
A Division of Course Technology
One Main Street
Cambridge, Massachusetts 02142

COURSE TECHNOLOGY

International Thomson Publishing
boyd & fraser publishing company is an ITP company.
The ITP logo is a registered trademark of International Thomson Publishing.

Printed in the United States of America

For more information, contact boyd & fraser publishing company:

boyd & fraser publishing company
A Division of Course Technology
One Main Street
Cambridge, Massachusetts 02142, USA

International Thomson Editores
Campos Eliseos 385, Piso 7
Colonia Polanco
11560 Mexico D.F. Mexico

International Thomson Publishing Europe
Berkshire House
168-173 High Holborn
London, WC1V 7AA, United Kingdom

International Thomson Publishing GmbH
Konigswinterer Strasse 418
53227 Bonn, Germany

Thomas Nelson Australia
102 Dodds Street
South Melbourne
Victoria 3205 Australia

International Thomson Publishing Asia
Block 211, Henderson Road #08-03
Henderson Industrial Park
Singapore 0315

Nelson Canada
1120 Birchmont Road
Scarborough, Ontario
Canada M1K 5G4

International Thomson Publishing Japan
Hirakawa-cho Kyowa Building, 3F
2-2-1 Hirakawa-cho, Chiyoda-ku
Tokyo 102, Japan

ISBN 0-7895-1167-3 (perfect bound)
ISBN 0-7895-1236-X (spiral bound)

PHOTO CREDITS: **Introduction to Computers** *Figure 1*, C-1 Photography; (A) Tony Stone Images-John Riley; (B) The Gamma Liason Network-James P. Wilson; (C) The National Institute of Industrial Ownership, Frederic Pitchal-Sygma; (D) Tony Stone-Images-Kevin Horan; (E) Gamma Liason, Shahn Kermani-Tot-Tech Computers; (F) Comshare; (G) Steve Reneker; (H) International Business Machines Corp.; (I) Sygma; *Figure 2*, Scott R. Goodwin Inc.; *Figure 3*, Tony Stone Images-Mitch Kezar; *Figure 4*, Scott R. Goodwin, Inc.; *Figure 5*, Epson (Manning, Selvege & Lee); *Figure 6*, Comshare; *Figure 7*, Comshare; *Figure 8*, Scott R. Goodwin Inc.; *Figure 9*, Hewlett Packard; *Figure 11*, Hewlett Packard; *Figure 12*, NEC Technology, Multisync; *Figure 13*, International Business Machines Corp.; *Figure 15*, Jerry Spagnoli; *Figure 16*, Greg Hadel; *Figure 19*, Jerry Spagnoli; *Figure 20*, Microscience International Corp.; *Figure 21*, 3M Corp.; Illustrations, Greg Herrington, Stephanie Nance. **Microsoft Windows 95** *Project 1, page WIN 1.4*, Bill Gates, © Matthew McVay, Stock Boston; Seattle Skyline, © Paul Conklin, PhotoEdit; *page WIN 1.5*, International Business Machines Corp.; *Project 2, page WIN 2.3*, Quantum Corp. **Microsoft Works 4 for Windows 95** *Project 1, page W 1.4*, Laptop Computer, Scott R. Goodwin Photography; *page W 1.5*, *Time Magazine* Cover © 1982 Time, Inc.; *Project 2, page W 2.2*, Albert Einstein provided by Brown Brothers; *Project 3, page W 3.2*, General Anthony McAuliffe provided by Brown Brothers; *page W 3.3*, Globe, Courtesy of Corel Professional Photos CD-ROM Image usage; *Project 5, pages W 5.2-3*, Workout and businessman images provided by PhotoDisc Inc. © 1996, Pie chart and bar graph, Courtesy of Corel Professional Photos CD-ROM Image usage; *Project 6, page W 6.2*, Bar graph, Courtesy of Corel Professional Photos CD-ROM Image usage; Business meeting image provided by PhotoDisc Inc. © 1996; *Project 7, pages W 7.2-3*, SoftKey photographs, Courtesy of SoftKey International Inc.; *Project 8, pages W 8.2-3*, Stream and student at computer provided by PhotoDisc Inc. © 1996; *Project 9, page W 9.2*, Hand with key image provided by PhotoDisc Inc. © 1996; *Project 10, page W 10.2*, James Bond provided by United Artists; Blender and flowers, Courtesy of Classic PIO Partners; Olive, Courtesy of Corel Professional Photos CD-ROM Image usage; Frame provided by PhotoDisc Inc. © 1996; *page W 10.3*, Graph and bar chart, Courtesy of Corel Professional Photos CD-ROM Image usage

4 5 6 7 8 9 10 BC 0 9 8 7

MICROSOFT WORKS 4
COMPLETE CONCEPTS AND TECHNIQUES

CONTENTS

▶ **PROJECT ONE**
**CREATING A FORMATTED DOCUMENT
WITH CLIP ART**

▶ PROJECT TWO

USING WORKS TASKWIZARDS TO CREATE DOCUMENTS

▶ PROJECT THREE

WRITING AND EDITING A RESEARCH REPORT WITH TABLES

▶ PROJECT FOUR

BUILDING A SPREADSHEET AND CHARTING DATA

▶ PROJECT FIVE

CREATING FORMULAS, SORTING, AND CHARTING DATA

▶ PROJECT EIGHT
MAINTAINING A DATABASE

▶ PROJECT NINE
DATABASE FILTERS AND REPORTS

 **Preface**

Shelly Cashman Series® Microsoft Windows 95 Books

The Shelly Cashman Series® Microsoft Windows 95 books reinforce the fact that you make the right choice when you use a Shelly Cashman Series book. The Shelly Cashman Series Microsoft Windows 3.1 books were used by more schools and more students than any other series in textbook publishing. Yet the Shelly Cashman Series team wanted to produce even better books for Windows 95, so the books were thoroughly redesigned to present material in an even easier to understand format. Features such as Other Ways and More Abouts were added to give in-depth knowledge to the student. The opening of each project provides a fascinating perspective of the subject covered in the project. Completely redesigned student assignments include the unique Cases and Places. This book provides the finest educational experience ever for a student learning about computer software.

Objectives of This Textbook

Microsoft Works 4: Complete Concepts and Techniques is intended for a three-unit course that presents Microsoft Works 4. The objectives of this book are:

- ▶ To teach the fundamentals of Microsoft Works 4
- ▶ To foster an appreciation of the integration package as a useful tool in the workplace and at home
- ▶ To give students an in-depth understanding of creating announcements, business letters, resumes, research papers, worksheets, and databases
- ▶ To provide a knowledge base of Microsoft Works 4 on which students can build
- ▶ To help students who are working on their own

When students complete the course using this textbook, they will have a firm knowledge and understanding of Works 4.

The Shelly Cashman Approach

Features of the Shelly Cashman Series Windows 95 books include:

- ▶ **Project Orientation:** Each project in the book uses the unique Shelly Cashman Series screen-by-screen, step-by-step approach.
- ▶ **Screen-by-Screen, Step-by-Step Instructions:** Each of the tasks required to complete a project is identified throughout the development of the project and is shown screen by screen, step by step.
- ▶ **Multiple Ways to Use the Book:** The book can be used in a variety of ways, including: (a) Lecture and textbook approach; (b) Tutorial approach; (c) Many teachers lecture on the material and then require their students to perform each step in the project, reinforcing the material lectured. The students then complete one or more of the In the Lab exercises; and (d) Reference: Each task in a project is clearly identified. Therefore, the material serves as a complete reference.
- ▶ **Other Ways Boxes for Reference:** Works 4 provides a wide variety of ways to carry out a given task. The Other Ways boxes displayed at the end of most of the step-by-step sequences specify the other ways to do the task completed in the steps.

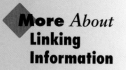 **More** *About* **Linking Information**

Use linking to transfer information between Works documents when you expect the source of the information to change. With linking, you copy the information and Works automatically updates the information when the source changes. You can link information into a Works document from any Windows program that supports linking.

Organization of This Textbook

Microsoft Works 4: Complete Concepts and Techniques consists of a brief introduction to computers, two projects on Microsoft Windows 95, and ten projects on Microsoft Works 4. A short description of each follows.

Introduction to Computers

Many students taking a course in the use of Microsoft Works 4 will have little previous experience with computers. For this reason, this textbook begins with a section titled Introduction to Computers that covers essential computer hardware and software concepts and information on how to purchase, install, and maintain a personal computer.

Microsoft Windows 95

To effectively use the Microsoft Works 4 application software, students need a practical knowledge of Windows 95. Thus, two Windows 95 projects are included as an introduction to the graphical user interface.

Project 1 – Fundamentals of Using Windows 95   In Project 1, students learn about user interfaces and Windows 95. Topics include using the Windows 95 desktop as a work area; using the mouse; the keyboard and keyboard shortcuts; using context-sensitive menus; sizing and scrolling windows; creating a document by starting an application program; saving a document on a disk; printing a document; closing a program; modifying a document; using Windows 95 Help; and shutting down Windows 95.

Project 2 – Using Windows Explorer   In Project 2, students are introduced to Windows Explorer. Topics include displaying the contents of a folder; expanding and collapsing a folder; creating a folder; changing the view; selecting and copying a group of files; creating, renaming, and deleting a folder; and renaming and deleting a file.

Microsoft Works 4 for Windows 95

The ten projects on Works 4 are divided into three projects on the Word Processor tool, three projects on the Spreadsheet tool, three projects on the Database tool, and one project on integrating the Word Processor, Spreadsheet, and Database tools.

Project 1 – Creating a Formatted Document with Clip Art   In Project 1, students are introduced to the Works Word Processor tool. Topics include starting and closing Works; entering and correcting text; centering text; creating a bulleted list; changing font, font size, and font style; inserting clip art; using print preview; opening and editing a word processing document; and using Works online Help.

Project 2 – Using Works TaskWizards to Create Documents   In Project 2, students create a cover letter using the Works Letter TaskWizard. Topics include setting margin indents to create a numbered list; creating and using a hanging indent; and spell checking a document. Students create a resume using the Works Resume TaskWizard. Topics include using the TAB key to align text vertically; working with multiple documents; and creating and using a custom template.

Project 3 – Writing and Editing a Research Report with Tables   In Project 3, students use the MLA style of documentation to create a research paper. Topics include changing margins; adjusting line spacing; using a header to number pages; indenting the first line of paragraphs; adding footnotes; inserting a page break; using the thesaurus; counting words in a document; using Find and Replace; creating a table using the Works Spreadsheet tool and OLE 2.0; and entering data into a Works table.

Project 4 – Building a Spreadsheet and Charting Data   In Project 4, students are introduced to the Works Spreadsheet tool. Topics include entering text and numeric values; summing columns and rows using the AutoSum button; copying cells using the fill handle; centering text across columns; coloring text; using the AutoFormat feature; changing column widths; saving a spreadsheet; printing a spreadsheet; charting the data in the spreadsheet using a 3-D Bar chart; opening a spreadsheet file; and correcting errors.

Project 5 – Creating Formulas, Sorting, and Charting Data   In Project 5, students use formulas and functions to create a spreadsheet and learn more about formatting and printing a spreadsheet. Topics include entering formulas using Point mode; copying formulas in single and multiple columns; using functions; using Easy Calc to create a formula; formatting text; formatting numbers; changing column widths; adding color to a spreadsheet; sorting rows in a spreadsheet; using Print Preview; printing in landscape orientation; creating a 3-D Pie chart; adding data labels to a chart from nonadjacent columns; and saving and printing a chart.

Project 6 – What-If Analysis, Functions, and Absolute Cell References   In Project 6, students learn to create a spreadsheet to answer what-if questions. Topics include creating a data sequence using the fill handle; using drag-and-drop to copy data to a nonadjacent area of a spreadsheet; rounding and the Round function, entering and copying relative and absolute cell references in a formula; creating a 3-D Stacked Bar chart; adding category labels to a chart; renaming a chart; changing series colors and patterns in a chart; and adding colors to chart text.

Project 7 – Using Form Design to Create a Database   In Project 7, students are introduced to the Works Database tool. Topics include an explanation of form design view; creating a form design view title using WordArt, entering fields and labels on the form; saving; formatting the database title; inserting clip art; positioning the fields on the form by dragging; and formatting fields and labels. The form view of the database is described; data is entered into the database; list view is explained; and the data is formatted in list view. Finally, the database is saved, printed in form view, and then printed in list view using landscape orientation.

Project 8 – Maintaining a Database   In Project 8, students learn maintaining a database in both list view and form view, including adding new records to the database, deleting records from the database, and changing data in database records. Using form design view, students learn to change the structure of the database by inserting fields, deleting fields, renaming fields, and resizing fields. The form view of the database is reformatted by deleting fields and moving other fields to produce a different database used to generate a report.

Project 9 – Database Filters and Reports   In Project 9, students learn to filter database records and create reports. Topics include working with filters; filtering for records that match exactly; showing all records in a database; filtering for records that are above or below a specific value; inverting filters; filtering for records that match in more than one field; filtering for records that meet one of several conditions; creating a filter using a formula; applying a filter; deleting a filter; renaming a filter; using Works ReportCreator to create database reports; modifying a report definition; creating reports with summary totals; duplicating a report definition; displaying a report definition; and grouping and filtering report information.

Project 10 – Integrating the Microsoft Works Tools   In Project 10, students learn to use all three Works tools (Word Processor, Spreadsheet, and Database) in an integrated project to create a form letter that includes both a spreadsheet and a chart. A database provides the names of the individuals to whom the letter is sent and other data that is incorporated into the letter. Topics include inserting placeholders; creating and entering a table using custom tabs; using Easy Formats to indent the first-line of paragraphs; linking and sizing a spreadsheet chart in the word processing document; inserting headers, printing form letters; and creating mailing labels.

Apppendix A – Works Functions   This appendix contains a summary of the functions available in Works and an example of their use.

End-of-Project Student Activities

A notable strength of the Shelly Cashman Series Windows 95 books is the extensive student activities at the end of each project. Well-structured student activities can make the difference between students merely participating in a class and students retaining the information they learn. These activities include:

▶ **What You Should Know** A listing of the tasks completed within a project together with the pages where the step-by-step, screen-by-screen explanations appear. This section provides a perfect study review for the student.

▶ **Test Your Knowledge** Four activities designed to determine the student's understanding of the material in the project. Included are true/false questions, multiple-choice questions, and two short-answer activities.

▶ **Use Help** Any user of Windows 95 must know how to use Help. Therefore, this book contains extensive exercises that require students to use Help. These exercises alone distinguish the Shelly Cashman Series from any other set of Windows 95 instructional materials.

▶ **Apply Your Knowledge** This exercise requires the student to open and manipulate a file from the Student Floppy Disk that accompanies this book.

▶ **In the Lab** Three in-depth assignments require the student to apply the knowledge gained in the project to solve problems on a computer.

▶ **Cases and Places** Seven unique case studies allow students to apply their knowledge to real-world situations.

Instructor's Resource Kit

A comprehensive Instructor's Resource Kit (IRK) accompanies this textbook in the form of a CD-ROM. The CD-ROM includes an electronic Instructor's Manual (called ElecMan) and teaching and testing aids. The CD-ROM (ISBN 0-7895-1168-1) is available through your Course Technology representative or by calling 1-800-648-7450. The contents of the CD-ROM are listed below.

▶ **ElecMan** (*Electronic Instructor's Manual*) ElecMan is made up of Microsoft Word files. The files include lecture notes, solutions to laboratory assignments, and a large test bank. The files allow you to modify the lecture notes or generate quizzes and exams from the test bank using your own word processor. Where appropriate, solutions to laboratory assignments are embedded as icons in the files. When an icon appears, double-click it and the application will start and the solution will display on the screen. ElecMan includes the following for each project: project objectives; project overview; detailed lesson plans with page number references; teacher notes and activities; answers to the end-of-project exercises; test bank of 110 questions for every project (50 true/false, 25 multiple-choice, and 35 fill-in-the blank) with page number references; and transparency references. The transparencies are available through the Figures on CD-ROM described below. The test bank questions are numbered the same as in Course Test Manager. Thus, you can print out a copy of the project and use the printed test bank to select your questions in Course Test Manager.

▶ **Figures on CD-ROM** Illustrations for every screen in the textbook are available. Use this ancillary to create a slide show from the illustrations for lecture or to print transparencies for use in lecture with an overhead.

▶ **Course Test Manager** This cutting edge Windows-based testing software helps instructors design and administer tests and pre-tests. The full-featured online program permits students to take tests at the computer where their grades are computed immediately following completion of the exam. Automatic statistics collection, student guides customized to the student's performance, and printed tests are only a few of the features.

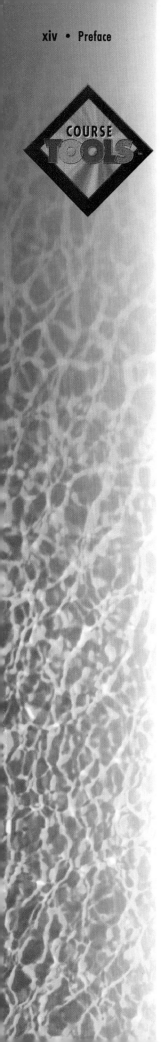

▶ **Lecture Success System** Lecture Success System files are for use with the application software, a personal computer, and projection device to explain and illustrate the step-by-step, screen-by-screen development of a project in the textbook without entering large amounts of data.

▶ **Lab Tests** Tests that parallel the In the Lab assignments are supplied for the purpose of testing students in the laboratory on the material covered in the project. You also can use these assignments as supplementary exercises.

▶ **Instructor's Lab Solutions** Solutions and required files for all the In the Lab assignments at the end of each project are available.

▶ **Student Files** All the files that are required by the student to complete the Apply Your Knowledge exercises or advanced projects are included.

▶ **Interactive Labs** Fourteen hands-on interactive labs that take the student from ten to fifteen minutes to step through help solidify and reinforce computer concepts. Student assessment is available in each interactive lab by means of a Print button. The assessment requires the student to answer questions about the contents of the interactive lab.

Shelly Cashman Online

Shelly Cashman Online is a World Wide Web service available to instructors and students of computer education. Visit Shelly Cashman Online at http://www.bf.com/scseries.html. Shelly Cashman Online is divided into four areas:

▶ **Series Information** Information on the Shelly Cashman Series products.

▶ **The Community** Opportunities to discuss your course and your ideas with instructors in your field and with the Shelly Cashman Series team.

▶ **Teaching Resources** This area includes password-protected data from Instructor's Floppy Disks that can be downloaded, course outlines, teaching tips, and ancillaries such as ElecMan.

▶ **Student Center** Dedicated to students learning about computers with Shelly Cashman Series textbooks and software. This area includes cool links, data from Student Floppy Disks that can be downloaded, and much more.

Acknowledgments

The Shelly Cashman Series would not be the leading computer education series without the contributions of outstanding publishing professionals. First, and foremost, among them is Becky Herrington, director of production and designer. She is the heart and soul of the Shelly Cashman Series, and it is only through her leadership, dedication, and tireless efforts that superior products are made possible. Becky created and produced the award-winning Windows 95 series of books.

Under Becky's direction, the following individuals made significant contributions to these books: Peter Schiller, production manager; Ginny Harvey, series administrator and manuscript editor; Ken Russo, senior illustrator and cover artist; Mike Bodnar, Stephanie Nance, Greg Herrington, and Dave Bonnewitz, Quark artists and illustrators; Patti Garbarino and Lora Wade, editorial assistants; Jeanne Black, Quark expert; Cristina Haley, indexer; Cherilyn King and Marilyn Martin, proofreaders; Susan Sebok, Tim Walker, Peggy Wyman, and Jerry Orton, contributing writers; Sarah Evertson of Image Quest, photo researcher; Henry Blackham, cover photographer; and Kent Lauer, cover glass work. Special mention must go to Suzanne Biron, Becky Herrington, and Michael Gregson for the outstanding book design, to Ken Russo for the cover design, and to Jim Quasney, series editor.

Gary B. Shelly
Thomas J. Cashman
Kathleen Shelly

Shelly Cashman Series – Traditionally Bound Textbooks

The Shelly Cashman Series presents computer textbooks across the entire spectrum including both Windows- and DOS-based personal computer applications in a variety of traditionally bound textbooks, as shown in the table below. For more information, see your Course Technology representative or call 1-800-648-7450.

COMPUTERS	
Computers	Using Computers: A Gateway to Information, World Wide Web Edition
	Using Computers: A Gateway to Information, World Wide Web Brief Edition
	Using Computers: A Gateway to Information, World Wide Web Edition and Exploring Computers: A Record of Discovery with CD-ROM
	Using Computers: A Gateway to Information
	Using Computers: A Gateway to Information, Brief Edition
	Exploring Computers: A Record of Discovery with CD-ROM
	A Record of Discovery for Exploring Computers
	Study Guide for Using Computers: A Gateway to Information, World Wide Web Edition
	Study Guide for Using Computers: A Gateway to Information
and Windows Apps	Using Computers: A Gateway to Information and Microsoft Office (also in spiral bound)
	Using Computers: A Gateway to Information and Microsoft Works 3.0 (also in spiral bound)
and Programming	Using Computers: A Gateway to Information and Programming in QBasic

WINDOWS APPLICATIONS	
Integrated Packages	Microsoft Office 95: Introductory Concepts and Techniques (also in spiral bound)
	Microsoft Office 95: Advanced Concepts and Techniques (also in spiral bound)
	Microsoft Office 4.3 running under Windows 95: Introductory Concepts and Techniques (also in spiral bound)
	Microsoft Office: Introductory Concepts and Techniques (also in spiral bound)
	Microsoft Office: Advanced Concepts and Techniques (also in spiral bound)
	Microsoft Works 4 for Windows 95*
	Microsoft Works 3.0 (also in spiral bound)* • Microsoft Works 2.0 (also in spiral bound)
	Microsoft Works 3.0—Short Course
Windows	Microsoft Windows 95: Introductory Concepts and Techniques (96-page)
	Introduction to Microsoft Windows 95 (224-page)
	Microsoft Windows 95: Complete Concepts and Techniques
	Microsoft Windows 3.1 Introductory Concepts and Techniques
	Microsoft Windows 3.1 Complete Concepts and Techniques
Windows Applications	Microsoft Word 2.0, Microsoft Excel 4, and Paradox 1.0 (also in spiral bound)
Word Processing	Microsoft Word 7* • Microsoft Word 6* • Microsoft Word 2.0
	WordPerfect 6.1* • WordPerfect 6* • WordPerfect 5.2
Spreadsheets	Microsoft Excel 7* • Microsoft Excel 5* • Microsoft Excel 4
	Lotus 1-2-3 Release 5* • Lotus 1-2-3 Release 4* • Quattro Pro 6 • Quattro Pro 5
Database Management	Microsoft Access 7* • Microsoft Access 2
	Paradox 5 • Paradox 4.5 • Paradox 1.0 • Visual dBASE 5/5.5
Presentation Graphics	Microsoft PowerPoint 7* • Microsoft PowerPoint 4*

DOS APPLICATIONS	
Operating Systems	DOS 6 Introductory Concepts and Techniques
	DOS 6 and Microsoft Windows 3.1 Introductory Concepts and Techniques
Integrated Package	Microsoft Works 3.0 (also in spiral bound)
Word Processing	WordPerfect 6.1 • WordPerfect 6.0
	WordPerfect 5.1 Step-by-Step Function Key Edition • WordPerfect 5.1 Function Key Edition
Spreadsheets	Lotus 1-2-3 Release 4 • Lotus 1-2-3 Release 2.4 • Lotus 1-2-3 Release 2.3
	Lotus 1-2-3 Release 2.2 • Lotus 1-2-3 Release 2.01
	Quattro Pro 3.0 • Quattro with 1-2-3 Menus (with Educational Software)
Database Management	dBASE 5 • dBASE IV Version 1.1 • dBASE III PLUS (with Educational Software)
	Paradox 4.5 • Paradox 3.5 (with Educational Software)

PROGRAMMING AND NETWORKING	
Programming	Introduction to Microsoft Visual Basic 4* (available with Student version of Visual Basic 4)
	Microsoft Visual Basic 3.0 for Windows*
	QBasic • QBasic: An Introduction to Programming • Microsoft BASIC
	Structured COBOL Programming
Networking	Novell NetWare for Users
	Business Data Communications: Introductory Concepts and Techniques
Internet	The Internet: Introductory Concepts and Techniques (UNIX)
	Netscape Navigator 3: An Introduction • Netscape Navigator 2 running under Windows 3.1
	Netscape Navigator: An Introduction (Version 1.1)
	Netscape Navigator Gold: Creating Web Pages

SYSTEMS ANALYSIS	
Systems Analysis	Systems Analysis and Design, Second Edition

*Also available as a Double Diamond Edition, which is a shortened version of the complete book

Shelly Cashman Series – Custom Edition® Program

If you do not find a Shelly Cashman Series traditionally bound textbook to fit your needs, the Shelly Cashman Series' unique **Custom Edition** program allows you to choose from a number of options and create a textbook perfectly suited to your course. Features of the **Custom Edition** program are:

▶ Textbooks that match the content of your course

▶ Windows- and DOS-based materials for the latest versions of personal computer applications software

▶ Shelly Cashman Series quality, with the same full-color materials and Shelly Cashman Series pedagogy found in the traditionally bound books

▶ Affordable pricing so your students receive the **Custom Edition** at a cost similar to that of traditionally bound books

The table on the right summarizes the available materials.

For more information, see your Course Technology representative or call 1-800-648-7450.

For Shelly Cashman Series information, visit Shelly Cashman Series Online at **http://www. bf.com/scseries.html**

COMPUTERS	
Computers	Using Computers: A Gateway to Information, World Wide Web Edition
	Using Computers: A Gateway to Information, World Wide Web Brief Edition
	Using Computers: A Gateway to Information
	Using Computers: A Gateway to Information, Brief Edition
	A Record of Discovery for Exploring Computers (available with CD-ROM)
	Study Guide for Using Computers: A Gateway to Information, World Wide Web Edition
	Study Guide for Using Computers: A Gateway to Information
	Introduction to Computers (32-page)
OPERATING SYSTEMS	
Windows	Microsoft Windows 95: Introductory Concepts and Techniques (96-page)
	Introduction to Microsoft Windows 95 (224-page)
	Microsoft Windows 95: Complete Concepts and Techniques
	Microsoft Windows 3.1 Introductory Concepts and Techniques
	Microsoft Windows 3.1 Complete Concepts and Techniques
DOS	Introduction to DOS 6 (using DOS prompt)
	Introduction to DOS 5.0 or earlier (using DOS prompt)
WINDOWS APPLICATIONS	
Integrated Packages	Microsoft Works 4 for Windows 95*
	Microsoft Works 3.0*
	Microsoft Works 3.0—Short Course
	Microsoft Works 2.0
Microsoft Office	Using Microsoft Office (16-page)
	Object Linking and Embedding (OLE) (32-page)
	Schedule+ 7
Word Processing	Microsoft Word 7* • Microsoft Word 6* • Microsoft Word 2.0
	WordPerfect 6.1* • WordPerfect 6* • WordPerfect 5.2
Spreadsheets	Microsoft Excel 7* • Microsoft Excel 5* • Microsoft Excel 4
	Lotus 1-2-3 Release 5* • Lotus 1-2-3 Release 4*
	Quattro Pro 6 • Quattro Pro 5
Database Management	Microsoft Access 7* • Microsoft Access 2*
	Paradox 5 • Paradox 4.5 • Paradox 1.0 • Visual dBASE 5/5.5
Presentation Graphics	Microsoft PowerPoint 7* • Microsoft PowerPoint 4*
DOS APPLICATIONS	
Integrated Package	Microsoft Works 3.0
Word Processing	WordPerfect 6.1 • WordPerfect 6.0
	WordPerfect 5.1 Step-by-Step Function Key Edition
	WordPerfect 5.1 Function Key Edition
	Microsoft Word 5.0
Spreadsheets	Lotus 1-2-3 Release 4 • Lotus 1-2-3 Release 2.4 • Lotus 1-2-3 Release 2.3
	Lotus 1-2-3 Release 2.2 • Lotus 1-2-3 Release 2.01
	Quattro Pro 3.0 • Quattro with 1-2-3 Menus
Database Management	dBASE 5 • dBASE IV Version 1.1 • dBASE III PLUS
	Paradox 4.5 • Paradox 3.5
PROGRAMMING AND NETWORKING	
Programming	Introduction to Microsoft Visual Basic 4* (available with Student version of Visual Basic 4) • Microsoft Visual Basic 3.0 for Windows*
	Microsoft BASIC
	QBasic
Networking	Novell NetWare for Users
Internet	The Internet: Introductory Concepts and Techniques (UNIX)
	Netscape Navigator 3: An Introduction
	Netscape Navigator 2 running under Windows 3.1
	Netscape Navigator: An Introduction (Version 1.1)
	Netscape Navigator Gold: Creating Web Pages

*Also available as a mini-module

INTRODUCTION TO COMPUTERS

Objectives

After completing this chapter, you will be able to:

- Define the term computer and discuss the four basic computer operations: input, processing, output, and storage
- Define data and information
- Explain the principal components of the computer and their use
- Describe the use and handling of floppy disks and hard disks
- Discuss computer software and explain the difference between system software and application software
- Describe several types of personal computer application software
- Discuss computer communications channels and equipment and LAN and WAN computer networks
- Explain how to purchase, install, and maintain a personal computer system

Every day, computers impact how individuals work and how they live. The use of personal computers continues to increase and has made computing available to almost anyone. In addition, advances in communication technology allow people to use personal computer systems to easily and quickly access and send information to other computers and computer users. At home, at work, and in the field, computers are helping people to do their work faster, more accurately, and in some cases, in ways that previously would not have been possible.

WHY STUDY COMPUTERS AND APPLICATION SOFTWARE?

Today, many people believe that knowing how to use a computer, is a basic skill necessary to succeed in business or to function effectively in society. As you can see in Figure 1, the use of computer technology is widespread in the world. It is important to understand that while computers are used in many different ways, there are certain types of common applications computer users need to know. It is this type of software that you will learn as you use this book. Given the widespread use and availability of computer systems, knowing how to use common application software on a computer system is an essential skill for practically everyone.

Figure 1
Computers in use in a wide variety of applications and professions. New applications are being developed every day.

Before you learn about application software, however, it will help if you understand what a computer is, the components of a computer, and the types of software used on computers. These topics are explained in this chapter. Also included is information that describes computer networks and a list of guidelines for purchasing, installing, and maintaining a personal computer.

WHAT IS A COMPUTER?

The most obvious question related to understanding computers is, "What is a computer?" A **computer** is an electronic device, operating under the control of instructions stored in its own memory unit, that can accept data (input), process data arithmetically and logically, produce output from the processing, and store the results for future use. Generally the term is used to describe a collection of devices that function together as a system. An example of the devices that make up a personal computer, or microcomputer, is shown in Figure 2.

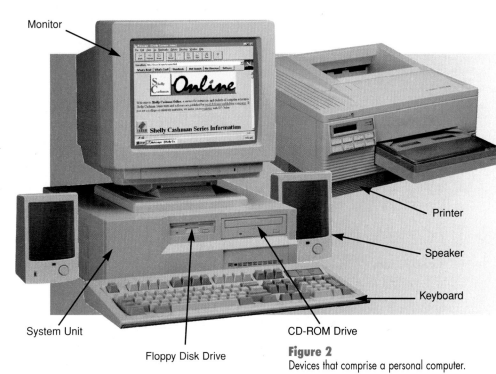

Monitor

Printer

Speaker

Keyboard

System Unit

CD-ROM Drive

Floppy Disk Drive

Figure 2
Devices that comprise a personal computer.

WHAT DOES A COMPUTER DO?

Whether small or large, computers can perform four general operations. These operations comprise the **information processing cycle** and are: input, process, output, and storage. Collectively, these operations describe the procedures a computer performs to process data into information and store it for future use.

All computer processing requires data. **Data** refers to the raw facts, including numbers, words, images, and sounds, given to a computer during the input operation. In the processing phase, the computer manipulates the data to create information. **Information** refers to data processed into a form that has meaning and is useful. During the output operation, the information that has been created is put into some form, such as a printed report, an invoice, or a paycheck. The information can also be placed in computer storage for future use.

These operations occur through the use of electronic circuits contained on small silicon chips inside the computer (Figure 3). Because these electronic circuits rarely fail and the data flows along these circuits at close to the speed of light, processing can be accomplished in billionths of a second. Thus, the computer is a powerful tool because it can perform these four operations reliably and quickly.

The people who either use the computer directly or use the information it provides are called **computer users**, **end users**, or sometimes, just **users**.

HOW DOES A COMPUTER KNOW WHAT TO DO?

For a computer to perform the operations in the information processing cycle, it must be given a detailed set of instructions that tell it exactly what to do. These instructions are called a **computer program**, or **software**. Before processing for a specific job begins, the computer program corresponding to that job is stored in the computer. Once the program is stored, the computer can begin to operate by executing the program's first instruction. The computer executes one program instruction after another until the job is complete.

WHAT ARE THE COMPONENTS OF A COMPUTER?

To understand how computers process data into information, you need to examine the primary components of the computer. The four primary components of a computer are: input devices, the processor unit, output devices, and auxiliary storage units (Figure 4).

Figure 3
Inside a computer are chips and other electronic components that process data in billionths of a second.

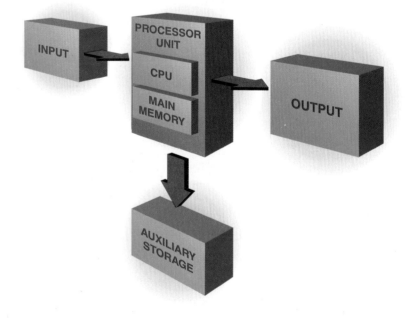

Figure 4
A computer is composed of input devices through which data is entered into the computer; the processor that processes data stored in main memory; output devices on which the results of the processing are made available; and auxiliary storage units that store data for future processing.

Input Devices

Input devices allow you to enter data into main memory. The two primary input devices used are the keyboard and the mouse.

The Keyboard

The most commonly used input device is the **keyboard**, on which data is entered by manually keying in or typing. The keyboard on most computers is laid out in much the same manner as the one shown in Figure 5. The alphabetic keys are arranged like those on a typewriter.

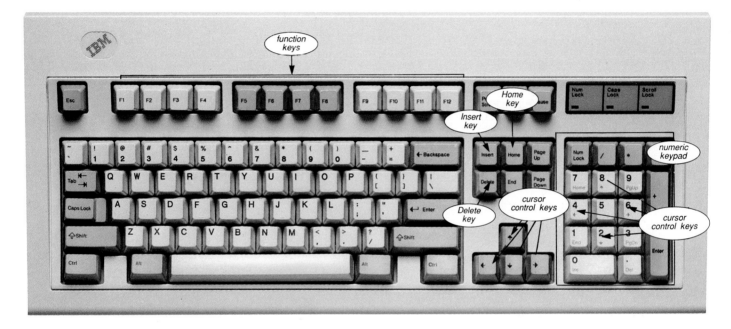

A **numeric keypad** or t is located on the right side of most keyboards. This arrangement of keys allows you to enter numeric data rapidly. To activate the numeric keypad you press and engage the NUMLOCK key located above the numeric keypad. The NUMLOCK key activates the numeric keypad so when the keys are pressed, numeric characters are entered into the computer memory and appear on the screen. A light turns on at the top right of the keyboard to indicate that the numeric keys are in use.

Figure 5
This keyboard represents most personal computer keyboards.

The **cursor** or **insertion point** is a symbol, such as a small vertical line, which indicates where you are working on the screen. The cursor **control keys**, or **arrow key**s, allow you to move the cursor around the screen. Pressing the **UP ARROW** (↑) key causes the cursor to move upward on the screen. The **DOWN ARROW** (↓) key causes the cursor to move down; the **LEFT ARROW** (←) and **RIGHT ARROW** (→) keys cause the cursor to move left and right on the screen. On the keyboard in Figure 5, there are two sets of cursor control keys. One set is included as part of the numeric keypad. The second set of cursor control keys is located between the typewriter keys and the numeric keypad. To use the numeric keypad for cursor control, the NUMLOCK key must be disengaged. If the NUMLOCK key is engaged (indicated by the fact that as you press any numeric keypad key, a number appears on the screen), you can return to the cursor mode by pressing the NUMLOCK key. On most keyboards, a NUMLOCK light will indicate when the numeric keypad is in the numeric mode or the cursor mode.

The other keys on the keypad-PAGE UP, PAGE DOWN, HOME, and END—have various functions depending on the software you use. Some programs make no use of these keys; others use the **PAGE UP** and **PAGE DOWN** keys, for example, to display previous or following pages of data on the screen. Some software uses the **HOME** key to move the cursor to the upper left corner of the screen. Likewise, the **END** key may be used to move the cursor to the end of a line of text or to the bottom of the screen, depending on the software.

Function keys on many keyboards can be programmed to accomplish specific tasks. For example, a function key might be used as a help key. Whenever that key is pressed, messages display that give instructions to help the user. The keyboard in Figure 5 has twelve function keys located across the top of the keyboard.

Other keys have special uses in some applications. The SHIFT keys have several functions. They work as they do on a typewriter, allowing you to type capital letters. The SHIFT key is always used to type the symbol on the upper portion of any key on the keyboard.

The keyboard has a **BACKSPACE** key, a **TAB** key, an **INSERT** key and a **DELETE** key that perform the functions their names indicate.

The **ESC** (**ESCAPE**) key is generally used by computer software to cancel an instruction or exit from a situation. The use of the ESC key varies between software packages.

As with the ESC key, many keys are assigned special meaning by the computer software. Certain keys may be used more frequently than others by one piece of software but rarely used by another. It is this flexibility that allows you to use the computer in so many different applications.

The Mouse

A **mouse** (Figure 6) is a pointing device you can use instead of the cursor control keys. You lay the palm of your hand over the mouse and move it across the surface of a pad that provides traction for a rolling ball on the bottom of the mouse. The mouse detects the direction of the ball movement and sends this information to the screen to move the cursor. You press buttons on top of the mouse to indicate your choices of actions from lists or icons displayed on the screen.

Figure 6
The mouse input device is used to move the cursor and choose selections on the computer screen.

The Processor Unit

The **processor unit** is composed of the central processing unit and main memory. The **central processing unit** (**CPU**) contains the electronic circuits that cause processing to occur. The CPU interprets instructions to the computer, performs the logical and arithmetic processing operations, and causes the input and output operations to occur. On personal computers, the CPU is designed into a chip called a **microprocessor** (Figure 7). The Pentium Pro microprocessor shown in Figure 7 can fit in the palm of your hand. It contains 5.5 million transistors and is able to perform 250 million instructions per second.

Main memory, also called **random access memory**, or **RAM**, consists of electronic components that store data including numbers, letters of the alphabet, graphics, and sound. Any data to be processed must be stored in main memory. The amount of main memory in computers is typically measured in kilobytes or megabytes. One **kilobyte** (**K** or **KB**) equals approximately 1,000 memory locations and one **megabyte** (**M** or **MB**) equals approximately 1 million memory locations. A memory location, or **byte**, usually stores one character. Therefore, a computer with 8MB of main memory can store approximately 8 million characters. One megabyte can hold approximately 500 pages of text information.

Figure 7
A Pentium Pro microprocessor from Intel Corporation. The microprocessor circuits are located in the center. Small gold wires lead from the circuits to the pins that fit in the microprocessor socket on the main circuit board of the computer.The pins provide an electronic connection to different parts of the computer.

Output Devices

Output devices make the information resulting from processing available for use. The output from computers can be presented in many forms, such as a printed report or color graphics. When a computer is used for processing tasks, such as word processing, spreadsheets, or database management, the two output devices most commonly used are the printer and the television-like display device.

Printers

Printers used with computers can be either impact printers or nonimpact printers. An **impact printer** prints by striking an inked ribbon against the paper. One type of impact printer used with personal computers is the dot matrix printer (Figure 8).

Figure 8
Dot matrix are the least expensive of the personal computer printers. Some can be purchased for less than $200. Advantages of dot matrix printers include the capability to handle wide paper and to print multipart forms.

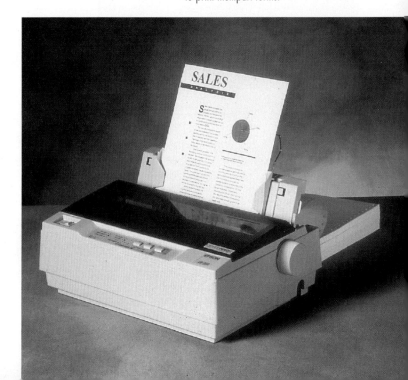

Nonimpact printers, such as inkjet printers and laser printers (Figure 9), form characters by means other than striking a ribbon against paper. One advantage of using a nonimpact printer is that it can print higher quality text and graphics than an impact printer, such as the dot matrix. Nonimpact printers also do a better job printing different font styles (Figure 10) and they are quiet.

The popular and affordable **inkjet printer** forms a character by using a nozzle that sprays drops of ink onto the page. Ink jet printers produce excellent images. They can print on average 3 pages (black) per minute and 1 page (color) per minute. Color inkjet printers are quite popular among personal computer users today.

Laser printers work similar to a copying machine by converting data from the computer into a beam of light that is focused on a photoconductor drum, forming the images to be printed (Figure 11). The photoconductor attracts particles of toner that are fused by heat and pressure onto paper to produce an image. Laser printers produce high-quality black or color output and are used for applications that combine text and graphics such as **desktop publishing** (Figure 12). Laser printers for personal computers can cost from $500 to more than $10,000. They can print four to sixteen pages of text and graphics per minute.

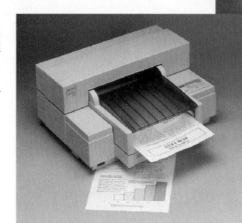

Figure 9
Two types of nonimpact printers are the laser printer (top) and the inkjet printer (left). Nonimpact printers are excellent for printing work that includes graphics.

Courier

Helvetica

Script

Times New Roman

Figure 10
Nonimpact printers do an excellent job of printing text in different typefaces, referred to as fonts. Technically, a font is a typeface in a particular size. It is common, however, to refer to the different typefaces as fonts. Dot matrix printers can print some fonts but usually at a slower rate and poorer quality than nonimpact printers. The names of four different typefaces (fonts) are shown.

Figure 11 ▶
Laser printers use a process similar to a copying machine. Data from the computer, such as the word DETAILS (1), is converted into a laser beam (2) that is directed by a mirror (3) to a photosensitive drum (4). The areas on the drum touched by the laser attract toner particles (5) that transferred to the paper (6). The toner is fused to the paper with feat and pressure(7).

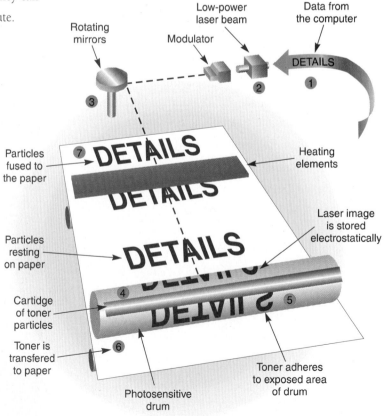

Computer Screens

Most full-size personal computers use a TV-like display device called a **screen**, **monitor**, or **CRT** (cathode ray tube) (Figure 13). Portable computers use a flat panel **liquid crystal display (LCD)** technology similar to a digital watch. The surface of the screen is made up of individual picture elements called **pixels**. Each pixel can be illuminated to form characters and graphic shapes (Figure 14). Color screens have three colored dots (red, green, and blue) for each pixel. These dots can be turned on to display different colors. Most color monitors today use super **VGA** (video graphics array) technology that improves the display significantly over older technology.

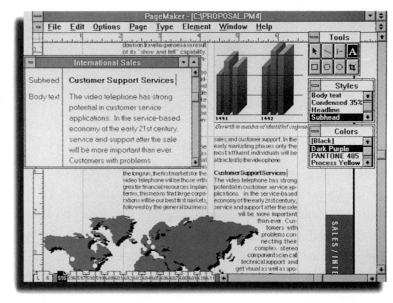

Figure 12
Desktop publishing software, such as PageMaker shown above, is used to produce high-quality documents that combine text and graphics. Such documents are often printed on laser printers.

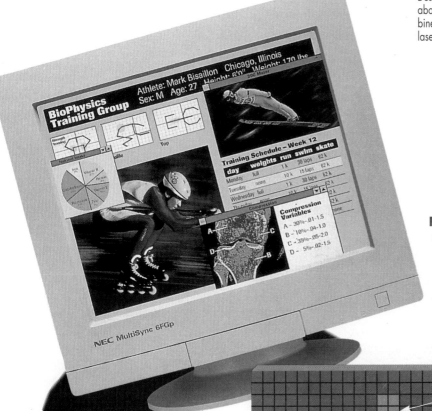

Figure 13
Almost all personal computer systems now come with color screens. Color can be used to enhance the information displayed so the user can understand it more quickly.

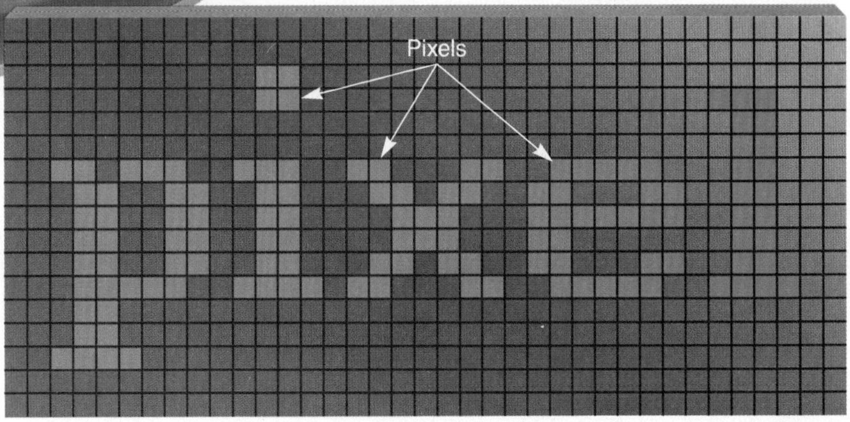

Figure 14
Pixel is an abbreviation of the words picture element, one of thousands of spots on a computer screen that can be turned on and off to form text and graphics

Auxiliary Storage

Auxiliary storage devices are used to store instructions and data when they are not being used in main memory. Two types of auxiliary storage most often used on personal computers are floppy disks and hard disks. CD-ROM disk drives are also becoming common.

Floppy Disks

A **floppy disk** is a circular piece of oxide-coated plastic that stores data as magnetic spots. Floppy disks are available in various sizes and storage capacities. Personal computers most commonly use floppy disks that are 3½-inches in diameter (Figure 15). The once dominant 5¼-inch floppy disk (Figure 15) is seldom used today.

To read data stored on a floppy disk or to store data on a floppy disk, you insert the floppy disk in a disk drive (Figure 16). You can tell that the computer is reading data on the floppy disk or writing data on it because a light on the floppy disk drive will come on while read/write operations are taking place. Do not try to insert or remove a floppy disk when the light is on as you could cause permanent damage to the data stored on it.

The storage capacities of floppy disk drives and the related floppy disks can vary widely (Figure 17). The number of characters that can be stored on a floppy disk depends on two factors: (1) the recording density of the bits on a track; and (2) the number of tracks on the floppy disk.

Figure 15
The most commonly used floppy disk for personal computers is the 3½-inch size on the right. The once-dominant 5¼-inch floppy disk on the left is seldom used today. Although they are smaller in size— the 3½-inch floppy disk can store more data.

Figure 16
A user inserts a 3½-inch floppy disk into the disk drive of a personal computer.

DIAMETER (INCHES)	DESCRIPTION	CAPACITY (BYTES)
5.25	Double-sided, double-density	360KB
5.25	Double-sided, high-density	1.25MB
3.5	Double-sided, double-density	720KB
3.5	Double-sided, high-density	1.44MB

Figure 17
Storage capacities of different size and type floppy disk

Disk drives found on most personal computers use 3½-inch floppy disks that can store 720,000 bytes or 1.44 million bytes of data. 3½-inch floppy disks have a rigid plastic housing that protects the magnetic surface of the floppy disk. Another type of disk drive often found on older computers uses 5¼-inch floppy disks. The 5¼-inch floppy disks can store from 360,000 bytes or 1.2 million bytes of data.

The recording density is stated in **bits per inch** (**bpi**)—the number of magnetic spots that can be recorded on a floppy disk in a one-inch circumference of the innermost track on the floppy disk. Floppy disks and disk drives used today are identified as being double-density or high-density. You need to be aware of the density of floppy disks used by your system because data stored on high-density floppy disks, for example, can not be processed by a computer that has only double-density disk drives.

The second factor that influences the number of characters that can be stored is the number of tracks on the floppy disk. A **track** is a very narrow recording band forming a full circle around the floppy disk (Figure 18).

The tracks are separated from each other by a very narrow blank gap. Each track on a floppy disk is divided into sectors. The term **sector** is used to refer to a pie-shaped section of the disk. It is also used to refer to a section of track. Sectors are the basic units for floppy disk storage. When data is read from a floppy disk, it reads a minimum of one full sector from a track. When data is stored on a floppy disk, it writes one full sector on a track at a time. The tracks and sectors on the floppy disk and the number of characters that can be stored in each sector are defined by a special formatting program that is used with the computer.

Data stored in sectors on a floppy disk must be retrieved and placed into main memory to be processed. The time required to access and retrieve data, called the **access time**, can be important in some applications. The access time for floppy disks varies from about 175 milliseconds (one millisecond equals 1/1000 of a second) to approximately 300 milliseconds. On average, data stored in a single sector on a floppy disk can be retrieved in approximately 1/15 to 1/3 of a second.

Floppy disk care is important to preserve stored data. Properly handled, floppy disks can store data indefinitely. However, the surface of the floppy disk can be damaged and the data stored can be lost if the floppy disk is handled improperly.

Figure 18
Each track on a floppy disk is a narrow, circular band. On a diskette containing 80 tracks, the outside track is called track 0 and the inside track is called track 79. The disk surface is divided into sectors.

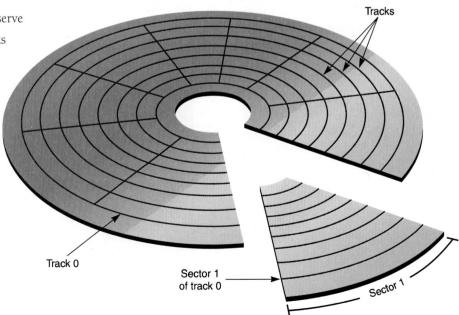

Tracks

Track 0

Sector 1 of track 0

Sector 1

A floppy disk will give you very good service if you follow a few simple procedures:

 Keep floppy disks in their original box or in a special floppy disk storage box to protect them from dirt and dust and prevent them from being accidentally bent. Store floppy disks in their protective containers. Store the container away from heat and direct sunlight. Magnetic and electrical equipment, including telephones, radios, and televisions, can erase the data on a floppy disk, so do not place floppy disks near such devices. Do not place heavy objects on a floppy disk, because the weight can pinch the covering, causing damage when the disk drive attempts to rotate.

 To affix one of the self-adhesive labels supplied with most floppy disks, it is best to write or type the information on the label before you place the label on the floppy disk. If the label is already on the floppy disk, use only a felt-tip pen to write on the label, and press lightly. Do not use ball point pens, pencils, or erasers on labels that are already on floppy disks.

 To use the floppy disk, grasp the floppy disk on the side away from the side to be inserted into the disk drive. Slide the floppy disk carefully into the slot on the disk drive.

The floppy disk write-protect feature (Figure 19) prevents the accidental erasure of the data stored on a floppy disk by preventing the disk drive from writing new data or erasing existing data.

On the 3½-inch floppy disk, a small switch can slide to cover and uncover the write-protection window. On a 3½-inch floppy disk, when the window is uncovered the data is protected.

Figure 19
Data cannot be written on the 3½-inch floppy disk on the left because the window in the corner of the floppy disk is open. A small piece of plastic covers the window of the 3½-inch floppy disk on the right, so data can be written on this floppy disk.

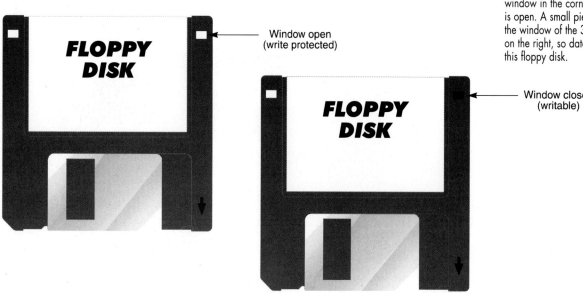

Window open
(write protected)

Window closed
(writable)

Hard Disk

Another form of auxiliary storage is a hard disk. A **hard disk** consists of one or more rigid metal platters coated with a metal oxide material that allows data to be magnetically recorded on the surface of the platters (Figure 20). Although hard disks are available in removable cartridge form, most disks cannot be removed from the computer. As with floppy disks, the data is recorded on hard disks on a series of tracks. The tracks are divided into sectors when the disk is formatted.

The hard disk platters spin at a high rate of speed, typically 3,600 revolutions per minute. When reading data from the disk, the read head senses the magnetic spots that are recorded on the disk along the various tracks and transfers that data to main memory. When writing, the data is transferred from main memory and is stored as magnetic spots on the tracks on the recording surface of one or more of the disk platters. When reading or writing, the read/write heads on a hard disk drive do not actually touch the surface of the disk.

The number of platters permanently mounted on the spindle of a hard disk varies. On most drives, each surface of the platter can be used to store data. Thus, if a hard disk drive uses one platter, two surfaces are available for data. If the drive uses two platters, four sets of read/write heads read and record data from the four surfaces. Storage capacities of internally mounted fixed disks for personal computers range from 240 million characters to more than one billion characters. Larger capacity, stand-alone hard disk units are also available that can store several billion bytes of information. One billion bytes is called a **gigabyte** (**GB**).

The amount of effective storage on both hard disks and floppy disks can be increased by the use of compression programs. **Compression programs** use sophisticated formulas to replace spaces and repeated text and graphics patterns with codes that can later be used to recreate the compressed data. Text files can be compressed the most; as much as an eighth of their original volume. Graphics files can be compressed the least. Overall, a 5-to-1 compression ratio is average.

CD-ROM

Compact disk read-only memory (**CD-ROM**) disks are increasingly used to store large amounts of prerecorded information (Figure 21). Each CD-ROM disk can store more than 600 million bytes of data-the equivalent of 300,000 pages of text. Because of their large storage capacity, CD-ROM is often used for multimedia material. **Multimedia** combines text, graphics, video (pictures), and audio (sound) (Figure 22 on the next page).

spindle   disk surface

read/write head

access arm

Figure 20
The protective cover of this hard disk drive has been removed. A read/write head is at the end of the access arm that extends over the recording surface, called a platter.

Figure 21
CD-ROM disk drives allow the user to access tremendous amounts of pre-recorded information—more than 600MB of data can be stored on one CD-ROM disk.

COMPUTER SOFTWARE

Computer software is the key to productive use of computers. With the correct software, a computer can become a valuable tool. Software can be categorized into two types: system software and application software.

System Software

System software consists of programs to control the operations of computer equipment. An important part of system software is a set of programs called the **operating system**. Instructions in the operating system tell the computer how to perform the functions of loading, storing, and executing an application and how to transfer data. For a computer to operate, an operating system must be stored in the computer's main memory. When a computer is started, the operating system is loaded into the computer and stored in main memory. This process is called **booting**.

Today, many computers use an operating system that has a **graphical user interface** (**GUI**) that provides visual clues such as icon symbols to help the user. Each **icon** represents an application, such as word processing, or a file or document where data is stored. Microsoft **Windows 95** (Figure 23) is a widely used graphical operating system. Apple Macintosh computers also have a graphical user interface operating system. **DOS** (**Disk Operating System**) is an older but still widely used operating system.

Application Software

Application software consists of programs that tell a computer how to produce information. The different ways people use computers in their careers or in their personal lives, are examples of types of application software. Business, scientific, and educational programs are all examples of application software.

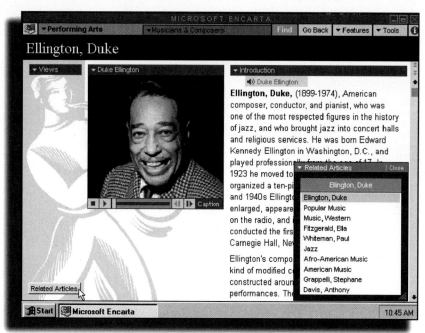

Figure 22
Microsoft Encarta is a multimedia encyclopedia available on a CD-ROM disk. Text, graphics, sound, video, and animation are all available. The speaker-shaped icon at the top of the text indicates that a sound item is available. In this topic, if the user clicks the speaker icon, a portion of Duke Ellington's music plays.

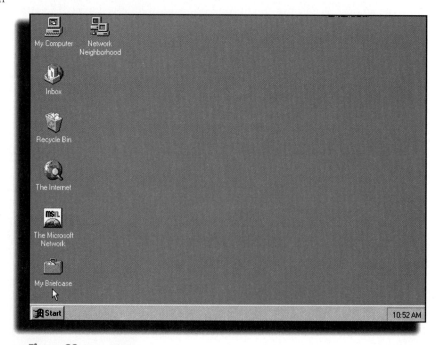

Figure 23
A graphical user interface such as Microsoft Windows 95 makes the computer easier to use. The small pictures, or symbols, on the screen are called icons. The icons represent different processing options that the user can choose.

PERSONAL COMPUTER
APPLICATION SOFTWARE PACKAGES

Personal computer users often use application software packages. Some of the most commonly used packages are: word processing, electronic spreadsheet, presentation graphics, database, communications, and electronic mail software.

Word processing software (Figure 24) is used to create and print documents. A key advantage of word processing software is its capability to make changes easily in documents, such as correcting spelling, changing margins, and adding, deleting, or relocating entire paragraphs. These changes would be difficult and time consuming to make using manual methods such as a typewriter. With a word processor, documents can be printed quickly and accurately and easily stored on a disk for future use. Word processing software is oriented toward working with text, but most word processing packages can also include numeric and graphic information.

Electronic spreadsheet software (Figure 25) allows the user to add, subtract, and perform user-defined calculations on rows and columns of numbers. These numbers can be changed and the spreadsheet quickly recalculates the new results. Electronic spreadsheet software eliminates the tedious recalculations required with manual methods. Spreadsheet information is frequently converted into a graphic form. Graphics capabilities are now included in most spreadsheet packages.

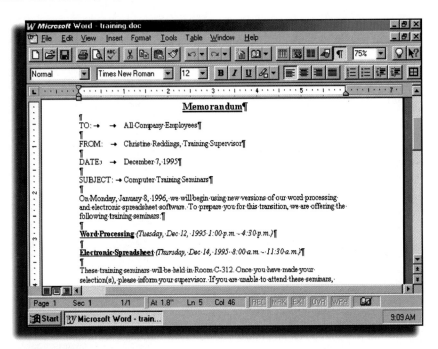

Figure 24
Word processing software is used to write letters, memos, and other documents. As the user types words and letters, they display on the screen. The user can easily add, delete, and change any text entered until the document looks exactly as desired. The user can then save the document on auxiliary storage and can also print it on a printer.

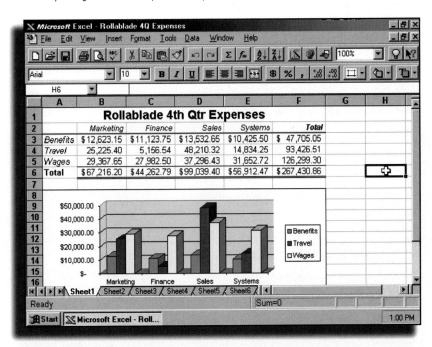

Figure 25
Electronic spreadsheet software is frequently used by people who work with numbers. The user enters the data and the formulas to be used on the data and the computer calculates the results. Most spreadsheet programs have the capability to use numeric data to generate charts, such as the above bar chart.

Database software (Figure 26) allows the user to enter, retrieve, and update data in an organized and efficient manner. These software packages have flexible inquiry and reporting capabilities that allow users to access the data in different ways and create custom reports that include some or all of the information in the database.

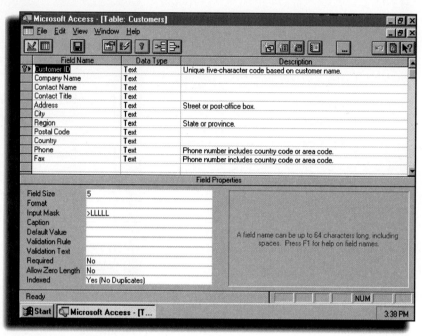

Figure 26
Database software allows the user to enter retrieve and update data in an organiszed and efficient manner. This database table illustrates how a business organized customer information. Once the table is defined, the user can add, delete, change, display, print, or reorganize the database records.

Presentation graphics software (Figure 27) allows the user to create documents called slides to be used in making presentations. Using special projection devices, the slides are projected directly from the computer. In addition, the slides can be printed and used as handouts, or converted into transparencies and displayed on overhead projectors. Presentation graphics software includes many special effects, color, and art that enhance information presented on a slide. Because slides frequently include numeric data, presentation graphics software includes the capability to convert the numeric data into many forms of charts.

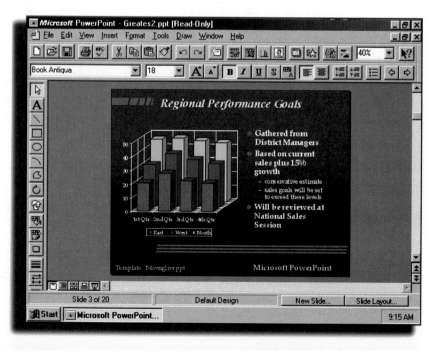

Figure 27
Presentation graphics software allows the user to create documents called slides for use in presentations. Using special projection devices, the slides display as they appear on the computer screen. The slides can also be printed and used as handouts or converted into transparencies to be used with overhead projectors.

Communications software (Figure 28) is used to transmit data and information from one computer to another. For the transfer to take place, each computer must have communications software. Organizations use communications software to transfer information from one location to another. Many individuals use communications software to access on-line databases that provide iinformation on current events, airline schedules, finances, weather, and hundreds of other subjects.

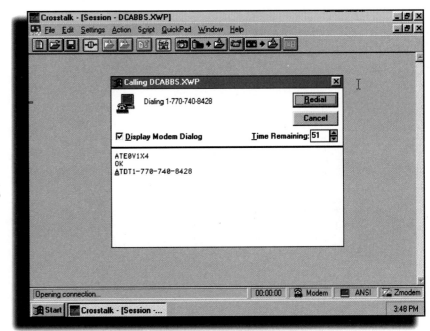

Figure 28
Communications software allows users to transmit data from one computer to another. This software enables the user to choose a previously entered phone number of another computer. Once the number is chosen, the communications software dials the number and establishes a communication link. The user can then transfer data or run programs on the remote computer.

Electronic mail software, also called **e-mail** (Figure 29), allows users to send messages to and receive messages from other computer users. The other users may be on the same computer network or on a separate computer system reached through the use of communications equipment and software.

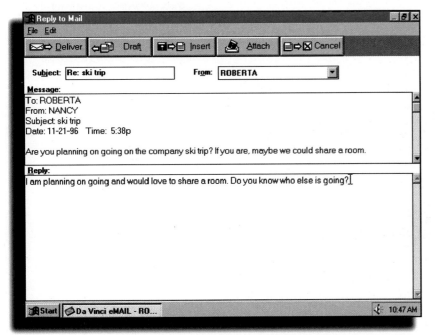

Figure 29
Electronic mail software allows users to send and receive messages with other computer users. Each user has an electronic mail box to which messages are sent. This software enables a user to add a reply to a received message and then send the reply back to the person who sent the original message.

WHAT IS COMMUNICATIONS?

Communications refers to the transmission of data and information over a communications channel, such as a standard telephone line, between one computer and another computer. Figure 30 shows the basic model for a communications system. This model consists of the following equipment:

- A computer
- Communications equipment that sends (and can usually receive) data
- The communications channel over which the data is sent
- Communications equipment that receives (and can usually send) data
- Another computer

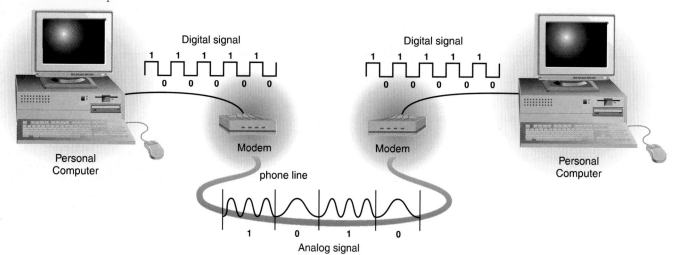

The basic model also includes communications software. When two computers are communicating with each other, compatible communications software is required on each system.

Communications is important to understand because of online services and the trend to network computers. With communications equipment and software, access is available to an increasing amount and variety of information and services. **Online information services** such as Prodigy and America On-Line offer the latest news, weather, sports, and financial information along with shopping, entertainment, and electronic mail.

Browsers such as Netscape Navigator (Figure 31) allow users to access information easily from thousands of computers around the world. The network of worldwide computers is called the **Internet**. A subset of the Internet is called the World Wide Web. The **World Wide Web** (**WWW**) allows users to visit sites that have text, graphics, video, and sound and have hypertext links to other information and Web sites. Electronic **bulletin boards** can be found in most cities with hundreds available in large metropolitan areas. An **electronic bulletin board system** (**BBS**) is a computer and at least one phone line that allows users to *chat* with the computer operator, called the **system operator** (**sys op**) or, if more than one phone line is available, with other BBS users. BBS users can also leave messages for other users. BBSs are often devoted to a specific subject area such as games, hobbies, or a specific type of computer or software. Many computer hardware and software companies operate BBSs so users of their products can share information.

Figure 30
The basic model of a communications system. Individual electrical pulses of the digital signal from the computer are converted into analog (electrical wave) signals for transmission over voice telephone lines. At the computer receiving end, another modem converts the analog signals back into digital signals that can be processed by the computer.

Communications Channels

A **communications channel** is the path the data follows as it is transmitted from the sending equipment to the receiving equipment in a communications system. These channels are made up of one or more **transmission media**, including twisted pair wire, coaxial cable, fiber optics, microwave transmission, satellite transmission, and wireless transmission.

Communications Equipment

If a personal computer is within approximately 1,000 feet of another computer, the two devices can usually be directly connected by a cable. If the devices are more than 1,000 feet, however, the electrical signal weakens to the point that some type of special communications equipment is required to increase or change the signal to transmit it farther. A variety of communications equipment exists to perform this task, but the equipment most often used is a modem.

Computers are designed to process data as **digital signals**, individual electrical pulses grouped together to represent characters. Telephone equipment was originally designed to carry only voice transmission, which is comprised of a continuous electrical wave called an **analog signal** (see Figure 30). Thus, a special piece of equipment called a modem converts between the digital signals and analog signals so telephone lines can carry data. A **modem** converts the digital signals of a computer to analog signals that are transmitted over a communications channel. A modem also converts analog signals it receives into digital signals used by a computer. The word modem comes from a combination of the words *mo*dulate, which means to change into a sound or analog signal, and *dem*odulate, which means to convert an analog signal into a digital signal. A modem is needed at both the sending and receiving ends of a communications channel. A modem may be an external stand-alone device that is connected to the computer and phone line or an internal circuit board that is installed inside the computer.

Modems can transmit data at rates from 1,200 to 28,800 bits per second (bps). Most personal computers use a 9,600 bps or higher modem. Business or heavier volume users would use faster and more expensive modems.

Figure 31
Use of the Internet has been made easier with browser programs such as Netscape Navigator. Browsers allow users to access World Wide Web (WWW or Web) sites that have text, graphics, video, and sound and have hypertext links to other information and Web sites. This screen shows how Netscape Navigator displays the first page of information (called a home page) located at the Web site of Netscape Communications Corporation, the developer of Netscape Navigator.

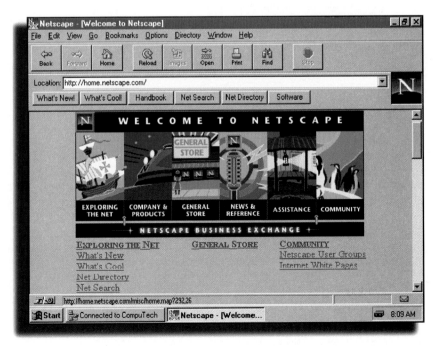

COMMUNICATION NETWORKS

A communication **network** is a collection of computers and other equipment using communications channels to share hardware, software, data, and information. Networks are classified as either local area networks or wide area networks.

Local Area Networks (LANs)

A **local area network**, or **LAN**, is a privately owned communications network and covers a limited geographic area, such as a school computer laboratory, an office, a building, or a group of buildings.

The LAN consists of a communications channel connecting a group of personal computers to one another. Very sophisticated LANs are capable of connecting a variety of office devices, such as word processing equipment, computer terminals, video equipment, and personal computers.

Three common applications of local area networks are hardware, software, and information resource sharing. **Hardware resource sharing** allows each personal computer in the network to access and use devices that would be too expensive to provide for each user or would not be justified for each user because of only occasional use. For example, when a number of personal computers are used on the network, each may need to use a laser printer. Using a LAN, the purchase of one laser printer serves the entire network. Whenever a personal computer user on the network needs the laser printer, it is accessed over the network. Figure 32 depicts a simple local area network consisting of four personal computers linked together by a cable. Three of the personal computers (computer 1 in the sales and marketing department, computer 2 in the accounting department, and computer 3 in the personnel department) are available for use at all times. Computer 4 is used as a server, which is dedicated to handling the communications needs of the other computers in the network. The users of this LAN have connected the laser printer to the server. Using the LAN, all computers and the server can use the printer.

Figure 32
A local area network (LAN) consists of multiple personal computers connected to one another. The LAN allows users to share software, hardware, and information.

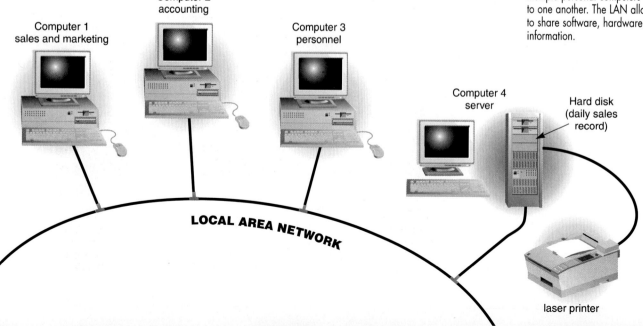

Computer 1
sales and marketing

Computer 2
accounting

Computer 3
personnel

Computer 4
server

Hard disk
(daily sales
record)

LOCAL AREA NETWORK

laser printer

Frequently used software is another type of resource sharing that often occurs on a local area network. For example, if all users need access to word processing software, the software can be stored on the hard disk of the server and accessed by all users as needed. This is more convenient and faster than having the software stored on a floppy disk and available at each computer.

Information resource sharing allows anyone using a personal computer on the local area network to access data stored on any other computer in the network. In actual practice, hardware resource sharing and information resource sharing are often combined. The capability to access and store data on common auxiliary storage is an important feature of many local area networks.

Information resource sharing is usually provided by using either the file server or client-server method. Using the **file server** method, the server sends an entire file at a time. The requesting computer then performs the processing. With the **client-server** method, processing tasks are divided between the server computer and the client computer requesting the information. Figure 33 illustrates how the two methods would process a request for information stored on the server system for customers with balances over $1,000. With the file server method, all customer records would be transferred to the requesting computer. The requesting computer would then process the records to identify the customers with balances over $1,000. With the client-server method, the server system would review the customers' records and only transfer records of customers meeting the criteria. The client-server method greatly reduces the amount of data sent over a network but requires a more powerful server system.

Figure 33
A request for information about customers with balances over $1,000 would be processed differently by the file server and client-server networks.

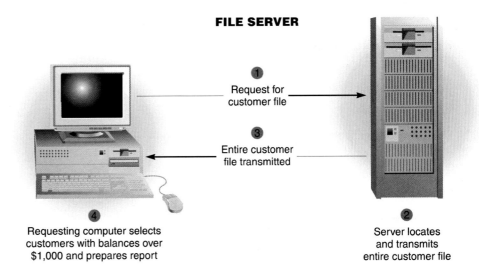

FILE SERVER

① Request for customer file

③ Entire customer file transmitted

④ Requesting computer selects customers with balances over $1,000 and prepares report

② Server locates and transmits entire customer file

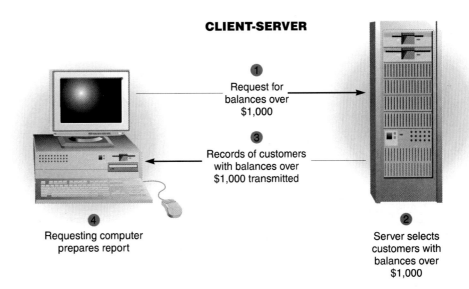

CLIENT-SERVER

① Request for balances over $1,000

③ Records of customers with balances over $1,000 transmitted

④ Requesting computer prepares report

② Server selects customers with balances over $1,000

Wide Area Networks (WANs)

A **wide area network**, or **WAN**, is geographic in scope (as opposed to local) and uses telephone lines, microwaves, satellites, or a combination of communications channels (Figure 34). Public wide area network companies include common carriers such as the telephone companies.

Telephone company deregulation has encouraged a number of companies to build their own wide area networks. Communications companies, such as MCI, have built WANs to compete with other communications companies.

HOW TO PURCHASE A COMPUTER SYSTEM

The personal computer (PC) is the most widely purchased type of system. The following guidelines assume you are purchasing an IBM compatible PC, to be used for home or light business use. That is not meant to imply that Macintosh or other types of computer systems are not worth considering. Software requirements and the need to be compatible with other systems you may work with should determine the type of system you purchase. Most businesses use IBM compatible PCs. A laptop (portable) computer would be an appropriate choice if your situation requires that you have a computer with you when you travel.

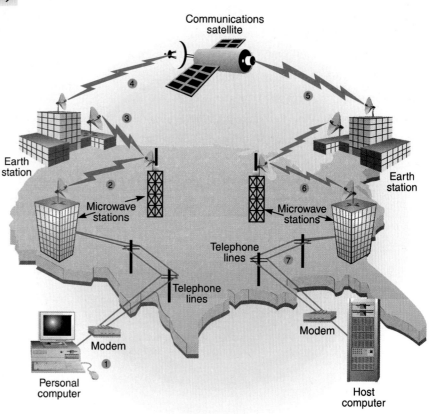

Figure 34
A wide area network (WAN) may use a number of different communications channels such as telephone lines, microwaves, and satellites.

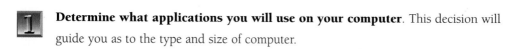

1. **Determine what applications you will use on your computer**. This decision will guide you as to the type and size of computer.

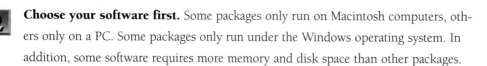

2. **Choose your software first.** Some packages only run on Macintosh computers, others only on a PC. Some packages only run under the Windows operating system. In addition, some software requires more memory and disk space than other packages.

3. **Be aware of hidden costs.** Realize that there will be some additional costs associated with buying a computer. Such costs might include; an additional phone line or outlet to use the modem, computer furniture, consumable supplies such as floppy disks and paper, floppy disk holders, reference manuals on specific software packages, and special training classes you may want to take. Depending on where you buy your computer, the seller may be willing to include some or all of these in the system purchase price.

Buy equipment that meets the *Energy Star* power consumption guidelines.
These guidelines require that computer systems, monitors, and printers, reduce electrical consumption if they have not been used for some period of time, usually several minutes. Equipment meeting the guidelines can display the *Energy Star* logo.

Use a spreadsheet like the one shown in Figure 35 to compare purchase alternatives. Use a separate sheet of paper to take notes on each vendor's system and then summarize the information on the spreadsheet.

Figure 35
A spreadsheet is an effective way to summarize and compare the prices and equipment offered by different system vendors.

Consider buying from local computer dealers and direct mail companies. Each has certain advantages. The local dealer can more easily provide hands-on support, if necessary. With a mail order company, you are usually limited to speaking to someone over the phone. Mail order companies usually, but not always, offer the lowest prices. The important thing to do when shopping for a system is to make sure you are comparing identical or similar configurations.

Consider more than just price. Don't necessarily buy the lowest cost system. Consider intangibles such as how long the vendor has been in business, its reputation for quality, and reputation for support.

Look for free software. Many system vendors now include free software with their systems. Some even let you choose which software you want. Such software only has value, however, if you would have purchased it if it had not come with the computer.

System Cost Comparison Worksheet

		Desired	#1	#2	#3	#4
Base System	Mfr	--				
	Model					
	Processor	Pentium				
	Speed	100MHz				
	Power supply	150watts				
	Expansion slots	5				
	Local bus video	yes				
	Operating System	Windows				
	Price					
Memory	RAM	16MB				
	L2 Cache	256K				
	Price					
Disk	Mfr					
	Size	1.0GB				
	Price					
Video Graphics	Mfr/Model					
	Memory	2MB				
	Price					
Floppy Disk Drive	3.5 inch	3.5 inch				
	Combo 3.5/5.25					
Color Monitor	Mfr/Model					
	Size	15 inch				
	Dot Pitch	0.28mm				
	Price					
Sound Card	Mfr/Model					
	Price					
Speakers	Mfr/Model					
	Watts					
	Size	2 inch				
	Price					
CD-ROM	Mfr/Model					
	Speed	Quad				
	Price					
Mouse	Mfr					
	Price					
Fax Modem	Mfr/Model					
	Speed	28.8kbps				
	Price					
Printer	Mfr/Model					
	Type	ink jet				
	Speed	6ppm				
	Price					
Surge Protector	Mfr/Model					
	Price					
Tape Backup	Mfr/Model					
	Price					
UPS	Mfr/Model					
	Price					
Other	Sales Tax					
	Shipping					
	1 YR Warranty	standard				
	1 YR On-Site Svc					
	3 YR On-Site Svc					
	TOTAL					
Software	List free software					

Buy a system compatible with the one you use elsewhere. If you use a personal computer at work or at some other organization, make sure the computer you buy is compatible. That way, if you need or want to, you can work on projects at home.

 Consider purchasing an on-site service agreement. If you use your system for business or otherwise can't afford to be without your computer, consider purchasing an on-site service agreement. Many of the mail order vendors offer such support through third-party companies. Such agreements usually state that a technician will be on-site within 24 hours. Some systems include on-site service for only the first year. It is usually less expensive to extend the service for two or three years when you buy the computer rather than waiting to buy the service agreement later.

 Use a credit card to purchase your system. Many credit cards now have purchase protection benefits that cover you in case of loss or damage to purchased goods. Some also extend the warranty of any products purchased with the card. Paying by credit card also gives you time to install and use the system before you have to pay for it. Finally, if you're dissatisfied with the system and can't reach an agreement with the seller, paying by credit card gives you certain rights regarding withholding payment until the dispute is resolved. Check your credit card agreement for specific details.

 Buy a system that will last you for at least three years. Studies show that many users become dissatisfied because they didn't buy a powerful enough system. Consider the following system configuration guidelines. Each of the components will be discussed separately:

Base System Components:	**Optional Equipment**
Pentium Processor, 100 megahertz,	28.8 Kbps fax modem
150 watt power supply	sound card and speakers
1.0 GB hard disk drive	4X CD-ROM drive
16 MB of RAM	color ink jet printer
3 open expansion slots	tape backup
1 open expansion bay	uninterruptable power supply
local bus video card with 2 MB of memory	
1 parallel and 2 serial ports	
3½-inch floppy disk drive	
15- or 17-inch SVGA color monitor	
mouse or other pointing device	
enhanced keyboard	
ink-jet or personal laser printer	
surge protector	
latest version of operating system	
FCC Class B approved	

Processor: A Pentium processor with a speed rating of 100 megahertz is needed for today's more sophisticated software, even word processing software. Buy a system that can be upgraded to the next generation processor.

Power Supply: 150 watts. If the power supply is too small, it will not be capable of supporting additional expansion cards you may want to add in the future. The power supply should be **UL** (Underwriters Laboratory) approved.

Hard Disk: 1 gigabyte (GB). Each new release of software requires more hard disk space. Even with disk compression programs, disk space is used up fast. Start with more space on your disk than you ever think you will need.

Memory (RAM): 16 megabytes (MB) Like disk space, the new applications are demanding more memory. It is easier and less expensive to obtain the memory when you buy the system than if you wait until later.

Expansion Slots: At least three open slots. Expansion slots are needed for a modem sound card, scanners, tape drives, video capture boards, and other equipment you may want to add in the future as your needs change and the price of this equipment becomes lower.

Expansion Bay: At least one open bay. An expansion (drive) bay will let you add another disk or floppy disk drive, a tape drive, or a CD-ROM drive.

Local Bus Video Card: Local bus video cards provide faster video performance than video cards that use the slower expansion bus. Make sure the video card has at least 2 MB of memory.

Ports: At least one parallel and two serial ports. The parallel port will be used for your printer. The serial ports can be used for additional printers, external modems, joysticks, a mouse, and some network connections.

Floppy Disk Drives: Most software is now distributed on 3½-inch floppy disks or CD-ROMs. If you need to read the older 5¼-inch floppy disks, consider buying a combination floppy disk drive, which is only slightly more expensive than a single 3½-inch floppy disk drive. The combination device has both 3½-inch and 5¼-inch floppy disk drives in a single unit.

Color Monitor: 15- or 17-inch. This is one device where it pays to spend a little more money. A 17-inch super VGA (SVGA) monitor with a dot pitch of 0.28mm or less will display graphics better than a 15-inch model. For health reasons, make sure you pick a low radiation model. Also, look for a monitor with an antiglare coating on the screen or consider buying an antiglare filter that mounts on the front of the screen.

Pointing Device: Most systems include a mouse as part of the base package. Some people prefer to use a trackball.

Enhanced Keyboard: Almost always included with the system. Check to make sure the keyboard is the *enhanced* and not the older *standard* model. The enhanced keyboard also is sometimes called the *101* keyboard because it has 101 keys (some enhanced keyboards have even more keys). If you are concerned about possible wrist injuries, get one of the ergonomically designed keyboards.

Printer: Inkjet and laser printers produce excellent graphic output and now are only slightly more expensive than dot matrix printers, which now are used primarily for multipart form printing applications. Inexpensive color inkjet printers also are available.

Surge Protecter: A voltage spike can literally destroy your system. It is low cost insurance to protect yourself with a surge protector. Do not merely buy a fused multiple plug outlet from the local hardware store. Buy a surge protector designed for computers with a separate protected jack for your phone (modem) line.

Operating System: Almost all new systems come with an operating system, but it is not always the most current version. Make sure the operating system is the one you want and is the latest version.

FFC Class B Approved: The Federal Communications Commission (FCC) provides radio frequency emission standards that computer manufacturers must meet. If a computer does not meet the FCC standards, it could cause interference with radio and television reception. Class B standards apply to computers used in a home. Class A standards apply to a business installation.

Fax Modem: 28.8 Kbps (Kilobytes per second) speed for both the modem and fax. Volumes of information are available via the Internet. In addition, many software vendors provide assistance and free software upgrades via bulletin boards. For the speed they provide, 28.8 Kbps modems are worth the extra money. Facsimile (fax) capability costs only a few dollars more and gives you additional communication options.

Sound Card and Speakers: More and more software and support materials are incorporating sound. For the best quality sound, buy amplified speakers with their own powered amplifier and a separate subwoofer.

CD-ROM Drive: Multimedia requires a CD-ROM drive. Also, many large software programs are now available on CD-ROM, which greatly reduces installation time. Get at least a quad speed model (transfer rate of 600 Kbps).

Tape Backup: Larger hard disks make backing up data on floppy disks impractical. Internal or external tape backup systems are the most common solution. Some portable units, great if you have more than one system, are designed to connect to your printer port. The small tapes can store the equivalent of hundreds of floppy disks.

Uninterruptable Power Supply (UPS): A UPS uses batteries to start or keep your system running if the main electrical power is turned off. The length of time they provide depends on the size of the batteries and the electrical requirements of your system but usually is at least 10 minutes. The idea of a UPS is to give you enough time to save your work. Get a UPS that is rated for your size system.

HOW TO INSTALL A COMPUTER SYSTEM

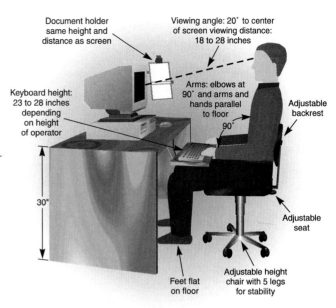

Document holder same height and distance as screen

Viewing angle: 20° to center of screen viewing distance: 18 to 28 inches

Keyboard height: 23 to 28 inches depending on height of operator

Arms: elbows at 90° and arms and hands parallel to floor
90°

Adjustable backrest

30"

Adjustable seat

Feet flat on floor

Adjustable height chair with 5 legs for stability

Figure 36
More than anything else, a well-designed work area should be flexible to allow adjustment to the height and build of different individuals. Good lighting and air quality should also be considered.

1 **Allow for adequate workspace around the computer**. A workspace of at least two feet by four feet is recommended.

2 **Install bookshelves.** Bookshelves above and/or to the side of the computer area are useful for keeping manuals and other reference materials handy.

3 **Install your computer in a well-designed work area.** The height of your chair, keyboard, monitor, and work surface is important and can affect your health. See Figure 36 for specific guidelines.

4 **Use a document holder.** To minimize neck and eye strain, obtain a document holder that holds documents at the same height and distance as your computer screen.

5 **Provide adequate lighting.**

6 **While working at your computer, be aware of health issues.** See Figure 37 for a list of computer user health guidelines.

7 **Install or move a phone near the computer.** Having a phone near the computer really helps if you need to call a vendor about a hardware or software problem. Oftentimes the vendor support person can talk you through the correction while you're on the phone. To avoid data loss, however, don't place floppy disks on the phone or any other electrical or electronic equipment.

Figure 37
All computer users should follow the Computer User Health Guidelines to maintain their health.

8 **Obtain a computer tool set.** Computer tool sets are available from computer dealers, office supply stores, and mail order companies. These sets will have the right-sized screwdrivers and other tools to work on your system. Get one that comes in a zippered carrying case to keep all the tools together.

9 **Save all the paperwork that comes with your system.** Keep it in an accessible place with the paperwork from your other computer-related purchases. To keep different-sized documents together, consider putting them in a plastic zip-lock bag.

10 **Record the serial numbers of all your equipment and software.** Write the serial numbers on the outside of the manuals that came with the equipment as well as in a single list that contains the serial numbers of all your equipment and software.

COMPUTER USER HEALTH GUIDELINES
1. Work in a well-designed work area. Figure 36 illustrates the guidelines
2. Alternate work activites to prevent physical and mental fatigue. If possible, change the order of your work to provide some variety.
3. Take frequent breaks. At least once per hour, get out of your chair and move around. Every two hours, take at least a 15 minute break.
4. Incorporate hand, arm, and body stretching exercises into your breaks. At lunch, try to get outside and walk.
5. Make sure your computer monitor is designed to minimize electromagnetic radiation.
6. Try to eliminate or minimize surrounding noise. Noisy environments contribute to stress and tension.
7. If you frequently have to use the phone and the computer at the same time, consider using a telephone headset. Cradling the phone between your head and shoulder can cause muscle strain.
8. Be aware of symptoms of repetitive strain injuries; soreness, pain, numbness, or weakness in neck, shoulders, arms, wrists, and hands. Don't ignore early signs; seek medical advice.

Keep the shipping containers and packing materials for all your equipment. This material will come in handy if you have to return your equipment for servicing or have to move it to another location.

 Look at the inside of your computer. Before you connect power to your system, remove the computer case cover and visually inspect the internal components. The user manual usually identifies what each component does. Look for any disconnected wires, loose screws or washers, or any other obvious signs of trouble. Be careful not to touch anything inside the case unless you are grounded. Static electricity can permanently damage the microprocessor chips on the circuit boards. Before you replace the cover, take several photographs of the computer showing the location of the circuit boards. These photos may save you from taking the cover off in the future if you or a vendor has a question about what equipment controller card is installed in what expansion slot.

 Identify device connectors. At the back of your system there are a number of connectors for the printer, the monitor, the mouse, a phone line, etc. If they aren't already identified by the manufacturer, use a marking pen to write the purpose of each connector on the back of the computer case.

 Complete and send in your equipment and software registration cards right away. If you're already entered in the vendors user database, it can save you time when you call in with a support question. Being a registered user also makes you eligible for special pricing on software upgrades.

 Install your system in an area where the temperature and humidity can be maintained. Try to maintain a constant temperature between 60 and 80 degrees fahrenheit when the computer is operating. High temperatures and humidity can damage electronic components. Be careful when using space heaters; their hot, dry air has been known to cause disk problems.

 Keep your computer area clean. Avoid eating and drinking around the computer. Smoking should be avoided also. Cigarette smoke can quickly cause damage to the floppy disk drives and floppy disk surfaces.

 Check your insurance. Some policies have limits on the amount of computer equipment they cover. Other policies don't cover computer equipment at all if it is used for a business (a separate policy is required).

HOW TO MAINTAIN YOUR COMPUTER SYSTEM

 Learn to use system diagnostic programs. If a set didn't come with your system, obtain one. These programs help you identify and possibly solve problems before you call for technical assistance. Some system manufacturers now include diagnostic programs with their systems and ask that you run the programs before you call for help.

2 **Start a notebook that includes information on your system.** This notebook should be a single source of information about your entire system, both hardware and software. Each time you make a change to your system, adding or removing hardware or software, or when you change system parameters, you should record the change in the notebook. Items to include in the notebook are the following:

✔Serial numbers of all equipment and software.

✔Vendor support phone numbers. These numbers are often buried in user manuals. Look up these numbers once and record all of them on a single sheet of paper at the front of your notebook.

✔Dates when software was installed or uninstalled.

✔Date and vendor for each equipment and software purchase.

✔Notes on discussions with vendor support personnel.

✔A chronological history of any equipment or software problems. This history can be helpful if the problem persists and you have to call several times.

3 **Periodically review disk directories and delete unneeded files**. Files have a way of building up and can quickly use up your disk space. If you think you may need a file in the future, back it up to a floppy disk.

4 **Any time you work inside your computer turn the power off and disconnect the equipment from the power source.** In addition, before you touch anything inside the computer, touch an unpainted metal surface such as the power supply. This will discharge any static electricity that could damage internal components.

5 **Reduce the need to clean the inside of your system by keeping the surrounding area dirt and dust free.** Floppy disk cleaners are available but should be used sparingly (some owners never use them unless they experience floppy disk problems). If dust builds up inside the computer it should be carefully removed with compressed air and a small vacuum. Don't touch the components with the vacuum.

6 **Backup key files and data.** Use the operating system or a utility program to create an emergency disk to help restart the computer if it crashes. Important data files should be copied regularly to floppy disks, tape, or another computer.

Figure 38
How a virus program can be transmitted from one computer to another.

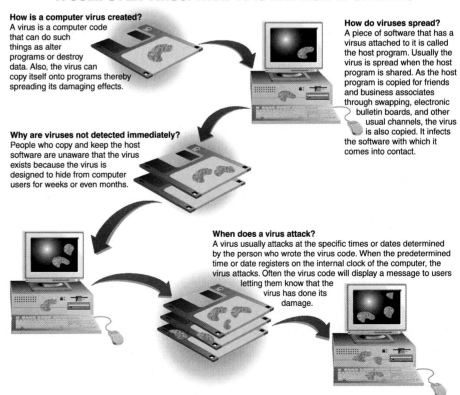

A COMPUTER VIRUS: WHAT IT IS AND HOW IT SPREADS

How is a computer virus created?
A virus is a computer code that can do such things as alter programs or destroy data. Also, the virus can copy itself onto programs thereby spreading its damaging effects.

How do viruses spread?
A piece of software that has a virsus attached to it is called the host program. Usually the virus is spread when the host program is shared. As the host program is copied for friends and business associates through swapping, electronic bulletin boards, and other usual channels, the virus is also copied. It infects the software with which it comes into contact.

Why are viruses not detected immediately?
People who copy and keep the host software are unaware that the virus exists because the virus is designed to hide from computer users for weeks or even months.

When does a virus attack?
A virus usually attacks at the specific times or dates determined by the person who wrote the virus code. When the predetermined time or date registers on the internal clock of the computer, the virus attacks. Often the virus code will display a message to users letting them know that the virus has done its damage.

Protect your system from computer viruses. Computer viruses are programs designed to *infect* computer systems by copying themselves into other computer files (Figure 38). The virus program spreads when the infected files are used by or copied to another system. On the previous page virus programs are dangerous because they are often designed to damage the files of the infected system. Protect yourself from viruses by installing an anti-virus program on your computer.

SUMMARY OF INTRODUCTION TO COMPUTERS

As you learn to use the software taught in this book, you will also become familiar with the components and operation of your computer system. When you need help understanding how the components of your system function, refer to this introduction. You can also refer to this section for information on computer communications and for guidelines when you decide to purchase a computer system of your own.

STUDENT ASSIGNMENTS

Student Assignment 1: True/False

Instructions: Circle T if the statement is true or F if the statement is false.

T F   1. A computer is an electronic device, operating under the control of instructions stored in its own memory unit, that can accept data (input), process data arithmetically and logically, produce output from the processing, and store the results for future use.

T F   2. Information refers to data processed into a form that has meaning and is useful.

T F   3. A computer program is a detailed set of instructions that tells a computer exactly what to do.

T F   4. A mouse is a communications device used to convert between digital and analog signals so telephone lines can carry data.

T F   5. The central processing unit contains the processor unit and main memory.

T F   6. A laser printer is an impact printer that provides high-quality output.

T F   7. Auxiliary storage is used to store instructions and data when they are not being used in main memory.

T F   8. A floppy disk is considered to be a form of main memory.

T F   9. CD-ROM is often used for multimedia material that combines text, graphics, video, and sound.

T F 10. The operating system tells the computer how to perform functions such as how to load, store, and execute an application program and how to transfer data between the input/output devices and main memory.

T F 11. Programs such as database management, spreadsheet, and word processing software are called system software.

T F 12. For data to be transferred from one computer to another over communications lines, communications software is required only on the sending computer.

T F 13. A communications network is a collection of computers and other equipment that use communications channels to share hardware, software, data, and information.

T   F   14.   Determining what applications you will use on your computer will help you to purchase a computer that is the type and size that meets your needs.

T   F   15.   The path the data follows as it is transmitted from the sending equipment to the receiving equipment in a communications system is called a modem.

T   F   16.   Computer equipment that meets the power consumption guidelines can display the *Energy Star* logo

T   F   17.   An on-site maintenance agreement is important if you cannot be without the use of your computer.

T   F   18.   An anti-virus program is used to protect your computer equipment and software.

T   F   19.   When purchasing a computer, consider only the price because one computer is no different from another.

T   F   20.   A LAN allows you to share software but not hardware.

Student Assignments 2: Multiple Choice

Instructions: Circle the correct response.

1.   The four operations performed by a computer include _____.
   a. input, control, output, and storage   c. input, output, processing, and storage
   b. interface, processing, output, and memory   d. input, logical/rational, arithmetic, and output

2.   A hand-held input device that controls the cursor location is _____.
   a. the cursor control keyboard   c. a modem
   b. a mouse   d. the CRT

3.   A printer that forms images without striking the paper is _____.
   a. an impact printer   c. an inkjet printer
   b. a nonimpact printer.   d. both b and c

4.   The amount of storage provided by a floppy disk is a function of _____.
   a. the thickness of the floppy disk   c. the number of recording tracks on the floppy disk
   b. the recording density of bits on the track   d. both b and c

5.   Portable computers use a flat panel screen called _____.
   a. a multichrome monitor   c. a liquid crystal display
   b. a cathode ray tube   d. a monochrome monitor

6.   When not in use, floppy disks should be _____.
   a. stored away from magnetic fields   c. stored in a floppy disk box or cabinet
   b. stored away from heat and direct sunlight   d. all of the above

7.   CD-ROM is a type of _____.
   a. main memory   c. communications equipment
   b. auxiliary storage   d. system software

8.   An operating system is considered part of _____.
   a. word processing software   c. system software
   b. database software   d. spreadsheet software

9.   The type of application software most commonly used to create and print documents is _____.
   a. word processing   b. electronic spreadsheet   c. database   d. none of the above

10.   The type of application software most commonly used to send messages to and receive messages from other computer users is _____.
   a. electronic mail   b. database   c. presentation graphics   d. none of the above

Student Assignment 3: Comparing Personal Computer Advertisements

Instructions: Obtain a copy of a recent computer magazine and review the advertisements for desktop personal computer systems. Compare ads for the least and most expensive desktop systems you can find. Discuss the differences.

Student Assignment 4: Evaluating On-Line Information Services

Instructions: Prodigy and America On-Line both offer consumer oriented on-line information services. Contact each company and request each to send you information on the specific services it offers. Try to talk to someone who actually uses one or both of the services. Discuss how each service is priced and the differences between the two on-line services.

Student Assignment 5: Visiting Local Computer Retail Stores

Instructions: Visit local computer retail stores and compare the various types of computers and support equipment available. Ask about warranties, repair services, hardware setup, training, and related issues. Report on the knowledge of the sales staff assisting you and their willingness to answer your questions. Does the store have standard hardware packages, or are they willing to configure a system to your specific needs? Would you feel confident buying a computer from this store?

INDEX

PHOTO CREDITS

Figure 1, C-1 Photography; (A) Tony Stone Images-John Riley; (B) The Gamma Liason Network-James P. Wilson; (C) The National Institute of Industrial Ownership, Frederic Pitchal-Sygma; (D) Tony Stone-Images-Kevin Horan; (E) Gamma Liason, Shahn Kermani-Tot-Tech Computers; (F) Comshare; (G) Steve Reneker; (H) International Business Machines Corp.; (I) Sygma; Figure 2, Scott R. Goodwin Inc.; Figure 3, Tony Stone Images-Mitch Kezar; Figure 4, Scott R. Goodwin,Inc.; Figure; 5, Epson (Manning, Selvege & Lee); Figure 6, Comshare; Figure 7, Comshare; Figure 8, Scott R. Goodwin Inc.; Figure 10, Hewlett Packard; Figure 11, Hewlett Packard; Figure 12, NEC Technology, Multisync; Figure 13, International Business Machines Corp.; Figure 15, Jerry Spagnoli; Figure 16, Greg Hadel; Figure 19, Jerry Spagnoli; Figure 20, Microscience International Corp.; Figure 21, 3M Corp.; Illustrations, Greg Herrington, Stephanie Nance.

▶ PROJECT ONE

FUNDAMENTALS OF USING WINDOWS 95

Objectives:

You will have mastered the material in this project when you can:

- Describe Microsoft Windows 95
- Describe a user interface
- Identify the objects on the Microsoft Windows 95 desktop
- Perform the basic mouse operations: point, click, right-click, double-click, drag, and right-drag
- Open a Windows 95 window
- Maximize, minimize, and restore a Windows 95 window
- Close a Windows 95 window
- Resize a window
- Scroll in a window
- Move a window on the Windows 95 desktop
- Understand keyboard shortcut notation
- Start an application program
- Create a written document
- Save a document on disk
- Print a document
- Close an application program
- Modify a document stored on disk
- Use Windows 95 Help
- Shut down Windows 95

▶ PROJECT TWO

USING WINDOWS EXPLORER

Objectives:

You will have mastered the material in this project when you can:

- Start Windows Explorer
- Understand the elements of the Exploring – My Computer window
- Display the contents of a folder
- Expand and collapse a folder
- Change the view
- Select and copy one file or a group of files
- Create, rename, and delete a folder
- Rename and delete a file

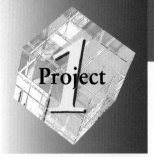

Project 1

A $14 Billion Mistake?

Digital Research officials would not yield to IBM's demands

Have you ever missed a meeting you should have attended but something else was more important? Did you lose $14 billion dollars because you were absent? Gary Kildall might have.

In the 1970s, Kildall's company, Digital Research, had developed an operating system called CP/M that was used on most microcomputers except the Apple II. Kildall was a leader in the microcomputer software business. Then, in 1980, IBM came calling.

Having decided to build a personal computer, IBM approached Bill Gates, president of a small company called Microsoft, in Redmond, Washington, to create the operating system. Gates demurred, suggesting IBM contact Kildall.

MICROSOFT

MS DOS

Bill Gates

SEATTLE COMPUTER PRODUCTS

When IBM arrived for the meeting in Pacific Grove, California, Kildall was off flying his airplane. The reasons are not entirely clear. Some say Kildall was a free spirit and not inclined to do business with the monolithic IBM. Kildall claimed he was flying to another important meeting.

Without Kildall at the meeting, IBM insisted on knowing everything about CP/M while disclosing nothing about its new computer. Fearing IBM would steal their secrets, Digital Research officials would not yield to IBM's demands. Rebuffed, IBM scurried back to Gates.

Sensing an opportunity, Gates agreed to provide an operating system to IBM even though he had no idea how. It just so happened, however, that a small company named Seattle Computer Products, almost next door to Microsoft, was writing an operating system called QDOS v0.110 (QDOS stood for Quick and Dirty Operating System).

Gates learned of QDOS and approached Seattle Computer Products to ask if the operating system was for sale. For a few favors and a little money, Microsoft, in December 1980, acquired non-exclusive rights to QDOS. Later, Microsoft acquired all rights and renamed the operating system MS-DOS. Seattle Computer Products received about $1 million.

Microsoft made substantial changes to MS-DOS and when IBM announced its personal computer in August 1981, MS-DOS was the operating system. The IBM machine was an instant hit. Microsoft sold millions of copies of MS-DOS and grew to be the largest software company in the world. Bill Gates became the world's richest man, with assets in excess of $14 billion dollars.

And Gary Kildall? He continued to develop software at Digital Research. Eventually, Digital Research was sold to Novell, Inc. In the summer of 1994, Kildall died. He left a legacy as an early pioneer who made a significant contribution to microcomputing, but perhaps his most memorable act was missing a meeting.

QDOS

```
Enter today's date (m-d-y): 8-4-1981

The IBM Personal Computer DOS
Version 1.00 (C)Copyright IBM Corp 1981

A>
```

Courtesy of Tim Paterson,
reprinted by permission of Microsoft Corporation.

The Microsoft Disk Operating System, or MS-DOS, was shipped as PC-DOS on the original IBM Personal Computer and later with many IBM compatible machines. Like other operating systems, MS-DOS oversees all the functions of a computer. Various upgrades to MS-DOS and further product refinements led to the release of Windows, an operating system that uses a graphical user interface. Microsoft's current version of Windows, released in August of 1995, is called Windows 95.

CP/M

GARY KILDALL

IBM

DIGITAL RESEARCH

Microsoft sold millions of copies of MS-DOS and grew to be the largest software company in the world

Project 1

Microsoft

Windows 95

Fundamentals of Using Windows 95

Case Perspective

Need: Each day millions of Windows 95 users turn on their computers, whether at home, in the office, at school, on an airplane, or at the beach. When the computer starts, the first image on the monitor is the Windows 95 desktop. If these users did not know how to start application programs from the desktop, manipulate files and images on the desktop, and preserve the work accomplished, their computers would be useless. You have just acquired a computer containing Windows 95. Your task is to learn the basics of Windows 95 so your computer will be useful to you.

Introduction

An **operating system** is the set of computer instructions, called a computer program, that controls the allocation of computer hardware such as memory, disk devices, printers, and CD-ROM drives, and provides the capability for you to communicate with your computer. The most popular and widely used operating system for personal computers is **Microsoft Windows**. **Microsoft Windows 95** (called Windows 95 for the rest of this book), the newest version of Microsoft Windows, allows you to easily communicate with and control your computer. Windows 95 is easier to use and more efficient than previous versions of Windows and can be customized to fit individual needs. Windows 95 simplifies the process of working with documents and applications, transferring data between documents, and organizing the manner in which you interact with your computer.

In Project 1, you will learn about Windows 95 and how to use the Windows 95 user interface.

Microsoft Windows 95

Microsoft Windows 95 is an operating system that performs every function necessary for you to communicate with and use your computer. Unlike previous versions of Windows, no associated operating system is required. Windows 95 is called a **32-bit operating system** because it uses 32 bits for addressing and other purposes, which means the operating system can address more than four gigabytes of RAM and perform tasks faster than older operating systems.

Windows 95 is designed to be compatible with all existing **application programs**, which are programs that perform an application-related function such as word processing. To use the application programs that can be executed under Windows 95, you must know about the Windows 95 user interface.

What Is a User Interface?

A **user interface** is the combination of hardware and software that you use to communicate with and control your computer. Through the user interface, you are able to make selections on your computer, request information from your computer, and respond to messages displayed by your computer. Thus, a user interface provides the means for dialogue between you and your computer.

Hardware and software together form the user interface. Among the hardware devices associated with a user interface are the monitor, keyboard, and mouse (Figure 1-1). The monitor displays messages and provides information. You respond by entering data in the form of a command or other response using the keyboard or mouse. Among the responses available to you are responses that specify what application program to run, what document to open, when to print, and where to store data for future use.

The computer software associated with the user interface consists of the programs that engage you in dialogue (Figure 1-1). The computer software determines the messages you receive, the manner in which you should respond, and the actions that occur based on your responses.

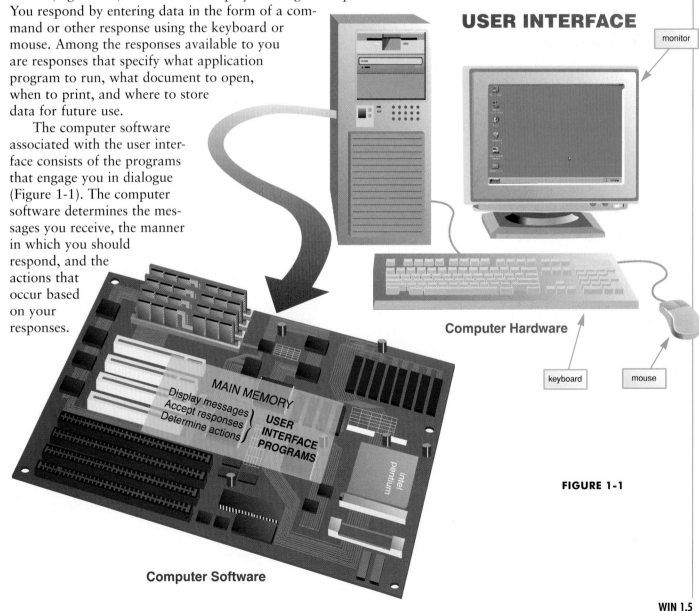

USER INTERFACE

monitor

Computer Hardware

keyboard   mouse

MAIN MEMORY
Display messages
Accept responses
Determine actions
} USER
INTERFACE
PROGRAMS

intel pentium

Computer Software

FIGURE 1-1

The goal of an effective user interface is to be **user friendly**, meaning that the software can be used easily by individuals with limited training. Research studies have indicated that the use of graphics can play an important role in aiding users to interact effectively with a computer. A **graphical user interface**, or **GUI** (pronounced gooey), is a user interface that displays graphics in addition to text when it communicates with the user.

The Windows 95 graphical user interface was carefully designed to be easier to set up, simpler to learn, and faster and more powerful than previous versions of Microsoft Windows.

Starting Microsoft Windows 95

When you turn on your computer, an introductory screen consisting of the Windows 95 logo and the Microsoft Windows 95 name displays on a blue sky and clouds background (Figure 1-2).

The screen clears and several items display on a background called the **desktop**. The default color of the desktop background is green, but your computer may display a different color. Your screen might display as shown in Figure 1-3. It also might display without the Welcome screen shown in Figure 1-3.

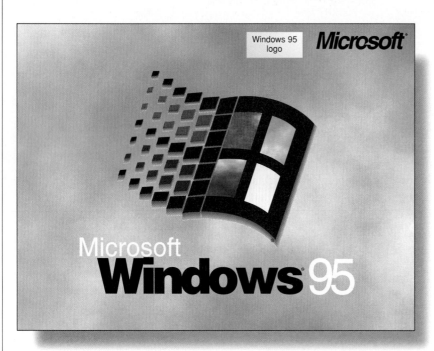

FIGURE 1-2

The items on the desktop in Figure 1-3 include six icons and their names on the left of the desktop, the Welcome screen in the center of the desktop, and the taskbar at the bottom of the desktop. Through the use of the six **icons**, you can view the contents of your computer (**My Computer**), work with other computers connected to your computer (**Network Neighborhood**), receive and send electronic faxes and mail (e-mail) from or to other computers (**Inbox**), discard unneeded objects (**Recycle Bin**), connect to the Microsoft online service (**The Microsoft Network**), and transfer data to and from a portable computer (**My Briefcase**). Your computer's desktop might contain more, fewer, or some different icons because the desktop of your computer can be customized.

The Welcome screen that might display on your desktop is shown in Figure 1-3. The **title bar**, which is dark blue in color at the top of the screen, identifies the name of the screen (Welcome) and contains the Close button, which can be used to close the Welcome screen. In the Welcome screen, a welcome message (Welcome to Windows 95) displays together with a helpful tip for using Windows 95, a check box containing a check mark, and several command buttons. The **check box** represents an option to display the Welcome screen each time Windows 95 starts that you can turn on or turn off. The **command buttons** allow you to perform different operations such as displaying the next tip or closing the screen.

Below the screen is the mouse pointer. On the desktop, the **mouse pointer** is the shape of a block arrow. The mouse pointer allows you to point to items on the desktop.

The **taskbar** at the bottom of the screen in Figure 1-3 contains the Start button, the Welcome button, and the Tray status area. The **Start button** provides an entry point to begin using the features of Windows 95, the Welcome button indicates the Welcome screen is open on the desktop, and the current time (6:06 PM) displays in the Tray status area.

Nearly every item on the Windows 95 desktop is considered an object. Even the desktop itself is an object. Every **object** has properties. The **properties** of an object are unique to that specific object and may affect what can be done to the object or what the object does. For example, the properties of an object may be the color of the object, such as the color of the desktop.

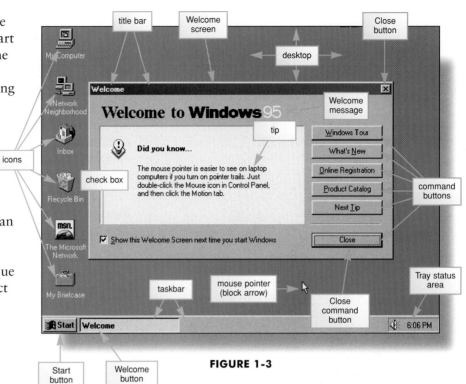

FIGURE 1-3

Closing the Welcome Screen

As noted, the Welcome screen might display when you start Windows 95. If the Welcome screen does display on the desktop, normally you should close it prior to beginning any other operations using Windows 95. To close the Welcome screen, complete the following step.

TO CLOSE THE WELCOME SCREEN

Step 1: Press the ESC key on the keyboard as shown in Figure 1-4.

The Welcome screen closes.

The Desktop as a Work Area

The Windows 95 desktop and the objects on the desktop were designed to emulate a work area in an office or at home. The Windows desktop may be thought of as an electronic version of the top of your desk. You can move objects around on the desktop, look at them and then put them aside, and so on. In Project 1, you will learn how to interact with and communicate with the Windows 95 desktop.

FIGURE 1-4

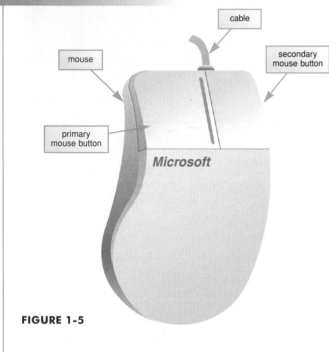

cable

mouse

secondary
mouse button

primary
mouse button

Microsoft

FIGURE 1-5

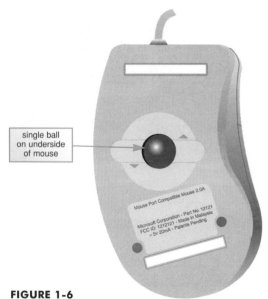

single ball
on underside
of mouse

FIGURE 1-6

Communicating with Microsoft Windows 95

The Windows 95 interface provides the means for dialogue between you and your computer. Part of this dialogue involves your requesting information from your computer and responding to messages displayed by your computer. You can request information and respond to messages using either a mouse or a keyboard.

Mouse Operations

A **mouse** is a pointing device used with Windows 95 that is attached to the computer by a cable. It contains two buttons — the primary mouse button and the secondary mouse button (Figure 1-5). The **primary mouse button** is typically the left mouse button and the **secondary mouse button** is typically the right mouse button although Windows 95 allows you to switch them. In this book, the left mouse button is the primary mouse button and the right mouse button is the secondary mouse button.

Using the mouse, you can perform the following operations: (1) point; (2) click; (3) right-click; (4) double-click; (5) drag; and (6) right-drag. These operations are demonstrated on the following pages.

Point and Click

Point means you move the mouse across a flat surface until the mouse pointer rests on the item of choice on the desktop. As you move the mouse across a flat surface, the movement of a ball on the underside of the mouse (Figure 1-6) is electronically sensed, and the mouse pointer moves across the desktop in the same direction.

Click means you press and release the primary mouse button, which in this book is the left mouse button. In most cases, you must point to an item before you click. To become acquainted with the use of a mouse, perform the following steps to point to and click various objects on the desktop.

Steps **To Point and Click**

1 **Point to the Start button on the taskbar by moving the mouse across a flat surface until the mouse pointer rests on the Start button.**

*The mouse pointer points to the Start button and a **ToolTip** (Click here to begin) displays (Figure 1-7). The ToolTip, which provides instructions, displays on the desktop for approximately five seconds.*

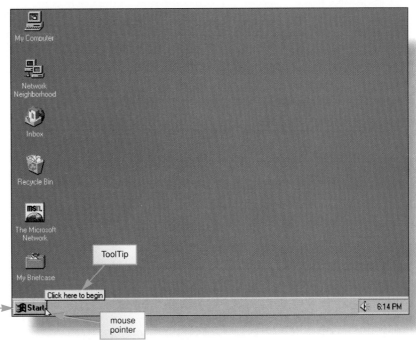

FIGURE 1-7

2 **Click the Start button on the taskbar by pressing and releasing the left mouse button.**

*Windows 95 opens the **Start menu** and indents the Start button (Figure 1-8). A **menu** is a list of related commands. Nine commands display on the Start menu. A **command** directs Windows 95 to perform a specific action such as opening another menu or shutting down the operating system. Each command consists of an icon and a command name. Some commands (Run and Shut Down) are followed by an **ellipsis** (...) to indicate Windows 95 requires more information before executing the command. Other commands (Programs, Documents, Settings, and Find) are followed by a **right arrow**. A right arrow indicates that pointing to the command will open a submenu containing more commands.*

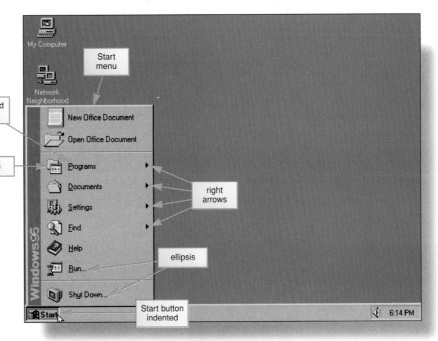

FIGURE 1-8

3 **Point to Programs on the Start menu.**

When you point to Programs, Windows 95 highlights the Programs command on the Start menu and opens the **Programs submenu** *(Figure 1-9). A* **submenu** *is a menu that displays when you point to a command that is followed by a right arrow.*

FIGURE 1-9

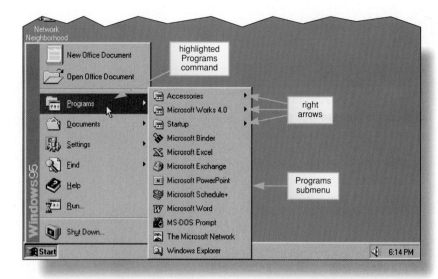

4 **Point to an open area of the desktop and then click the open area of the desktop.**

Windows 95 closes the Start menu and the Programs submenu (Figure 1-10). The mouse pointer points to the desktop. To close a menu anytime, click anywhere on the desktop except the menu itself. The Start button is not indented.

FIGURE 1-10

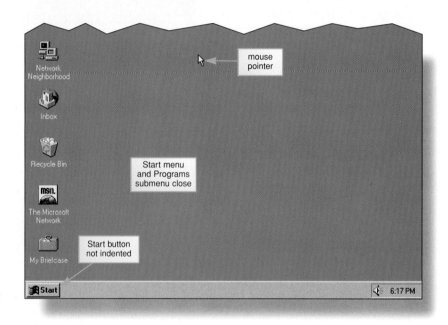

More *About* **Buttons**

Buttons on the desktop and in programs are in integral part of Windows 95. When you point to them, their function displays in a ToolTip. When you click them, they appear to indent on the screen to mimic what would happen if you pushed an actual button. All buttons in Windows 95 behave in the same manner.

Notice in Figure 1-9 that whenever you point to a command on a menu, the command is highlighted.

When you click an object such as the Start button in Figure 1-8 on the previous page, you must point to the object before you click. In the steps that follow, the instruction that directs you to point to a particular item and then click is, Click the particular item. For example, Click the Start button, means point to the Start button and then click.

Right-Click

Right-click means you press and release the secondary mouse button, which in this book is the right mouse button. As when you use the primary mouse button, normally you will point to an object on the screen prior to right-clicking. Perform the following steps to right-click the desktop.

Steps To Right-Click

1 **Point to an open area on the desktop and press and release the right mouse button.**

Windows 95 displays a context-sensitive menu containing six commands (Figure 1-11). Right-clicking an object, such as the desktop, opens a **context-sensitive menu** *(also referred to as a* **shortcut menu** *or an* **object menu***) that contains a set of commands specifically for use with that object. The Paste command in Figure 1-11 is dimmed, meaning that command cannot be used at the current time.*

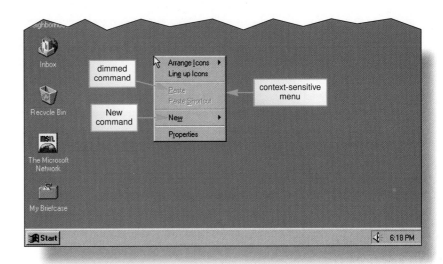

FIGURE 1-11

2 **Point to New on the context-sensitive menu.**

When you move the mouse pointer to the New command, Windows 95 highlights the New command and opens the **New submenu** *(Figure 1-12). The New submenu contains a variety of commands. The number of commands and the actual commands that display on your computer might be different.*

3 **Point to an open area of the desktop and click the open area to remove the context-sensitive menu and the New submenu.**

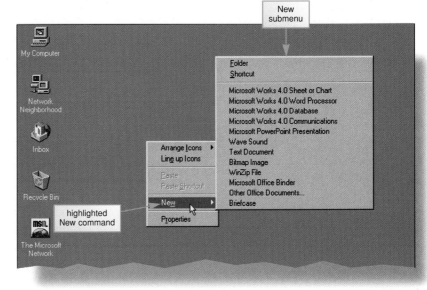

FIGURE 1-12

Whenever you right-click an object, a context-sensitive, or shortcut, menu will display. As you will see, the use of shortcut menus speeds up your work and adds flexibility to your interface with the computer.

Double-Click

Double-click means you quickly press and release the left mouse button twice without moving the mouse. In most cases, you must point to an item before you double-click. Perform the step on the next page to open the My Computer window on the desktop by double-clicking the My Computer icon.

Steps To Open a Window by Double-Clicking

1 **Point to the My Computer icon on the desktop and double-click by quickly pressing and releasing the left mouse button twice without moving the mouse.**

*Windows 95 opens the My Computer window and adds the My Computer button to the taskbar (Figure 1-13). The My Computer window is the active window. The **active window** is the window currently being used. Whenever you double-click an object that can be opened, Windows 95 will open the object; and the open object will be identified by a button on the taskbar. The active window is identified by the indented button.*

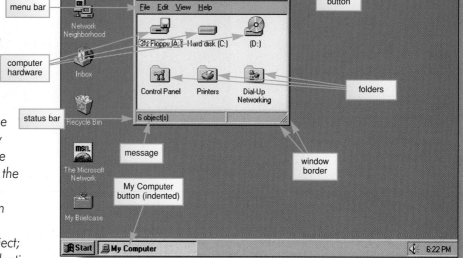

FIGURE 1-13

More *About* Double-Clicking

Double-clicking is the most difficult mouse skill to learn. Many people have a tendency to move the mouse before they click a second time, even when they do not want to move the mouse. You should find, however, that with a little practice double-clicking becomes quite natural.

More *About* My Computer

The trade press and media have poked fun at the icon name, My Computer. One wag said no one should use Windows 95 for more than five minutes without changing the name (which is easily done). Microsoft responds that in its usability labs, My Computer was the most easily understood name by beginning computer users.

My Computer Window

The thin line, or **window border**, surrounding the My Computer window in Figure 1-13 determines its shape and size. The **title bar** at the top of the window contains a small icon that is the same as the icon on the desktop and the **window title** (My Computer) that identifies the window. The color of the title bar (dark blue) and the indented My Computer button on the taskbar indicate the My Computer window is the active window. The color of the active window on your computer might be different from the dark blue color.

Clicking the icon at the left on the title bar will open the Control menu, which contains commands to carry out actions associated with the My Computer window. At the right on the title bar are three buttons, the Minimize button, the Maximize button, and the Close button, that can be used to specify the size of the window and can close the window.

The **menu bar**, a horizontal bar below the title bar of a window (see Figure 1-13), contains a list of menu names for the My Computer window: File, Edit, View, and Help. One letter in each menu name is underlined. You can open a menu by clicking the menu name on the menu bar.

Six icons display in the My Computer window. A name below each icon identifies the icon. The three icons in the top row represent a 3½ floppy disk drive (3½ Floppy [A:]), a hard disk drive (Hard disk [C:]), and a CD-ROM drive ([D:]). The contents of the My Computer window on your computer might be different than shown in Figure 1-13.

The icons in the second row are folders. A **folder** is an object created to contain related documents, applications, and other folders. A folder in Windows 95 contains items in much the same way a folder on your desk contains items. If you

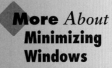

double-click a folder, the items within the folder display in a window. A message at the left of the **status bar** located at the bottom of the window indicates the window contains six objects (see Figure 1-13).

Minimize Button

Two buttons on the title bar of a window, the Minimize button and the Maximize button, allow you to control the way a window displays or does not display on the desktop. When you click the **Minimize button** (see Figure 1-13), the My Computer window no longer displays on the desktop and the indented My Computer button on the taskbar changes to a non-indented button. A minimized window or application program is still open but it does not display on the screen. To minimize and then redisplay the My Computer window, complete the following steps.

 To Minimize and Redisplay a Window

1 **Point to the Minimize button on the title bar of the My Computer window.**

The mouse pointer points to the Minimize button on the My Computer window title bar (Figure 1-14). The My Computer button on the taskbar is indented.

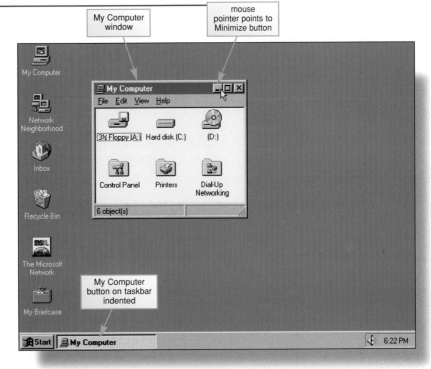

FIGURE 1-14

2 **Click the Minimize button.**

The My Computer window disappears from the desktop and the My Computer button on the taskbar changes to a non-indented button (Figure 1-15).

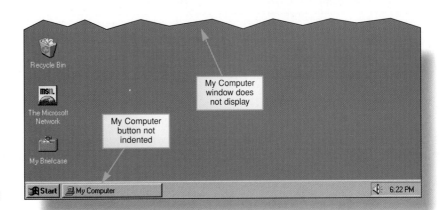

FIGURE 1-15

3 **Click the My Computer button on the taskbar.**

The My Computer window displays on the desktop in the same place and size as before it was minimized (Figure 1-16). In addition, the My Computer window is the active window because it contains the dark blue title bar and the My Computer button on the taskbar is indented.

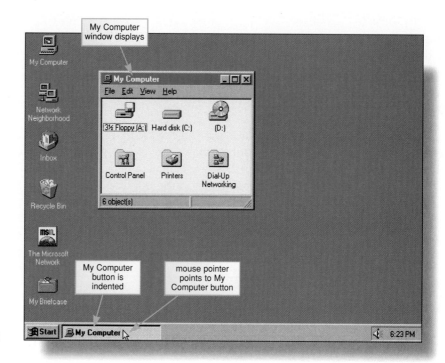

FIGURE 1-16

Whenever a window is minimized, it does not display on the desktop but a non-indented button for the window does display on the taskbar. Whenever you want a window that has been minimized to display and be the active window, click the window's button on the taskbar.

Maximize and Restore Buttons

The **Maximize button** maximizes a window so the window fills the entire screen, making it easier to see the contents of the window. When a window is maximized, the **Restore button** replaces the Maximize button on the title bar. Clicking the Restore button will return the window to its size before maximizing. To maximize and restore the My Computer window, complete the following steps.

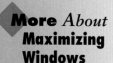

More *About* Maximizing Windows

Many application programs run in a maximized window by default. Often you will find that you want to work with maximized windows.

 Steps To Maximize and Restore a Window

1 **Point to the Maximize button on the title bar of the My Computer window.**

The mouse pointer points to the Maximize button on the title bar of the My Computer window (Figure 1-17).

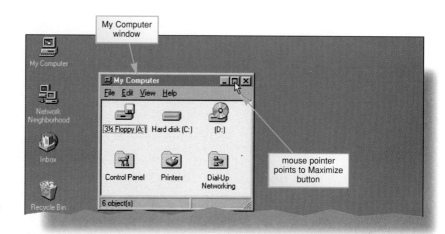

FIGURE 1-17

2 **Click the Maximize button.**

The My Computer window expands so it and the taskbar fill the entire screen (Figure 1-18). The Restore button replaces the Maximize button. The My Computer button on the taskbar does not change. The My Computer window is still the active window.

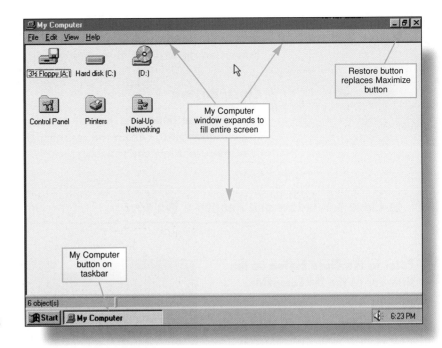

FIGURE 1-18

3 **Point to the Restore button on the title bar of the My Computer window.**

The mouse pointer points to the Restore button on the title bar of the My Computer window (Figure 1-19).

FIGURE 1-19

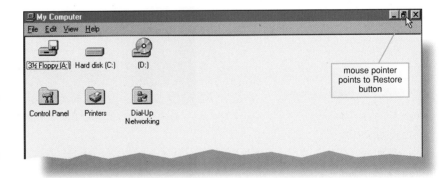

4 **Click the Restore button.**

The My Computer window returns to the size and position it occupied before being maximized (Figure 1-20). The My Computer button on the taskbar does not change. The Maximize button replaces the Restore button.

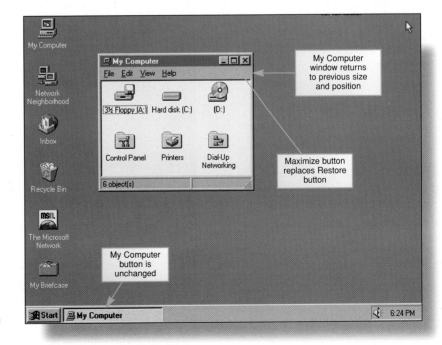

FIGURE 1-20

More *About* the Close Button

The Close button is a new innovation for Windows 95. In previous versions of Windows, the user had to either double-click a button or click a command from a menu to close the window.

When a window is maximized, you can also minimize the window by clicking the Minimize button. If, after minimizing the window, you click the window button on the taskbar, the window will return to its maximized size.

Close Button

The **Close button** on the title bar of a window closes the window and removes the window button from the taskbar. To close and then reopen the My Computer window, complete the following steps.

Steps To Close a Window and Reopen a Window

1 Point to the Close button on the title bar of the My Computer window.

The mouse pointer points to the Close button on the title bar of the My Computer window (Figure 1-21).

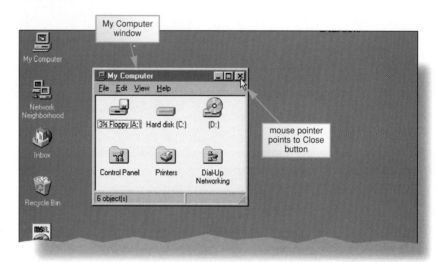

FIGURE 1-21

2 Click the Close button.

The My Computer window closes and the My Computer button no longer displays on the taskbar (Figure 1-22).

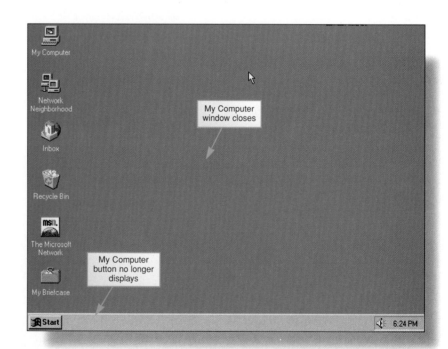

FIGURE 1-22

③ Point to and double-click the My Computer icon on the desktop.

The My Computer window opens and displays on the screen (Figure 1-23). The My Computer button displays on the taskbar.

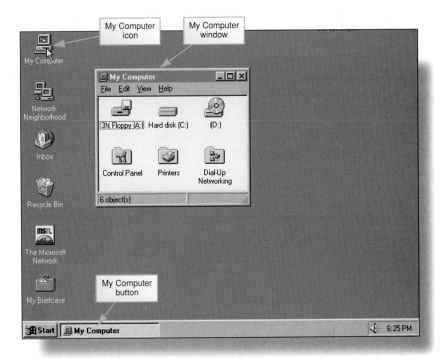

FIGURE 1-23

Drag

Drag means you point to an item, hold down the left mouse button, move the item to the desired location on the screen, and then release the left mouse button. You can move any open window to another location on the desktop by pointing to the title bar of the window and dragging the window. To drag the My Computer window, perform the following steps.

  Steps **To Move an Object by Dragging**

① Point to the My Computer window title bar.

The mouse pointer points to the My Computer window title bar (Figure 1-24).

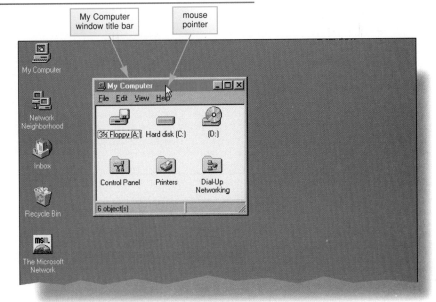

FIGURE 1-24

2 Hold down the left mouse button and then move the mouse so the window outline moves to the center of the desktop (do not release the left mouse button).

As you drag the My Computer window, Windows 95 displays an outline of the window (Figure 1-25). The outline, which can be positioned anywhere on the desktop, specifies where the window will display when you release the left mouse button.

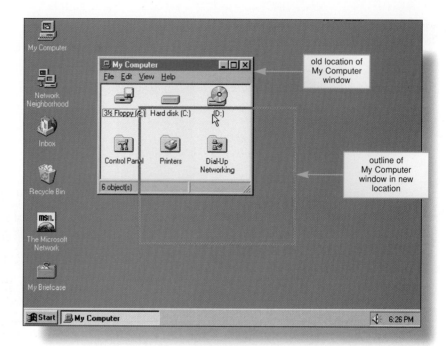

FIGURE 1-25

3 Release the left mouse button.

Windows 95 moves the My Computer window to the location the outline occupied prior to releasing the left mouse button (Figure 1-26).

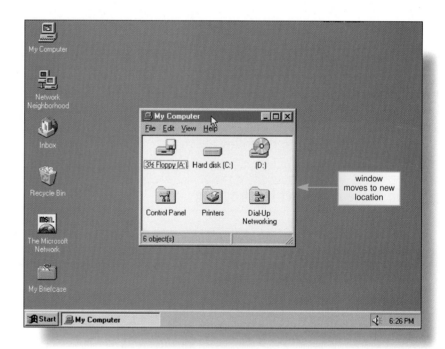

FIGURE 1-26

Sizing a Window by Dragging

You can use dragging for more than just moving an item or object. For example, you can drag the border of a window to change the size of the window. To change the size of the My Computer window, complete the following step.

 Steps **To Size a Window by Dragging**

1 **Position the mouse pointer over the lower right corner of the My Computer window until the mouse pointer changes to a two-headed arrow. Drag the lower right corner upward and to the left until the window on your desktop resembles the window in Figure 1-27.**

As you drag the lower right corner, the My Computer window changes size and a vertical scroll bar displays (Figure 1-27). A scroll bar is a bar that displays at the right edge and/or bottom edge of a window when the window contents are not completely visible. A vertical scroll bar contains an up scroll arrow, a down scroll arrow, and a scroll box.

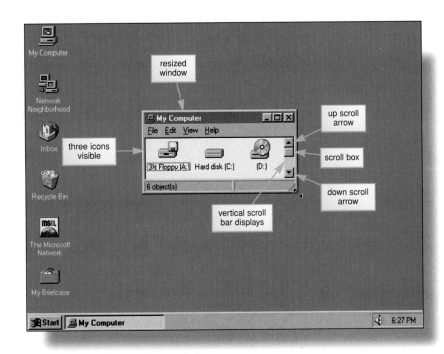

FIGURE 1-27

More *About*
Window Sizing

Windows 95 remembers the size of a window when you close the window. When you reopen the window, it will display in the same size as when you closed it.

The size of the scroll box in any window is dependent on the amount of the window that is not visible. The smaller the scroll box, the more of the window that is not visible. In addition to dragging a corner of a window, you can also drag any of the borders of a window.

Scrolling in a Window

You can use the scroll bar to view the contents of a window that are not visible. Scrolling can be accomplished in three ways: click the scroll arrows; click the scroll bar; and drag the scroll box.

To display the contents of the My Computer window by scrolling using scroll arrows, complete the steps on the next page.

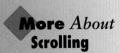

More *About*
Scrolling

Most people will either maximize a window or size it so all the objects in the window are visible to avoid scrolling because scrolling takes time. It is more efficient not to have to scroll in a window.

Steps To Scroll a Window Using Scroll Arrows

1 **Point to the down scroll arrow on the vertical scroll bar.**

The mouse pointer points to the down scroll arrow on the scroll bar (Figure 1-28).

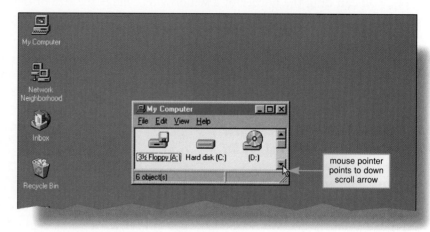

FIGURE 1-28

2 **Click the down scroll arrow one time.**

The window scrolls down (the icons move up in the window) and displays the tops of icons not previously visible (Figure 1-29). Because the window size does not change when you scroll, the contents of the window will change, as seen in the difference between Figure 1-28 and Figure 1-29.

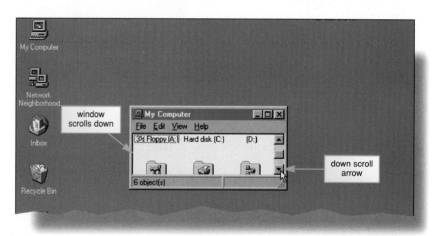

FIGURE 1-29

3 **Click the down scroll arrow two more times.**

The scroll box moves to the bottom of the scroll bar and the icons in the last row of the window display (Figure 1-30).

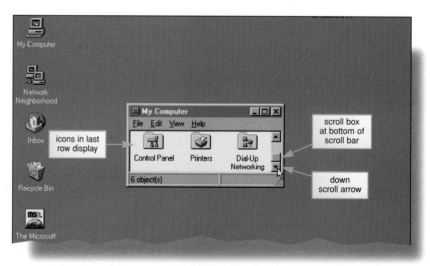

FIGURE 1-30

You can continuously scroll through a window using scroll arrows by clicking the up or down scroll arrow and holding down the left mouse button. The window continues to scroll until you release the left mouse button or you reach the top or bottom of the window.

You can also scroll by clicking the scroll bar itself. When you click the scroll bar, the window moves up or down a greater distance than when you click the scroll arrows.

A third way in which you can scroll through a window to view the window's contents is by dragging the scroll box. When you drag the scroll box, the window moves up or down as you drag.

Being able to view the contents of a window by scrolling is an important Windows 95 skill because the entire contents of a window may not be visible.

Resizing a Window

You might want to return a window to its original size. To return the My Computer window to about its original size, complete the following steps.

TO RESIZE A WINDOW

Step 1: Position the mouse pointer over the lower right corner of the My Computer window border until the mouse pointer changes to a two-headed arrow.

Step 2: Drag the lower right corner of the My Computer window until the window is the same size as shown in Figure 1-26 on page WIN 1.18, and then release the mouse button.

The My Computer window is about the same size as before you changed it.

Closing a Window

After you have completed your work in a window, normally you will close the window. To close the My Computer window, complete the following steps.

TO CLOSE A WINDOW

Step 1: Point to the Close button on the right of the title bar in the My Computer window.

Step 2: Click the Close button.

The My Computer window closes and the desktop contains no open windows.

Right-Drag

Right-drag means you point to an item, hold down the right mouse button, move the item to the desired location, and then release the right mouse button. When you right-drag an object, a context-sensitive menu displays. The context-sensitive menu contains commands specifically for use with the object being dragged. To right-drag the My Briefcase icon to the center of the desktop, perform the steps on the next page. If the My Briefcase icon does not display on your desktop, you will be unable to perform Step 1 through Step 3 on the next page.

◆ **M**ore *About*
the Scroll Bar

In many application programs, clicking the scroll bar will move the window a full screen's worth of information up or down. You can step through a word processing document screen by screen, for example, by clicking the scroll bar.

◆ **M**ore *About*
the Scroll Box

Dragging the scroll box is the most efficient technique to scroll long distances. In many application programs, such as Microsoft Word 7, as you scroll using the scroll box, the page number of the document displays next to the scroll box.

◆ **M**ore *About*
Scrolling Guidelines

General scrolling guidelines: (1) To scroll short distances (line by line), click the scroll arrows; (2) To scroll one screen at a time, click the scroll bar; (3) To scroll long distances, drag the scroll box.

Steps To Right-Drag

1 **Point to the My Briefcase icon on the desktop, hold down the right mouse button, drag the icon diagonally toward the center of the desktop, and then release the right mouse button.**

The dragged My Briefcase ghosted icon and a context-sensitive menu display in the center of the desktop (Figure 1-31). The My Briefcase icon remains at its original location on the left of the screen. The context-sensitive menu contains four commands: Move Here, Copy Here, Create Shortcut(s) Here, and Cancel. The Move Here command in bold (dark) type identifies what happens if you were to drag the My Briefcase icon with the left mouse button.

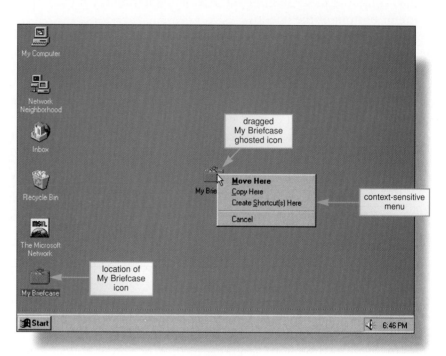

FIGURE 1-31

2 **Point to Cancel on the context-sensitive menu.**

The mouse pointer points to Cancel on the context-sensitive menu (Figure 1-32). The Cancel command is highlighted.

3 **Click Cancel on the context-sensitive menu.**

The context-sensitive menu and the dragged My Briefcase icon disappear from the screen.

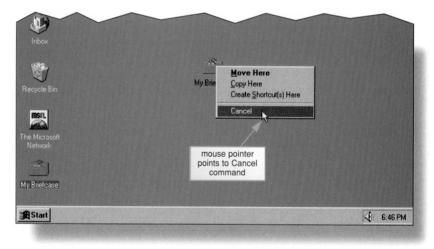

FIGURE 1-32

More About Right-Dragging

Right-dragging was not even available on earlier versions of Windows, so you might find people familiar with Windows not even considering right-dragging. Because it always produces a context-sensitive menu, however, right-dragging is the safest way to drag.

Whenever you begin an operation but do not want to complete the operation, click Cancel on a context-sensitive menu or click the Cancel button in a dialog box. The Cancel command will reset anything you have done.

If you click Move Here on the context-sensitive menu shown in Figure 1-31, Windows 95 will move the icon from its current location to the new location. If you click the Copy Here command, the icon will be copied to the new location and two icons will display on the desktop. Windows 95 automatically will give the second icon and the associated file a different name. If you click the Create Shortcut(s) Here command, a special object called a shortcut will be created.

Although you can move icons by dragging with the primary (left) mouse button and by right-dragging with the secondary (right) mouse button, it is strongly suggested you right-drag because a menu displays and you can specify the exact operation you want to occur. When you drag using the left mouse button, a default operation takes place and the operation may not do what you want.

The Keyboard and Keyboard Shortcuts

FIGURE 1-33a

The **keyboard** is an input device on which you manually key, or type, data. Figure 1-33a shows the enhanced IBM 101-key keyboard and Figure 1-33b shows a Microsoft keyboard designed specifically for use with Windows 95. Many tasks you accomplish with a mouse also can be accomplished using a keyboard.

To perform tasks using the keyboard, you must understand the notation used to identify which keys to press. This notation is used throughout Windows 95 to identify **keyboard shortcuts**.

Keyboard shortcuts consist of: (1) pressing a single key (example: press F1); or, (2) holding down one key and pressing a second key, as shown by two key names separated with a plus sign (example: press CTRL+ESC). For example, to obtain Help about Windows 95, you can press the F1 key. To open the Start menu, hold down the CTRL key and press the ESC key (press CTRL+ESC).

Often, computer users will use keyboard shortcuts for operations they perform frequently. For example, many users find pressing the F1 key to start

FIGURE 1-33b

Windows 95 Help easier than using the Start menu as shown later in this project. As a user, you will likely find your own combination of keyboard and mouse operations that particularly suit you, but it is strongly recommended that generally you use the mouse.

Creating a Document by Starting an Application Program

A **program** is a set of computer instructions that carries out a task on your computer. An **application program** is a program that allows you to accomplish a specific task for which that program is designed. For example, a word processing program is an application program that allows you to create written documents, a spreadsheet program is an application program that allows you to create spreadsheets and charts, and a presentation graphics application program allows you to create graphic presentations for display on a computer or as slides.

More *About*
Application Programs

Some application programs, such as Notepad, are part of Windows 95. Most application programs, however, such as Microsoft Office 95, Lotus SmartSuite 96, and others must be purchased separately from Windows 95.

The most common activity on a computer is to run an application program to accomplish tasks using the computer. You can start an application program by using the Start button on the taskbar.

To illustrate the use of an application program to create a written document, assume each morning you create a daily reminders list so you will remember the tasks you must accomplish throughout the day. You print the document containing the reminders for your use. On occasion, you must update the daily reminders list as events occur during the day. You have decided to use **Notepad**, a popular application program available with Windows 95, to create your list.

To create the list, one method you can use with Windows 95 is to start the Notepad application program using the Start button on the taskbar. After the Notepad program is started, you can enter your daily reminders.

To start the Notepad program, perform the following steps.

Steps **To Start a Program**

1 **Click the Start button on the taskbar. Point to Programs on the Start menu. Point to Accessories on the Programs submenu. If you happen to point to another command on one of the menus or submenus, a different submenu might display. Merely move the mouse so it points to Programs and then Accessories to display the correct menu and submenus.**

Windows 95 opens the Start menu, the Programs submenu, and the Accessories submenu (Figure 1-34). The mouse pointer points to Accessories on the Programs submenu. The Accessories submenu contains the Notepad command to start the Notepad program. Notice that whenever you point to a menu name that has a right arrow following it, a submenu displays. You might find more, fewer, or different commands on the submenus on your computer.

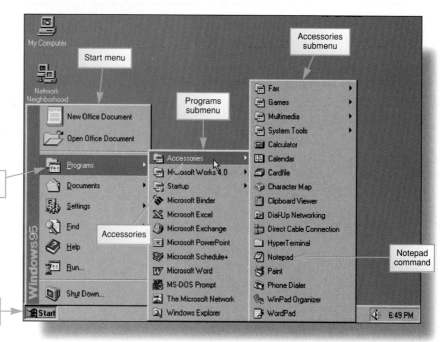

FIGURE 1-34

2 Point to Notepad on the Accessories submenu.

When the mouse pointer points to Notepad on the Accessories submenu, the Notepad command is highlighted (Figure 1-35).

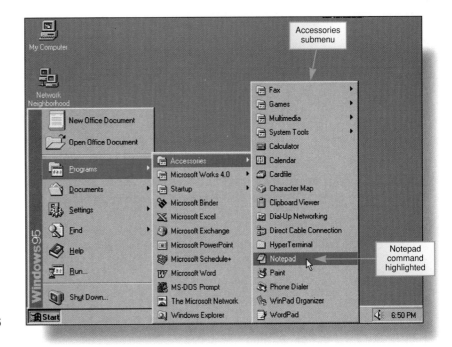

FIGURE 1-35

3 Click Notepad.

Windows 95 starts the Notepad program by opening the Notepad window on the desktop and adding an indented Notepad button to the taskbar (Figure 1-36). Notepad is the active window (dark blue title bar). The word Untitled in the window title (Untitled - Notepad) and on the Notepad button indicates the document has not been saved on disk. The menu bar contains the following menu names: File, Edit, Search, and Help. The area below the menu bar contains an insertion point and two scroll bars. The **insertion point** *is a flashing vertical line that indicates the point at which text typed on the keyboard will be displayed. The scroll bars do not contain scroll boxes, indicating the document is not large enough to allow scrolling.*

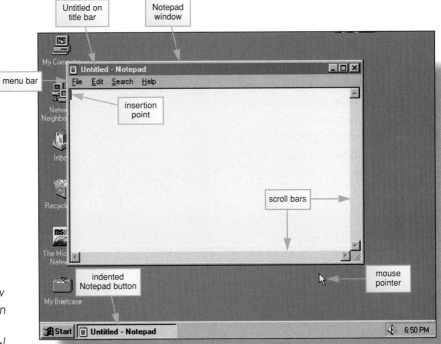

FIGURE 1-36

OtherWays

1. Right-click desktop, point to New, click Text Document, double-click the New Text Document icon
2. Click Start button, click Run, type Notepad, click OK button
3. Press CTRL+ESC, press R, type Notepad, press ENTER key

After you have started an application program such as Notepad, you can use the program to prepare your document.

Windows 95 provides a number of ways in which to accomplish a particular task. When a task is illustrated by a series of steps in this book, those steps may not be the only way in which the task can be done. If you can accomplish the same task using other methods, the Other Ways box specifies the other methods. In each case, the method shown in the steps is the preferred method, but it is important you are aware of all the techniques you can use.

Creating a Document

To create a document in Notepad, you must type the text you want in the document. After typing a line of text, press the ENTER key to indicate the end of the line. If you press the ENTER key when the insertion point is on a line by itself, Notepad inserts a blank line in the document. To create the Daily Reminders document, perform the following step.

Steps **To Create a Document**

1 **Type** Daily Reminders - Wednesday **and press the ENTER key twice. Type** 1. Call Tim Hoyle - Photoshop retouch due **and press the ENTER key. Type** 2. Memo to Linda Tomms - Meeting next week **and press the ENTER key. Type** 3. Lunch with Harris - Noon, Remmington's **and press the ENTER key.**

The first five lines of the document are entered (Figure 1-37). A blank line is inserted following the first line. The insertion point is positioned on the sixth line of the document.

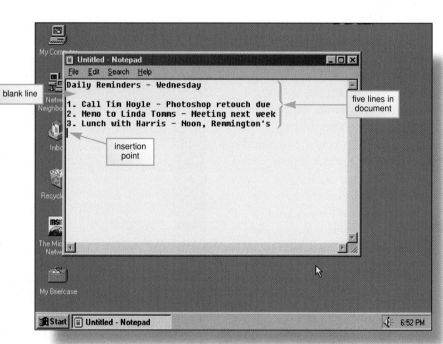

FIGURE 1-37

Saving a Document on Disk

When you create a document using a program such as Notepad, the document is stored in the main memory (RAM) of your computer. If you close the program without saving the document or if your computer accidentally loses electrical power, the document will be lost. To protect against the accidental loss of a document and to allow you to easily modify the document in the future, you can save the document on disk.

When you save a document, you must assign a filename to the document. All documents are identified by a filename. Typical filenames are Daily Reminders - Wednesday, Mileage Log, and Automobile Maintenance. A filename can contain up to 255 characters, including spaces. Any uppercase or lowercase character is valid when creating a filename, except a backslash (\), slash (/), colon (:), asterisk (*), question mark (?), quotation mark ("), less than symbol (<), greater than symbol (>), or vertical bar (|). Filenames cannot be CON, AUX, COM1, COM2, COM3, COM4, LPT1, LPT2, LPT3, PRN, or NUL.

To associate a document with an application, Windows 95 assigns an extension of a period and up to three characters to each document. All documents created using the Notepad program, which are text documents, are saved with the .TXT extension. To save the document you created using Notepad on a floppy disk in drive A of your computer using the filename, Daily Reminders - Wednesday, perform the following steps.

 Steps **To Save a Document on Disk**

1 **Insert a formatted floppy disk into drive A on your computer. Click File on the menu bar.**

Windows 95 highlights the File menu name on the menu bar and opens the File menu in the Notepad window (Figure 1-38). The mouse pointer points to File on the menu bar.

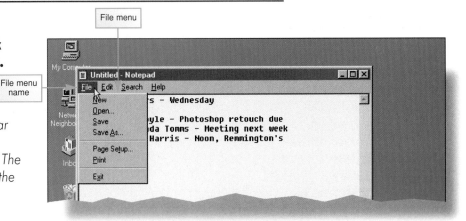

FIGURE 1-38

2 **Point to Save As on the File menu.**

*The mouse pointer points to the Save As command on the File menu (Figure 1-39). The ellipsis (...) following the Save As command indicates Windows 95 requires more information to carry out the Save As command and will open a dialog box when you click Save As. A **dialog box** displays whenever Windows 95 needs to supply information to you or wants you to enter information or select among several options.*

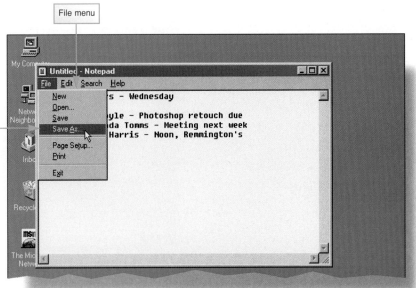

FIGURE 1-39

3 Click Save As.

*Windows 95 displays the Save As dialog box (Figure 1-40). The Save As dialog box becomes the active window (dark blue title bar) and the Notepad window becomes the **inactive window** (light blue title bar). The Save As dialog box contains the Save in drop-down list box. A **drop-down list box** is a rectangular box containing text and a down arrow on the right. The Save in drop-down list box displays the Desktop icon and Desktop name. The entry in the Save in drop-down list box indicates where the file will be stored. At the bottom of the dialog box is the File name text box. A **text box** is a rectangular area in which you can enter text. The File name text box contains the highlighted entry, Untitled. When you type the filename from the keyboard, the filename will replace the highlighted entry in the File name text box.*

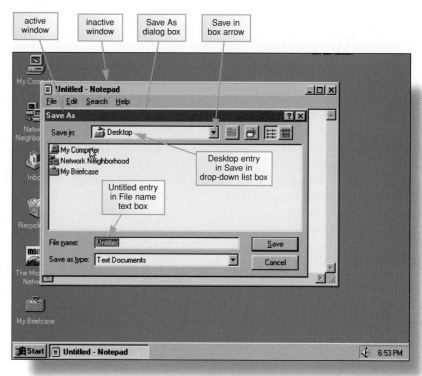

FIGURE 1-40

4 Type Daily Reminders - Wednesday in the File name text box. Point to the Save in box arrow.

The filename, Daily Reminders – Wednesday, and an insertion point display in the File name text box (Figure 1-41). When you save this document, Notepad will automatically add the .TXT extension. The mouse pointer points to the Save in box arrow.

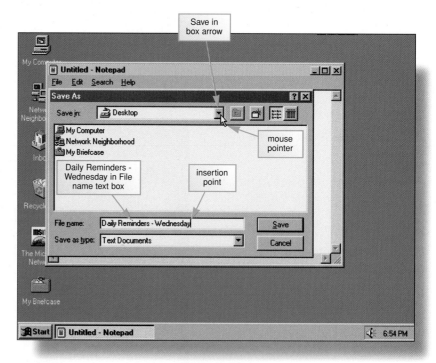

FIGURE 1-41

5 Click the Save in box arrow and then point to the 3½ Floppy [A:] icon.

Windows 95 displays the Save in drop-down list (Figure 1-42). The list contains various elements of your computer, including the Desktop, My Computer, Network Neighborhood, and My Briefcase. Within My Computer are 3½ Floppy [A:], Hard disk [C:], and [D:]. When you point to the 3½ Floppy [A:] icon, the entry in the list is highlighted.

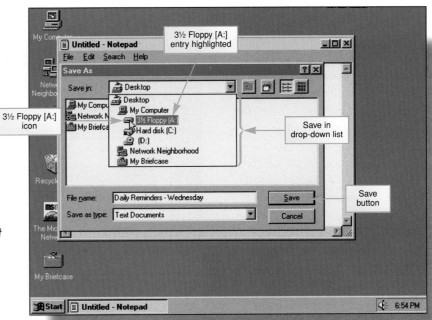

FIGURE 1-42

6 Click the 3½ Floppy [A:] icon and then point to the Save button.

The 3½ Floppy [A:] entry displays in the Save in drop-down list box (Figure 1-43). This specifies that the file will be saved on the floppy disk in drive A using the filename specified in the File name text box. The mouse pointer points to the Save button.

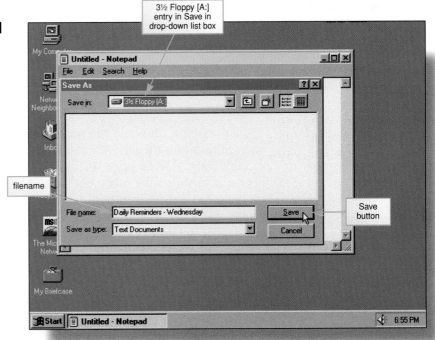

FIGURE 1-43

⑦ Click the Save button.

*Windows 95 displays an **hourglass icon** while saving the Daily Reminders - Wednesday document on the floppy disk in drive A, closes the Save As dialog box, makes the Notepad window the active window, and inserts the filename on the Notepad window title bar and on the button on the taskbar (Figure 1-44). The filename on the title bar may or may not display the .TXT extension, depending on the setting on your computer. The hourglass icon indicates Windows 95 requires a brief interval of time to save the document. The filename on the button on the taskbar (Daily Reminders - We...) contains an ellipsis to indicate the entire button name does not fit on the button. To display the entire button name for a button on the taskbar, point to the button.*

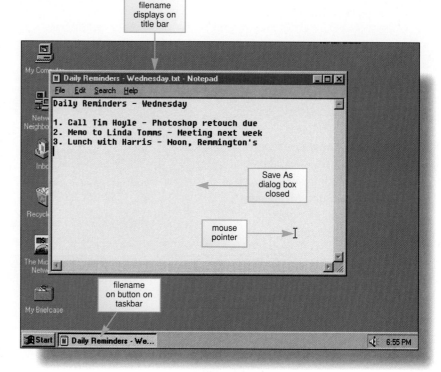

FIGURE 1-44

The method shown in the previous steps for saving a file on a floppy disk can be used to save a file on a hard disk, such as drive C, or even on the desktop.

In Figure 1-38 on page WIN 1.27, the File menu displays. Once you have opened a menu on the menu bar, you need merely point to another menu name on the menu bar to open that menu. Thus, in Figure 1-38, if you point to Edit on the menu bar, the Edit menu will display. If you accidentally move the mouse pointer off the menu you want to display, point back to the menu name to display the desired menu. To close a menu without carrying out a command, click anywhere on the desktop except on the menu.

Printing a Document

Quite often, after creating a document and saving it, you will want to print it. Printing can be accomplished directly from an application program. To print the Daily Reminders – Wednesday document, perform the following steps.

Steps **To Print a Document**

1 **Click File on the menu bar and then point to Print on the File menu.**

The File menu displays and the mouse pointer points to the Print command (Figure 1-45). As with all menu commands when you point to them, the Print command is highlighted. **FIGURE 1-45**

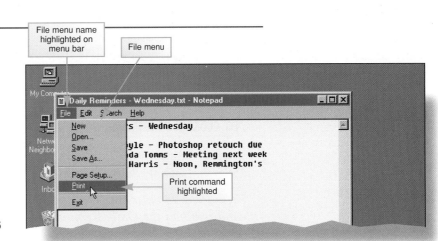

2 **Click Print.**

A Notepad dialog box briefly displays with a message that indicates the Daily Reminders document is being printed (Figure 1-46). The dialog box disappears after the report has been printed. To cancel printing, you can click the Cancel button. The printed report is shown in Figure 1-47. Notepad automatically places the filename at the top of the page and a page number at the bottom of the page.

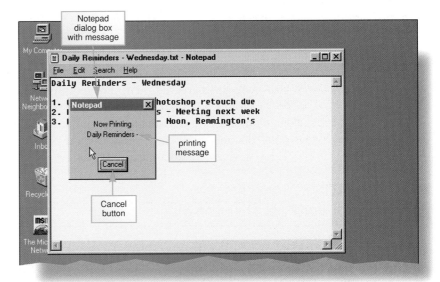

FIGURE 1-46

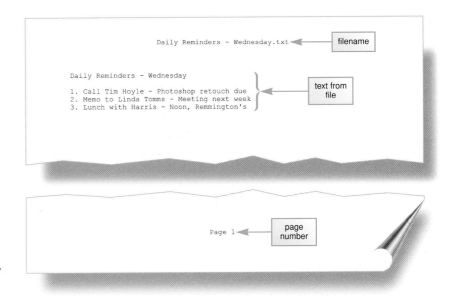

FIGURE 1-47

Closing a Program

After creating the Daily Reminders – Wednesday document, saving the document on the floppy disk in drive A, and printing it, your use of the Notepad program is complete. Therefore, the Notepad program should be closed by performing the following steps.

TO CLOSE A PROGRAM

Step 1: Point to the Close button on the Notepad title bar.
Step 2: Click the Close button.

Windows 95 closes the Daily Reminders – Wednesday.txt – Notepad window and removes the Daily Reminders – Wednesday.txt – Notepad button from the taskbar.

Modifying a Document Stored on Disk

Many documents you create will need to be modified at some point in time after you have created them. For example, the Daily Reminders - Wednesday document should be modified each time you determine another task to be done. To modify an existing document, you can start the application program and open the document. To start the Notepad program and open the Daily Reminders – Wednesday document, complete the following steps.

Steps To Open a Document Stored on Disk

1 **Click the Start button on the taskbar. Point to Programs. Point to Accessories. Point to Notepad.**

The Start menu, Programs sub-menu, and Accessories submenu display (Figure 1-48). The mouse pointer points to the Notepad command.

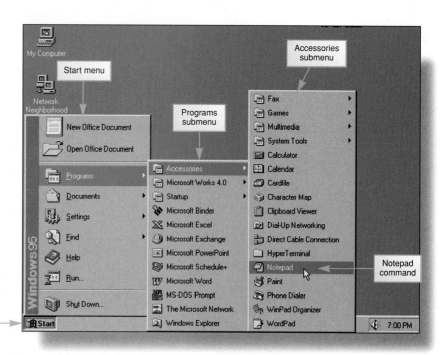

FIGURE 1-48

2 **Click Notepad. When the Notepad window opens, click File on the menu bar and then point to Open on the File menu.**

Windows 95 starts the Notepad program (Figure 1-49). The Untitled – Notepad button on the taskbar indicates no document has been opened. The File menu displays and the mouse pointer points to the Open command.

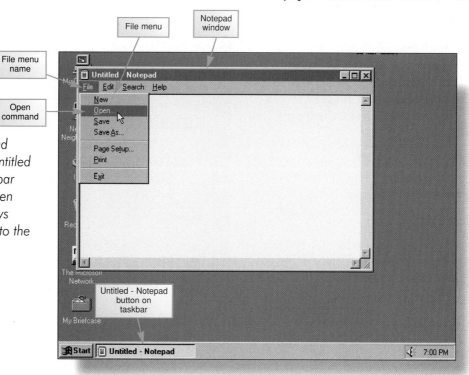

FIGURE 1-49

3 **Click Open. Click the Look in box arrow. Point to the 3½ Floppy [A:] icon.**

Windows 95 displays the Open dialog box (Figure 1-50). When you click the Look in box arrow, the Look in drop-down list displays. The mouse pointer points to the 3½ Floppy [A:] icon. The 3½ Floppy [A:] entry is highlighted.

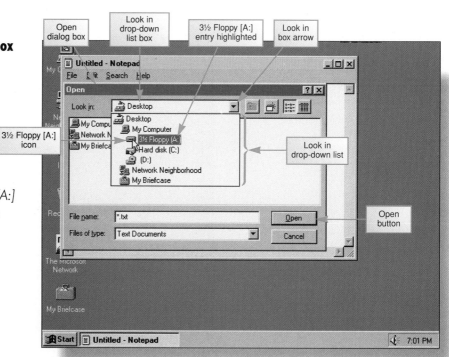

FIGURE 1-50

4 Click the 3½ Floppy [A:] icon. When the filenames display in the window, click Daily Reminders – Wednesday.txt and then point to the Open button.

Windows 95 places the 3½ Floppy [A:] icon and entry in the Look in drop-down list box, indicating that the file to be opened is found on the floppy disk in drive A (Figure 1-51). The names of folders and/or text document files stored on the floppy disk in drive A are displayed in the window below the Look in drop-down list box. The Daily Reminders - Wednesday.txt file is selected, as indicated by the highlight, and the mouse pointer points to the Open button. Notice that the Daily Reminders – Wednesday.txt filename displays in the File name text box, indicating this is the file that will be opened.

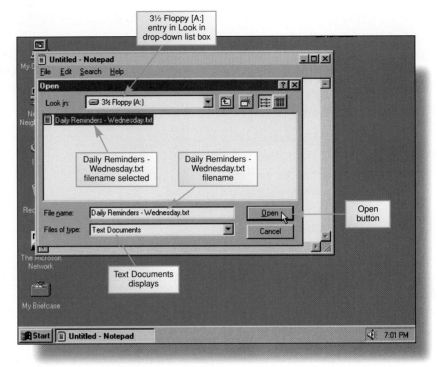

FIGURE 1-51

5 Click the Open button.

Windows 95 opens the Daily Reminders – Wednesday.txt file and displays it in the Notepad window (Figure 1-52). The filename displays on the title bar of the Notepad window and on the button on the taskbar.

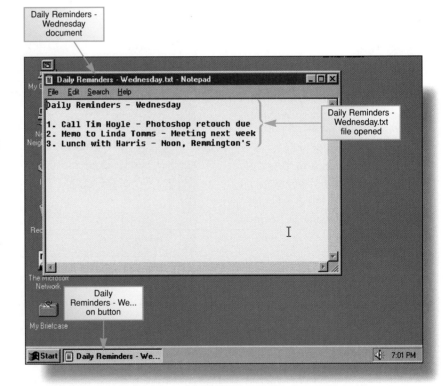

FIGURE 1-52

After opening the Daily Reminders – Wednesday document, perform the following step to modify the document by adding another line.

TO MODIFY A DOCUMENT

Step 1: Press the DOWN ARROW key five times, type 4. E-Mail Sue Wells - Adobe Illustrator drawing as the new line, and then press the ENTER key.

After modifying the Daily Reminders – Wednesday document, you should save the modified document on the floppy disk in drive A using the same file-name. To save the modified document on the disk, complete the following steps.

Steps To Save a Modified Document on Disk

1 **Click File on the menu bar and then point to Save.**

The File menu opens and the mouse pointer points to the Save command (Figure 1-53). The Save command is used to save a file that has already been created.

2 **Click Save.**

The modified document is stored on the floppy disk in drive A and the Notepad window remains open. Whenever you use the Save command, the document is stored using the same filename in the same location from which it was opened.

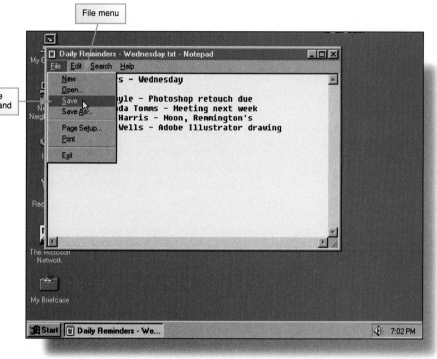

FIGURE 1-53

If you want to print the modified document, click File on the menu bar and then click Print on the File menu in the same manner as shown in Figure 1-45 and Figure 1-46 on page WIN 1.31.

OtherWays

1. Press ALT+F, press S

Closing the Notepad Program

After modifying the document and storing the modified document on the floppy disk in drive A, normally you will close the Notepad program. To close the Notepad program, complete the step on the next page.

TO CLOSE A PROGRAM

Step 1: Click the Close button on the right of the Notepad title bar.

The Notepad window closes and the Notepad button on the taskbar disappears.

Modifying an existing document is a common occurrence and should be well understood when using Windows 95.

Using Windows Help

One of the more powerful application programs for use in Windows 95 is Windows Help. Windows Help is available when using Windows 95, or when using any application program running under Windows 95, to assist you in using Windows 95 and the various application programs. It contains answers to virtually any question you can ask with respect to Windows 95.

Contents Sheet

Windows 95 Help provides a variety of ways in which to obtain information. One method to find a Help topic involves using the Contents sheet to browse through Help topics by category. To illustrate this method, you will use Windows 95 Help to determine how to find a topic in Help. To start Help, complete the following steps.

Steps **To Start Help**

1 **Click the Start button on the taskbar. Point to Help on the Start menu.**

Windows 95 opens the Start menu (Figure 1-54). Because the mouse pointer points to the Help command, the Help command is highlighted.

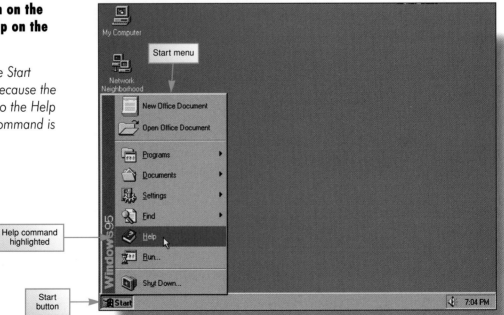

FIGURE 1-54

2 **Click Help on the Start menu. If the Contents sheet does not display, click the Contents tab.**

Windows 95 opens the Help Topics: Windows Help window (Figure 1-55). The window contains three tabs (Contents, Index, and Find). The Contents sheet is visible in the window. Clicking either the Index tab or the Find tab opens the Index or Find sheet, respectively. The Contents sheet contains two Help topics preceded by a question mark icon and five books. Each book consists of a closed book icon followed by a book name. The first Help topic, Tour: Ten minutes to using Windows, is highlighted. Three command buttons (Display, Print, and Cancel) display at the bottom of the window.

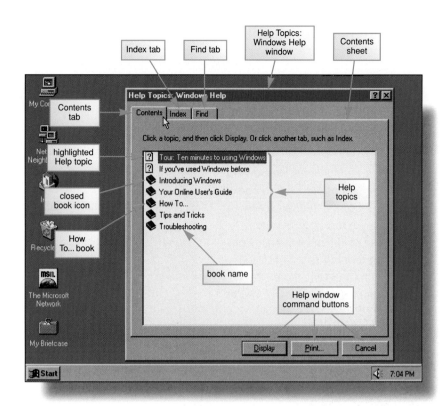

FIGURE 1-55

In the Help window shown in Figure 1-55, the closed book icon indicates Help topics or more books are contained within the book. The question mark icon indicates a Help topic without any further subdivisions.

In addition to starting Help by using the Start button, you can also start Help by pressing the F1 key.

After starting Help, the next step is to find the topic in which you are interested. To find the topic that describes how to find a topic in Help, complete the steps on the next two pages.

OtherWays

1. Press F1, press CTRL+TAB or CTRL+SHIFT+TAB to highlight desired sheet

Steps To Use Help to Find a Topic in Help

1 **Double-click How To... in the Help Topics: Windows Help window. Point to the Use Help closed book.**

Windows 95 highlights the How To book and opens the How To book (Figure 1-56). The ellipsis following the How To book indicates additional books will display when you open the book. The list of closed book icons indicates more Help information is available. The mouse pointer points to the Use Help closed book icon. The Close button in Figure 1-56 replaces the Display button in Figure 1-55. If you click the Close button, the How To book will close and the list of books below the How To book disappears.

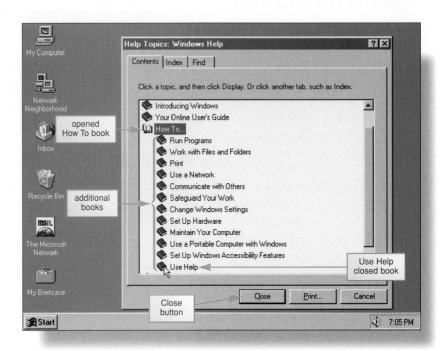

FIGURE 1-56

2 **Double-click the Use Help closed book icon and then point to Finding a topic in Help in the opened Use Help book.**

Windows 95 opens the Use Help book and displays several Help topics in the book (Figure 1-57). The mouse pointer points to Finding a topic in Help.

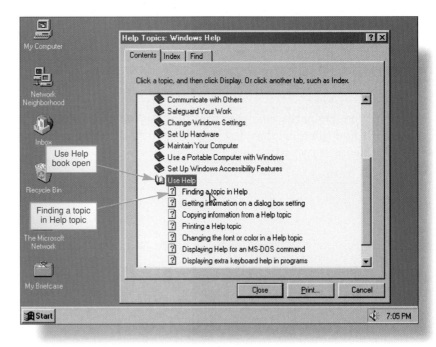

FIGURE 1-57

3 **Double-click Finding a topic in Help.**

Windows 95 closes the Help Topics: Windows Help window and opens the Windows Help window (Figure 1-58). The window contains three buttons (Help Topics, Back, and Options), steps to find a topic in Help, and a Tip. The Windows Help button displays on the taskbar.

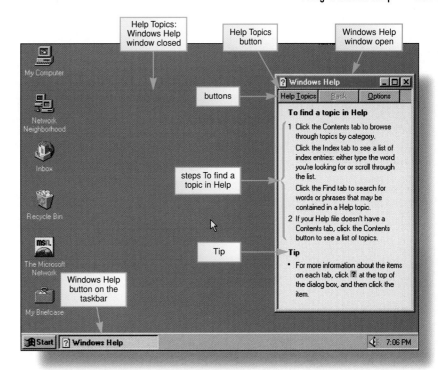

FIGURE 1-58

4 **After reading the information in the Windows Help window, click the Help Topics button in the Windows Help window.**

The Help Topics: Windows Help window displays together with the Windows Help window (Figure 1-59).

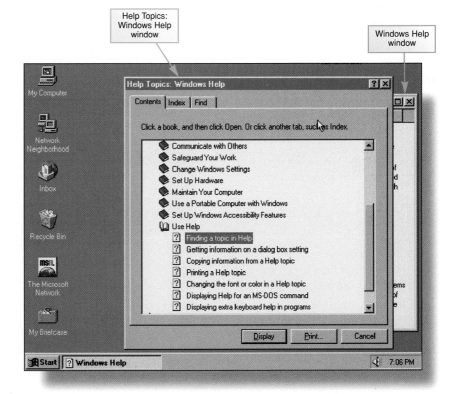

FIGURE 1-59

> ### Other**Ways**
>
> 1. Press DOWN ARROW until book or topic highlighted, press ENTER, continue until Help topic displays, read Help topic, press T

More *About*
the Index Sheet

The Index sheet is probably the best source of information in Windows Help because you can enter the subject you are interested in. Sometimes, however, you will have to be creative to discover the index entry that answers your question because the most obvious entry will not always lead to your answer.

Clicking the Help Topics button in the Windows Help window will always display the Help Topics: Windows Help window.

In Figure 1-58 on the previous page, if you click the Back button in the Windows Help window (when the button is not dimmed), Windows 95 will display the previously displayed Help topic. Clicking the Options button in the Windows Help window allows you to annotate a Help topic, copy or print a Help topic, change the font and color scheme of Help windows, and control how Help windows display in relation to other windows on the desktop.

Notice also in Figure 1-58 that the Windows Help title bar contains a Minimize button, a Maximize button, and a Close button. You can minimize and maximize the Windows Help window, and you can also close the Windows Help window without returning to the Help Topics: Windows Help window.

Index Sheet

A second method to find answers to your questions about Windows 95 or application programs is the Index sheet. The **Index sheet** lists a large number of index entries, each of which references one or more Help screens. To learn more about Windows 95 basic skills by using the Index sheet, and to see an example of animation available with Help, complete the following steps.

Steps **To Use the Help Index Sheet**

1 **Click the Index tab. Type** basic skills **(the flashing insertion point is positioned in the text box). Point to the Display button.**

The Index sheet displays, including a list of entries that can be referenced (Figure 1-60). When you type an entry, the list automatically scrolls and the entry you type, such as basic skills, is highlighted. To see additional entries, use the scroll bar at the right of the list. To highlight an entry in the list, click the entry. On some computers, the basic skills entry may not be present. On those machines, select another topic of interest to you.

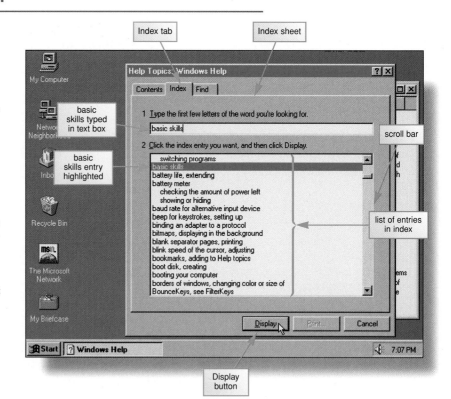

FIGURE 1-60

2 Click the Display button. Click the Maximize button in the Windows Help title bar. Point to the Sizing windows button.

The Windows Help window opens and a screen titled, The Basics, displays (Figure 1-61). The window is maximized and the Restore button displays in place of the Maximize button. The screen includes six buttons to learn Windows essentials and a picture of the Windows 95 desktop. When the mouse pointer is positioned on one of the buttons, it changes to a hand with a pointing finger. The Windows Help button displays on the taskbar.

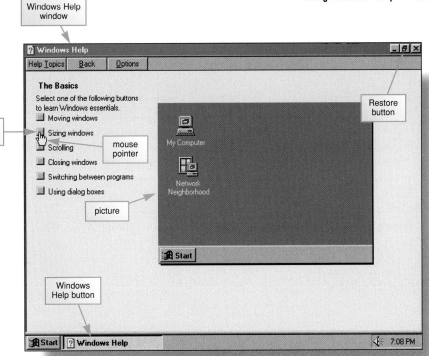

FIGURE 1-61

3 Click the Sizing windows button. Point to the Play button (the button with the right arrow) below the picture on the right.

The words, Sizing windows, display in bold, the My Computer window is added to the picture on the right, and the controls to play the animation display (Figure 1-62). The Play button will play the animation, the Option button displays a series of options regarding the animation, and the slide indicates progress when the animation plays. Text that explains how to accomplish the task, such as sizing windows, displays above the picture. On some computers, the animation might not be available. On those computers, instead of displaying the animation picture, the message, Unable to display graphic, will display on the screen. The text above the picture that explains how to perform the task still displays.

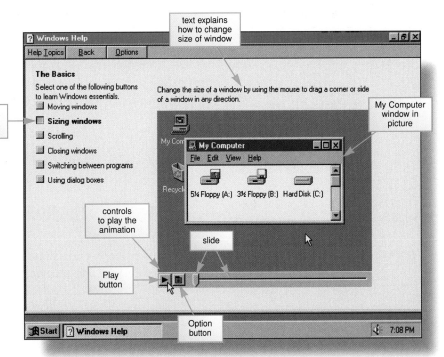

FIGURE 1-62

4 **Click the Play button if it displays on the screen.**

The Play button changes to a Stop button and the animation plays (Figure 1-63). The slide indicates the progress of the animation.

5 **When the animation is complete, click any buttons you wish to view other animations.**

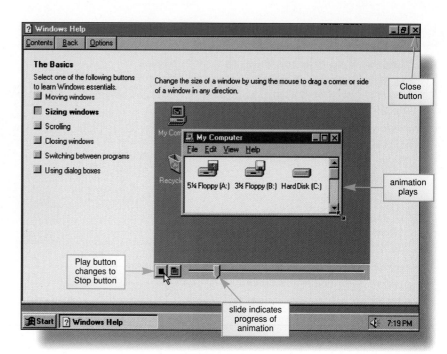

FIGURE 1-63

After viewing Help topics, normally you will close Windows Help. To close Windows Help, complete the following step.

TO CLOSE WINDOWS HELP

Step 1: Click the Close button on the title bar of the Windows Help window.

Windows 95 closes the Windows Help window.

Shutting Down Windows 95

After completing your work with Windows 95, you might want to shut down Windows 95 using the **Shut Down command** on the Start menu. If you are sure you want to shut down Windows 95, perform the steps on the next page. If you are not sure about shutting down Windows 95, read the following steps without actually performing them.

Steps **To Shut Down Windows 95**

1 **Click the Start button on the taskbar and then point to Shut Down on the Start menu.**

Windows 95 displays the Start menu (Figure 1-64). The Shut Down command is highlighted because the mouse pointer points to it.

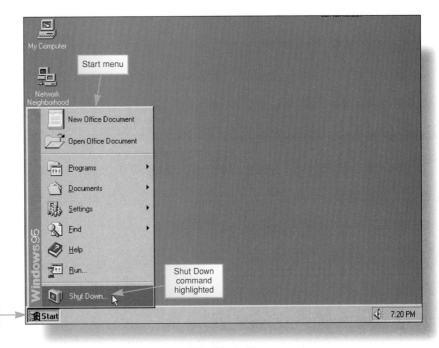

FIGURE 1-64

2 **Click Shut Down. Point to the Yes button in the Shut Down Windows dialog box.**

Windows 95 darkens the entire desktop and opens the Shut Down Windows dialog box (Figure 1-65). The dialog box contains four option buttons. The selected option button, Shut down the computer?, indicates that clicking the Yes button will shut down Windows 95.

3 **Click the Yes button.**

Two screens display while Windows 95 is shutting down. The first screen containing the text, Shutting down Windows, displays momentarily while Windows 95 is being shut down. Then, a second screen containing the text, It is okay to turn off your computer, displays. At this point you can to turn off your computer. When shutting down Windows 95, you should never turn off your computer before this last screen displays.

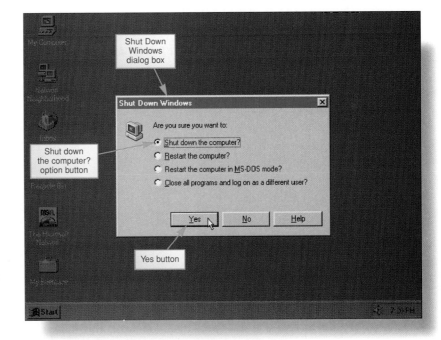

FIGURE 1-65

Other Ways

1. Press CTRL+ESC, press U, press UP ARROW or DOWN ARROW until option button selected, press ENTER

2. Press ALT+F4, press UP ARROW or DOWN ARROW until option button selected, press ENTER

If you accidentally click Shut Down on the Start menu and you do not want to shut down Windows 95, click the No button in the Shut Down Windows dialog box to return to normal Windows 95 operation.

Project Summary

Project 1 illustrated the Microsoft Windows 95 graphical user interface. You started Windows 95, learned the parts of the desktop, and learned to point, click, right-click, double-click, drag, and right-drag. You created a document by starting Notepad, entering text, saving the document on a floppy disk, and printing the document. You then modified the Notepad document and saved the modified document. Using both the Help Content and the Help Index sheets you obtained Help about Microsoft Windows 95. You shut down Windows 95 using the Shut Down command on the Start menu.

What You Should Know

Having completed this project, you should now be able to perform the following tasks:

▶ Close a Program *(WIN 1.32, WIN 1.36)*
▶ Close the Welcome Screen *(WIN 1.7)*
▶ Close a Window *(WIN 1.20)*
▶ Close a Window and Reopen a Window *(WIN 1.16)*
▶ Close Windows Help *(WIN 1.42)*
▶ Create a Document *(WIN 1.26)*
▶ Maximize and Restore a Window *(WIN 1.14)*
▶ Minimize and Redisplay a Window *(WIN 1.13)*
▶ Modify a Document *(WIN 1.35)*
▶ Move an Object by Dragging *(WIN 1.17)*
▶ Open a Document Stored on Disk *(WIN 1.32)*
▶ Open a Window by Double-Clicking *(WIN 1.12)*
▶ Point and Click *(WIN 1.9)*

▶ Print a Document *(WIN 1.31)*
▶ Resize a Window *(WIN 1.21)*
▶ Right-Click *(WIN 1.11)*
▶ Right-Drag *(WIN 1.22)*
▶ Save a Document on Disk *(WIN 1.27)*
▶ Save a Modified Document on Disk *(WIN 1.35)*
▶ Scroll a Window Using Scroll Arrows *(WIN 1.20)*
▶ Shut Down Windows 95 *(WIN 1.43)*
▶ Size a Window by Dragging *(WIN 1.19)*
▶ Start a Program *(WIN 1.24)*
▶ Start Help *(WIN 1.36)*
▶ Use Help to Find a Topic in Help *(WIN 1.38)*
▶ Use the Help Index Sheet *(WIN 1.40)*

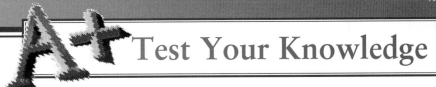

Test Your Knowledge

1 True/False

Instructions: Circle T if the statement is true or F if the statement is false.

T   F   1. A user interface is a combination of computer hardware and computer software.

T   F   2. Click means press the right mouse button.

T   F   3. When you drag an object on the desktop, Windows 95 displays a context-sensitive menu.

T   F   4. You can resize a window by dragging the title bar of the window.

T   F   5. Daily Reminders - Friday and Mileage Log are valid filenames.

T   F   6. To save a new document created using Notepad, click Save As on the File menu.

T   F   7. To print a document, click Print on the File menu.

T   F   8. To open a document stored on a floppy disk, click Open on the Start menu.

T   F   9. You can start Help by clicking the Start button and then clicking Help on the Start menu.

T   F   10. To find an item in the Windows Help Index, type the first few characters of the item in the text box on the Contents sheet.

2 Multiple Choice

Instructions: Circle the correct response.

1. Through a user interface, the user is able to _____.
   a. control the computer
   b. request information from the computer
   c. respond to messages displayed by the computer
   d. all of the above

2. A context-sensitive menu opens when you _____ a(n) _____.
   a. right-click, object
   b. click, menu name on the menu bar
   c. click, submenu
   d. double-click, indented button on the taskbar

3. In this book, a dark blue title bar and an indented button on the taskbar indicate a window is _____.
   a. inactive
   b. minimized
   c. closed
   d. active

4. To view contents of a window that are not currently visible in the window, use the _____.
   a. title bar
   b. scroll bar
   c. menu bar
   d. Restore button

(continued)

A+ Test Your Knowledge

Multiple Choice (*continued*)

5. _____ is holding down the right mouse button, moving an item to the desired location, and then releasing the right mouse button.
   a. Double-clicking
   b. Right-clicking
   c. Right-dragging
   d. Pointing

6. The Notepad command used to start the Notepad application program is located on the _____ (sub)menu.
   a. Start
   b. Accessories
   c. Programs
   d. Help

7. To quit the Notepad application and close its window, _____.
   a. click the Close button on the Notepad title bar
   b. click File on the menu bar
   c. double-click the Notepad title bar
   d. click the Minimize button on the Notepad title bar

8. To save a Notepad document after modifying the document, _____.
   a. click the Close button on the Notepad title bar
   b. click the Minimize button on the Notepad title bar
   c. click Save on the File menu
   d. click Exit on the File menu

9. For information about an item on the Index sheet of the Help Topics: Windows Help window, _____.
   a. press the F1 key
   b. click the Question Mark button in the top right corner of the dialog box and then click the item
   c. click the Find tab in the Help Topics: Windows Help window
   d. press CTRL+F3

10. To shut down Windows 95, _____.
    a. click the Start button, click Shut Down on the Start menu, click the Shut down the computer? option button, and then click the Yes button
    b. click the Shut Down button on the Windows 95 File menu
    c. click the taskbar, click Close down Windows 95, and then click the Yes button
    d. press the F10 key and then click the Yes button

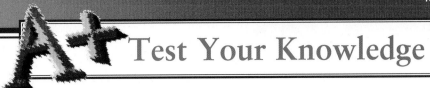

3 Identifying Objects on the Desktop

Instructions: On the desktop in Figure 1-66, arrows point to several items or objects on the desktop. Identify the items or objects in the spaces provided.

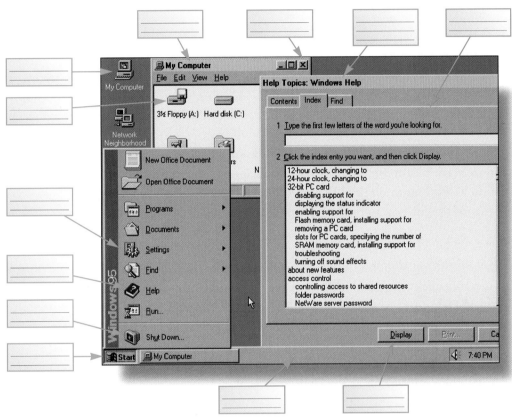

FIGURE 1-66

4 Saving a Document

Instructions: List the steps in the spaces provided to save a new Notepad file on a floppy disk in drive A using the filename, This is my file.

Step 1: _____

Step 2: _____

Step 3: _____

Step 4: _____

Step 5: _____

Step 6: _____

Step 7: _____

? Use Help

1 Using Windows Help

Instructions: Use Windows Help and a computer to perform the following tasks.

Part 1: Using the Question Mark Button

1. Start Microsoft Windows 95 if necessary.
2. Click the Start button. Click Help on the Start menu to open the Help Topics: Windows Help window. If the Contents tab sheet does not display, click the Contents tab.
3. Click the Question Mark button on the title bar. The mouse pointer changes to a block arrow with question mark pointer. Click the list box containing the Help topics and Help books. A pop-up window explaining the list box displays. Click an open area of the list box to remove the pop-up window.
4. Click the Question Mark button on the title bar and then click the Display button.
5. Click the Question Mark button on the title bar and then click the Print button.
6. Click the Question Mark button on the title bar and then click the Cancel button.
7. Click an open area of the list box to remove the pop-up window.

Part 2: Finding What's New with Windows 95

1. Double-click the Introducing Windows book to open the book. Double-click the Welcome book to open the book. Double-click the A List of What's New book to open the book. Double-click the A new look and feel Help topic to open the Windows Help window. Click the first button (Start button and taskbar) and read the contents of the What's New window.
2. Click the Close button in the What's New window.
3. Click the Help Topics button in the Windows Help window to open the Help Topics: Windows Help window. Click the Print button in the Help Topics: Windows Help window. Click the OK button in the Print dialog box to print the Help topic (A new look and feel).
4. Click the Help Topics button in the Windows Help window.
5. Double-click the Welcome book to close the book.

Part 3: Learning About Getting Your Work Done

1. Double-click the Getting Your Work Done book to open the book. Double-click the Saving your work Help topic. Click the Save button and read the pop-up window.
2. Click other items in the Save As dialog box and read the pop-up windows.
3. Click the Help Topics button in the Windows Help window to open the Help Topics: Windows Help window. Click the Print button in the Help Topics: Windows Help window. Click the OK button in the Print dialog box to print the Saving your work Help topic.
4. Click the Close buttons in the Windows Help windows to close the windows.

? Use Help

2 Using Windows Help to Obtain Help

Instructions: Use Windows Help and a computer to perform the following tasks.

1. Find Help about viewing the Welcome screen that displays when you start Windows 95 by looking in the Tips of the Day book within the Tips and Tricks book in the Help Topics: Windows Help window. Answer the following questions in the spaces provided.
   a. How can you open the Welcome screen? _____
   b. How can you see the list of tips in the Welcome screen? _____
   c. Open the Welcome screen. Cycle through the tips in the Welcome screen. How can you set your computer's clock? _____
   d. Click the What's New button in the Welcome screen. According to Help, how do you start a program? _____
   e. Close the Welcome screen. Click the Help Topics button in the Windows Help window.

2. Find Help about keyboard shortcuts by looking in the Keyboard Shortcuts book. Answer the following questions in the spaces provided.
   a. What keyboard shortcut is used to quit a program? _____
   b. What keyboard shortcut is used to display the Start menu? _____
   c. What keyboard shortcut is used to view the shortcut menu for a selected item? _____
   d. What keyboard shortcut is used to rename an item? _____
   e. What keyboard shortcut is used to open the Save in list box (drop-down list box)? _____
   f. Click the Help Topics button in the Windows Help window.

3. Find Help about Notepad by looking in the For Writing and Drawing book. Answer the following questions in the spaces provided.
   a. Can you create or edit a text file that requires formatting using Notepad? _____
   b. What size file can you create using Notepad? _____
   c. Which program can you use to create a larger file? _____
   d. What is the only format used by Notepad to store a file? _____

4. Find Help about the Internet by looking in the Welcome to the Information Highway book. Answer the following questions in the spaces provided.
   a. List one source of online information available on the Internet. _____
   b. How do you use The Microsoft Network to sign up for the Internet?
   c. Where else can you find information about connecting to the Internet? _____

5. Find Help about what to do if you have a problem starting Windows 95. The process of solving such a problem is called troubleshooting. Answer the following questions in the spaces provided.
   a. What size floppy disk do you need to create a startup disk? _____
   b. To start Windows in safe mode, what do you do when you see the message "Starting Windows 95?" _____

6. Answer the following questions in the spaces provided.
   a. List two ways you can get Help in a dialog box: _____; _____.
   b. How can you print information displayed in a Help pop-up window?
   _____

(continued)

Use Help

Use Help *(continued)*

7. You have been assigned to obtain information on software licensing. Answer the following questions, and find and print information from Windows Help that supports your answers.
   a. How is computer software protected by law?
   b. What is software piracy? Why should you be concerned?
   c. Can you use your own software on both your desktop and your laptop computers?
   d. How can you identify illegal software?
8. Close all open Windows Help windows.

In the Lab

1 Improving Your Mouse Skills

Instructions: Use a computer to perform the following tasks:

1. Start Microsoft Windows 95 if necessary.
2. Click the Start button on the taskbar, point to Programs on the Start menu, point to Accessories on the Programs submenu, point to Games on the Accessories submenu, and click Solitaire on the Games submenu.
3. Click the Maximize button in the Solitaire window.
4. Click Help on the Solitaire menu bar.
5. Click Help Topics on the Help menu.
6. If the Contents sheet does not display, click the Contents tab.
7. Review the How to play Solitaire and Scoring information Help topics on the Contents sheet.
8. After reviewing the topics, close all Help windows.
9. Play the game of Solitaire.
10. Click the Close button on the Solitaire title bar to close the game.

2 Starting an Application, Creating a Document, and Modifying a Document

Instructions: Perform the following steps to start the Notepad application and create and modify a document.

Part 1: *Creating a Document*

1. Start Microsoft Windows 95 if necessary.
2. Click the Start button. Point to Programs on the Start menu. Point to Accessories on the Programs submenu. Click Notepad on the Accessories submenu.

In the Lab

3. Enter the document shown in Figure 1-67 in the Notepad document.

4. Insert a formatted floppy disk in drive A of your computer.

5. Click File on the menu bar. Click Save As on the File menu.

6. Type Office Supplies Shopping List - Tuesday in the File name text box.

```
Office Supplies Shopping List - Tuesday

1. Staples
2. 2 boxes of copier paper
3. Toner for computer printer
4. Box of formatted floppy disks
```

FIGURE 1-67

7. Click the Save in box arrow. Click the 3½ Floppy [A:] icon. Click the Save button.

8. Click File on the menu bar. Click Print on the File menu.

9. Click the Close button on the Notepad title bar.

10. If you are not completing Part 2 of this assignment, remove your floppy disk from drive A.

Part 2: *Modifying a Document*

1. Click the Start button, point to Programs on the Start menu, point to Accessories on the Programs submenu, and then click Notepad on the Accessories submenu.

2. Click File on the menu bar and then click Open on the File menu. Click the Look in box arrow and then click the 3½ Floppy [A:] icon. Click Office Supplies Shopping List - Tuesday. Click the Open button.

3. Press the DOWN ARROW key six times. Type 5. Two boxes of black ink pens and then press the ENTER key.

4. Click File on the menu bar and then click Save on the File menu.

5. Click File on the menu bar and then click Print on the File menu.

6. Click the Close button on the Notepad title bar.

7. Remove the floppy disk from drive A of your computer.

3 Creating a Document

Instructions: As a student, you would like to give a copy of your daily schedule to your parents and friends so you can be contacted in an emergency. To do this, you want to create a document for each weekday (Monday through Friday). Each document will have an appropriate title and contain your daily school and personal schedule. Each course in the document will contain the start and finish time for the course, course number, course title, room number, and instructor name. Other entries for extracurricular activities, sporting events, or personal events also will be included in the documents. Print the five documents on the printer and follow directions from your instructor for turning in this assignment. Store the five documents on a floppy disk.

Cases and Places

The difficulty of these case studies varies:

▶ Case studies preceded by a single half moon are the least difficult. You can complete these case studies using your own computer or a computer in the lab.

▶▶ Case studies preceded by two half moons are more difficult. You must research the topic presented using the Internet, a library, or another resource, and then prepare a brief written report.

▶▶▶ Case studies preceded by three half moons are the most difficult. You must visit a store or business to obtain the necessary information, and then use it to create a brief written report.

1 ▶ Your employer is concerned that some people in the company are not putting enough thought into software purchases. She has prepared a list of steps she would like everyone to follow when acquiring software (Figure 1-68).

You have been asked to use WordPad to prepare a copy of this list that can be posted in every department. Use the concepts and techniques presented in this project to start WordPad and create, save, and print the document. After you have printed one copy of the document, try experimenting with different WordPad features to make the list more eye-catching. If you like your changes, save and print a revised copy of the document. If WordPad is not available on your machine, use Notepad.

Steps in Software Acquisition

1. *Summarize your requirements*
2. *Identify potential vendors*
3. *Evaluate alternative software packages*
4. *Make the purchase*

FIGURE 1-68

2 ▶ The local community center has asked you to teach an introductory class on Windows 95 to a group of adults with little previous computer experience. The center director has sent you a note about one of his concerns (Figure 1-69).

Think of two topics about which people in the class may have questions. Use online Help to find answers to the questions. Consider how you would find answers to the same questions using a book. Write a response to the center director describing the advantages and disadvantages of using online Help instead of a book. Explain why you feel the class does or does not need a resource book. To make the director aware of online Help's limitations, tell how you think Microsoft could improve Help in Windows 95.

Is online Help enough for this group?

These people are pretty traditional and are used to having a printed text. Do we need to buy some kind of "help resource book" for everyone? We don't have much money, but on the other hand we don't want people to be disappointed.

Please think about it and get back to me.

FIGURE 1-69

Cases and Places

3 ▶▶ Early personal computer operating systems were adequate, but they were not user-friendly and had few advanced features. Over the past several years, however, personal computer operating systems have become increasingly easy to use, and some now offer features once available only on mainframe computers. Using the Internet, a library, or other research facility, write a brief report on four personal computer operating systems. Describe the systems, pointing out their similarities and differences. Discuss the advantages and disadvantages of each. Finally, tell which operating system you would purchase for your personal computer and explain why.

4 ▶▶ Many feel that Windows 95 was one of the most heavily promoted products ever released. Using the Internet, current computer magazines, or other resources, prepare a brief report on the background of Windows 95. Explain why Windows 95 was two years behind schedule and how it was promoted. Discuss the ways in which Windows 95 is different from earlier versions of Windows (such as Windows 3.1). Based on reviews of the new operating system, describe what people like and do not like about Windows 95. Finally, from what you have learned and your own experience, explain how you think Windows 95 could be improved.

5 ▶▶▶ Software must be compatible with (able to work with) the operating system of the computer on which it will be used. Visit a software vendor and find the five application packages (word processing programs, spreadsheet programs, games, and so on) you would most like to have. List the names of the packages and the operating system used by each. Make a second list of five similar packages that are compatible (meaning they use the same operating system). Using your two lists, write a brief report on how the need to purchase compatible software can affect buying application packages and even the choice of an operating system.

6 ▶▶▶ Because of the many important tasks it performs, most businesses put a great deal of thought into choosing an operating system for their personal computers. Interview people at a local business on the operating system they use with their personal computers. Based on your interviews, write a brief report on why the business chose that operating system, how satisfied they are with it, and under what circumstances they might consider switching to a different operating system.

7 ▶▶▶ In a recent television commercial from Apple Computers, a frustrated father tries to use Windows 95 to display pictures of dinosaurs for his young son. After waiting impatiently, the boy tells his father he is going next door to the neighbor's because they have a Mac. Visit a computer vendor and try an operating system with a graphical user interface other than Windows 95, such as Macintosh System 7.5 or OS/2. Write a brief report comparing the operating system to Windows 95, and explain which operating system you would prefer to have on your personal computer.

Putting the Squeeze on DATA

1978

320K

In 1994, a federal district court ruled that Microsoft violated the rights of Stac Electronics in the data compression software component of MS-DOS 6.2, Microsoft's operating system. In response, Microsoft paid Stac a royalty of $43 million and replaced MS-DOS 6.2 with version 6.21, which did not contain the offending code.

Why the lawsuit? Data compression software, which allows you to store more data on your hard disk, is an important component of your computer's software and is so valuable to its developers that they will sue to protect their rights.

Disk storage capacity has not always been critical. Indeed, the first personal computers did not have disk storage. Instead, they used slow, unreliable tape cassettes. Then, in 1978, Apple demonstrated its first working prototype of the Apple

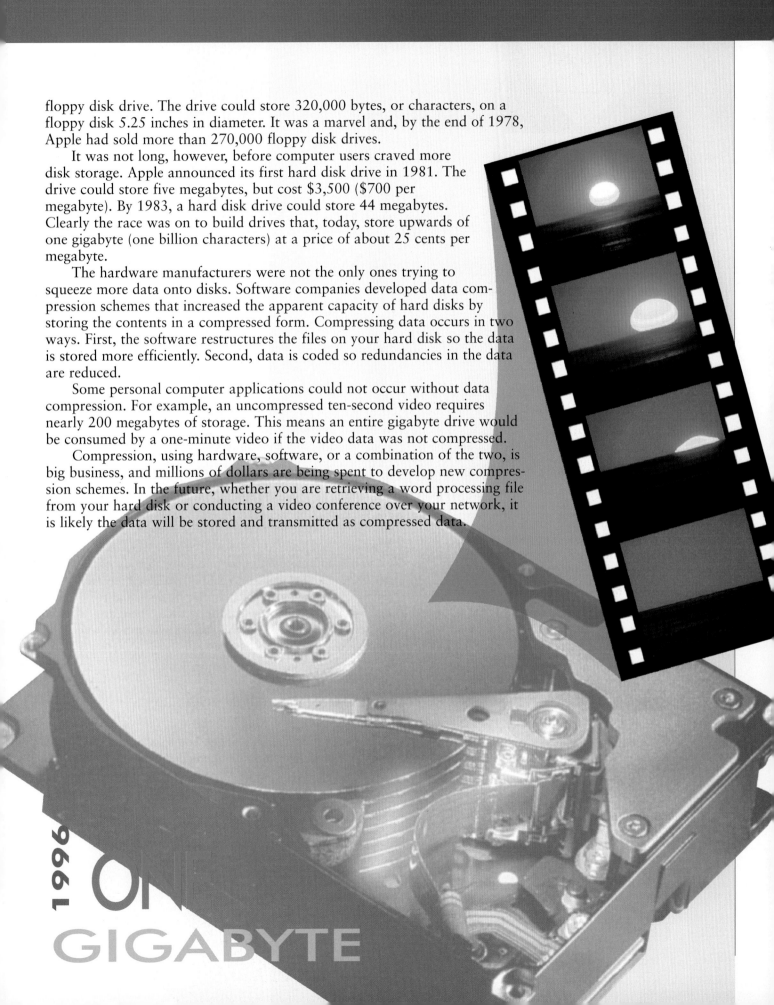

floppy disk drive. The drive could store 320,000 bytes, or characters, on a floppy disk 5.25 inches in diameter. It was a marvel and, by the end of 1978, Apple had sold more than 270,000 floppy disk drives.

It was not long, however, before computer users craved more disk storage. Apple announced its first hard disk drive in 1981. The drive could store five megabytes, but cost $3,500 ($700 per megabyte). By 1983, a hard disk drive could store 44 megabytes. Clearly the race was on to build drives that, today, store upwards of one gigabyte (one billion characters) at a price of about 25 cents per megabyte.

The hardware manufacturers were not the only ones trying to squeeze more data onto disks. Software companies developed data compression schemes that increased the apparent capacity of hard disks by storing the contents in a compressed form. Compressing data occurs in two ways. First, the software restructures the files on your hard disk so the data is stored more efficiently. Second, data is coded so redundancies in the data are reduced.

Some personal computer applications could not occur without data compression. For example, an uncompressed ten-second video requires nearly 200 megabytes of storage. This means an entire gigabyte drive would be consumed by a one-minute video if the video data was not compressed.

Compression, using hardware, software, or a combination of the two, is big business, and millions of dollars are being spent to develop new compression schemes. In the future, whether you are retrieving a word processing file from your hard disk or conducting a video conference over your network, it is likely the data will be stored and transmitted as compressed data.

1996

ONE

GIGABYTE

Project

2

Microsoft

Windows 95

Using Windows Explorer

Case Perspective

Need: Your organization has finally made the decision to switch to Windows 95 from Windows 3.1. Although most everyone is excited about the change, many are apprehensive about file management. Few of them ever felt comfortable with Windows 3.1 File Manager and, as a result, hardly ever used it. Your boss has read in computer magazines that in order to effectively use Windows 95, people must learn Windows Explorer. She has asked you to teach a class with an emphasis on file management to all employees who will be using Windows 95. Your goal in Project 2 is to become competent using Windows Explorer so you can teach the class.

Introduction

Windows Explorer is an application program included with Windows 95 that allows you to view the contents of the computer, the hierarchy of folders on the computer, and the files and folders in each folder.

Windows Explorer also allows you to organize the files and folders on the computer by copying and moving the files and folders. In this project, you will use Windows Explorer to (1) work with the files and folders on your computer; (2) select and copy a group of files between the hard drive and a floppy disk; (3) create, rename, and delete a folder on floppy disk; and (4) rename and delete a file on floppy disk. These are common operations that you should understand how to perform.

Starting Windows 95

As explained in Project 1, when you turn on the computer, an introductory screen consisting of the Windows 95 logo and the Microsoft Windows 95 name displays on a blue sky and clouds background. The screen clears and Windows 95 displays several items on the desktop.

If the Welcome to Windows screen displays on your desktop, click the Close button on the title bar to close the screen. Six icons (My Computer, Network Neighborhood, Inbox, Recycle Bin, The Microsoft Network, and My Briefcase) display along the left edge of the desktop, the Microsoft Office Manager toolbar displays in the upper right corner of the desktop, and the taskbar displays along the bottom of the desktop (Figure 2-1).

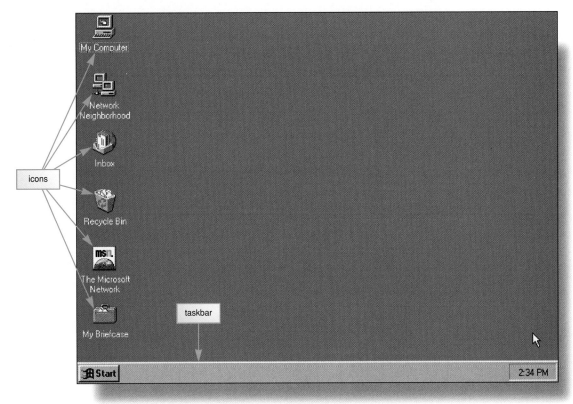

FIGURE 2-1

Starting Windows Explorer and Maximizing Its Window

To start Windows Explorer and explore the files and folders on the computer, right-click the My Computer icon on the desktop, which opens a context-sensitive menu, and then click the Explore command on the menu to open the Exploring – My Computer window. To maximize the Exploring – My Computer window, click the Maximize button on the title bar.

Steps To Start Windows Explorer and Maximize Its Window

1 **Right-click the My Computer icon to open a context-sensitive menu, and then point to the Explore command on the menu.**

Windows 95 highlights the My Computer icon, opens a context-sensitive menu, and highlights the Explore command on the menu (Figure 2-2). The mouse pointer points to the Explore command on the menu.

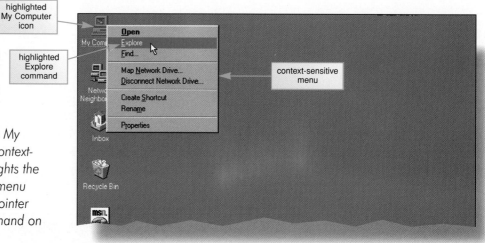

FIGURE 2-2

2 **Click Explore on the context-sensitive menu, and then click the Maximize button on the Exploring – My Computer title bar.**

Windows 95 opens and maximizes the Exploring – My Computer window and adds the indented Exploring – My Compu... button to the taskbar (Figure 2-3).

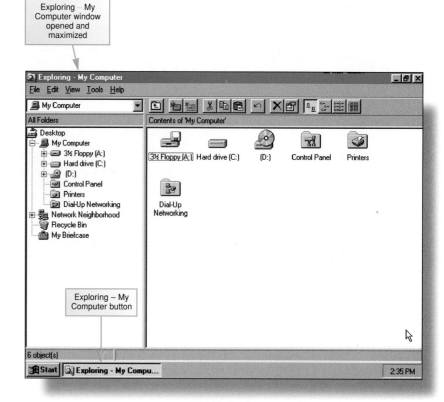

FIGURE 2-3

OtherWays

1. Right-click Start button, click Explore on context-sensitive menu

2. Click Start button, point to Programs, click Windows Explorer on the Programs submenu

3. Right-click Network Neighborhood icon, or Inbox icon, or Recycle Bin icon, or The Microsoft Network icon, or My Briefcase icon, click Explore on context-sensitive menu

4. Right-click Start button or any icons in 3 above, press E

Windows Explorer

When you start Windows Explorer by right-clicking the My Computer icon, Windows 95 opens the Exploring – My Computer window (Figure 2-4). The menu bar contains the File, Edit, View, Tools, and Help menu names.

These menus contain commands to organize and work with the drives on the computer and the files and folders on those drives.

Below the menu bar is a toolbar. The **toolbar** contains a drop-down list box and thirteen buttons. The drop-down list box contains an icon and the My Computer folder name. The entry in the drop-down list box, called the **current folder**, indicates Windows Explorer was started by right-clicking the My Computer icon. The buttons on the toolbar provide a quick way to perform commonly used tasks in Windows Explorer. Many of the buttons correspond to the commands available from the menu bar. Pointing to a button on the toolbar displays a ToolTip identifying the button. If the toolbar does not display in the Exploring – My Computer window on your computer, click View on the menu bar and then click Toolbar on the View menu.

The window is divided into two areas separated by a bar. The left side of the window, identified by the All Folders title, contains a **hierarchy** of folders on the computer. The right side of the window, identified by the Contents of 'My Computer' title, displays the contents of the current folder (My Computer). In Figure 2-4, the Contents side contains the icons and folder names of six folders (3½ Floppy [A:], Hard drive [C:], and [D:], Control Panel, Printers, and Dial-Up Networking). These folders may be different on your computer. You change the size of the All Folders and Contents sides of the window by dragging the bar that separates the two sides.

Each folder in the All Folders side of the window is represented by an icon and folder name. The first folder, consisting of an icon and the Desktop folder name, represents the desktop of the computer. The four folders indented and aligned below the Desktop folder name (My Computer, Network Neighborhood,

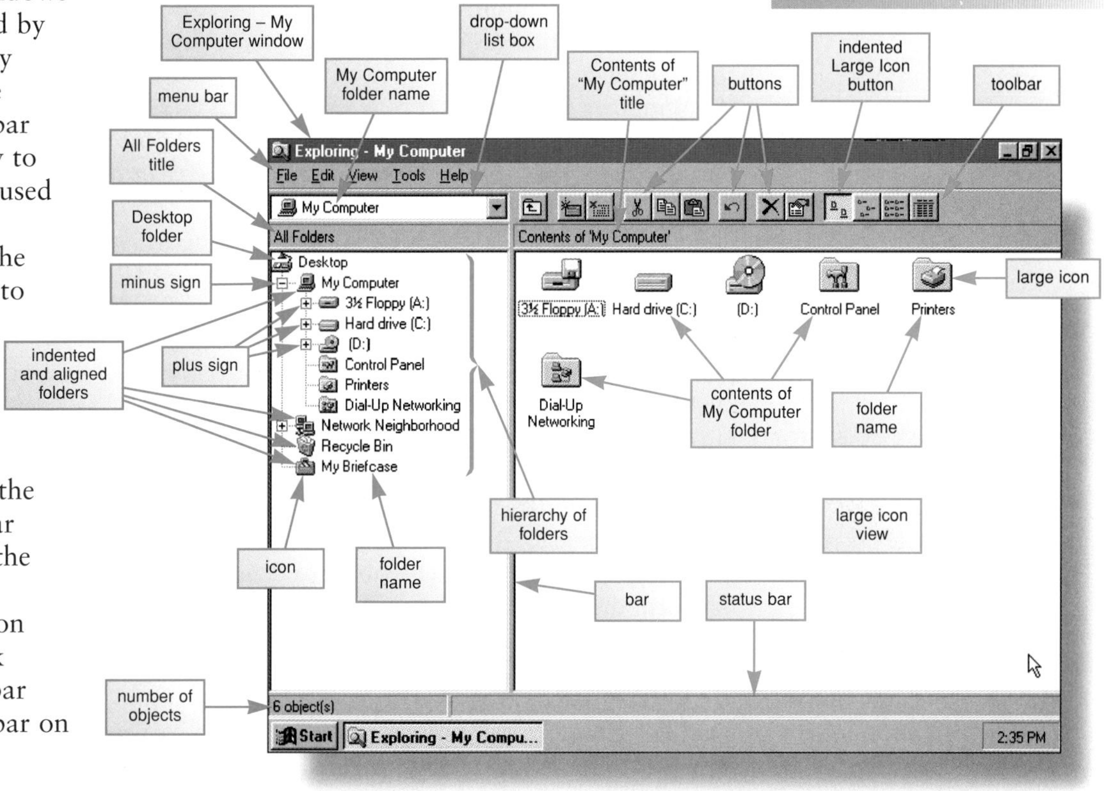

FIGURE 2-4

More About Explorer

For those familiar with Windows 3.1, Windows 95 Explorer bears some resemblance to File Manager. Microsoft, however, made significant improvements and changed the basic way the program works. Those who passionately disliked File Manager might find Explorer a better way to perform file maintenance.

More About a Hierarchy

One definition of hierarchy in Webster's Ninth New Collegiate Dictionary is, "a division of angels." While no one would argue angels have anything to do with Windows 95, some preach that working with a hierarchical structure as presented by Explorer is less secular ("of or relating to the worldly") and more spiritual ("of or relating to supernatural phenomena") than the straight-forward showing of files in windows. What do you think?

Recycle Bin, and My Briefcase) are connected to the vertical line below the Desktop icon. These folders correspond to four of the six icons displayed on the left edge of the desktop (see Figure 2-1 on page WIN 2.5). These folders may be different on your computer.

Windows 95 displays a minus sign (–) in a box to the left of any icon in the All Folders side to indicate the corresponding folder contains one or more folders that are visible in the All Folders side. These folders, called **subfolders**, are indented and aligned below the folder name.

In Figure 2-4 on the previous page, a minus sign precedes the My Computer icon, and six subfolders are indented and display below the My Computer folder name. The six subfolders (3½ Floppy [A:], Hard drive [C:], [D:], Control Panel, Printers, and Dial-Up Networking) correspond to the six folders in the Contents side. Clicking the minus sign, referred to as **collapsing the folder**, removes the indented subfolders from the hierarchy of folders in the All Folders side and changes the minus sign to a plus sign.

Windows 95 displays a plus sign (+) in a box to the left of an icon to indicate the corresponding folder consists of one or more subfolders that are not visible in the All Folders side of the window. In Figure 2-4, a plus sign precedes the first three icons indented and aligned below the My Computer name (3½ Floppy [A:], Hard drive [C:], [D:]) and the Network Neighborhood icon. Clicking the plus sign, referred to as **expanding the folders**, displays a list of indented subfolders and changes the plus sign to a minus sign.

If neither a plus sign nor a minus sign displays to the left of an icon, the folder does not contain subfolders. In Figure 2-4, the Control Panel, Printers, Dial-Up Networking, Recycle Bin, and My Briefcase icons are not preceded by a plus or minus sign and do not contain subfolders.

The status bar at the bottom of the Exploring – My Computer window indicates the number of folders, or objects, displayed in the Contents side of the window (6 object(s)). Depending upon the objects displayed in the Contents side, the amount of disk space the objects occupy and the amount of unused disk space may also display on the status bar. If the status bar does not display in the Exploring – My Computer window on your computer, click View on the menu bar and then click Status Bar on the View menu.

In addition to using Windows Explorer to explore your computer by right-clicking the My Computer icon, you can also use Windows Explorer to explore different aspects of your computer by right-clicking the Start button on the taskbar and the Network Neighborhood, Inbox, Recycle Bin, The Microsoft Network, and My Briefcase icons on the desktop.

Displaying the Contents of a Folder

In Figure 2-4 on the previous page, the current folder (My Computer) displays in the drop-down list box on the toolbar and the Contents side of the window contains the subfolders in the My Computer folder. In addition to displaying the contents of the My Computer folder, the contents of any folder in the All Folders side can be displayed in the Contents side. Perform the following steps to display the contents of the Hard drive [C:] folder.

Steps **To Display the Contents of a Folder**

1 **Point to the Hard drive [C:] folder name in the All Folders side of the Exploring – My Computer window (Figure 2-5).**

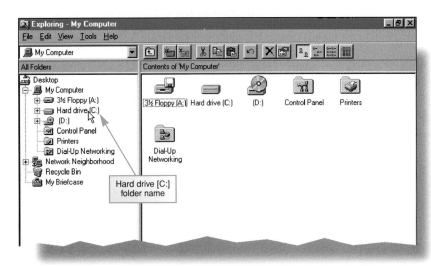

FIGURE 2-5

2 **Click the Hard drive [C:] folder name.**

Windows 95 highlights the Hard drive [C:] folder name in the All Folders side, changes the current folder in the drop-down list box to the Hard drive [C:] folder, displays the contents of the Hard drive [C:] folder in the Contents side, changes the window title to contain the current folder name (Exploring – Hard drive [C:]), changes the button on the taskbar to contain the current folder name, and changes the messages on the status bar (Figure 2-6). The status bar messages indicate there are 82 objects and 19 hidden objects in the Hard drive [C:] folder, the objects occupy 25.9MB of disk space, and the amount of unused disk space is 12.5MB. The contents of the Hard drive [C:] folder may be different on your computer.

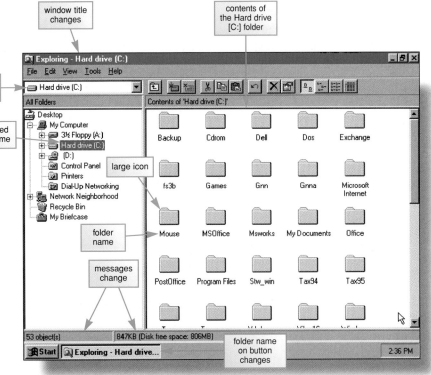

FIGURE 2-6

OtherWays

1. Double-click Hard disk [C:] icon in Contents side

2. Press TAB until any icon in All Folders side highlighted, press DOWN ARROW or UP ARROW until Hard disk [C:] highlighted in Contents side

In addition to displaying the contents of the Hard drive [C:] folder, you can display the contents of the other folders by clicking the corresponding icon or folder name in the All Folders side. The contents of the folder you click will then display in the Contents side of the window.

Expanding a Folder

Currently, the Hard drive [C:] folder is highlighted in the All Folders side of the Exploring – Hard drive [C:] window and the contents of the Hard drive [C:] folder display in the Contents side of the window. Windows 95 displays a plus sign (+) to the left of the Hard drive [C:] icon to indicate the folder contains subfolders that are not visible in the hierarchy of folders in the All Folders side of the window. To expand the Hard drive [C:] folder and display its subfolders, click the plus sign to the left of the Hard drive [C:] icon. Perform the following steps to expand the Hard drive [C:] folder.

Steps **To Expand a Folder**

1 Point to the plus sign to the left of the Hard drive [C:] icon in the All Folders side of the Exploring – Hard drive [C:] window (Figure 2-7).

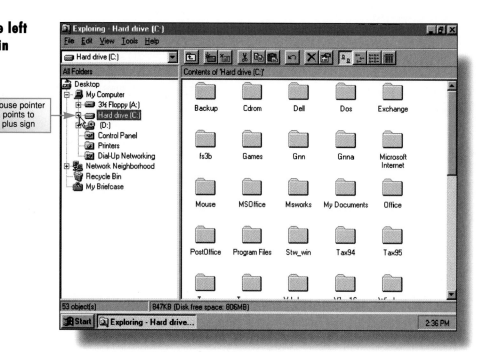

FIGURE 2-7

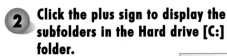
2 **Click the plus sign to display the subfolders in the Hard drive [C:] folder.**

Windows 95 replaces the plus sign preceding the Hard drive [C:] icon with a minus sign, displays a vertical scroll bar, and expands the Hard drive [C:] folder to include its subfolders, indented and aligned below the Hard drive [C:] folder name, (Figure 2-8). Each subfolder in the Hard drive [C:] folder is identified by a closed folder icon and folder name. The window title, current folder in the drop-down list box on the toolbar, and the files and folders in the Contents side of the window remain unchanged.

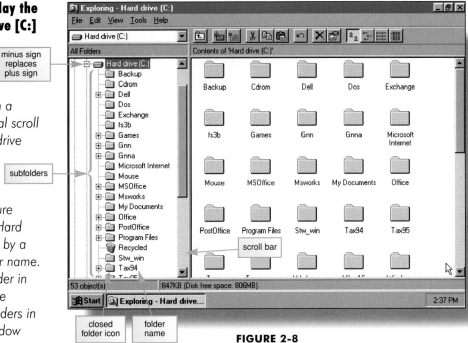

FIGURE 2-8

Collapsing a Folder

Currently, the subfolders in the Hard drive [C:] folder display indented and aligned below the Hard drive [C:] folder name (see Figure 2-8). Windows 95 displays a minus sign (–) to the left of the Hard drive [C:] icon to indicate the folder is expanded. To collapse the Hard drive [C:] folder and then remove its subfolders from the hierarchy of folders in the All Folders side, click the minus sign preceding the Hard drive [C:] icon. Perform the following steps to collapse the Hard drive [C:] folder.

 Steps **To Collapse a Folder**

1 **Point to the minus sign preceding the Hard drive [C:] icon in the All Folders side of the Exploring – Hard drive [C:] window (Figure 2-9).**

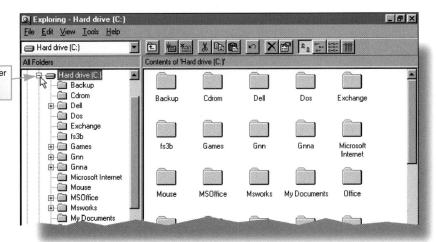

FIGURE 2-9

2 Click the minus sign to display the Hard drive [C:] folder without its subfolders.

Windows 95 replaces the minus sign preceding the Hard drive [C:] icon with a plus sign and removes the subfolders in the Hard drive [C:] folder from the hierarchy of folders (Figure 2-10).

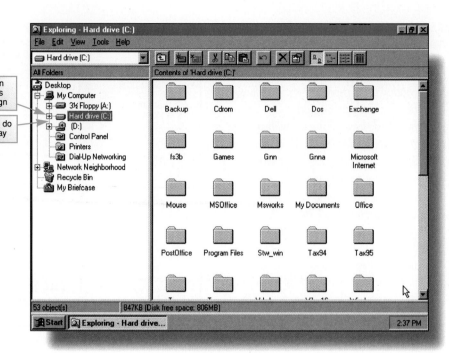

FIGURE 2-10

Other Ways

1. Highlight folder icon, press MINUS SIGN on numeric keypad
2. Double-click the folder icon
3. Select folder to collapse, press LEFT ARROW

Copying Files to a Folder on a Floppy Disk

One common operation that every student should understand how to perform is copying a file or group of files from one disk to another disk or from one folder to another folder. On the following pages, you will create a new folder, named My Files, on the floppy disk in drive A, select a group of files in the Windows folder on drive C, and copy the files from the Windows folder on drive C to the My Files folder on drive A.

When copying files, the drive and folder containing the files to be copied are called the **source drive** and **source folder**, respectively. The drive and folder to which the files are copied are called the **destination drive** and **destination folder**, respectively. Thus, the Windows folder is the source folder, drive C is the source drive, the My Files folder is the destination folder, and drive A is the destination drive.

Creating a New Folder

In preparation for selecting and copying files from a folder on the hard drive to a folder on the floppy disk in drive A, a new folder with the name of My Files will be created on the floppy disk. Perform the following steps to create the new folder.

Steps **To Create a New Folder**

1 **Insert a formatted floppy disk into drive A on your computer.**

2 **Click the 3½ Floppy [A:] folder name in the All Folders side of the Exploring – Hard drive [C:] window and then point to an open area of the Contents side of the window.**

Windows 95 highlights the 3½ Floppy [A:] folder name, changes the current folder to 3½ Floppy [A:], displays the contents of the 3½ Floppy [A:] folder in the Contents side, and changes the messages on the status bar (Figure 2-11). The window title, Contents side title, and button on the taskbar change to include the 3½ Floppy [A:] folder name. Currently, no files or folders display in the Contents side. The files and folders may be different on your computer. The mouse pointer points to an open area of the Contents side.

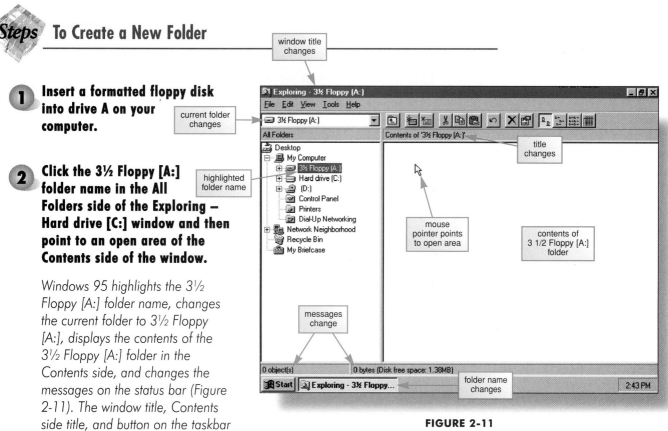

FIGURE 2-11

3 **Right-click the open area of the Contents side of the window to open a context-sensitive menu and then point to New on the menu.**

Windows 95 opens a context-sensitive menu and the New sub-menu, highlights the New command in the context-sensitive menu, and displays a message on the status bar (Figure 2-12). The message, Contains commands for creating new items., indicates the New submenu contains commands that allow you to create new items in the Contents side. The mouse pointer points to the New command. Although no subfolders display in the Contents side and no plus sign should precede the 3½ Floppy [A:] icon in the All Folders area, a plus sign precedes the icon.

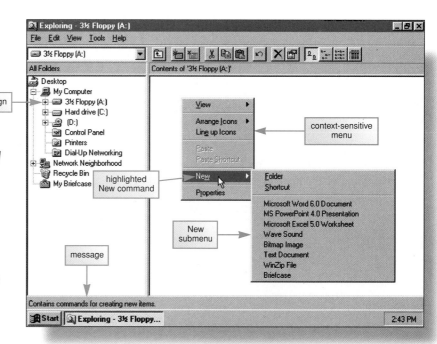

FIGURE 2-12

④ Point to Folder on the New submenu.

Windows 95 highlights the Folder command on the New submenu and displays the message, Creates a new, empty folder., on the status bar (Figure 2-13). The mouse pointer points to the Folder command. Clicking the Folder command will create a folder in the Contents side of the window using the default folder name, New Folder.

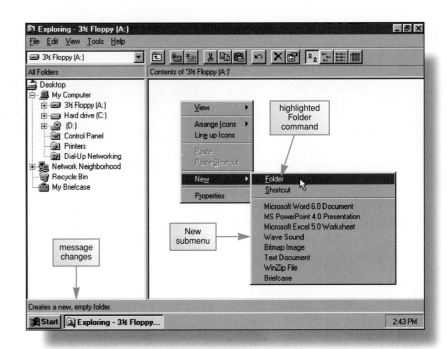

FIGURE 2-13

⑤ Click Folder on the New submenu.

Windows 95 closes the context-sensitive menu and New submenu, displays the highlighted New Folder icon in the Contents side, and changes the message on the status bar (Figure 2-14). The text box below the icon contains the highlighted default folder name, New Folder, followed by the insertion point. A plus sign continues to display to the left of the 3½ Floppy [A:] icon to indicate the 3½ Floppy [A:] folder contains the New Folder subfolder. The message on the status bar indicates one object is selected in the Contents side.

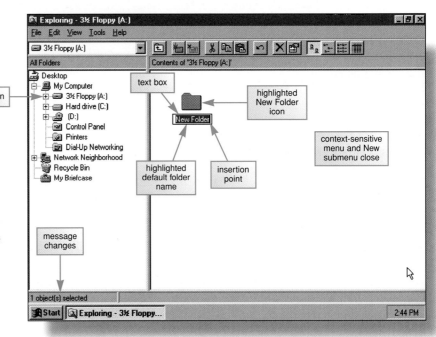

FIGURE 2-14

6 **Type** My Files **in the text box and then press the ENTER key.**

The new folder name, My Files, is entered and Windows 95 removes the text box (Figure 2-15).

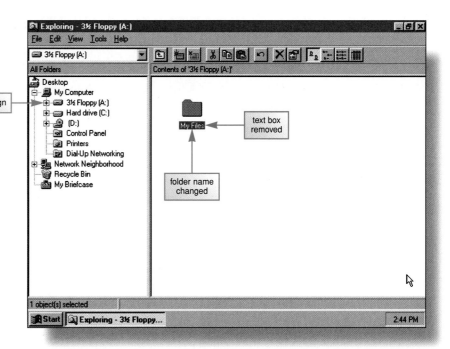

FIGURE 2-15

After creating the My Files folder on the floppy disk in drive A, you can save files in the folder or copy files from other folders to the folder. On the following pages, you will copy a group of files consisting of the Black Thatch, Bubbles, and Circles files from the Windows folder on drive C to the My Files folder on drive A.

Displaying the Destination Folder

To copy the three files from the Windows folder on drive C to the My Files folder on drive A, the files to be copied will be selected in the Contents side and right-dragged to the My Files folder in the All Folders side. Prior to selecting or right-dragging the files, the destination folder (My Files folder on drive A) must be visible in the All Folders side and the three files to be copied must be visible in the Contents side.

Currently, the plus sign (+) to the left of the 3½ Floppy [A:] icon indicates the folder contains one or more subfolders that are not visible in the All Folders side (see Figure 2-15). Perform the steps on the next page to expand the 3½ Floppy [A:] folder to display the My Files subfolder.

Other Ways

1. Select drive, click File on the menu bar, on File menu click New, click Folder on New submenu

TO EXPAND THE 3½ FLOPPY [A:] FOLDER

Step 1: Point to the plus sign to the left of the 3½ Floppy [A:] icon in the All
Folders side of the Exploring – 3½ Floppy [A:] window.
Step 2: Click the plus sign to display the subfolders in the 3½ Floppy [A:]
folder.

*Windows 95 replaces the plus sign preceding the 3½ Floppy [A:] folder with
a minus sign, highlights the 3½ Floppy [A:] folder name, and displays the
subfolders in the 3½ Floppy [A:] folder, indented and aligned below the 3½
Floppy [A:] folder name (Figure 2-16). Currently, only one subfolder (My
Files) displays.*

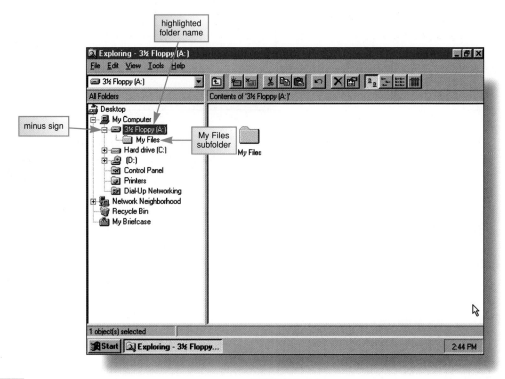

FIGURE 2-16

OtherWays

1. Right-click 3½ Floppy [A:]
   icon, click Explore

Displaying the Contents of the Windows Folder

Currently, the My Files folder displays in the Contents side of the Exploring –
3½ Floppy [A:] window. To copy files from the source folder (Windows folder on
drive C) to the My Files folder, the Windows folder must be visible in the All
Folders side. To make the Windows folder visible, you must expand the Hard
drive [C:] folder, scroll the All Folders side to make the Windows folder name
visible, and then click the Windows folder name to display the contents of the
Windows folder in the Contents side. Perform the following steps to display the
contents of the Windows folder.

Steps To Display the Contents of a Folder

1 **Click the plus sign to the left of the Hard drive [C:] icon in the All Folders side of the Exploring – 3½ Floppy [A:] window, scroll the All Folders side to make the Windows folder name visible, and then point to the Windows folder name.**

*Windows 95 replaces the plus sign to the left of the Hard drive [C:] icon with a minus sign, displays the subfolders in the Hard drive [C:] folder, and scrolls the hierarchy of folders in the All Folders side to make the Windows folder visible (Figure 2-17). In addition to folders and other files, the Windows folder contains a series of predefined graphics, called **clip art files**, that can be used with application programs. The mouse pointer points to the Windows folder name. The plus sign to the left of the Hard drive [C:] icon is not visible in Figure 2-17.*

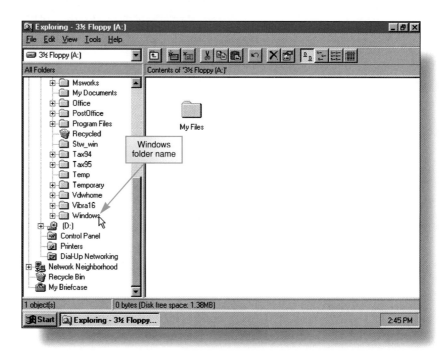

FIGURE 2-17

2 **Click the Windows folder name to display the sub-folders in the Windows folder.**

Windows 95 highlights the Windows folder name in the All Folders side of the window, changes the closed folder icon to the left of the Windows folder name to an open folder icon, and displays the contents of the Windows folder in the Contents side (Figure 2-18).

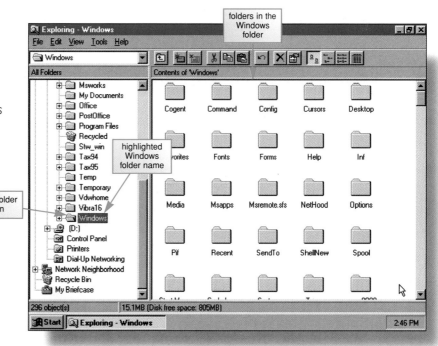

FIGURE 2-18

3 **Scroll the Contents side to make the files in the Windows folder visible.**

One folder (Wordview folder) and several files display in the Contents side of the window (Figure 2-19). Each file is identified by a large icon and a filename. The files and folders in the Windows folder may be different and the file extensions may not display on your computer.

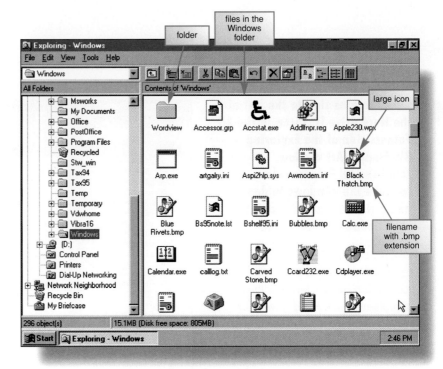

FIGURE 2-19

Changing the View

In Figure 2-19, the files and folder in the Contents side of the Exploring – Windows window display in large icons view. In **large icons view**, each file and folder is represented by a large icon and a filename or folder name. Other views include the small icons, list, and details views. The list view is often useful when copying or moving files from one location to another location. In **list view**, each file or folder is represented by a smaller icon and name, and the files and folders are arranged in columns. Perform the following steps to change from large icons view to list view.

Steps To Change to List View

① Right-click any open area in the Contents side of the Exploring – Windows window to open a context-sensitive menu, point to View on the context-sensitive menu, and then point to List on the View submenu.

Windows 95 opens a context-sensitive menu, highlights the View command on the context-sensitive menu, opens the View submenu, and highlights the List command on the View submenu (Figure 2-20). A large dot to the left of the Large Icons command on the View submenu indicates files and folders in the Contents side display in large icons view. The mouse pointer points to the List command. Clicking the List command will display the files and folders in the Contents side in list view.

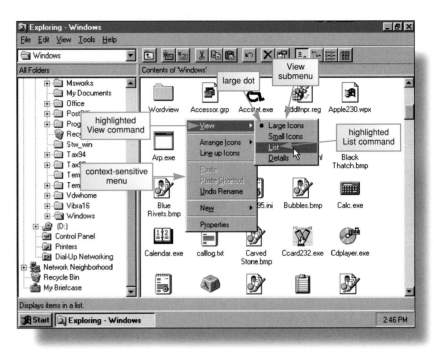

FIGURE 2-20

② Click List on the View submenu.

Windows 95 displays the files and folders in the Contents side of the window in list view, indents the List button on the toolbar, and returns the Large Icons button to normal (Figure 2-21).

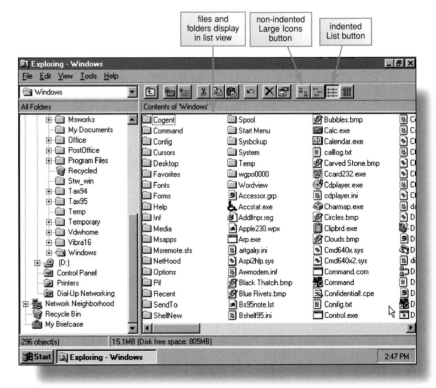

FIGURE 2-21

▶OtherWays

1. On View menu click List
2. Click List button on toolbar
3. Press ALT+V, press L

Selecting a Group of Files

You can easily copy a single file or group of files from one folder to another folder using Windows Explorer. To copy a single file, select the file in the Contents side of the window and right-drag the highlighted file to the folder in the All Folders side where the file is to be copied. Group files are copied in a similar fashion. Select the first file in a group of files by clicking its icon or filename. You select the remaining files in the group by pointing to each file icon or filename, holding down the CTRL key, and clicking the file icon or filename. Perform the following steps to select the group of files consisting of the Black Thatch.bmp, Bubbles.bmp, and Circles.bmp files.

 To Select a Group of Files

1 Select the Black Thatch.bmp file by clicking the Black Thatch.bmp filename, and then point to the Bubbles.bmp filename.

Windows highlights the Black Thatch.bmp file in the Contents side and displays two messages on the status bar (Figure 2-22). The messages indicate that one file is selected (1 object(s) selected) and the size of the file (182 bytes). The mouse pointer points to the Bubbles.bmp filename.

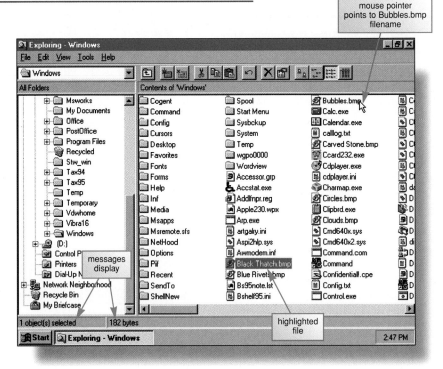

FIGURE 2-22

2 Hold down the CTRL key, click the Bubbles.bmp filename, release the CTRL key, and then point to the Circles.bmp filename.

The Black Thatch.bmp and Bubbles.bmp files are highlighted, and the two messages on the status bar change to reflect the additional file selected (Figure 2-23). The messages indicate that two files are selected (2 object(s) selected) and the size of the two files (2.24KB). The mouse pointer points to the Circles.bmp filename.

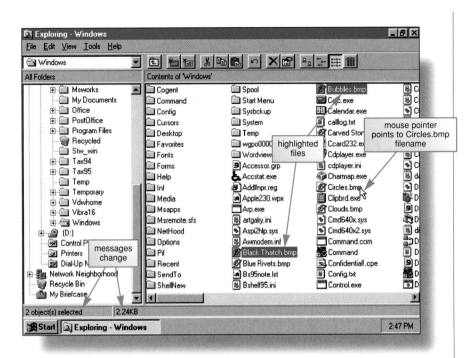

FIGURE 2-23

3 Hold down the CTRL key, click the Circles.bmp filename, and then release the CTRL key.

The group of files consisting of the Black Thatch.bmp, Bubbles.bmp, and Circles.bmp files is highlighted, and the messages on the status bar change to reflect the selection of a third file (Figure 2-24). The messages indicate that three files are selected (3 object(s) selected) and the size of the three files (2.43KB).

FIGURE 2-24

> **Other Ways**
>
> 1. Use arrow keys to select first file, hold down SHIFT key to move to next file, press SPACEBAR
>
> 2. To select contiguous files, select first filename, hold down SHIFT key, click last filename
>
> 3. To select all files, click Edit on menu bar, click Select All

Copying a Group of Files

After selecting a group of files, copy the files to the My Files folder on drive A by pointing to any highlighted filename in the Contents side, and right-dragging the filename to the My Files folder in the All Folders side. Perform the following steps to copy a group of files.

 Steps **To Copy a Group of Files**

---

1 **Scroll the All Folders side of the Exploring – Windows window to make the My Files folder visible and then point to the highlighted Black Thatch.bmp filename in the Contents side.**

Windows 95 scrolls the All Folders side to make the My Files folder visible (Figure 2-25). The mouse pointer points to the highlighted Black Thatch.bmp filename in the Contents side.

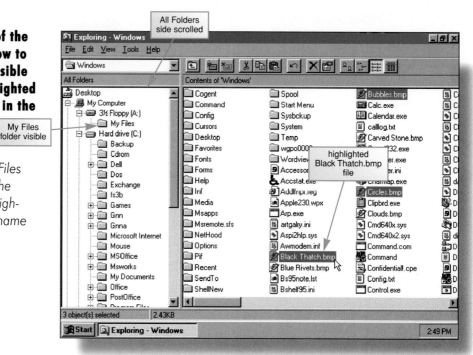

FIGURE 2-25

2 **Right-drag the Black Thatch.bmp file over the My Files folder name in the All Folders side of the Exploring – Windows window.**

As you drag the file, Windows 95 displays an outline of an icon and a horizontal line of one or more of the three files being copied and highlights the My Files folder name (Figure 2-26). The mouse pointer contains a plus sign to indicate the group of files is being copied, not moved.

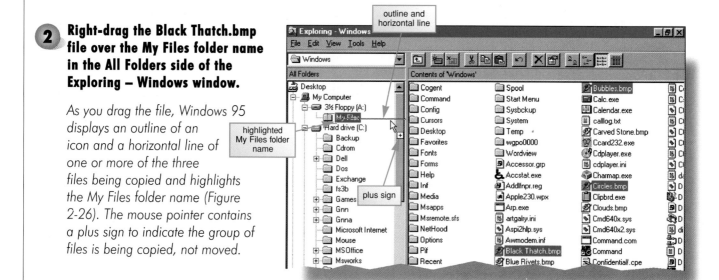

3 **Release the right mouse button to open a context-sensitive menu, and then point to the Copy Here command on the menu.**

Windows 95 opens a context-sensitive menu and highlights the Copy Here command on the menu (Figure 2-27). The mouse pointer points to the Copy Here command. Clicking the Copy Here command will copy the three files to the My Files folder.

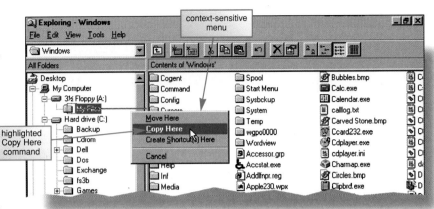

FIGURE 2-27

4 **Click Copy Here on the context-sensitive menu.**

Windows 95 opens the Copying dialog box, and the dialog box remains on the screen while Windows 95 copies each file to the My Files folder (Figure 2-28). The Copying dialog box shown in Figure 2-28 indicates the Black Thatch.bmp file is currently being copied.

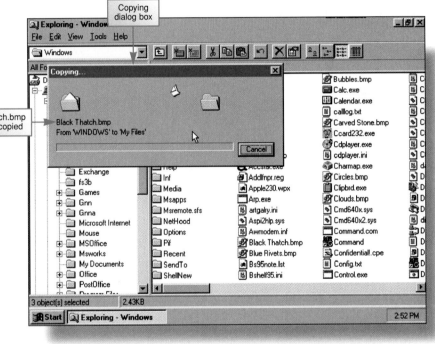

FIGURE 2-28

OtherWays

1. Right-drag file to copy from Contents side to folder icon in All Folders side, click Copy on context-sensitive menu

2. Select file to copy in Contents side, click Edit on menu bar, click Copy on Edit menu, select folder icon to receive copy, click Edit on menu bar, click Paste on Edit menu

Displaying the Contents of the My Files Folder

After copying a group of files, you should verify that the files were copied into the correct folder. To view the files that were copied to the My Files folder, click the My Files folder name in the All Folders side.

More *About* **Copying and Moving**

"Copying, moving, it's all the same to me," you might be tempted to say. They're not the same at all! When you copy a file, it will be located at two different places - the place it was copied to and the place it was copied from. When a file is moved, it will be located at only one place - where it was moved to. Many users have been sorry they did not distinguish the difference when a file they thought they had copied was moved instead.

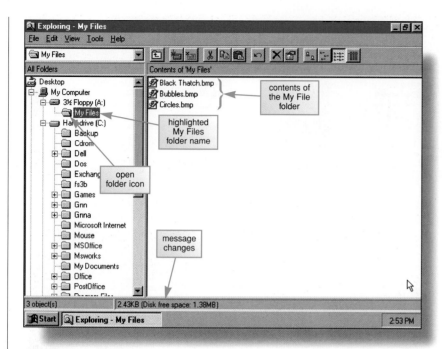

FIGURE 2-29

TO DISPLAY THE CONTENTS OF A FOLDER

Step 1: Point to the My Files folder name in the All Folders side of the Exploring – Windows window.

Step 2: Click the My Files folder name in the All Folders side.

Windows 95 highlights the My Files folder name in the All Folders side, replaces the closed folder icon to the left of the My Files folder name with an open folder icon, displays the contents of the My Files folder in the Contents side, and changes the message on the status bar (Figure 2-29). The status bar message indicates 1.38MB of free disk space on the disk in drive A.

More *About*
Renaming a File or Folder

A file or folder name can contain up to 255 characters, including spaces. But, they cannot contain any of the following characters: \ /:*?"<>|.

Renaming a File or Folder

Sometimes, you may want to rename a file or folder on disk. You change the filename by clicking the filename twice, typing the new filename, and pressing the ENTER key. Perform the following steps to change the name of the Circles.bmp file on drive A to Blue Circles.bmp.

Steps **To Rename a File**

1 **Point to the Circles.bmp filename in the Contents side.**

The mouse pointer points to the Circles.bmp filename (Figure 2-30).

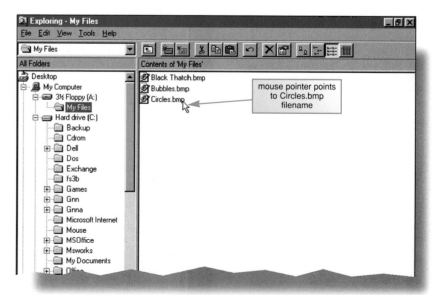

FIGURE 2-30

2 **Click the Circles.bmp filename twice (do not double-click the filename).**

Windows 95 displays a text box containing the highlighted Circles.bmp filename and insertion point (Figure 2-31).

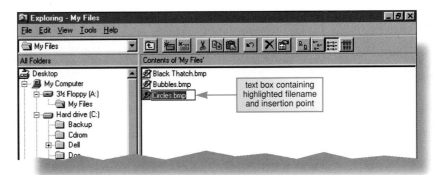

FIGURE 2-31

3 **Type** Blue Circles.bmp **and then press the ENTER key.**

Windows 95 changes the filename to Blue Circles.bmp and removes the box surrounding the filename (Figure 2-32).

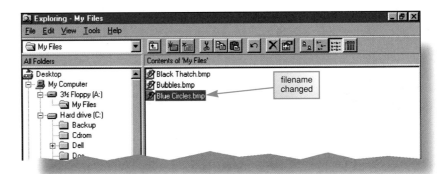

FIGURE 2-32

To change a folder name, click the folder name twice, type the new folder name, and press the ENTER key. Perform the steps below and on the next page to change the name of the My Files folder to Clip Art Files.

Steps **To Rename a Folder**

1 **Point to the My Files folder name in the All Folders side of the Exploring – My Files window.**

The mouse pointer points to the My Files folder name (Figure 2-33).

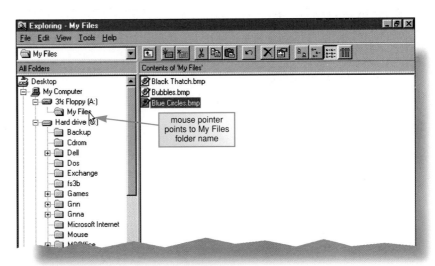

FIGURE 2-33

2 Click the My Files folder name twice (do not double-click the folder name).

Windows 95 displays a text box containing the highlighted My Files name and insertion point (Figure 2-34).

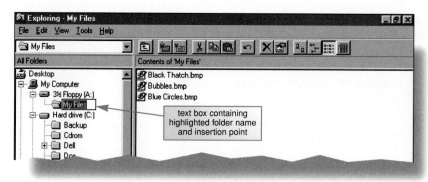

FIGURE 2-34

3 Type Clip Art Files and then press the ENTER key.

Windows 95 changes the folder name to Clip Art Files and removes the box surrounding the folder name (Figure 2-35). The new folder name replaces the old folder name in the window title, drop-down list box, Contents side title, and button on the taskbar.

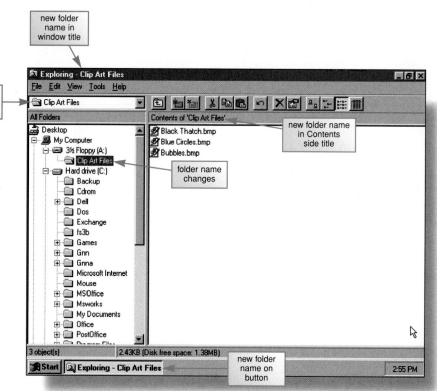

FIGURE 2-35

OtherWays

1. Click folder name, press F2, type new name, press ENTER
2. Click folder name, click File on menu bar, click Rename, type new name, press ENTER

Deleting a File or Folder

When you no longer need a file or folder, you can delete it. Two methods are commonly used to delete a file or folder. One method uses the Delete command on the context-sensitive menu that opens when you right-click the filename or folder name. Another method involves right-dragging the unneeded file or folder to the **Recycle Bin**. The Recycle Bin icon is located at the left edge of the desktop (see Figure 2-1 on page WIN 2.5).

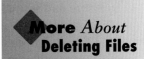
When you delete a file or folder on the hard drive using the Recycle Bin, Windows 95 stores the deleted file or folder temporarily in the Recycle Bin until you permanently discard the contents of the Recycle Bin by emptying the Recycle Bin. Until the Recycle Bin is emptied, you can retrieve the files and folders you deleted in error. Unlike deleting files or folders on the hard drive, when you delete a file or folder located on a floppy disk, the file or folder is deleted immediately and not stored in the Recycle Bin.

On the following pages, you will delete the Bubbles.bmp and Black Thatch.bmp files. The Bubbles.bmp file will be deleted by right-clicking the Bubbles.bmp filename and then clicking the Delete command on a context-sensitive menu. Next, the Black Thatch.bmp file will be deleted by dragging the Black Thatch.bmp file to the Recycle Bin.

Deleting a File by Right-Clicking Its Filename

To delete a file using the Delete command on a context-sensitive menu, right-click the filename in the Contents side to open a context-sensitive menu and then click the Delete command on the menu. To illustrate how to delete a file by right-clicking, perform the steps below and on the next page to delete the Bubbles.bmp file.

> ### More *About* Deleting Files
>
> A few years ago, someone proposed that the Delete command be removed from operating systems. It seems an entire database was deleted by an employee who thought he knew what he was doing, resulting in a company that could not function for more than a week while the database was rebuilt. Millions of dollars in revenue were lost. The Delete command is still around, but it should be considered a dangerous weapon.

Steps To Delete a File by Right-Clicking

1 **Right-click the Bubbles.bmp filename in the Contents side of the Exploring – Clip Art Files window and then point to the Delete command on the context-sensitive menu.**

Windows 95 opens a context-sensitive menu and highlights the Bubbles.bmp filename (Figure 2-36). The mouse pointer points to the Delete command on the menu.

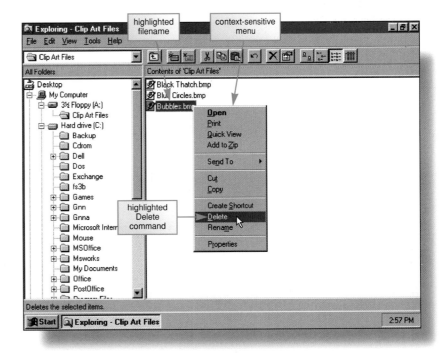

FIGURE 2-36

2 **Click Delete on the context-sensitive menu. When the Confirm File Delete dialog box opens, point to the Yes button.**

Windows 95 opens the Deleting dialog box and then opens a Confirm File Delete dialog box on top of the Deleting dialog box (Figure 2-37). The Confirm File Delete dialog box contains the message, Are you sure you want to delete 'Bubbles.bmp'?, and the Yes and No command buttons. The mouse pointer points to the Yes button. Clicking the Yes button confirms the deletion of the Bubbles.bmp file and causes the file to be deleted.

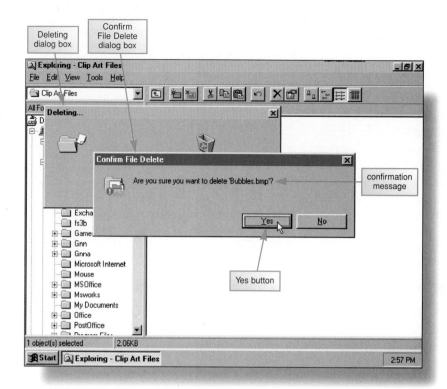

FIGURE 2-37

3 **Click the Yes button in the Confirm File Delete dialog box.**

Windows 95 closes the Confirm File Delete dialog box, displays the Deleting dialog box while the file is being deleted, and then removes the Bubbles.bmp file from the Contents side (Figure 2-38).

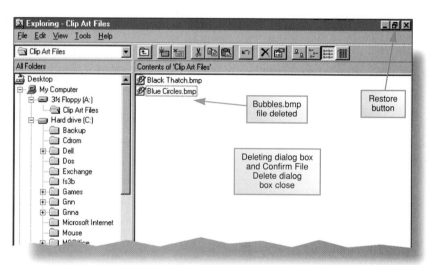

FIGURE 2-38

*Other***Ways**

1. Click filename, press DELETE

More *About* **Deleting Files**

Warning! This is your last warning! Be EXTREMELY careful when deleting files. Hours and weeks of hard work can be lost with one click of a button. If you are going to delete files or folders from your hard disk, consider making a backup of those files so that if you inadvertently delete something you need, you will be able to recover.

Deleting a File by Right-Dragging Its Filename

Another method to delete a file is to right-drag the filename from the Contents side of the window to the Recycle Bin icon on the desktop to open a context-sensitive menu, and then click the Move Here command on the context-sensitive menu. Currently, the Exploring – Clip Art Files window is maximized and occupies the entire desktop. With a maximized window, you cannot right-drag a file to the Recycle Bin. To allow you to right-drag a file, restore the Exploring – Clip Art Files window to its original size by clicking the Restore button on the title bar. Perform the following steps to delete the Black Thatch.bmp file by right-dragging its filename.

Steps **To Delete a File by Right-Dragging**

1 **Click the Restore button on the Exploring – Clip Art Files window title bar and then point to the Black Thatch.bmp filename in the Contents side of the window.**

Windows 95 restores the Exploring – Clip Art Files window to its original size before maximizing the window and replaces the Restore button on the title bar with the Maximize button (Figure 2-39). The mouse pointer points to the Black Thatch.bmp filename in the Contents side of the window.

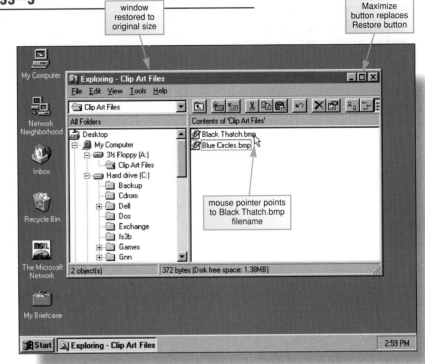

FIGURE 2-39

2 **Right-drag the Black Thatch.bmp filename over the Recycle Bin icon, and then point to the Move Here command on the context-sensitive menu.**

Windows 95 opens a context-sensitive menu and highlights the Move Here command on the menu (Figure 2-40). The Black Thatch.bmp filename displays on top of the Recycle Bin icon on the desktop and the mouse pointer points to the Move Here command on the menu.

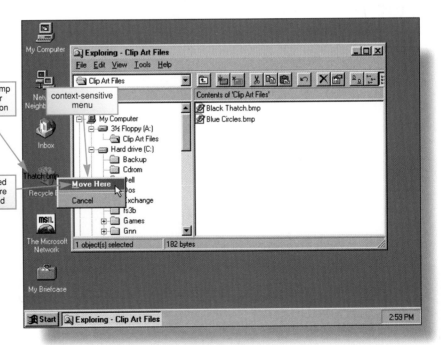

FIGURE 2-40

3 **Click Move Here on the context-sensitive menu. When the Confirm File Delete dialog box opens, point to the Yes button.**

Windows 95 opens the Deleting dialog box and then opens the Confirm File Delete dialog box on top of the Deleting dialog box (Figure 2-41). The Confirm File Delete dialog box contains the message, Are you sure you want to delete 'Black Thatch.bmp'?, and the Yes and No command buttons. The mouse pointer points to the Yes button. Clicking the Yes button confirms the deletion of the Black Thatch.bmp file and causes the file to be deleted.

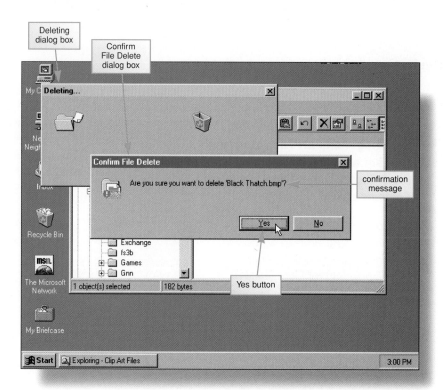

FIGURE 2-41

4 **Click the Yes button in the Confirm File Delete dialog box.**

Windows 95 closes the Confirm File Delete dialog box, displays the Deleting dialog box while the file is being deleted, and then removes the Black Thatch.bmp file from the Contents side (Figure 2-42).

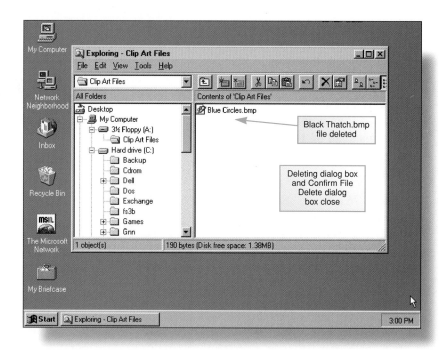

FIGURE 2-42

More *About* **the Recycle Bin**

Once you delete a file or folder, it's gone forever – True or False? Windows stores deleted files and folders in the Recycle Bin. You can recover files or folders you delete in error using the Recycle Bin.

Whether you delete a file by right-clicking or right-dragging, you can use the file selection techniques illustrated earlier in this project to delete a group of files. When deleting a group of files, click the Yes button in the Confirm Multiple File Delete dialog box to confirm the deletion of the group of files.

Deleting a Folder

When you delete a folder, Windows 95 deletes any files or subfolders in the folder. You can delete a folder using the two methods shown earlier to delete files (right-clicking or right-dragging). Perform the steps below and on the next page to delete the Clip Art Files folder on drive A by right-dragging the folder to the Recycle Bin.

 Steps To Delete a Folder

<table>
<tr><td>**More** *About* **Deleting Folders**</td></tr>
<tr><td>If you drag a folder to the Recycle Bin, only the files in that folder appear in the Recycle Bin. If you restore a file that was originally located in a deleted folder, Windows recreates the folder, and then restores the file to it.</td></tr>
</table>

1 **Point to the Clip Art Files folder name in the All Folders side of the Exploring – Clip Art Files window (Figure 2-43).**

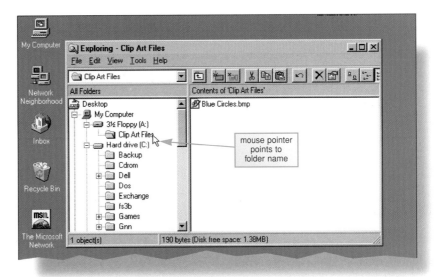

FIGURE 2-43

2 **Right-drag the Clip Art Files icon in the All Folders side to the Recycle Bin icon, and then point to the Move Here command on the context-sensitive menu.**

Windows 95 opens a context-sensitive menu (Figure 2-44). The mouse pointer points to the highlighted Move Here command on the menu.

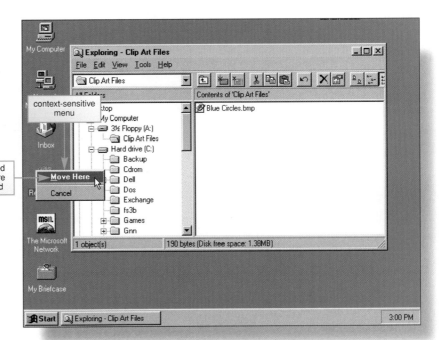

FIGURE 2-44

3 Click Move Here on the context-sensitive menu. When the Confirm Folder Delete dialog box opens, point to the Yes button.

Windows 95 opens the Deleting dialog box and then opens the Confirm Folder Delete dialog box on top of the Deleting dialog box (Figure 2-45). The Confirm Folder Delete dialog box contains the message, Are you sure you want to remove the folder 'Clip Art Files' and all its contents?, and the Yes and No command buttons. The mouse pointer points to the Yes button. Clicking the Yes button confirms the deletion of the Clip Art Files folder and causes the folder and its contents to be deleted.

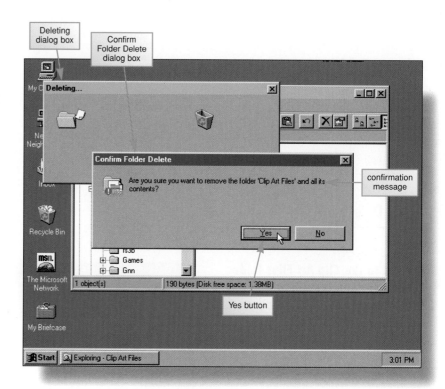

FIGURE 2-45

4 Click the Yes button in the Confirm Folder Delete dialog box.

Windows 95 closes the Confirm Folder Delete dialog box, displays the Deleting dialog box while the folder is being deleted, removes the Clip Art Files folder from the All Folders side, and replaces the minus sign preceding the 3½ Floppy [A:] icon with a plus sign (Figure 2-46).

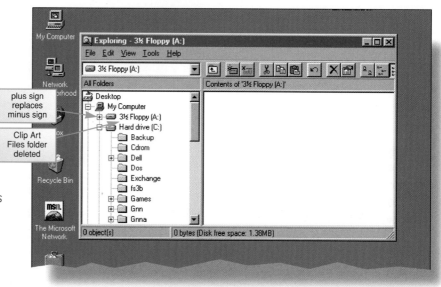

5 Remove the floppy disk from drive A.

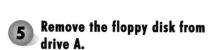

FIGURE 2-46

> **Other Ways**
> 1. Click folder name, press DELETE

Quitting Windows Explorer and Shutting Down Windows 95

After completing work with Windows Explorer, quit Windows Explorer using the Close button on the Windows Explorer title bar, and then shut down Windows using the Shut Down command on the Start menu.

Perform the following steps to quit Windows Explorer.

TO QUIT AN APPLICATION

Step 1: Point to the Close button in the Exploring window.
Step 2: Click the Close button.

Windows 95 closes the Windows Explorer window and quits Windows Explorer.

Perform the following steps to shut down Windows 95.

TO SHUT DOWN WINDOWS 95

Step 1: Click the Start button on the taskbar.
Step 2: Click Shut Down on the Start menu.
Step 3: Click the Yes button in the Shut Down Windows dialog box.
Step 4: Turn off the computer.

Project Summary

In this project, you used Windows Explorer to select and copy a group of files, change views, display the contents of a folder, create a folder, expand and collapse a folder and rename and delete a file and a folder.

What You Should Know

Having completed this project, you should now be able to perform the following tasks:

- Change to List View *(WIN 2.19)*
- Collapse a Folder *(WIN 2.11)*
- Copy a Group of Files *(WIN 2.22)*
- Create a New Folder *(WIN 2.13)*
- Delete a File by Right-Clicking *(WIN 2.27)*
- Delete a File by Right-Dragging *(WIN 2.29)*
- Delete a Folder *(WIN 2.31)*
- Display the Contents of a Folder *(WIN 2.9, WIN 2.17, WIN 2.24)*
- Expand a Folder *(WIN 2.10)*
- Expand the 3½ Floppy [A:] Folder *(WIN 2.16)*
- Quit an Application *(WIN 2.33)*
- Rename a File *(WIN 2.24)*
- Rename a Folder *(WIN 2.25)*
- Select a Group of Files *(WIN 2.20)*
- Shut Down Windows 95 *(WIN 2.33)*
- Start Windows Explorer and Maximize Its Window *(WIN 2.6)*

 Test Your Knowledge

1 True/False

Instructions: Circle T if the statement is true or F if the statement is false.

T F   1. Windows Explorer is an application you can use to organize and work with the files and folders on the computer.

T F   2. Double-clicking the My Computer icon is the best way to open Windows Explorer.

T F   3. The contents of the current folder are displayed in the All Folders side.

T F   4. To display the contents of drive C on your computer in the Contents side, click the plus sign in the small box next to the drive C icon.

T F   5. A folder that is contained within another folder is called a subfolder.

T F   6. To display the contents of a folder, right-click its folder name.

T F   7. Collapsing a folder removes the subfolders from the hierarchy of folders in the All Folders side.

T F   8. After you expand a drive or folder, the information in the Contents side is always the same as the information displayed below the drive or folder icon in the All Folders side.

T F   9. The source folder is the folder containing the files to be copied.

T F 10. You select a group of files in the Contents side by pointing to each icon or filename and clicking the left mouse button.

2 Multiple Choice

Instructions: Circle the correct response.

1. The drop-down list box in the Exploring - My Computer window contains the
   _____.
   a. hierarchy of folders
   b. source folder
   c. files in the current folder
   d. current folder

2. The _____ contains the hierarchy of folders on the computer.
   a. Contents side
   b. status bar
   c. All Folders side
   d. toolbar

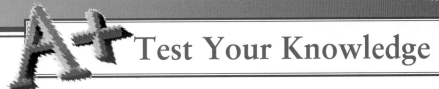

Test Your Knowledge

3. To display the contents of a folder in the Contents side, _____.
   a. double-click the plus sign next to the folder icon
   b. right-click the folder icon in the All Folders side
   c. click the folder icon in the Contents side
   d. click the folder icon in the All Folders side

4. You _____ the minus sign preceding a folder icon to expand a folder.
   a. click
   b. drag
   c. double-click
   d. point to

5. When an expanded file is collapsed in the All Folders side, _____.
   a. the expansion closes and the contents of the folder display in the Contents side
   b. the entire Exploring - My Computer window closes
   c. the computer beeps at you because you cannot perform this activity
   d. the My Computer window opens

6. To select multiple files in the Contents side, _____.
   a. right-click each file icon
   b. hold down the SHIFT key and then click each file icon you want to select
   c. hold down the CTRL key and then click each file icon you want to select
   d. hold down the CTRL key and then double-click each file icon you want to select

7. After selecting a group of files, you _____ the group to copy the files to a new folder.
   a. click
   b. right-drag
   c. double-click
   d. none of the above

8. In _____ view, each file or folder in the Contents side is represented by a smaller icon, and the files or folders are arranged in columns.
   a. large icons
   b. small icons
   c. list
   d. details

9. A file or folder can be renamed by _____.
   a. right-dragging its filename
   b. double-clicking its filename
   c. dragging its filename
   d. clicking its filename twice

(continued)

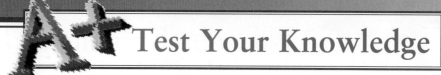

Test Your Knowledge

Multiple Choice *(continued)*

10. A file can be deleted by right-dragging the filename from the Contents side of the window to the _____ icon on the desktop.
    a. My Computer
    b. Network Neighborhood
    c. Recycle Bin
    d. My Briefcase

3 Understanding the Exploring - My Computer Window

Instructions: In Figure 2-47 arrows point to several items in the Exploring - My Computer window. Identify the items or objects in the spaces provided.

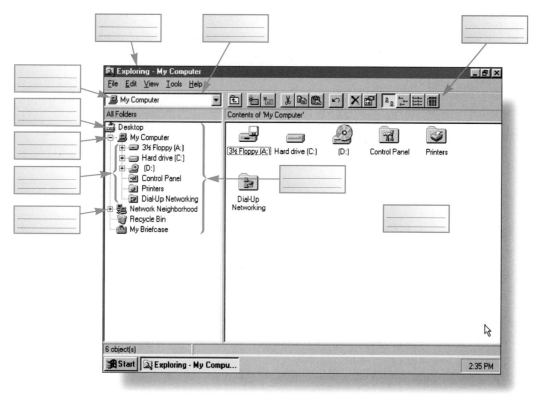

FIGURE 2-47

Use Help

1 Using Windows Help

Instructions: Use Windows Help and a computer to perform the following tasks.

1. Start Microsoft Windows 95 if necessary.
2. Answer the following questions about paths.
   a. What is a path? _____
   b. What does a path include? _____
   c. How do you specify a path? _____
   d. What do you do if your filename contains more than eight characters? _____
3. Open the Help Topics: Windows Help window. Click the Index tab if necessary and then type `windows explorer` in the text box. Click demo in the Windows Explorer list and then click the Display button. In the Windows Help window, play the demonstration.
   a. How does the demonstration open Windows Explorer? _____
   b. What folders are contained on drive C in the demonstration? _____
4. How can you cause Explorer to start each time you start Windows 95? _____
5. You have recently written a business letter to a manager named Lori Hill. You explained CD-ROM drives to her. You want to see what else you said in the letter, but you can neither remember the name of the file nor where you stored the file on your computer. You read something in your Windows 95 manual that the Find command could be used to find lost files. Using Help, determine what you must do to find your letter. Write those steps in the spaces provided.

   _____
   _____

   _____
6. You and a friend both recently bought computers. She was lucky and received a color printer as her birthday gift. You would like to print some of your more colorful documents on her color printer. You have heard that for not too much money you can buy a network card and some cable and hook up your computers on a network. Then, you can print documents stored on your computer on her color printer. Using Windows Help, determine if you can share her printer. If so, what must you do in Windows 95 to make this become a reality. Print the Help pages that document your answer.
7. You can hardly believe that last week you won a laptop computer at a charity dance. The application programs on the laptop are the same as those on your desktop computer. The only trouble is that when you use your laptop computer to modify a file, you would like the same file on your desktop also to be modified. In that way, you can work on the file either on your desktop computer or on your laptop computer. A friend mentioned that the My Briefcase feature of Windows 95 allows you to do what you want to do. Using Windows Help, find out all you can about My Briefcase. Print the Help pages that specify how to keep files on both your desktop and laptop computers synchronized with each other.

In the Lab

1 File and Program Properties

Instructions: Use a computer to perform the following tasks and answer the questions.

1. Start Microsoft Windows 95 if necessary.
2. Open the My Computer window.
3. Open the drive C window on your computer.
4. Scroll until the Windows icon is visible in the drive C window.
5. Right-click the Windows icon.
6. Click Open on the context-sensitive menu.
7. Scroll until the Black Thatch icon is visible. If the Black Thatch icon does not display on your computer, find another Paint icon.
8. Right-click the Black Thatch icon.
9. Click Properties on the context-sensitive menu.
10. Answer the following questions about the Black Thatch file:
    a. What type of file is Black Thatch? _____
    b. What is the path for the location of the Black Thatch file? (Hint: Point to the location of the file)
    _____
    c. What is the size (in bytes) of the Black Thatch file? _____
    d. What is the MS-DOS name of the Black Thatch file? _____ The tilde (~) character is placed in the MS-DOS filename when the Windows 95 filename is greater than 8 characters. Windows 95 uses the first six characters of the long filename, the tilde character, and a number to distinguish the file from other files that might have the same first six characters.
    e. When was the file created? _____
    f. When was the file last modified? _____
    g. When was the file last accessed ? _____
11. Click the Cancel button in the Black Thatch Properties dialog box.
12. Scroll in the Windows window until the Notepad icon displays.
13. Right-click the Notepad icon.
14. Click Properties on the context-sensitive menu.
15. Answer the following questions:
    a. What type of file is Notepad? _____
    b. What is the path of the Notepad file? _____
    c. How big is the Notepad file? _____
    d. What is the file extension of the Notepad file? What does it stand for?
    _____
    e. What is the file version of the Notepad file? _____
    f. What is the file's description? _____
    g. Who is the copyright owner of Notepad? _____
    h. What language is Notepad written for? _____
16. Click the Cancel button in the Notepad Properties dialog box.
17. Close all open windows.

In the Lab

2 Windows Explorer

Instructions: Use a computer to perform the following tasks:

1. Start Microsoft Windows 95.
2. Right-click the My Computer icon.
3. Click Explore on the context-sensitive menu.
4. Maximize the Exploring window.
5. Drag the bar between the All Folders side and the Contents side to the center of the Exploring window. What difference do you see in the Window? _____

   _____

6. Return the bar to its previous location.
7. Click Tools on the menu bar.
8. Click Go to on the Tools menu.
9. Type c:\windows and then click the OK button in the Go To Folder dialog box. What happened in the Exploring window? _____

10. Click View on the menu bar and then click Small Icons on the View menu.
11. Click View on the menu bar and then click Options on the View menu.
12. Drag the Options dialog box so you can see the Contents side of the Exploring window. Click Show all files. Click the Apply button. Do any more folders display? If so, what new folders display? Did more files display?

    _____

    _____

13. Click Hide files of these types. Click Hide MS-DOS file extensions for file types that are registered. Click the Apply button. Did the filenames displayed in the Contents area change? If so, what are the changes? Give three examples of filenames that are different:

    _____

    _____

14. Click Hide MS-DOS file extensions for file types that are registered. Click Hide files of these types. Click the OK button.
15. Click View on the menu bar and then click Details on the View menu.
    a. In the Contents side, scroll until you see only file icons and then click the Name button below the Contents of 'Windows' bar. Did the sequence of file icons change? How?

       _____

    b. Click the Size button. How did the sequence of file icons change? _____
    c. Click the Type button. How did the sequence of file icons change? _____
    d. Click the Modified button. How did the sequence of folder and file icons change?

       _____

    e. Click the Name button.

(continued)

In the Lab

Windows Explorer *(continued)*

16. Click Edit on the menu bar. Click Select All on the Edit menu. If the Select All dialog box displays, click the OK button. What happened? _____

17. Click Edit on the menu bar. Click Invert Selection on the Edit menu. Was there any change?
_____

18. Click File on the menu bar. Point to New on the File menu and then click Bitmap Image on the New submenu. What happened? _____

19. Type In the Lab Image and then press the ENTER key. What is the name of the bitmap image?
_____

20. Right-click the In the Lab Image icon. Click Delete on the context-sensitive menu. Click the Yes button in the Confirm File Delete dialog box.

21. Close the Exploring window.

3 Window Toolbars

Instructions: Use a computer to perform the following tasks:

1. Open the My Computer window.
2. Maximize the My Computer window.
3. Click View on the menu bar. Click Large icons on the View menu.
4. Click View on the menu bar. If a check does not display to the left of the Toolbar command, click Toolbar on the View menu. A toolbar displays in the My Computer window (Figure 2-48).
5. Click the down arrow next to the drop-down list box containing the My Computer icon and name.
6. Click the drive C icon in the drop-down list. How did the window change? _____
_____
7. Double-click the Windows icon. What happened? _____
_____
8. In the Windows window, if the toolbar does not display, click View on the menu bar and then click Toolbar on the View menu.
9. Scroll down if necessary until the Argyle icon displays in the window. If the Argyle icon does not display on your computer, find another Paint icon. Click the Argyle icon and then point to the Copy button on the toolbar (Hint: To determine the function of each button on the toolbar, point to the button).
10. Click the Copy button. Do you see any change? If so, what? _____

In the Lab

11. Insert a formatted floppy disk in drive A of your computer.
12. Click the down arrow next to the drop-down list box containing the Windows icon and name.
13. Click the 3½ Floppy [A:] icon in the drop-down list. What happened? _____
14. If the toolbar does not display in the 3½ Floppy [A:] window, click View on the menu bar and then click Toolbar on the View menu.
15. In the 3½ Floppy [A:] window, click the Paste button on the toolbar. The Argyle icon displays in the 3½ Floppy [A:] window.
16. With the Argyle icon highlighted in the 3½ Floppy [A:] window, click the Delete button on the toolbar and then click the Yes button in the Confirm File Delete dialog box.
17. In the 3½ Floppy [A:] window, return the toolbar status to what it was prior to step 8. Close the 3½ Floppy [A:] window.
18. In the drive C window, click the Small Icons button and then describe the screen. _____
_____
19 Click the List button and then describe the screen. _____
20. Click the Details button and then describe the screen. _____
21. Click the Large Icons button on the toolbar
22. Click the Up One Level button on the toolbar. What is the difference between clicking the Up One Level button and clicking My Computer in the drop-down list box? _____
23. Return the toolbar status to what it was prior to step 4. Close the My Computer and drive C windows.

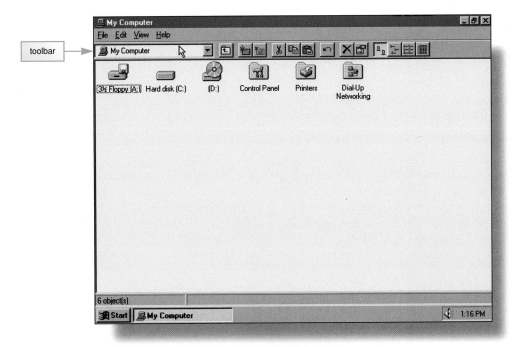

FIGURE 2-48

Cases and Places

The difficulty of these case studies varies:

◗ Case studies preceded by a single half moon are the least difficult. You can complete these case studies using your own computer in the lab.

◗◗ Case studies preceded by two half moons are more difficult. You must research the topic presented using the Internet, a library, or another resource, and then prepare a brief written report.

◗◗◗ Case studies preceded by three half moons are the most difficult. You must visit a store or business to obtain the necessary information, and then use it to create a brief written report.

1 ◗ A key feature of Windows 95 is the capability to modify the view of a window to suit individual preferences and needs. Using Windows Explorer, display the Hard drive [C:] folder in the Contents side and then experiment with the different commands on the View menu. Describe the effects of the Large Icons, Small Icons, List, and Details commands on the icons in the Contents side. When using details view, explain how clicking one of the buttons at the top of the Contents side (such as Name or Type) changes the window. Try out diverse arrangements of icons on the Contents side by pointing to the Arrange Icons command on the View menu and then clicking various commands on the Arrange Icons submenu. Finally, specify situations in which you think some of the views you have seen would be most appropriate.

2 ◗ When the Hard disk [C:] folder is displayed in the Contents side of the Exploring window, it is clear that an enormous number of folders and files are stored on your computer's hard disk. Imagine how hard it would be to manually search through all the folders and files to locate a specific file! Fortunately, Windows 95 provides the Find command to perform the search for you. Click Tools on the Exploring window menu bar, point to Find, and then click Files or Folders on the Find submenu. Learn about each sheet in the Find: All Files dialog box by clicking a tab (Name & Location, Date Modified, or Advanced), clicking the Help menu, clicking What's This? on the Help menu, and then clicking an item on a sheet. Try finding a file using each sheet. Finally, explain how the Find command is used and describe a circumstance in which each sheet would be useful. When you are finished, click the Close button on the window title bar to close the Find: All Files dialog box.

3 ◗◗ Backing up files is an important way to protect data and ensure it is not inadvertently lost or destroyed. File backup on a personal computer can use a variety of devices and techniques. Using the Internet, a library, personal computer magazines, or other resources, determine the types of devices used to store backed up data, the schedules, methods, and techniques for backing up data, and the consequences of not backing up data. Write a brief report of your findings.

Cases and Places

4 ▶▶ A hard disk must be maintained in order to be used most efficiently. This maintenance includes deleting old files, defragmenting a disk so it is not wasteful of space, and from time to time finding and attempting to correct disk failures. Using the Internet, a library, Windows 95 Help, or other research facilities, determine the maintenance that should be performed on hard disks, including the type of maintenance, when it should be performed, how long it takes to perform the maintenance, and the risks, if any, of not performing the maintenance. Write a brief report on the information you obtain.

5 ▶▶▶ The quest for more and faster disk storage continues as application programs grow larger and create sound and graphic files. One technique for increasing the amount of data that can be stored on a disk is disk compression. Disk compression programs, using a variety of mathematical algorithms, store data in less space on a hard disk. Many companies sell software you can load on your computer to perform the task. Windows 95 has disk compression capabilities as part of the operating system. Visit a computer store and find two disk compression programs you can buy. Write a brief report comparing the two packages to the disk compression capabilities of Windows 95. Discuss the similarities and differences between the programs and identify the program that claims to be the most efficient in compressing data.

6 ▶▶▶ Some individuals in the computer industry think both the Windows 3.1 and the Windows 95 operating systems are deficient when it comes to ease of file management. Therefore, they have developed and marketed software that augments the operating systems to provide different and, they claim, improved services for file management. Visit a computer store and inquire about products such as Symantec's Norton Navigator for Windows 95. Write a brief report comparing the products you tested with Windows 95. Explain which you prefer and why.

7 ▶▶▶ Data stored on disk is one of a company's more valuable assets. If that data were to be stolen, lost, or compromised so it could not be accessed, the company could literally go out of business. Therefore, companies go to great lengths to protect their data. Visit a company or business in your area. Find out how it protects its data against viruses, unauthorized access, and even against such natural disasters as fire and tornadoes. Prepare a brief report that describes the procedures. In your report, point out any areas where you see the company has not adequately protected its data.

Index

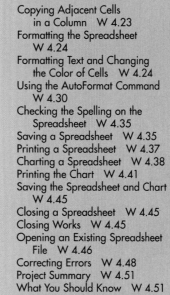

Microsoft Works 4 Windows 95

(continued)

Microsoft Works 4

Creating a Formatted Document with Clip Art

Objectives

You will have mastered the material in this project when you can:

▶ Start Microsoft Works for Windows 95
▶ Start the Word Processor tool
▶ Identify the features of the Works word processing window
▶ Enter text
▶ Highlight a character, word, line, or paragraph
▶ Center one or more words
▶ Change fonts, font sizes, and font styles
▶ Create a bulleted list
▶ Change the color of text
▶ Insert clip art in a document
▶ Use the Print Preview feature
▶ Save a document
▶ Print a document
▶ Close a document
▶ Close Works
▶ Open an existing document
▶ Delete and insert data
▶ Use online Help

Project 1

Four Score and Seven Years Ago . . .

How did Abe ever get by without a Word Processor?

What if Abraham Lincoln had owned a laptop computer? While he might not have improved the Gettysburg Address, he could have saved himself a case of writer's cramps from handwriting the multiple copies requested by friends and historians.

Today, writers are more fortunate than Mr. Lincoln. Whether facing a term paper for Poly Sci or writing home for more money, the word processor of Microsoft Works, with its built-in Task Wizards for letters, resumés, and other documents gives anyone a running start.

In college and in virtually any career thereafter— engineer, scientist, movie writer, journalist, or U.S. President—it is essential that you present the ideas and products of your work in clear, accurate written form. In fact, just getting a start in a chosen profession may depend on how well you are represented by your stand-in: a well-prepared resumé.

Making a favorable first impression is not only important, it is vital.

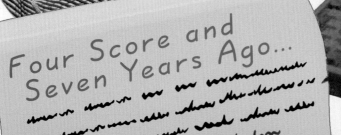

Four Score and
Seven Years Ago...

Once you have a job, you are likely to find that companies no longer provide secretarial assistance for creating and revising documents. Now employers expect professionals to come to the workplace armed with these skills.

Fortunately, technology has risen to the challenge. In the days of typewriters, every change and every mistake meant retyping a page or sometimes the whole document. Today's tools permit words, sentences, pages, and even whole sections of text to be added, deleted, or reordered with the click of a mouse before using a single page of printer paper. With the built-in spelling checker and thesaurus, capabilities are included for searching out spelling errors and finding those elusive synonyms.

Why the emphasis on accuracy? Because errors are expensive. Consider *Time* magazine's $100,000 missing "r." The presses had already begun rolling out the covers for the March 21, 1983 issue when someone discovered the letter r missing from the word "Control" in the headline: "A New Plan for Arms Contol." This mistake cost the publication $100,000 and a day's delay to add back the letter r. Spelling checker would have spotted this.

In the same manner, written errors can become legend. In 1631, an authorized edition of the *Holy Bible* came off the presses in London with the "not" missing from the seventh of the Ten Commandments. The result: "Thou shalt commit adultery." The book's publishers were fined 3,000 English pounds and went down in history as the creators of the *Wicked Bible*. This illustrates that even the best tools cannot replace careful proofreading.

Though the Works Word Processor is not a substitute for original thought and careful review, it can remove many of the artificial barriers to completing a quality education and later on, getting a quality job.

In the Beginning... ¶

Project 1

Microsoft
Works 4
Windows 95

Creating a Formatted Document with Clip Art

Case Perspective

The National Business Training Seminars has grown rapidly in the last four years — primarily as a provider of continuing business education on leadership skills. Management feels that by the year 2000, more than one million companies will be disseminating information and services on the Internet. To instruct businesses how to effectively use the Internet as a business tool, management has designed a new workshop. They have asked you to design and create an announcement advertising the company's new comprehensive, one-day seminar on how businesses can gain desktop access to the world. In addition, Victor Lebar, marketing director, has asked you to insert an illustration in the announcement to make it more visually appealing and draw attention to the global opportunities of using the Internet.

You are to create an attractive, informative advertisement that will convey the importance of attending the seminar. You are to enter the text and format the document with color and clip art so it is suitable for mailing to businesses.

Introduction to Microsoft Works for Windows 95

Microsoft Works for Windows 95 is application software that provides word processing, spreadsheet, database, and communications capabilities in a single package.

The applications within Microsoft Works for Windows 95, called **tools**, work together to help you create your documents. These tools are briefly described in the following paragraphs.

1. **Word Processor Tool** — Use the Word Processor tool to prepare all forms of personal and business communications, including letters, business and academic reports, and other types of written documents.
2. **Spreadsheet Tool** — Use the Spreadsheet tool for applications that require you to enter, calculate, manipulate, and analyze data. You can also use the Spreadsheet tool to display data graphically in the form of charts, such as bar charts and pie charts.
3. **Database Tool** — Use the Database tool for creating, sorting, retrieving, displaying, and printing data such as names and addresses of friends or customers, company inventories, employee payroll records, or other types of business or personal data. You can use the Database tool for virtually any type of record keeping activity that requires you to create, sort, display, retrieve, and print data.

4. **Communications Tool** — Use the Communications tool with a modem to communicate computer to computer with other computer users, information services, and special-interest bulletin board services. You can use the Communications tool to send and receive messages through electronic mail or fax.

Microsoft Works Accessories

Additional software features, called **accessories**, are a part of the software package that helps you work more effectively with the various tools. These accessories include Spelling Checker, which allows you to check the spelling in documents; ClipArt Gallery, which contains illustrations you can insert in documents; a WordArt feature, which allows you to change plain text into artistically designed text; Note-It, which allows you to insert pop-up notes in a document, and Microsoft Draw, which allows you to create and modify drawings that can be inserted into a Word Processor document or a Database form. These accessories will be explained in detail as they are used throughout the book.

Templates and TaskWizards

In addition to the Microsoft Works tools and accessories, Works includes templates and TaskWizards to help you create professional-looking documents. **Templates** are documents that contain all the settings, text, and formats that you can reuse. For example, when you create a thank you letter for a job interview, you can save it as a template and reuse it as a basis for writing other thank you letters for interviews.

TaskWizards permit you to create a letter, design a database, create a newsletter, and similar activities by asking you what you want to do. Based on your responses, TaskWizard performs the task. For example, when creating a resume, Works will ask if you want to add a letterhead to the resume, what type of professionally designed layout you want to use, or what category headings you want to include in the resume. Based on your responses, Works inserts the elements you specify and designs the resume automatically for you. When the TaskWizard is finished, you can add or remove text and make any changes you want.

Mouse Usage

In this book, the mouse is used as the primary way to communicate with Microsoft Works. You can perform five operations with a mouse: point, click, right-click, double-click, and drag.

Point means you move the mouse across a flat surface until the mouse pointer rests on the item of choice on the screen. As you move the mouse, the mouse pointer moves across the screen in the same direction. **Click** means you press and release the left mouse button. The terminology used in this book to direct you to point to a particular item and then click is, Click the particular item. For example, Click the Bold button, means point to the Bold button and then click.

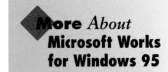

More *About*
Microsoft Works for Windows 95

Microsoft Works for Windows 95 combines four of the most popular types of PC programs in one package – a word processor, a spreadsheet program, a database management program, and a communications program. Each of the four tools is not as sophisticated as the larger and more sophisticated stand-alone products like Microsoft Word for Windows or Lotus 1-2-3. Works' big advantage is that it offers a package that includes the most important features of the stand-alone products at a fraction of the cost.

Right-click means you press and release the right mouse button. As with the left mouse button, you normally will point to an item on the screen prior to right-clicking. When you right-click in Microsoft Works for Windows 95, a context-sensitive menu displays. The **context-sensitive menu** contains frequently used commands you can use with the current selection.

Double-click means you quickly press and release the left mouse button twice without moving the mouse. In most cases, you must point to an item before double-clicking. **Drag** means you point to an item, hold down the left mouse button, move the item to the desired location on the screen, and then release the left mouse button.

The use of the mouse is an important skill when working with Microsoft Works for Windows 95.

Project One

Because word processing is widely used in both the academic and business world, the Word Processor is the first of the Works tools presented. To illustrate the use and power of the Word Processor, the steps necessary to create the document shown in Figure 1-1 are explained on the following pages. This announcement advertises a one-day seminar, Doing Business on the Internet.

To create the announcement, you must type the text, center selected lines, use several different fonts and font styles, enlarge the fonts, change the font styles to bold, add bullets to the list, insert an illustration into the document, and display the last three lines in red. You can accomplish these tasks easily using the Microsoft Works for Windows 95 Word Processor.

DOING BUSINESS ON THE INTERNET

A ONE-DAY SEMINAR

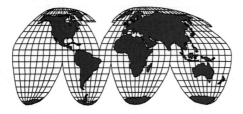

Discover how you can tap into the Internet marketplace to successfully promote your company's products and services. Ride the information superhighway to greater profits.

Learn to:

- **Identify business opportunities on the Internet**
- **Use the Internet's tools to attract customers**
- **Publish Home Pages that introduce your business to potential prospects**
- **Safeguard information and ensure confidentiality for your company and your clients**

Register Now

CALL (714) 555-3567
FAX (714) 555-2468
E-MAIL seminar@email.com

FIGURE 1-1

Starting Microsoft Works for Windows 95

To start Works, Windows 95 must be running and Microsoft Works version 4.0 must be installed on your computer. Perform the following steps to start Works.

Steps **To Start Microsoft Works for Windows 95**

1 **Click the Start button on the taskbar, point to Programs, point to the Microsoft Works 4.0 folder on the Programs submenu, and then point to Microsoft Works 4.0 on the Microsoft Works 4.0 submenu.**

When you click the Start button on the taskbar, the Start menu displays (Figure 1-2). The right-pointing arrow to the right of Programs indicates a submenu is associated with the menu. When you point to Programs, the Programs submenu displays. When you point to the Microsoft Works 4.0 folder on the Programs submenu, the Microsoft Works 4.0 submenu displays. The mouse pointer points to the application name, Microsoft Works 4.0.

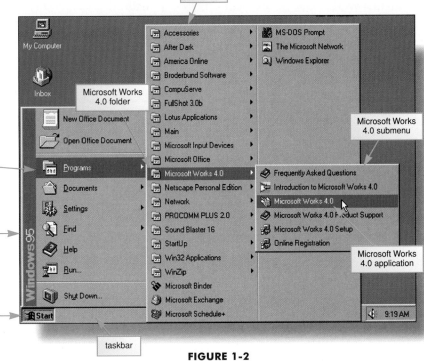

FIGURE 1-2

2 **Click Microsoft Works 4.0. When the Works Task Launcher dialog box displays, point to the Works Tools tab.**

*Works briefly displays a message on the screen about Works and the software license. Then, the Microsoft Works application window containing a dialog box with the title, **Works Task Launcher**, displays (Figure 1-3). The Works Task Launcher dialog box contains three tabbed sheets; TaskWizards, Existing Documents, and Works Tools. The **TaskWizards sheet** currently displays on the screen. A list of wizard categories displays in the list box. The **Common Tasks category** displays six TaskWizards you can use to quickly create a document. The*

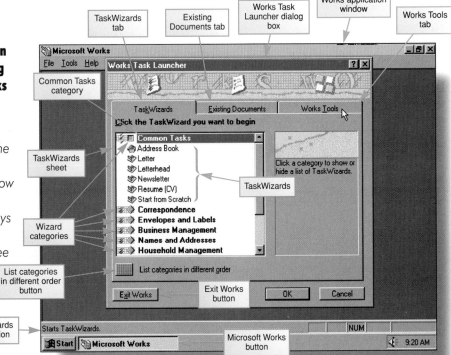

FIGURE 1-3

List categories in different order button *located below the list of wizard categories rearranges the TaskWizards list. The **Exit Works button** located in the lower left corner of the Works Task Launcher dialog box closes all open Works documents and closes Works. A brief description of the TaskWizard sheet displays below the Works Task Launcher dialog box. The **Microsoft Works button** displays on the taskbar. The mouse pointer points to the **Works Tools tab**.*

3 **Click the Works Tools tab.**

When you click the Works Tools tab, the **Works Tools sheet** *moves forward and the TaskWizards sheet that was on top moves behind the Works Tools sheet (Figure 1-4). The buttons in the Works Tools sheet allow you to start any of the Works tools.*

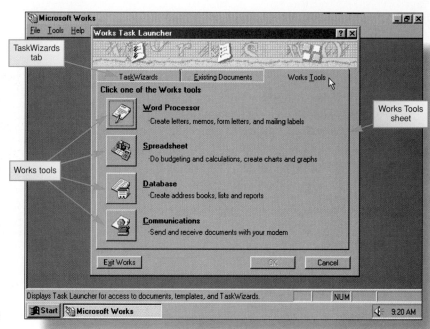

FIGURE 1-4

You have now started Works and are ready to choose the tool you want to use. To create the document in Figure 1-1 on page W 1.8, use the Word Processor tool.

Starting the Word Processor

Start the Word Processor by choosing the appropriate button in the Works Task Launcher dialog box. The following steps explain this process.

 To Start the Word Processor

1 **Point to the Word Processor button on the Works Tools sheet (Figure 1-5).**

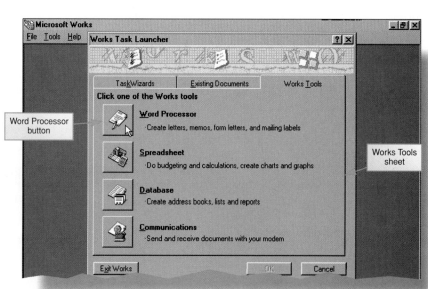

FIGURE 1-5

2 **Click the Word Processor button.**

Works displays the Word Processor document window containing the document name, Unsaved Document 1, within the Microsoft Works application window (Figure 1-6). The Help window displays next to the document window. The Word Processor Menu displays in the Help window because the Word Processor tool was chosen. Be aware the Help window may or may not display to the right of the document. The display of the Help window depends on the status of the Help window the last time the Word Processor was used.

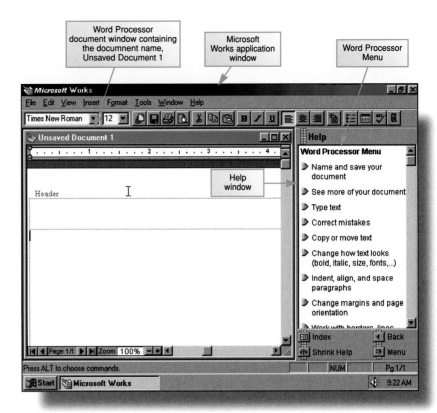

FIGURE 1-6

3 **Point to the Shrink Help button located below the Word Processor Menu in the Help window (Figure 1-7).**

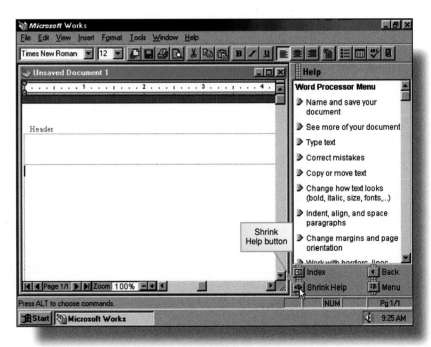

FIGURE 1-7

4 **Click the Shrink Help button.**

Works minimizes the Help window in a vertical bar to the right of the document window and increases the working space of the document window (Figure 1-8).

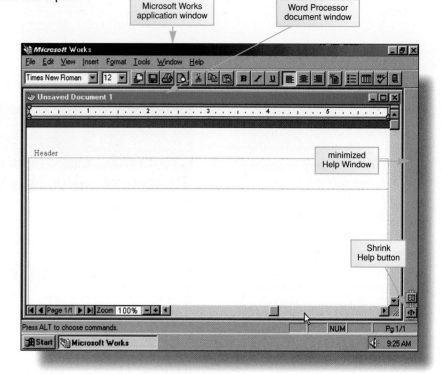

FIGURE 1-8

When you minimize the Help window (Figure 1-8), you can see more of your document. To display the Help window to the right of the document window, click the Shrink Help button located at the bottom right corner of the Works window.

The large window is the Microsoft Works application window, and the smaller window is the Word Processor document window. The blank area in the document window is the area where Works displays the text as you type. The document window contains the title, Unsaved Document 1. Unsaved Document 1 is the name assigned by Works to the first word processing document you create. Works uses this name until you name the document and save it on disk.

Each window has its own border, title bar, Minimize, Maximize or Restore, and Close buttons. It is recommended that both the application window and the document window be maximized when you use the Word Processor tool.

Maximizing the Document Window

When you start the Word Processor, the Microsoft Works application window is maximized by default. The document window, however, is not maximized. To maximize the document window, complete the following steps.

To Maximize The Document Window

1 **Point to the Maximize button in the document window (Figure 1-9).**

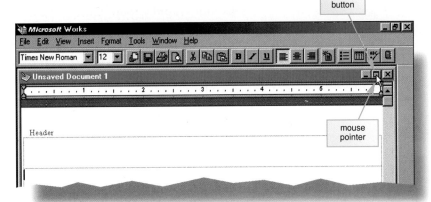

FIGURE 1-9

2 **Click the Maximize button.**

The document window is maximized (Figure 1-10). The document name, Unsaved Document 1, now displays in the application window title bar at the top of the screen.

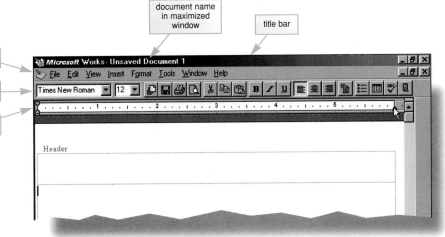

FIGURE 1-10

The Word Processor Window

The Word Processor window has many of the features common to all window screens. The following section describes these features.

Title Bar

The **title bar** (see Figure 1-10) contains the title of the application window, Microsoft Works, and the document name, Unsaved Document 1.

Menu Bar

The **menu bar** displays menu names. Each menu name represents a menu that contains commands you choose when you open, close, save, or print documents, or otherwise manipulate data in the document you are creating.

Toolbar

The **toolbar** contains buttons that allow you to perform frequently required tasks more rapidly than when using the commands in the menus. Each button on the toolbar has a pictorial representation in a small square box that helps you identify its function. Figure 1-11 illustrates the toolbar and describes the function of each of the buttons. The use of the toolbar is explained in more detail as you use the buttons in the projects in this book.

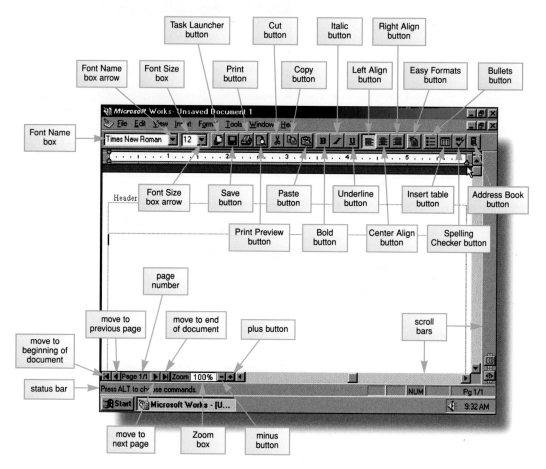

FIGURE 1-11

To choose any of these buttons, position the mouse pointer on the button and click. Any button you choose appears recessed or light gray. When you position the mouse pointer on a button on the toolbar, a ToolTip displays. A **ToolTip** is a small rectangular box that contains a word or words describing the purpose of the button. A more complete description of the button function displays in the status bar. You can control when the toolbar displays by clicking the Toolbar command on the View menu. You can also control the display of the ToolTip. On the Tools menu, click the Customize Toolbar command, and then click Enable ToolTips. Works displays a check mark in the box. Removing the check mark from the Enable ToolTips check box prevents a ToolTip from displaying when the mouse pointer is positioned on a button on the toolbar.

Ruler

In the area below the toolbar is a numbered bar called the **ruler** (Figure 1-10 on page W 1.13). The zero point is at the left edge of the ruler and it indicates the left edge of your text. Toward the right side of the ruler is the 6-inch mark that indicates the right edge of your text. The numbers in between show the distance in inches on the document. Thus, a line approximately six inches in length is represented on the screen. As you type characters on the screen, the characters display in the blank area below the ruler. By comparing the characters typed to the ruler, it is easy to see the number of inches occupied by the typed characters.

You can use the small triangles on the left and right sides of the ruler to control paragraph indents. When the ruler is displayed, you can change paragraph indents by dragging the small triangles. Tab stops are set by default at each half inch on the ruler and are denoted by the small vertical line on the ruler line.

Scroll Bars

When the text you enter occupies a length or width greater than the size of the display screen, you can use the **scroll bars** to move through the document (Figure 1-11). The left side of the scroll bar contains page arrows that assist you in moving through a document that consists of more than a single page. Clicking the left-pointing page arrow that is preceded by a vertical line will move the insertion point to the beginning of the document. Click the left-pointing page arrow without a vertical line to move the insertion point to the beginning of the previous page. Clicking the right-pointing page arrow without the vertical line will move the insertion point forward to the beginning of the next page in the document. When you click the right-pointing page arrow with a vertical line, the insertion point will move to the end of the document. The page number and total number of pages in a document display between the page arrows.

The **Zoom box** is located to the right of the page arrows. The Zoom box controls how much of a page displays at one time in the document window. Clicking the Zoom box displays a list of available zoom percentages to magnify or reduce your document on the screen. You can also use the plus or minus buttons next to the Zoom box to control the document display. To magnify your document, click the plus button. To reduce your document, click the minus button.

Status Bar

The **status bar** is located at the bottom of the Works window (Figure 1-11). The left side of the status bar displays comments that assist you in using Works. Keyboard indicators such as NUM display on the right side of the status bar. NUM indicates that Works will display numbers if you press the keys on the numeric keypad that is located to the right of the standard keyboard. The page number and total number of pages in a document display in the lower right corner of the status bar.

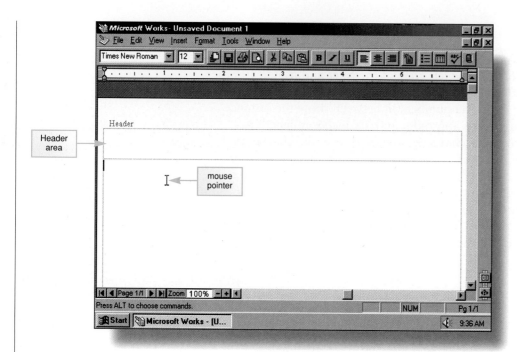

FIGURE 1-12

Mouse Pointer

The **mouse pointer** is used to point to various parts of the screen and indicates which area of the screen will be affected when you click or right-click (Figure 1-12). The mouse pointer changes shape in different parts of the screen. Within the blank area of the screen, called the **document workspace**, the mouse pointer takes the shape of an I-beam. An **I-beam** is a vertical line with short crossbars on the top and bottom.

On the menu bar, the ruler, and the scroll bar areas, the mouse pointer takes the shape of a block arrow. Other forms and uses of the mouse pointer are explained as required in the development of various documents.

View Modes

You can work with a Word Processor document in one of two **view modes**; page layout view or normal view. **Page layout view** displays each page of your document as it will look when printed. Figure 1-12 displays a blank document in page layout view. The **Header area** displays at the top of the document. Any text typed in this area will appear at the top of every page.

Normal view displays your document close to the way it looks when it is printed. In normal view, however, more of your document displays on the screen at one time. When you first start the Works Word Processor, the initial view mode setting is page layout view.

Changing View Modes

Project 1 uses the normal view to create the document in Figure 1-1 on page W1.8. To change the view from page layout to normal view, click the **Normal command** on the **View menu**. Complete the steps on the next page to change views in the Word Processor.

Steps **To Change Views in the Word Processor**

1 Point to View on the menu bar.

The mouse pointer points to the View menu name (Figure 1-13).

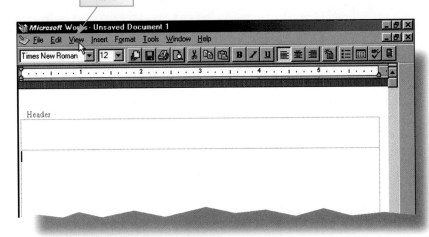

FIGURE 1-13

2 Click View on the menu bar. When the View menu displays, point to Normal.

Works displays the View menu and the mouse pointer is positioned on the Normal command (Figure 1-14). A check mark displays to the left of the Page Layout command indicating the command is in effect.

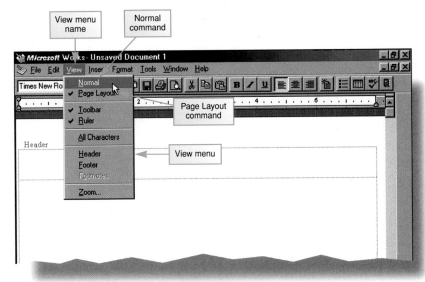

FIGURE 1-14

3 Click Normal.

Works displays the document in Normal view (Figure 1-15).

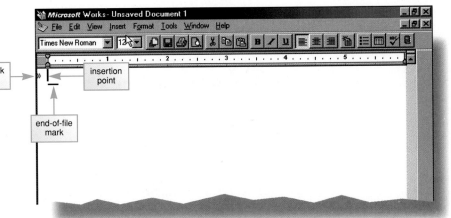

FIGURE 1-15

After you click Normal, a check mark appears to the left of this command the next time you display the View menu, indicating the command is in effect.

Page Break Mark, Insertion Point, and End-of-File Mark

In the upper left corner of the blank workspace in normal view (Figure 1-15 on the previous page), two small arrows, called a **chevron character**, point to the right. The chevron character is the **page break mark** that appears on the first line of a new document. The mark also appears in the left margin of the screen when a page break occurs after you have entered a full page of text.

The **insertion point** is a blinking vertical bar that indicates where the next character you type will appear on the screen. The insertion point also indicates the beginning position in a document where you can insert text, delete text, or change the appearance of text. The insertion point is controlled by the movement of the mouse.

The short horizontal line below the insertion point in Figure 1-15 is the **end-of-file** mark. This mark displays as the last character in every document and indicates where the document ends. You can move the insertion point throughout the document you create, but you cannot move it beyond the end-of-file mark.

Word Processor Defaults

Before you enter the text to create a document, you should know about the predefined settings for the Word Processor, called **defaults**, that affect the way your screen appears and the way a document prints. Consider the following important defaults.

1. Margins – When printing a document, Works places a one-inch top margin and a one-inch bottom margin on each page. The right and left margins are 1.25 inches each.
2. Spacing – Text is single-spaced.
3. Line width – Line width is six inches, based on a paper size of 8.5 inches by 11 inches.
4. Tab stops – Tab stops are set along the ruler at one-half inch intervals.
5. Default drive – Drive C, the hard disk, is the default drive for saving and retrieving documents.

You can change these defaults by using the commands from various Works menus.

Understanding Fonts, Font Styles, and Font Sizes

To create the announcement in Figure 1-1 on page W1.8, you must format the page. Formatting refers to the process of controlling the appearance of the characters that appear on the screen and in the printed document. With Works you can specify the font, font size, font style and color of one or more characters, words, sentences, or paragraphs in a document.

Fonts

A **font** is a set of characters with a specific design. Each font is identified by a name. Some of the commonly used fonts are **Times New Roman, Courier New**, and **Arial** (Figure 1-16).

Each of the fonts in Figure 1-16 has a unique design. When using Windows 95, a variety of fonts become available that you can use with Works.

Most fonts fall into one of two major categories: (1) serif, or (2) sans serif. **Serif** fonts have small curved finishing strokes in the characters. The Times New Roman and Courier New fonts are examples of a serif font. Serif fonts are considered easy to read when large blocks of text are involved and normally are used in books and magazines for the main text material.

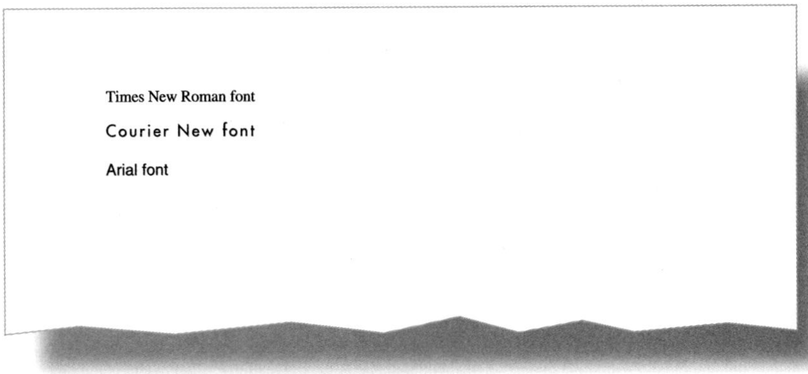

Sans serif fonts are relatively plain, straight letter forms. The Arial font in Figure 1-16 is a sans serif font. Sans serif fonts are commonly used in headlines and short titles.

Times New Roman font

Courier New font

Arial font

FIGURE 1-16

Font Style

In Works, **font style** is the term used to describe the special appearance of text and numbers. Widely used font styles include bold, italic, and underlined (Figure 1-17). You can choose bold, italic, and underlined font styles using toolbar buttons. All three styles can be applied to a set of characters.

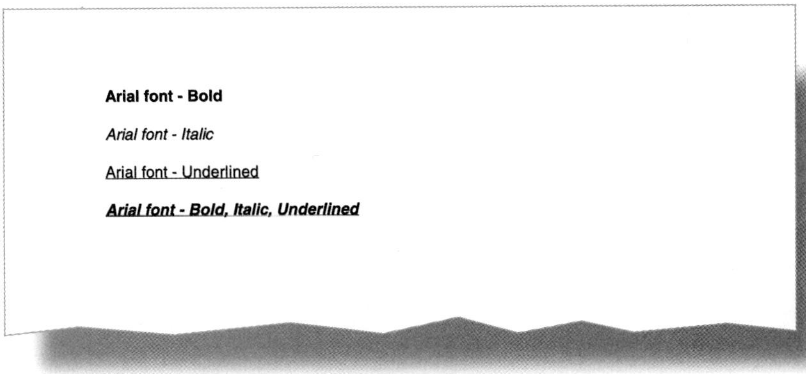

Arial font - Bold

Arial font - Italic

Arial font - Underlined

Arial font - Bold, Italic, Underlined

FIGURE 1-17

Font Sizes

Font sizes are measured in **points**. One inch consists of seventy-two points. Thus, a font size of thirty-six points is approximately one-half inch in height. The measurement is based on measuring from the top of the tallest character in a font (such as a lowercase l) to the bottom of the lowest character (such as a lowercase g, which extends below a line). Figure 1-18 illustrates the Arial font in various sizes.

The fonts and font sizes you choose sometimes depend on the printer you are using and the fonts available within your software. Available fonts can vary from system to system. In the Works Word Processor, the default font is 12-point Times New Roman.

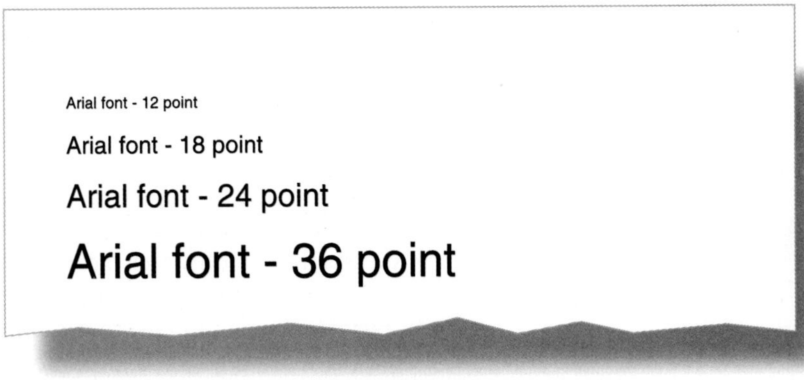

Arial font - 12 point

Arial font - 18 point

Arial font - 24 point

Arial font - 36 point

FIGURE 1-18

Formatting Requirements for Project One

The announcement used in this project is again illustrated in Figure 1-19. Before typing the text, you must understand the fonts, font styles, font sizes, and colors you will use in creating the announcement.

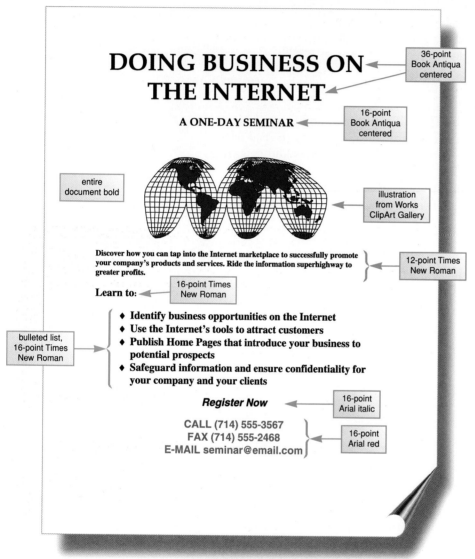

FIGURE 1-19

In this document, the first heading displays on the first two lines of the document, is centered on the page, and displays in 36-point Book Antiqua font. The second heading is centered on the page and displays using 16-point Book Antiqua font. An illustration from the Works ClipArt Gallery is placed after the second heading. The next three lines are single-spaced and display in 12-point Times New Roman font. These lines are followed by a blank space and then another line displays in 16-point Times New Roman. The next four entries are indented one-half inch, contain a bullet (solid diamond) before the beginning of each entry, and display in 16-point Times New Roman. The line following the bulleted list is centered on the page and displays in 16-point Arial italic font. The last three lines in the document are centered and display in red using 16-point Arial font. The entire document displays in bold.

When you understand the format of the document, you are ready to use the word processing software to create the document.

Creating a Document

The following tasks will be completed in this project.

1. Type the text line by line.
2. Begin each line at the left margin.
3. Leave three blank lines before the illustration, one blank line for the illustration, and one blank line after the illustration.
4. Format the document; that is, center lines, change fonts, font sizes, font styles, and color as required to produce the document.

5. Insert the clip art illustration.
6. Save the document.
7. Print the document.

The following pages contain a detailed explanation of these tasks.

All Characters Command

When using the Works Word Processor, each time you press a key on the keyboard a character is entered, and each character becomes part of the document. For example, pressing the SPACEBAR between words creates a small black dot, called a **space mark**, in the space between the words. Pressing the ENTER key creates a character called the **paragraph mark**. These characters do not print, but it is recommended that you display these special characters as you type. The following steps explain how to display on the screen all the characters you type.

Steps To Display All Characters

1 **Click View on the menu bar. Point to All Characters.**

Works displays the View menu and the mouse pointer is positioned on the All Characters command (Figure 1-20).

FIGURE 1-20

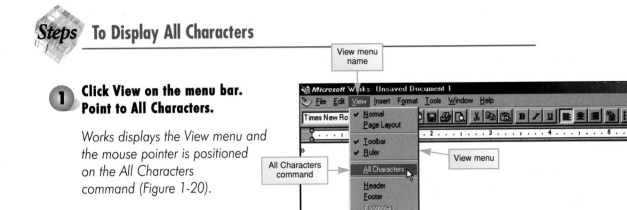

2 **Click All Characters on the View menu.**

A paragraph mark now appears after the insertion point (Figure 1-21).

FIGURE 1-21

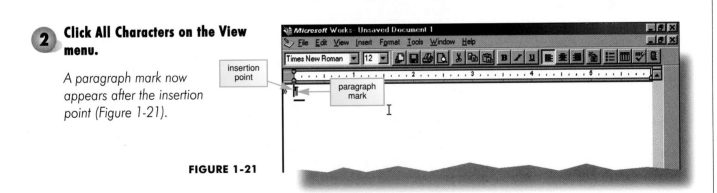

Works automatically inserts a paragraph mark at the end of every document. Because you have not yet entered text, a paragraph mark appears after the insertion point because it is the end of the document at this time. As you type, a small dot appears when you press the SPACEBAR, and a paragraph mark will appear whenever you press the ENTER key.

More *About*
Entering Text

Oftentimes when you first enter a heading in a document, you have no idea how the formatting of the text will affect the display of the text. When increasing the font size at a later time, the one-line heading may display on multiple lines.

After you click the All Characters command, a check mark appears to the left of this command the next time you display the View menu, indicating the command is in effect. Clicking the left mouse button again when pointing to this command will turn off the All Characters command and remove the check mark.

You are now ready to enter the text to create the document.

Entering Text

Perform the following steps to enter the text of the document.

Steps **To Enter Text**

1 **Press the CAPS LOCK key on the keyboard and type** DOING BUSINESS ON THE INTERNET **as the first line of text.**

As you type, the characters display in capital letters and the insertion point and paragraph mark move to the right one character at a time (Figure 1-22). If you make an error while typing, press the BACKSPACE key to delete the character or characters you have just typed and then type the characters correctly.

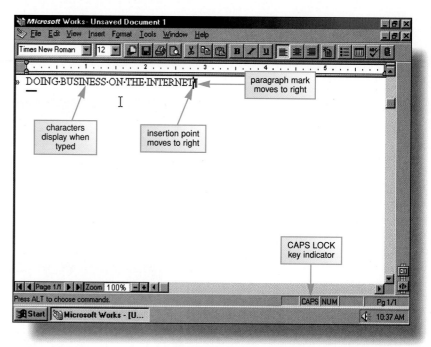

FIGURE 1-22

2 **Press the ENTER key to end the first line.**

When you press the ENTER key, Works inserts a paragraph mark immediately after the last character typed (Figure 1-23). The insertion point moves to the beginning of the next line followed by a paragraph mark, and the end-of-file mark moves down one line.

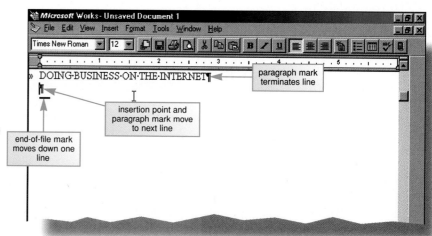

FIGURE 1-23

3 Press the ENTER key to create a blank line. Type A ONE-DAY SEMINAR as the second line of text, and then press the ENTER key once to end the second line of text. Press the ENTER key five more times to create three blank lines before the clip art illustration, a line for the illustration, and a blank line following the illustration. The insertion point now displays on the line where you will type the next line of text.

Only one line needs to be allowed for the clip art illustration (Figure 1-24). When Works inserts the illustration in the document, the space is expanded to allow the illustration to be placed between the lines of text.

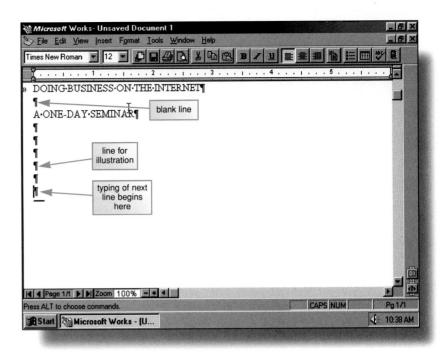

FIGURE 1-24

Paragraph Marks

It is important to understand the purpose of the paragraph mark. The term paragraph, when using the Works Word Processor, can mean a blank line, a single character, a word, a single line, or many sentences. You create a paragraph by pressing the ENTER key. When you are typing and then press the ENTER key, Works inserts a paragraph mark after the last character typed.

A paragraph is a section of text treated as a unified group of characters to which various types of formatting can be applied. Once you have established the characteristics of a paragraph, text you add to the paragraph will take on the characteristics of that paragraph.

Using the Wordwrap Feature

Wordwrap allows you to type multiple lines without pressing the ENTER key at the end of each line. When typing text that requires more than one line, the insertion point continues to the right margin and then automatically drops down to the beginning of the next line. In addition, when you type a line and a word extends beyond the right margin, the word is automatically placed on the next line. Thus, as you enter text, do not press the ENTER key when the insertion point reaches the right margin.

Perform the following step to use the wordwrap feature.

Steps To Use Wordwrap

1 **Press the CAPS LOCK key to remove this feature. Type** Discover how you can tap into the Internet marketplace to successfully promote your company's products and services. Ride the information superhighway to greater profits. **as the first paragraph in the body of the announcement. Press the ENTER key.**

The CAPS LOCK indicator on the status bar is turned off (Figure 1-25). Works automatically wraps the word, company's, to the beginning of the next line because it is too long to fit on the first line. Your document may wordwrap on a different word, depending on the type of printer you are using.

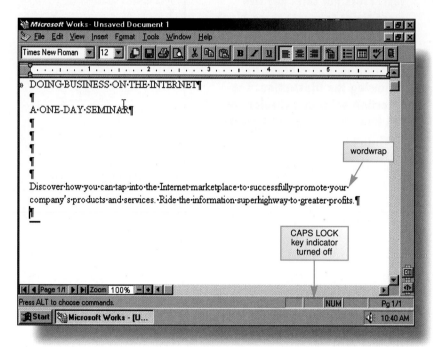

FIGURE 1-25

Wordwrap is an important feature of the Word Processor because it facilitates rapid entry of data and allows Works to easily rearrange characters, words, and sentences within a paragraph when you make changes.

Entering Text that Scrolls Through the Document Window

As you type more lines of text than Works can display in the text area, Works scrolls the top portion of the document upward off of the screen. Although you cannot see the text once it scrolls off the screen, it still remains in the document.

Perform the steps on the next page to enter text that scrolls through the document window.

Steps To Enter Text that Scrolls Through the Document Window

1 Press the ENTER key to enter a blank line. Type the text paragraph in the announcement: Learn to: and then press the ENTER key twice (Figure 1-26).

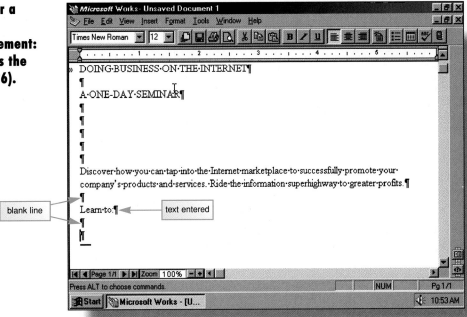

FIGURE 1-26

2 Type the remaining lines of text. Press the ENTER key to end each paragraph.

As you type the paragraph beginning, Safeguard, Works scrolls the beginning of the announcement off the screen (Figure 1-27). All the text in the announcement has been entered.

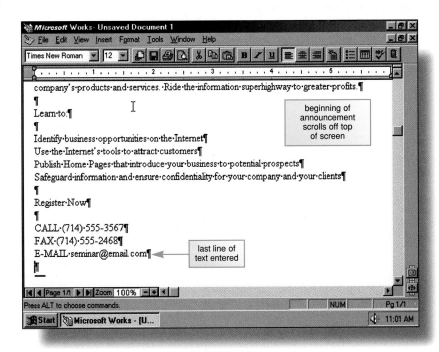

FIGURE 1-27

More *About* **Long Filenames**

One of Works 95 new features is the ability to support long filenames. Using long filenames can save you time because you can give your files names that mean something even months after they have been created.

Saving a Document

When you create a document, the document is stored only in your computer's random access memory. If the computer is turned off or a power loss occurs before you save a document, your work will be lost. You should save all documents either on the hard disk or on a floppy disk. When saving a document, you must select a filename. The filename is the name that is used to reference the file (document) when it is stored on a hard disk or floppy disk. The complete path to the file, including drive letter and filename, can contain up to 255 characters. Filenames cannot include any of the following characters: forward slash (/), backslash (\), greater-than sign (>), less-than sign (<), asterisk (*), question mark (?), quotation mark ("), pipe symbol (|), colon (:), or semicolon (;). To save the document created in Project 1 on a floppy disk in drive A using the filename, Business on the Internet Seminar, perform the following steps.

Steps **To Save a New Document**

① **Insert a formatted floppy disk into drive A. Point to the Save button on the toolbar.**

The mouse button points to the ***Save button*** *(Figure 1-28). Works displays the ToolTip for the button. The description of the Save button displays on the status bar.*

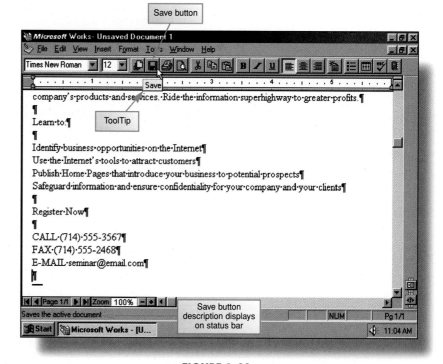

FIGURE 1-28

2 Click the Save button on the toolbar. When the Save As dialog box displays, type Business on the Internet Seminar in the File name text box. Point to the Save in box arrow.

The Save As dialog box displays on the screen (Figure 1-29). A blinking insertion point displays in the File name text box when the Save As dialog box first displays on screen. The filename you typed displays in the File name text box. The mouse pointer points to the Save in box arrow.

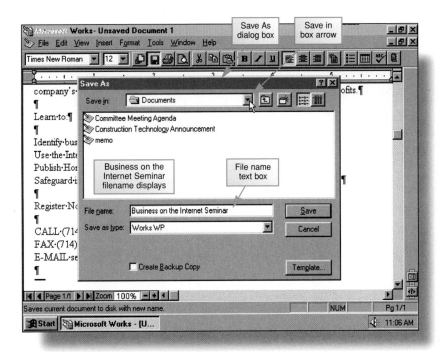

FIGURE 1-29

3 Click the Save in box arrow and then point to the 3½ floppy [A:] icon. (If necessary, use the up scroll arrow to bring the icon into view.)

The Save in drop-down list displays a list of available drives and folders (Figure 1-30). The list of available drives may be different on your system.

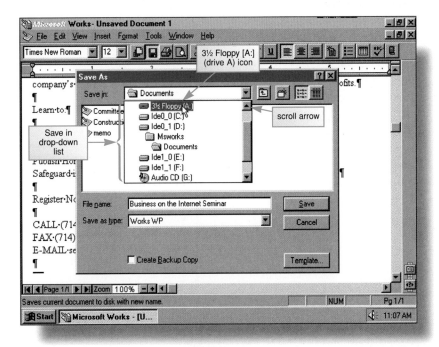

FIGURE 1-30

4 **Click the 3½ floppy [A:] icon. Point to the Save button.**

Drive A (3½ Floppy [A:]) becomes the selected drive (Figure 1-31). The mouse pointer points to the Save button.

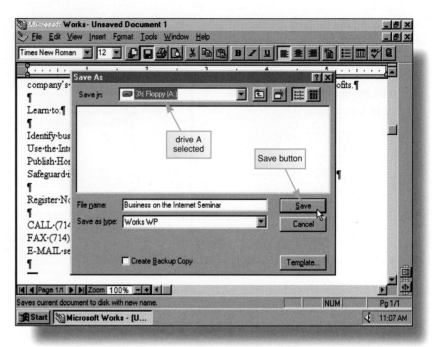

FIGURE 1-31

5 **Click the Save button.**

The dialog box disappears and the document remains displayed on the screen (Figure 1-32). Works saves the document on the floppy disk in drive A. The name changes in the title bar from Unsaved Document 1 to the name of the document saved (Business on the Internet Seminar).

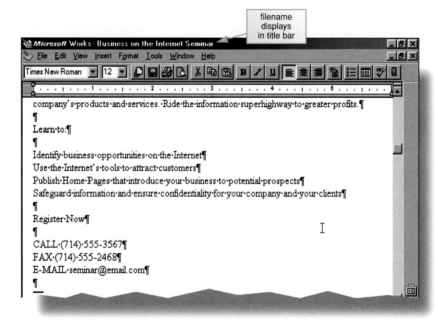

FIGURE 1-32

Formatting the Document

The next step in preparing the announcement is to format the document, which involves centering selected lines, specifying the font and font size for each of the lines, and applying the proper font style and color to the lines.

Highlighting Characters, Words, Lines, and Paragraphs

Before you can change the format of a document, you must **highlight** the text you want to change. Highlighted text displays as white text on a black background on the screen. Figure 1-33 illustrates a highlighted word in a sentence.

Works provides a variety of ways to highlight text. One method of highlighting is to move the mouse pointer to the first character of the text to format and then drag the mouse pointer across the text you want to highlight.

Table 1-1 explains other techniques you can use to highlight text.

When highlighting more than one word, Works automatically highlights all of the next word as you drag through that word. If you prefer to highlight character by character, you can turn off the automatic word selection feature by removing the X from the Automatic word selection check box on the Editing sheet in the Options dialog box. The Options dialog box can be displayed by clicking Options on the Tools menu.

If you have highlighted text and want to remove the highlighting for any reason, click anywhere within the workspace area of the screen. The highlighting will be removed. You also may press any arrow key to remove highlighting.

FIGURE 1-33

Table 1–1	
TO HIGHLIGHT	*ACTION TO BE PERFORMED*
A word	Double-click when the mouse pointer is located anywhere within the word.
A line	Click in the left margin of the document window beside the line. The I-beam pointer changes to a block arrow in this area.
A sentence	Drag the mouse pointer over the sentence, or press the CTRL key and click with the mouse pointer located anywhere within the sentence.
A paragraph	Double-click in the left margin of the document window beside the paragraph.
Several lines	Position the mouse pointer in the left margin of the document window and drag the pointer up or down.
An entire document	Hold down the CTRL key and click in the left margin of the document window or click the Select All command from the Edit menu.

Centering Paragraphs

The first two heading lines of the announcement are centered within the margins of the document. Several approaches can be taken when centering these two lines. You can center one line at a time, or by highlighting both lines, you can center both lines at once with a single click of the mouse button. It is more efficient to center both lines at once, so this approach is illustrated in the following steps.

Perform the steps on the next page to center the paragraphs.

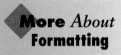

More *About* Formatting

Be cautious when using multiple fonts, font styles, and colors in a document. Beginning designers usually use too many special features that make reading a document difficult. Most experts advise using no more than three fonts in a document so you do not overtax and confuse the reader. Use color to draw attention to an important fact in the document.

Steps **To Center Paragraphs**

1 **Click the beginning of document button at the lower left of the document window to display the top portion of the document on the screen. Position the mouse pointer in the left margin of the document window next to the first line of the paragraphs you want to center.**

The insertion point is moved to the beginning of the document (Figure 1-34). The mouse pointer becomes a block arrow pointing to the right.

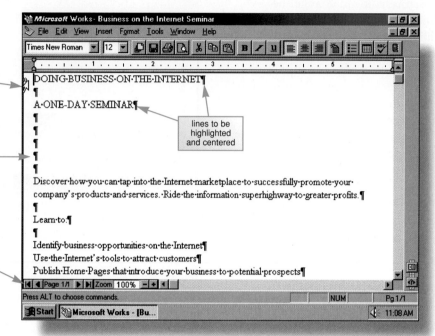

FIGURE 1-34

2 **Drag the mouse pointer down the left margin of the document window until the lines you want to center are highlighted. Release the left mouse button.**

The lines are highlighted (Figure 1-35).

FIGURE 1-35

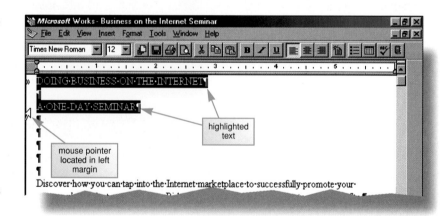

3 **Click the Center Align button on the toolbar.**

Works centers the two heading lines between the page margins (Figure 1-36). Notice the Center Align button on the toolbar is recessed, indicating the paragraphs are centered.

FIGURE 1-36

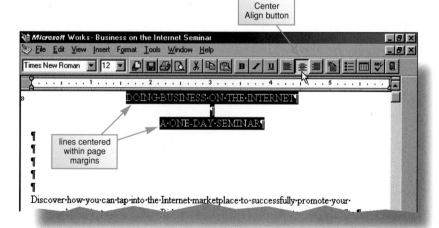

Changing Fonts

When Works is started, the default font is Times New Roman and the default font size is 12 points. Works displays this information on the left side of the toolbar.

The text in the announcement now displays in 12-point Times New Roman font. The first two heading lines should display in Book Antiqua font. To change from Times New Roman font to Book Antiqua font, perform the following steps.

Steps **To Change Fonts**

1 **Highlight the paragraphs you want to change to Book Antiqua font. Click the Font Name box arrow.**

Works displays the Font Name drop-down list box containing a list of font names (Figure 1-37). The font list displays the fonts as the way they will look on screen. The font names on your computer may be different from the font names shown in Figure 1-37.

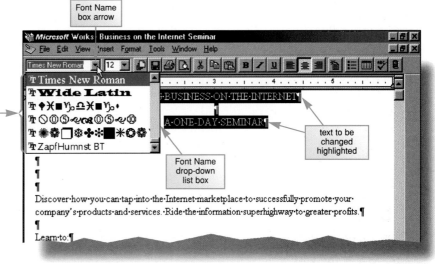

FIGURE 1-37

2 **Position the mouse pointer on the up scroll arrow and scroll to display additional names until the Book Antiqua font name appears in the Font Name drop-down list.**

Additional font names display as you scroll through the Font Name drop-down list (Figure 1-38). The Book Antiqua font name displays near the top of the list.

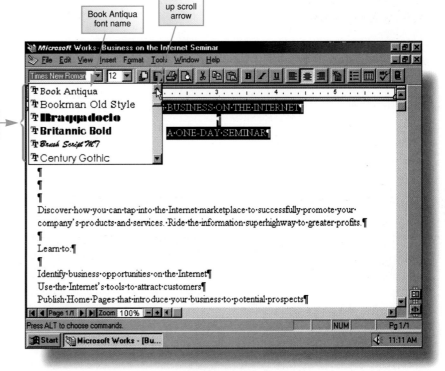

FIGURE 1-38

3 **Point to the Book Antiqua font name in the Font Name drop-down list.**

The Book Antiqua font name is highlighted in the list of font names and displays highlighted in the Font Name box on the toolbar (Figure 1-39).

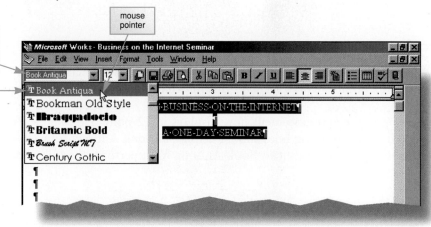

FIGURE 1-39

4 **Click Book Antiqua.**

The two heading lines display in Book Antiqua font (Figure 1-40). The Book Antiqua font name appears in the Font Name box on the toolbar.

FIGURE 1-40

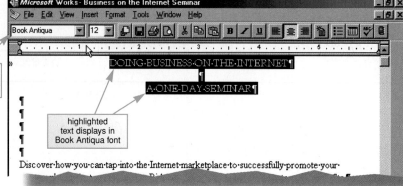

After choosing the font, the changed lines remain highlighted. To remove the highlighting, click anywhere in the workspace area of the screen.

Changing Font Size

The next step in formatting the document is to change the font size of the heading lines. The words, DOING BUSINESS ON THE INTERNET, should display in 36-point font size.

Perform the following steps to change the font size.

Steps **To Change Font Size**

1 **Highlight the line of text to enlarge (DOING BUSINESS ON THE INTERNET) by clicking in the left margin of the document window on the same line as the text.**

Works highlights the words, DOING BUSINESS ON THE INTERNET (Figure 1-41).

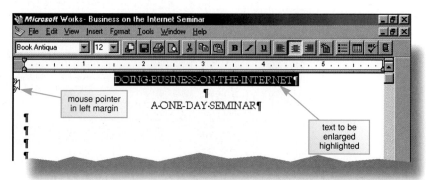

FIGURE 1-41

2 **Click the Font Size box arrow on the toolbar.**

A list of font sizes displays (Figure 1-42). The current font size (12) is highlighted in the list.

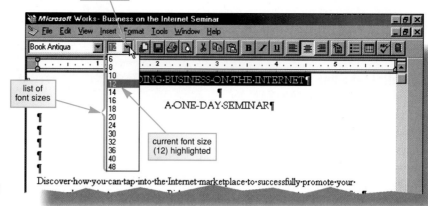

FIGURE 1-42

3 **Point to the number 36, which indicates 36-point font size (Figure 1-43).**

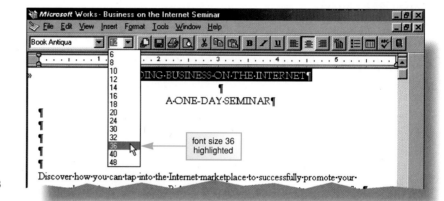

FIGURE 1-43

4 **Click 36.**

Works changes the first heading line to 36-point Book Antiqua font (Figure 1-44). The number 36 displays in the Font Size box on the toolbar. Because the heading line is increased to 36 points, Works automatically wraps the word, THE, to the beginning of the next line and centers the text.

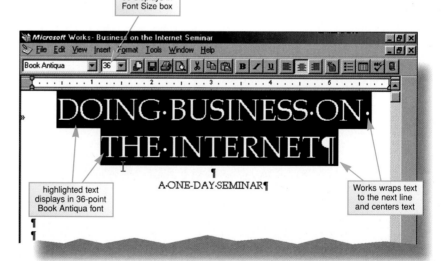

FIGURE 1-44

Formatting the Remaining Heading Lines

The heading line, A ONE-DAY SEMINAR, should display in 16-point Book Antiqua font. Perform the steps on the next page to accomplish this formatting.

Other Ways

1. Right-click selected text, click Font and Style on context-sensitive menu, click desired font size in Size list, click OK button

2. On Format menu click Font and Style, click desired font size in Size list, click OK button

3. Press CTRL+SHIFT+P

Steps **To Change Font Size**

1 Highlight the line of text to change (A ONE-DAY SEMINAR) by clicking the left margin of the document window on the same line as the text. Click the Font Size box arrow on the toolbar. Point to the number 16, which indicates 16-point font size.

Works highlights the words, A ONE-DAY SEMINAR, a list of font sizes displays, and the mouse pointer points to the number 16 in the Font Size drop-down list box (Figure 1-45).

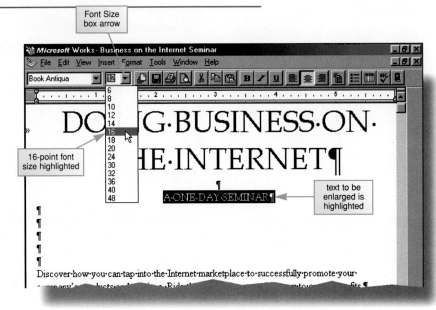

FIGURE 1-45

2 Click 16.

Works changes the second heading line to 16 point Book Antiqua font (Figure 1-46). The number 16 displays in the Font Size box on the toolbar.

FIGURE 1-46

The heading lines are now formatted in the proper font and font size.

Formatting Additional Text

The three lines following the heading lines display in 12-point Times New Roman. Because the default font and font size are 12-point Times New Roman, no additional steps are necessary. The five lines following the body of the announcement beginning with the words, Learn To:, are to display in 16-point Times New Roman. Because the default font and font size are 12-point Times New Roman, the only step necessary is to change the font size for the lines to 16-point. To accomplish this formatting, perform the following steps.

Steps **To Change Font Size**

1 Scroll the document to view the line containing the words, Learn to:. Highlight the five lines of text to be formatted by dragging down in the left margin of the document window the words, Learn to:. Click the Font Size box arrow on the toolbar. Point to the number 16, which indicates 16-point font size.

five lines of text highlighted

Works highlights the five lines, a list of font sizes appears, and the mouse pointer points to the number 16 in the drop-down list box (Figure 1-47).

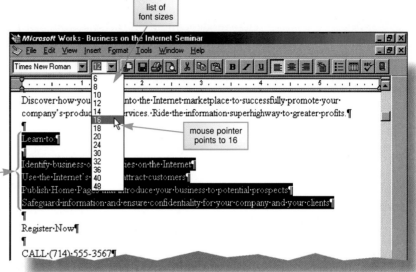

FIGURE 1-47

2 Click 16.

Works changes the five lines to 16-point font size. The number 16 displays in the Font Size box on the toolbar (Figure 1-48). When Works increases the font size of the high-lighted lines, the last two lines auto-matically wrap to the next line down.

lines of text display in 16-point Times New Roman font

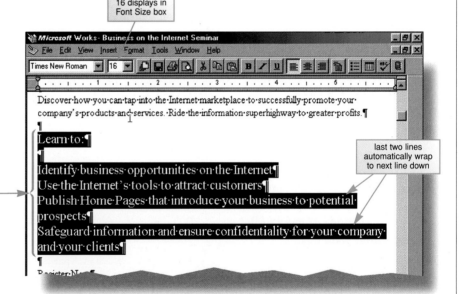

FIGURE 1-48

The first part of the announcement is now formatted with the proper fonts and font sizes.

Creating a Bulleted List

The four paragraphs following the words, Learn to:, are indented one-half inch from the left margin and appear as a bulleted list. A **bulleted list** consists of a word or words on one or more lines that are preceded by a special character at the beginning of the line. The purpose is to have the list stand out from the rest of the text.

More *About* **Context-sensitive menus**

Right-clicking any selection causes Works to display a context-sensitive menu with com-mands you can use. In addition to clicking any command on the context-sensitive menu, you can also right-click any command to carry out a task.

You can create a bulleted list by clicking **Bullets** on the context-sensitive menu. The context-sensitive menu contains frequently used commands you can use with the current selection. The commands available on the context-sensitive menu change, depending on the selection. For example, the list of commands available when text is selected is different from the list available when an object is selected. You activate the context-sensitive menu by right-clicking the selection. To create a bulleted list using the context-sensitive menu, complete the following steps.

Steps To Create a Bulleted List

1 Highlight the lines that are to comprise the bulleted list. Point to the selection and right-click. When the context-sensitive menu displays, point to Bullets.

Works highlights the lines and displays the context-sensitive menu (Figure 1-49). The mouse pointer points to the Bullets command. The context-sensitive menu contains the most frequently used commands you can use with the current selection.

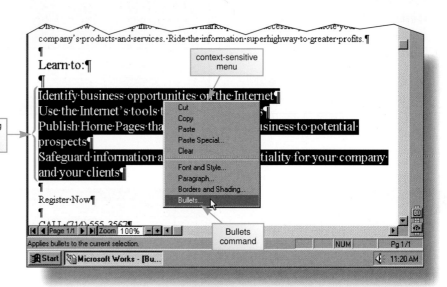

FIGURE 1-49

2 Click Bullets. When the Format Bullets dialog box displays, click the solid diamond-shaped bullet in the Bullet style box.

Works displays the Format Bullets dialog box (Figure 1-50). Twenty-four different styles of bullets you can insert at the beginning of each highlighted paragraph display in the Bullet style box. The solid diamond-shaped bullet in the Bullet Style box is highlighted, indicating it is selected. The Bullet size box displays 12, indicating the bullet style will display in 12-point size. A check mark displays in the Hanging indent check box, indicating that the first line of each highlighted paragraph will begin farther to the left than the rest of the lines in the paragraph. The Sample box shows how the bulleted list will display.

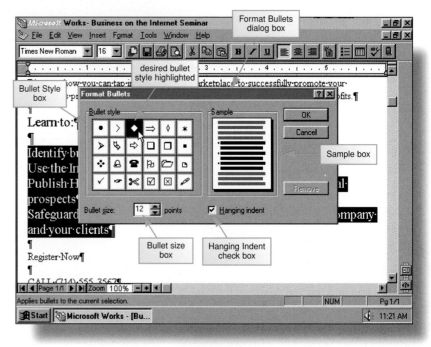

FIGURE 1-50

3 **Point to the Bullet size box up arrow and click four times until 16 displays in the Bullet size box. Point to the OK button.**

The Bullet size box displays 16, indicating the bullet style will display in 16, point size (Figure 1-51). The mouse pointer points to the OK button.

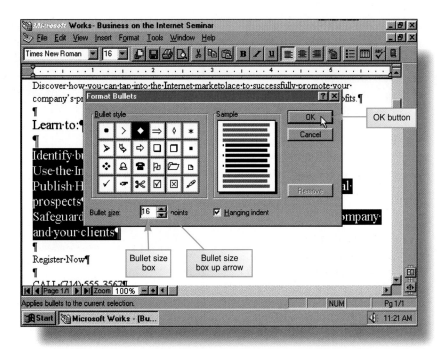

FIGURE 1-51

4 **Click the OK button.**

*A 16-point solid black diamond shaped bullet displays in front of the text (Figure 1-52). The text moves to the right one-quarter of an inch. The bottom triangle on the left side of the ruler, called the **left indent marker,** moves to the right one-quarter of an inch. The Bullets button on the tool-bar is recessed indicating the highlighted text contains bullets.*

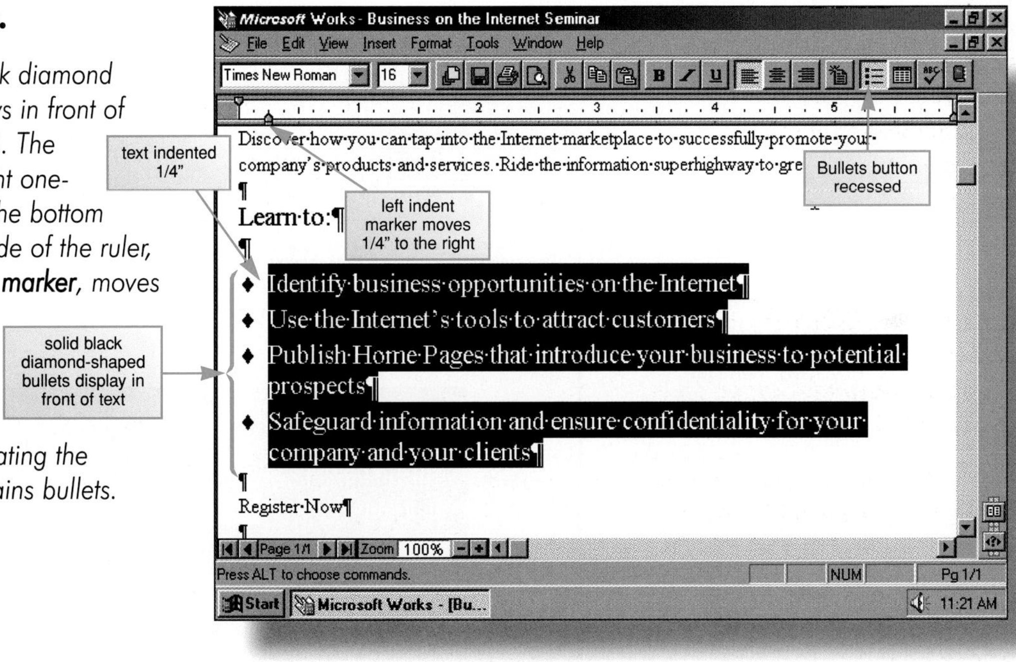

FIGURE 1-52

5 Point to the small rectangle marker beneath the left indent marker and click. When the First-time Help dialog box displays, point to the OK button.

The first time you click the ruler in each session, Works displays the First-time Help dialog box (Figure 1-53). Clicking the To set a custom indent button displays the Help window to the right of the document screen with step-by-step instructions on setting a custom indent. Clicking the To set a tab stop button displays the Help window with step-by-step instructions on setting a tab stop. The First-time Help dialog box will not display if you have previously clicked the Don't display this message in the future check box. The mouse pointer points to the OK button.

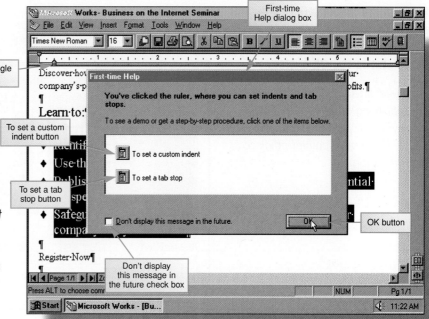

FIGURE 1-53

6 Click the OK button. Drag the rectangle marker under the left indent marker to the three-quarter inch mark on the ruler.

*When you click the OK button in the First-time help dialog box, the dialog box is removed from the screen. The bullets and related text indent an additional one-half inch (Figure 1-54). The top triangle on the left side of the ruler, called the **first-line indent marker,** moves to the right one-half an inch, and the left indent marker moves to the right an additional one-half inch. The bullets are indented one-half inch from the left margin. The text begins three-quarters of an inch from the left margin.*

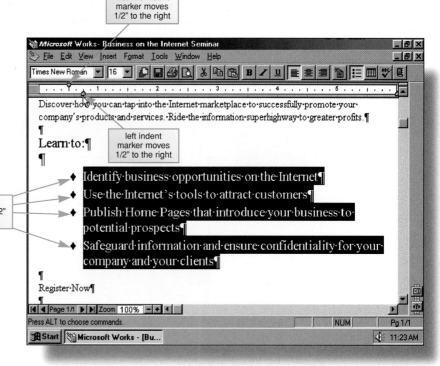

FIGURE 1-54

> ▶ *Other***Ways**
>
> 1. On Format menu click Paragraph, click Indents and Alignment tab, click Bulleted, click OK button
> 2. On Format menu click Bullets, click desired bullet style, click OK button
> 3. On toolbar click Bullet button

Be aware that using the Bullet button or the Paragraph command creates a bulleted list using the special character that was last chosen in the Format Bullets dialog box.

To remove the highlighting, position the mouse pointer anywhere in the workspace area and click.

To remove the bullets from the bulleted list, highlight the bulleted list and click the Bullet button on the toolbar. If you want to change the bulleted list to standard text at the left margin, highlight the bulleted list and press the CTRL+Q keys.

The document is now formatted with the proper font and font sizes except for the last four lines. The lines following the bulleted list should be centered within the margins of the document and display in 16-point Arial. To center the last four lines and then change the font to Arial and the font size to 16, complete the following steps.

TO CENTER TEXT AND CHANGE FONT AND FONT SIZE

Step 1: Highlight the last four lines in the document.
Step 2: Click the Center Align button on the toolbar.
Step 3: Click the Font Name box arrow to display the list of fonts. Scroll the list to bring the Arial font name into view.
Step 4: Click Arial.
Step 5: Click the Font Size box arrow to display the list of font sizes.
Step 6: Click 16.

The last four lines are centered and display in 16-point Arial font (Figure 1-55)

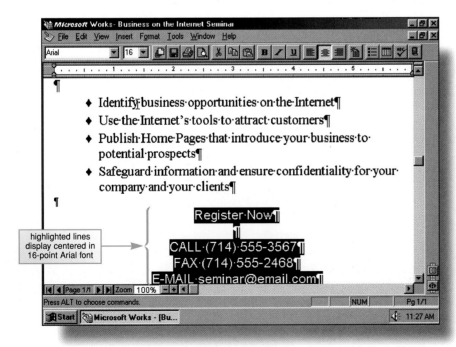

FIGURE 1-55

Displaying Text in Italics

The next step is to select the first line after the bulleted list and italicize the characters in it. Perform the step on the next page to italicize text.

Steps **To Italicize Text**

1 **Highlight the line to be italicized. Click the Italic button on the toolbar.**

The first line after the bulleted list displays in italics (Figure 1-56).

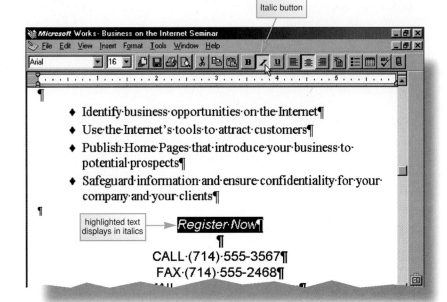

FIGURE 1-56

When the selected text is italicized, the Italic button on the toolbar is recessed. If you want to remove the italic format from the selected text, click the Italic button a second time.

Displaying Text in Color

The last three lines are to display in red. To format these lines, use the Font and Style command on the context-sensitive menu as shown in the following steps.

 Steps **To Display Text In Color**

1 **Highlight the last three lines in the document. Point to the highlighted lines and right-click. Then, point to Font and Style on the context-sensitive menu.**

The last three lines in the document are highlighted (Figure 1-57). Works displays the context-sensitive menu and the mouse pointer is positioned on Font and Style.

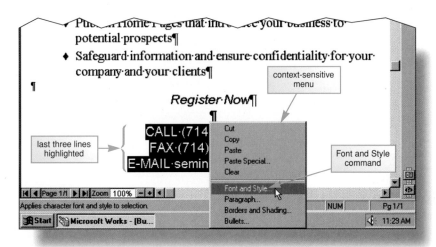

FIGURE 1-57

2 Click Font and Style on the context-sensitive menu. When the Format Font and Style dialog box displays, click the Color box, scroll through the list until the Red color box displays, and then point to the Red color box.

Works displays the Format Font and Style dialog box (Figure 1-58). In the Format Font and Style dialog box, Arial displays in the Font box, 16 displays in the Size box, indicating the font for the highlighted text is 16-point Arial. The mouse pointer points to the red rectangle in the Color drop-down list box.

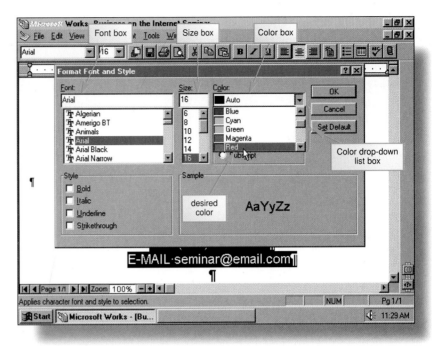

FIGURE 1-58

3 Click Red and then point to the OK button.

Text in the Sample box displays in red 16-point Arial font (Figure 1-59). The mouse pointer points to the OK button.

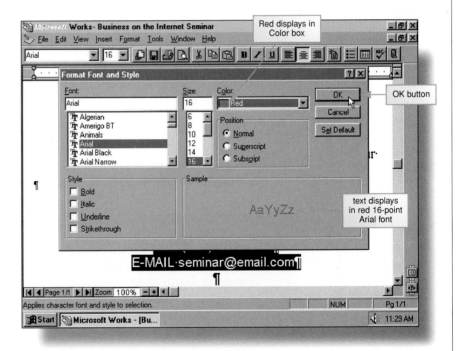

FIGURE 1-59

4 **Click the OK button. Click anywhere in the blank workspace area to remove the highlighting.**

Works displays the last three lines in red 16-point Arial font (Figure 1-60). The paragraph mark for the next paragraph retains the formatting from the previous paragraph.

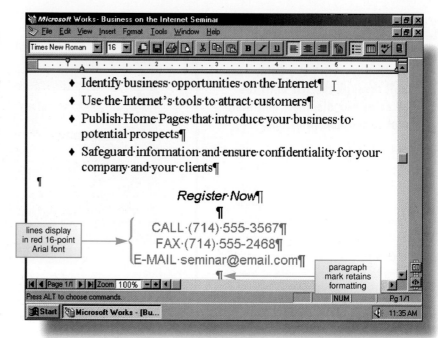

FIGURE 1-60

Other Ways
1. On Format menu click Font and Style, click desired color in Color drop-down list box, click OK button

When you format the last paragraph in a document, the formatting remains in place for subsequent paragraphs unless you change it. That is the reason the paragraph mark on the last line in Figure 1-60 displays centered in red 16-point Arial font.

The Format Font and Style dialog box in Figure 1-59 on the previous page contains check boxes and option buttons. A **check box** represents options that you can turn on or off. A check in a check box indicates the option is turned on. To place a check mark in a box, click the box. In Figure 1-59, the Style box contains four check boxes; Bold, Italic, Underline, and Strikethrough. None of the boxes contains a check mark, indicating the options are turned off. You can select more than one check box at a time.

Option buttons also represent options that you can turn on or off. You can select only one option button at a time, however. To select an option button, click the option button. Choosing a new option automatically turns off the previous option. In Figure 1-59, the Position box contains three option buttons; Normal, Superscript, and Subscript. The option button containing the black dot, (Normal), is the selected button. The Normal option positions highlighted characters on the line with other text.

Bold Style

To further emphasize the contents of the announcement, the entire document should display in bold. To do this, you must first highlight the entire document, and then click the Bold button on the toolbar. To display the document in bold, perform the steps on the next page.

Steps **To Display an Entire Document in Bold**

1 **Hold down the CTRL key and then click in the left margin.**

The entire document is highlighted (Figure 1-61).

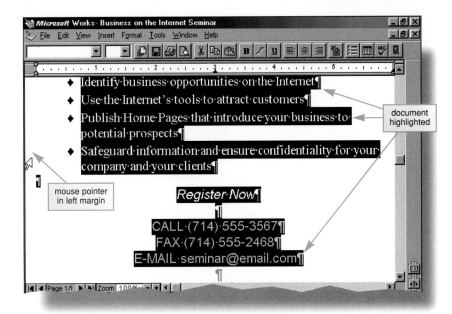

FIGURE 1-61

2 **Click the Bold button on the toolbar.**

Works changes all text to bold (Figure 1-62).

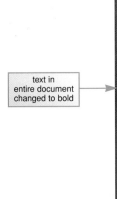

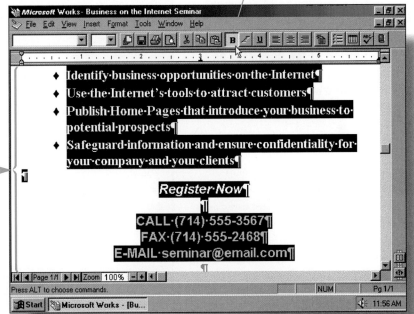

FIGURE 1-62

The document is now formatted except for the illustration that must be inserted in the document.

Using Clip Art in a Document

The next step in preparing the announcement is to insert an illustration related to the seminar in the document (see Figure 1-1 on page W1.8). To accomplish this, you must use the Microsoft **clip art** (predrawn illustrations) that is available for use as a part of the Word Processor.

Inserting Clip Art in a Word Processing Document

You insert clip art into a document by clicking **ClipArt** on the **Insert menu**. The steps to insert clip art into the announcement are explained below and on the next three pages.

Steps **To Insert Clip Art into a Document**

1 **Click the beginning of document button at the lower left of the document window to display the top portion of the document on the screen. Click the line in the document where you want to place the clip art.**

When you click the beginning of document button, Works moves the insertion point to the beginning of the document and displays the first lines of the docu-ment on the screen. The insertion point is positioned on the line where you will insert the clip art (Figure 1-63).

FIGURE 1-63

2 Because you want to center the clip art, click the Center Align button on the toolbar.

Works centers the insertion point and the paragraph mark on the screen (Figure 1-64).

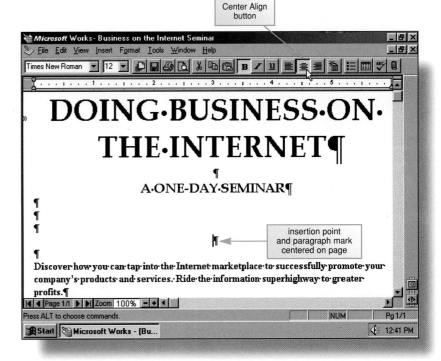

FIGURE 1-64

3 Click Insert on the menu bar and point to ClipArt.

Works displays the Insert menu (Figure 1-65). The mouse pointer points to ClipArt.

FIGURE 1-65

4 **Click ClipArt. When the Microsoft ClipArt Gallery 2.0 dialog box displays, click Maps - International in the Categories list. Then, point to the clip art illustrating the world map. The clip art on your computer may appear in a different sequence than shown in Figure 1-66. If so, scroll until the world map displays.**

Works displays the Microsoft ClipArt Gallery 2.0 dialog box (Figure 1-66). The dialog box displays clip art that you can place in a document. The filename and a description of the selected clip art display at the bottom of the Microsoft ClipArt Gallery 2.0 dialog box. You can click a different category name to display a particular type of clip art.

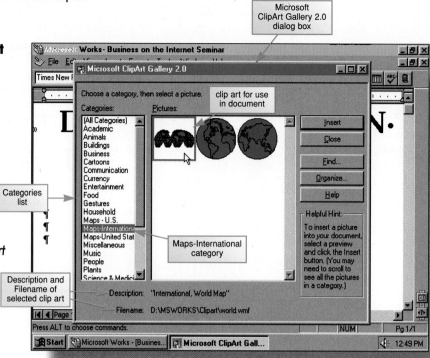

FIGURE 1-66

5 **Click the world map clip art to highlight the clip art for the document, and then point to the Insert button.**

The clip art with the illustration of the world map is highlighted as indicated by the blue outline around the clip art (Figure 1-67). The mouse pointer points to the Insert button.

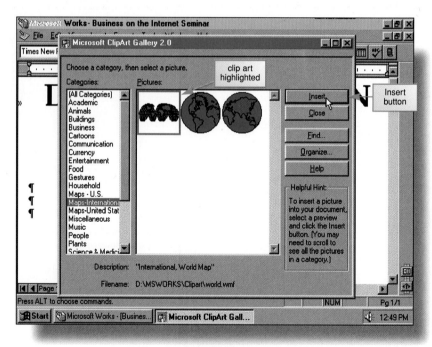

FIGURE 1-67

6 **Click the Insert button.**

Works inserts the clip art in the word processing document at the location of the insertion point (Figure 1-68). A rectangular border that contains small dark squares, called **resize handles,** *displays around the border of the clip art. This border indicates the clip art is selected.*

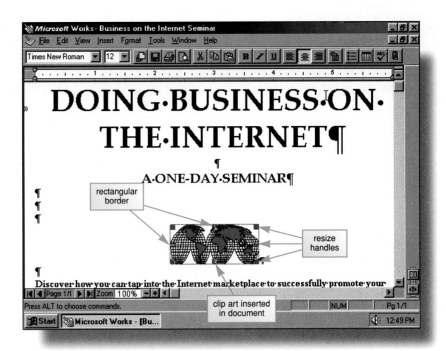

FIGURE 1-68

To remove the border around the clip art, click anywhere outside the clip art.

The Microsoft ClipArt Gallery 2.0 dialog box that displays on your computer may contain additional images. Many different clip art images may be purchased and added to Works.

The clip art that is placed in the word processing document is called an **object.** Once in the word processing document, the object may be resized, that is, made larger or smaller, as required.

Changing the Size of Clip Art

After adding the clip art to the document, the size of the clip art must be changed to correspond to Figure 1-1 on page W1.8. To change the size of the clip art, complete the steps on the next two pages.

Steps   To Resize Clip Art

1 **If the clip art is not selected, click the clip art object. Position the mouse pointer over the resize handle in the upper right corner of the border that surrounds the clip art.**

When the mouse pointer is positioned inside a selected object, it changes to a block arrow with the word DRAG beneath it. This indicates you can drag the clip art to any position within the document. A border surrounds the clip art indicating the object is selected (Figure 1-69). Positioning the mouse pointer on a resize handle causes the mouse pointer to change to a small square with a two-headed arrow intersecting the square. The word RESIZE displays beneath the square.

FIGURE 1-69

2 **With the mouse pointer pointing to the resize handle in the upper right corner of the clip art, drag upward and to the right until the scaling percentage displayed on the status bar is 263% high and 263% wide.**

As you drag upward and to the right, the entire rectangular border around the clip art enlarges (Figure 1-70). As you drag the resize handle upward and to the right, Works displays the percentage of the object's original width and height on the status bar.

FIGURE 1-70

3 **Release the mouse button. Scroll down to view the entire illustration.**

The illustration expands to fill the enlarged rectangular border (Figure 1-71). Works also recenters the enlarged illustration.

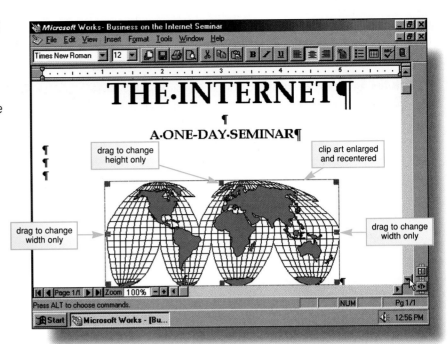

FIGURE 1-71

For objects in a Word Processor document, when you drag one of the corner resize handles, the entire rectangular border increases or decreases proportionately in size. If you drag a resize handle in the middle of a vertical border, only the width of the illustration changes. Similarly, if you drag a resize handle in the middle of a horizontal border, only the height of the illustration changes. Be aware that dragging a resize handle in the middle of a vertical or horizontal border will change the original proportions of the object.

If you ever need to clear a clip art image from a Microsoft Works Word Processor document, select the image and then press the DELETE key. You also can select the image and then click Clear on the context-sensitive menu or the Edit menu.

If an object has been previously selected, clicking anywhere in the document workspace except the selected object will remove the rectangular border.

Saving an Existing Document with the Same Filename

The announcement for Project 1 is now complete. To save the formatting changes and clip art to your floppy disk in drive A, you must save the document again. When you saved the document the first time, you assigned a filename to it (Business on the Internet Seminar). When you make changes to an already saved document and want to save the modified document without changing the filename, use the **Save button** on the toolbar. Works will save the modified document without displaying the Save As dialog box and asking you for a new filename. Perform the step on the next page to save the existing document with the same filename.

More *About* **Saving a Document**

You have struggled so hard to create the perfect paper on the computer for an English class. Suddenly, a student trips over your power cord and your monitor goes blank. It has been 30 minutes since you last saved your work. Horror stories such as this have happened to most people who have used a computer. There is no such thing as saving too often to protect the work you have completed.

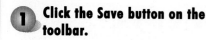 **To Save an Existing Document with the Same Filename**

1 **Click the Save button on the toolbar.**

Works saves the document on a floppy disk inserted in drive A using the currently assigned filename, Business on the Internet Seminar. When the save is finished, the document remains in main memory and displays on the screen (Figure 1-72).

FIGURE 1-72

Other Ways

1. On File menu click Save
2. Press CTRL+S

If you want to save the modified document using a filename different from the name under which the file is currently saved, then you must use the **Save As command** from the File menu. When you use the Save As command, Works will display the Save As dialog box, and then you must enter the new filename, drive, and location. Works will save the document using the new filename in the location you specify. Note, however, that the file saved using the old filename still resides on disk. The file using the new name does not replace the file with the old name.

Print Preview

After you create and save a Word Processor document, you often will want to print the document. To view the document in reduced size on the screen, use the **print preview** feature of the Word Processor. To use print preview, perform the following steps.

To Use Print Preview

1 **Point to the Print Preview button on the toolbar (Figure 1-73).**

FIGURE 1-73

2 **Click the Print Preview button.**

Works opens the print preview window, and you can see the entire document as it will print (Figure 1-74).

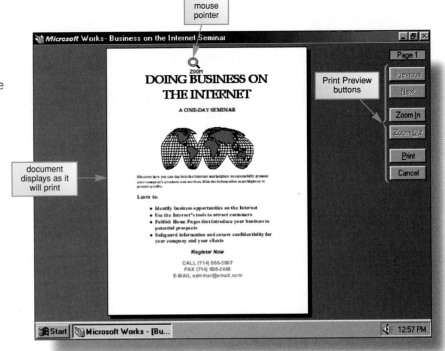

mouse pointer

document displays as it will print

Print Preview buttons

FIGURE 1-74

OtherWays

1. On File menu click Print Preview
2. Press CTRL+F+V

At the top right side of the print preview window, a box contains the page number of the page displayed. Below the page number box is a series of buttons, called **Print Preview buttons**, you can use to control what you want to display. Clicking the Previous button will display a previous page, if there is one. Clicking the Next button will display the next page, if there is one.

The document image that Works displays is reduced in size. It is possible enlarge the image. Clicking the Zoom In button once will enlarge the image approximately one-half the size displayed in the document window where you enter text. Clicking the Zoom In button twice will enlarge the image to the full size displayed in the document window where you enter text. Use the Zoom Out button to reduce the size of the image after you have enlarged it.

Clicking the Print button will cause Works to print the document. Clicking the Cancel button returns you to the document window where you can enter text.

If you position the mouse pointer in the print preview image area, the mouse pointer shape changes to a magnifying glass and you can use the mouse to enlarge the print preview image. Clicking the print preview image area one time will enlarge the image one-half its normal screen size. Clicking a second time will enlarge the image to approximately full-size. Clicking a third time will reduce the image to its original size as shown in Figure 1-74.

If you have a color printer, the document will display as illustrated in Figure 1-74. If you do not have a color printer, the document will display in black and white and the clip art appears in black and green.

Printing a Document

The following steps explain how to print a document that appears in the document window by clicking the **Print command** on the File menu. The Print command available from the File menu should be used the first time you print a document on a given computer to ensure the print options are properly selected.

Steps **To Print a Document**

1 **Click the Cancel button in the print preview window to return to the document window. Click File on the menu bar and point to Print.**

The File menu displays (Figure 1-75). The mouse pointer points to Print.

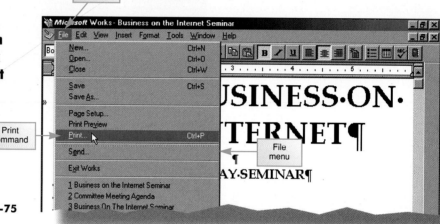

FIGURE 1-75

2 **Click Print. When the First-time Help dialog box displays, point to the OK button.**

The first time you click Print in each session, Works displays the First-time Help dialog box (Figure 1-76). Click the Quick tour of printing button to display the Help window to the right of the document window and view an overview of printing. To view step-by-step instructions on printing your document, click the To print your document button. To view step-by-step instructions on printing a specific page or range of pages, click the To print a specific page or range of pages button. The First-time Help dialog box will not display if you have previously clicked the Don't display this message in the future check box. The mouse pointer points to the OK button.

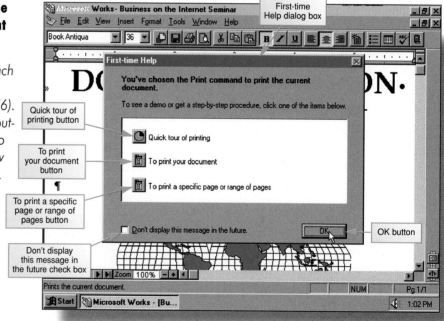

FIGURE 1-76

3 **Click the OK button in the First-time Help dialog box. When the Print dialog box displays, point to the OK button.**

The Print dialog box displays on the screen (Figure 1-77). Review the Print dialog box to ensure the Number of copies box contains 1 and All is selected (a small black circle appears within the All option button when it is selected). This indicates all pages will print. In the What to Print box, make sure Main Document is selected.

FIGURE 1-77

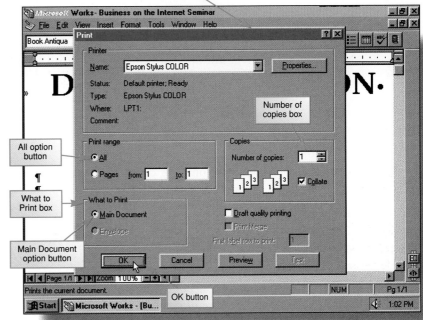

4 **Click the OK button.**

The Printing dialog box displays a brief message on the screen describing the status of the printing operation. The document is then printed on your printer (Figure 1-78).

DOING BUSINESS ON THE INTERNET

A ONE-DAY SEMINAR

Discover how you can tap into the Internet marketplace to successfully promote your company's products and services. Ride the information superhighway to greater profits.

Learn to:

♦ **Identify business opportunities on the Internet**
♦ **Use the Internet's tools to attract customers**
♦ **Publish Home Pages that introduce your business to potential prospects**
♦ **Safeguard information and ensure confidentiality for your company and your clients**

Register Now

**CALL (714) 555-3567
FAX (714) 555-2468
E-MAIL seminar@email.com**

FIGURE 1-78

▶*Other***Ways**

1. On toolbar, click Print button
2. Press CTRL+P

After you have made entries in the Print dialog box to assure that printing will occur as you want, you can use the Print button on the toolbar to print the document. When you click the Print button on the toolbar, the Print dialog box will not appear. Printing will result based on previous entries in the Print dialog box.

More *About*
The Close Button

The Close button is a new innovation for Works. In previous versions of Works, the user had to click a command from a menu or a button in the Works Startup dialog box to close the window. Clicking the Close button is the fastest way to close a document or application.

Closing a Document

When you have completed working on a document, normally you will close the document and begin work on another document or close Works. Closing a document you are working on removes the document from the screen and from random access memory. If you close a document and no other documents are open, Works displays the Works Task Launcher dialog box, which allows you to continue using Works.

You should close a document when you no longer want to work on that document, but want to continue using Works. Complete the following steps to close the document.

Steps To Close a Document

1 **Point to the Close button in the upper right corner of the document window.**

The mouse pointer points to the Close button in the upper right corner of the document window (Figure 1-79).

FIGURE 1-79

2 Click the Close button.

The text on the screen disappears and the Works Task Launcher dialog box displays, allowing you to continue to use Works (Figure 1-80).

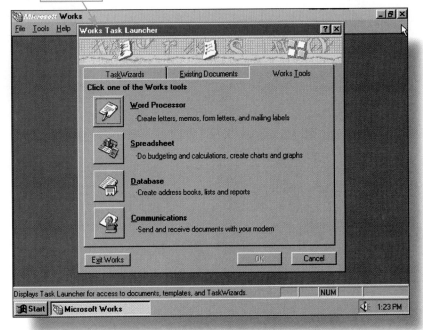

FIGURE 1-80

OtherWays

1. On File menu click Close
2. Press CTRL+W
3. Press CTRL+F4

If you have made any changes to a document after it has been saved, a dialog box appears asking you if you want to save the changes before closing the document. Click the Yes button in the dialog box to save changes.

Closing Works

If you are finished using Works, you should **close** Works. It is important to close Works and not just turn off the machine after completing a document. The steps on the next page explain how to close Works.

Steps **To Close Works**

1 **Point to the Close button in the upper right corner of the application window.**

The mouse pointer points to the Close button in the upper right corner of the application window (Figure 1-81).

2 **Click the Close button.**

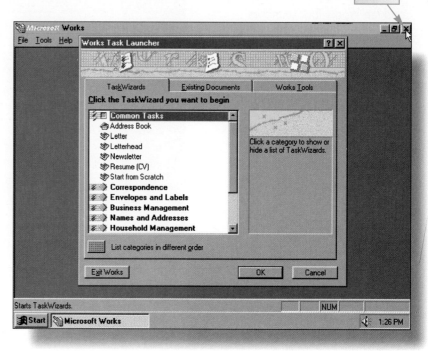

FIGURE 1-81

Works is terminated, and the Microsoft Windows 95 desktop will again display. If you have made any changes to a document after it has been saved, a dialog box appears asking you if you want to save the changes before exiting. Click the Yes button in the dialog box to save changes.

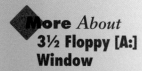

**More About
3½ Floppy [A:]
Window**

In addition to opening a file in the 3½ Floppy window, you can accomplish other tasks. Right-click any file in the window and Works displays a context-sensitive menu with commands you can use to print, copy, delete, or rename a file.

Opening an Existing Document

Often after creating, saving, and printing a document and closing Works, you may want to open an existing document to make changes to that document. The easiest way to open an existing document is to use the **My Computer icon** located in the upper left corner of the desktop. My Computer allows you to access files stored on your hard disk or a floppy disk. To open the file you created in Project 1, Business on the Internet Seminar, double-click the My Computer icon, double-click the 3½ floppy [A:] icon, where the document is located, and then double-click the filename. Windows 95 will start Microsoft Works for Windows 95 and then open Business on the Internet Seminar. Perform the steps on the next two pages to open an existing document.

Steps **To Open An Existing Document**

1 **Point to the My Computer icon in the upper left corner of the desktop.**

The mouse pointer points to the My Computer icon on the desktop (Figure 1-82).

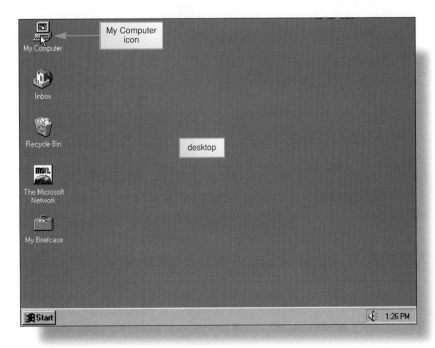

FIGURE 1-82

2 **Double-click the My Computer icon. When the My Computer window opens, point to the 3½ Floppy [A:] icon.**

When you double-click the My Computer icon, Windows 95 opens the My Computer window (Figure 1-83). The My Computer window contains icons representing the hard disk, floppy disk drive, and CD-ROM drive, and two folder icons. The icons that display on your screen may be different. The mouse pointer points to the 3½ Floppy [A:] icon.

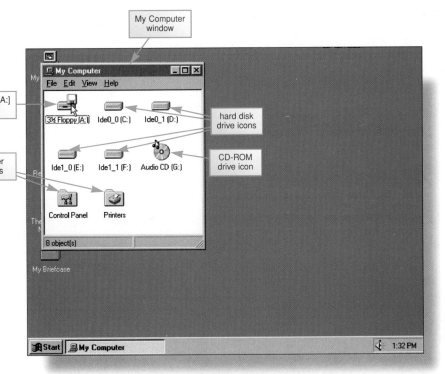

FIGURE 1-83

3 Double-click the 3½ Floppy [A:] icon. When the 3½ Floppy [A:] window opens, point to the Business on the Internet Seminar file icon.

When you double-click the 3½ Floppy [A:] icon, Windows 95 opens the 3½ Floppy [A:] window (Figure 1-84) and displays the filenames on drive A. The mouse pointer points to the Business on the Internet Seminar file icon.

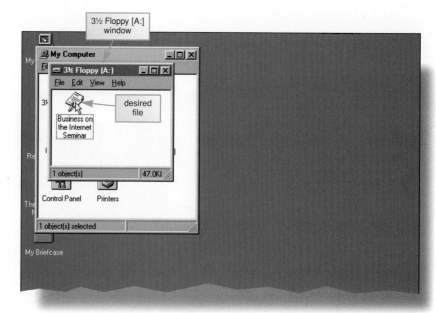

FIGURE 1-84

4 Double-click the Business on the Internet Seminar file icon.

Windows 95 first starts Works and then opens the document, Business on the Internet Seminar, and displays it on the screen (Figure 1-85). You can revise or print the document as required.

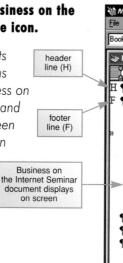
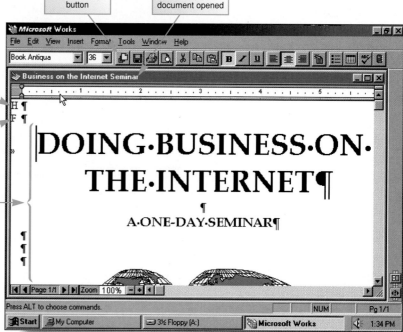

FIGURE 1-85

When you open an existing document in the Word Processor, Works displays a header line (H) and footer line (F) above the first line of the document (Figure 1-85). Text you type in the header line will display at the top of the first page of the document on the screen and print at the top of each page when the document is printed. Text you type in the footer line will display at the bottom of the first page on the screen of the document and print at the bottom of each page when the document is printed. The header line and footer line display at the top of the first page of a document in Normal view only.

Another method of opening a file uses filenames displayed at the bottom of the File menu (Figure 1-86). Works saves the names of the last four documents on which you have worked and lists their names at the bottom of the File menu. If you want to open one of these documents, click the filename. The document will open and display on the screen.

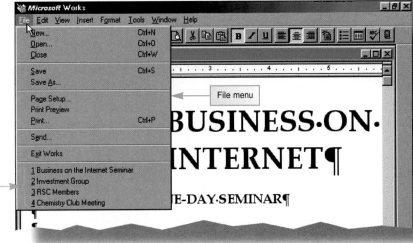

FIGURE 1-86

Moving Around in a Word Processor Document

When you modify a document, you often will have to place the insertion point at different locations within the document. When using the mouse, you can place the insertion point at any location on the screen by pointing to the location and clicking. To place the insertion point at a location in the document that does not display on the screen, use the scroll bars to move the document until the desired location displays and then point and click the desired location in the document.

In some instances, you may want to use keystrokes to move larger distances in a document. Table 1-2 summarizes useful keystrokes for moving around in a document.

You can also use the UP, DOWN, LEFT, and RIGHT ARROW keys to move the insertion point through a document.

Table 1-2	
TASK	KEYSTROKES
Move to the beginning of a document	CTRL+HOME
Move to the end of a document	CTRL+END
Move up one screen	PAGE UP
Move down one screen	PAGE DOWN
Move to the beginning of a line	HOME
Move to the end of a line	END

Deleting and Inserting Text in a Document

When modifying a document, you may find it necessary to delete certain characters, words, sentences, or paragraphs or to insert additional characters, words, or paragraphs. You can use a variety of methods to delete and insert text. Table 1-3 summarizes methods of deleting text.

Table 1-3	
METHOD	RESULT
Press the DELETE key	Deletes the character to the right of the insertion point
Press the BACKSPACE key	Deletes the character to the left of the insertion point
Highlight words, sentences, or paragraphs and press the DELETE key or click Clear command from the Edit menu	Deletes highlighted information

Inserting Text

The Word Processor is initially set to allow you to insert new text between characters, words, lines, and paragraphs without deleting any of the existing text. To insert text in an existing document, place the insertion point where you want the text to appear and then type. The text to the right of the text you type will be adjusted to accommodate the insertion. For example, to insert the word, potential, before the word, customers, in the second bulleted paragraph of the announcement in Figure 1-1 on page W 1.8, place the insertion point in the space before the word, customers, by pointing and clicking and then typing the word, potential, followed by a space. Works inserts the word, potential, in the paragraph.

Overtyping Existing Text

Sometimes you may need to type over existing text. One method of doing this is to press the INSERT key on the keyboard, which causes the letters OVR to display on the status bar, and then type the new text.

When you type, the existing text will be typed over. For example, if a document contains 213, and it should contain 802, position the insertion point immediately to the left of the 2 in 213, press the INSERT key, and type 802. The number 802 will replace the number 213. To remove the overtyping status, press the INSERT key again.

You also can implement overtyping by clicking the **Options command** from the **Tools menu**. When the Options dialog box displays, click the **Editing tab** to display the **Editing sheet**. When the Editing sheet displays, click the Overtype check box and click the OK button.

Replacing Text with New Text

Another method you can use to replace existing text with new text is to highlight all the text you want to replace. When you start typing new text, the highlighted text is deleted and the new text takes its place.

Undo Command

You can use the **Undo Editing command** to reverse a typing, editing, or formatting change. For example, if you accidentally delete a paragraph, you can restore the paragraph by immediately clicking Undo. Undo Editing is effective only if you use it immediately after making a change and before taking any other action. Undo Editing is found on the Edit menu (Figure 1-87).

FIGURE 1-87

Undo Paragraph Formatting

To undo all paragraph formatting changes at any time and revert to the default formatting, highlight the text you want to undo, hold down the CTRL key, and press the letter Q key. For example, if several lines are centered and you no longer want the lines centered, highlight the lines, hold down the CTRL key, and press the Q key. You also can change and undo paragraph formatting by clicking Paragraph on the Format menu and making the appropriate entries in the Paragraph dialog box that displays.

Undo Font Styles

To undo font styles and revert to the default font and styles, highlight the text you want to undo, hold down the CTRL key, and press the SPACEBAR. For example, if a word displays in bold, italics, and underlined, and you want to remove these font styles from the word, highlight the word, hold down the CTRL key, and press the SPACEBAR. You also can click the Bold, Italic, and Underline buttons on the toolbar to undo their effect when they have been selected. Another method is to click the Font and Style command from the Format menu and make the appropriate entries in the Format Font and Style dialog box that displays.

Online Help

To assist you in learning and referencing Works, Works provides extensive online Help. At any time as you create or edit a document, you can display the Help window on the right side of your screen. In Figure 1-88, the Word Processor Menu displays in the Help window because a word processing document displays on the screen. The Word Processor Menu provides a list of common tasks you may want help on when creating or editing a document.

If you need help with a task, find the topic in the Help menu list and then click the topic icon. Works displays a numbered procedure on the Step-by-Step sheet (Figure 1-89 on the next page) you can follow as you complete the task in the document window. Some Step-by-Step topics contain green underlined text that you can click to see a definition of the term. The More Info tab displays overview information and troubleshooting information or tips.

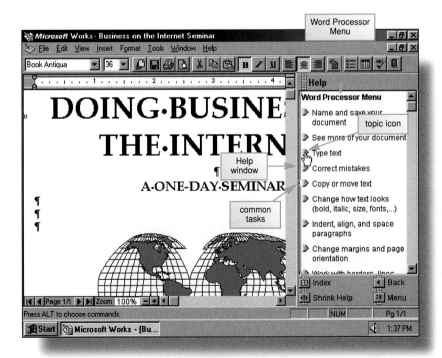

FIGURE 1-88

FIGURE 1-89

If the topic you want is not listed in the Help menu, you can search for other Help topics by clicking the Index button at the bottom of the Help window. Works displays a Help Topics: Microsoft Works dialog box (Figure 1-90). The dialog box contains two tabbed sheets, Index and Contents. On the Index tabbed sheet, type a word or words for the task or item about which you wish information. Works displays the topic in the Help window. To see a listed topic, click the topic.

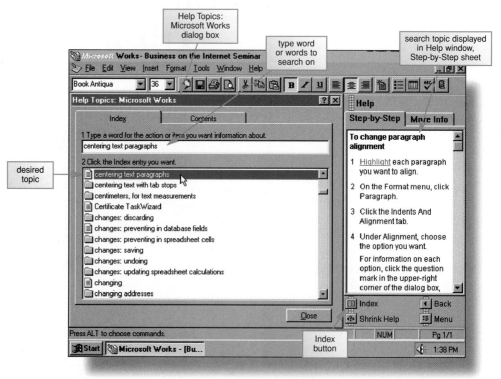

FIGURE 1-90

You also can get specific help for each option in a dialog box by clicking the question mark button in the upper right corner of the dialog box, and then clicking an option (Figure 1-91) Works displays information concerning the option.

More *About*
Help in a Dialog box

Want the fastest way to get additional help on any Works dialog box option? Just right-click the dialog box option you want help for and Works displays a short explanation. Right-click the explanation and Works displays a context-sensitive menu with commands that allow you to copy or print the explanation.

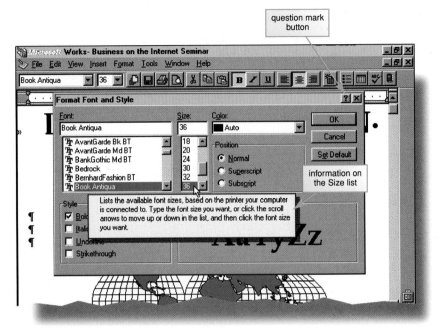

FIGURE 1-91

To learn how to use online Help, perform the following steps.

Steps **To Learn Online Help**

1 **Click Help from the menu bar, and then point to How to use Help.**

*Works displays the **Help menu** (Figure 1-92). The mouse pointer points to How to use Help.*

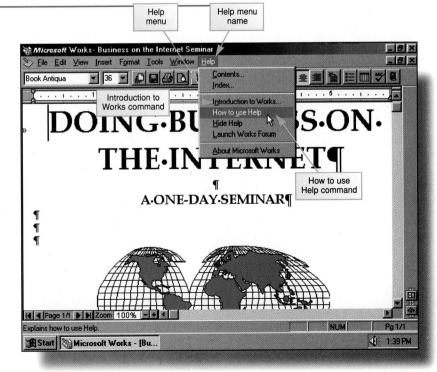

FIGURE 1-92

2 Click How to use Help. Point to any topic.

Works displays the Help window to the right of the document window and displays the Using Help topic (Figure 1-93). When you point to a topic, the mouse pointer changes to a hand with a pointing finger.

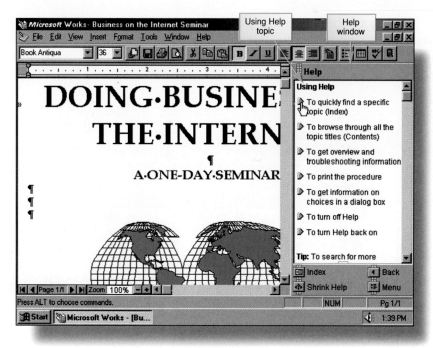

FIGURE 1-93

Reading the topics listed in Using Help provides you with the information you need to further explore online Help.

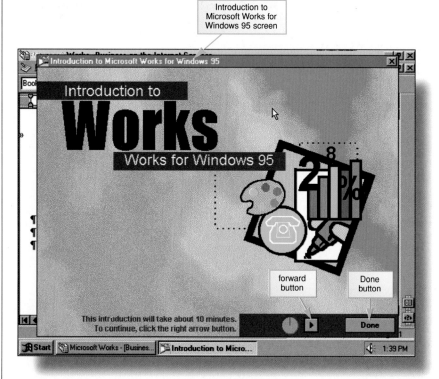

FIGURE 1-94

Viewing Introduction to Works

You can view a ten-minute demonstration of the features in Works by clicking **Introduction to Works** (see Figure 1-92 on the previous page) on the Help menu. When you click Introduction to Works, the screen shown in Figure 1-94 displays. Click the forward button to go to the next screen. Click the Done button to exit the Introduction to Works demonstration.

Project Summary

This project taught you many of the capabilities of the Works Word Processor. Important subject matter included starting Works, entering text, centering text, using fonts, increasing font size, using different font styles, previewing documents, saving a document, closing a document, closing Works, opening an existing document, inserting and deleting data, and using online Help. With a knowledge of these features of the Word Processor, you are now capable of creating a variety of documents.

What You Should Know

Having completed this project, you should now be able to perform the following tasks:

- Center Paragraphs *(W 1.29)*
- Change Fonts *(W 1.31)*
- Change Font Size *(W 1.32)*
- Change Views in the Word Processor *(W 1.17)*
- Close a Document *(W 1.54)*
- Close Works *(W 1.55)*
- Create a Bulleted List *(W 1.35)*
- Display All Characters *(W 1.21)*
- Display an Entire Document in Bold *(W 1.43)*
- Display Text in Color *(W 1.40)*
- Enter Text *(W 1.22)*
- Enter Text that Scrolls Through the Document Window *(W 1.25)*
- Insert Clip Art into a Document *(W 1.44)*
- Italicize Text *(W 1.39)*
- Maximize the Document Window *(W 1.12)*
- Open an Existing Document *(W 1.56)*
- Print a Document *(W 1.52)*
- Resize Clip Art *(W 1.47)*
- Save an Existing Document with the Same Filename *(W 1.49)*
- Save a New Document *(W 1.26)*
- Start Microsoft Works for Windows 95 *(W 1.9)*
- Start the Word Processor *(W 1.10)*
- Use Online Help *(W 1.61)*
- Use Print Preview *(W 1.50)*
- Use Wordwrap *(W 1.23)*

Test Your Knowledge

1 True/False

Instructions: Circle T if the statement is true or F if the statement is false.

T F   1. Microsoft Works for Windows 95 is application software that provides word processing, spreadsheet, database, and communications capabilities in a single package.

T F   2. The applications within Microsoft Works for Windows 95 are called applets.

T F   3. To start Works, click the Start button on the taskbar, point to Programs on the Start menu, point to Microsoft Works 4.0 on the Programs submenu, and click Microsoft Works 4.0.

T F   4. The ClipArt Gallery, which contains illustrations you can insert in documents, is an additional accessory to Works.

T F   5. The title bar in the document window contains the application name, Microsoft Works, and the name of the document you are creating.

T F   6. With Works, the default font is 12-point Arial.

T F   7. To highlight a word to be formatted, right-click the word.

T F   8. When using the Works Word Processor, the term paragraph can mean a blank line, a single character, a word, a single line, or many sentences.

T F   9. You must use print preview to make insertions or deletions in a document.

T F   10. When you close a document, click the Close button in the upper right corner of the application window.

2 Multiple Choice

Instructions: Circle the correct response.

1. When the mouse pointer is located in the document workspace area of the screen, it appears as a(n) _____.
   a. hourglass   b. I-beam   c. vertical bar   d. block arrow

2. By default, Works uses _____-inch left and right margins and _____-inch top and bottom margins.
   a. 1, 1.25   b. 1.25, 1   c. 1.25, 1.25   d. 1.50, 1.25

3. When nonprinting characters display in the document window, spaces are indicated by _____.
   a. periods   b. right-pointing arrows   c. raised dots   d. ¶

4. Before you change the format of a word, you must _____.
   a. highlight the first character in the word to be formatted   b. right-click the word to be formatted
   c. highlight the word to be formatted   d. underline the word to be formatted

5. To activate the context-sensitive menu, point to the selection and _____.
   a. double-click   b. click   c. right-click   d. drag

6. To create a bulleted list, highlight the text, right-click the selection, and click _____.
   a. Bullets   b. Style   c. Font and Style   d. Paragraph

7. Selected objects display _____ handles at the corners and middle points of the rectangular border.
   a. selection   b. resize   c. sizing   d. scaling

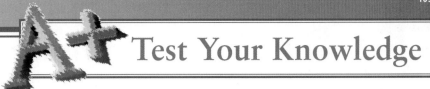

Test Your Knowledge

8. To save an existing document using a filename different from the name under which the file is currently saved, use the _____.
   a. Save button on the toolbar
   b. Close button in the upper right corner of the document window
   c. Save As command on the File menu
   d. Save command on the File menu

9. When you close a document, _____.
   a. you close Works
   b. the document remains on the screen
   c. the document is erased from disk
   d. the Works Task Launcher dialog box displays on the screen

10. To erase a character to the right of the insertion point, press the _____.
    a. DELETE key
    b. BACKSPACE key
    c. SPACEBAR
    d. INSERT key

3 Fill In

Instructions: In Figure 1-95, a series of arrows points to the major components of the Microsoft Works Word Processor window. Identify the parts of the window in the space provided.

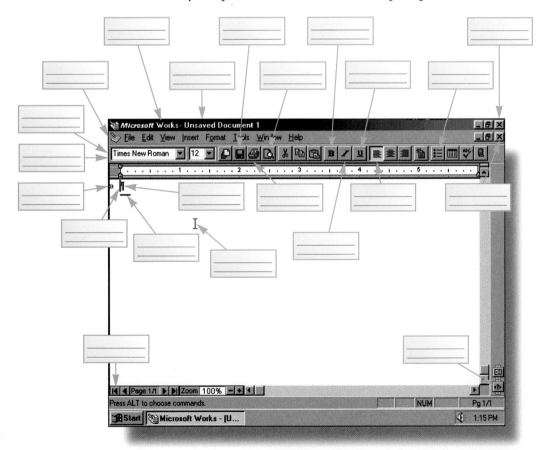

FIGURE 1-95

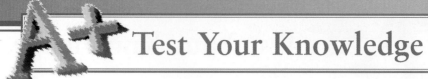

Test Your Knowledge

4 Fill In

Instructions: Write the appropriate command or button name to accomplish each task.

TASK	COMMAND OR BUTTON NAME
View a document in normal view	_____
Display special characters in the document window	_____
Save a new document	_____
Center a paragraph	_____
Create a bulleted list	_____
Remove bullets from a bulleted list	_____
Change text color	_____
Bold text	_____
Insert clip art	_____
Save an existing document with a different filename	_____
Print preview a document	_____
Print a document	_____
Close a document	_____
Close Works	_____
Open an existing document	_____
Reverse a deletion before taking any other action	_____

Use Help

1 Reviewing Project Activities

Instructions: Use your computer to perform the following tasks to obtain experience using online Help.

1. Start the Microsoft Works Word Processor tool.
2. Click How to use Help on the Help menu.
3. The Using Help topic displays in the Help window.
4. Click the topic, To quickly find a specific topic (Index).
5. A numbered procedure on the topic, To quickly find a specific topic (Index), displays on the Step-by-Step sheet.

Use Help

6. Read the topic. Use the down scroll arrow to read the entire topic. In Step 4 at the bottom of the Step-by-Step sheet, several words display in green. Click the green underlined word, drag. Read the information in the pop-up definition box. Click the box to remove it from the screen. Print this topic by clicking the Print this topic icon.

7. Click the More Info tab. On the More Info sheet, click Overview. Read the Overview topic. Click Print this topic in the Overview topic. Click the Done button to close the Overview dialog box.

8. Click the Index button at the bottom of the Help window. When the Help Topics: Microsoft Works dialog box displays, type help in the 1 Type a word for the action or item you want information about text box. Below the text box, click the topic, Help: dialog box choices. Read the topic that displays in the Step-by-Step sheet. Use the down scroll arrow to view the entire screen. Click the Show an example icon. Click the Close button at the bottom of the Help Topics: Microsoft Works dialog box.

9. Click the Close button in the application window to exit Works.

2 Expanding on the Basics

Instructions: Use Works online Help to better understand the topics listed below. Print the topic or topics that substantiate your answer. If there is no Print this topic icon, then answer the question on a separate piece of paper.

1. Using the term, bullet, and the Index sheet in the Help Topics: Microsoft Works dialog box, answer the following questions.
    a. What is the definition of a bullet?
    b. How do you change the size of a bullet from 12 points to 14 points?
    c. List two ways to remove a bullet from a paragraph.
    d. How would you change the spacing between a bullet and text in a bulleted list?

2. Click Font and Style on the Format menu. When the Format Font and Style dialog box displays, use the question mark icon located in the upper right corner of the dialog box to answer the following questions.
    a. Why would you click the Set Default button in the Format Font and Style dialog box?
    b. What is the difference between the OK button and the Cancel button in the Format Font and Style dialog box?
    c. What does a check mark specify in the Strikethrough check box in the Format Font and Style dialog box?

Apply Your Knowledge

1 Creating a Bulleted List and Inserting Clip Art

Instructions: Start the Microsoft Works Word Processor tool. Open the document, Suburban Renewal, on the Student Floppy Disk that accompanies this book. The formatted document is illustrated in Figure 1-96. Create a bulleted list for the two sections of flower names and one section of vegetable names. Drag the left indent marker of each bulleted list to the 2.75-inch mark on the ruler. Change the bullet style to display an asterisk. Then, insert the clip art of a daffodil from the Microsoft ClipArt Gallery, Plants category, in the document after the second heading line. Center the clip art. Resize the clip art until the status bar reads 132% high and 132% wide. Use Save As on the File menu to save the completed document with the filename, Fall Planting. Print the completed document.

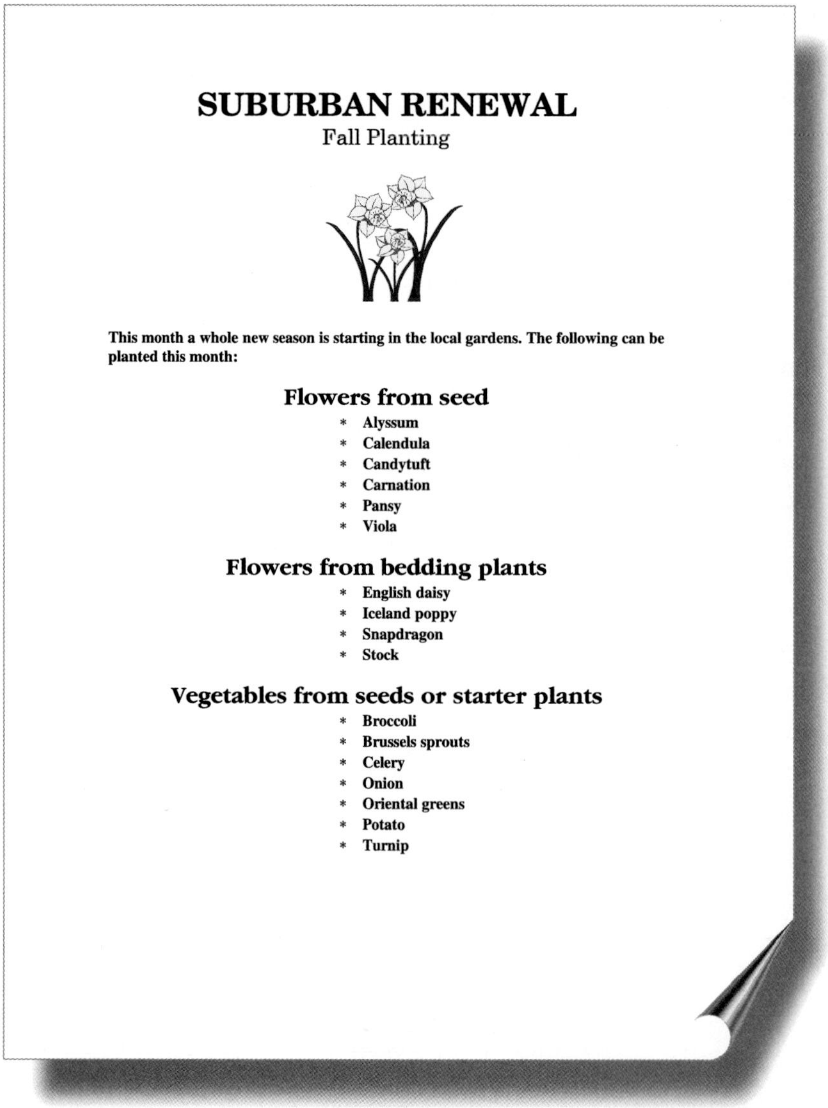

SUBURBAN RENEWAL
Fall Planting

This month a whole new season is starting in the local gardens. The following can be planted this month:

Flowers from seed
* Alyssum
* Calendula
* Candytuft
* Carnation
* Pansy
* Viola

Flowers from bedding plants
* English daisy
* Iceland poppy
* Snapdragon
* Stock

Vegetables from seeds or starter plants
* Broccoli
* Brussels sprouts
* Celery
* Onion
* Oriental greens
* Potato
* Turnip

FIGURE 1-96

In the Lab

1 Creating and Formatting a Document Using Clip Art

Problem: As the president of the Chemistry Club, you have been asked by the club's advisor to create a flyer announcing the monthly meeting. The flyer is shown in Figure 1-97.

Instructions: Display the first heading line, CHEMISTRY CLUB, in 36-point Algerian font. Display the second heading line in 18-point Book Antiqua. The picture is clip art from the Microsoft ClipArt Gallery, Science & Medicine category. The next two lines display in 14-point Times New Roman font. Display the bulleted list with a three-quarter inch margin in 12-point Arial font. The first line after the bulleted list displays in 12-point Arial font. The last two lines display in dark magenta 14-point Times New Roman font. Display the entire document in bold.

After you have typed and formatted the document, save the document on a floppy disk. Use the filename Chemistry Club Meeting. Print the document, and then follow directions from your instructor for turning in the assignment.

CHEMISTRY CLUB

Monthly Meeting

Professor Gutnekov will lecture from his recently published book on the molecular structure of organic compounds.

➤ This month's meeting is scheduled for Tuesday, September 10, 1996, at 5:00 p.m. in Atom Hall.

➤ Food will be served at 5:00 p.m. Dr. Gutnekov will begin promptly at 6:30 p.m.

➤ Question and answer period to follow the lecture.

Don't miss this opportunity to interact with this recognized chemist.

Please e-mail your reservation
gardner@nexus.university.edu

FIGURE 1-97

In the Lab

2 Creating and Formatting a Document Using Clip Art

Problem: As an employee of the Public Relations department, you have been asked by your supervisor to create a flyer advertising the college. The flyer is shown in Figure 1-98.

Instructions: Display the first heading line, MID-WESTERN BUSINESS COLLEGE, in 30-point Arial font. Choose the illustration from the clip art in the Microsoft ClipArt Gallery, Academic category. Display the first line below the clip art in red 20-point Times New Roman font. The next three lines display in 12-point Times New Roman font. Display the bulleted list with a one and one-half-inch margin in 14-point Arial font. The line following the bulleted list displays in 16-point Arial font. The last two lines display in 10-point Times New Roman font. Display the entire document in bold.

After you have typed and formatted the document, save the document on a floppy disk. Use the filename Mid-Western Flyer. Print the document, and then follow directions from your instructor for turning in the assignment.

MID-WESTERN BUSINESS COLLEGE

Design a New Career Path and Become a Leader

The true measure of any program is the success of its students. At MWBC, our students have real-world leadership skills and know how to succeed ethically.

Our program includes the following:

Leadership classes
Research on the Internet
Academically and professionally experienced faculty
Weekend and evening classes
Financial aid and counseling services

Fall classes begin September 6th

For further information call
(405) 555-3835

FIGURE 1-98

In the Lab

3 Creating and Formatting a Document Using Clip Art

Problem: The Home Buyers Fair Committee has asked you to create a flyer announcing Home Buyers Fair. The flyer is shown in Figure 1-99.

Instructions: Create the document illustrated in Figure 1-99 using the appropriate fonts, font styles, sizes, colors, and clip art. Note the proportions of the clip art have been changed. Use Help to determine how to change the proportions of a clip art object.

After you have typed and formatted the document, save the document on a floppy disk. Use the filename Home Buyers Fair. Print the document, and then follow directions from your instructor for turning in the assignment.

BUYING A HOUSE?
Home Buyers Fair

If you are in the market for a new home, now is the time to attend the informative Home Buyers Fair on May 1, 1996, in the West Coast Convention Center. You will find everything you need to know about buying a home.

You'll learn:

✓ **Finding the best mortgage rate**
✓ **Negotiating low closing costs**
✓ **Identifying excellent school districts**
✓ **Locating real estate agents to work for you**

Please call Marie Marlin, (714) 555-7445, to make your reservation.

Don't Miss This Opportunity
Reservations Required!

FIGURE 1-99

Cases and Places

The difficulty of these case studies varies:

▶ Case studies preceded by a single half moon are the least difficult. You can complete these case studies using your own computer or a computer in the lab.

▶▶ Case studies preceded by two half moons are more difficult. You must research the topic presented using the Internet, a library, or another resource, and then prepare a brief written report.

▶▶▶ Case studies preceded by three half moons are the most difficult. You must visit a store or business to obtain the necessary information, and then use it to create a brief written report.

1 ▶ The Social Work Club on your campus is sponsoring a winter coat and blanket drive for low-income community residents. The project is one of several undertaken annually by this active Club having 75 members. Most of the students are social work majors. The Club president is Betsy Mans, and she can be reached at (802) 555-2829 for additional information. You have offered to help their efforts by producing a one-page flyer to hang on campus bulletin boards and a press release for the campus and local newspapers. Create the following document:

Line 1: Help warm a life. (36-point Times New Roman bold centered)
Line 2: Donate a winter coat or blanket. (24-point Times New Roman centered)
Line 3: *Insert and center an appropriate graphic from the Microsoft ClipArt Gallery.*
Line 4: Bring your donation to the Student Union (18-point, Arial centered)
Line 5: on Monday, November 18 (18-point, Arial centered)
Line 6: from 8:00 a.m. to 8:00 p.m. (18-point Arial centered)
Line 7: The Social Work Club will distribute your articles to needy families on Thanksgiving. (14-point Arial)
Line 8: Share the warmth of the holidays. (24-point Times New Roman italic centered)

Enter blank lines where appropriate to properly space the document. Use this information to write a press release to promote the winter coat and blanket drive.

Cases and Places

2 ▶ Time is in short supply for most college students, so they find waiting in line to be particularly frustrating. While you were in line at the post office this morning, you heard the clerks answering the same questions repeatedly. You think that displaying a poster with these clerks' advice might accelerate the process and shorten the lines. You discuss this idea with the Postmaster, and he recruits you to develop the poster. Design and create the following document:

Line 1: Help us deliver for you. (40-point Arial bold underlined centered)
Line 2: How you can help us: (36-point Arial bold centered)
(Lines 3 through 9 should be bulleted, 18-point Times New Roman)
Line 3: Address your letters with block capital letters.
Line 4: Do not use punctuation marks.
Line 5: Use ZIP + 4 Codes.
Line 6: Print the sender's address and your return address on the same side of the envelope.
Line 7: Insure precious packages inexpensively. For example, $100 worth of insurance is just $1.60.
Line 8: Pack fragile items in sturdy boxes filled with such cushioned packing material as newspaper or popcorn.
Line 9: Buy your money orders here for only 85 cents.
Line 10: *Insert and center an appropriate graphic from the Microsoft ClipArt Gallery.*

Enter blank lines where appropriate to properly space the document.

3 ▶▶ Now that you are using a personal computer to complete many of your assignments, you have been suffering from a tingling sensation in your wrists, numbness in your fingers, and difficulty opening and closing your hands. During your next visit to the doctor, you mention these ailments. Your doctor informs you that you are suffering from repetitive stress, or strain, injury (RSI). This term is applied to injuries resulting from repeated movements that irritate nerves and tendons. He describes various actions you can take to alleviate or prevent RSI. They include taking short, frequent breaks of at least 10 minutes every hour, stretching the entire body, shrugging your shoulders, and rubbing your hands. You can perform some simple exercises at your desk, such as stretching your fingers, rotating your wrists, and squeezing your thumbs and fingers together. He tells you to adapt your computer work-station to fit your needs, just as you adjust the rearview mirror and seat in your car. For example, you can tilt your monitor so the top line of print on the screen is slightly below eye level and sit 14 to 24 inches away from it. Use ergonomically correct furniture that can be adjusted so the home row of keys is 29 to 31 inches above the floor and your feet are flat on the floor at a 90-degree angle. Have a good desk lamp that illuminates your work, not the screen.

You decide to summarize the doctor's advice by making a reminder list to hang on the side of your monitor. Using this information, create a one-page bulleted list of the 10 major steps you can take to help alleviate or prevent RSI. Title the document "How I can prevent RSI." Add appropriate clip art from the Microsoft ClipArt Gallery. Be certain to spell check your reminder list.

Cases and Places

4 ▶▶ Every year you are faced with writing thank you notes to your relatives for the birthday gifts they send you. This year you want to expedite the process by using your computer to generate the notes. You create the following form letter:

Dear [Name],
Thank you so much for the nice [gift]. I am certain I will think of you every time I use it at [place]. It was very thoughtful of you to remember my birthday. I will [action] you soon.

For each relative, use search and replace to change the words, Name, gift, place, and action to those in Figure 1-100. In addition, use the thesaurus to find a synonym for the word, nice, in each letter.

NAME	GIFT	PLACE	ACTION
Grandma	sweater	the ski resort	call
Aunt Karen	dictionary	school	see
Uncle Rich	basketball	the gym	visit
Cousin Jim	CD	my apartment	talk with you

FIGURE 1-100

5 ▶▶▶ Stress management allows you to use your awareness and mind to control your physical reactions to stress. You can learn to relieve tension and anxiety by relaxing. In turn, you can decrease your heart rate, blood pressure, and total cholesterol level. Obtain one article at least three pages long that discusses stress management. Using the concepts and techniques presented in this project, write a one-page summary of this article using the Modern Language Association's style for writing research reports. Include a footnote that cites your source and a bulleted list of the benefits of practicing stress management. Attach a cover page listing your name, your instructor's name, the course name, and current date.

6 ▶▶▶ Many students are unaware of various deadlines that occur during the semester, such as the last day for dropping a class, the first day of advanced registration, the last day of late registration, midterm week, final exam week, and holidays. You see the registrar in the cafeteria one day and propose that he create a one-half page flyer to distribute at registration. He suggests you provide him with a prototype. Design and create this document, listing important dates during the semester. Be creative in your design. If useful, add appropriate clip art from the Microsoft ClipArt Gallery.

7 ▶▶▶ Some campus organizations have difficulties with public relations. While the members are dedicated and talented, they simply do not know how to communicate their messages effectively to the student body and community. You have decided to use your computer expertise to help one of these groups. Locate a club on campus that seems to need assistance, whether it be in recruiting new members, promoting an event, or announcing a new program. Talk to the organization's officers and suggest how you can help. Design and create a document advertising one facet of the club. Be creative in your design. Use appropriate clip art from the Microsoft ClipArt Gallery.

Microsoft Works 4

Windows 95

Using Works TaskWizards to Create Documents

Objectives:

You will have mastered the material in this project when you can:

▶ Explain the parts of a business letter
▶ Create a letter using the Letter TaskWizard
▶ Replace selected text with new text
▶ Highlight characters with SHIFT+click
▶ Set margin indents to create a numbered list
▶ Create and use a hanging indent
▶ Use the Works spelling checker
▶ Open two document windows
▶ Describe the contents of a resume
▶ Create a resume using the Resume TaskWizard.
▶ Use the TAB key to align text vertically
▶ Use the Window menu
▶ Create and use a custom template

"Letters and Résumés *toGo*"

"Young physicist seeks teaching position at the university level. Ph.D. thesis submitted, awaiting acceptance. Works include papers on particle theory, quantum theory, and special theory of relativity. Family man, enjoys playing the violin and sailing. Contact A. Einstein."

Yes, *that* A. Einstein, who, in 1905, wrote by hand literally dozens of letters seeking employment as a teacher while he labored in relative obscurity at the Swiss patent office. That same year, he published three studies that set the world of science on its ear. Fame eventually helped, but persistence in his search paid off when he finally landed a teaching appointment at the University of Zurich after years as a patent clerk.

No one can tell whether Einstein might have met his goals more quickly if he would have had the benefit of a modern word processor, but certainly Microsoft Works would have made his life easier. Beginning with a Letter TaskWizard, a writer can easily create a personalized letter-head, and then draft a letter guided by the TaskWizard's capabilities to manage margins and take care of details, such as automatically placing the inside address, salutation, close, and the name of the writer. Changes

SHARON LAMM

21 Sycamore Avenue, West Chester, PA

An International **ORGANIZATION DEVE**
with over ten years diverse experience. Sp
building, team/group facilitation and proble
program development, action learning, an
and development. A business partner wit
presentation skills.

PROFESSIONAL EXPERIENCE

Lamm Associates, LTD., West Chester

can be made quickly, so the same letter can be used, with minor differences, for many addressees taken from a database of recipients, such as possible employers. Résumé templates provide a similar advantage for those who are unfamiliar with the mechanics of writing out their personal work histories, establishing a good starting point from which changes can be made.

Imitation is the sincerest form of flattery.
Amateur writers imitate; mature writers steal.
Originality is only undiscovered plagiarism.

These three famous puns share a common thread of practicality: if good guidelines exist for doing something, use them. This same practicality is built into Microsoft Works. Through TaskWizards and templates, Works provides the framework that eliminates the need to start from scratch every time, while the writer supplies the substance.

To understand the importance of using these guidelines, consider the meaning of the word *represent*: "to bring clearly before the mind." When creating letters and résumés, which are two elements of business life that are fundamental to success, it is critical to bring a *favorable* image to mind. These documents must be crisp, to the point, and good-looking, because usually they are the first glimpse a prospective employer gets of a job-seeker.

Even if an individual's personal trip through the universe does not include physics or violins, a good résumé and cover letter may be the launch vehicles that start the journey.

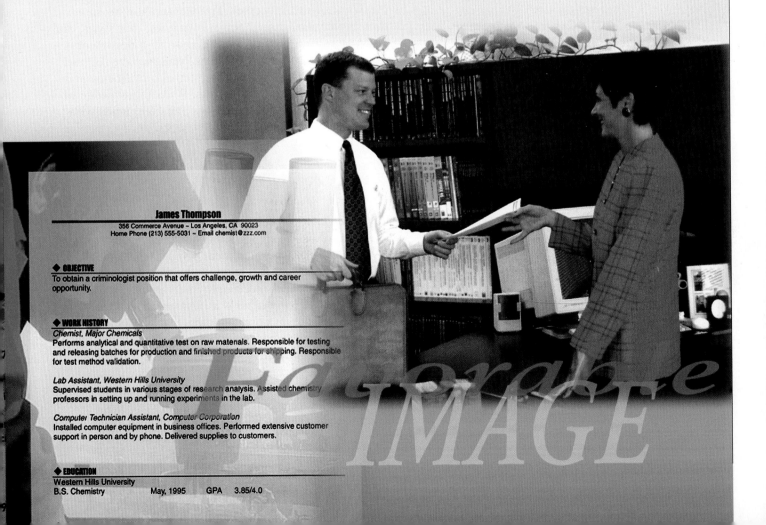

James Thompson
356 Commerce Avenue ~ Los Angeles, CA 90023
Home Phone (213) 555-5031 ~ Email chemist@zzz.com

◆ **OBJECTIVE**
To obtain a criminologist position that offers challenge, growth and career opportunity.

◆ **WORK HISTORY**
Chemist, Major Chemicals
Performs analytical and quantitative test on raw materials. Responsible for testing and releasing batches for production and finished products for shipping. Responsible for test method validation.

Lab Assistant, Western Hills University
Supervised students in various stages of research analysis. Assisted chemistry professors in setting up and running experiments in the lab.

Computer Technician Assistant, Computer Corporation
Installed computer equipment in business offices. Performed extensive customer support in person and by phone. Delivered supplies to customers.

◆ **EDUCATION**
Western Hills University
B.S. Chemistry   May, 1995   GPA   3.85/4.0

Microsoft

Works 4

Windows 95

Using Works TaskWizards to Create Documents

Case Perspective

You currently are employed as a graphic artist in a small family-owned business. Although you are happy with the position, you feel you could be doing more challenging tasks and taking on greater responsibilities. In the local Sunday paper, you browse the employment section and notice a job listing that sounds challenging. You decide to create a resume and send it to the personnel manager with a cover letter stating your interest in the position.

You are to use Works TaskWizards to create a personalized cover letter and resume.

Introduction

In Project 1, you learned how to use many features of the Works Word Processor. You learned how to enter text, center text, change fonts, font sizes, font styles, and font colors, and how to insert clip art in a document. You also learned about the Print Preview, Save As, and Print commands, as well as the methods of closing and opening a file and exiting Works. With a knowledge of these word processing techniques and commands, you can create a wide variety of documents.

Project Two

In Project 2, you will learn how to use Works TaskWizards to create a resume and a cover letter. A **resume** is a printed document given to potential employers. It contains information about an applicant's educational background, employment experience, and related data. A **cover letter** is a business letter that allows you to elaborate on positive points in your resume. A cover letter also provides you with the opportunity to show the potential employer your written communication skills. This project presents the Works commands and word processing techniques required to create the cover letter and resume shown in Figure 2-1.

Angelica Baker

61 Beacon Street ᵣ Boston, MA 02215
Home Phone (619) 555-9112 ᵣ Email student@zzz.com

March 18, 1997

Ms. Leanne Brown
Personnel Department
Graphics Design, Inc.
49 Commonwealth Street
Boston, MA 02115

Dear Ms. Brown,

I believe my experience and solid record of achievement make me an ideal candidate for the graphic designing position in your firm advertised in the *Boston News* February 23.

I have over four years of professional graphic designing experience, with a two-year career base established with East Coast Design. As my enclosed resume indicates, I have successfully performed needs assessments for clients and designed corporate logos. My experience includes designing ads, assisting in photo shoots, and writing technical manuals.

Please consider the following relevant highlights of my qualifications:

1. Served as a student representative to the Massachusetts Graphic Design Board and assisted in developing standards that are currently followed in the graphics industry.

2. Maintained a 4.0 grade point average in my major field of study and a 3.85 overall grade point average while a student at Boston Arts College.

Please call me at (619) 555-9112 after 6 p.m. if you need further information about my experience.

Sincerely,

Angelica Baker

AB

Enc: 1

Angelica Baker

◆◆◆

61 Beacon Street
Boston, MA 02215
◆
Home Phone (619) 555-9112
Email student@zzz.com

◆ OBJECTIVE

A career position with a progressive organization in the field of graphic design where opportunities for growth and advancement exist.

◆ WORK HISTORY

1995-1997   *Graphic Designer, East Coast Design*
Design brochures, posters, stationery packages, and corporate identity systems. Assist production supervisor at photo shoots and other aspects of the business. Responsible for designing ads for newspaper publications as well as layout and execution of newsletters.

1994-1995   *Art Director, MSL Design, Inc.*
Solely responsible for tasks in the art department including: communicating with clientele and assessing their needs, creating corporate brochures, newsletters, and posters, production layout and design, as well as aiding customers in preparing their work for the press.

1993-1994   *Intern, Eastern Advertising Agency*
Designed presentation pieces on a PC. Assisted Art Director in writing a graphics standards manual and performing photo shoots.

◆ EDUCATION

Boston Arts College, Boston, MA
B.A. Graphic Design   May, 1994   GPA   3.85/4.0
A.A. Desktop Publishing   June, 1992   GPA   3.75/4.0

◆ COMPUTER SKILLS

- QuarkXPress for Windows 95
- Adobe Illustrator and Aldus PageMaker for Windows
- Adobe Photoshop
- Microsoft Word 7 for Windows 95
- Experienced with Macintosh and PC systems

◆ AWARDS RECEIVED

- Best Graphic Design of a Corporate Logo, 1996
- Student of the Year, 1994

◆ PROFESSIONAL AFFILIATIONS

Association for Art Direction and Design of Boston
National Association for Graphic Designers

◆ **More** *About* **TaskWizards**

Works TaskWizards allow you to create professional looking documents quickly and easily. The TaskWizards are divided into ten categories. Each category contains TaskWizards appropriate to the type of work you do in that category. For example, if you are a student, choose the Students and Teachers category. The available TaskWizards in this category include Bibliography, Schedule, School Reports/Thesis, and Student & Membership Information. In just a matter of seconds, these TaskWizards step you through the process of creating a professional document.

The cover letter in Figure 2-1 is a response to an advertisement in a newspaper for an employment opportunity with a company. The resume to accompany the cover letter also is illustrated in Figure 2-1. Because composing cover letters and resumes from scratch can be difficult for many people, Works provides TaskWizards to assist you in preparing these documents.

FIGURE 2-1

Document Preparation Steps

The following steps give you an overview of how the cover letter and resume in Figure 2-1 on the previous page will be developed in this project. If you are preparing the documents in this project on a personal computer, read these steps without doing them.

1. Start Works.
2. Use the Letter TaskWizard to create a cover letter.
3. Personalize the cover letter.
4. Check the spelling of the cover letter using the Works spelling checker.
5. Save the cover letter on a floppy disk using the filename, Cover Letter.
6. Print the cover letter.
7. Use the Resume TaskWizard to create a resume.
8. Personalize the resume.
9. Check the spelling of the resume using the Works spelling checker.
10. Save the resume on a floppy using the filename, Resume.
11. Print the resume.
12. Use the entries in the Window menu to view either the cover letter or the resume.

The following pages contain a detailed explanation of each of these steps.

Format of a Cover Letter

At the top of the cover letter is the letterhead. A **letterhead** contains the name, address, city, state, zip code, and telephone number of the individual creating the letter. The letter is typed below the letterhead. A variety of letter styles may be used when creating a business letter. The style illustrated in Figure 2-2 is called a block letter. In a **block letter**, all the components of the letter begin at the left margin except the numbered list of items below the third paragraph. Figure 2-2 identifies the components of a basic business letter and the recommended spacing for a long (full page) letter.

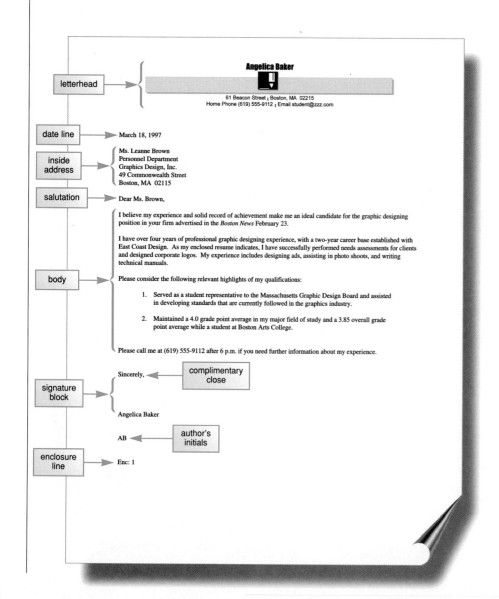

A business letter contains a **date line** below the letterhead. The next element is the inside address. The **inside address** contains the name of the person to whom the letter is being sent, followed by the person's title, the name of the company, and the address of the company. Following the inside address is the **salutation** (Dear Ms. Brown,). A comma is placed after the name in the salutation.

The next element of the letter is the message, which is called the **body** of the letter. After the body of the letter is the **complimentary close**, which consists of the word, Sincerely, a comma, three blank lines, and then the name of the individual sending the letter. The initials of the author (AB) are entered below the name followed by the number of enclosures (Enc:1).

Page Setup and Margins

Recall from Project 1, Works places 1-inch top and bottom margins and 1.25-inch right and left margins as defaults for printing the document. When using a TaskWizard to create a letter and a resume, Works changes these default margin values. Works provides a .5-inch top margin and 1-inch left, right, and bottom margins. These values can be reviewed and changed by clicking Page Setup on the File Menu. The Page Setup dialog box will contain the page setup values currently in effect.

Starting Works

To start Works, follow the procedures explained in Project 1. These procedures are summarized below.

TO START WORKS

Step 1: Click the Start button on the taskbar, point to Programs, point to the Microsoft Works 4.0 folder on the Programs submenu, and click Microsoft Works 4.0 on the Microsoft Works 4.0 submenu.
Step 2: The Works Task Launcher dialog box will display.

You are now ready to use a Works TaskWizard to create a cover letter.

Using the Letter TaskWizard to Create a Cover Letter

To create the cover letter illustrated in Figure 2-1 on page W 2.5, you will use the Letter TaskWizard. The Letter TaskWizard provides a quick and convenient way to create and format the letter with appropriate spacing and layout. With a TaskWizard, you can instruct Works to prewrite the letter for you. Then, you personalize the letter by selecting and replacing text. Follow the steps on the next several pages to use the Letter TaskWizard to create a cover letter.

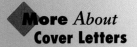

More *About*
Cover Letters

In a job search, your cover letter should be tailored to a particular reader you have contacted or to a specific job target. Link your skills to the employer's advertised needs, point by point in a graphic way, such as using bullets or numbered lists. One page maximum length is appropriate for a cover letter.

Steps To Use the Letter TaskWizard to Create a Cover Letter

1 **Ensure the TaskWizards sheet displays in the Works Task Launcher dialog box. Then point to Letter in the Common Tasks category. If the TaskWizards are not arranged in category order, click the List categories in different order button below the TaskWizard list. Click List by category.**

The TaskWizards sheet displays and the mouse pointer points to the Letter TaskWizard in the Common Tasks category (Figure 2-3). The TaskWizards are listed according to categories by default. You can click a category to show or hide the list of TaskWizards in that particular category. Click the List categories in different order button below the TaskWizard list to rearrange

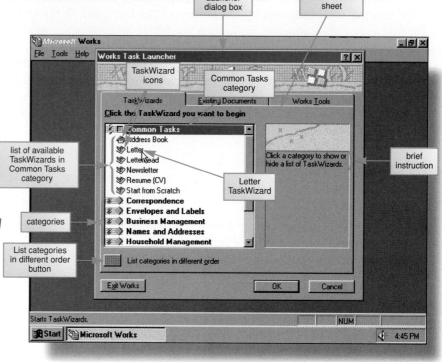

FIGURE 2-3

the categories alphabetically, those most recently used, or by document type. The icons located to the left of the TaskWizards indicate which Works tool will create the document. For example, the icon associated with the Letter TaskWizard indicates the Word Processor tool is used to create the document.

2 **Click Letter and point to the OK button in the Works Task Launcher dialog box.**

Works highlights the Letter Task-Wizard and the mouse pointer points to the OK button (Figure 2-4). A brief description of the highlighted TaskWizard displays to the right of the TaskWizard list.

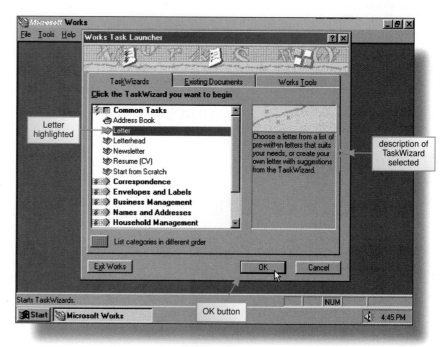

FIGURE 2-4

3 **Click the OK button in the Works Task Launcher dialog box. When Works displays the Works Task Launcher dialog box, point to the Yes, run the TaskWizard button.**

Works displays the Works Task Launcher dialog box asking you to confirm that you want to run the TaskWizard (Figure 2-5). Be aware Works will not display this confirmation dialog box if the Always display this message check mark was previously removed.

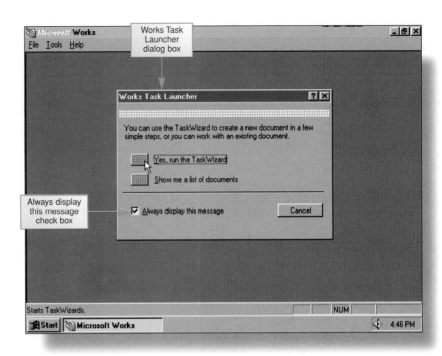

FIGURE 2-5

4 **Click the Yes, run the TaskWizard button in the Works Task Launcher dialog box. When the Letter TaskWizard displays, click Simple. Point to the Next button.**

After a few seconds, Works displays the first in a series of Letter TaskWizard dialog boxes instructing you to click the document layout you want, and then click the Next button to go on (Figure 2-6). Three letter layouts (Professional, Simple, and Formal) display. The Simple layout displays with a border indicating it is selected. A sample of the Simple layout displays to the right of the document layouts. Below the sample, a description of the selected layout explains its

FIGURE 2-6

benefits. Clicking the Instructions button in the lower left portion of the dialog box displays additional information about TaskWizards. The mouse pointer points to the Next button in the lower right portion of the screen. Clicking this button will display the next Letter TaskWizard dialog box. Clicking the Cancel button located to the left of the Next button closes the Letter TaskWizard and returns to the Works Task Launcher dialog box.

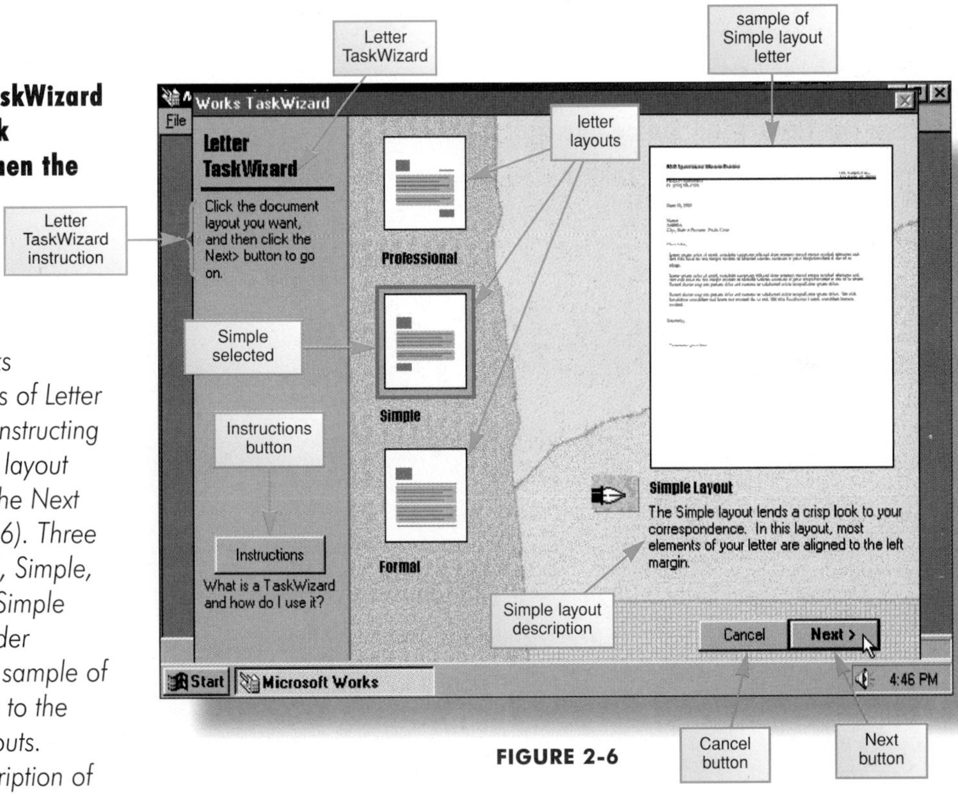

5 **Click the Next button. When the next Letter TaskWizard dialog box displays, point to the Letterhead button.**

A new dialog box displays with additional instructions and five buttons (Letterhead, Address, Content, Text Style, and Extras) you can use to modify different elements of the letter (Figure 2-7). You can click the Create It! button at any time to create your document with the choices you have made. Clicking the Back button will move you to the preceding dialog box. The mouse pointer points to the Letterhead button.

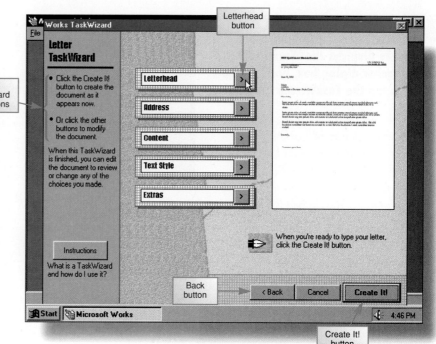

FIGURE 2-7

6 **Click the Letterhead button. When the Letterhead dialog box displays, click I want to design my own. Point to the Next button.**

The Letterhead dialog box displays in front of the Letter TaskWizard dialog box asking, What kind of letterhead do you want to use? (Figure 2-8). A small dark circle within the option button indicates the I want to design my own option button has been selected. If you select the I want to use my pre-printed letterhead stationery option, Works allows space at the top of the letter for the preprinted letterhead. The mouse pointer points to the Next button.

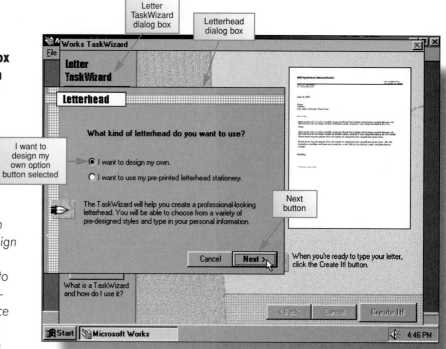

FIGURE 2-8

7 **Click the Next button. When the next Letterhead dialog box displays, click Symbol. Point to the Next button.**

The next Letterhead dialog box displays allowing you to select one of seven letterhead styles (Figure 2-9). You can click each option button to display a sample of the selected style to the right of the style list. The small dark circle within the Symbol option button indicates the Symbol style is selected. A sample of the Symbol letterhead style displays to the right of the styles list. The text that displays in the sample letterhead on your screen may be different. The mouse pointer points to the Next button.

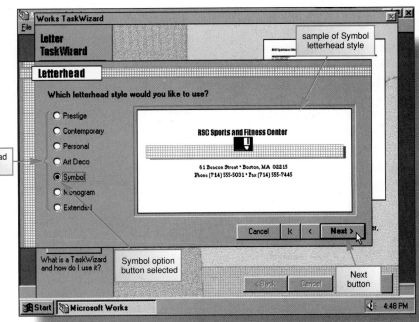

FIGURE 2-9

8 **Click the Next button. When the next Letterhead dialog box displays, click Company name to remove the X. Click Personal name. Type** `Angelica Baker` **in the Personal name text box. Point to the Next button.**

The next Letterhead dialog box displays the question, Which name do you want to use? (Figure 2-10). The X no longer displays in the Company name check box. Personal name is selected and the name, Angelica Baker, displays in the Personal name text box. The mouse pointer points to the Next button. To the left of the Next button is a button identified by a single arrowhead pointing to the left. Clicking this button will return you to the preceding dialog box. The button with the single arrowhead pointing to the left preceded by a vertical line is used to move to the first Letterhead dialog box.

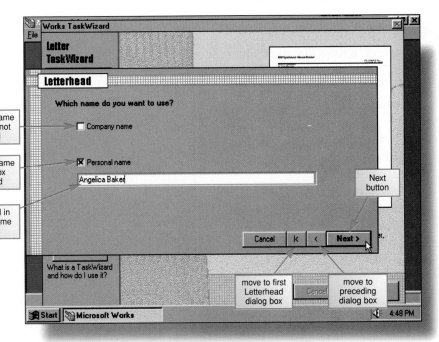

FIGURE 2-10

9 Click the Next button. When the next Letterhead dialog box displays, type 61 Beacon Street in the Address Line 1 text box. Press the TAB key to move to the Address Line 2 text box. Make no entry in the Address Line 2 text box. Press the TAB key again to move to the City, State/Province, Postal Code text box. Type Boston, MA 02215 in the city, State,/Province, Postal Code text box. Point to the Next button.

The Letterhead dialog box displays allowing you to enter information that is to appear in the letterhead (Figure 2-11). The mouse pointer points to the Next button.

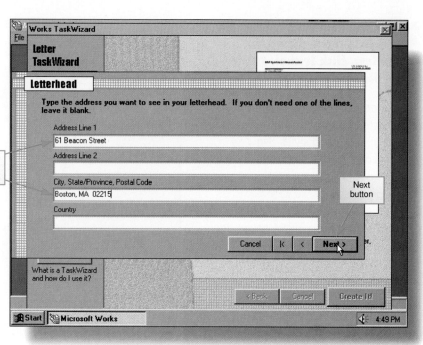

FIGURE 2-11

10 Click the Next button. When the next Letterhead dialog box displays, ensure the Work phone number and Fax number check boxes do not display an X. Click Home phone number and type (619) 555-9112 in the Home phone number text box. Then click E-mail address and type student@zzz.com in the E-mail address text box. Point to the Next button.

The dialog box contains the information that is to appear in the letterhead (Figure 2-12). The mouse pointer points to the Next button.

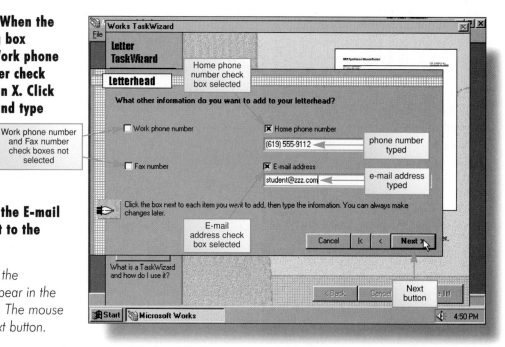

FIGURE 2-12

11 **Click the Next button. When the next Letterhead dialog box displays, point to the OK button.**

The Letterhead dialog box displays indicating the letterhead element of the letter is completed (Figure 2-13). A sample of the letterhead created from the options given in the Letterhead dialog boxes displays. The mouse pointer points to the OK button.

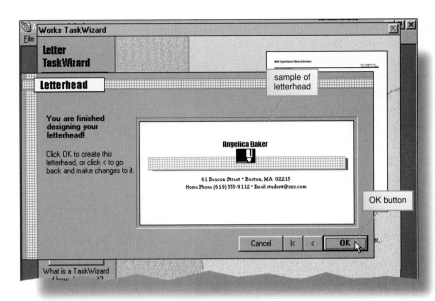

FIGURE 2-13

12 **Click the OK button in the Letterhead dialog box. When the Letter TaskWizard dialog box displays, point to the Address button.**

The Letterhead dialog box closes and the Letter TaskWizard dialog box remains on the screen (Figure 2-14). The letterhead you designed displays in the sample letter. The mouse pointer points to the Address button.

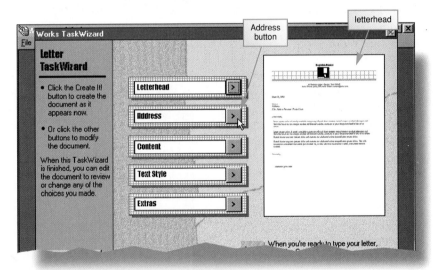

FIGURE 2-14

13 **Click the Address button. When the Address dialog box displays, ensure that the I want to type a single address option button is selected. Point to the Next button.**

The Address dialog box displays with the question, How do you want to address your letter? (Figure 2-15). The I want to type a single address option button is selected. The mouse pointer points to the Next button.

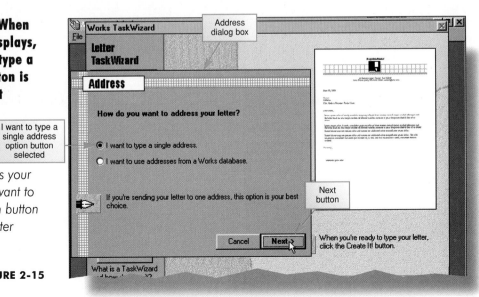

FIGURE 2-15

14 **Click the Next button. When the next Address dialog box displays, type** Ms. Leanne Brown **in the recipient's name and address text box and press the ENTER key. Type** Personnel Department **and press the ENTER key. Type** Graphics Design, Inc. **and press the ENTER key. Type** 49 Commonwealth Street **and press the ENTER key. Type** Boston, MA 02115 **and point to the Next button.**

Works displays the next Address dialog box (Figure 2-16). The recipient's name and address display in the text box. The TaskWizard will insert the recipient's name and address into the letter. The mouse pointer points to the Next button.

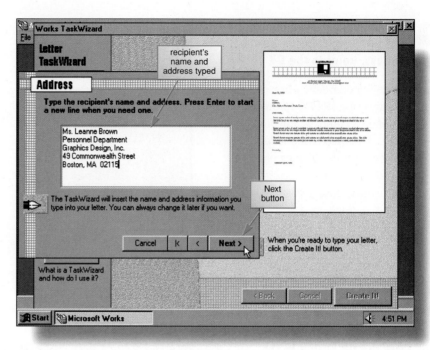

FIGURE 2-16

15 **Click the Next button. When the next Address dialog box displays, type** Ms. Brown **in the text box and point to the Next button.**

When you click the Next button, Works displays the Address dialog box with the text, Dear, in the text box. The name you typed displays in the text box (Figure 2-17). The TaskWizard will insert the salutation into the letter. The mouse pointer points to the Next button.

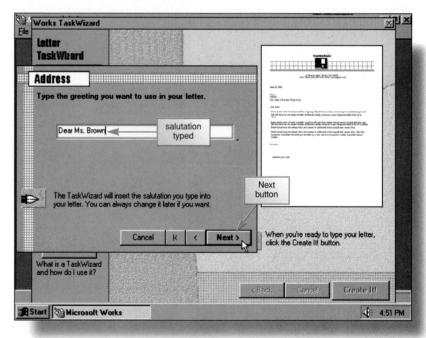

FIGURE 2-17

16 Click the Next button. When the next Address dialog box displays, point to the OK button.

The last Address dialog box displays a message stating that you are finished addressing the letter (Figure 2-18). The mouse pointer points to the OK button.

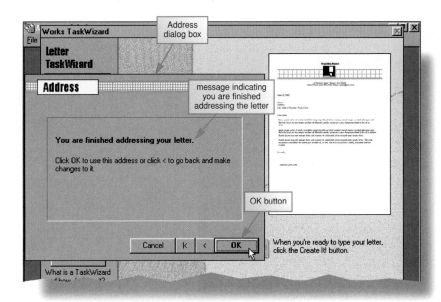

FIGURE 2-18

17 Click the OK button in the Address dialog box. When the Letter TaskWizard dialog box displays, point to the Content button.

The Address dialog box closes and the Letter TaskWizard dialog box remains on the screen (Figure 2-19). The address and salutation you typed display in the sample letter. The mouse pointer points to the Content button.

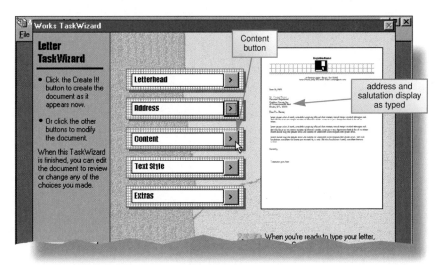

FIGURE 2-19

18 Click the Content button. When the Content dialog box displays, scroll down to view Resume cover letter in the list. Click Resume cover letter. Point to the OK button.

The Content dialog box displays (Figure 2-20). Approximately one hundred prewritten letters display in the list.

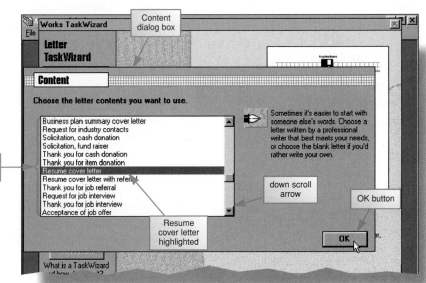

FIGURE 2-20

19 Click the OK button in the Content dialog box. When the Letter TaskWizard dialog box displays, point to the Text Style button.

The Content dialog box closes and the Letter TaskWizard dialog box remains on the screen (Figure 2-21). The mouse pointer points to the Text Style button.

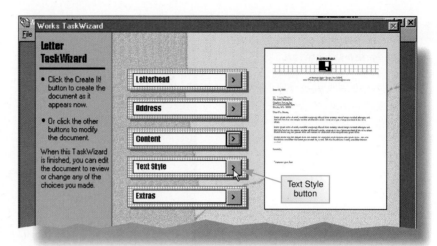

FIGURE 2-21

20 Click the Text Style button. When the Text Style dialog box displays, click Prestige. Point to the OK button.

The Text Style dialog box displays (Figure 2-22). You may select one of four text styles: Prestige, Contemporary, Typewriter, or Whimsical. A brief description of the selected text style displays to the right. The sample area displays the selected text style. The mouse pointer points to the OK button.

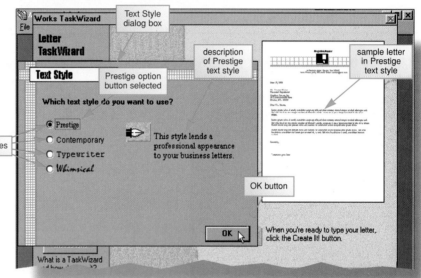

FIGURE 2-22

21 Click the OK button in the Text Style dialog box. When the Letter TaskWizard dialog box displays, point to the Extras button.

The Letter TaskWizard displays and the mouse pointer points to the Extras button (Figure 2-23).

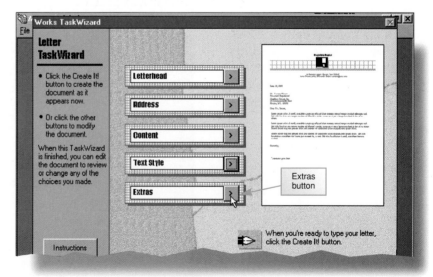

FIGURE 2-23

22 **Click the Extras button. When the Extras dialog box displays, click Enclosures and type** 1 **in the Enclosures text box. Click Author's initials and type** AB **in the Author's initials text box. Point to the OK button.**

The Extras dialog box displays (Figure 2-24). The TaskWizard will enter the number of enclosures and the author's initials in the letter. The mouse pointer points to the OK button.

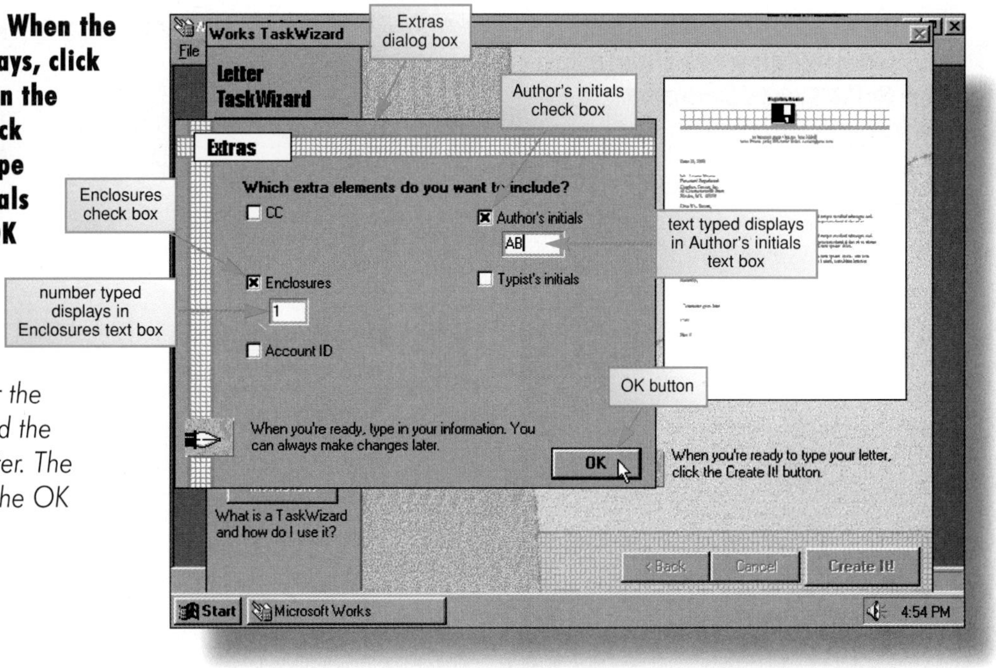

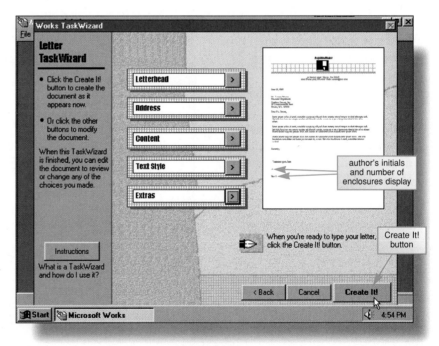

FIGURE 2-24

23 **Click the OK button in the Extras dialog box. When the Letter TaskWizard displays, point to the Create It! button.**

The TaskWizard dialog box displays and the mouse pointer points to the Create It! button (Figure 2-25). The extra elements you selected display in the sample letter.

FIGURE 2-25

24 **Click the Create It! button. When the Checklist dialog box displays, point to the Create Document button.**

The Checklist dialog box displays and the mouse pointer points to the Create Document button (Figure 2-26). The Checklist displays the choices you made using the Letter TaskWizard. You can click the Return to Wizard button to make any changes to the letter.

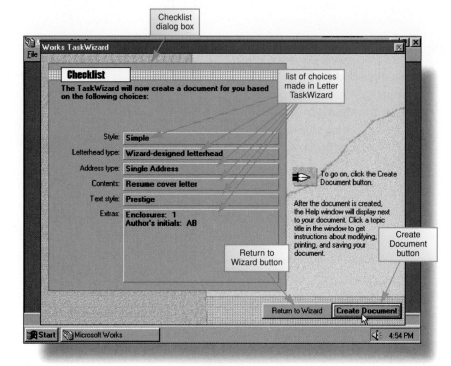

FIGURE 2-26

25 **Click the Create Document button in the Checklist dialog box. When the Works application window and the Unsaved Document 1 window display, maximize the window if necessary. If the Help window displays to the right of the document window, click the Shrink Help button.**

After a few seconds, Works displays the cover letter in the document window (Figure 2-27). Works displays the document in Page Layout view. Because Works displays the current date in the letter, your date may display differently.

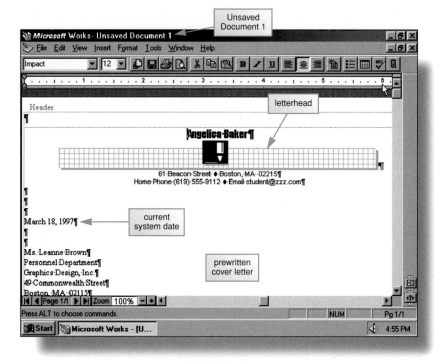

FIGURE 2-27

26 **Click View on the menu bar. When the View menu displays, click Normal.**

Works displays the document in Normal view (Figure 2-28). Notice the right margin has scrolled off the screen. Use the right scroll arrow to view the right margin.

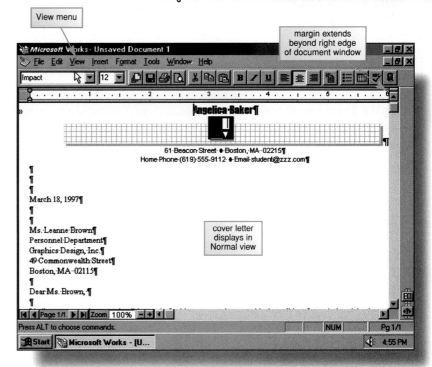

FIGURE 2-28

In addition to the Letter TaskWizard, Works provides over thirty-eight TaskWizards in ten categories to assist you in creating a variety of documents. Table 2-1 below lists the TaskWizards and the Works tools that create each document. Later in this project you will use the Resume TaskWizard.

Zooming Margin Width

The Letter TaskWizard changes the left and right margins of the cover letter from the default of 1.25 inches to 1 inch. Because this allows a line width of 6.5 inches, the right margin moved beyond the right edge of the document window (see Figure 2-28). Thus, some of the text at the right side of the document will not display in the document window. For this reason, Works enables you to **Zoom** a document, meaning you can control how much of it displays in the document window. That is, you can magnify or **zoom** in on a document, or you can reduce or **zoom out** on a document.

Because you often want to see both margins in the document window at the same time, Works provides **margin width zoom** option as shown in the steps on the next page.

TABLE 2-1		
WORD PROCESSOR TASKWIZARDS	*SPREADSHEET TASKWIZARDS*	*DATABASE TASKWIZARDS*
Bibliography	Bids Create From Scratch	Accounts
Brochure	Employee Time Sheet	Address Book
Certificate	FAX Cover Sheet	Business Inventory
Envelopes	Grade Book	Customers or Clients
Flyer	Invoice	Employee Profile
Form Letter	Mortgage/Loan Analysis	Home Inventory
Labels	Order Form	Phone List
Letter	Price List	Sales Contacts
Letterhead	Quotations	Student & Membership Information
Memo	Schedule	Supplies & Vendors
Newsletter		
Proposal Forms		
Proposal Letters		
Resume		
School Reports/Thesis		
Statements		
Tests		

Steps To Zoom Margin Width

1 **Click the Zoom box at the bottom of the Works window. Point to Margin Width.**

Works displays a list of available zoom percentages (Figure 2-29). The mouse pointer points to Margin Width.

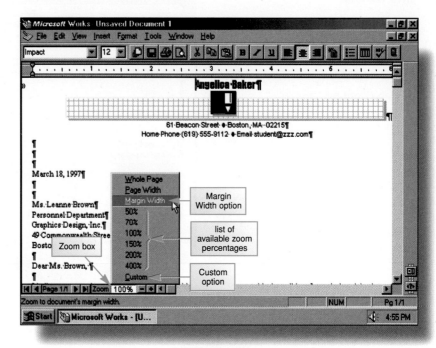

FIGURE 2-29

2 **Click Margin Width.**

Works reduces the size of the document, bringing both the left and right margins into view in the document window (Figure 2-30). The Zoom box now displays 89% which Works computes based on your margin settings.

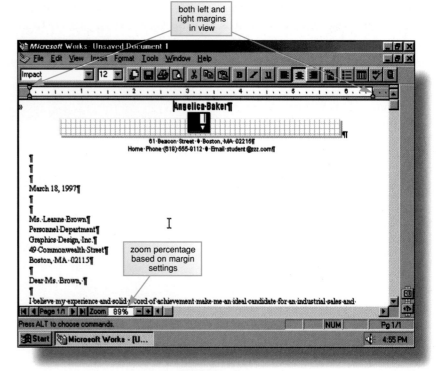

FIGURE 2-30

*Other*Ways

1. On View menu click Zoom, click desired zoom option, click OK

If you wish to zoom to a percentage not displayed in the Zoom list, you can click Custom on the Zoom list (see Figure 2-29) and enter any zoom percentage you desire. To return the document to its normal size on the screen, click 100% on the Zoom list. The zoom setting of a document has no effect on how the document will look when it is printed.

Printing the Cover Letter Created by the Letter TaskWizard

You may wish to print the cover letter created by the Letter TaskWizard so you can review it and identify words, phrases, and sentences you need to revise. To print the cover letter created by the Letter TaskWizard, click the Print button on the toolbar. The resulting printout is shown in Figure 2-31.

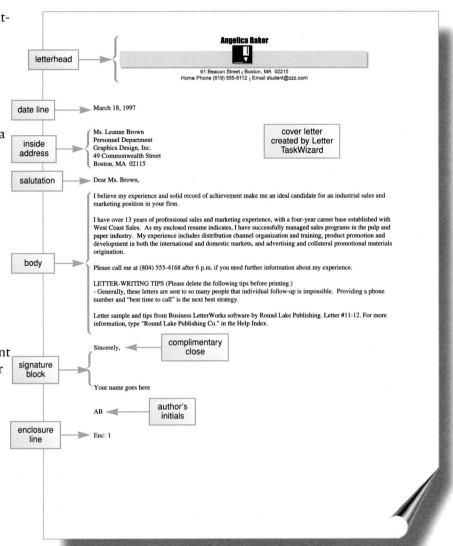

FIGURE 2-31

Modifying the Prewritten Cover Letter

If you compare the printout in Figure 2-31 to the cover letter in Figure 2-1 on page W2.5, you will notice several modifications still need to be made. The first two paragraphs must be changed to address the applicant's experiences. Next, a numbered list must be inserted highlighting the applicant's qualifications. Finally, the Letter-Writing Tips included at the bottom of the cover letter must be deleted.

Entering Information in the Cover Letter

The Letter TaskWizard has supplied default text that you must change. To enter information in the cover letter, you must first highlight the text you wish to replace, and then type the new information to replace the existing text. The easiest way to accomplish this is to use the word processing feature called **typing replaces selection**. Typing replaces selection means when you highlight text and then type, the text you type replaces the highlighted text. This feature, which is turned on by default, can be turned on or off by clicking the appropriate check box in the **Options dialog box**. The Options dialog box can be displayed by clicking **Options** on the Tools menu.

To enter personalized information in the cover letter, complete the following steps.

Steps **To Enter Information in the Cover Letter**

1 **Press the PAGE DOWN key to scroll down one screenful. Click to left of the second occurrence of the word, an, in the first sentence. Hold down the SHIFT key and click to the right of the word, marketing. Position the mouse pointer to the right of the paragraph mark so you can easily see the highlighted words.**

The words, an industrial sales and marketing, are highlighted (Figure 2-32).

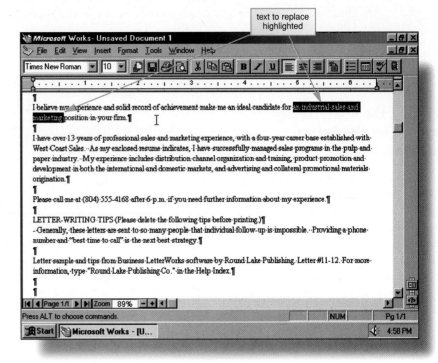

FIGURE 2-32

2 **Type the graphic designing and press the SPACEBAR. Click to the right of the word, firm, press the SPACEBAR, and type the remainder of the sentence as shown in Figure 2-33. When you reach the words, Boston News, click the Italics button on the toolbar. Type *Boston News*. Click the Italics button on the toolbar and complete the sentence.**

Works enters the text in the first sentence (Figure 2-33). When you click the Italics button on the tool-bar and type text, Works italicizes each character you type until you click the Italics button a second time.

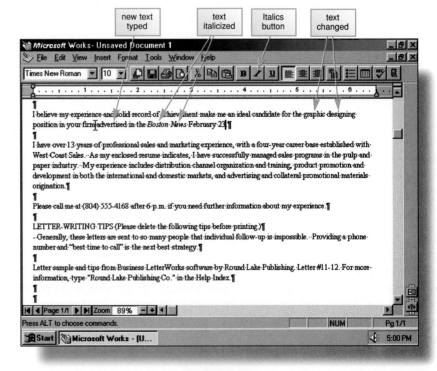

FIGURE 2-33

The next step in customizing the cover letter is to replace the remaining words and phrases in the cover letter, as shown in the following steps.

TO REPLACE TEXT IN THE COVER LETTER

Step 1: In the first sentence in the second paragraph of the cover letter, double-click the text, 13, type four and press the SPACEBAR. Highlight the text, sales and marketing, and type graphic designing and press the SPACEBAR. Highlight the text, four, and type two. Highlight the text, West Coast Sales, and type East Coast Design.

Step 2: In the second sentence of the second paragraph of the cover letter, highlight the text, managed sales programs in the pulp and paper industry, and type performed needs assessments for clients and designed corporate logos. Highlight the last sentence in the second paragraph of the cover letter, and type My experience includes designing ads, assisting in photo shoots, and writing technical manuals. Press the ENTER key twice.

Step 3: Type Please consider the following relevant highlights of my qualifications: as the beginning of the third paragraph. Press the ENTER key twice.

The cover letter displays as shown in Figure 2-34.

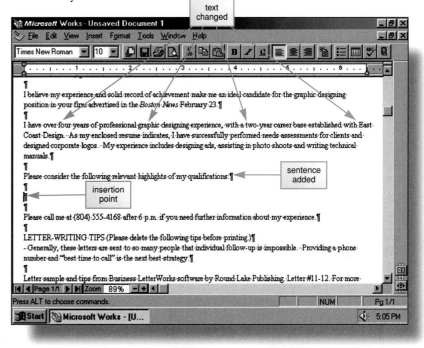

FIGURE 2-34

Differences in Document Displays

The screen shown in Figure 2-34 displays the first paragraphs of the letter. You should be aware that the number of words displayed per line in the document and printed per line on the printer can vary slightly from computer to computer. This occurs because the screen shows text exactly as it will print on your printer and, even though the font and font size are the same, some printers will print a different number of characters per line than other printers. Do not be concerned, therefore, if a line on your screen does not correspond exactly to the screen shown in Figure 2-34.

Hanging Indents

Following the first two paragraphs of the cover letter is a numbered list (Figure 2-35). In a numbered list, you type a number followed by period, press the TAB key to create blank space, and then type the text. When the text reaches the end of the line, the text does not wrap back to the margin of the first line. Instead, it aligns vertically with the first word following the number. This is called a **hanging indent**.

It is recommended that you indent the numbered list one-half inch from the left and right margins, and indent the text one-quarter inch from the beginning of the number.

The following steps explain how to create a hanging indent and the numbered list in the letter using the first-line indent marker, the left-margin indent marker, and the right-margin indent marker.

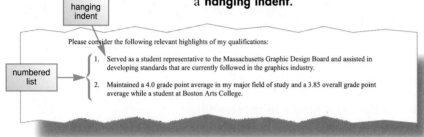

FIGURE 2-35

To Create a Hanging Indent and a Numbered List

1 **Make sure the insertion point is positioned at the location in the letter where you wish to type the numbered list. Point to the left-margin indent marker, which is the lower of the two leftmost triangles on the ruler.**

The mouse pointer points to the left-margin indent marker on the ruler (Figure 2-36).

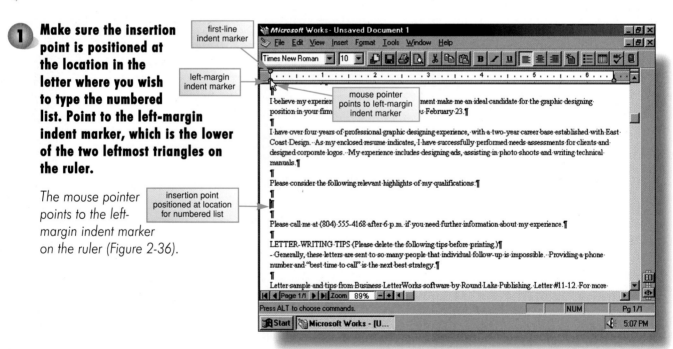

FIGURE 2-36

2 Hold down the SHIFT key and drag the left-margin indent marker right to the 3/4-inch mark on the ruler. Then release the mouse button and the SHIFT key. This establishes the left margin for the text in the numbered list. If the First-time Help dialog box displays, click the OK button.

The left-margin indent marker is positioned at the ¾-inch mark on the ruler (Figure 2-37). Holding down the SHIFT key informs Works you want to drag only the left-margin indent marker. If you do not hold down the SHIFT key, both the left-margin indent marker and the first-line indent marker will move.

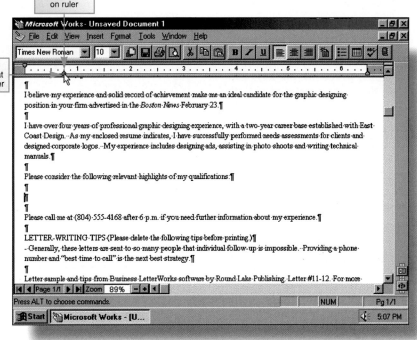

FIGURE 2-37

3 Point to the first-line indent marker, which is the upper left-most triangle on the ruler, and drag the first-line indent marker to the 1/2-inch mark on the ruler. This establishes the leftmost position of the numbers in the numbered list.

The left-margin indent marker is set at the 3/4-inch mark and the first-line indent marker is set at the 1/2-inch mark on the ruler (Figure 2-38). The paragraph mark and the insertion point move 1/2 inch to the right.

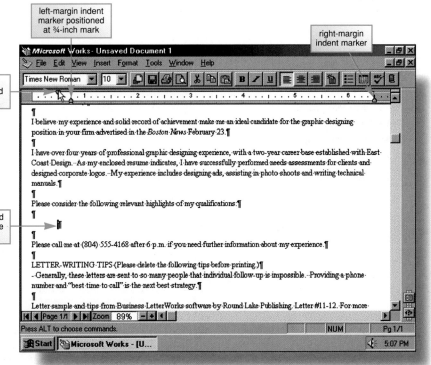

FIGUE 2-38

4 **Drag the right-margin indent marker from the 6½-inch mark to the 6-inch mark on the ruler. Type 1., press the TAB key, and type the text associated with the number as shown in Figure 2-39. Press the ENTER key when the paragraph is completed.**

The right-margin indent marker is positioned at the 6-inch mark, which indents the right margin of the numbered list ½-inch (Figure 2-39). The number 1 begins ½-inch to the right of the 0 position on the ruler. Works inserts a right-pointing arrow to indicate the TAB key has been pressed. The text begins at the left-margin indent marker (¾-inch mark). The text on the second line indents automatically to the left-margin indent marker, aligning the text on the first and second lines.

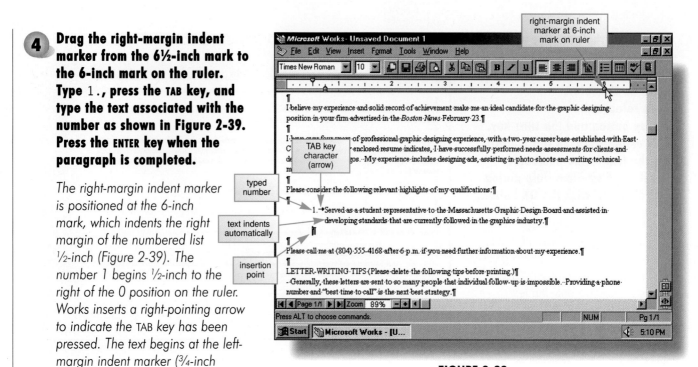

FIGURE 2-39

5 **Press the ENTER key to create a blank line. Then type the remainder of the numbered list as shown in Figure 2-40. Press the ENTER key.**

The numbered list displays (Figure 2-40). Works indents the insertion point and the paragraph mark following the numbered list.

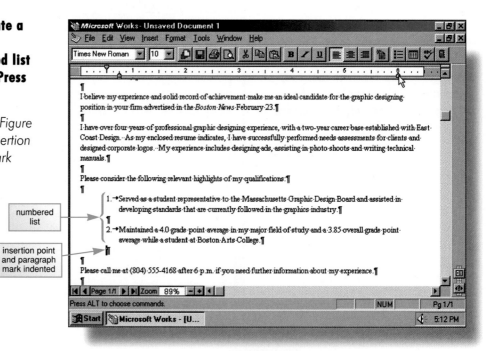

FIGURE 2-40

6 **To return the left-margin indent marker and the first-line indent marker to the 0-inch position on the ruler and the right-margin indent marker to the 6½-inch mark on the ruler, press the CTRL+Q keys.**

The left-margin indent marker and the first-line indent marker return to the 0-inch position on the ruler (Figure 2-41). The right-margin indent marker returns to the 6 ½-inch mark on the ruler. The insertion point and the paragraph mark are located at the 0-inch position also.

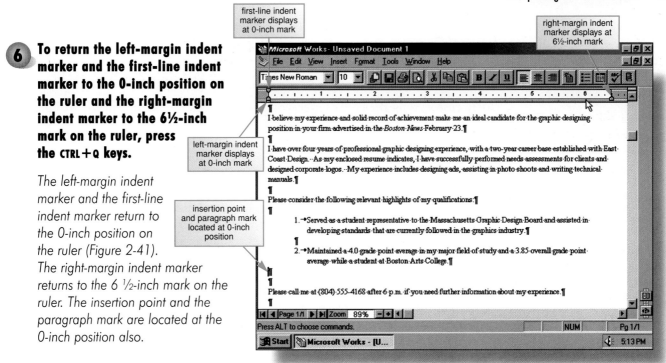

FIGURE 2-41

Use the CTRL+Q key combination any time you want to remove all paragraph formatting from a paragraph at one time.

> **Other Ways**
>
> 1. On Format menu click Paragraph, on Indents and Alignment tab enter desired indentation in Indentation box, click OK
> 2. Press CTRL+SHIFT+H

Completing the Cover Letter

To complete the cover letter, perform the following steps (see Figure 2-42).

TO COMPLETE THE LETTER

Step 1: In the paragraph following the numbered list, highlight the phone number and type (619) 555-9112.

Step 2: Press the PAGE DOWN key if necessary, to view the Letter-Writing Tips. Highlight the Letter-Writing Tips and press the DELETE key. Highlight the text, Your name goes here, and type Angelica Baker.

The completed cover letter displays as shown in Figure 2-42.

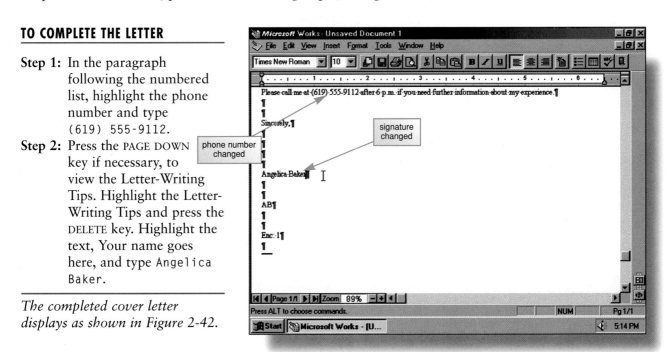

FIGURE 2-42

More *About*
Spelling Checker

You can check a single word for correct spelling as you are typing a document. Highlight the word or words you want to check for accuracy and click the Spelling Checker button on the toolbar. Works will check only the words in the selection.

Using the Spelling Checker

After customizing the cover letter, you should check the document for spelling or typing errors. Works provides the capability of checking the spelling of all words in a document through the use of its spelling checker. To use the spelling checker, you can click the Spelling Checker button on the toolbar. When checking spelling, Works compares the words in a document to the words in a 113,664-word dictionary. When Works finds a word in a document it does not find in the dictionary, Works displays the word in the Spelling: American English dialog box and provides a list of suggested spellings for the word if available. You can add specialized words to the dictionary if you wish, or you can ignore words that Works identifies as misspelled.

To illustrate the use of the Works spelling checker, the word, personnel, has been deliberately misspelled as personnell for the following steps only. Perform the steps to use the spelling checker to find the incorrectly spelled word.

Steps To Check Spelling

1 **Click the beginning of document button on the scroll bar to position the insertion point at the beginning of the document, and then click the Spelling Checker button on the toolbar.**

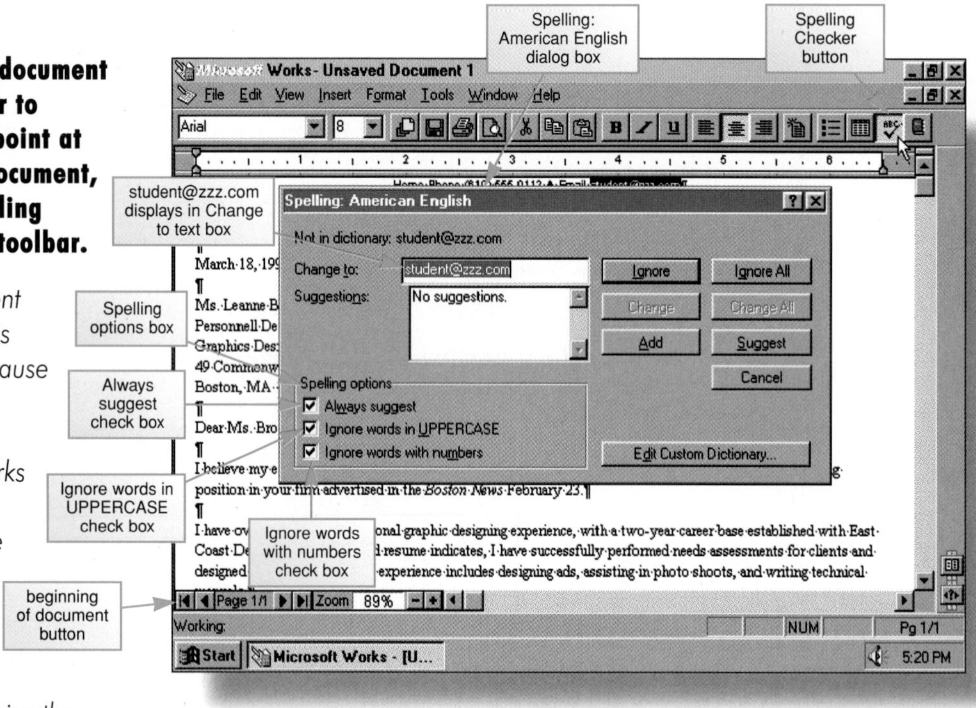

FIGURE 2-43

Works scans the document until it finds a word that is not in the dictionary. Because the e-mail address, student@zzz.com, is not in the dictionary, Works highlights the text, student@zzz.com, on the screen and also displays the Spelling: American English dialog box (Figure 2-43). The Change to text box contains the highlighted text, student@zzz.com. No suggestions to replace the highlighted text display in the Suggestions box. The Always suggest check box, Ignore words in UPPERCASE check box, and Ignore words with numbers check box in the Spelling options box contain check marks. The Always suggest option specifies that Works always will display a list of proposed spellings in the Suggestions box. The Ignore words in UPPERCASE option specifies that Works will ignore words containing all capital letters. The Ignore words with numbers option specifies that Works will ignore words containing numbers.

2 Because student@zzz.com is an e-mail address and is not misspelled, point to the Ignore All button in the Spelling: American English dialog box (Figure 2-44).

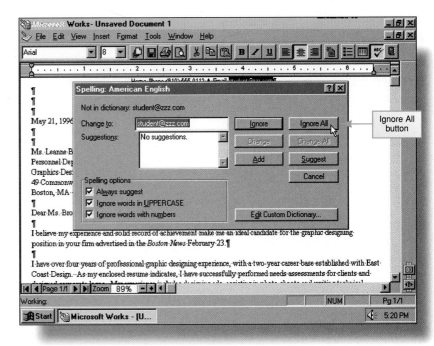

FIGURE 2-44

3 Click the Ignore All button in the Spelling: American English dialog box. When Works highlights the word, Personnell, in the document, point to the Change button.

Works ignores all future uses of the e-mail address student@zzz.com. Works continues to search for words not in the dictionary. Works highlights the word, Personnell, in the letter on the screen (Figure 2-45). Works displays suggested spellings for the word, Personnell, and places the most likely spelling (Personnel) in the Change to text box. The mouse pointer points to the Change button.

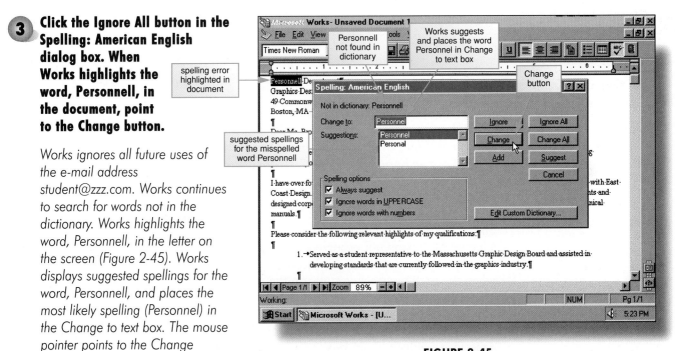

FIGURE 2-45

4 To accept the suggested spelling, click the Change button in the Spelling: American English dialog box.

Works inserts the word, Personnel, in the letter, and immediately continues checking the spelling of each subsequent word. Additional words not found in the dictionary will include the initials, ab, and the abbreviation, Enc. Click the Ignore All button after each occurrence to continue. After checking the entire document, Works displays the Microsoft Works dialog box with a message indicating the spelling check is finished (Figure 2-46).

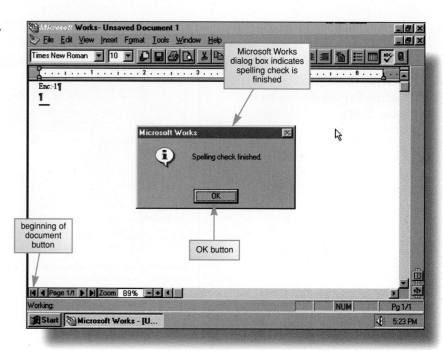

FIGURE 2-46

5 Click the OK button to remove the dialog box from the screen.

OtherWays

1. On Tools menu click Spelling
2. Press F7

When using the spelling checker, you also can type a word in the Change to text box to change a highlighted word, or you can correct a word that is placed in the Change to text box by adding or deleting one or more characters.

The spelling checker also looks for repeated words, such as for for, in a document. You can choose either the Ignore button to ignore the repeated words or the Change button to delete the second occurrence of the repeated word.

If you choose the Ignore button for a misspelled word, Works will ignore only that occurrence of the word, while if you choose the Ignore All button, all occurrences of the word will be ignored. Similarly, if you choose the Change button, only that occurrence of the word is changed, while if you choose the Change All button, all occurrences of the word will be changed.

If you want to add a word to the spelling dictionary, choose the Add button when the spelling checker stops on the word.

For most efficient use of the spelling checker you should place the insertion point at the beginning of the document before you begin to check the spelling. To terminate the spelling check operation, click the Cancel button in the Spelling: American English dialog box.

Saving the Cover Letter on Disk

After checking the spelling of the cover letter, the next step is to save the cover letter on a floppy disk inserted in drive A using the filename, Cover Letter. The steps to save the cover letter are summarized on the next page.

TO SAVE THE COVER LETTER

Step 1: Click the Save button on the toolbar.
Step 2: In the Save As dialog box, type the filename, Cover Letter, in the File name text box.
Step 3: Select drive A from the Save in list box, if necessary.
Step 4: Click the Save button in the Save As dialog box.

The cover letter displays on the screen with the filename, Cover Letter, in the title bar (Figure 2-47).

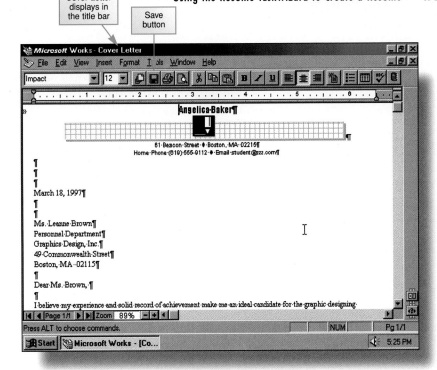

Cover Letter displays in the title bar

Save button

FIGURE 2-47

Printing the Letter

The next step is to print the letter. If the entries you have used previously in the Print dialog box apply to the document you are going to print currently, click the Print button on the toolbar to print the letter. If you want to display the Print dialog box before printing, you must click Print on the File menu.

TO PRINT THE COVER LETTER

Step 1: Click the Print button on the toolbar.

The cover letter will print as shown in Figure 2-1 on page W 2.5.

Using the Resume TaskWizard to Create a Resume

After typing the cover letter, checking the spelling, and saving and printing the cover letter, the next step is to create the resume. Instead of closing the file containing the cover letter or quitting Works, leave the letter displayed on the screen and proceed to the next step, which involves creating the resume.

With Works 4 for Windows 95, you can have up to eight documents open at one time. This technique allows you to switch among documents and display them on the screen with a few clicks of the mouse. For example, when creating the resume, you may wish to switch to a screen that displays the cover letter to assist you in creating the resume, or you may wish to make changes to the letter as you develop the resume.

Works supplies a **Resume TaskWizard** to assist you in building your resume. Once the Resume TaskWizard creates the resume, you will need to customize it as you did the cover letter. If you are not familiar with the content or format of a resume, the Works Resume TaskWizard can be a valuable tool. The techniques for creating a resume and switching between open documents (the cover letter and the resume) are explained on the following pages.

More *About* **Resumes**

More and more large companies rely on high-tech machines to read resumes and create databases that hiring managers search to fill positions. As resumes come in, they are scanned into a database. When jobs need to be filled, a computer is fed a list of key words and phrases. The computer searches through the database and prints out a list of candidates with the most matches. Contact the human resources department of the company to which you are applying to ask if you need to send a scannable resume. If the company scans resumes, include job-specific jargon and other detail phrases you think the company will search for.

Creating the Resume

The Resume TaskWizard will ask you several questions necessary to building a resume, as shown in the following steps.

Steps To Create a Resume Using the Resume TaskWizard

1 Point to the Task Launcher button on the toolbar (see Figure 2-48).

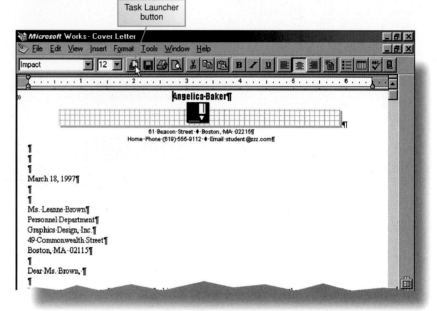

FIGURE 2-48

2 Click the Task Launcher button. When the Works Task Launcher dialog box displays, ensure the TaskWizards sheet displays, and click Resume (CV) in the Common Tasks category. Point to the OK button.

Works displays the Task Launcher dialog box (Figure 2-49). The Resume TaskWizard is highlighted and the mouse pointer points to the OK button.

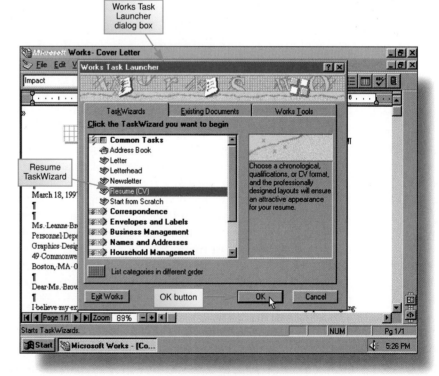

FIGURE 2-49

3 Click the OK button in the Works Task Launcher dialog box. If the Works Task Launcher dialog box displays confirming that you want to run the TaskWizard, click the Yes, run the TaskWizard button. When the Resume TaskWizard dialog box displays, ensure the Chronological layout is selected, and then point to the Next button.

After a few seconds, Works displays the first in a series of Resume TaskWizard dialog boxes instructing you to Click the document layout you want, and then click the Next button to go on (Figure 2-50). Three resume layouts (Chronological, Qualifications, and Curriculum Vitae) display. The Chronological layout displays with a border indicating it is selected. A sample of the Chronological layout displays on the right. Below the sample, a description of the selected layout describes its advantages and disadvantages. The mouse pointer points to the Next button.

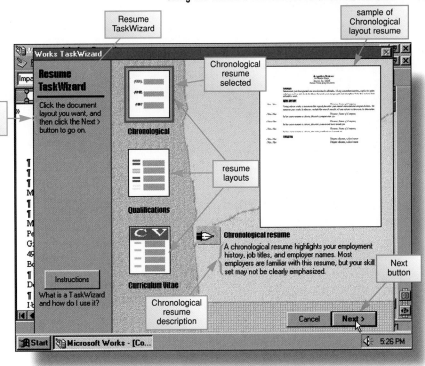

FIGURE 2-50

4 Click the Next button in the Resume TaskWizard dialog box. When the second Resume TaskWizard dialog box displays, point to the Letterhead button.

The second Resume TaskWizard dialog box displays with four buttons (Letterhead, Layout, Headings, and Entries) you can use to modify the resume (Figure 2-51). The mouse pointer points to the Letterhead button.

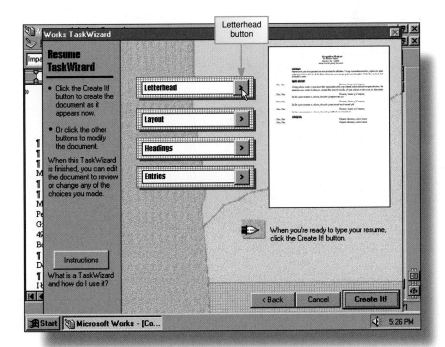

FIGURE 2-51

5 Click the Letterhead button. Using the techniques previously explained in Steps 6 through 9 beginning on page W 2.10, step through the five Letterhead dialog boxes to create the letterhead. That is, click I want to design my own as the kind of letterhead you want to use and click the Next button. Click Art Deco as the letterhead style to use and click the Next button. Click Personal name and type Angelica Baker as the name you want to use and click the Next button. Type 61 Beacon Street, Boston, MA 02215 as the address you want to use and click the Next button. Type (619) 555-9112 in the Home phone number text box and type student@zzz.com in the E-mail address text box and click the Next button. Point to the OK button in the Letterhead dialog box.

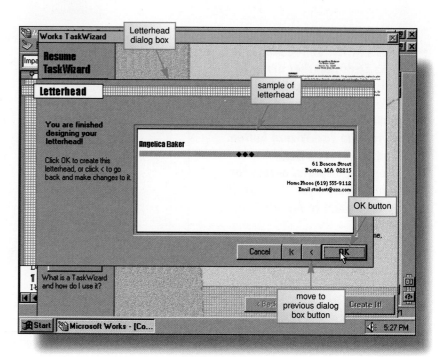

FIGURE 2-52

The completed letterhead displays in the Letterhead dialog box (Figure 2-52). Click the move to the previous dialog box button to return to the Letterhead TaskWizard to make any necessary changes.

6 Click the OK button in the Letterhead dialog box. When the Resume TaskWizard dialog box displays, click the Layout button (refer to Step 4 on page W2.33). When the Layout dialog box displays, click Art Deco Headings and point to the OK button.

When you click the OK button in the Letterhead dialog box, the Resume TaskWizard dialog box displays. When you click the Layout button, the Layout dialog box displays and allows you to select one of four layout styles (Figure 2-53). The Art Deco Headings layout style is selected. A sample of the Art Deco Headings layout style displays to the right of the dialog box. The mouse pointer points to the OK button.

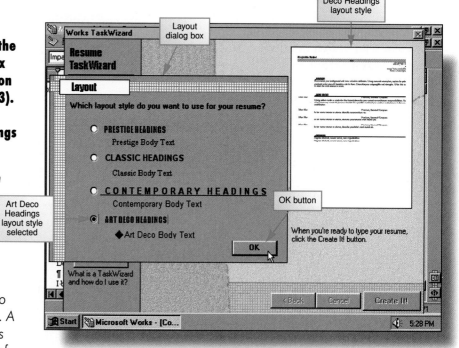

FIGURE 2-53

7 Click the OK button in the Layout dialog box. When the Resume TaskWizard dialog box displays, click the Headings button. When the Headings dialog box displays, place an X in the check boxes by the headings you want to include; that is, click Objective, Work History, Education, Computer Skills, and Awards received. Click I want to type one of my own and type Professional Affiliations in the text box. If an X displays in the Summary, Interests & Activities, or the Licenses & Certificates check boxes, remove each X by clicking each check box. Point to the OK button.

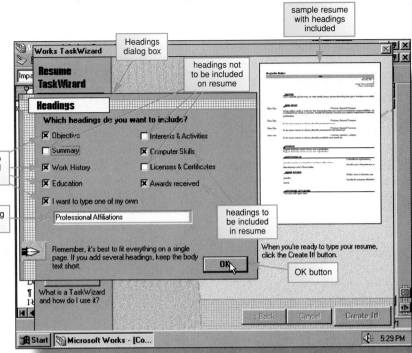

FIGURE 2-54

When you click the OK button in the Layout dialog box, the Resume TaskWizard dialog box displays. When you click the Headings button, the Headings dialog box displays allowing you to select the headings you wish to include (Figure 2-54). When you click the I want to type one of my own check box, a text box displays. You can enter up to 35 characters, including spaces, for a heading. The mouse pointer points to the OK button.

8 Click the OK button in the Headings dialog box. When the Resume TaskWizard displays, click the Entries button. When the Entries dialog box displays, click the 3 option button below the question, How many jobs do you want to show on your resume? Click the 1 option button below the question, How many education entries do you want to show on your resume? Point to the OK button.

When you click the OK button in the Headings dialog box, the Resume TaskWizard dialog box displays. When you click the Entries button, the Entries dialog box displays, allowing you to choose how many jobs entries will show on the resume and how many education entries will show on the resume (Figure 2-55). The mouse pointer points to the OK button.

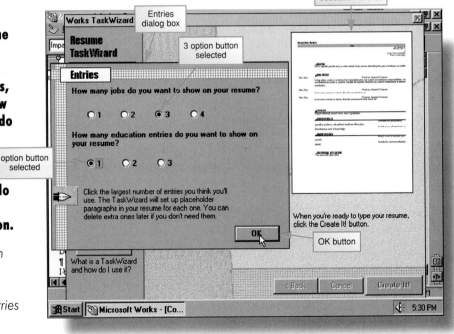

FIGURE 2-55

9 Click the OK button in the Entries dialog box. When the Resume Task Wizard displays, click the Create It! button. When the Checklist dialog box displays listing the choices you made, point to the Create Document button.

The Checklist dialog box displays and the mouse pointer points to the Create Document button (Figure 2-56). The Checklist displays the choices you made using the Resume TaskWizard.

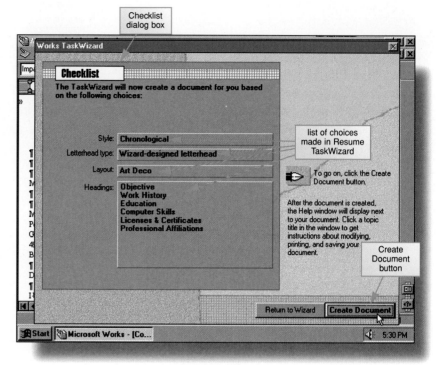

FIGURE 2-56

10 Click the Create Document button in the Checklist dialog box. When the resume displays, click Normal on the View menu. Then click the Zoom box at the bottom of the Works window and click Margin Width.

Works creates a chronological resume layout (Figure 2-57). When you click Margin Width in the Zoom list, Works brings both the left and right margins into view in the document window.

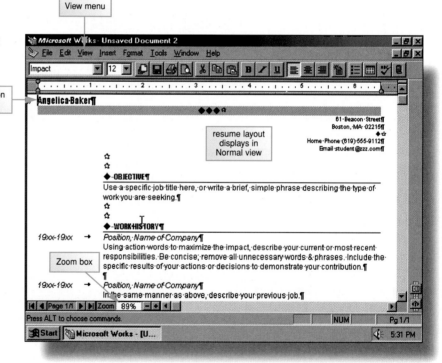

FIGURE 2-57

You are now ready to enter personalized information in the resume.

Entering Information in the Resume

To enter information in the resume, highlight each line or paragraph that you want to replace, and then type the new information to replace the existing text as shown in the following pages.

Steps **To Enter Information into the Resume**

1 **Position the mouse pointer on the word, Use, in the first line under the Objective heading of the resume and highlight the sentence by holding down the CTRL key and clicking. Move the mouse pointer to the right of the paragraph mark so you can easily see the highlighted sentence.**

Holding the CTRL key and clicking in the first line of the Objective section, highlights the sentence (Figure 2-58). Notice the paragraph mark at the end of the highlighted sentence is not highlighted. You should not highlight this mark, because if you do, it will be deleted when you type.

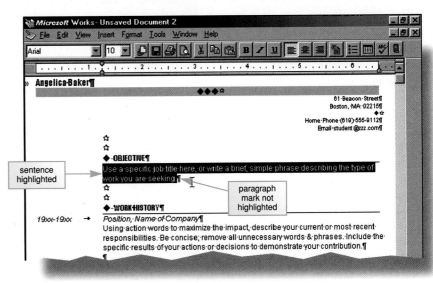

FIGURE 2-58

2 **Type** A career position with a progressive organization in the field of graphic design where opportunities for growth and advancement exist.

As you type, Works replaces the original text with the text you type (Figure 2-59).

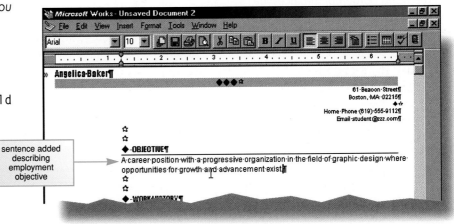

FIGURE 2-59

3 **Click the down scroll arrow to view the three placeholders for employment in the Work History section of the resume. In the Work History section, highlight xx in the first 19xx.**

Works highlights the text (Figure 2-60). Notice the right-pointing arrows to the right of the second 19xx, indicating the TAB key has been pressed in the resume. You should not highlight the right pointing arrows, because if you do, they will be deleted when you type.

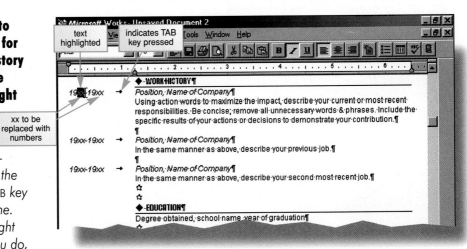

FIGURE 2-60

4 Type 95 **and highlight the xx in the second 19xx. Type** 97. **Click to the left of P in Position, hold down the** SHIFT **key, and click to the right of the y in Company to highlight the text, Position, Name of Company. Type** Graphic Designer, East Coast Design.

The dates, position, and name of company are entered for the first work history (Figure 2-61).

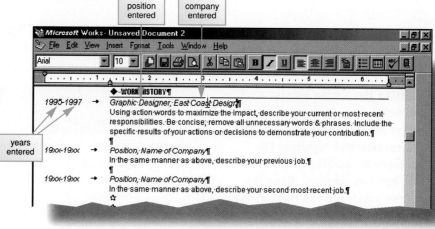

FIGURE 2-61

5 **Highlight the paragraph under the text, Graphic Designer; East Coast Design. Type a paragraph explaining Angelica Baker's most recent job responsibilities as shown in Figure 2-62.**

The typed paragraph replaces the previous paragraph (Figure 2-62).

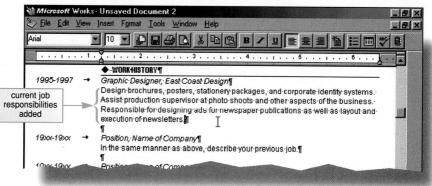

FIGURE 2-62

6 **Following the techniques previously explained, type the dates, positions, companies, and remaining entries that tell about Angelica's work history as shown in Figure 2-63.**

As you type, previously entered text is replaced with the text you type (Figure 2-63).

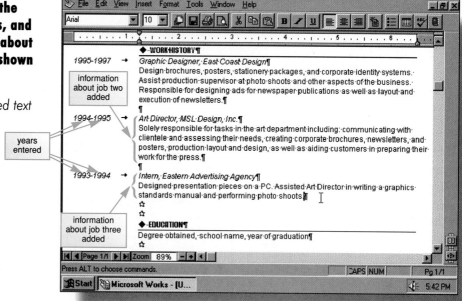

FIGURE 2-63

More *About*
CTRL Vs SHIFT Keys

The fastest way to highlight text in a document is to use the CTRL key or SHIFT key. Holding down the CTRL key and clicking anywhere in a sentence highlights the sentence. Using the CTRL key to highlight a sentence containing additional periods (e.g., abbreviations) will highlight text up to the first period in the abbreviation. Holding down the CTRL key and clicking in the left margin highlights the document. Using SHIFT + click highlights all text between mouse clicks.

The resume data now has been entered for the Objective and Work History sections.

Using the TAB Key to Align Text Vertically

The next step is to enter the resume data in the Education section. Notice in Figure 2-64 that the degree award dates, GPA, and grade point averages are aligned vertically. That is, the letter in M in May 1994 is directly above the letter J in June 1992; the two letter Gs in GPA are aligned; and the number 3 in 3.85 is directly above the number 3 in 3.75. The right-pointing arrows indicate the TAB key has been pressed.

Works presets tab stops every one-half inch. These preset, or default, tabs are indicated on the horizontal ruler by small tick marks (see Figure 2-64). Perform the following steps to align text vertically with the TAB key.

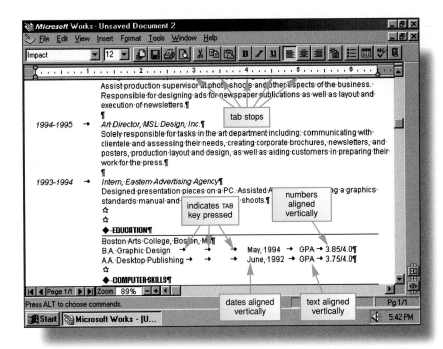

FIGURE 2-64

Steps To Vertically Align Text with the TAB Key

1 **Highlight the line below the Education heading and type** Boston Arts College, Boston, MA. **Be careful not to highlight the paragraph mark at the end of the line. Press the ENTER key.**

The college's name, city, and state display (Figure 2-65)

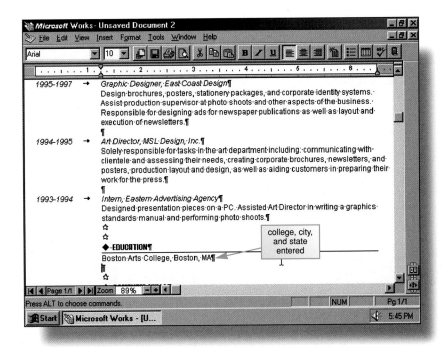

FIGURE 2-65

2 **Type** B.A. Graphic Design.

The text you typed displays (Figure 2-66).

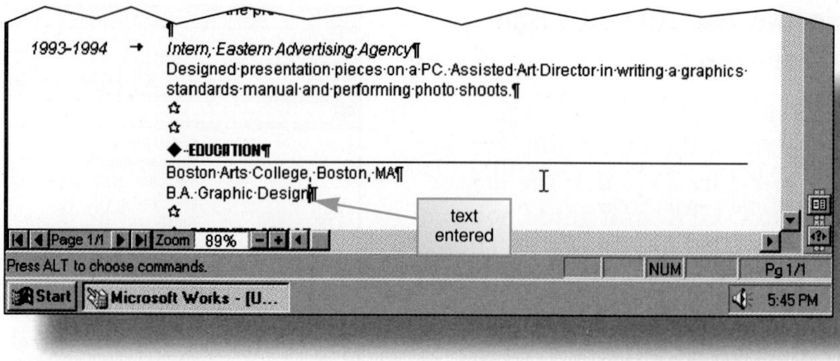

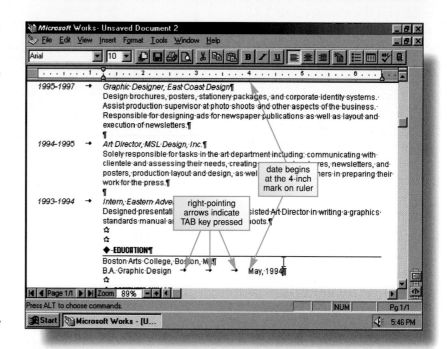

FIGURE 2-66

3 **Press the TAB key three times and type** May, 1994.

Each time you press the TAB key, the insertion point moves one-half inch to the right and a right-pointing arrow displays (Figure 2-67). The date begins at the 4-inch mark on ruler.

FIGURE 2-67

4 **Press the TAB key once. Type** GPA **and press the TAB key once again. Type** 3.85/4.0.

The first degree information is entered (Figure 2-68). GPA is aligned at the 5-inch mark and 3.85 is aligned at the 5.5-inch mark.

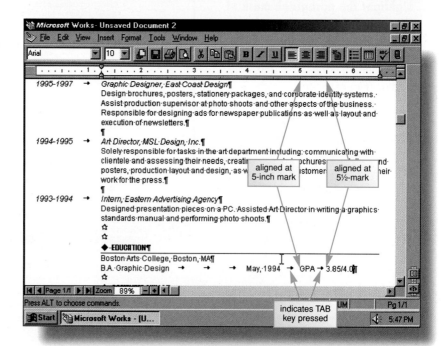

FIGURE 2-68

5 **Press the ENTER key. Type** A.A. Desktop Publishing **and press the TAB key three times. Type** June, 1992 **and press the TAB key once. Type** GPA **and press the TAB key once. Type** 3.75/4.0.

The Education section of the resume is complete (Figure 2-69).

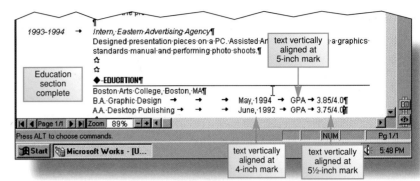

FIGURE 2-69

6 **Press the PAGE DOWN key. Highlight the first bulleted sentence under the Computer Skills heading by holding down the CTRL key and clicking anywhere in the sentence. Type** QuarkXPress for Windows 95. **CTRL click the second bulleted sentence and type** Adobe Illustrator and Aldus PageMaker for Windows. **Press the ENTER key.**

The text you typed displays (Figure 2-70). When you press the ENTER key, Works inserts a bullet to the left of the insertion point.

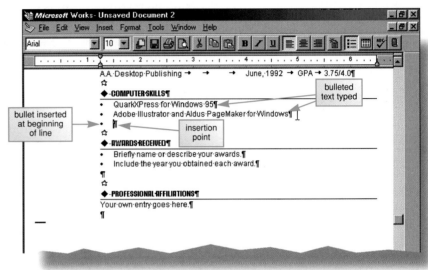

FIGURE 2-70

7 **Complete the remaining entries under the Computer Skills, Awards Received, and Professional Affiliations headings in the resume using the techniques previously explained (see the resume in Figure 2-1 on page W 2.5). After all entries are completed, click the beginning of document button on the scroll bar to return to the beginning of the resume.**

The first portion of the resume displays (Figure 2-71).

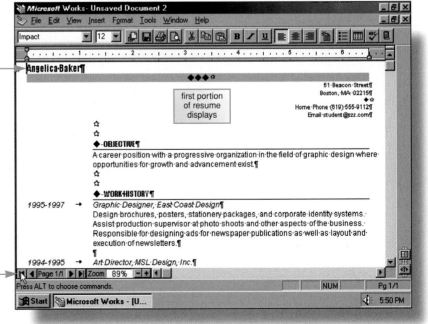

FIGURE 2-71

Checking Spelling and Using Print Preview

The resume is now complete. You should check the spelling of the document using the Works spelling checker and make any needed corrections using the steps specified below.

TO CHECK SPELLING

Step 1: Position the insertion point at the beginning of the document.
Step 2: Click the Spelling Checker button on the toolbar.
Step 3: If the spelling checker stops at any word, take the appropriate action either to correct the word or accept the word.
Step 4: When the Microsoft Works dialog box displays a message informing you the spelling check is finished, click the OK button.

After checking the spelling, follow the steps below to preview the completed document to ensure it will print properly.

TO USE PRINT PREVIEW

Step 1: Click the Print Preview button on the toolbar.
Step 2: If necessary, zoom in on the document to review the document.
Step 3: Click the Cancel button in the Print Preview screen to return to the document.

Saving the Resume Document

After you create the resume, you should save the resume on a floppy disk. To save the resume, complete the following steps.

TO SAVE THE RESUME

Step 1: Click the Save button on the toolbar.
Step 2: In the Save As dialog box, type the filename, Resume.
Step 3: Select drive A from the Save in drop-down list box, if necessary.
Step 4: Click the Save button in the Save As dialog box.

Printing the Resume

Printing the resume is the final step in creating the document. If the entries you have previously used in the Print dialog box apply to the resume, complete the following step to print the resume.

TO PRINT THE RESUME

Step 1: Click the Print button on the toolbar.

The resume will print as formatted. Figure 2-72 illustrates the completed resume.

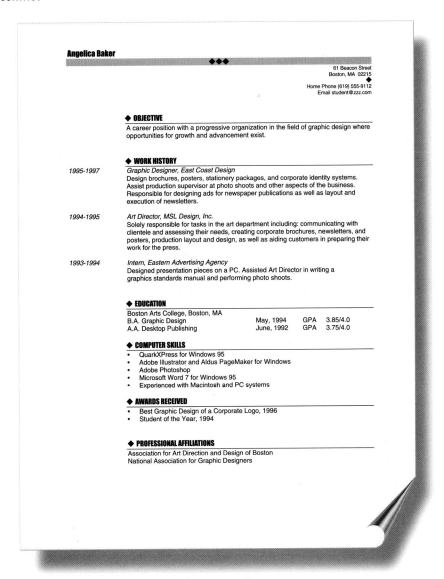

FIGURE 2-72

If you want to display the Print dialog box to make print control changes before printing, you must use the Print command from the File menu.

Working with Multiple Documents

As you create the resume, you may want to review the cover letter you wrote regarding the employment opportunity. This can be accomplished using entries in the Window menu. To display the letter again, perform the steps on the next page.

More *About*
Multiple Documents

Works let you view and work on up to eight documents at once. However, due to memory limitations on your computer, the actual number and size of files you can open simultaneously depends on the size of the files.

Steps To View Multiple Documents

1 **Click Window on the menu bar and point to Cover Letter at the bottom of the menu.**

Works displays the names of open documents at the bottom of the Window menu (Figure 2-73).

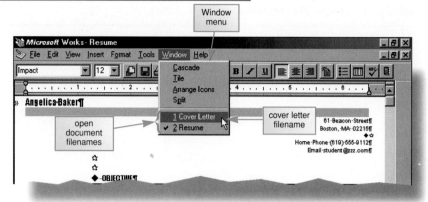

FIGURE 2-73

2 **Click Cover Letter.**

Works displays the document named Cover Letter (Figure 2-74). You may review or change the letter as necessary.

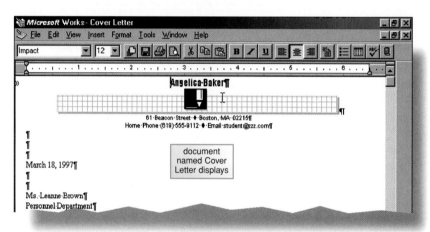

FIGURE 2-74

3 **To display the resume again, click Window on the menu bar and point to Resume.**

Works displays the Window menu (Figure 2-75)

4 **Click Resume.**

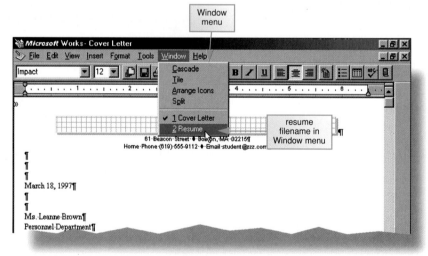

FIGURE 2-75

OtherWays

1. Press CTRL+ F6

The resume again will display. The capability to work with multiple documents is an important feature of Works. This feature can be useful when there is a need to review quickly on the screen two or more documents that contain related information.

Quitting Works

After you have saved the cover letter and the resume and have printed the cover letter and the resume, you can quit Works. Complete the following step to quit Works.

TO QUIT WORKS

Step 1: Click the Close button in the upper right corner of the application window.

The Microsoft Windows 95 desktop again will display.

Creating User Defined Templates

Works allows you to design and save user defined templates. **User defined templates** are documents that you create containing the settings, text, and formats that you can reuse. To create a user defined template, first prepare a document using the Word Processor until it is exactly as you want. Then, use the Template button in the Save As dialog box to save the document as a template. For example, you can save the letterhead you created using the Letter TaskWizard earlier in this project as a user defined template. Then, you can use the letterhead template whenever you need a letterhead in a letter without recreating it.

To save the letterhead created earlier in this project as a user defined template, complete the following steps.

> **More** *About*
> **User Defined Templates**
>
> The TaskWizard category User Defined Templates will not display as a category in the TaskWizards sheet until you create a document and save it as a template. If you want Works to use a user defined template as the default template for that tool, click the Use this template for new Word Processor documents check box in the Save As Template dialog box.

 To Create a User Defined Template

1 **Double-click the My Computer icon. When the My Computer window opens, double-click the 3½ Floppy [A:] icon. When the 3½ Floppy window opens, double-click the Cover Letter file you saved on a floppy disk in drive A. After opening the file, highlight all the text below the letterhead. Press the Delete key. Click the beginning of document button on the scroll bar to return to the beginning of the document.**

The Cover Letter document opens and displays on the screen. When you highlight the text below the letterhead and press the Delete key, only the letterhead remains (Figure 2-76).

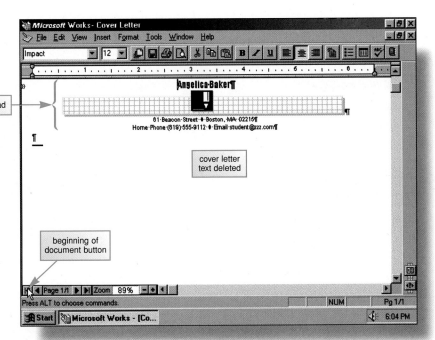

FIGURE 2-76

2 **Click File on the menu bar and point to Save As.**

The File menu displays and the mouse pointer points to the Save As command (Figure 2-77).

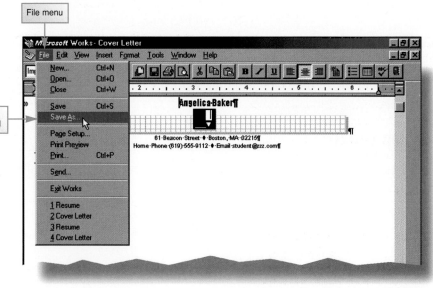

FIGURE 2-77

3 **Click Save As. When the Save As dialog box displays, point to the Template button.**

The Save As dialog box displays and the mouse pointer points to the Template button (Figure 2-78).

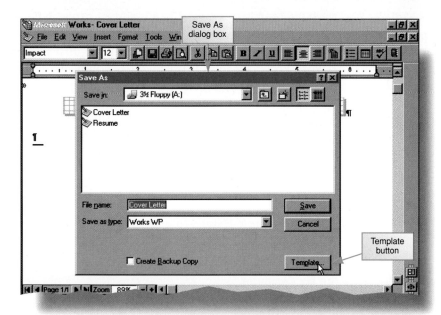

FIGURE 2-78

4 **Click the Template button in the Save As dialog box. When the Save As Template dialog box displays, type** Personal Letterhead **in the Type a name for the template below text box. Point to the OK button.**

Works displays the Save As Template dialog box (Figure 2-79). The name of the template, Personal Letterhead, displays in the Type a name for the template below text box. The mouse pointer points to the OK button.

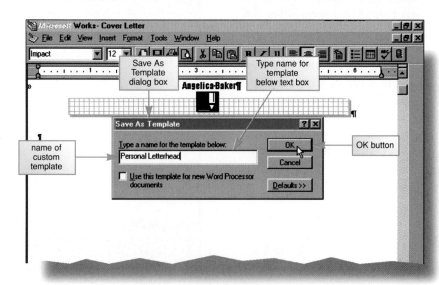

FIGURE 2-79

5 Click the OK button in the Save As Template dialog box.

The template is saved in the User Defined Templates group and control returns to the open document, which is the altered Cover Letter document (Figure 2-80). The template is saved on the hard disk drive in the Works' Template folder.

6 Click the Close button in the upper right corner of the application window to close Works. When the Microsoft Works dialog box displays a warning asking you to save changes to the cover letter, click the No button.

control returns to open document

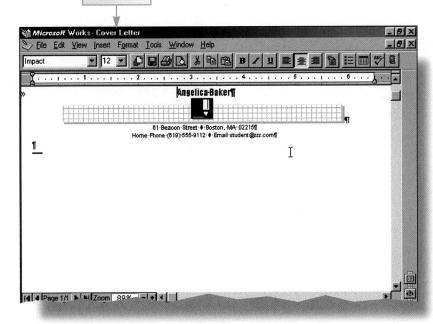

FIGURE 2-80

Using a User Defined Template

Once you have created a custom template, you can use the template provided by Works. To use the user defined template, complete the following steps.

Steps **To Use a User Defined Template**

1 If Works is not currently active, start Works using the techniques explained previously. When the Works Task Launcher dialog box displays, ensure the TaskWizards sheet displays. Use the down scroll arrow to view the User Defined Templates category. Click the User Defined Templates icon. Then click Personal Letterhead. Point to the OK button.

Works displays the Works Task Launcher dialog box (Figure 2-81). The User Defined Templates icon is recessed and the Personal Letterhead template is highlighted. The mouse pointer points to the OK button.

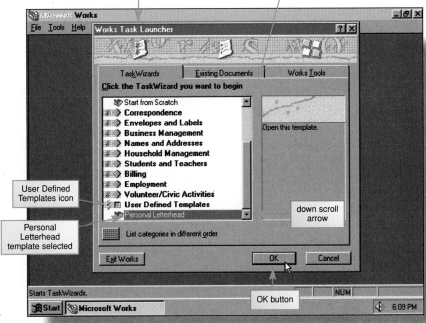

FIGURE 2-81

2 **Click the OK button in the Works Task Launcher dialog box.**

The Personal Letterhead template displays on the screen (Figure 2-82). Note that the document name is Unsaved Document 1, not Personal Letterhead. A template is not the same as a document file.

FIGURE 2-82

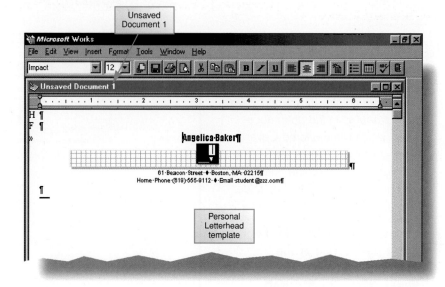

You can create user defined templates for any need you have. User defined templates also can be created for the Spreadsheet and Database tools within Works.

Project Summary

In this project, you learned how to create a cover letter and a resume using Works TaskWizards. You used the Letter Wizard to create a cover letter. In the cover letter, you learned how to type a numbered list with a hanging indent. This required the use of the left-margin indent marker and the first-line indent marker. To check the spelling of a document, you used the Spelling Checker button on the toolbar. You then used the Resume TaskWizard to create a resume. In the resume, you learned how to use the TAB key to vertically align text.

Using the steps and techniques presented in this project, you also learned how to create and use a user defined template. In addition, you learned how to view two open documents using the Window menu.

What You Should Know

Having completed this project, you should now be able to perform the following tasks:

▸ Align Text Vertically with the TAB Key *(W 2.39)*
▸ Check Spelling *(W 2.28, W 2.42)*
▸ Complete the Cover Letter *(W 2.27)*
▸ Create a Cover Letter Using the Letter TaskWizard *(W 2.8)*
▸ Create a Hanging Indent and a Numbered List *(W 2.24)*
▸ Create a Resume Using the Resume TaskWizard *(W 2.32)*
▸ Create a User Defined Template *(W 2.45)*
▸ Enter Information in a Cover Letter *(W 2.22)*

▸ Enter Information into the Resume *(W 2.37)*
▸ Print the Cover Letter *(W 2.31)*
▸ Print the Resume *(W 2.43)*
▸ Quit Works *(W 2.45)*
▸ Save the Resume *(W 2.42)*
▸ Start Works *(W 2.7)*
▸ Use a User Defined Template *(W 2.47)*
▸ Use Print Preview *(W 2.42)*
▸ Vertically align Text with Tab Key *(W 2.39)*
▸ View Multiple Documents *(W 2.44)*
▸ Zoom Margin Width *(W 2.20)*

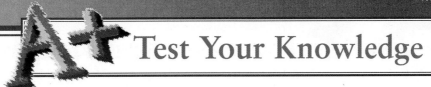

1 True/False

Instructions: Circle T if the statement is true or F if the statement is false.

T F   1. Works provides TaskWizards to assist you in document preparation.

T F   2. To create a document using a TaskWizard, click the New button on the toolbar.

T F   3. To create a hanging indent in a document, press the TAB key.

T F   4. To set the left-margin indent marker, click the ruler where you want the left margin to begin.

T F   5. The zoom setting of a document has no effect on how the document will look when it is printed.

T F   6. Use the CTRL+Q key combination any time you want to remove all paragraph formatting from a paragraph at one time.

T F   7. Click the Check Spelling button on the toolbar to cause Works to check the spelling of a document.

T F   8. If Works detects a word that is not in the dictionary, you can ignore all further occurrences of the word in the document by clicking the Ignore button in the Spelling: American English dialog box.

T F   9. The Works spelling checker ignores duplicate adjacent words in a document.

T F   10. To move between two open windows, click Switch on the Window menu.

2 Multiple Choice

Instructions: Circle the correct response.

1. Instead of dragging the mouse to highlight text, position the insertion point at the beginning of the text to highlight it and then _____ at the end of the text to stop highlighting the text.
   a. click
   b. CTRL+click
   c. SHIFT+click
   d. ALT+click

2. To highlight a sentence, _____ in the sentence.
   a. SHIFT+click
   b. CTRL+click
   c. double-click
   d. triple-click

3. One method of creating a hanging indent is to use the _____ .
   a. Page Setup command from the File menu
   b. first-line indent marker and the right-margin indent marker on the ruler
   c. TAB key
   d. first-line indent marker and the left-margin indent marker on the ruler

(continued)

A+ Test Your Knowledge

Multiple Choice *(continued)*

4. The first-line indent marker is positioned by _____.
   a. pressing the CTRL+Q keys
   b. clicking the left mouse button on the ruler
   c. dragging the first-line indent marker on the ruler
   d. pressing the TAB key

5. The character that displays on the screen indicating the TAB key has been pressed is a _____.
   a. raised dot
   b. right-pointing arrow
   c. left-pointing arrow
   d. paragraph mark

6. To check the spelling in a document, use the _____.
   a. Spelling Checker button on the toolbar
   b. CTRL+Q keys
   c. Spelling Checker command on the Format menu
   d. SHIFT+S keys

7. When using the Works spelling checker, a word that is not found in the dictionary can be _____.
   a. changed
   b. ignored
   c. added to the dictionary
   d. all of the above

8. To remove all paragraph formatting, use the _____.
   a. SHIFT+Q keys
   b. CTRL+Q keys
   c. DELETE key
   d. Cut command from the Edit menu

9. To save a user defined template, _____.
   a. click the Template button in the Save As dialog box
   b. click the Template button on the toolbar
   c. click the Template command on the File menu
   d. click the Save button on the toolbar

10. To use a user defined template, _____.
    a. click the Open button on the toolbar
    b. click the desired template in the User Defined Template category in the Works Task Launcher dialog box
    c. click the desired template in the Existing Documents list
    d. click the Template button on the toolbar

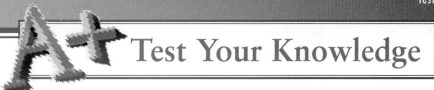

Test Your Knowledge

3 Fill In

Instructions: In the spaces provided, identify each of the marks on the ruler in Figure 2-83.

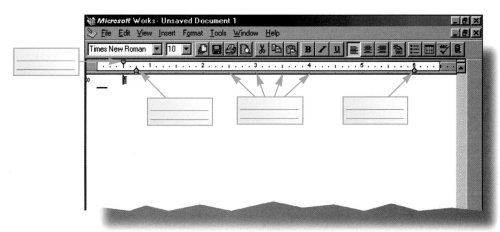

FIGURE 2-83

4 Fill In

Instructions: In the space provided, explain the steps necessary to create the numbered list in the letter illustrated in Figure 2-84.

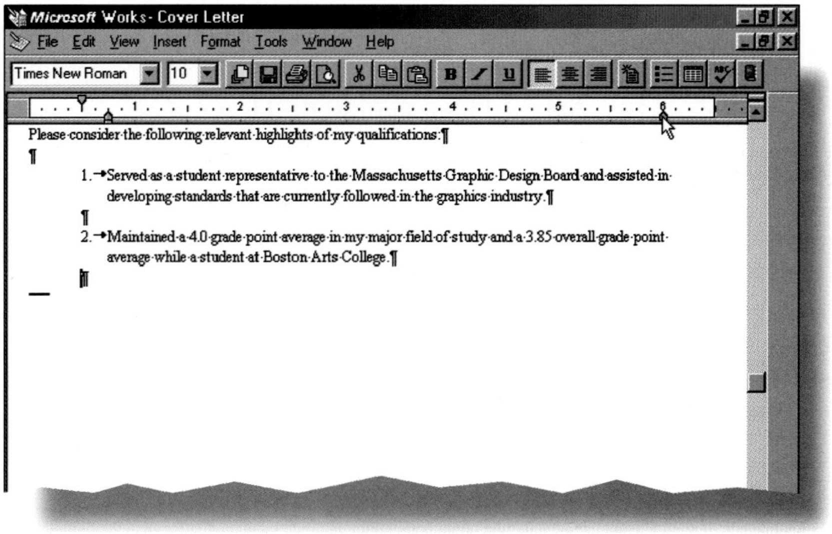

FIGURE 2-84

Steps: _____

_____

? Use Help

1 Reviewing Project Activities

Instructions: Use your computer to perform the following tasks to obtain experience using online Help.

1. Start the Microsoft Works Word Processor tool.
2. Display the Help window to the right of the document window. Click the Index button below the Help window to display the Help Topics: Microsoft Works dialog box.
3. Click the Index tab in the Help Topics: Microsoft Works dialog box.
4. Type check spelling in the Index text box.
5. Click the topic, check spelling, in the list box.
6. Read the numbered procedure on the topic, To check spelling, on the Step-by-Step sheet. Print this topic by clicking the Print this topic icon at the bottom of the numbered procedure.
7. Click the More Info tab. On the More Info sheet, click Overview. Read and print the Overview topic. Click the Done button to close the Overview dialog box.
8. Click the What if you don't want to check the entire document? topic. Read the topic and briefly summarize the steps required if you do not wish to check the spelling of the entire document.

   _____

9. Click the Close button in the application window to exit Works.

2 Expanding on the Basics

Instructions: Use Works online Help to better understand the topics listed below. Print the topic or topics that substantiate your answer. If there is no Print this topic icon, then answer the question on a separate piece of paper.

1. Using the key term, templates, and the Index sheet in the Help topics: Microsoft Works dialog box, answer the following questions.
   a. Explain how to modify an existing template.
   b. How do you specify a user defined template as the default template for the Word Processor tool? Explain how to stop using the user defined template as the default template for the Word Processor tool.
   c. List the steps necessary to delete a user defined template.
   d. List the steps necessary to rename a user defined template.

Apply Your Knowledge

1 Spell Checking a Document

Instructions: Start the Microsoft Works Word Processor Tool. Open the document, Anderson Cover Letter, on the Student Floppy Disk that accompanies this book. The document is illustrated in Figure 2-85. One or more spelling errors have been incorporated into the cover letter. Perform the following tasks.

1. Use the spelling checker to check the spelling of the cover letter.
2. Make corrections as required.
3. Print a copy of the corrected cover letter.
4. Turn in a copy of the incorrect and the corrected cover letters to your instructor.

Lynn Anderson

89523 Point Drive † Los Angeles, CA 90025
Home Phone (619) 555-1903 † Email student@zzz.com

March 19, 1997

Mr. John Leroy
Personnel Director
4256 Harbor Boulevard
Costa Mesa, CA 92626

Dear Mr. Leroy,

I believe my experience and solid record of achievment make me an ideal candidate for the position of of Payroll Clerk. This employment opportunity was advertised in the the March 1 edition of the *Costa Mesa News*.

I have over five years experience working in Accounts Receivable, with a two-year base established with Whitman and Evans Accounting firm. As my enclosed resume indicates, I have had recent work expereince in the accounting department of AlphaMicro Corporation.

My interest in pursueing a career in the accounting profession and my leadership skills are highlighed in the following acomplishments while attending West Lake College:

1. Served as President of the Student Accountant's Asociation for two years.

2. Maintained a grade point average of 3.85 whild a student at West Lake College.

Please call me at (619) 555-1903 after 6 p.m. if you need further information about my experience.

Sincerely,

Lynn Anderson

Enc:1

FIGURE 2-85

In the Lab

1 Using the Letter TaskWizard to Create a Cover Letter

Problem: You have recently graduated from college and are seeking employment in the city of Los Angeles. Prepare the cover letter shown in Figure 2-86.

Instructions: Perform the tasks below.

1. Create a cover letter using the Letter TaskWizard. Refer to Figure 2-86 for the letterhead and the address information requested by the Letter TaskWizard.

2. Modify the cover letter so the revised cover letter matches Figure 2-86.

3. Create the numbered list.

4. Check the spelling in the cover letter using the Works spelling checker.

5. Save the cover letter on a floppy disk in drive A. Use the filename, Thompson Cover Letter.

6. Print the cover letter.

James Thompson

◆◆◆

356 Commerce Avenue
Los Angeles, CA 90023
◆
Phone (213) 555-5031
Email chemist@zzz.com

March 14, 1997

Ms. Susan Hoffmyers
Personnel Director
7852 North Center Street
Los Angeles, CA 92678

Dear Ms. Hoffmyers,

I believe my experience and solid record of achievement make me an ideal candidate as a criminologist for the city of Los Angeles.

I have over three years of experience working with analytical instrumentation, wet chemistry techniques, and blood alcohol samples. As my enclosed resume indicates, I have successfully supervised students working in the laboratory on various research projects.

Please consider the following important highlights of my qualifications:

1. I have taken the following relevant chemistry courses as a student at Western Hills University: Analytical Chemistry, Organic Chemistry, and Quantitative Analysis.

2. During my four years of college at Western Hills University, I maintained a grade point average of 4.0 in my major.

Please call me at (213) 555-5031 after 6 p.m. if you need further information about my experience.

Sincerely,

James Thompson

JT

Enc: 1

FIGURE 2-86

In the Lab

7. Follow directions from your instructor for turning in this assignment.

2 Using the Resume TaskWizard to Create a Resume

Problem: You have prepared the cover letter in Figure 2-86 and would like to prepare an accompanying resume. The resume is shown in Figure 2-87.

Instructions: Perform the following tasks.

1. Use the Resume TaskWizard to create a resume. Use the name and address information shown in Figure 2-87.

2. Personalize the resume, as shown in Figure 2-87.

3. Check the spelling in the resume using the Works spelling checker.

4. Save the resume on a floppy disk in drive A using the filename, Thompson Resume.

5. Print a copy of the resume.

6. Follow directions from your instructor for turning in this assignment.

James Thompson

356 Commerce Avenue ~ Los Angeles, CA 90023
Home Phone (213) 555-5031 ~ Email chemist@zzz.com

◆ **OBJECTIVE**

To obtain a criminologist position that offers challenge, growth and career opportunity.

◆ **WORK HISTORY**

1995-1997 *Chemist, Major Chemicals*
Performs analytical and quantitative tests on raw materials. Responsible for testing and releasing batches for production and finished products for shipping. Responsible for test method validation.

1992-1995 *Lab Assistant, Western Hills University*
Supervised students in various stages of research analysis. Assisted chemistry professors in setting up and running experiments in the lab.

1991-1991 *Computer Technician Assistant, Computer Corporation*
Installed computer equipment in business offices. Performed extensive customer support in person and by phone. Delivered supplies to customers.

◆ **EDUCATION**

Western Hills University
B.S. Chemistry   May, 1995   GPA   3.85/4.0

◆ **INTERESTS & ACTIVITIES**

·   Participated in 1995 and 1996 LA Marathons
·   Avid cyclist - biked across United States, summer 1994

◆ **RESEARCH PROJECT**

Authored research paper in 1995 entitled *Modifying Water Determination Techniques Using Karl Fisher Reagent and Refractive Index*

FIGURE 2-87

In the Lab

3 Using TaskWizards to Create a Cover Letter and Resume

Problem: You are currently in the market for a new job. You want to use Works TaskWizards to prepare a cover letter and resume from a recent want ad.

Instructions:

1. Using Works TaskWizards, prepare a cover letter and your personal resume for response to an employment opportunity advertised in your local newspaper.
2. Spell check the cover letter and resume.
3. Save the cover letter and resume on a floppy disk.
4. Print the cover letter and resume.
5. Follow directions from your instructor for turning in this assignment.

Cases and Places

The difficulty of these case studies varies:

▶ Case studies preceded by a single half moon are the least difficult. You are asked to create the required document based on information that already has been placed in an organized form.
▶▶ Case studies preceded by two half moons are more difficult. You must organize the information presented before using it to create the required document.
▶▶▶ Case studies preceded by three half moons are the most difficult. You must decide on a specific topic, obtain the information, and then organize these facts before creating the required document.

1 ▶ Use the Resume TaskWizard to revise the resume on the next page. Create an appropriate letter-head. Select the Chronological and Classic Headings layout styles.

Cases and Places

Carl L. Richards · 804 Wilshire Road · Crystal, IN 47978
(219) 555-4233

Objective
To gain employment as a computer software specialist or trainer.
Work History
1995 - present. Computer Lab Consultant, Northeast City College,
Chicago, IL
Assist students with personal computers. Install software. Answer technical
questions. Repair hardware.
1993 - 1994. BJ's Hot Dogs. Chicago, IL
Sold a variety of food and drink items. Designed carryout menu. Trained
employees. Increased sales by 35 percent.
Education
Northeast City College, Chicago, IL.
Computer Technology major. B.A. expected May 1998. GPA 3.31/4.0.
Awards Received
Outstanding student, Computer Technology, Northeast City College, Chicago,
IL. December 1996.
Certificate in Personal Computer Software, Northeast City College,
Chicago, IL. May 1996.

2 ▶ Using the information in Case Study 1 above, modify the cover letter in Figure 2-1 on page W 2.5.

3 ▶▶ Mary Ann Sims has performed volunteer work for your company for the past three years under your supervision. Now a permanent, full-time position is available for a child-care attendant, and she has applied for the opening. She has asked you to write a letter of recommendation to the company president. You believe Mary Ann's strengths are her patience, creativity, and strong work ethic. She has helped organize children's activities at several company picnics and the annual holiday party, and recently she was in charge of entertainment at the employee recognition banquet honoring those employees with five, ten, fifteen, and twenty years of service. She is an elementary education major at the university and has earned high honors for the past four semesters. She will graduate with a bachelor's degree in May. Create a letter using the Works Letter TaskWizard. Send the letter to Robert Shepard at the Atlantic Coast Corporation, 765 Front Street, Riverton, NJ 08076.

Cases and Places

4 ▶▶▶ Your best friend wants to work in the campus library. He asks you to help him design a resume. Interview him to obtain information about his education, work experience, honors, and activities. Create a sample document.

5 ▶▶▶ The following advertisement appeared in today's edition of the *Chicago Tribune*:

> **Help Wanted:** Trainee with knowledge of Microsoft applications, particularly Works 4 for Windows 95. Responsibilities include designing documents, building spreadsheets, and creating databases. Additional experience will be gained through attendance at a structured training program. Must be able to work in a team environment and on weekends. Respond to XPJ Technologies, Human Resources Department, 165 N. Wabash Ave., Chicago, IL 60601. Please include a resume.

Prepare a cover letter with a letterhead to respond to this employment opportunity.

6 ▶▶▶ Prepare a resume to respond to the advertisement in Case Study 5 above. Use the same letterhead used for the cover letter.

7 ▶▶▶ Your college studies have included classes in public relations and speech, and you are considering a career in the communications field. You know that one of the ways to gain valuable experience is through an internship, so you plan to send a cover letter and resume to several companies to inquire about summer internships. In an effort to test your marketability, you want to apply at Fortune 500 companies and at not-for-profit organizations. Create two user-defined templates: one should use a professional style for corporate correspondence and be saved as Corporate Letterhead; and the second should use a creative style for the not-for profit organization and be saved as Not-For-Profit Letterhead. Use the two templates on documents you created in Project 2 exercises.

Microsoft Works 4

Windows 95

Writing and Editing a Research Report with Tables

Objectives

You will have mastered the material in this project when you can:

▶ Describe the format of a research report
▶ Use the Page Setup command
▶ Create a report header
▶ Create a footnote using the Footnote command
▶ Close a footnote pane
▶ Insert a page break in a document
▶ Use the Go To command
▶ Use the Find command
▶ Replace a word in a document using the Replace command
▶ Use the Undo command
▶ Move a paragraph using drag-and-drop
▶ Use the Thesaurus command
▶ Use the Word Count command
▶ Create a table using OLE 2.0

NUTS!

The Art of Conveying Information

During the Battle of the Bulge in World War II, the 101st Airborne Division took refuge in the strategic crossroads town of Bastogne, Belgium. Several divisions of the German army surrounded them and fought for days trying to oust the Americans. Then, General Lüttwitz, the German commander, sent a white-flag courier to demand the surrender of the holdouts. General Anthony ("Mad Anthony") McAuliffe, commander of the 101st, replied, "You may report back to your general that my response is a single word: NUTS!" Ultimately, the Germans backed down and McAuliffe's single-word report became one of the more famous in the annals of military history.

Most reports are not so succinct, though brevity and clarity should always be the key criteria when writing reports or presenting them orally. This is easier to do if you keep in mind the main purpose of a report: to convey information. Information is words and numbers placed in a meaningful context. When General McAuliffe uttered

Effective Communication

SOCIAL SECURITY

HUMAN SERVICES-USA

123-45-6789

THIS NUMBER HAS BEEN ESTABLISHED FOR

JOHN Q. PUBLIC

SIGNATURE

his famous retort, he was not offering the Germans a snack. The word, Nuts, conveyed information that the Americans would not surrender. Even a simple string of numbers, such as 123456789, can become information in the proper context. For example, with hyphens, the number becomes 123-45-6789, a Social Security number, which is *information*. By adding a zero and shifting the hyphens, 123-456-7890 becomes a telephone number.

Sometimes it is enough to merely convey information through the use of words and numbers in a report. Often, however, the person rendering the report is expected to state conclusions based on an analysis of the information in the report. This process, which is a more advanced form of writing, is the norm for modern researchers.

The manner of presentation of information in a report often will determine the effectiveness of the communication. You can bet the German envoy had no doubt as to General McAuliffe's meaning. For written reports, the powerful Word Processor within Microsoft Works makes the presentation of information far easier than older methods. Works allows you to create custom styles for research reports that can be reused as templates, bypassing the need to set up each new report and freeing the writer to concentrate on content rather than form. Another big plus is the capability to incorporate tables directly into the body of the document, allowing mathematical and sorting operations on the data itself, independent of text.

In aiming for a career goal, students should recognize that the nature of the workplace is far different from what it was twenty, or even five, years ago. Most of the new, higher-paying jobs require the ability to write meaningful reports. In a recent issue of *Newsweek,* one company states that it no longer uses librarians simply to look up facts; instead, it employs teams of consultants to research and assemble analyses for scientists and market researchers. These positions pay twice what the former jobs paid.

Writing a report is a necessary skill. Whether rejecting a demand for surrender, analyzing the crime statistics for the *Daily Planet* in the city of Metropolis, or conveying the excitement of searching for the Loch Ness monster, the report must be clearly written and presented.

Project

Microsoft
Works 4
Windows 95

Writing and Editing a Research Report with Tables

*C*ase *P*erspective

You are currently enrolled in Computer Information Systems 201. Your professor has asked you to research the World Wide Web and prepare a research report. This report is to follow one of the recommended MLA styles. The paper must contain footnotes and a table. The professor has requested that the footnotes be placed at the end of the report.

You are to use Microsoft Works 4.0 for Windows 95 to prepare the research report.

More *About* **Documentation Styles**

A research paper presents the results of your investigations on a selected topic. You should adhere to some form of documentation style when writing research papers. Two of the most widely used styles are the MLA, illustrated in Project 3, and the American Psychological Association (APA). The MLA style is the standard in the humanities; whereas, the APA style is preferred in the sciences and education.

Introduction

In both the business world and the academic world, writing research reports is an important task. In the business world, you may prepare reports for sales representatives, management personnel, and stockholders. In the academic world, instructors require you to write research reports as a part of course work.

Whether you are preparing a report for the business world or for class work, you should use a standard format, or style, when preparing the report. Specific standards and recommendations for writing research reports have been proposed by various professional associations. The **Modern Language Association of America (MLA)** recommends several styles that you may use when you write research reports. These styles are used by many instructors and schools throughout the United States. Project 3 uses one of the recommended MLA styles. The style used is explained in the following paragraphs.

Project Three

A complete, brief research report, entitled World Wide Web, is illustrated in Figure 3-1. The research report contains approximately 500 words, fills two pages of text, and includes a table. The third page contains a section entitled NOTES. The references (names of the books or other material) used in preparing the research report are contained in the NOTES section of the paper. The raised numbers in the text and in the NOTES section are called **superscripts**. The numbers associate portions of the text with the individual references cited on the NOTES page of the research report.

Ramera 3

NOTES

[1]William Peterson, *Beginner's Guide to Surfing the World Wide Web* (New York: Computer Network Press, 1997) 125-130.

[2]T. S. Cobb, "Managing Web Information Services on the World Wide Web." http://www.university.edu/home/cis.html (5 September 1997).

[3]USA Wireservice, "Designing Home Pages on the World Wide Web." *Daily News*, 19 August 1997, Morning ed., Sec. Business: 3+.

Ramera 2

The World Wide Web consists of a large collection of documents that are stored on computers around the world. These documents, known as Web pages, provide an unlimited amount of information and are connected, or linked, to each other so you can move easily from one to another. These pages can include graphics, sound, and video.[2]

A Web site is a business, government agency, or university that stores Web pages you can view. A home page is typically the starting point for a World Wide Web site. For this reason, many sites try to make their home page as spectacular as possible by combining eye-catching graphics and specially formatted text.[3]

Table 1 shows the projected growth of World Wide Web sites from 1997 to 2000.

Table 1 WWW Sites - Growth Projections	1997	2000
Commercial	245,000	735,000
Education	11,000	30,000
	250	6,500
	500	35,000
	025	3,500
	500	120,250

he Web will be phenomenal. With
is expanding rapidly into a global

Ramera 1

Lenora Ramera

Professor Christine Sfeir

Computer Information Systems 201

September 22, 1997

World Wide Web

The World Wide Web is the newest and most powerful information provider on the Internet. While the Internet is a web of interconnecting computer networks, the World Wide Web is a graphical, easy-to-use system on the Internet that offers a vast amount of information. Almost every large corporation, university, government, organization, and business around the world has a presence on the Web.

The World Wide Web was first developed in 1990 by a physics researcher, Tim Berners-Lee, and a programming team at the European Particle Physics Laboratory (known by its French initials, CERN) in Geneva, Switzerland. The developers first designed the World Wide Web as a means of sharing information and research papers between physicists all over the world. The important goal of the original developers was to ensure that networked information would be accessible in any country from any type of computer, with one easy-to-use program. This would make the World Wide Web the ultimate research tool.[1]

Although the Web has been in existence for only a short time, it is already being used in a variety of ways by both public and private institutions. Businesses are using the Web to advertise their products to potential customers and provide information on the company. Educational institutions also are making information available on the Web, and students are discovering that they can perform research more quickly and easily on the Web than in the library. Electronic magazines and newspapers are being delivered on the Web. You can make travel plans, look up the latest stock quotes, apply for a job, electronically visit a museum, research the latest health issue, and make new friends on the World Wide Web. As a system, the Web is governed and regulated cooperatively without actual laws. It is operated based on codes of individual conduct and ethic.

FIGURE 3-1

Superscripts and their corresponding references are called **footnotes**. Footnotes may appear at the bottom of the page or at the end of the document. Footnotes at the end of the document are sometimes called **endnotes**. At other times, they are called notes, depending on the MLA format chosen.

In the research report prepared in this project, the footnotes are placed at the end of the document as illustrated in Figure 3-1 on the previous page. This is one of the widely used MLA styles. This MLA style specifies that the title, NOTES, and related references in the form of footnotes be placed on a separate page at the end of the research report.

In this project, you will learn the word processing techniques and Works commands necessary to create the research report in Figure 3-1. You will first create the research report without the table. The table will be added later in the project.

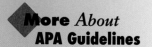

More *About*
APA Guidelines

To follow the APA style, double-space all pages of the paper with 1.5" top, bottom, left, and right margins. The APA style requires a title page and a header placed in the upper right margin of each page of the report. The header consists of the page number double-spaced below a summary of the paper title.

Formatting Standards for the Research Report

When creating the research report, you should follow a number of important standards relating to formatting the document. These standards, specified by the MLA, are described in the following paragraphs and are illustrated in Figure 3-2. Follow these standards when you type the research report.

1. Double-space the research report.
2. Number all pages consecutively in the upper right corner of the manuscript, .5-inch from the top of the page. Type your last name before the page number. Leave one space between your name and the page number. This is called the report **header**.
3. A brief research report does not require the use of a title page. Instead, begin 1 inch down from the top of the first page at the left margin. On separate lines, type your name, the instructor's name, the course title and number, and the date.
4. Provide a 1-inch margin at the bottom of the page.
5. Provide 1-inch left and right margins.
6. Indent the first line in each paragraph .5-inch.
7. Single-space after a period when using Times New Roman font or any proportional spacing font.
8. Print the research report on standard-sized paper, 8.5 inches wide by 11 inches long.

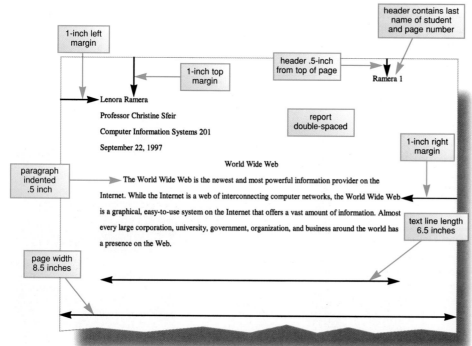

FIGURE 3-2

Starting Works

To create the research report, start the Works Word Processor using the procedures learned in Project 1 and Project 2. These procedures are summarized below.

TO START WORKS

Step 1: Click the Start button on the taskbar, point to Programs, point to the Microsoft Works 4.0 folder on the Programs sub menu, point to Microsoft Works 4.0 to view the Microsoft Works 4.0 submenu, and then click Microsoft Works 4.0.

Step 2: When the Works Task Launcher dialog box displays, click the Works Tools tab.

Step 3: Click the Word Processor button on the Works Tools sheet.

Step 4: Maximize the application and document windows.

Step 5: Click Normal on the View menu.

Setting Margins and Controlling the Placement of Footnotes

Before typing the research report, you must set margins as specified by the preceding MLA standards and indicate to Works that you wish to place the footnotes at the end of the report. These tasks are accomplished using the **Page Setup command** on the File menu.

Works normally provides a .5-inch header margin, a 1-inch top margin, a 1-inch bottom margin, a 1.25-inch left margin and a 1.25-inch right margin. These header, top, bottom, left, and right margin sizes are Works **default** values; that is, the values are set when you start Works.

Because the standards for the research report require a 1-inch left margin and a 1-inch right margin, you must change the Works default values. In addition, when you double-space a report, Works inserts a blank line before printing the first line on each page. The blank line occupies approximately .17 inch on the page. Therefore, to obtain a true one-inch top margin, you must specify a top margin of .83 inches. The blank line (.17 inch) and the .83-inch top margin will give you a 1-inch top margin when your document is printed. The bottom margin is not affected. To set the margins, perform the following steps.

 To Set Margins

1 **Click File on the menu bar and point to Page Setup.**

Works displays the File menu (Figure 3-3). The mouse pointer points to the Page Setup command.

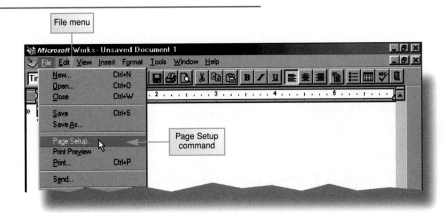

FIGURE 3-3

2 Click Page Setup. If necessary, click the Margins tab in the Page Setup dialog box.

Works displays the Margins sheet in the Page Setup dialog box (Figure 3-4). Default values for the Top margin, Bottom margin, Left margin, Right margin, Header margin, and Footer margin display in their respective text boxes.

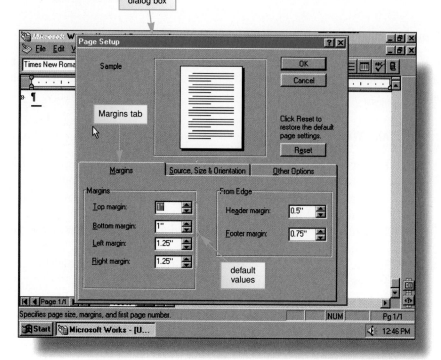

FIGURE 3-4

3 Type .83 in the Top margin text box, press the TAB key two times to move the insertion point to the Left margin text box, and type 1" in the Left margin text box. Press the TAB key and type 1" in the Right margin text box.

The Top margin text box now contains .83", and both the Left margin text box and the Right margin text box contain 1" (Figure 3-5). Other default values are not changed. The Bottom margin text box contains the default value of 1", which is the correct value. The Header margin text box contains 0.5", which is the correct value for a one-half inch top margin for the header.

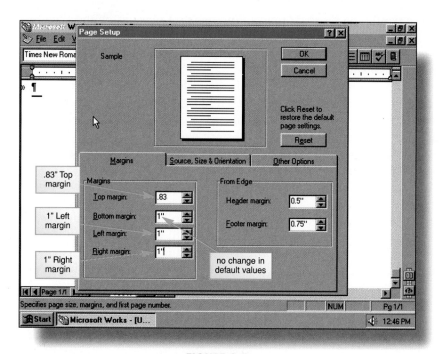

FIGURE 3-5

More *About*
Page Setup Dialog Box

If your printer has more than one paper source, you can select your printer's paper source on the Source, Size, & Orientation sheet.

The Page Setup dialog box contains three separate **sheets** you can display by clicking the **tabs** at the top of each sheet within the dialog box. These tabs resemble the tabs on a standard file folder. Clicking the Source, Size and Orientation tab will cause a sheet to display that allows you to specify the paper size and how text will display when printed. Clicking the Other Options tab will display a screen that allows you to direct Works to print footnotes at the end of the report. The following steps explain how to cause footnotes to print at the end of a document.

Steps **To Print Footnotes at the End of a Document**

1 **Point to the Other Options tab in the Page Setup dialog box.**

The Page Setup dialog box displays on the screen (Figure 3-6). The mouse pointer points to the Other Options tab.

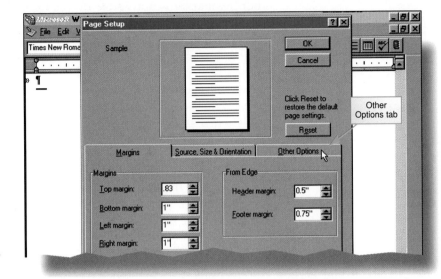

FIGURE 3-6

2 **Click the Other Options tab in the Page Setup dialog box. When the Other Options sheet displays, click Print footnotes at end. Point to the OK button.**

Works displays the Other Options sheet (Figure 3-7). Clicking the check box causes a check mark (✓) to appear in the Print footnotes at end check box. The mouse pointer points to the OK button.

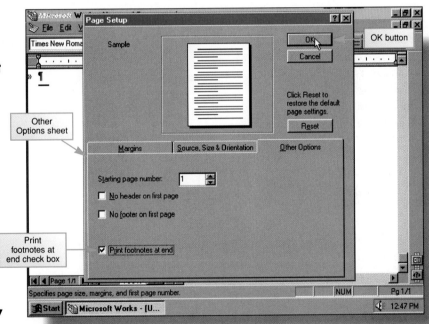

FIGURE 3-7

3 **Click the OK button in the Page Setup dialog box. Click anywhere in the document window.**

The Works Word Processor document screen displays; however, the right-margin indent marker is not visible (Figure 3-8).

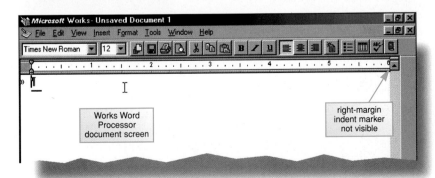

FIGURE 3-8

The right margin is no longer set at 6 inches because a 1-inch left margin and a 1-inch right margin (two inches total) provide a 6.5-inch space for text on an 8.5-inch wide document. Works sets the right-margin indent marker at 6.5 inches, but the marker is not visible on the right side of the screen because of the size of the screen display.

The margin settings you entered on the Margins sheet of the Page Setup dialog box, and the entry in the Print footnotes at end check box on the Other Options sheet of the Page Setup dialog box, stay in effect when you create the research report. When you save the document and then open the document again, these values continue to be in effect. The original default values will be in effect only when you create a new document.

Using the Scroll Bar

To verify the proper setting of the right margin and to view the right-margin indent marker, you must use the scroll bar and the right scroll arrow at the bottom of the screen.

Steps To Scroll The Screen Horizontally

1 Point to the right scroll arrow and click.

The entire screen moves approximately one-half inch to the left, displaying the right portion of the screen previously not visible (Figure 3-9). The right-margin indent marker is set at 6.5 inches.

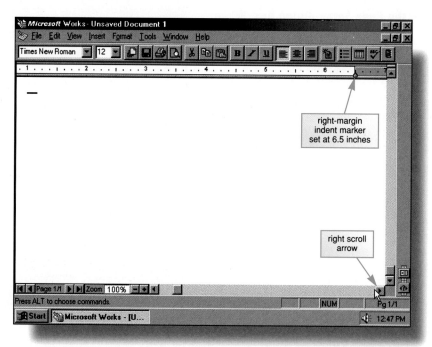

right-margin
indent marker
set at 6.5 inches

right scroll
arrow

FIGURE 3-9

To return the screen to its normal position, position the mouse pointer on the left scroll arrow and click.

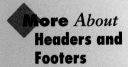

Typing the Research Report

After setting the margins and the location for printing the footnotes, the next step in preparing the research report is to type the report header. The header consists of the student's last name on the top right side of the page, followed by a blank space and then the page number (see Figure 3-2 on page W 3.6).

Headers and Footers

A **header** is special text that appears at the top of every printed page in a document. A **footer** is special text that appears at the bottom of every printed page in a document. You use headers and footers to number pages and/or add a title or other types of information to the pages in a document. In the research report, you use a header to identify the student and number the pages in the report. According to MLA standards, you are to print the header one-half inch from the top of the page. In this document, you are not using a footer. In Normal view, headers and footers display on screen only at the top of the first page of a document.

A header or footer prints in the top or bottom page margin areas and can be a single line or multiple lines of text. The research report in this project contains a single line header.

To create the header, you will use the Header command on the View menu to display the header line at the top of the document. You will type the student's last name followed by a blank space. Then, use the Page Number command on the Insert menu to instruct Works to print the page number. The Page Number command inserts the placeholder, *page*, in the header line. A **placeholder** marks the location where information is inserted when you print or preview your document. For example, when you print or preview the document, Works replaces the placeholder, *page*, with the correct page number.

Follow these steps to create a header for the research report.

More *About*
Headers and Footers

You can have only one header and one footer in a document. Once they are entered, they will appear on every page in the document. In a word processing document, headers and footers can occupy multiple lines.

Steps **To Create a Header**

1 **Click View on the menu bar and point to Header.**

Works displays the View menu (Figure 3-10). The mouse pointer points to the Header command.

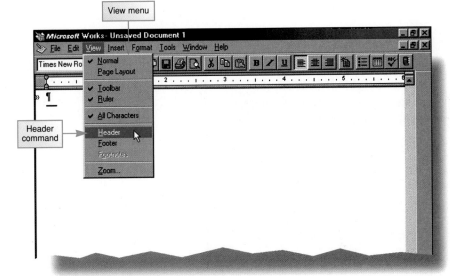

FIGURE 3-10

2 **Click Header. If the First-time help dialog box displays, click the OK button in the First-time help dialog box.**

Works displays the header (H) line and the footer (F) line at the top of the page and moves the insertion point to the right of the H on the header line (Figure 3-11). Text typed on the header (H) line displays at the top of each page when you print or preview the document. Text typed on the footer (F) line displays at the bottom of each page when you print or preview the document. In a multi-page document, text typed on either the header or footer lines displays on the screen only on the first page of the document.

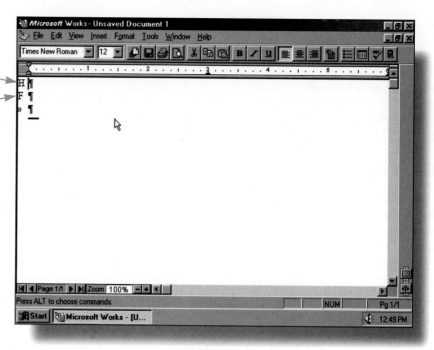

FIGURE 3-11

3 **Click the Right Align button on the toolbar. Type** Ramera **and press the SPACEBAR to enter a space.**

When you click the Right Align button, Works moves the insertion point to the right margin. As you type, the text moves to the left (Figure 3-12).

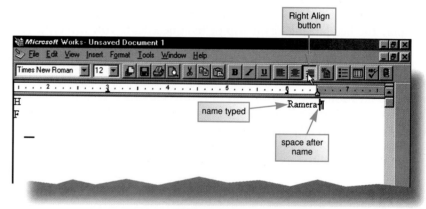

FIGURE 3-12

4 **Position the mouse pointer between the paragraph mark and the spacemark in the header (H) line and right-click. When the context-sensitive menu displays, point to Insert Page Number.**

When you right-click, Works places the insertion point to the left of the paragraph mark and displays the context-sensitive menu (Figure 3-13). The mouse pointer points to the Insert Page Number command.

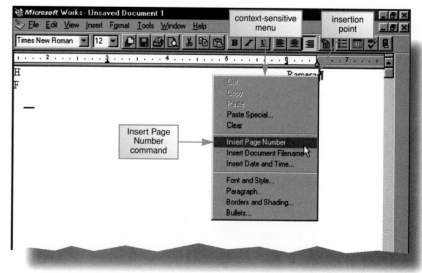

FIGURE 3-13

5 **Click Insert Page Number.**

Works inserts the *page* place-holder in the header (H) line (Figure 3-14). When you print or preview the document, Works replaces *page* with the correct page number.

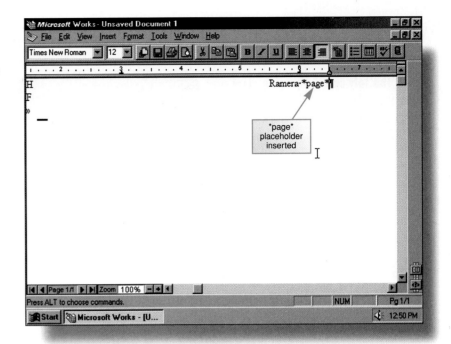

FIGURE 3-14

The header information will print one-half inch down from the top of each page when you print the research report. The header information will display on the screen only on the first page of the research report.

When using placeholders in a header or footer, you can type any text, spaces, or punctuation before or after the placeholder to produce the required output. You must, however, use the Insert Page Number command to insert this place-holder. If you type the placeholder name and the asterisks yourself, Works will not insert the page number in the header when it prints the document.

Entering Text

According to the MLA style, the first step in entering the text comprising the research report is to type the name of the student on the first line, followed by the name of the instructor on the second line, the course title on the third line, and the date on the fourth line. Because all lines on the report are double-spaced, you also must specify double-spacing. Perform the following step to accomplish these tasks.

Steps To Double-Space and Type Identifying Information

1 Use the left scroll arrow to view the page break mark. Click to the left of the paragraph mark on the first line of the document. Press the CTRL+2 keys to double-space the document. Then type the name of the student on the first line, the name of the instructor on the second line, the course title on the third line, and the date on the fourth line as shown in Figure 3-15. Press the ENTER key after typing each line.

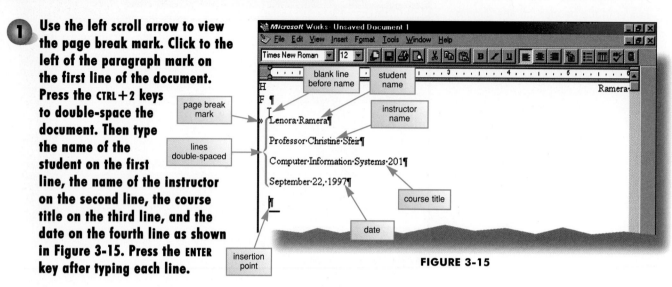

FIGURE 3-15

The student name displays on the second line of the screen because of the double-space mode (Figure 3-15). The instructor name, course title, and date are double-spaced below the student name. The insertion point is positioned at the left margin of the next double-spaced line.

Centering the Report Title

After typing the heading information, the next step is to type the title of the research report, which is to be centered on the document. To center a single line (the title) on a document, complete the following steps.

Steps To Center a Report Title

1 Click the Center Align button on the toolbar.

The insertion point and paragraph mark display in the center of the line (Figure 3-16).

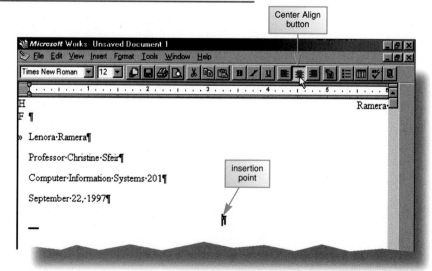

FIGURE 3-16

2 **Type the report title,** World Wide Web, **and then press the** ENTER **key.**

Works centers the title (Figure 3-17). The insertion point remains in the center of the report, double-spaced below the report title.

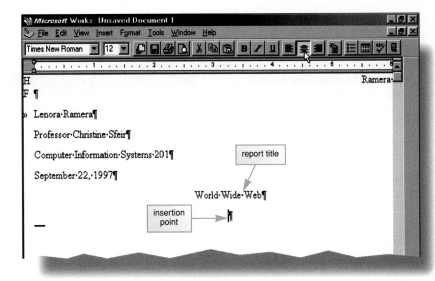

FIGURE 3-17

3 **Click the Left Align button on the toolbar.**

The insertion point moves to the left margin (Figure 3-18).

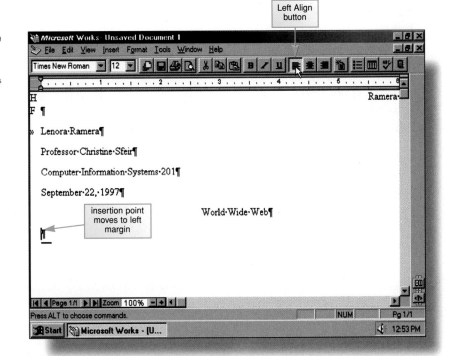

FIGURE 3-18

Indenting Paragraphs

In the report, the first line of each paragraph is indented one-half inch. You can use the TAB key to indent each paragraph, or you can use the Works **first-line indent** feature when there is a need to indent the first line of numerous paragraphs, such as in the research report. The following steps explain how to use the first-line indent marker to indent the first line of each paragraph one-half inch from the left margin.

Other Ways

1. On Format menu click Paragraph, click Indents and Alignment tab, click Center in Alignment box, click OK button

2. On context-sensitive menu click Paragraph, click Indents and Alignment tab, click Center in Alignment box, click OK button

Steps To Use First-Line Indent

1 **Point to the first-line indent marker on the ruler.**

The mouse pointer points to the first-line indent marker (Figure 3-19).

FIGURE 3-19

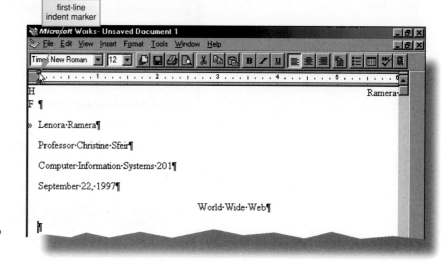

2 **Drag the first-line indent marker to the .5-inch mark on the ruler. If the First-time Help dialog box displays, click the OK button.**

As you drag the mouse, a vertical dotted line displays in the document window, indicating the location of the first-line indent marker (Figure 3-20).

FIGURE 3-20

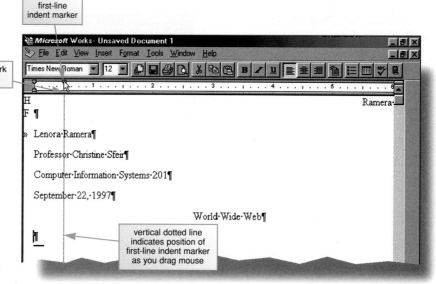

3 **Release the left mouse button.**

Works indents the insertion point for the first paragraph .5-inch (Figure 3-21).

FIGURE 3-21

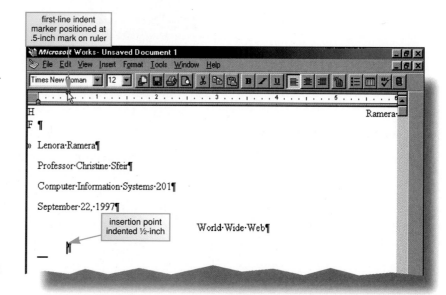

④ **Begin typing the report as shown in Figure 3-22.**

As you type the report, the first line of each paragraph will automatically be indented one-half inch after you press the ENTER key (Figure 3-22).

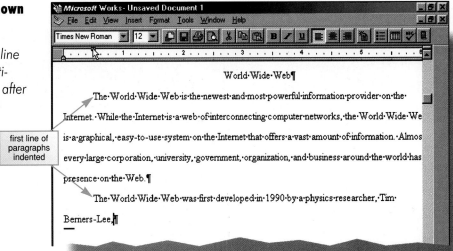

first line of paragraphs indented

FIGURE 3-22

Creating a Custom Zoom

When you changed the margins earlier in this project, the right margin moved beyond the right edge of the document window. Thus, some of the text at the right edge of the document does not display in the document window (Figure 3-22).

Recall in Project 2, you used the Margin Width option to zoom the document display between margins. When using the Margin Width option, Works automatically determines the zoom percentage necessary to properly display all the text between the left and right margins. Works also allows you to set a **custom zoom** for a document, meaning you can control how much of the document displays in the document window. In this Project, you are to use a custom zoom percentage of 95%. To use the Custom Zoom feature in Works, follow the steps below.

 Steps **To Create a Custom Zoom**

① **Click the Zoom box at the bottom of the Works window. When the Zoom list displays, point to Custom.**

Works displays a list of available zoom options and zoom percentages (Figure 3-23). The mouse pointer points to the Custom option.

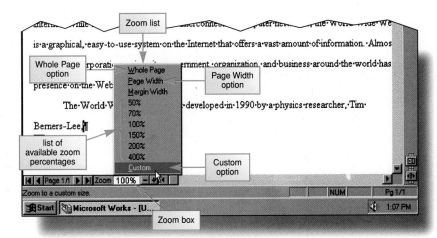

Zoom list

Whole Page option

Page Width option

list of available zoom percentages

Custom option

Zoom box

FIGURE 3-23

2 **Click Custom. When the Zoom dialog box displays, type** 95 **in the Custom text box. Point to the OK button.**

Works displays the Zoom dialog box (Figure 3-24). The desired custom display percentage, 95, displays in the Custom text box. This percentage instructs Works to display the document at 95% of the original size. The Zoom dialog box contains five preset magnification/reduction percentages. The Page width option button displays the document between the left and right margins, regardless of the window size. This option is useful if the Help menu is displayed to the right of the document window. The Whole Page option displays the document in the width of the document window. The mouse pointer points to the OK button.

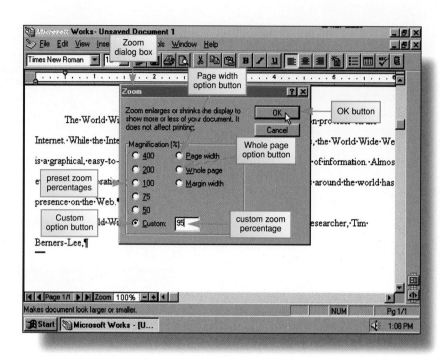

FIGURE 3-24

3 **Click the OK button in the Zoom dialog box.**

Works reduces the display of the document to 95% of the original size (Figure 3-25). The Zoom box now displays 95%. The zoom size of a document has no effect on how the document will look when it is printed.

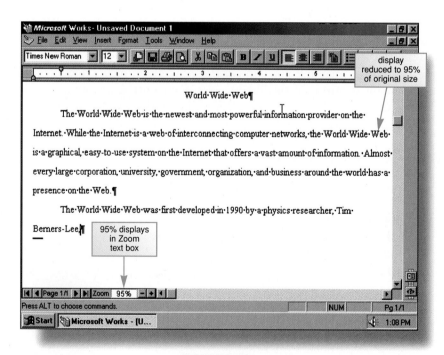

FIGURE 3-25

Other Ways

1. On View menu click Zoom, type desired percentage in Custom text box, click OK button

Entering Text

Continue entering text, as specified in the following step (Figure 3-26).

Steps **To Enter Text**

1 **Type the remaining six lines in the second paragraph as shown in Figure 3-26.**

As you continue typing the report and the screen fills with text, the text will scroll upward (Figure 3-26).

second paragraph in report

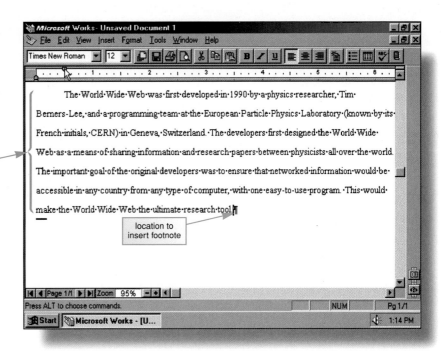

location to insert footnote

FIGURE 3-26

Creating Footnotes

The second paragraph in the research report describes the historical development of the World Wide Web. This description was taken from a book that was used as a source of information when preparing the report. When you use information from a book or other reference source, you must identify the source and also credit the author by including a footnote or endnote in the report. When you create a footnote, Works places a **footnote mark** in your document. The footnote mark can be a raised number, called a **superscript** or other characters, such as an asterisk.

When you create a footnote, Works opens an area at the bottom of the screen called the **footnote pane**. When you create a footnote, Works automatically places the footnote mark and the text in the footnote pane.

In a research report, the footnote text will vary depending upon whether the reference is a book, newspaper, magazine, or other source. However, the information in the footnote commonly consists of the name of the author of the reference work, the title of the work, the location of the publisher, the publisher, the year of publication of the work, and the page number or numbers you reference in the work (see Figure 3-1 on page W 3.5).

The first line of each footnote should be indented one-half inch from the left margin and double-spaced.

The steps on the following pages explain how to include a footnote that will be an endnote in a report.

▼ **More** *About* **Footnotes**

Footnotes are an important part of research papers. Typing and numbering footnotes can be a chore without a computer. Works makes creating a footnote and keeping track of each footnote simple. You can display footnotes at the bottom of the page that contains a footnote mark or display all the footnotes at the end of the document. To display footnotes only at the bottom of the page on which they are referenced, remove the check mark in the Print footnotes at end check box on the Page Setup dialog box.

Steps To Create a Footnote

1 Position the insertion point where you want the footnote mark to appear. Click Insert on the menu bar and point to Footnote.

The Insert menu displays and the mouse pointer points to the Footnote command (Figure 3-27).

FIGURE 3-27

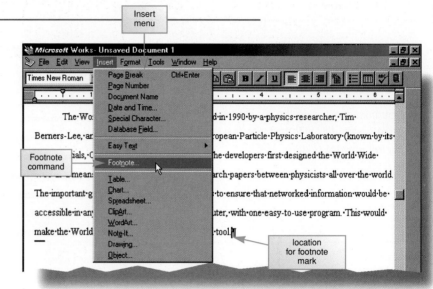

2 Click Footnote. When the Insert Footnote dialog box displays, click Numbered in the Footnote style box, and then point to the Insert button.

Works displays the Insert Footnote dialog box (Figure 3-28). The Numbered option button in the Footnote style box is selected, as indicated by the dark circle in the button. This is the Works default selection. This selection causes a number to display as the footnote mark. The mouse pointer points to the Insert button.

FIGURE 3-28

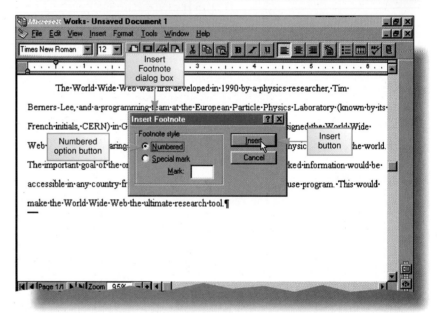

3 Click the Insert button in the Insert Footnote dialog box.

*The screen scrolls upward and displays a single line of text containing the footnote mark 1 at the top of the screen (Figure 3-29). Works opens an area at the bottom of the screen called the footnote pane. The footnote displays at the left margin of the footnote pane. Footnote are, by default, **superscripted**; that is, they are raised above other letters.*

FIGURE 3-29

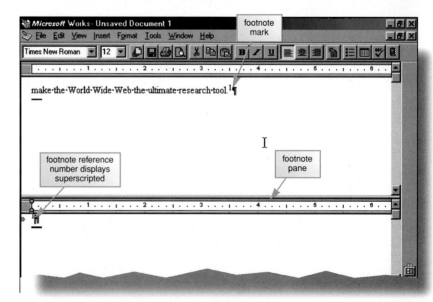

④ **Point to the first-line indent marker on the footnote pane ruler and drag the marker to the .5-inch mark. Press the CTRL+2 keys to double-space the footnote.**

The footnote reference number is indented one-half inch and a blank line displays above the footnote reference nember (Figure 3-30).

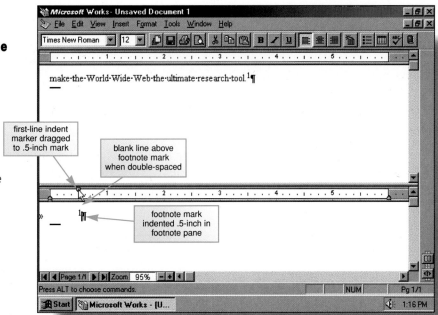

FIGURE 3-30

⑤ **Type** William Peterson **and press the SPACEBAR once. Then press the CTRL+I keys. Type** Beginner's Guide to Surfing the World Wide Web, **and press the CTRL+I keys. Press the SPACEBAR once and type the remaining footnote information as shown in Figure 3-31.**

The first footnote displays in the footnote pane with the book name italicized (Figure 3-31). When you press CTRL+I the first time, the Italic button on the toolbar is recessed and Works italicizes each character as you type them. When you press the CTRL+I keys after typing the book name, the Italics button on the toolbar no longer is recessed and Works no longer italicizes text as you type. CTRL+I *is a **toggle**. That is, the keyboard shortcut is typed once to activate the button and typed again to deactivate the button. When your fingers are on the keyboard, it is more efficient to use a keyboard shortcut, instead of using the mouse.*

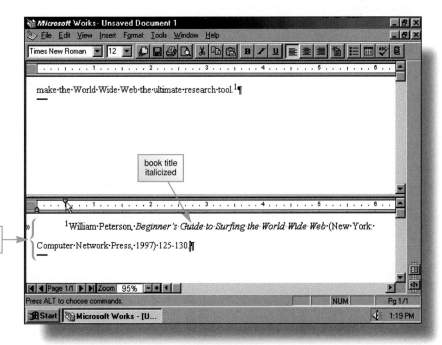

FIGURE 3-31

Each time you create a footnote, it is necessary to indent the first line of the footnote in the footnote pane and double-space the footnote.

When a report contains a large number of footnotes, the footnotes can be single-spaced. When only a few footnotes appear in the report, it is recommended that the footnotes be double-spaced.

Closing the Footnote Pane

After creating the footnote, you should close the footnote pane. Closing the footnote pane will remove the footnote pane from the screen. Perform the following steps to close the footnote pane.

Steps To Close the Footnote Pane

1 **Position the mouse pointer on the narrow split bar above the ruler in the footnote pane.**

The mouse pointer becomes an equal sign with small arrows on the top and bottom on the split bar, with the word ADJUST below (Figure 3-32).

FIGURE 3-32

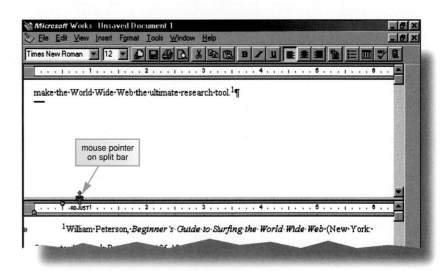

2 **Double-click.**

The footnote pane closes and the line of text containing the footnote reference number displays at the top of the screen (Figure 3-33).

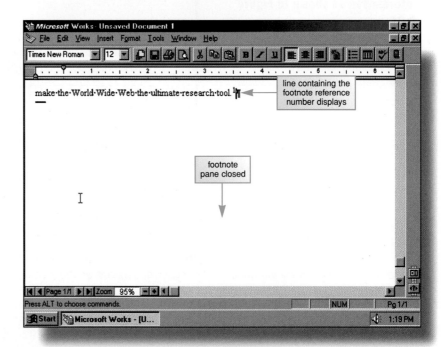

FIGURE 3-33

▶**Other**Ways
1. On View menu click Footnotes

To view the footnote in the footnote pane, click Footnotes on the View menu. You also can display the footnote by clicking Page Layout on the View menu. In page layout view, the footnote displays as a part of the document instead of inside the footnote pane. You can correct or otherwise change the footnote as required.

To correct a footnote, click Footnotes on the View menu, and make the correction. To enlarge or resize the footnote pane, position the mouse pointer on the split bar above the footnote pane ruler and drag up or down.

To delete a footnote, highlight the footnote mark in the document window and press the DELETE key. If there are multiple footnotes, Works renumbers them.

Saving the Document

A good practice is to periodically save the information you are typing on a floppy disk or the hard disk to eliminate retyping information in the event of a power or computer failure. To save the document on a floppy disk in drive A using the filename, World Wide Web Report, complete the steps below.

TO SAVE A DOCUMENT

Step 1: Click the Save button on the toolbar.
Step 2: Type the filename, World Wide Web Report, in the File name text box of the Save As dialog box.
Step 3: If necessary, select drive A from the Save in drop-down list box.
Step 4: Click the Save button in the Save As dialog box.

Entering Text

After creating the first footnote, continue to type the remainder of the research report, as specified below.

 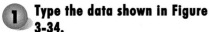 **To Enter Text**

1 **Type the data shown in Figure 3-34.**

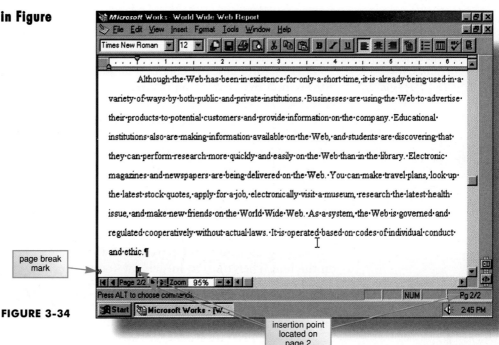

page break mark

insertion point located on page 2

FIGURE 3-34

2 Type the data shown in Figure 3-35. As you continue typing, the text scrolls upward when the screen is filled. Create footnote 2 and footnote 3. To obtain the data required for the footnote information, refer to Figure 3-1 on page W 3.5. If necessary, when creating footnotes or when viewing footnotes after clicking Footnotes on the View menu, use the scroll bar and scroll arrows in the footnote pane to display the footnotes.

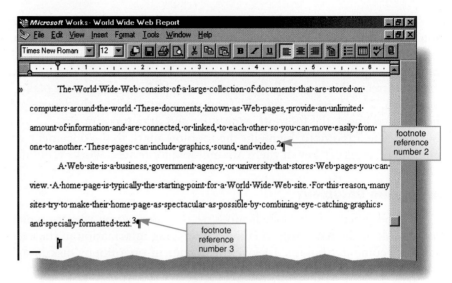

FIGURE 3-35

3 Type the end of the research paper as shown in Figure 3-36.

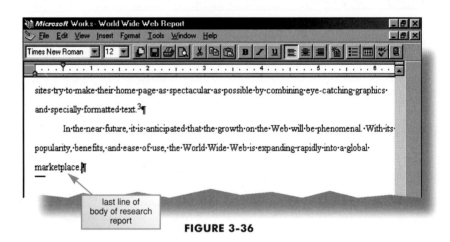

FIGURE 3-36

Automatic Page Break

Works automatically creates a **page break** in a document if you type more information than can fit on one page of a printed report. The automatic page break mark displays as a chevron character in the left margin (see Figure 3-34). The line to the right of the page break mark will print as the first line on the next page of the report. You can control where the page break occurs by specifying a value in the Bottom margin text box on the Margins sheet in the Page Setup dialog box. The Works default value is a 1-inch bottom margin.

Inserting a Manual Page Break and Formatting the Footnotes Page

According to the MLA style, the footnotes (endnotes) should print on a separate page at the end of the report with the heading, NOTES, centered horizontally on the line. Therefore, to format the footnote page, you must: (1) create a manual page break; and (2) center the word, NOTES, on the new page. The footnotes will then print after the word, NOTES, because the word is the last line of the report.

To accomplish these tasks, perform the following steps.

Steps **To Insert a Manual Page Break and Center a Word on the New Page**

1 **Press the ENTER key to position the insertion point on the next line where the page break is to occur. Press the CTRL+ENTER keys.**

The insertion point is positioned immediately after the last line in the report (Figure 3-37). A dotted line indicating a manual page break displays on the screen immediately above the insertion point. The page break mark displays below the dotted line and the new page number (3) displays in the scroll bar and the status bar.

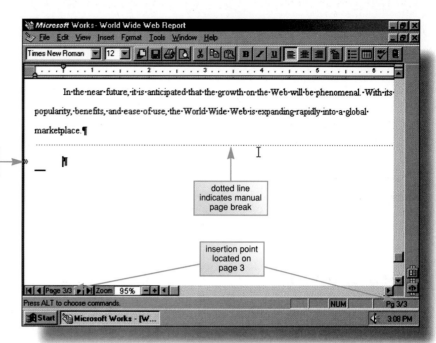

FIGURE 3-37

2 **Drag the first-line indent marker to the left margin on the ruler. Click the Center Align button on the toolbar. Type** NOTES.

The first-line indent marker is located at the left margin on the ruler (Figure 3-38). The word NOTES displays centered between the document margins.

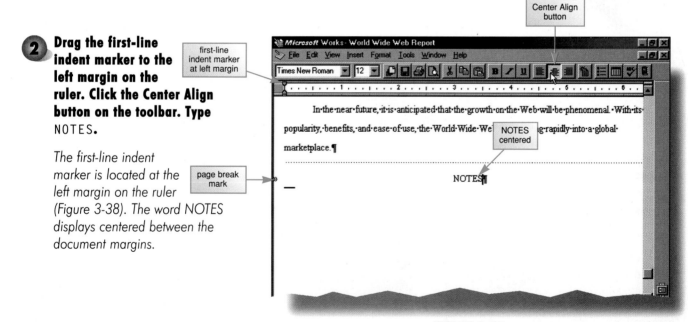

FIGURE 3-38

OtherWays

1. On Insert menu click Page Break

If you insert a page break by mistake, you can delete it by moving the insertion point to the beginning of the line that immediately follows the page break and pressing the BACKSPACE key; or you can highlight the dotted line and press the DELETE key.

When you print the research report, Works places the information you typed in the footnote pane below the word NOTES on the last page of the report (see Figure 3-1 on page W 3.5).

Editing the Research Report

After typing the research report, you should save it using the Save button on the toolbar. Next, you should edit the research report; that is, review the report for any additions, deletions, or changes. You can edit the report while it displays on the screen, or you may find it useful to print a copy of the report and edit the printed copy. When making changes to a report, you may wish to move quickly to a certain page on the report or to a certain word or words. You also may have a need to replace certain words in the document, or move words, sentences, or paragraphs. Works provides a number of useful commands to assist you in performing these editing tasks.

Using the Go To Command

If the insertion point is at the beginning of a document and you want to move to page 2 of the document, you can use the scroll bar or scroll arrow to move through the document. To move from page to page, you also can use the next page button and the previous page button on the scroll bar. Another particularly useful method to move through a document when the document consists of many pages is using the **Go To command** on the Edit menu. To use the Go To command, perform the following steps.

Steps **To Use the Go To Command**

① **Click the beginning of document button on the scroll bar to position the insertion point at the beginning of the document. Click Edit on the menu bar and point to Go To.**

Works displays the Edit menu and the mouse pointer points to the Go To command (Figure 3-39)

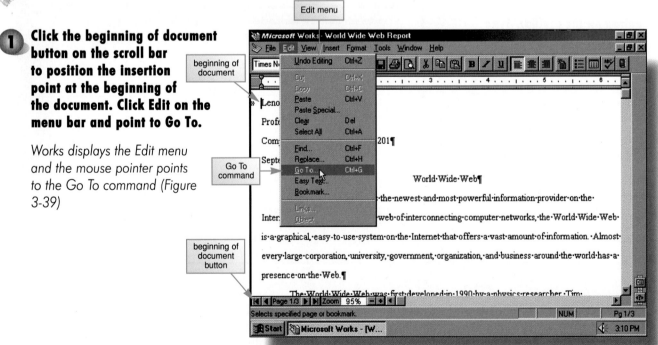

FIGURE 3-39

2 **Click Go To. When the Go To dialog box displays, type 2 in the Go to text box, and then point to the OK button.**

Works displays the Go To dialog box (Figure 3-40). The number 2 displays in the Go to text box. The mouse pointer points to the OK button.

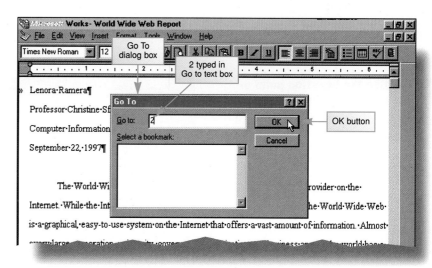

FIGURE 3-40

3 **Click the OK button in the Go To dialog box.**

Page 2 of the research report displays (Figure 3-41). Works places the insertion point at the leftmost position on the first line of page 2 at the top of the screen.

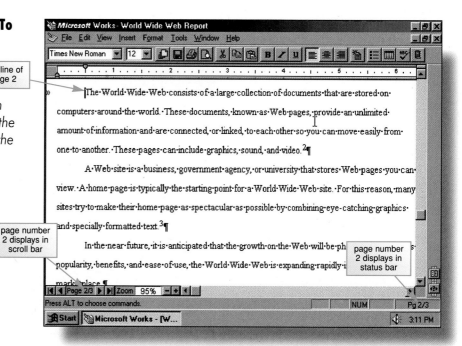

FIGURE 3-41

The Go To command provides a quick way to move to a specific page in a document. Once the page is reached, you can click to move to a specific location in the document, or you can use the scroll bar and scroll arrows or the arrow keys to move through the document to find a specific paragraph.

Using the Find Command

Another command you can use to move quickly to a specific area in a document is the **Find command**. The Find command allows you to specify one or more words you wish to locate in a document. In the following example, assume the insertion point is located at the beginning of the document and you want to find the words, Web pages, which are located somewhere within the research report. To use the Find command, perform the steps on the next page.

▶ **Other Ways**

1. Press CTRL+G, type desired page number in Go to text box, click OK button

Steps To Use the Find Command

1 **Position the insertion point at the beginning of the document. Click Edit on the menu bar and point to Find.**

Works displays the Edit menu and the mouse pointer points to the Find command (Figure 3-42).

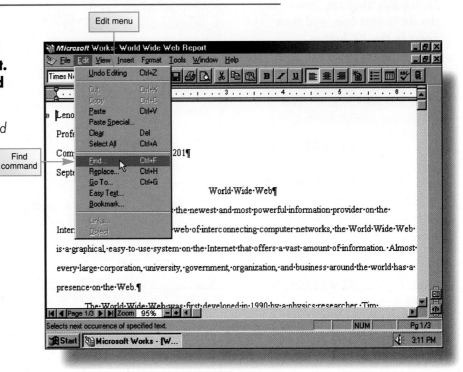

FIGURE 3-42

2 **Click Find. When the Find dialog box displays, type** Web pages **in the Find what text box. Click the Match case check box and then point to the Find Next button.**

*Works displays the Find dialog box (Figure 3-43). The words, Web pages, display in the Find what text box. The **Match case check box** is selected, which means the case of the characters in the document must match the case of the characters you type in the Find what text box. Clicking the Tab mark button inserts a tab mark code in the Find what text box to identify and find tab marks in your document. Clicking the Paragraph mark button inserts a paragraph mark code in the Find what text box to identify and find paragraph marks in your document. The mouse pointer points to the Find Next button.*

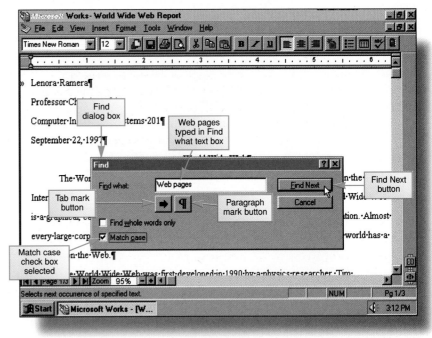

FIGURE 3-43

3 Click the Find Next button in the Find dialog box.

Works locates the first location where the words, Web pages, occur and highlights the words (Figure 3-44). The Find dialog box remains on the screen.

4 Click the Find Next button to search for the next occurrence of the words, or click the Cancel button to exit from the Find dialog box and return to the word processing document. If you click the Find Next button and no additional occurrence of the words is found, a Microsoft Works dialog box displays indicating the search has reached the end of the document. Click the OK button in the Microsoft Works dialog box and then click the Cancel button in the Find dialog box to return to the document. If the Microsoft Works dialog box displays, "Continue searching from beginning of document?" click No.

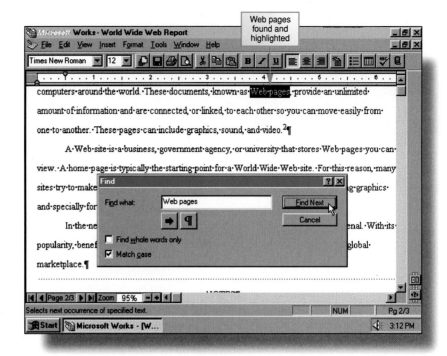

FIGURE 3-44

Other Ways

1. Press CTRL+F, type desired word or words in Find what box, click Find Next button

When you click the Match case check box, Works matches the case of the characters you type exactly. Case refers to uppercase or lowercase letters of the alphabet. For example, if you type WEB PAGES and click the Match case check box, Works will not find the words, Web pages. The Find dialog box also contains the **Find whole words only check box**. If you click this box, Works searches only for whole words. For example, if you click this box and type Web pages, Works would find Web pages, but would not find Web page.

Using the Replace Command

Another powerful Works editing feature is the **Replace command**. The Replace command searches a document, including the header (H) and footer (F) lines, for specified text and replaces it with new text. When using the Replace command, Works searches the text from the insertion point to the end of the document. If the insertion point is not initially positioned at the top of the first page, that is, in the header (H) line when the search begins, at the end of the search Works displays a dialog box offering to continue the search from the top of the first page. For this reason, it is easier to use the CTRL+HOME keys to move the insertion point to the top of the first page. Using the CTRL+HOME keys moves the insertion point to the header (H) line on the first page. Recall that clicking the beginning of document button moves the insertion point to the beginning of the document, not the header (H) line. In this project, clicking the beginning of document button moves the insertion point to the left of the word, Lenora, in the first line of the report.

In the research report, assume you would like to replace the word, documents, with the word, files. To accomplish this task, use the Replace command as shown in the following steps.

Steps **To Use the Replace Command**

1 Press the **CTRL + HOME** keys to move the insertion point to the top of the first page. Then, click Edit on the menu bar and point to Replace.

When you press the CTRL+HOME keys, Works moves the insertion point to the header (H) line (Figure 3-45). Works displays the Edit menu and the mouse pointer points to the Replace command.

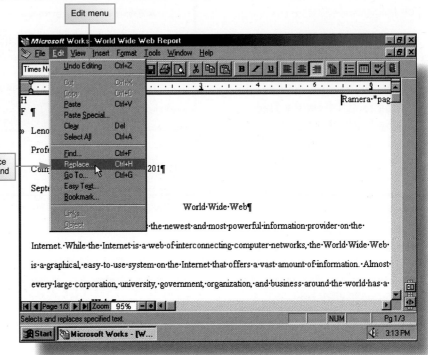

FIGURE 3-45

2 Click Replace. When the Replace dialog box displays, type documents in the Find what text box. Press the **TAB** key and type files in the Replace with text box. Click the Match case check box to remove the check mark. Point to the Find Next button.

Works displays the Replace dialog box (Figure 3-46). The word, documents, and the word, files, display in the appropriate text boxes. The Match case check box is not selected in this example because if the word, documents, began a sentence, it would be capitalized. Because the Match case check box is not selected, Works will search for instances of the word, Documents, as well.

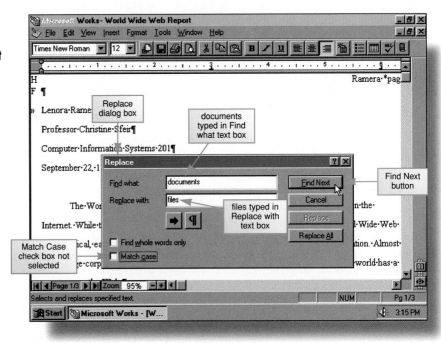

FIGURE 3-46

3 Click the Find Next button in the replace dialog box. When a match is found, point to the Replace button.

Works highlights the first occurrence of the word, documents, in the research report (Figure 3-47).

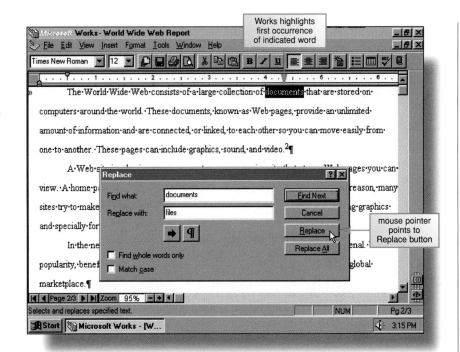

FIGURE 3-47

4 Click the Replace button in the Replace dialog box. When the next occurrence of the word, documents, is found, click the Replace button again. If the Microsoft Works dialog box displays, "Continue searching from beginning of document?" click No. Then click the Close button. Use the down scroll arrow to view page 2 of the report.

Works replaces the word documents with the word files in all occurrences (Figure 3-48).

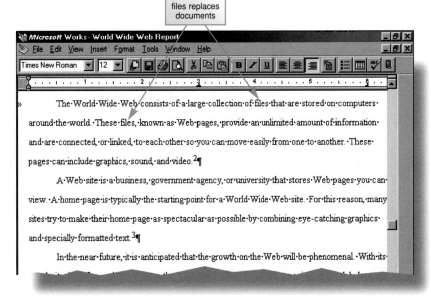

FIGURE 3-48

▶*Other***Ways**

1. Press CTRL+H, type desired words in Find What text box and Replace With text box, click Find Next button, click Close button

After Works highlights the first occurrence of the word, documents, you can replace the word with the text in the Replace with text box by clicking the Replace button, or you can find the next occurrence of the word by clicking the Find Next button. Continue this process until Works returns to the top of the first page. At any time you can exit from the Replace dialog box by clicking the Cancel button. Once you replace a word or words, the Cancel button in the Replace dialog box changes to a Close button. When you click the Close button in the Replace dialog box, the Replace dialog box will be removed from the screen.

The Replace dialog box also contains a Replace All button. If you choose the Replace All button, Works replaces all occurrences of the word in the Find what text box without the need to choose the Replace button each time.

When the Replace All operation is complete, Works displays the page where you began the search.

Undo Editing Command

If you make an editing change in a document and you want to restore the document to its form before the change, Works provides an **Undo Editing command**. This command allows you to undo the last editing that has taken place on a document. Assume you would like to return the research paper to its original form so that the word, documents, again appears where the word, files, now displays. Perform the following steps to undo the editing.

Steps To Undo Editing

1 **Click Edit on the menu bar and point to Undo Editing.**

The Edit menu displays and the mouse pointer points to the Undo Editing command (Figure 3-49).

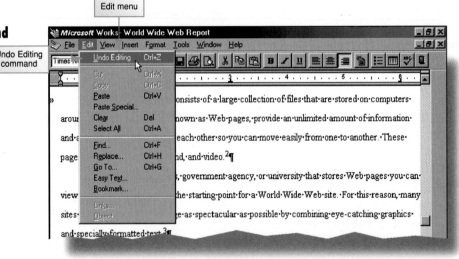

FIGURE 3-49

2 **Click Undo Editing. Scroll to the top of page 2 of the document.**

Works undoes the editing that was performed and moves the insertion point to the top of page 1 of the document. When you scroll to the top of page 2, note that Works returns the research paper to its original form (Figure 3-50).

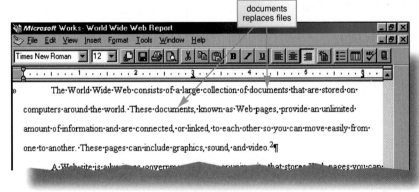

FIGURE 3-50

Other Ways

1. Press CTRL+Z

The Undo Editing command is a useful command and is especially valuable when you delete words or paragraphs accidentally and want to restore them. Note, however, that you must click Undo on the Edit menu immediately after you have performed the editing, without any intervening operations.

Redo Command

If you undo an editing operation using the Undo Editing command, you can click **Redo Editing** on the Edit menu to restore the document so it once again contains the editing. The Redo Editing command appears on the Edit menu after the Undo Editing command is used.

Moving Words, Sentences, or Paragraphs

Upon reviewing a document, you may want to move certain text to other locations within the document. With Works, you can move a single character, a single word or words, a sentence or sentences, or one or more paragraphs or sections of text within a document. Works provides three techniques that can be used to move data previously typed in a document.

These techniques are: (1) use the **Cut button** and the **Paste button** on the toolbar; (2) use the **Cut command** and the **Paste command** on the Edit menu; and (3) use the **drag-and-drop** method.

To use the Cut button and the Paste button to move text, highlight the text you wish to move and then click the Cut button on the toolbar. The text will be removed from the document and will be placed in an area of memory called the **Clipboard**. Then, position the insertion point at the location in the document where you wish to place the text you just *cut* from the document and click the Paste button. The text on the Clipboard will be *pasted* into the document at the insertion point.

Instead of using the Cut and Paste buttons, you can highlight the text you wish to move, click Cut on the Edit menu, position the insertion point where you wish to place the text, and click Paste on the Edit menu.

Using Drag-and-Drop to Move Text

In this project, you will learn to use the drag-and-drop method. The general steps to move text in a document using drag-and-drop are given below.

1. Highlight the text you wish to move.
2. Position the mouse pointer within the highlighted text. The mouse pointer becomes the shape of a block arrow and the word DRAG displays below the arrow.
3. Drag the insertion point to the location where you wish to move the text.

To illustrate the drag-and-drop method, assume you decide to move the second paragraph on page 2 that begins with the words, A Web site, to a location above the first paragraph on page 2 that begins with the words, The World Wide Web (Figure 3-51).

> **M**ore *About*
> **Drag-and-Drop**
>
> For short moves from one part of the screen to another, use drag-and-drop to move or copy data. As you drag the high-lighted text, the insertion point moves with the mouse pointer, allowing you to place the text precisely. The drag-and-drop method does not store the high-lighted text on the Clipboard.

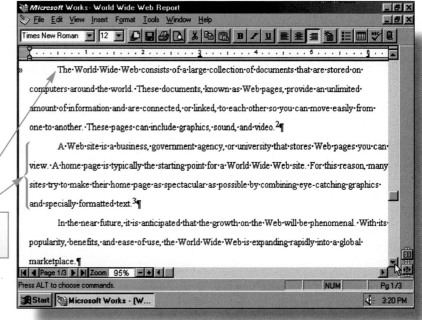

paragraph beginning with a Web site to be moved above paragraph beginning with The World Wide Web

To move a paragraph using the drag-and-drop method, perform the following steps.

Steps To Move a Paragraph Using Drag and Drop

1 **Position the research report using the scroll arrows, page buttons, or the Go To command so the first line of page 2 displays at the top of the screen. Double-click to the left of the second paragraph to highlight it. Position the mouse pointer within the highlighted area of the paragraph.**

The second paragraph is high-lighted (Figure 3-52). The mouse pointer displays with the word DRAG below the arrow.

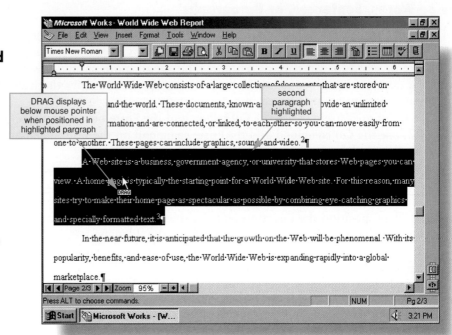

FIGURE 3-52

2 **Drag upward until the dragged insertion point is positioned just above the word, The, which is the first word in the first paragraph on the second page.**

An insertion point follows the tip of the mouse pointer being dragged (Figure 3-53). The dragged inser-tion point is positioned in front of the word, The, where the high-lighted paragraph will be moved.

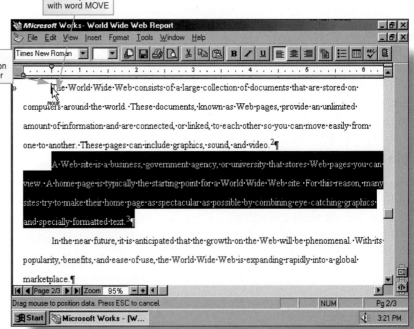

FIGURE 3-53

3 **Release the mouse button.**

Works moves the high-lighted paragraph and places it at the top of page 2 (Figure 3-54). Note that the footnote reference numbers have been changed so they are correctly sequenced in the document. The related footnotes in the NOTES section of the report also will be repositioned.

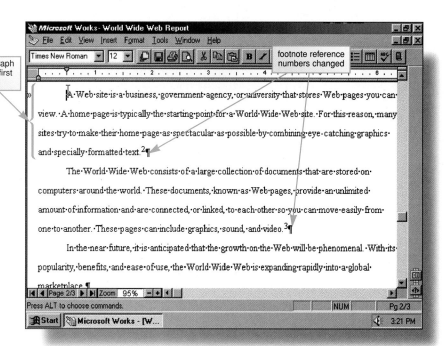

FIGURE 3-54

Copying Data in a Word Processing Document

In addition to moving text within a word processing document, you can also copy data. **Copying data** means to duplicate the data at another location within the document. To copy data, first highlight the data to be copied. Then, use one of three methods: (1) click the Copy button on the toolbar, place the insertion point at the location where you wish the copied data to appear, and click the Paste button on the toolbar; (2) click Copy on the Edit menu, place the insertion point at the location where you wish the copied data to appear, and click Paste on the Edit menu; or (3) position the mouse pointer in the highlighted text, press the CTRL key and at the same time drag the mouse pointer (displayed as a block arrow with the word COPY below it) and the accompanying insertion point to the location where you wish the copied data to appear. Release the mouse button and the CTRL key. This is called the drag-and-drop method of copying data.

Undoing a Drag-and-Drop Operation

You can undo a move or copy operation by clicking Undo Drag and Drop on the Edit menu. For example, in Figures 3-52 through 3-54, paragraphs were moved, but the paragraphs in this project should actually remain in their original sequence. Therefore, perform the steps on the next page to undo the drag-and-drop operation.

*Other***Ways**

1. Highlight desired information, on Edit menu click Cut, position insertion point where you wish to move desired information, on Edit menu click Paste

2. Highlight desired information, click Cut button on toolbar, position insertion point where you wish to move desired information, click Paste button on toolbar

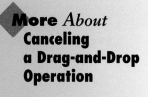

More *About*
**Canceling
a Drag-and-Drop
Operation**

If you wish to cancel a drag-and-drop operation in the middle of the process of copying or moving data, press the ESC key. Works will leave the highlighted text in its original location.

TO UNDO A DRAG-AND-DROP OPERATION

Step 1: Click Edit on the menu bar and point to Undo Drag and Drop.
Step 2: Click Undo Drag and Drop.
Step 3: The text will appear in the report in the same order as it was prior to the drag-and-drop operation.

For the Undo Drag and Drop command to be effective, you must click the command before any other intervening steps occur.

Using the Thesaurus

When writing a research report, you may find instances where you want to replace certain words in the document with words of similar meaning. Such words are called **synonyms**. To do this, you can use the Works **thesaurus**. A thesaurus is a dictionary of synonyms. The Works thesaurus contains 200,000 words.

To illustrate the use of the thesaurus, you are to replace the word, using, in the research report. The word using is found in the third paragraph on page 1. To replace the word using the thesaurus, perform the following steps.

Steps To Use the Thesaurus

1 **Display page 1 of the research report. Scroll down to display the third paragraph. Highlight the word for which you need a synonym (using), click Tools on the menu bar, and point to Thesaurus.**

*The word, using, is highlighted in the research report (Figure 3-55). The mouse pointer points to the **Thesaurus command** on the Tools menu.*

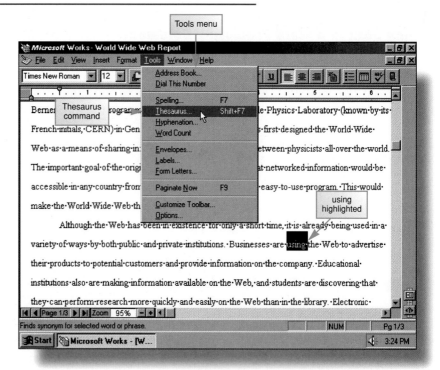

FIGURE 3-55

2 **Click Thesaurus. When the Thesaurus: American English dialog box displays, point to the Replace button.**

Works displays the Thesaurus: American English dialog box (Figure 3-56). In the Meanings list box, Works displays a list of meanings for the word, using. The synonym, utilizing, is highlighted in the Meanings list box and displays in the Replace with synonym text box. This is the synonym Works will insert into the document. Below the Replace with synonym text box is a list of synonyms for the word, using. The word, utilizing, is highlighted. The mouse pointer points to the Replace button.

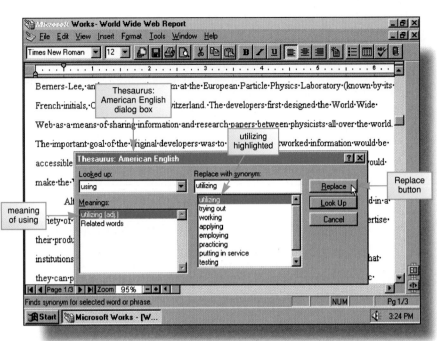

FIGURE 3-56

3 **Click the Replace button in the Thesaurus: American English dialog box.**

Works replaces the word, using, in the document with the word, utilizing (Figure 3-57).

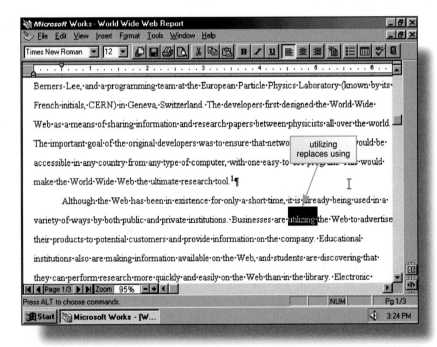

FIGURE 3-57

When using the Works thesaurus, you can click words from either the Meanings list box or the Replace with synonym list box. Clicking the Look Up button in the Thesaurus: American English dialog box will display additional words in the thesaurus.

▶**Other****Ways**

1. Highlight desired word, press SHIFT+F7, click desired synonym, click OK button

Counting Words

Works provides the capability to count the number of words in your document. When the words are counted, the count includes the words in the headers, footers, and footnotes. You also can count only the words in a highlighted portion of a document. To count all the words in a document, perform the following steps.

Steps To Use Word Count

1 **Position the insertion point anywhere in the document. Click Tools on the menu bar and point to Word Count.**

The Tools menu displays and the mouse pointer points to the Word Count command (Figure 3-58).

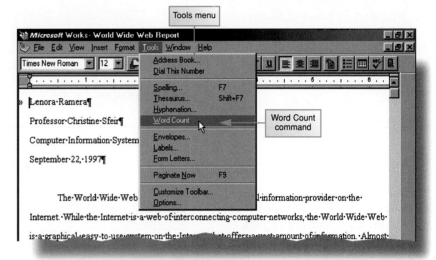

FIGURE 3-58

2 **Click Word Count.**

Works displays the Microsoft Works dialog box that contains the number of words in the document (Figure 3-59).

3 **Click the OK button in the Microsoft Works dialog box to remove it from the screen.**

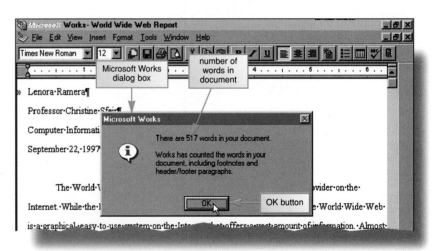

FIGURE 3-59

To count the number of words in the research report excluding the heading information and the footnotes, highlight the entire document beginning with the first paragraph and ending with the last paragraph, and then click Word Count on the Tools menu.

Checking Spelling, Saving, and Printing the Research Report

After you enter and edit the report, check the spelling of the research report using the Spelling Checker button on the toolbar. When you create documents, you should, as a final step, check the spelling to ensure no errors have occurred.

After checking the spelling, save the document on a floppy disk inserted in drive A, and then print the document using the Print button on the toolbar. The completed research report appears in Figure 3-60.

Ramera 3

NOTES

[1]William Peterson, *Beginner's Guide to Surfing the World Wide Web* (New York: Computer Network Press, 1997) 125-130.

[2]T. S. Cobb, "Managing Web Information Services on the World Wide Web." http://www.university.edu/home/cis.html (5 September 1997).

[3]USA Wireservice, "Designing Home Pages on the World Wide Web." *Daily News*, 19 August 1997, Morning ed., Sec. Business: 3+.

Ramera 2

The World Wide Web consists of a large collection of documents that are stored on computers around the world. These documents, known as Web pages, provide an unlimited amount of information and are connected, or linked, to each other so you can move easily from one to another. These pages can include graphics, sound, and video.[2]

A Web site is a business, government agency, or university that stores Web pages you can view. A home page is typically the starting point for a World Wide Web site. For this reason, many sites try to make their home page as spectacular as possible by combining eye-catching graphics and specially formatted text.[3]

In the near future, it is anticipated that the growth on the Web will be phenomenal. With its popularity, benefits, and ease of use, the World Wide Web is expanding rapidly into a global marketplace.

Ramera 1

Lenora Ramera

Professor Christine Sfeir

Computer Information Systems 201

September 22, 1997

World Wide Web

The World Wide Web is the newest and most powerful information provider on the Internet. While the Internet is a web of interconnecting computer networks, the World Wide Web is a graphical, easy-to-use system on the Internet that offers a vast amount of information. Almost every large corporation, university, government, organization, and business around the world has a presence on the Web.

The World Wide Web was first developed in 1990 by a physics researcher, Tim Berners-Lee, and a programming team at the European Particle Physics Laboratory (known by its French initials, CERN) in Geneva, Switzerland. The developers first designed the World Wide Web as a means of sharing information and research papers between physicists all over the world. The important goal of the original developers was to ensure that networked information would be accessible in any country from any type of computer, with one easy-to-use program. This would make the World Wide Web the ultimate research tool.[1]

Although the Web has been in existence for only a short time, it is already being used in a variety of ways by both public and private institutions. Businesses are utilizing the Web to advertise their products to potential customers and provide information on the company. Educational institutions also are making information available on the Web, and students are discovering that they can perform research more quickly and easily on the Web than in the library. Electronic magazines and newspapers are being delivered on the Web. You can make travel plans, look up the latest stock quotes, apply for a job, electronically visit a museum, research the latest health issue, and make new friends on the World Wide Web. As a system, the Web is governed and regulated cooperatively without actual laws. It is operated based on codes of individual conduct and ethic.

FIGURE 3-60

Tables in Word Processing Documents

After reviewing the research report shown in Figure 3-60 on the previous page, the next step is to add a table to the report to depict the growth projections for World Wide Web sites. Tables provide a method of presenting information that may be conveniently displayed in columns and rows. Figure 3-61 illustrates the table.

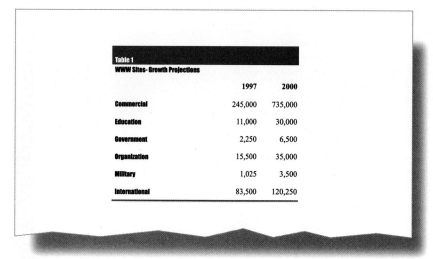

Table 1		
WWW Sites- Growth Projections		
	1997	2000
Commercial	245,000	735,000
Education	11,000	30,000
Government	2,250	6,500
Organization	15,500	35,000
Military	1,025	3,500
International	83,500	120,250

FIGURE 3-61

When writing research reports, use the following general guidelines for creating a table.

1. Begin the table with the table heading. The heading should start with the word Table and be followed by the number of the table. The first table should be labeled Table 1.
2. The next line should contain the title of the table.
3. Column labels should appear on the next line, followed by row labels and the data comprising the table.
4. The table should be double-spaced.
5. The columns should be wide enough to display the information in a visually appealing form that can be easily read.
6. The table should be centered horizontally on the document.
7. A blank line should separate the table from the text, both at the beginning of the table and at the end of the table.

It is important to follow these guidelines when creating a table for use in a research report.

Creating the Table

Works provides several ways in which you can create a table. One method uses tab stops placed at locations on the ruler to allow information to be typed in columns. The other method uses the **Insert Table button** on the toolbar. This method allows a table to be placed within the word processing document for entering data in columns and rows. The table in the research report will be created using the Insert Table button on the toolbar.

Works provides twenty-eight predefined formats you can apply to the table. These predefined formats enable you to format a table in a variety of styles without going through a series of individual steps to select color, font and font styles, borders, and so forth.

When you use the Insert Table button to insert a table in a word processing document, first specify the number of rows and columns in the table and then specify a predesigned table format. Works inserts the table into the word processing document. Fill in the rows and columns with your data.

Before creating the table, you should determine where in the report the table will be placed and create space for the table. The table in the research report in this project is to be placed following the second paragraph on page 2 and is to be preceded by a sentence explaining the contents of the table.

Thus, the first steps in creating a table are to enter an explanatory sentence, create space in the word processing document for the table, and insert the table into the document. To accomplish these tasks, complete the following steps.

Steps **To Create Space for a Table and Insert a Table**

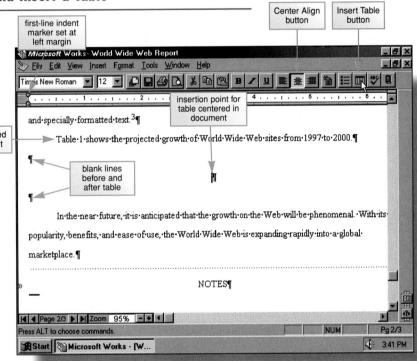

FIGURE 3-62

1 **Use the scroll arrows to position the text in the document so the last line of the second paragraph on page 2 (the line ending with footnote reference number 3) displays at the top of the screen. Then place the insertion point at the end of the line following the footnote reference number and press the ENTER key. Type** Table 1 shows the projected growth of World Wide Web sites from 1997 to 2000. **Press the ENTER key once. Move the first-line indent marker to the left margin on the ruler. Press the ENTER key two additional times. Position the insertion point in front of the second paragraph mark and click the Center Align button on the toolbar. Point to the Insert Table button on the toolbar.**

The sentence introducing the table displays near the top of the screen (Figure 3-62). The insertion point and paragraph mark for the table are centered in the document. The first paragraph mark provides space before the table. The last paragraph mark provides space after the table. The mouse pointer points to the Insert Table button on the toolbar.

2 Click the Insert Table button on the toolbar.

Works displays the Insert Table dialog box (Figure 3-63). The number 5 displays in the Number of rows text box and the number 3 displays in the Number of columns text box by default. This instructs Works to insert a table with five rows and three columns. The Select a format list box displays a list of predesigned styles. You can click the down scroll arrow to display additional styles. The Plain style is the default format. A sample of this style displays in the Example box. The Example box shows how the table will display based on the selection in the Select a format list box.

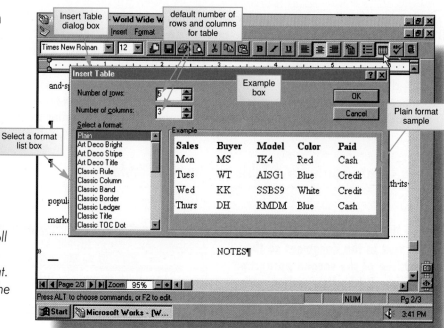

FIGURE 3-63

3 Click the Number of rows up arrow four times so that the number 9 displays in the Number of rows text box. In the Select a format list box, use the down scroll arrow to view Prestige Rule format. Click Prestige Rule. Point to the OK button.

The number 9 displays in the Number of rows text box and the number 3 displays in the Number of columns text box (Figure 3-64). This information instructs Works to insert a table with nine rows and three columns in the document. Works displays a sample of Prestige Rule in the Sample box. The mouse pointer points to the OK button.

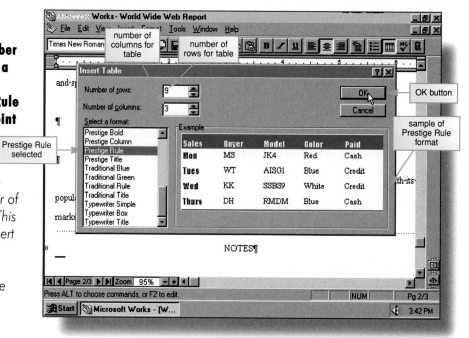

FIGURE 3-64

4 **Click the OK button in the Insert Table dialog box.**

Works inserts the table in the document and extends the table from the left margin to the right margin (Figure 3-65). A solid border surrounds the table indicating the table is active and you can enter data into the table. The upper left cell of the table is selected and the insertion point displays in the cell. Works applies the predefined format style, Prestige Rule, to the table. The toolbar now displays the buttons associated with a spreadsheet; the Font and Font Size boxes change; and the menu bar changes to contain spreadsheet commands. Thus, within the word processing document, you have the capability of using the full power of the Works Spreadsheet tool to create a table. Notice the right side of the table has scrolled off the screen.

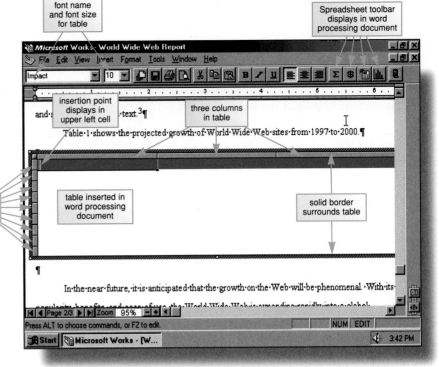

FIGURE 3-65

Other Ways

1. On Insert menu click Table, enter desired rows and columns, click desired format, click OK button

The table consisting of three **columns** and nine **rows** organized in **cells**, like a spreadsheet displays. A cell is a rectangular box located at the intersection of a column and a row.

When creating a table, information is entered into specific cells in the table. To enter data into a cell, you must first highlight the cell. When you highlight a cell, the cell is outlined by a dark border. In Figure 3-65, the upper left cell in the table is highlighted. A variety of methods exist to highlight a cell, including clicking the cell, pressing the arrow keys, and pressing the TAB key.

Entering Data into the Table

The next step is to enter data into the table. This is accomplished by highlighting the cell in which you want to enter data and typing the data. One method to highlight a cell is to click the cell. An alternative method is to use the arrow keys that are located to the left of the numeric keypad. After you press an arrow key, the adjacent cell in the direction of the arrow on the key becomes the highlighted cell. Do not press the ENTER key. The ENTER key is used to begin new paragraphs within a cell.

To enter the table title and the column labels into the table, perform the steps on the next page.

More *About* Tables

To select a single cell in a table, click anywhere inside the cell. To select an entire column, click the column's top border. To add a row or column to the middle of a table, highlight the row below or the column to the right, right-click the selection, and then click Insert Row or Insert Column on the context-sensitive menu.

Steps To Enter a Title and Column Labels Into a Table

1 **If necessary, highlight the upper left cell in the table by clicking the cell. Type** Table 1 **in the cell.**

The entry, Table 1, displays in the row 1 column 1 cell of the table (Figure 3-66). The text displays in white 10-point Impact font.

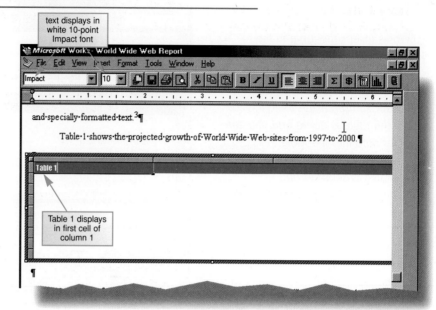

FIGURE 3-66

2 **Press the DOWN ARROW key, and then type** WWW Sites - Growth Projections **in the row 2 column 1 cell of the table.**

When you press the DOWN ARROW key, Works confirms the entry in the row 1 column 1 cell and left-aligns the text in the cell (Figure 3-67). Because you pressed the DOWN ARROW key, the cell immediately below the first cell becomes the highlighted cell. As you type, the table title displays in the cell. Notice the entire table displays on the screen.

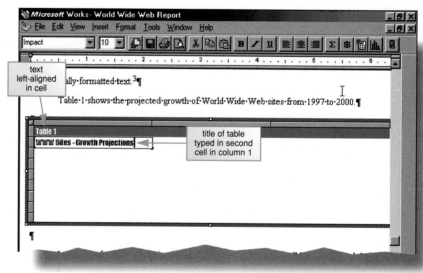

FIGURE 3-67

3 **Press the DOWN ARROW key. Press the TAB key once to position the mouse pointer in the row 3 column 2 cell. Type** 1997.

Works confirms the entry in the row 2 column 1 cell (Figure 3-68). The column label, 1997, displays in the row 3 column 2 cell.

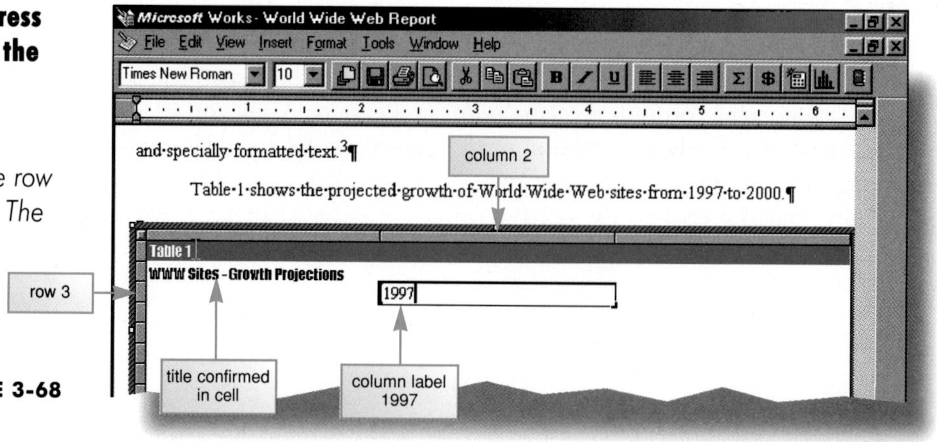

FIGURE 3-68

4 **Press the TAB key. Type the column label, 2000, in the row 3 column 3 cell. Press the TAB key.**

When you press the TAB key, the entry in the in row 3 column 2 cell is confirmed and is right-aligned in the cell because 1997 is a numeric value (Figure 3-69). The value you typed displays in the row 3 column 3 cell. The row 4 column 1 cell is highlighted.

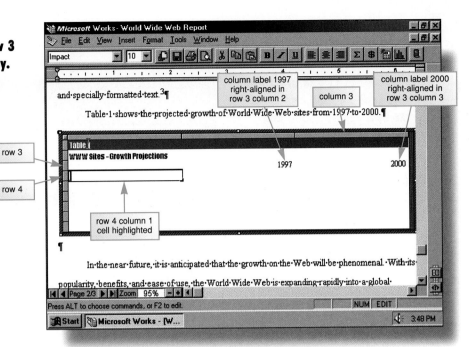

FIGURE 3-69

When you confirm an entry in a cell, a series of events occurs. First, when non-numeric data, called **text**, is confirmed, Works positions the text left-aligned in the cell. When you confirm the entry of numeric data into a cell, the data is right-aligned in the cell. Second, when you confirm an entry using the arrow keys or the TAB key, the adjacent cell is then highlighted.

Correcting a Mistake while Typing

If you make a mistake while typing and notice the error before confirming the entry, use the BACKSPACE key to erase all the characters back to and including the ones that are incorrect. The insertion point will indicate where the next character you type will display. Then type the remainder of the entry correctly.

To cancel the entire entry before confirming the entry, press the ESC key.

If you see an error in data you have already entered into a cell, highlight the cell, use the mouse pointer to highlight the text, and then retype the entire entry.

Entering Row Labels and Numeric Data into the Table

The next step in developing the table is to enter the row labels and numeric data into the table. Numbers can include the digits zero through nine and any of the following characters: + - ( ) , / . $ %. If a cell entry contains any other character from the keyboard, Works interprets the entry as text and treats it accordingly.

To enter row labels and the data into the table, perform the steps on the next page.

Steps **To Enter Row Labels and Numeric Data Into a Table**

1 **Type** Commercial **and press the TAB key. Type** 245000 **and press the TAB key. Type** 735000 **and press the TAB key.**

The row label and numeric values display in row 4 of the table (Figure 3-70).

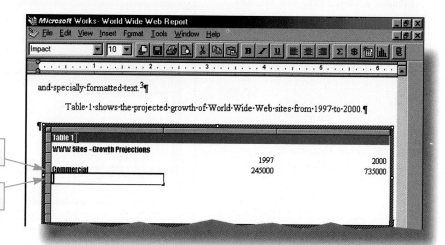

data entered in row 4

row 5 column 1 cell highlighted

FIGURE 3-70

2 **Type** Education. **Press the TAB key. Continue entering the appropriate data in each cell using techniques previously explained as shown in Figure 3-71. After typing the value in the last cell, do not press the TAB key.**

You have now entered all the information required for the table (Figure 3-71). The table consisting of three columns and nine rows displays in the word processing document.

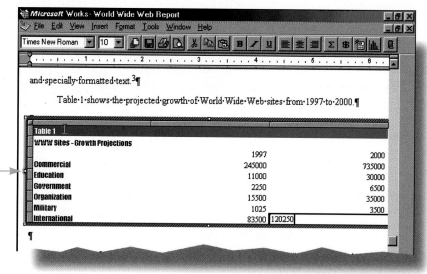

all data entered in table

FIGURE 3-71

3 **Click outside the table.**

When you click outside the table, Works removes the solid border from the table and confirms the entry in the last cell in the table (Figure 3-72). The Word Processor toolbar and menu bar display.

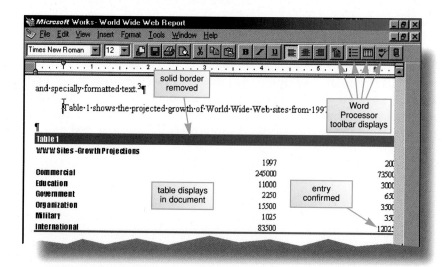

solid border removed

Word Processor toolbar displays

table displays in document

entry confirmed

FIGURE 3-72

Changing Column Width

When you insert a table in a document, Works automatically extends the table from the left margin to the right margin and adjusts the width of the columns to the best fit. Because the table you inserted contains three columns, Works set the column widths to 29. Approximately 28 average-width letters of the alphabet, numbers, or special characters can be placed in a column with a width of 29. The column widths of column 2 and column 3 should be decreased to 12. To change the width of column 2 and column 3 in the table to 12, perform the following steps.

 Steps **To Change Column Width**

1 **Position the mouse pointer in the table and double-click to activate the table. Then, position the mouse pointer in the row 1 column 2 cell and drag through the row 1 column 3 cell. Click Format on the menu bar and point to Column Width.**

When you double-click the table, the Spreadsheet menu bar, toolbar, and solid border around the table display (Figure 3-73). Works high-lights the row 1 column 2 cell and the row 1 column 3 cell. The Format menu displays and the mouse pointer points to the Column Width command.

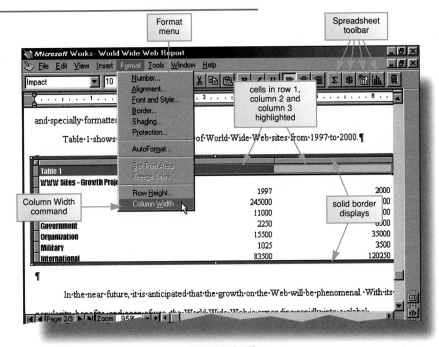

FIGURE 3-73

2 **Click Column Width. When the Column Width dialog box displays, type 12 in the Column width text box. Point to the OK button.**

The Column Width dialog box displays (Figure 3-74). The mouse pointer points to the OK button.

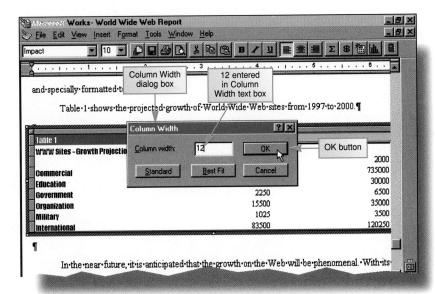

FIGURE 3-74

3 Click the OK button in the Column Width dialog box.

The table displays with the width of column 2 and column 3 decreased to 12 (Figure 3-75). The table is centered between the margins because you clicked the Center Align button earlier in the project.

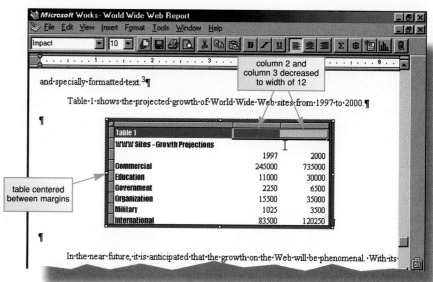

FIGURE 3-75

Increasing Row Height

As specified in the guidelines for creating a table, the table should be double-spaced, that is, each line of text should be separated by a blank line. It is recommended, therefore, that you increase the height of each row to in effect create a blank line between each line of text and/or numbers.

To increase the row height to achieve the appearance of double-spacing in the table, complete the following steps.

Steps To Increase Row Height

1 Drag row 1 column 1 cell through the row 9 column 1 cell. Click Format on the menu bar and point to Row Height.

Works highlights the cells in rows 1 through 9 (Figure 3-76). The first cell in the highlighted row has a border around it. The Format menu displays and the mouse pointer points to the Row Height command.

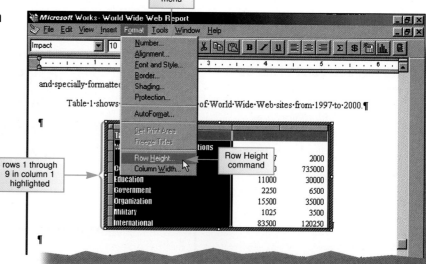

FIGURE 3-76

2 **Click Row Height. When the Format Row Height dialog box displays, type 26 in the Row Height text box. Then point to the OK button.**

The Format Row Height dialog box displays (Figure 3-77). Initially, the box contains the number 12. The 12 indicates a standard row height that will properly display 10 point Impact fonts. You more than double the height of the row when you type 26 in the Row Height text box. The mouse pointer points to the OK button.

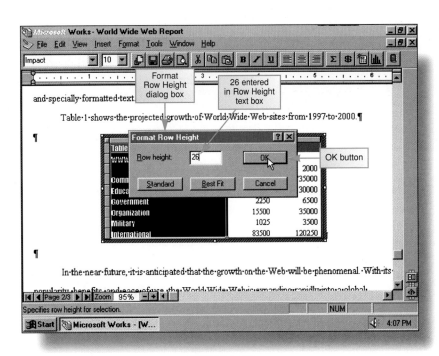

FIGURE 3-77

3 **Click the OK button in the Format Row Height dialog box. Click any cell in the table to remove the highlight.**

Works displays the table with the row height increased (Figure 3-78). A blank area displays above each line, so the table appears to be double-spaced.

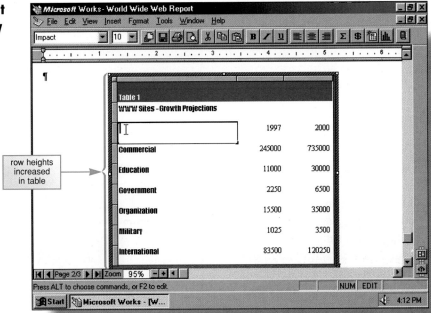

FIGURE 3-78

Other Ways

1. Highlight row 3, on Format menu click Row Height, type desired height in Row Height text box, click OK button

Formatting the Table

After typing the information comprising the table and adjusting the column widths and row heights, it is frequently desirable to format the table. Formatting involves such tasks as inserting dollar signs, commas, and decimal points in the numeric data entered; changing font styles; and similar tasks.

In the research report, you should bold the column labels in row 3 and insert commas in the numbers so they are easier to read.

Complete the following steps to bold the text and format the numbers to display with commas.

Steps **To Bold Text and Format Numbers with Commas**

1 **Highlight the column labels in row 3 by positioning the mouse pointer in the row 3 column 2 cell and dragging across to the row 3 column 3 cell. Click the Bold button on the toolbar.**

Works highlights the column labels in row 3 and displays the text in bold (Figure 3-79).

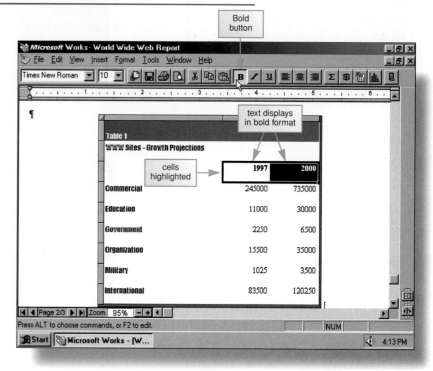

FIGURE 3-79

2 **Highlight the numbers in the table by positioning the mouse pointer in the row 4 column 2 cell and dragging across and down to the row 9 column 3 cell. Point to the selection and right-click. When the context-sensitive menu displays, point to Format.**

Works highlights the cells and displays the context-sensitive menu (Figure 3-80). The mouse pointer points to the Format command on the context-sensitive menu.

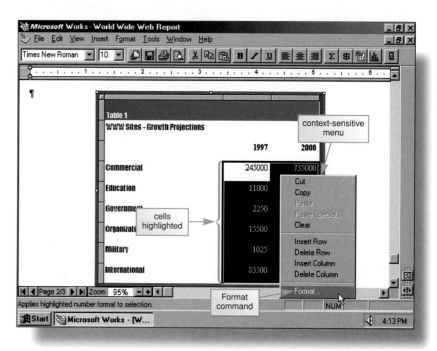

FIGURE 3-80

3 **Click Format. When the Format Cells dialog box displays, ensure the Number sheet displays, and then click Comma in the Format box. Type** 0 **in the Decimal places text box. Point to the OK button.**

The Format Cells dialog box displays (Figure 3-81). The Comma option button is selected. The value 0 displays in the Decimal places text box and the mouse pointer points to the OK button. A sample of the format displays in the Sample box.

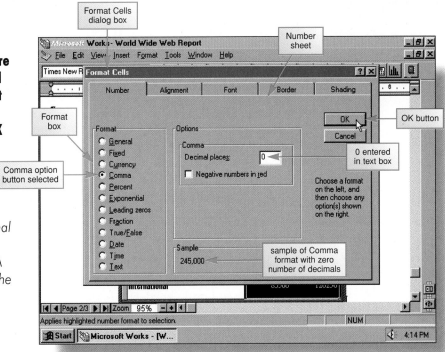

FIGURE 3-81

4 **Click the OK button in the Format Cells dialog box. Click anywhere outside the table in the word processing document.**

The table border disappears and the table in the word processing document displays with the numbers formatted using commas (Figure 3-82).

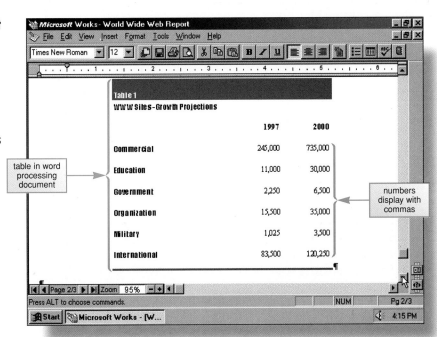

FIGURE 3-82

The research report is now complete with the table as illustrated in Figure 3-1 on page W 3.5. Save the completed research report and table using the Save button on the toolbar.

Other Ways

1. On Format menu click Number, click Comma, type 0 in Decimal places text box, click OK button

Objects and Object Linking and Embedding (OLE) 2.0

Switching back and forth between the word processing document and the table uses a method available in Works 4.0 and Windows 95 called **object linking and embedding** (**OLE**, pronounced oh-lay). The version of OLE being used is 2.0. OLE 2.0 allows you to use one software application, such as the Spreadsheet application, to create an object that resides within a document created by another software application, such as the Word Processor. In this case, the Spreadsheet application was used to create the table, which is an **object** that resides within the word processing document.

You can highlight an object, such as the table, at any time by clicking anywhere in the object. When you do so, the object displays with a dotted line around it and resize handles on the corners and sides (see Figure 3-83). When positioned on the border of a highlighted object, the mouse pointer changes to a block arrow with the word DRAG below it, indicating you can drag the object to other locations within the word processing document.

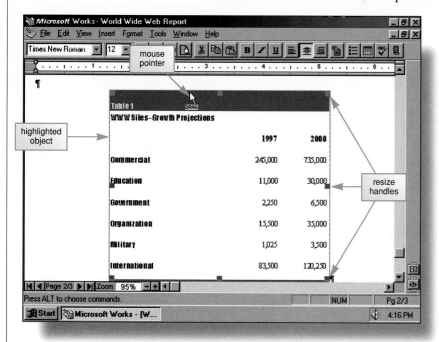

FIGURE 3-83

Because the object was created using another software application, in this case the Spreadsheet application, you must use that application to make any changes in the object. For example, if you wanted to change the row label, Commercial, to Business, you would have to make the change using the Spreadsheet application. To invoke the application used to create an object, such as the Spreadsheet application used to create the table, place the mouse pointer anywhere within the object and double-click. The document and the object remain on the screen, but the menu bar and the toolbar change to the commands and buttons available with the application that created the object. Changing the menu bar and the toolbar when the object is double-clicked is called **visual editing** when using OLE 2.0.

After you have made any desired changes, click anywhere in the document except on the object to change the menu bar and the toolbar back to those for the application that made the document in which the object resides.

When the object is highlighted, it displays with a dotted line and resize handles around it. The object can be resized by dragging the resize handles.

To delete an object, highlight the object and press the DELETE key on the keyboard, or click Clear on the Edit menu or the context-sensitive menu.

Project Summary

When you master the skills presented in Project 3, you are capable of writing a research report using the recommended style of the Modern Language Association. In this project, you learned how to set top, bottom, left, and right margins using the Page Setup command on the File menu. Next, you learned to create a header for each page using the header (H) line at the top of a document in Normal page view.

When writing the body of the report, you learned how to create a footnote and create a manual page break.

To assist in editing a research report, you learned the use of the Go To, Find, and Replace commands, and how to use the drag-and-drop method to move a paragraph. You also learned to use the Works thesaurus and how to use the Word Count command on the Tools menu to determine the number of words in a document. To conclude the project, you learned how to incorporate a table in a word processing document using OLE 2.0.

What You Should Know

Having completed this project, you should now be able to perform the following tasks:

▶ Bold Text and Format Numbers with Commas *(W 3.50)*

▶ Center a Report Title *(W 3.14)*

▶ Change Column Width in a Table *(W 3.47)*

▶ Close the Footnote Pane *(W 3.22)*

▶ Create a Custom Zoom *(W 3.17)*

▶ Create a Footnote *(W 3.20)*

▶ Create a Header *(W 3.11)*

▶ Create Space for a Table *(W 3.41)*

▶ Enter a Title and Column Labels into a Table *(W 3.44)*

▶ Enter Row Labels and Numeric Data into a Table *(W 3.46)*

▶ Enter Text *(W 3.19, W 3.23)*

▶ Increase Row Height *(W 3.48)*

▶ Insert a Manual Page Break and Center a Word on the New Page *(W 3.25)*

▶ Insert a Table *(W 3.41)*

▶ Move Text Using Drag and Drop *(W 3.34)*

▶ Print Footnotes at the End of a Document *(W 3.9)*

▶ Save a Document *(W 3.23)*

▶ Scroll the Screen Horizontally *(W 3.10)*

▶ Set Margins *(W 3.7)*

▶ Start Works *(W 3.9)*

▶ Undo a Drag-and-Drop Operation *(W 3.36)*

▶ Undo Editing *(W 3.32)*

▶ Use the Find Command *(W 3.28)*

▶ Use First-line Indent *(W 3.16)*

▶ Use the Go To Command *(W 3.26)*

▶ Use the Replace Command *(W 3.30)*

▶ Use the Thesaurus *(W 3.36)*

▶ Use Word Count *(W 3.38)*

Test Your Knowledge

1 True/False

Instructions: Circle T if the statement is true or F if the statement is false.

T F 1. A research report should have a 1.25-inch left margin and 1.25-inch right margin, which are the Works default values for left and right margins.

T F 2. In a multi-page document, text typed on the header (H) line displays on the screen in Normal view only on the first page of the document.

T F 3. To insert the page number in a header in a word processing document, type *page* in the header (H) line.

T F 4. When using placeholders in a header or a footer, you can type any text, spaces, or punctuation before or after the placeholder to produce the required output.

T F 5. The zoom size of a document affects how the document will look when it is printed.

T F 6. In Normal view, you view footnotes in a footnote pane.

T F 7. The only character that may be used to identify a footnote in a report is a raised number called a superscript.

T F 8. You can use the drag-and-drop method to copy a paragraph and move it to another location.

T F 9. Use the Word Count command to count the total number of words in a document, including headers, footers, and footnotes.

T F 10. To insert a table in a word processing document, click the Insert Table button on the toolbar.

2 Multiple Choice

Instructions: Circle the correct response.

1. To set the top, bottom, left, and right margins in a word processing document, use the _____.
   a. Margins command on the File menu
   b. Paragraph command on the Format menu
   c. Header command on the File menu
   d. Page Setup command on the File menu

2. The Header command is found on the _____ menu.
   a. File
   b. Edit
   c. View
   d. Format

3. In Normal view, text typed in the header (H) line will _____.
   a. display at the top of each screen
   b. display at the top of each screen only when there is a page break mark on the screen
   c. display at the top of page 1 only
   d. display at the top of each page

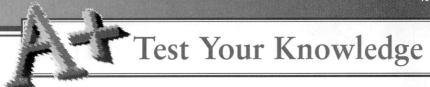

4. Dragging the first-line indent marker on the ruler one-half inch to the right will cause _____.

   a. the first line of each paragraph to be indented one-half inch if you press the TAB key

   b. all lines typed to be indented one-half inch

   c. the first line of each paragraph to be indented one-half inch

   d. all lines typed to be indented one-half inch except the first line of each paragraph

5. To set the spacing of a document to double spacing, use the _____ keys.

   a. CTRL+2

   b. SHIFT+2

   c. CTRL+SHIFT+2

   d. CTRL+ENTER+2

6. When you click Footnote on the Insert menu in Normal view, _____.

   a. a Footnote dialog box displays in the footnote pane

   b. a Footnote dialog box displays in the center of the screen allowing you to select a numbered footnote or special character

   c. a footnote pane appears at the top of the screen allowing you to type the footnote

   d. a footnote pane appears at the end of the document allowing you to type the footnote

7. To insert a manual page break in a document, press the _____ keys.

   a. CTRL+ENTER

   b. CTRL+SHIFT

   c. CTRL+P

   d. SHIFT+P

8. To replace one or more words at a time in a document with another word or words use the _____ command.

   a. Find .

   b. Replace

   c. Go To

   d. Thesaurus

9. Use the drag-and-drop method to _____.

   a. copy paragraphs from one location to another location in a document

   b. move paragraphs from one location to another location in a document

   c. move sentences from one location to another location in a document

   d. a, b, and c

10. To insert a table in a word processing document, click the _____.

   a. Spreadsheet button in the Works Task Launcher dialog box

   b. Insert Table button on the toolbar

   c. Insert Spreadsheet button on the toolbar

   d. Object button on the toolbar

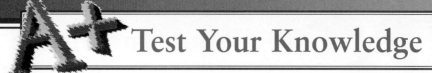

Test Your Knowledge

3 Fill In

Instructions: In the spaces provided, explain what happens when you click the options or buttons identified by the arrows in Figure 3-83.

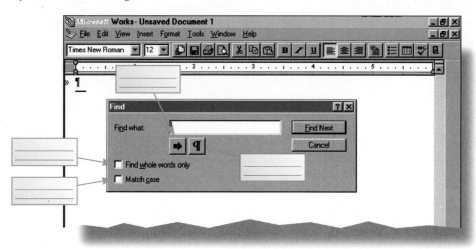

FIGURE 3-84

4 Fill In

Instructions: In Figure 3-85, arrows point to the major components of a table. Identify the various parts of the table in the space provided.

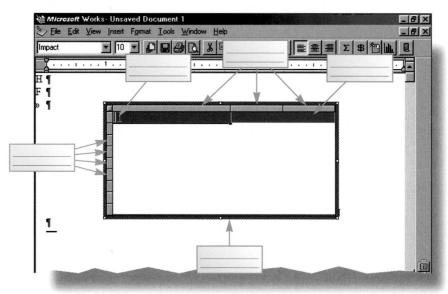

FIGURE 3-85

? Use Help

1 Reviewing Project Activities

Instructions: Use your computer to perform the following tasks to obtain experience using online Help.

1. Start the Microsoft Works Word Processor tool.
2. Display the Help window to the right of the document window. Click the Index button below the Help window to display the Help Topics: Microsoft Works dialog box.
3. Click the Index tab in the Help Topics: Microsoft Works dialog box.
4. Type `headers for text documents: creating` in the 2 Click the Index entry you want list box.
5. Click the topic, To add a header or footer WP.
6. Read the numbered procedure on the topic, To add a header or footer, in the Step-by-Step sheet. Print this topic by clicking the Print this topic icon at the bottom of the numbered procedure.
7. Click the More Info tab. On the More Info sheet, click Overview. Read the Overview topic. Print the document. Click the Done button to close the Overview dialog box.
8. Click the Quick Tour button on the More Info sheet. When the Works Quick Tour: Headers and footers window displays, read the information. To continue, click the right arrow button located at the bottom of the window. To close the window, click the Done button.
9. Click the Close button in the application window to exit Works.

2 Expanding on the Basics

Instructions: Use Works online Help to better understand the topics listed below. Print the topic or topics that substantiate your answer. If there is no Print this topic icon, then answer the question on a separate piece of paper.

1. Using the key term, *tables: creating blank tables for new data*, and the Index sheet in the Help Topics: Microsoft Works dialog box, answer the following questions.
   a. Explain how to add a column to a table.
   b. Explain how to add a row to a table.
   c. List the steps necessary to change the size of a table.
   d. List the steps necessary to change the format of a table.

Apply Your Knowledge

1 Using the Word Count Command

Instructions: Start the Works Word Processor. Open the word processing document with the filename Research Report on the Student floppy disk that accompanies this book. This file contains three paragraphs of a research report. After opening the document, complete the following tasks.

1. Use the Word Count command to count the number of words in the first two paragraphs. Begin the count starting with the report title. How many words are in the first two paragraphs?
   _____

2. Use the Word Count command to count the number of words in the third paragraph of the report. How many words are in the second paragraph? _____

3. Use the Word Count command to count the number of words in the document. How many words are in the document? _____

4. Use the Word Count command to count the number of words in the document excluding the header. How many words are in the document excluding the header?_____

In the Lab

1 Preparing a Research Report

Part 1: Typing the Research Report

Problem: You have been asked by a friend to retype the research report shown in Figure 3-86 using the Modern Language Association's style for writing research reports as illustrated in this project.

Instructions: Type the research report using 12-point Times New Roman font. The student's name is Matthew Hill. The professor's name is Ranger M. Long. The class is Management Systems 201. Use the current date in the report heading.

After you type the research report, save the document on a floppy disk. Use the filename, Temporary Workers Report. Retain the disk for use in Part 2 of this lab assignment. Print the research report. Follow directions from your instructor for turning in the assignment.

In the Lab

Temporary Workers in the Workforce

The use of temporary workers in the United States workforce has nearly doubled over the past five years from 1.2 million to more than two million; a record of job creation that beats just about every other industry in the country.

The temporary help industry has been functioning as an agency bringing workers and companies together since the early 1900's. In the beginning, most of the people filling temporary positions were filling low wage clerical, secretarial, and light industrial blue collar positions. Today, some of the fastest growing segments of the temporary job market are in professional and technical fields. These high skill areas already make up about 20% of the total temporary worker payroll. It is predicted that the growth in the low wage clerical and administrative temp jobs will slow, but the rate of creation of higher paid positions will increase.[1]

Temporary workers are actually employees of a temporary agency who are recruited, trained, assigned, and paid by the temporary agency. This temporary agency has the responsibility to pay all payroll and social security taxes for the temporary employees and to arrange for fringe benefits, vacation pay, and 401K plans.

Temporary work can be good for many people seeking even full-time employment. These workers can experience a number of positions to gain new skills that are currently needed in the workforce. At the same time, the temporary employee can make valuable networking contacts and demonstrate their talents to a number of potential employers. Many temporary employees find that their jobs lead to full-time employment. Indeed, approximately 38% of temporary workers are offered full-time jobs as a result of a temporary assignment.[2]

For many people in the job market for a full-time position, temporary work can relieve some of the financial and emotional stress of a job search. Working as a temporary employee while looking for the ideal job relieves enough financial pressure to give the worker better bargaining power to hold out for higher wages or a better job.

Working as a temporary employee means being able to come into a new work environment with unfamiliar surroundings and be productive immediately. Not all people have the necessary skills to catch on quickly to unfamiliar material, office procedures, and work styles. Because you are constantly changing work sites, feeling part of a team will be difficult to attain.

In today's economy of downsizing and restructuring, if you find yourself out of a job, give serious consideration to registering with several temporary agencies. You just may temp yourself to a new job.

---

[1]Charles W. Jaspers, *The Direction of Temporary Workers in America* (New York: Communications Publishing Company, 1996) 123-150.

[2]John C. Masters, *From Temp to Full-Time in No Time* (San Francisco: Quick Press Publishing Company, 1997) 95-102.

FIGURE 3-86

(continued)

In the Lab

Preparing a Research Report *(continued)*

Part 2: Editing the Research Report

Problem: You are to edit the research report you typed in Part 1 of this lab assignment. Follow the instructions below to edit the report.

Instructions: Use the Replace command to replace the word, stress, in the research report with the word, pressures, where appropriate. Use the thesaurus to replace the word, valuable, in the fourth paragraph with a word recommended by the thesaurus. Use the drag-and-drop method to place the sixth paragraph in the research report immediately after the fourth paragraph. Check the spelling of the entire document, and then use the Word Count command to count the number of words in the research report.

After you edit the research report, save the document on a floppy disk. Use the filename, Temporary Workers Report - Edited. Print the research report. Write the total number of words in the research report above the student name on the report. Follow directions from your instructor for turning in the assignment.

Part 3: Adding a Table

Problem: You are to insert the following table in the research report.

Instructions: The table should be inserted after the sixth paragraph. Format the table using the Art Deco Bright format. Label the table Table 1. Include the following sentence before the table: Table 1 lists the top four temporary agencies in the United States and the number of temporary workers placed by each agency.

Table 1	
TEMPORARY AGENCY	NUMBER OF EMPLOYEES
Hire A Temp	175,890
Tech Temps	162,700
Employees on the Move	157,450
People Handlers	125,450

The table should be created in the word processing document using the style presented in this project.

After you add the table to the research report, save the document on a floppy disk. Use the filename, Temporary Workers Report - Final. Print the research report.

Follow directions from your instructor for turning in the assignment.

2 Preparing a Research Report

Part 1: Typing the Research Report

Problem: You have been asked by a friend to retype the research report in Figure 3-87 using the Modern Language Association's style for writing research reports as illustrated in this project.

Instructions: Type the research report using 12-point Times New Roman font. The student's name is John A. Greenwald. The professor's name is Susan Q. White. The class is Introduction to Computers 201. Use the current date in the report heading.

After you type the research report, save the document on a floppy disk. Use the filename, Computer Viruses Report. Retain the disk for use in Part 2 of this lab assignment. Print the research report. Follow directions from your instructor for turning in the assignment.

In the Lab

The Threat of Computer Viruses

The computer virus is a threat to the effective use of computers in homes and businesses. A computer virus is a computer program that is specifically designed to become part of an operating system or an application program and adversely affect computer processing when executed.

Computer viruses have only been in existence for the past ten years. Today, with the rising popularity of the Internet, viruses of all types are traveling in the fast lane of the superhighway. Strains multiply as more computer users trade disks, download files from the Internet, and join computer networks. Even corporate networks and electronic mail provide fertile breeding grounds for the computer viruses. Once you run the program on your computer, a virus program may be stored on your disk. If you give a copy of the program that contains the virus to another person, the virus is effectively transmitted from one computer to another.

Research indicates that Western countries lost almost $1 billion last year from viruses that brought down systems and destroyed data. American companies alone, lost at least $100 million last year from viruses.[1]

Viruses may be activated based upon a date or the time. Viruses of this type allow application programs to execute properly until a predetermined date or time of the day. Then, the virus will execute, causing the program or data to be adversely affected in some manner. A number of programs on the market can scan software prior to execution to detect virus instructions placed in the software. These are called anti-virus programs.[2]

Today, many corporations designing anti-virus programs are working on the next frontier in the virus world: They are creating an immune strategy for eradicating viruses. Researchers hope the new system, different from existing software that relies largely on fighting known viruses, will be available in about two years.[3]

All programs obtained from any source should be scanned for a virus with an anti-virus program to protect your computer system.

---

[1]William G. Daniels, *The Destructive Nature of Computer Viruses* (New York: Computer Press, 1996) 15.

[2]John D. Carpenter, *Introduction to Computer System Security* (San Francisco: Network Press, 1995) 56.

[3]Susan Lee Briginton, *Inoculating Computer Systems* (Boston: Computer Publishing Company, 1996) 125.

FIGURE 3-87

(continued)

In the Lab

Preparing a Research Report *(continued)*

Part 2: Editing the Research Report

Problem: You are to edit the research report you typed in Part 1 of this lab assignment. Follow the instructions below to edit the report.

Instructions: Use the Replace command to replace the word, virus, in the research report with the words, computer virus, where appropriate. Use the thesaurus to replace the word, indicates, in the third paragraph with a word recommended by the thesaurus. Use the drag-and-drop method to place the third paragraph in the research report immediately after the first paragraph. Check the spelling of the entire document, and then use the Word Count command to count the number of words in the research report.

After you edit the research report, save the document on a floppy disk. Use the filename, Computer Viruses Report - Edited. Print the research report. Write the total number of words in the research report above the student name on the report. Follow directions from your instructor for turning in the assignment.

Part 3: Adding a Table

Problem: You are to insert the following table in the research report.

Instructions: The table should be inserted after the third paragraph. Format the table using an appropriate format. Label the table Table 1. Include the following sentence before the table: Table 1 lists the names of the top five computer viruses found on computer systems and the effect of each virus.

Table 1	
VIRUS NAME	*EFFECT*
Green Caterpillar	**Destroys data on disk**
Doom Slayer	**Destroys games on disk**
Time Bomb	**Destroys data based on time**
Slug	**Displays random messages**
Trojan Horse	**Destroys a computer system**

The table should be created in the word processing document using the style presented in this project.

After you add the table to the research report, save the document on a floppy disk. Use the filename, Computer Viruses Report - Final. Print the research report.

Follow directions from your instructor for turning in the assignment.

3 Preparing a Research Report

Part 1: Typing the Research Report

Problem: You have been asked by a friend to retype the research report shown in Figure 3-88 using the Modern Language Association's style for writing research reports as illustrated in this project.

Instructions: Type the research report using 12-point Times New Roman font. The student's name is Cathy E. Wain. The professor's name is Daniel P. Adibi. The class is Computer Science 101. Use the current date in the report heading.

After you type the research report, save the document on a floppy disk. Use the filename, Internet Report. Retain the disk for use in Part 2 of this lab assignment. Print the research report. Follow directions from your instructor for turning in the assignment.

In the Lab

Using the Internet

One of the most popular and fastest growing areas in computing today is the Internet. Using the Internet, you can do research, shop for services and merchandise, display weather maps, get stock quotes, converse with people worldwide, and obtain information stored on computers around the world.

The Internet is a collection of networks funded by commercial and governmental organizations that allows computer-to-computer communication by millions of users throughout the world. These networks are connected with high-, medium-, and low-speed data lines that allow data to move from one computer to another.

The Internet began in 1969 under the name ARPANET. The first system involved four computers designed to demonstrate the feasibility of creating networks that would allow computers to transmit data over communications lines dispersed throughout a wide area. The network was originally designed to support users involved in research for the military. An important goal was to design networks that would not fail.[1]

The four computers forming the original ARPANET were located at the University of California at Santa Barbara, the University of California at Los Angeles, Stanford Research Institute, and the University of Utah. During the 1970s, numerous other computers and networks were added to the system. Some were privately funded and others were funded by the government. Eventually many of the privately and publicly funded networks merged to form a comprehensive interconnected network called Internet. Today, the Internet consists of many different intercommunicating networks. The Internet now operates in more than 70 countries throughout the world. Most large corporations, newspapers, television stations, and even the White House, are on the Internet.

All types of people use the Internet, including students, librarians, scientists, engineers, university researchers, and individuals in governmental agencies. Their purpose is to communicate, exchange ideas, and gain access to knowledge.[2]

The Internet has a variety of uses. The main uses include electronic mail, electronic file transfer, searching files and databases, and game playing with other users.

With its popularity and benefits, it is anticipated that the Internet will be as common as a telephone line in the home. The Internet will become an integral tool in the global marketplace as well.

_____

[1]Lynn R. Burleson, *History of the Internet* (New York: Computer Network Press, 1996) 13-15.

[2]Robert C. Conrad, "Who Is Using the Internet Today?" *Internet Today* (17 July 1995) 12-20.

FIGURE 3-88

(continued)

In the Lab

Preparing a Research Report (continued)

Part 2: Editing the Research Report

Problem: You are to edit the research report you typed in Part 1 of this lab assignment. Follow the instructions below to edit the report.

Instructions: Use the Replace command to replace the word, ARPANET, in the research report with the words, Advanced Research Projects Agency Network, where appropriate. Use the thesaurus to replace the word, transmit, in the third paragraph with a word recommended by the thesaurus. Use the drag-and-drop method to place the sixth paragraph in the research report immediately after the fourth paragraph. Check the spelling of the entire document, and then use the Word Count command to count the number of words in the research report.

After you edit the research report, save the document on a floppy disk. Use the filename, Internet Report - Edited. Print the research report. Write the total number of words in the research report above the student name on the report. Follow directions from your instructor for turning in the assignment.

Part 3: Adding a Table

Problem: You are to insert the following table in the research report.

Instructions: The table should be inserted after the sixth paragraph. Format the table using an appropriate format. Label the table Table 1. Include the following sentence before the table: Table 1 shows the projected growth of the Internet from 1997 to the year 2000.

Table 1		
INTERNET GROWTH PROJECTIONS	1997	2000
Networks	10,000	200,000
Computers	1,500,000	50,000,000
Service Providers	3,000	7,500
Direct Users	50,000,000	100,000,000

The table should be created in the word processing document using the style presented in this project.

After you add the table to the research report, save the document on a floppy disk. Use the filename, Internet Report - Final. Print the research report.

Follow directions from your instructor for turning in the assignment.

Cases and Places

The difficulty of these case studies varies:

▶ Case studies preceded by a single half moon are the least difficult. Create a brief research paper (about 500 words) using resources that probably are available in the classroom setting.
▶▶ Case studies preceded by two half moons are more difficult. Write a brief research paper (about 500 words) using information from resources outside the classroom, such as the library or the Internet.
▶▶▶ Case studies preceded by three half moons are the most difficult. Prepare a brief research paper (about 500 words) based on conventional resources, such as the library and the Internet and on your own experiences beyond the college environment.

1 ▶ The Learning Pyramid depicts how various teaching methods affect retention rates.

Learning Pyramid

Teaching Method	Average Retention Rate
Lecture	5%
Reading	10%
Audio-Visual	20%
Demonstration	30%
Discussion Group	50%
Practice by Doing	75%
Teach Others/Immediate Use of Learning	90%

To demonstrate this concept, write a brief research paper describing one task that can be accomplished using Microsoft Works 4. Possible examples are creating a formatted document with clip art, writing a cover letter and resume using TaskWizards, using templates, and writing a research paper with footnotes and tables. Use your textbook, Works online Help, and any other resources available. Include at least two footnotes and a bibliography.

2 ▶ Graphical user interfaces, such as Windows 95, claim to be easy to learn, consistent among various applications, and user-friendly. Write a brief research paper describing how well Microsoft Works 4 reflects these characteristics. Use your textbook, Works online Help, and any other resources available. Explain why Works 4 is (or is not) easy to master, how working with Works 4 is similar to (or different from) using Windows 95 or other applications, and how Works 4 compensates for (or penalizes) user errors. Include at least two footnotes and a bibliography.

3 ▶▶ The invention of movable type resulted in books, once available only to the clergy and nobility, becoming accessible to a broad segment of the population. Their content changed from esoteric religious tomes to practical texts that helped spread secular knowledge. Some people believe word processing software, such as Microsoft Works 4, will result in a similar revolution by making documents easier to create, edit, and format. Others insist, however, that word processors merely help people produce just what their name implies – processed words devoid of imagination and originality. In addition, critics fear that word processors fuel plagiarism through such features as cut and paste and search and replace. Using the library or other resources (such as the Internet), prepare a brief research paper on the effect word processors have had, and are likely to have, on the written word. Include footnotes and a bibliography.

Cases and Places

4 ▶▶ The first word processing software, introduced in the late 1970s, was slightly more sophisticated than electronic typewriters. Although documents could be created and edited, formatting and stylistic enhancements were limited. To produce attractive output, desktop publishing (DTP) software was used to embellish documents produced with word processing software. Modern word processing packages, such as that found in Microsoft Works 4, however, have many of the capabilities once found only in DTP software. Using the library or other resources (such as the Internet), prepare a brief research paper comparing word processing and desktop publishing software. Describe the similarities and differences. Discuss the future of DTP software in light of the growing sophistication of word processing software. Include footnotes and a bibliography.

5 ▶▶▶ Computers have had a tremendous effect on all aspects of the workplace. Perhaps the employee most affected by word processing software, however, is the office secretary. Once responsible for almost all of an office's written correspondence, a secretary today has new duties because many professionals now use word processing software to create and store their documents. Using the library or other resources (such as the Internet), research how word processing software has transformed the office. Then, visit an office and talk to people whose jobs have been changed by these programs. Prepare a brief research paper on the effect word processing software has had on the modern office. Include footnotes and a bibliography.

6 ▶▶▶ Word processing software has affected the appearance of documents and has altered the writing process. People can write without the fear of making a mistake. The editing capabilities of word processors coupled with such tools as an online thesaurus, dictionary, and spell checker make revising and correcting documents easier than using a typewriter or pen and paper. Some educators now are using a different methodology to teach writing. Using the library or other resources (such as the Internet), research how word processing software has altered the way educators teach composition skills. Then, visit a school and talk to teachers and students about how word processing software is used. Prepare a brief research paper on the effect word processing software has had in the English classroom. Include footnotes and a bibliography.

7 ▶▶▶ Today, many word processing software packages are available. Some of the more popular are Microsoft Word, WordPerfect, and Ami Pro. Also popular are programs that are part of other packages, such as Windows WordPad, Q & A Write, and this Microsoft Works Word Processor. Using the library or other resources (such as the Internet), compare at least one word processor to Microsoft Works 4. Visit a software vendor to use this alternate package. Note the similarities, differences, strengths, and weaknesses. Then, prepare a brief research paper comparing Works 4 to the other word processing package you tested. Include footnotes and a bibliography.

Microsoft *Works 4*

Building a Spreadsheet and Charting Data

Objectives:

You will have mastered the material in this project when you can:

▶ Start the Microsoft Works Spreadsheet tool
▶ List the steps required to build a spreadsheet
▶ Describe the spreadsheet
▶ Highlight a cell or range of cells
▶ Enter text
▶ Enter numbers
▶ Use the AutoSum button to sum a range of cells in a row or column
▶ Copy a cell to a range of adjacent cells
▶ Format a spreadsheet
▶ Center text in a range of cells
▶ Add color to a spreadsheet
▶ Use the AutoFormat feature
▶ Change column widths
▶ Save a spreadsheet
▶ Print a spreadsheet
▶ Create a 3-D Bar chart
▶ Print a chart
▶ Close a spreadsheet
▶ Close Works
▶ Open a spreadsheet file
▶ Correct errors in a spreadsheet
▶ Clear cells and clear the entire spreadsheet

Crunching Numbers Can Be Fun

It just takes the right tool

Into the crowded lecture hall strides a man in a blue suit, carrying an official-looking leather portfolio. At the podium, he calls out a name. One of the students cheers and rushes forward to receive a one million dollar check for winning the lottery! She is the same student who claimed to have created a spreadsheet for picking winning lottery numbers. If only her friends had listened... .

For now anyway, such a scene exists only in fantasy, but for lottery winners and everyone else, a spreadsheet can make many real-life situations easier to handle. Appearing on your computer monitor as a table of rows and columns, a computer spreadsheet is similar to the accountant's ledger sheet. Aided by the speed and power of the PC, a user can construct a spreadsheet to quickly and easily perform "what-if" analysis for interdependent sets of numerical data; for example, "what if the projected sales figures for July increase by 10%, how will that affect gross profit?" For the same analysis, an accountant without a computer might need hours to manually recalculate and re-enter the resulting figures on paper.

$40.2

$42.4

$9.0

$13.6 $12.3

Ten Busiest Airports
by total number of passengers

Chicago O'Hare Int'l
Dallas/Ft. Worth Int'l
Los Angeles Int'l
Hartsfield Atlanta Int'l
Heathrow Airport
Tokyo Haneda Int'l
J.F. Kennedy Int'l
San Francisco Int'l
Stapleton Int'l
Frankfurt, West

Almost everyone, especially a student on a tight budget, needs an efficient way to manage personal finances. For some, keeping track of classes and activities is a hassle that gets in the way of an education. For still others, buying a car — new or used — on a time payment plan is the beginning of major heartburn. In these three examples, the Microsoft Works Spreadsheet TaskWizards come to the rescue with ready-made templates — Accounts, Schedules, and Loan Analysis — that can be used as-is or personalized to an individual's own needs, helping to organize time and finances. Spelling checker and Easy Calc are also available to ensure spelling accuracy and to speed simple math operations.

Of course, the capabilities of spreadsheets extend beyond college into business, science, and many other fields, including managing personal affairs. Business applications are numerous and familiar, from creating business plans to calculating actuarial tables, from forecasting sales to tracking and comparing airline traffic at airports. Going beyond these traditional uses, geographic data is being merged with statistics to create color-coded maps that track such diverse factors as global warming, health care needs, criminal justice, risk of damage by flood, even maps of what is selling where. For personal use, a number of sophisticated spreadsheet programs help to manage investment portfolios, balance checkbooks, and track house-hold inventories for insurance purposes.

Spreadsheets also have become an important tool for improving productivity in law enforcement, an area that reaches everyone. In one application, the Los Angeles Police Department uses a system based on spreadsheets to save the equivalent of 368 additional police officers by speeding the paperwork — up to 37 forms for a single incident — required of those already on the force. For certain crimes, such as car theft, spreadsheet data can be used to create maps showing crime frequency, helping police establish stakeout points.

With embedded multimedia sound and video, the expanding technology of spreadsheets opens a wide new vista of applications. For hundreds of thousands who daily use these electronic marvels, the world of "what-if?" has become the world of "what next?" Perhaps someone, someday, will even crack the lottery.

Microsoft
Works 4
Windows 95

Building a Spreadsheet and Charting Data

Case Perspective

RSC Sports and Fitness Centers has experienced explosive growth since its inception three years ago. The management would like a report showing the memberships at each of their clubs. They have asked you to prepare a spreadsheet that specifies the clubs' current memberships. In particular, they want to know the total memberships for students, singles, families, and executives in the following four cities: Anaheim, Irvine, Fullerton, and Yorba Linda. They want the totals by type of memberships (Student, Single, Family, and Executive).

Your task is to develop a spreadsheet to show these memberships. In addition, the director of membership has asked to see a graphical representation of the memberships to easily illustrate this data to her sales force.

The Works Spreadsheet Tool

A **spreadsheet** is a software tool that is useful when you have a need to enter and calculate data that can be conveniently displayed in rows and columns. The Microsoft Works for Windows Spreadsheet tool allows you to enter data in a spreadsheet, perform calculations on that data, ask what-if questions regarding the data in the spreadsheet, make decisions based on the results found in the spreadsheet, chart data in the spreadsheet, and share these results with other tools within Works.

As a result of the capabilities of the Works for Windows Spreadsheet tool, you can accomplish such tasks as accounting and record keeping, financial planning and budgeting, sales forecasting and reporting, or keeping track of your basketball team's scoring averages. In addition, once you have determined the information you require, you can present it as a spreadsheet or as a chart in printed reports.

Works also allows you to change data and automatically recalculate your spreadsheet. You can place data in the spreadsheet that simulates given conditions, which then you can test and determine the results. For example, you can enter the monthly payment you want to make on a house and then determine the price of the house you can afford based on various interest rates.

Project Four

To illustrate the use of the Microsoft Works for Windows 95 Spreadsheet tool, this section of the book presents a project similar to the one you created for the Works Word Processor. Project 4 uses the Works Spreadsheet tool to produce the spreadsheet and 3-D Bar chart shown in Figure 4-1.

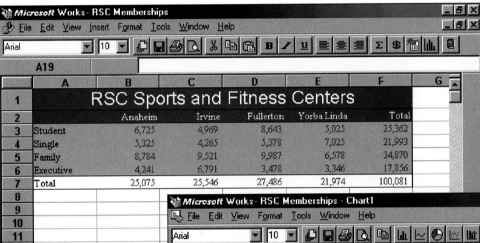

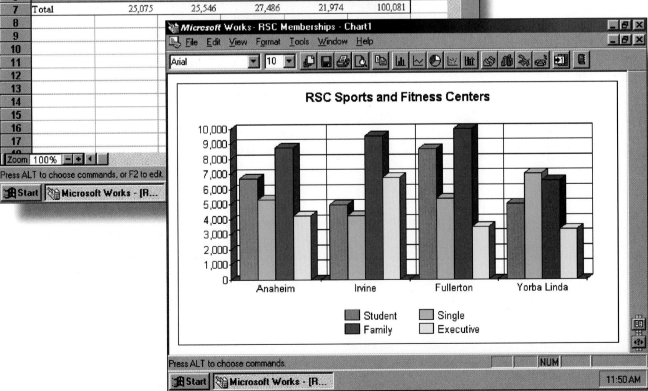

FIGURE 4-1

The spreadsheet contains RSC Sports and Fitness Centers memberships for Anaheim, Irvine, Fullerton, and Yorba Linda. Memberships fall into four categories: Student, Single, Family, and Executive. Works calculates the total memberships for each city, the total memberships for each category, and the total of all memberships in each city. The spreadsheet in this project also demonstrates the use of the various fonts, font sizes, styles, and colors in the spreadsheet. Proper spreadsheet formatting as shown in this project is an important factor in modern spreadsheet design.

The bar chart, called a 3-D Bar chart, displays the membership categories by city. Works creates the 3-D Bar chart based on the data in the spreadsheet. Each category is represented by the color indicated by the legend below the chart.

Spreadsheet Preparation Steps

The following tasks will be completed in this project.

1. Start the Works Spreadsheet.
2. Enter the report title (RSC Sports and Fitness Centers), the column titles (Anaheim, Irvine, Fullerton, Yorba Linda, and Total), and the row titles (Student, Single, Family, Executive, and Total).
3. Enter the Student, Single, Family, and Executive memberships for each of the four cities (Anaheim, Irvine, Fullerton, and Yorba Linda).
4. Enter the formulas to calculate the memberships for each city, for each category of membership, and for the total memberships.
5. Format the spreadsheet title, including adding color to the title.
6. Format the body of the spreadsheet. The membership data, city totals, and category totals are to contain commas.
7. Save the spreadsheet on disk.
8. Print the spreadsheet.
9. Create the 3-D Bar chart based on data in the spreadsheet.
10. Print the 3-D Bar chart.
11. Save the spreadsheet and chart.
12. Close Works.

The following pages contain a detailed explanation of these steps.

Starting the Works Spreadsheet

To start the Works Spreadsheet, follow the steps you used in the word processing project to open the Microsoft Works Task Launcher dialog box (Figure 4-2). Then perform the steps on the next two pages.

Steps **To Start the Works Spreadsheet**

1 Click the Works Tools tab, and then point to the Spreadsheet button in the Works Task Launcher dialog box (Figure 4-2).

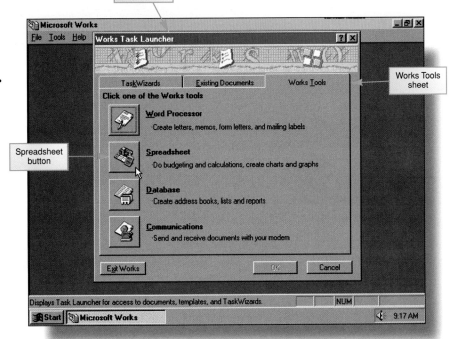

FIGURE 4-2

2 Click the Spreadsheet button. When the Microsoft Works window displays, maximize the window if necessary. If the Help window displays, click the Shrink Help button. Then point to the Unsaved Spreadsheet 1 Maximize button.

Works displays an empty spreadsheet titled Unsaved Spreadsheet 1 (Figure 4-3). The mouse pointer points to the Maximize button.

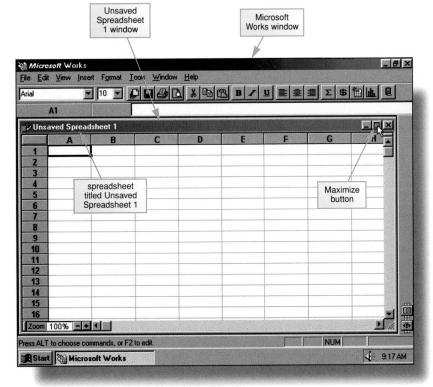

FIGURE 4-3

3 **Click the Maximize button in the Unsaved Spreadsheet 1 window.**

Works maximizes the spreadsheet and places the spreadsheet title, Unsaved Spreadsheet 1, in the main title bar (Figure 4-4).

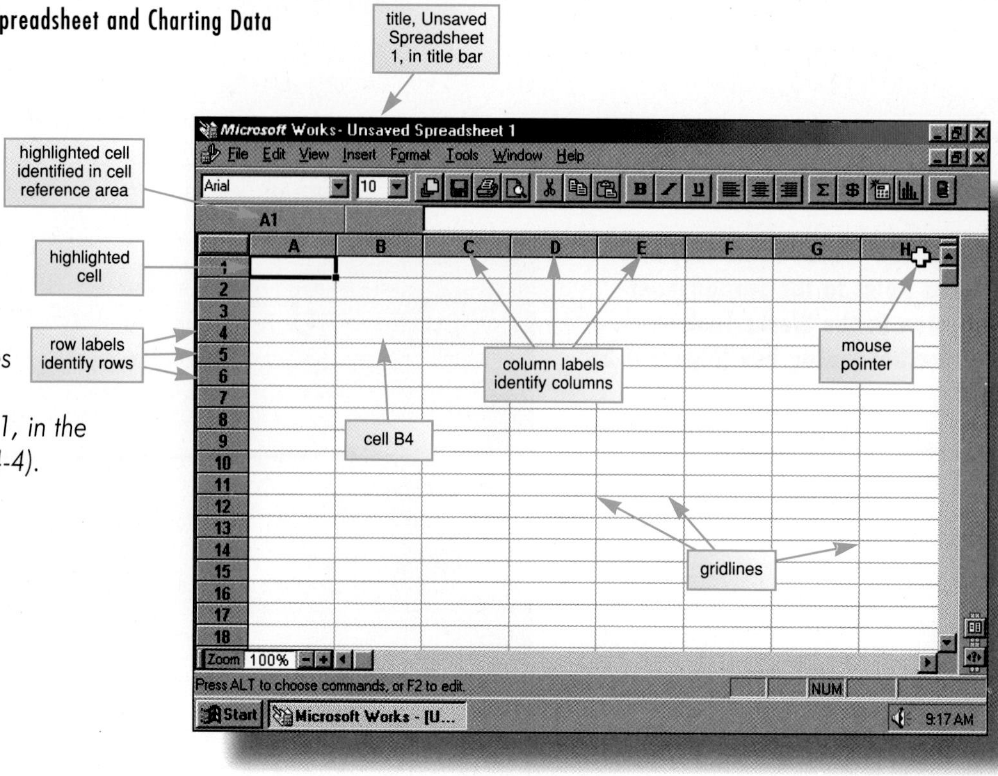

title, Unsaved Spreadsheet 1, in title bar

highlighted cell identified in cell reference area

highlighted cell

row labels identify rows

column labels identify columns

mouse pointer

cell B4

gridlines

FIGURE 4-4

The following paragraphs describe the elements of the spreadsheet screen identified in Figure 4-4.

The Spreadsheet

The spreadsheet is organized into a rectangular grid containing columns (vertical) and rows (horizontal). A **column label**, which is a letter of the alphabet above the grid, identifies each **column**. A **row label**, which is a number down the left side of the grid, identifies each **row**. Eight columns (letters A through H) and eighteen rows (numbered 1 through 18) appear on the screen when the spreadsheet is maximized.

Cell, Highlighted Cell, and Mouse Pointer

The intersection of each column and each row is a **cell**. A cell is the basic unit of a spreadsheet into which you enter data. A cell is referred to by its **cell reference**, which is the coordinate of the intersection of a column and a row. To identify a cell, specify the column label (a letter of the alphabet) first, followed by the row label (a number). For example, cell reference B4 refers to the cell located at the intersection of column B and row 4 (Figure 4-4).

The horizontal and vertical lines on the spreadsheet itself are called **gridlines**. Gridlines are intended to make it easier to see and identify each cell on the spreadsheet. If desired, you can remove the gridlines from the spreadsheet but it is recommended that you use the gridlines in most circumstances.

One cell in the spreadsheet, designated the **highlighted cell**, is the one into which you can enter data. The highlighted cell in Figure 4-4 is cell A1. Works identifies the highlighted cell in two ways. First, Works places a heavy border around it. Second, the cell reference area, which is above the column labels on the left side of the screen, contains the cell reference of the highlighted cell (Figure 4-4).

The **mouse pointer** can become a number of shapes when used with the Works Spreadsheet, depending on the activity in Works and the location of the mouse pointer on the spreadsheet window. In Figure 4-4, the mouse pointer has the shape of a block plus sign. Normally, the mouse pointer displays as a block plus sign whenever it is located in a cell on the spreadsheet.

Another common mouse pointer shape is the block arrow. The mouse pointer turns into a block arrow whenever you move it outside the spreadsheet window. Other mouse pointer shapes will be described when they appear on the screen.

Spreadsheet Window

The Works Spreadsheet contains 256 columns and 16,384 rows for a total of 4,194,304 cells. The column labels begin with A and end with IV. The row labels begin with 1 and end with 16384. Only a small fraction of the spreadsheet displays on the screen at one time. You view the portion of the spreadsheet displayed on the screen through the spreadsheet window (Figure 4-5). Scroll bars, scroll arrows, and scroll boxes that you can use to move the window around the spreadsheet are located below and to the right of the spreadsheet window.

More *About* **Scroll Boxes**

Dragging the scroll box is the most efficient way to scroll long distances. Drag the scroll boxes in the vertical or horizontal scroll bar to move the spreadsheet view up and down, or left and right, through the document.

More *About* **Scroll Bars**

Clicking the scroll bar will move the spreadsheet window a full screen up or down.

More *About* **Scroll Arrows**

To move the spreadsheet up or down one cell at a time click the scroll arrows at the ends of the vertical scroll bars. Use the scroll arrows on the horizontal scroll bar to move the spreadsheet left or right one cell at a time.

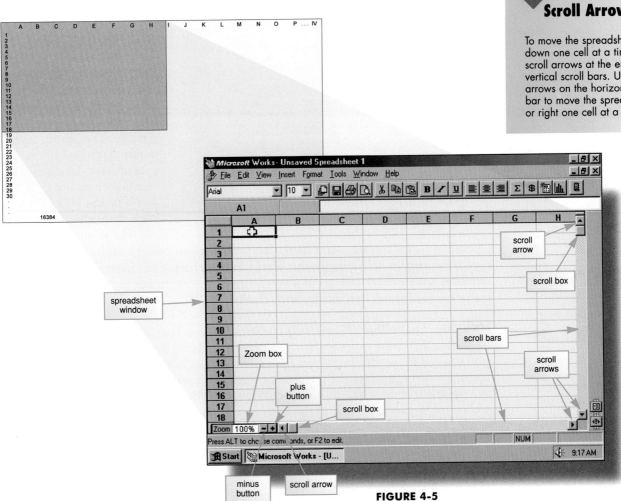

FIGURE 4-5

The **Zoom box** is located at the bottom left corner of the spreadsheet window. The Zoom box controls how much of a spreadsheet displays at one time in the spreadsheet window. Clicking the Zoom box displays a list of available zoom percentages to magnify or reduce your spreadsheet on the screen. You can also use the plus or minus buttons next to the Zoom box to control the display. To magnify your spreadsheet, click the plus button; to reduce your spreadsheet, click the minus button. The zoom size of the display has no effect on how the spreadsheet will look when it is printed.

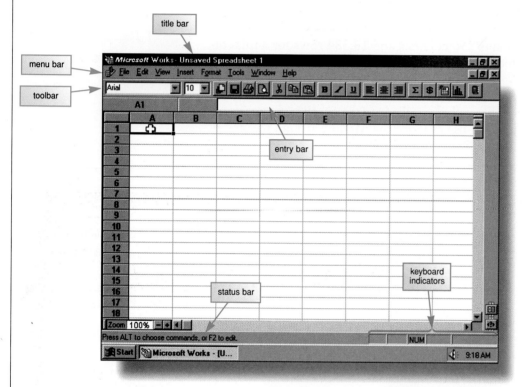

FIGURE 4-6

Menu Bar, Toolbar, Entry Bar, and Status Bar

The menu bar, toolbar, and entry bar display at the top of the screen just below the title bar (Figure 4-6). The status bar displays at the bottom of the screen.

MENU BAR The **menu bar** displays the Works Spreadsheet menu names (Figure 4-6). Each menu name represents a menu of commands that can retrieve, save, print, and manipulate data in the spreadsheet. To display a menu such as the File menu or the Edit menu, click the menu name.

The menu bar can change to include other menu names and other menu choices depending on the type of work you are doing in the Works Spreadsheet. For example, if you are working with a chart instead of a spreadsheet, the menu bar consists of a list of menu names for use specifically with charts.

TOOLBAR The **toolbar** (Figure 4-6) contains buttons that allow you to perform frequent tasks more quickly than you can when using the menu bar. Each button contains a picture that helps you remember its function. If you point to the button, a description of the purpose of the button will display beneath the button in a yellow rectangle and also in the status bar. You click a button to cause a command to execute. Each of the buttons on the toolbar is explained when used in the projects.

As with the menu bar, Works displays a different toolbar when you work with charts. The buttons on the Charting toolbar are explained when charts are used.

ENTRY BAR Below the toolbar, Works displays the **entry bar** (Figure 4-6). Data that you type appears in the entry bar. Works also displays the highlighted cell reference in the cell reference area on the left side of the entry bar.

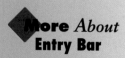

More About Scrolling Guidelines

Follow these general scrolling guidelines for viewing your spreadsheet: (1) To scroll short distances (one cell at a time), click the scroll arrows; (2) To scroll one screen at a time, click the scroll bar; (3) To scroll long distances, drag the scroll box.

More About Entry Bar

When you enter more characters in a cell than will fit in the width of the entry bar, the entry bar's text display area drops down so that you see all of the characters you are typing.

STATUS BAR The left side of the **status bar** at the bottom of the screen displays brief instructions, a brief description of the currently selected command, a brief description of the function of a toolbar button, or one or more words describing the current activity in progress.

Keyboard indicators indicating which keys are engaged, such as NUM (NUM LOCK key active) and CAPS (CAPS LOCK key active), display on the right side of the status bar within the small rectangular boxes.

Highlighting a Cell

To enter data into a cell, you must first **highlight** the cell. The easiest method to highlight a cell is to position the block plus sign mouse pointer in the desired cell and click.

An alternative method is to use the arrow keys that are located to the right of the typewriter keys on the keyboard. After you press an arrow key, the adjacent cell in the direction of the arrow on the key becomes the highlighted cell. You also can use the **TAB key** to move from one cell to another in a row.

You know a cell is highlighted when a heavy border surrounds the cell and the cell reference of the highlighted cell displays in the cell reference area in the entry bar (Figure 4-7).

Entering Text in a Spreadsheet

In the Works Spreadsheet, any set of characters containing a letter is **text**. Text is used for titles, such as spreadsheet titles, column titles, and row titles. In Project 4, the spreadsheet title, RSC Sports and Fitness Centers, identifies the spreadsheet. The column titles consist of the words Anaheim, Irvine, Fullerton, Yorba Linda, and Total. The row titles (Student, Single, Family, Executive, and Total) identify each row in the spreadsheet (Figure 4-7).

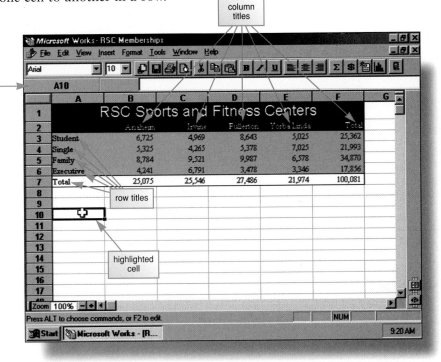

FIGURE 4-7

More *About* Labels

Whenever possible, arrange your spreadsheet so that similar items are grouped together, and label your cells as though you will not remember what they are later. Then, you won't spend as much time figuring out what you did.

Entering the Spreadsheet Title

The first task to build the spreadsheet is to complete the following steps to enter the spreadsheet title into cell A1.

Steps **To Enter the Spreadsheet Title**

1 **Click cell A1 to highlight it.**

A heavy border surrounds cell A1, and cell A1 displays in the cell reference area (Figure 4-8).

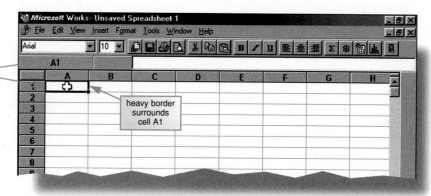

FIGURE 4-8

2 **Type** RSC Sports and Fitness Centers **in cell A1.**

*When you type the first character, the heavy border surrounding the cell changes and a new message displays on the status bar (Figure 4-9). Works displays three boxes; the **Cancel box**, the **Enter box**, and the **Help box** in the entry bar. As you type characters, each character displays in the cell followed immediately by a blinking vertical bar called the **insertion point**. The insertion point indicates where the next character typed will display. Works also displays the data in the entry bar as it is typed. Notice that the mouse pointer changes from a block plus sign to an I-beam. Whenever the mouse pointer is located in the current cell when you enter data, it will change to an I-beam. If you make a typing mistake, press the BACKSPACE key until the error is erased, and then retype the text. Clicking the Help box displays the Help window to the right of the spreadsheet window.*

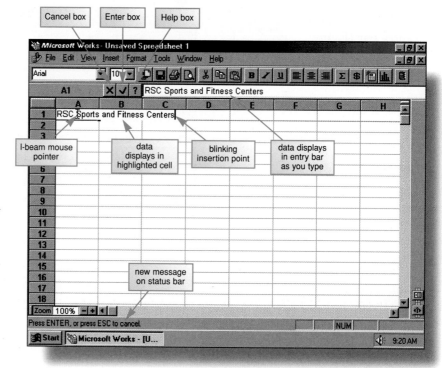

FIGURE 4-9

3 **After you type the text, point to the Enter box (Figure 4-10).**

FIGURE 4-10

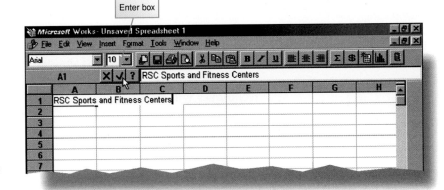

4 **Click the Enter box to confirm the entry.**

When you confirm the entry, Works enters the text in cell A1 (Figure 4-11).

FIGURE 4-11

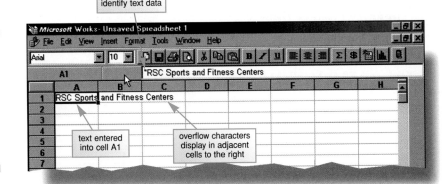

In the example in Figure 4-11, instead of using the mouse to confirm the entry, you can press the ENTER key after typing the text. Pressing the ENTER key replaces Step 3 and Step 4.

When you confirm a text entry into a cell, a series of events occurs. First, when text displays in the entry bar, it displays preceded by a double quotation mark, which indicates the entry is text and not a number or other value.

Second, Works positions the text left-aligned in the highlighted cell. Therefore, the R in the abbreviation RSC begins in the leftmost position of cell A1.

Third, when the text you enter contains more characters than can be displayed in the width of the cell, Works displays the overflow characters in adjacent cells to the right as long as these adjacent cells contain no data. In Figure 4-11, cell A1 is not wide enough to contain twenty-six characters plus four blank spaces. Thus, Works displays the overflow characters in cells B1 and C1 because the cells are empty.

Fourth, when you confirm an entry into a cell by clicking the Enter box or pressing the ENTER key, the cell into which the text is entered remains the highlighted cell.

Correcting a Mistake While Typing

If you type the wrong letter and notice the error before clicking the Enter box or pressing the ENTER key, use the BACKSPACE key to erase all the characters back to and including the ones that are wrong. The insertion point will indicate where in the text the next character you type will display. Then retype the remainder of the text entry.

To cancel the entire entry before confirming the entry, click the Cancel box or press the ESC key.

If you see an error in data you have already entered into a cell, highlight the cell and retype the entire entry. Later in this project, additional error-correction techniques will be explained.

Entering Column Titles

The next step is to enter the column titles consisting of the words, Anaheim, Irvine, Fullerton, Yorba Linda, and Total. To enter the column titles, select the appropriate cell and then enter the text, as illustrated in the following steps.

 Steps **To Enter Column Titles**

1 **Click cell B2 to highlight it.**

A heavy border surrounds cell B2, and B2 displays in the cell reference area (Figure 4-12).

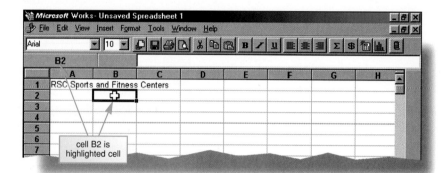

FIGURE 4-12

2 **Type** Anaheim **as the column title.**

Works displays Anaheim in the entry bar and in cell B2, which is the highlighted cell (Figure 4-13). Because the mouse pointer is located in the highlighted cell while data is entered, it changes to an I-beam.

FIGURE 4-13

3 **Press the RIGHT ARROW key.**

Works highlights cell C2 (Figure 4-14). When you press an arrow key to confirm an entry, Works enters the data and then makes the adjacent cell in the direction of the arrow (up, down, left, or right) the highlighted cell.

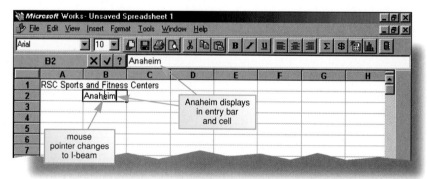

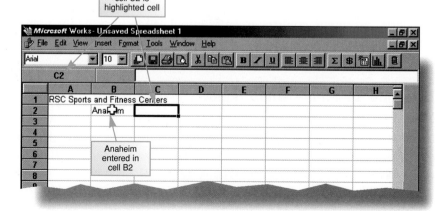

FIGURE 4-14

4 Repeat Step 2 and Step 3 for the remaining column titles. That is, enter Irvine **in cell C2,** Fullerton **in cell D2,** Yorba Linda **in cell E2, and** Total **in cell F2. Confirm the last column title entry in cell F2 by clicking the ENTER box or pressing the ENTER key.**

The column titles display as shown in Figure 4-15.

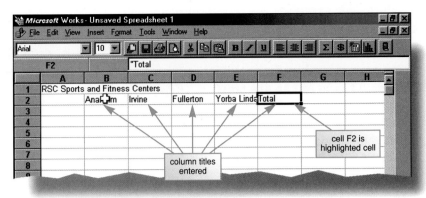

FIGURE 4-15

When confirming an entry in a cell, use the arrow keys if the next entry is in an adjacent cell. If the next entry is not in an adjacent cell, click the Enter box in the entry bar or press the ENTER key, and then use the mouse to select the appropriate cell for the next entry.

Entering Row Titles

The next step in developing the spreadsheet is to enter the row titles in column A. Complete the following steps to enter the row titles.

 To Enter Row Titles

1 **Click cell A3 to highlight it (Figure 4-16).**

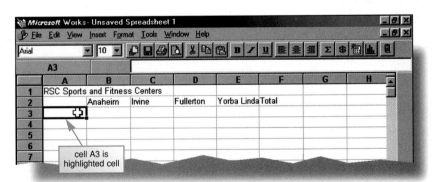

FIGURE 4-16

2 **Type the row title** Student **and then press the DOWN ARROW key.**

When you press the down arrow key, Works enters the row title, Student, in cell A3 and makes cell A4 the highlighted cell (Figure 4-17).

FIGURE 4-17

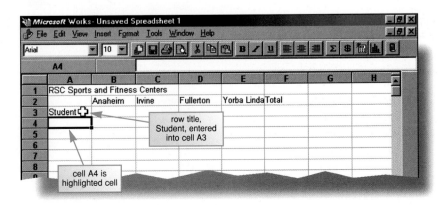

3 Type `Single` **in cell A4 and press the DOWN ARROW key. Type** `Family` **in cell A5 and press the DOWN ARROW key. Type** `Executive` **in cell A6 and press the DOWN ARROW key. Type** `Total` **in cell A7, and then confirm the entry by clicking the ENTER box or pressing the ENTER key.**

The row titles display as shown in Figure 4-18. The row titles are left-aligned in each cell. Cell A7 is the highlighted cell.

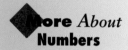

FIGURE 4-18

Entering Numbers

You can enter numbers into cells to represent amounts and other numeric values. Numbers can include the digits zero through nine and any one of the following characters:

( ) , . / $ % E e

The use of these characters is explained when they are required in a project. If a cell entry contains any other character from the keyboard, Works interprets the entry as text or a date and treats it accordingly.

In Project 4, you must enter the memberships for Anaheim, Irvine, Fullerton, and Yorba Linda for each of the categories, Student, Single, Family, and Executive in rows 3, 4, 5, and 6. The steps below and on the next two pages illustrate how to enter these values one row at a time.

To Enter Numeric Data

1 **Click cell B3 to highlight it (Figure 4-19).**

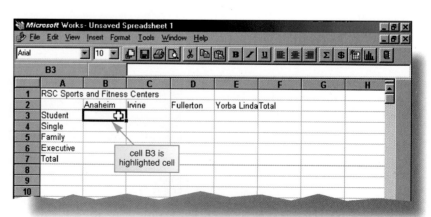

FIGURE 4-19

2 **Type** 6725 **into cell B3.**

The number 6725 displays in the entry bar and in the highlighted cell (Figure 4-20). Enter the number without a comma. You will format the numbers in the spreadsheet with commas in a later step. The mouse pointer changes from a block plus sign to an I-beam.

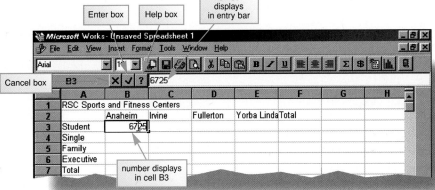

FIGURE 4-20

3 **Press the RIGHT ARROW key.**

Works enters the number 6725 into cell B3 and makes cell C3 the highlighted cell (Figure 4-21).

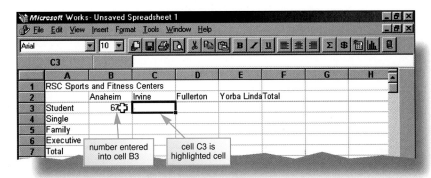

FIGURE 4-21

4 **Type** 4969 **into cell C3 and then press the RIGHT ARROW key. Type** 8643 **into cell D3 and then press the RIGHT ARROW key. Type** 5025 **into cell E3 and then press the ENTER key.**

Row 3 contains the Student memberships and cell E3 is highlighted (Figure 4-22).

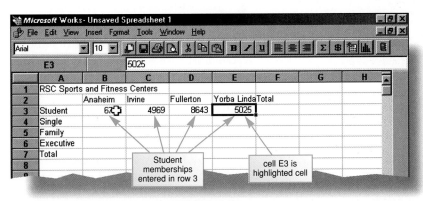

FIGURE 4-22

5 **Click cell B4 to highlight it (Figure 4-23).**

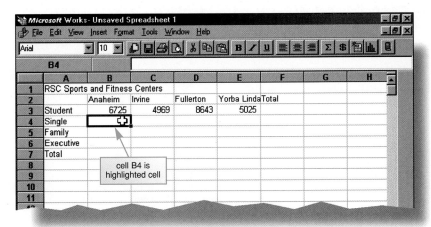

FIGURE 4-23

6 **Repeat the procedures used in Step 2 through Step 4 to enter the Single memberships, Family memberships, and Executive memberships.**

The Single, Family, and Executive memberships are entered in rows 4, 5, and 6, respectively (Figure 4-24).

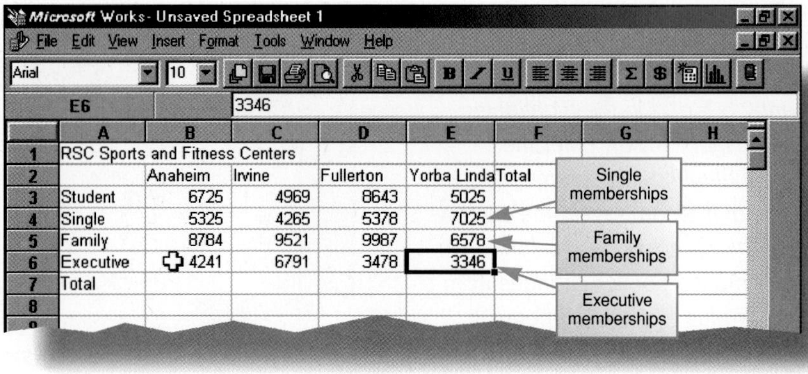

FIGURE 4-24

You now have entered all the numbers required for this spreadsheet. Notice several important points. First, commas, which are used to separate every third digit, are not required when you enter numbers. You will add them in a later step.

Second, Works enters numbers **right-aligned** in the cells, which means they occupy the rightmost positions in the cells.

Third, Works will calculate the totals in row 7 and column F. The capability of the Works Spreadsheet tool to perform calculations is one of its major features.

Calculating a Sum

The next step in creating the RSC Sports and Fitness Centers spreadsheet is to calculate the total memberships for Anaheim. To calculate this value and enter it into cell B7, Works must add the numbers in cells B3, B4, B5, and B6. The SUM function available in the Works Spreadsheet tool provides a convenient means to accomplish this task.

To use the SUM function, you must first identify the cell into which the sum will be entered after it is calculated. Then, you can use the **AutoSum button** on the toolbar to actually sum the numbers.

The following steps illustrate how to use the AutoSum button to sum the sales for Anaheim in cells B3, B4, B5, and B6 and enter the answer in cell B7.

Steps **To Sum a Column of Numbers Using the Autosum Button**

1 **Click cell B7 to highlight the cell that will contain the sum for Anaheim – cell B7.**

Cell B7 is highlighted (Figure 4-25).

FIGURE 4-25

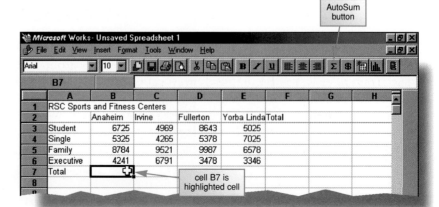

2 **Click the AutoSum button on the toolbar.**

Works responds by displaying =SUM(B3:B6) in the entry bar and in the highlighted cell (Figure 4-26). The =SUM entry identifies the SUM function. The B3:B6 entry within parentheses following the function name SUM is the way Works identifies cells B3, B4, B5, and B6 as the cells containing the values to be summed. Works also places a dark background behind the proposed cells to sum. The word POINT displays on the status bar indicating the SUM function is pointing to a range to be summed.

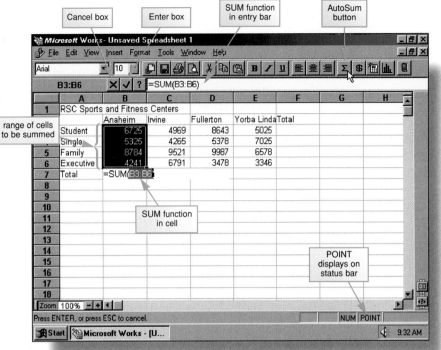

FIGURE 4-26

3 **Click the AutoSum button a second time.**

Works displays the sum of the memberships for Anaheim (6725 + 5325 + 8784 + 4241 = 25075) in cell B7 (Figure 4-27). Although the SUM function assigned to cell B7 is not displayed in the cell, it remains in the cell and displays in the entry bar when the cell is highlighted.

FIGURE 4-27

> **Other Ways**
>
> 1. Press CTRL+M

To display the SUM function in a cell instead of the sum, click the cell and then click in the entry bar area.

When you enter the SUM function using the AutoSum button, Works automatically highlights what it considers to be your choice of the group of cells to sum. The group of cells, B3, B4, B5, and B6, is called a range. A **range** is a block of adjacent cells in a spreadsheet. Ranges can be as small as a single cell and as large as an entire spreadsheet. Once you define a range, you can work with all the cells in the range instead of one cell at a time. In Figure 4-26, clicking the Auto-Sum button defines the range, which consists of cells B3 through B6 (designated B3:B6 by Works).

> ◆ **More** *About*
> **AutoSum**
>
> Consider how fast Works completes the following sophisticated operations after clicking the AutoSum button twice: (1) Works enters the equal sign and function name; (2) scans the spreadsheet and highlights cells to be summed; (3) calculates the total; and (4) displays the result of the calculation.

When highlighting the range of cells to sum using the AutoSum button, Works first looks for a range with numbers above the highlighted cell, and then to the left. If Works highlights the wrong range, drag the correct range any time prior to clicking the AutoSum button a second time. You also can enter the correct range in the highlighted cell to receive the sum by typing the beginning cell reference, a colon (:), and the ending cell reference, followed by clicking the AutoSum button a second time. A third method to fix an incorrect range specified by Works is to enter the correct range in the entry bar by dragging over the range specified in the entry bar and then typing the beginning cell reference, a colon (:), and the ending cell reference, followed by clicking the AutoSum button a second time.

When using the AutoSum button, you can click it once and then click the Enter box or press the ENTER key to complete the entry. Clicking the AutoSum button a second time, however, is the quickest way to enter the SUM function.

Copying a Cell to Adjacent Cells

In the RSC Sports and Fitness Centers spreadsheet, Works also must calculate the totals for Irvine, Fullerton, and Yorba Linda. For the Irvine memberships, the total is the sum of the values in the range C3:C6. Similarly, for the Fullerton memberships, the range to sum is D3:D6 and for the Yorba Linda memberships, the range is E3:E6.

To calculate these sums, you can follow the steps shown in Figures 4-25 through 4-27 on the previous two pages. A more efficient method, however, is to copy the SUM function from cell B7 to the range C7:E7. The copy cannot be an exact duplicate, though, because different columns must be referenced for each respective total. Therefore, when you copy cell references, Works adjusts the cell references for each column. As a result, the range in the SUM function in cell C7 will be C3:C6, the range in the SUM function in cell D7 will be D3:D6, and the range in SUM function in cell E7 will be E3:E6.

The easiest way to copy the SUM function from cell B7 to cells C7, D7, and E7 is to use the fill handle. The **fill handle** is the small rectangular dot located in the lower right corner of the heavy border around the highlighted cell. To copy using the fill handle, first highlight the cell that includes the data you want to copy. Then drag the fill handle to highlight the range you want to copy to. Complete the following steps to perform this operation.

Steps   To Copy One Cell to Adjacent Cells in a Row

1 **Click the cell to copy – cell B7 – and position the mouse pointer on the fill handle located in the lower right hand corner of cell B7.**

Cell B7 is highlighted (Figure 4-28). When you position the mouse pointer on the fill handle, the mouse pointer changes to the word FILL with a cross indicating the fill handle is selected.

	A	B	C	D	E	F	G	H
1	RSC Sports and Fitness Centers							
2		Anaheim	Irvine	Fullerton	Yorba Linda	Total		
3	Student	6725	4969	8643	5025			
4	Single	5325	4265	5378	7025			
5	Family	8784	9521	9987	6578			
6	Executive	4241	6791	3478	3346			
7	Total	25075						
8								
9								
10								

B7 = SUM(B3:B6)

cell to be copied is highlighted

FILL

mouse pointer changes shape

FIGURE 4-28

2 **Drag the range you want to copy into (cells C7, D7, and E7).**

When you drag the fill handle through the cells, Works places a border around the cell you want to copy (B7) and an outline around the range you want to copy into (C7:E7) (Figure 4-29). The contents of cell B7 display in the entry bar.

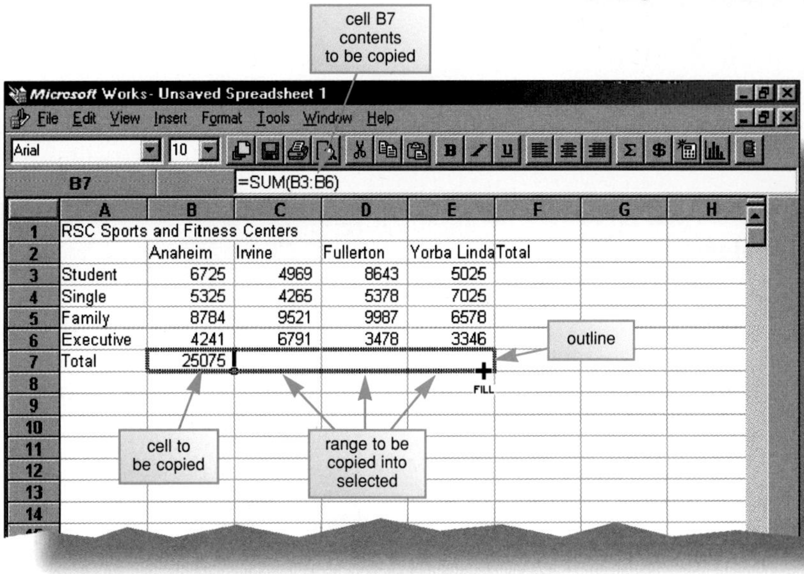

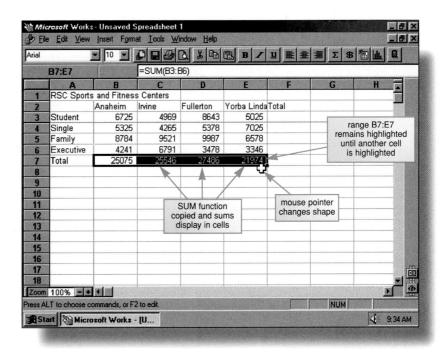

cell B7 contents to be copied

outline

cell to be copied

range to be copied into selected

FILL

FIGURE 4-29

3 **Release the mouse button.**

When you release the mouse button, the mouse pointer changes to a block plus sign (Figure 4-30). Works copies the SUM function from cell B7 into the range C7:E7. In addition, Works performs calculations based on the formula in each of the cells and displays sums in cells C7, D7, and E7.

range B7:E7 remains highlighted until another cell is highlighted

SUM function copied and sums display in cells

mouse pointer changes shape

FIGURE 4-30

OtherWays
1. On Edit menu click Fill Right
2. Press CTRL+R

After Works has copied the contents of a cell into a range, the range remains highlighted. To remove the range highlight, click any cell in the spreadsheet.

Summing a Row Total

The next step in building the RSC Sports and Fitness Centers spreadsheet is to total the Student memberships, the Single memberships, the Family memberships, and the Executive memberships, and then to calculate the Total memberships for the centers. These totals will be entered in column F. The SUM function is used in the same manner as totaling the memberships in row 7. Perform the steps on the next page to sum the row numbers.

Steps To Sum a Row of Numbers Using the AutoSum Button

1 **Click the cell to contain the total for Student – cell F3.**

Cell F3 is highlighted (Figure 4-31).

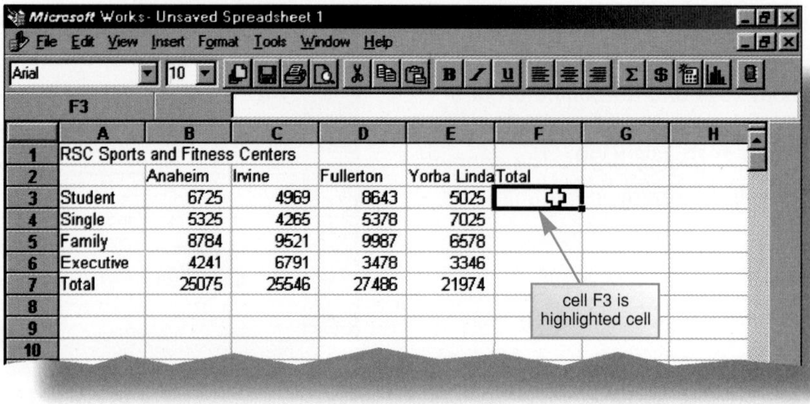

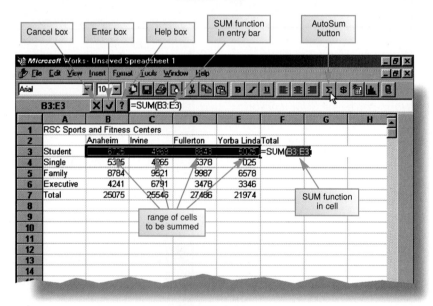

cell F3 is highlighted cell

FIGURE 4-31

2 **Click the AutoSum button on the toolbar.**

Works responds by displaying =SUM(B3:E3) in the entry bar and in the highlighted cell (Figure 4-32). Works also places a dark background behind the proposed cells to sum. The =SUM entry identifies the SUM function. The B3:E3 entry within parentheses following the function name SUM is the way Works identifies cells B3, C3, D3, and E3 as the cells containing the values to be added.

Cancel box — Enter box — Help box — SUM function in entry bar — AutoSum button

range of cells to be summed

SUM function in cell

FIGURE 4-32

3 **Click the AutoSum button a second time.**

Works enters the formula in cell F3, displays the sum in the cell, and displays the SUM function from cell F3 in the entry bar (Figure 4-33).

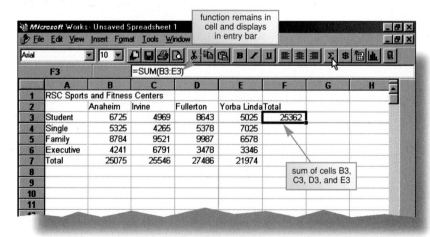

function remains in cell and displays in entry bar

sum of cells B3, C3, D3, and E3

FIGURE 4-33

Other Ways

1. Press CTRL+M

As shown previously, you can accomplish Step 3 by clicking the ENTER box or pressing the ENTER key.

Copying Adjacent Cells in a Column

The next task is to copy the SUM function from cell F3 to the range F4:F7 to obtain the Total memberships for Single, Family, Executive, and the Total memberships for RSC Sports and Fitness Centers. The steps to accomplish this task follow.

 Steps **To Copy One Cell to Adjacent Cells in a Column**

① Click cell F3. Position the mouse pointer on the fill handle located in the lower right-hand corner of cell F3. When the mouse pointer changes to the word FILL with a cross, drag the range to cell F7.

When you drag the fill handle through the cells, Works places a border around the cell you want to copy (F3) and an outline around the range you want to copy into (F4:F7) (Figure 4-34). The contents of cell F3 display in the entry bar.

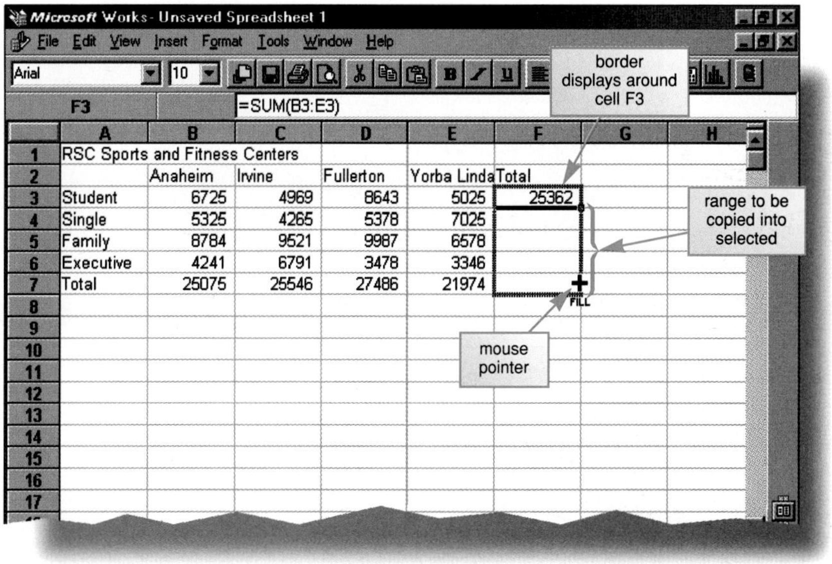

FIGURE 4-34

② Release the mouse button.

When you release the mouse button, the mouse pointer changes to a block plus sign (Figure 4-35). Works fills the highlighted range with the SUM function and displays the calculated sums in each of the cells. When Works copies the function, each range reference in the function is adjusted to reflect the proper rows of numbers to sum.

OtherWays

1. On Edit menu click Fill Down
2. Press CTRL+D

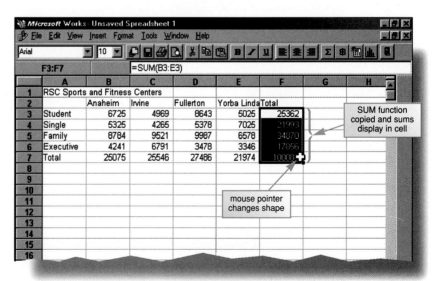

FIGURE 4-35

After Works copies the cell contents, the range F3:F7 remains highlighted. You can remove this highlight by clicking any cell in the spreadsheet.

Formatting the Spreadsheet

You have now entered all the text, numeric entries, and functions for the spreadsheet. The next step is to format the spreadsheet. You **format** a spreadsheet to emphasize certain entries and make the spreadsheet attractive to view and easy to read and understand.

With Works, you have the ability to change fonts, font sizes, and font styles such as bold and italic, and to color the font and cells containing the data in the spreadsheet. On the following pages you will learn how to format the spreadsheet in Project 4 as shown in Figure 4-36 and as described in the list on Page W 4.6.

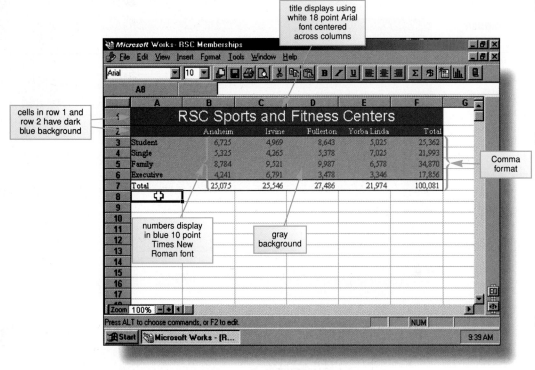

FIGURE 4-36

1. The spreadsheet title displays in white 18-point Arial font. The cell background is dark blue. The title is centered over the columns in the spreadsheet.
2. The color of the column titles (white), row titles (black) and the remainder of the spreadsheet display as illustrated. The fonts, font sizes, styles, and colors are determined by the AutoFormat feature of Works.
3. The membership numbers, column totals, and row totals display with commas.

The following paragraphs explain how to format the spreadsheet.

Formatting Text and Changing the Color of Cells

The first step in formatting the spreadsheet is to format the title of the spreadsheet in cell A1. The spreadsheet title displays in white 18 point Arial font and is centered over columns A through F. The cell background is dark blue. Formatting can be accomplished using the Format command from the context-sensitive menu. Complete the following steps to format the title.

Steps **To Format Cells**

1 **Highlight the range of cells A1:F1. Point to the highlighted cells and right-click. When the context-sensitive menu displays, point to Format.**

Cells A1 through F1 are highlighted (Figure 4-37). The context-sensitive menu displays and the mouse pointer points to the Format command.

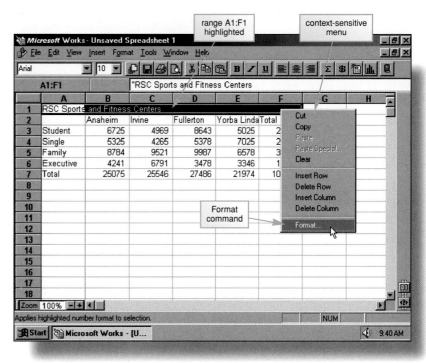

FIGURE 4-37

2 **Click Format on the context-sensitive menu. When the Format Cells dialog box displays, point to the Alignment tab.**

Works displays the Format Cells dialog box (Figure 4-38). The Format Cells dialog box contains five tabbed sheets; Number, Alignment, Font, Border, and Shading. The Number sheet displays in front of the other tabbed sheets. The mouse pointer points to the Alignment tab.

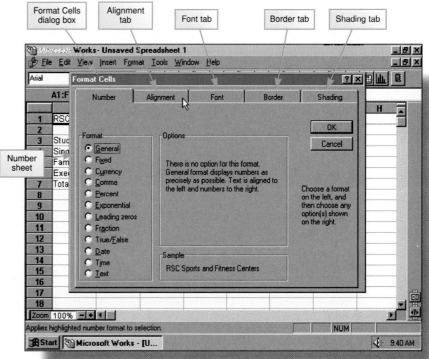

FIGURE 4-38

3 Click the Alignment tab in the Format Cells dialog box. When the Alignment sheet displays, click Center across selection in the Horizontal box. Click Center in the Vertical box. Then, point to the Font tab in the Format Cells dialog box.

When you click the Alignment tab, the Alignment sheet moves to the front (Figure 4-39). Selecting the Center across selection option button in the Horizontal box indicates the title should be centered horizontally across the selected columns. The selection of the Center option button in the Vertical box indicates that the title is to be centered vertically in the cells. The mouse pointer points to the Font tab.

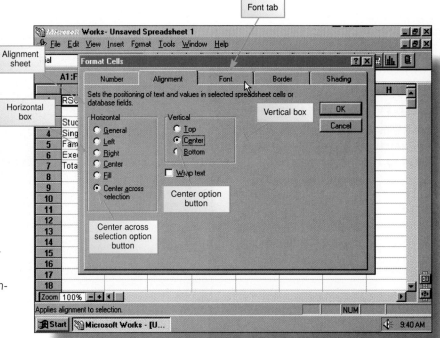

FIGURE 4-39

4 Click the Font tab. When the Font sheet displays, point to the number 18 in the Size list box.

Works displays the Font sheet (Figure 4-40). The default values are Arial font, 10 point size, Auto color, and no selections in the Style box. The Sample box displays an example of the text with these options in effect. Auto color displays text in black.

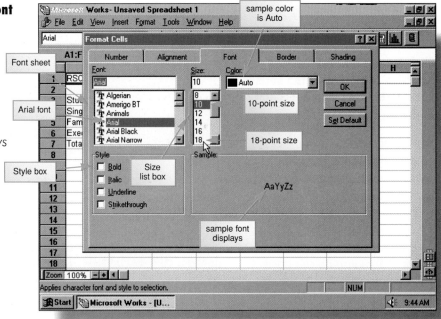

FIGURE 4-40

More *About*
Right-Clicking

Right-clicking highlighted cells was not even available on earlier versions of Works, so you may find people familiar with Works not even considering right-clicking. Because it always produces a context-sensitive menu containing frequently used commands, however, right-clicking can be the fastest way to access commands on the menu bar.

5 **Click 18 in the Size list box. Point to the Color drop-down list box arrow.**

Works displays a preview of 18-point Arial text in the Sample box (Figure 4-41). The mouse pointer points to the Color drop-down list box arrow.

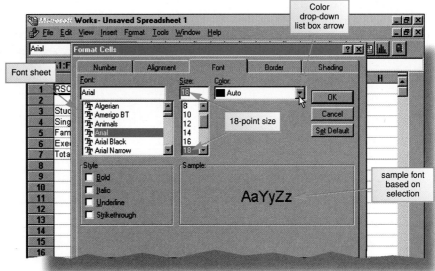

FIGURE 4-41

6 **Click the Color drop-down list box arrow. Scroll down to view the color White. Point to the color White.**

The Color drop-down list box displays and the mouse pointer points to the color White (Figure 4-42).

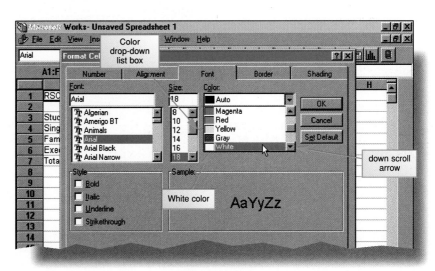

FIGURE 4-42

7 **Click White. Then, point to the Shading tab in the Format Cells dialog box.**

The color white and the word White display in the Color drop-down list box (Figure 4-43). The Sample box displays text with the current selections in effect. The mouse pointer points to the Shading tab.

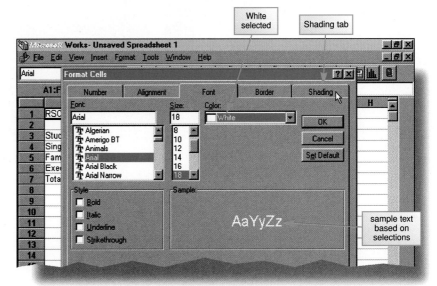

FIGURE 4-43

8 **Click the Shading tab. When the Shading sheet displays, point to the solid pattern in the Pattern list box.**

Works displays the Shading sheet (Figure 4-44). A series of rectangular boxes displays in the Pattern list box. The first rectangular box is highlighted and contains the word None. This box is followed by a series of boxes with various patterns you can select. The first pattern below None is the solid pattern. Below the Pattern list box the description of the selected pattern displays None, indicating no pattern is selected. The mouse pointer points to the solid pattern.

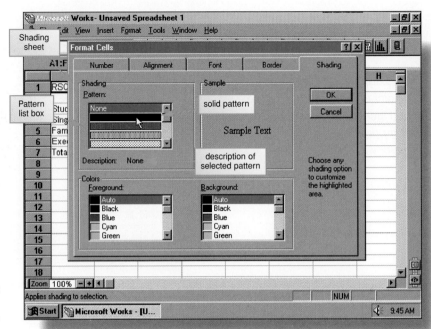

FIGURE 4-44

9 **Click the solid pattern in the Pattern list box. In the Foreground list box, scroll down and point to the color Dark Blue.**

The solid pattern in the Pattern list box is selected (Figure 4-45). The description of the selected pattern displays Solid (100%) below the Pattern list box. The foreground color is the color that will display in the highlighted cells. The mouse pointer points to the color Dark Blue.

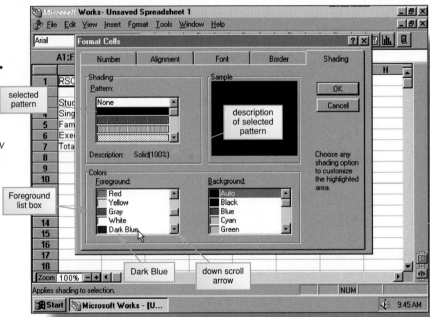

FIGURE 4-45

10 **Click Dark Blue. Point to the OK button in the Shading sheet.**

Dark Blue is highlighted in the Foreground list box (Figure 4-46). The solid pattern selected in the Pattern list box changes to dark blue. A preview of the solid pattern, Dark Blue, displays in the Sample box of the Shading sheet. The mouse pointer points to the OK button.

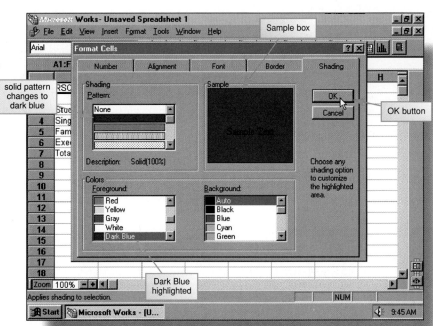

FIGURE 4-46

11 **Click the OK button in the Format Cells dialog box. Click any cell to remove the highlight.**

Works displays the foreground color in cells A1 through F1 in dark blue (Figure 4-47). The title displays in white 18-point Arial font and is centered across columns A through F. Notice that when the font size is increased to 18 point, Works automatically increases the height of row 1 so the enlarged text displays properly.

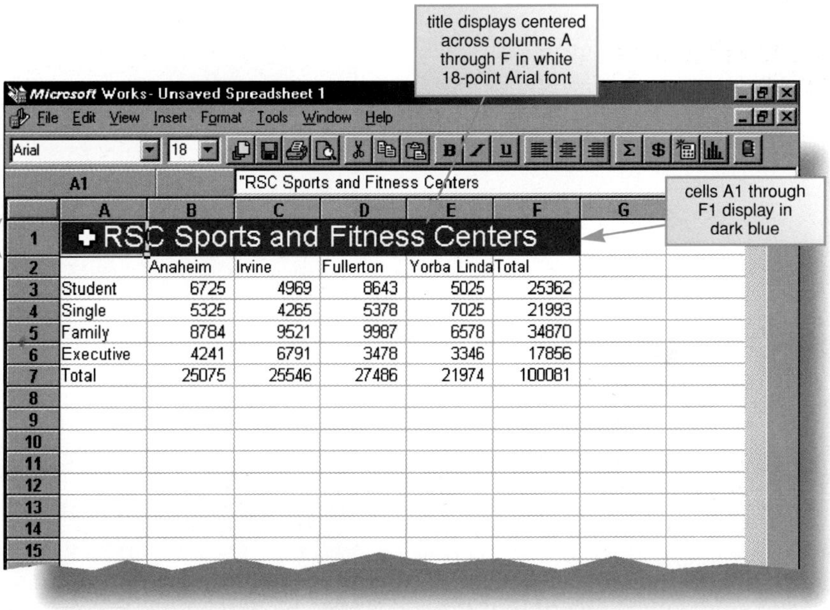

FIGURE 4-47

Other Ways

1. On Format menu click Alignment, Font and Style, Border, or Shading, click OK button

The background color in the Colors box of the Shading sheet (see Figure 4-45) can be used when a pattern other than solid is selected. Patterns other than solid may use both a foreground and background color.

More *About*
AutoFormat

After you apply a format to a highlighted range with the Auto-Format command, you can apply additional formatting. For example, you can increase the thickness of a border or change the foreground shading color of the cells.

Using the AutoFormat Command

Works provides an AutoFormat feature that enables you to format a spreadsheet in a variety of styles without going through a series of individual steps to select color, font and font styles, borders, and so forth. AutoFormat allows you to select one of fifteen different, predefined formats to apply to a spreadsheet. AutoFormat sets the alignment, fonts, patterns, column width, cell height, and borders automatically to match the style option you select.

The following steps explain how to use the Works AutoFormat feature.

Steps **To Use AutoFormat**

① **Highlight cells A2:F7 by dragging the mouse pointer from cell A2 through cell F7. Click Format on the menu bar and then point to AutoFormat.**

Cells A2 through F7 are highlighted (Figure 4-48). The Format menu displays. The mouse pointer points to the AutoFormat command.

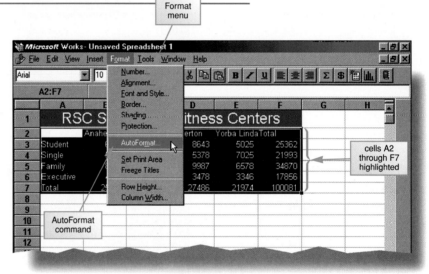

FIGURE 4-48

② **Click AutoFormat.**

Works displays the AutoFormat dialog box (Figure 4-49). The Select a format list box displays a list of preformatted styles. You can click the down scroll arrow to display additional formats. The Plain style is the default format. A sample of this style displays in the Example box. The Example box shows how the highlighted cells in the spreadsheet will display based on the selection in the Select a format list.

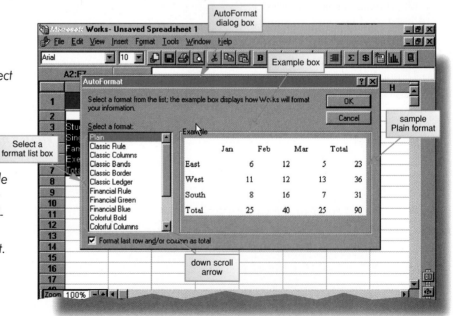

FIGURE 4-49

3 **In the Select a format list box, click Classic Bands. Ensure the Format last row and/or column as total check box displays a check mark. Point to the OK button.**

Works displays a sample of Classic Bands in the Sample box (Figure 4-50). A check mark in the Format last row and/or column as total check box specifies that you want Works to format the last row of the selected range as a total row for easy identification.

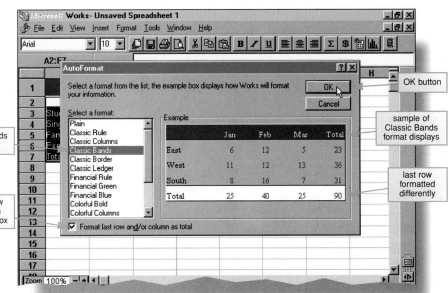

FIGURE 4-50

4 **Choose the OK button in the AutoFormat dialog box. Click any cell to remove the highlight.**

Works applies the predefined format style Classic Bands to the highlighted spreadsheet (Figure 4-51). The spreadsheet displays with the fonts, font styles, colors, and borders as illustrated. Works formats row 7 with a white background color for easy identification.

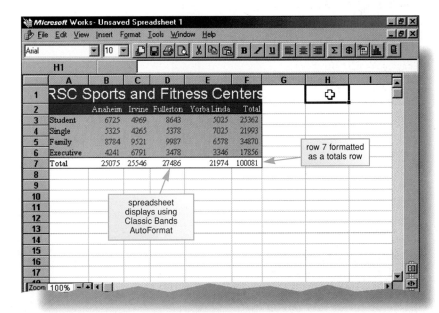

FIGURE 4-51

You can apply additional formatting to the spreadsheet. In Project 4, the numbers in cells B3 through F7 are to contain commas if necessary. This requires additional formatting.

Comma Format

The numeric values in rows 3, 4, 5, 6, and 7 are to be formatted with commas. In Works this requires the use of the Comma format. When you use the **Comma format**, by default, Works places two digits to the right of the decimal point (including zeroes), and a comma separates every three digits to the left of the decimal point. Because the numeric values in rows 3 through 7 are whole numbers, you will apply the Comma format and specify zero digits to the right of the decimal point and a comma separating every three digits to the left of the decimal point. To format numeric values in the Comma format, complete the following steps.

Steps ## To Display Numbers with the Comma Format

1 **Highlight the range of cells B3:F7 by dragging from cell B3 through cell F7. Right-click the selected range and point to Format on the context-sensitive menu.**

Cells B3 through F7 are high-lighted (Figure 4-52). The context-sensitive menu displays and the mouse pointer points to the Format command.

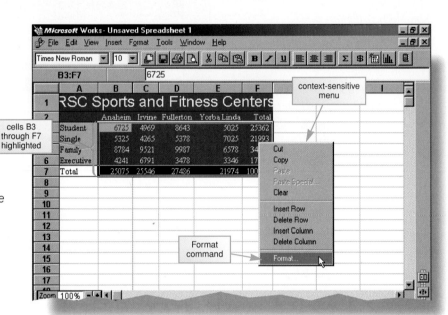

FIGURE 4-52

2 **Click Format on the context-sensitive menu. When the Format Cells dialog box displays, ensure the Number sheet displays and click Comma in the Format box. Type 0 in the Decimal places text box in the Comma box of the Options box. Then, point to the OK button.**

The Comma option button is selected and the mouse pointer points to the OK button (Figure 4-53). The value 0 displays in the Decimal places text box. The Sample box shows how the numbers will display in the cells formatted with the Comma format. The mouse pointer points to the OK button.

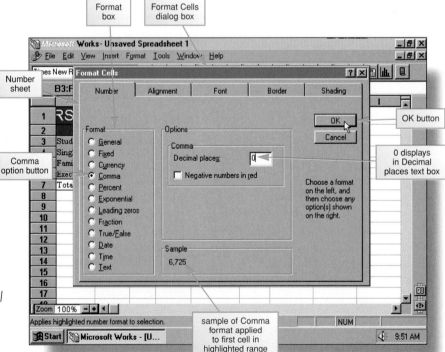

FIGURE 4-53

3 **Click the OK button in the Format Cells dialog box. Click any cell to remove the highlight.**

Works formats the range of cells B3:F7 using the Comma format with commas every three digits to the left (Figure 4-54).

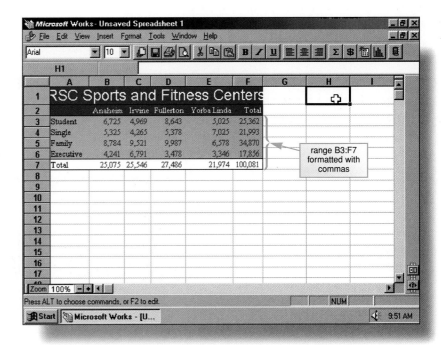

range B3:F7 formatted with commas

FIGURE 4-54

Changing Column Widths

The next step in formatting the spreadsheet is to change the column widths. The default column width is ten characters. You change column widths for several reasons. First, changing the column width increases the space between each column and often makes the spreadsheet easier to read. Also, in some instances the values you enter into a cell or the values Works calculates in a cell will not fit in a ten-character wide cell. When this occurs, you must change the width of the column to a size that can accommodate the entry in the cell.

The AutoFormat feature changes column width to a best fit to accommodate the numbers in each of the columns. Adding formatting such as the Comma format may require increasing the column width. In this project when the formatting was changed by adding commas, the columns became too narrow for good readability. Therefore, the column width of columns A through F should be changed to twelve to improve the readability of the spreadsheet.

Works provides the capability to change each column individually or you can change the width of a group of columns. In the following example, the columns will be changed as a group, which requires highlighting all columns to be changed and then choosing the Column Width command from the context-sensitive menu. To complete the task, perform the steps on the next two page.

Other Ways

1. On Format menu click Number, click Comma, click OK button

2. Press CTRL+, (comma)

Steps To Change Column Widths

1 **Position the mouse pointer on column heading A and drag across column headings B, C, D, E, and F to highlight columns A through F. Right-click the selection and point to Column Width on the context-sensitive menu.**

Columns A through F are highlighted (Figure 4-55). The context-sensitive menu displays and the mouse pointer points to the Column Width command.

FIGURE 4-55

2 **Click Column Width. When the Column Width dialog box displays, type 12 in the Column width text box. Point to the OK button.**

Works displays the Column Width dialog box (Figure 4-56). The number 12 has been typed in the Column width text box. The mouse pointer points to the OK button.

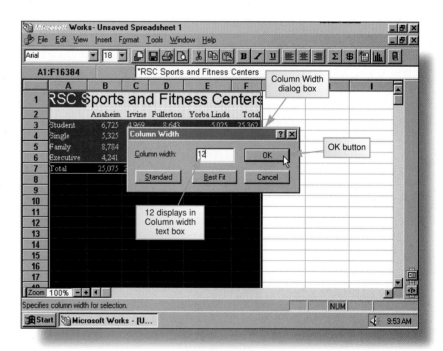

FIGURE 4-56

3 **Click the OK button in the Column Width dialog box. Click any cell to remove the highlight.**

Works makes columns A through F twelve characters wide (Figure 4-57). Notice most of column G and all of columns H and I have moved off the screen.

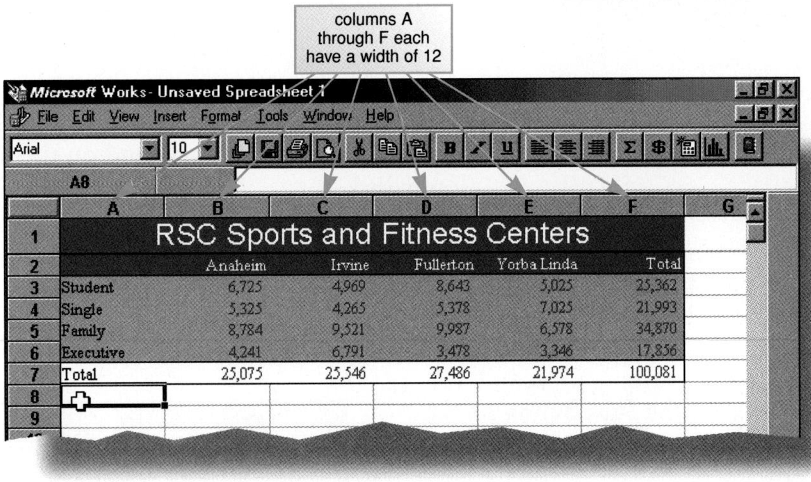

columns A through F each have a width of 12

FIGURE 4-57

Other Ways

1. On Format menu click Column Width, type desired width in Column width text box, click OK button

Works provides a number of methods that can be used to change the column width. To quickly change the width of a single column, place the mouse pointer over the column border (the right or left vertical line in the column label area) and drag. When the column is as large or small as you want, release the mouse button.

To quickly adjust the column width for best fit, double-click the column letter. This will adjust the column width to fit the longest entry in the column. To obtain best fit, you also can click the Best Fit button in the Column Width dialog box. If more than one column is highlighted, Works applies an appropriate width to each column.

If, at a later time, you want to change these columns back to the default value, highlight the desired columns, right-click the selected columns, click Column-Width command, and then click the Standard button in the Column Width dialog box.

Checking the Spelling on the Spreadsheet

The spreadsheet is now complete. All the data is entered and the formatting is complete. You should now check the spelling on the spreadsheet using the **Spelling command** on the Tools menu. To check the spelling, complete the following steps.

TO CHECK SPELLING

Step 1: Click Tools on the menu bar.
Step 2: Click Spelling.
Step 3: If any errors are found, perform the steps to correct the errors.

Saving a Spreadsheet

If you accidentally turn off your computer or if electrical power fails, you will lose all your work on the spreadsheet unless you have saved it on disk. Therefore, after you have worked on a spreadsheet for a period of time, or when you complete the spreadsheet, you should save it on hard disk or a floppy disk. When saving the spreadsheet for the first time, use the **Save button** on the toolbar.

More *About*
The Undo Feature

Remember the Undo feature from the Word Processor tool? It is available with the Spreadsheet tool as well. Click Undo on the Edit menu immediately after performing the operation you want to undo.

You can save a spreadsheet on hard disk or on a floppy disk. In Project 4, you are to save the spreadsheet on a floppy disk located in drive A. You can use the procedure explained below and on the next page, however, for either hard disk or floppy disk.

Steps   To Save a Spreadsheet

1 **Point to the Save button on the toolbar (Figure 4-58).**

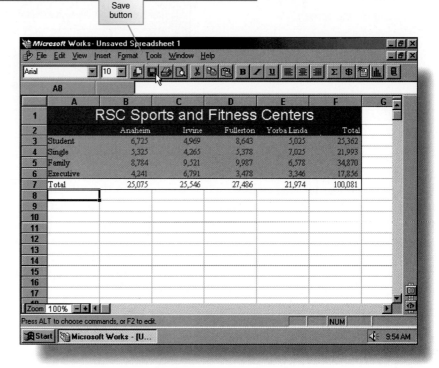

FIGURE 4-58

2 **Click the Save button on the toolbar. When the Save As dialog box displays, type** RSC Memberships **in the File name text box. Click the Save in box arrow. Click the 3½ floppy [A:] icon in the Save in list and then point to the Save button.**

Works displays the Save As dialog box (Figure 4-59). The filename you type displays in the File name text box. This is the name Works will use to store the file. Drive A (3½ Floppy [A:]) is selected in the Save In box. The mouse pointer points to the Save button.

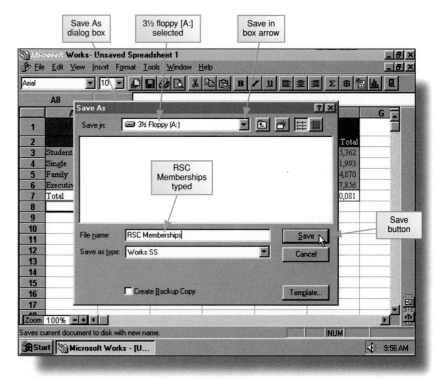

FIGURE 4-59

3 **Click the Save button in the Save As dialog box.**

Works saves the file on the designated disk drive, drive A, and places the filename in the title bar (Figure 4-60).

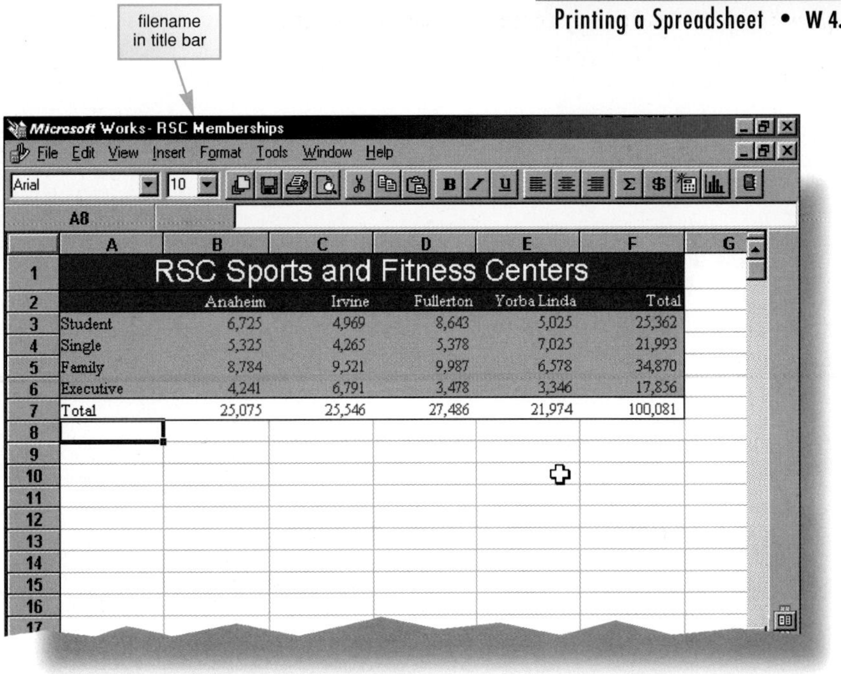

filename in title bar

FIGURE 4-60

Other Ways

1. On File menu click Save As, enter filename, click OK button

2. Press CTRL+S

Printing a Spreadsheet

After you save the spreadsheet, the next step is to print the spreadsheet. To print a spreadsheet, click Print on the File menu, as explained in the steps below and on the next page.

Steps **To Print a Spreadsheet**

1 **Click File on the menu bar and then point to Print.**

Works displays the File menu and the mouse pointer points to the Print command (Figure 4-61).

File menu

Print command

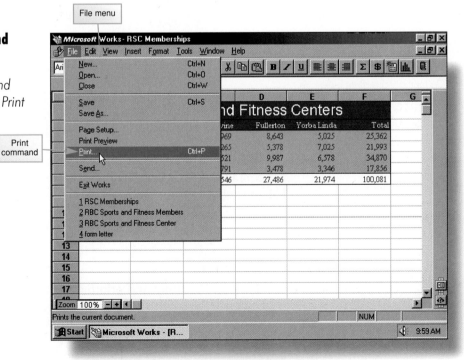

FIGURE 4-61

2 **Click Print. When the Print dialog box displays, point to the OK button.**

Works displays the Print dialog box (Figure 4-62). The default for the dialog box is that one copy of the spreadsheet is to print and all pages in the document are to print.

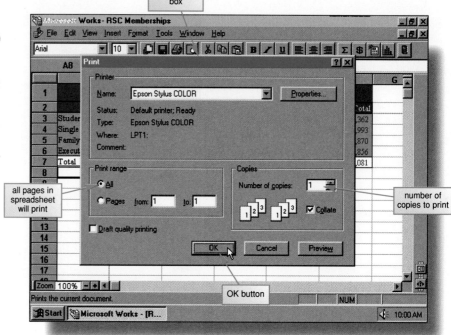

FIGURE 4-62

3 **Click the OK button in the Print dialog box.**

Works momentarily displays a Printing dialog box. Then, the document is printed on the printer (Figure 4-63).

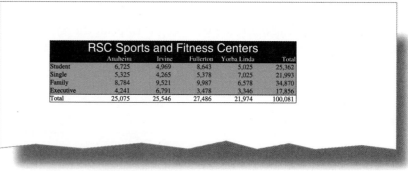

FIGURE 4-63

Other Ways

1. On toolbar, click Print button
2. Press CTRL+P

If a color printer is used, the output will appear as illustrated. If a black and white printer is used, the spreadsheet will print in shades of black, gray, and white.

If you have used the Print command previously and know that proper entries are contained in the Print dialog box, you can click the Print button on the toolbar to cause the spreadsheet to print.

Charting a Spreadsheet

In addition to creating and printing the spreadsheet, Project 4 requires a portion of the data in the spreadsheet to be charted. A **chart** is a graphical representation of the data in the spreadsheet. You are to create a 3-D Bar chart of the memberships for Anaheim, Irvine, Fullerton, and Yorba Linda for each of the four categories (Student, Single, Family, and Executive). With a 3-D Bar chart, memberships are represented by a series of vertical bars that are shaded to give a three-dimensional effect.

To create the 3-D Bar chart, perform the steps below and on the next page.

Steps **To Create a 3-D Bar Chart**

1 **Highlight the cells to be charted (A2:E6) and then point to the New Chart button on the toolbar.**

The highlighted cells include the column titles, row titles, and memberships for Anaheim, Irvine, Fullerton, and Yorba Linda (Figure 4-64). The totals are not included because they do not present meaningful comparisons on a Bar chart. The mouse pointer points to the New Chart button.

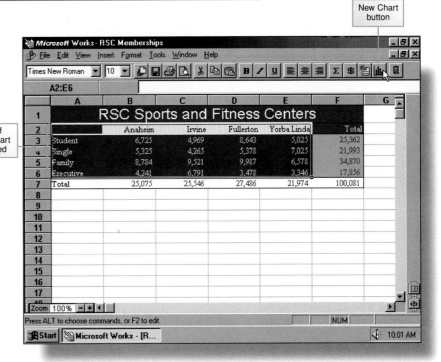

FIGURE 4-64

2 **Click the New Chart button on the toolbar. When the New Chart dialog box displays, point to the 3-D Bar chart in the What type of chart do you want? box located on the Basic Options sheet.**

Works displays the New Chart dialog box (Figure 4-65). Twelve types of charts display in the What type of chart do you want? box on the Basic Options sheet. The Works default chart (Bar chart) is selected. The chart name that is selected (Bar) displays above the chart types. A sample of the chart that will display is shown in the Your Chart box. The mouse pointer points to the 3-D Bar chart.

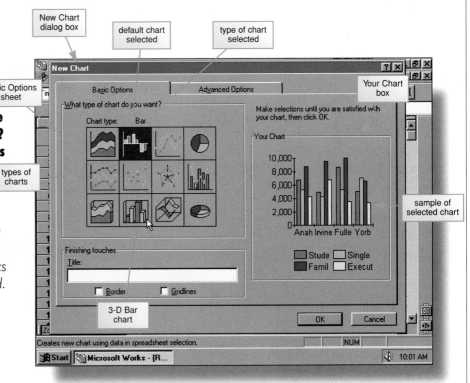

FIGURE 4-65

3 Click 3-D Bar chart. Press the TAB key and type RSC Sports and Fitness Centers in the Title text box. Click Border, and then click Gridlines located in the Finishing touches box. Point to the OK button.

The 3-D Bar chart is selected in the What type of chart do you want? box (Figure 4-66). The title for the chart displays in the Title box. The check mark in the Border check box instructs Works to place a border around the chart. The check mark in the Gridlines check box informs Works to include gridlines on the chart. The Your Chart box contains a sample of the chart that will display. You can enter a maximum of 39 characters including spaces in the Title box.

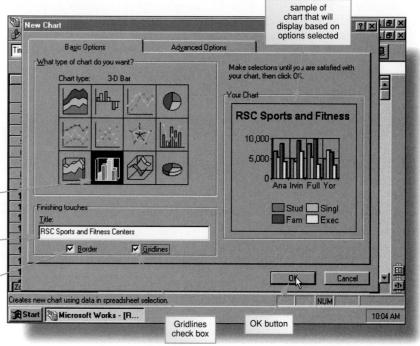

FIGURE 4-66

4 Click the OK button in the New Chart dialog box.

Works displays the chart with the title, RSC Memberships - Chart1, in the title bar (Figure 4-67). The chart title displays centered above the chart. The cluster of bars for each city (Anaheim, Irvine, Fullerton, and Yorba Linda) is called a **category**. All the category labels together are called the **category (X) series**. Each bar (red for Student, green for Single, blue for Family, and yellow for Executive) represents the memberships for each item in the spreadsheet and is called the **Y-series**, or the **value series**. The chart legend indicates the item each color represents. The Charting toolbar displays below the menu bar. The horizontal gridlines originate from each number on the y-axis. The vertical gridlines separate each category on the x-axis. A border displays around the chart.

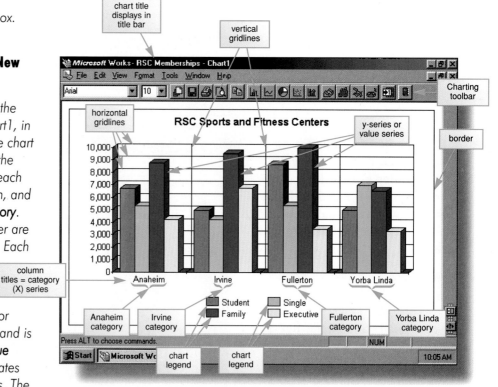

FIGURE 4-67

Other Ways

1. On Tools menu click Create New Chart, click 3-D Bar button, click desired options, click OK button

A spreadsheet file can contain a total of eight charts.

To remove the vertical gridlines from the chart, click the Vertical (Y) axis command on the Format menu in the chart window. In the Format Vertical Axis dialog box, remove the check mark from the Show gridlines check box. To remove the horizontal gridlines from the chart, click the Horizontal (X) axis command on the Format menu in the chart window. In the Format Horizontal Axis dialog box, remove the check mark from the Show gridlines check box.

To remove the border around the chart, click the Border command on the Format menu.

Printing the Chart

You can print the chart by clicking the Print button on the Charting toolbar. By default, Works attempts to fill the entire page with the chart when printing. Therefore, if you want to print a chart with proper proportions, you should first click the **Page Setup command** on the File menu and click Screen Size. Works reduces the chart to the size of your computer screen, which is approximately one-quarter page. Then click the Print button on the toolbar. Perform the steps below and on the next two pages to print the chart with the proper proportions.

More About Printing a Chart

If you work with a color monitor but print in black and white, the colors you see on screen are replaced with patterns in black and white. To view the chart as it will appear when printed, click Display as Printed on the View menu. Works displays the chart as it will appear when printed in black and white.

Steps To Print a Chart

1 **Click File on the menu bar and then point to Page Setup.**

Works displays the File menu and the mouse pointer points to the Page Setup command (Figure 4-68).

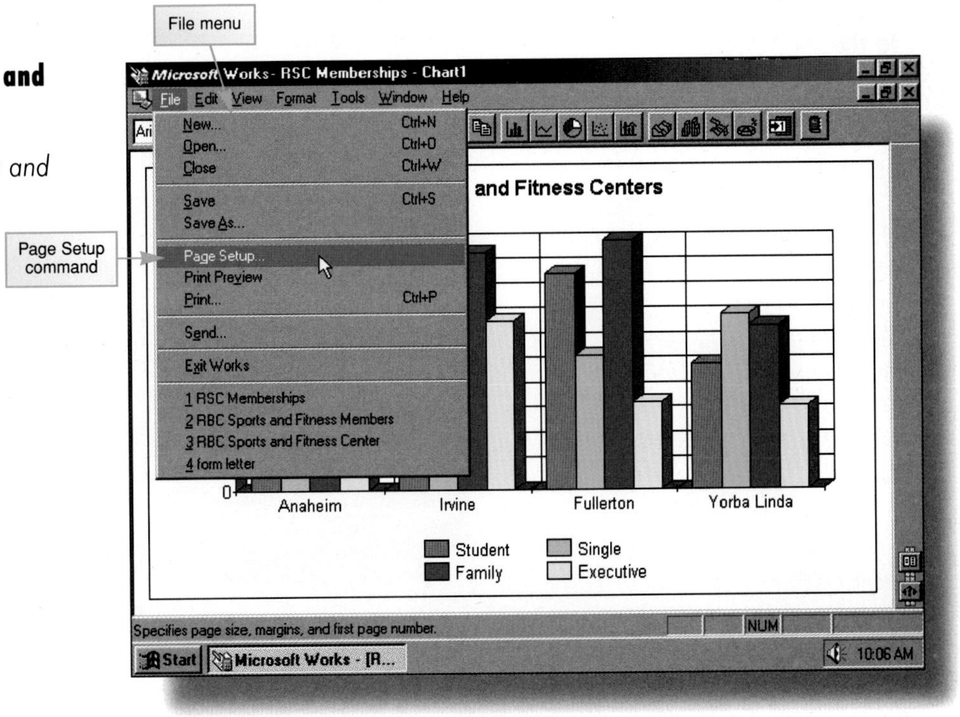

FIGURE 4-68

2 **Click Page Setup. When the Page Setup dialog box displays, point to the Other Options tab.**

The Page Setup dialog box displays and the mouse pointer points to the Other Options tab (Figure 4-69).

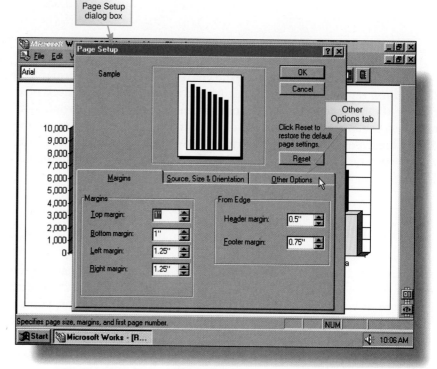

FIGURE 4-69

3 **Click the Other Options tab in the Page Setup dialog box. Click Screen size in the Size box. Point to the OK button.**

Works displays the Other Options sheet (Figure 4-70). The Screen size option button is selected. This option instructs Works to reduce the chart from the default size of full page to the size of your computer screen, which is approximately one-quarter of a page.

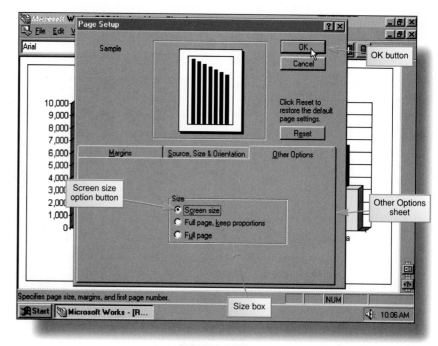

FIGURE 4-70

4 Click the OK button in the Page Setup dialog box. Point to the Print button on the toolbar.

Works removes the Page Setup dialog box (Figure 4-71). The mouse pointer points to the Print button on the toolbar.

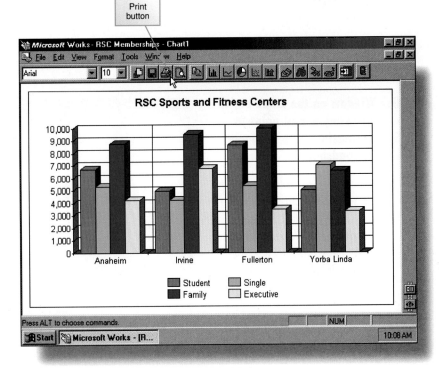

FIGURE 4-71

5 Click the Print button on the toolbar.

Works prints the chart on the top one-quarter of the page (Figure 4-72).

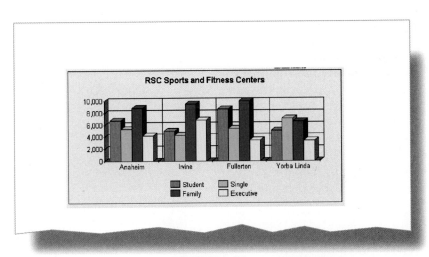

FIGURE 4-72

Other Ways
1. On File menu in the chart window, click Print
2. Press CTRL+P

Viewing the Spreadsheet

When you create a chart, Works displays the chart window on top of the spreadsheet. To view the spreadsheet, click the filename of the spreadsheet on the Window menu in the chart window as illustrated in the steps on the next page.

Steps To View the Spreadsheet

1 **Click Window on the menu bar in the chart window and point to RSC Memberships, the filename of the spreadsheet.**

The Window menu displays and lists the open windows in the application (Figure 4-73). The chart is the active window and Works indicates this by the check mark next to the chart name RSC Memberships - Chart1.

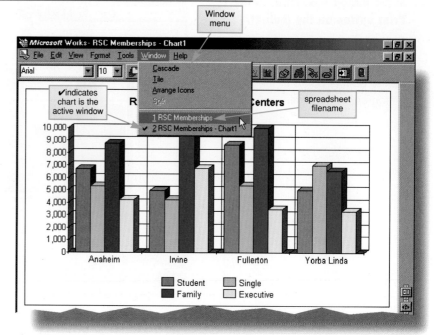

FIGURE 4-73

2 **Click RSC Memberships. Click any cell to remove the highlight from the cells.**

Works displays the spreadsheet and makes the spreadsheet window the active window (Figure 4-74).

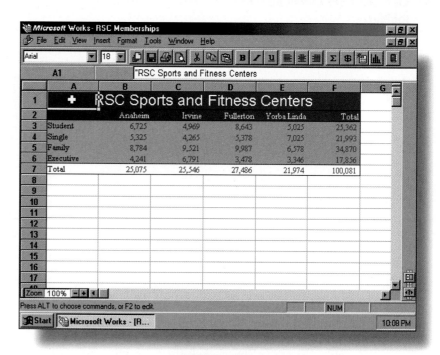

FIGURE 4-74

To move back to the chart window, click the chart name on the Window menu.

Saving the Spreadsheet and Chart

If you want to save the chart with the spreadsheet, save the spreadsheet again using techniques previously explained. The chart will be saved with the spreadsheet. To view the chart at a later time (for example, after you have closed the spreadsheet file), open the spreadsheet file and then choose the Chart command from the View menu.

Closing a Spreadsheet

Once you complete the spreadsheet and chart, you can close the spreadsheet and work on another spreadsheet or another Works project. To close the spreadsheet, perform the following steps.

Steps To Close the Spreadsheet

1. **Point to the Close button in the upper right-hand corner of the spreadsheet window.**

   The mouse pointer points to the Close button in the upper right-hand corner of the spreadsheet window (Figure 4-75).

2. **Click the Close button.**

   The spreadsheet closes and the Works Task Launcher dialog box displays, allowing you to continue to use Works.

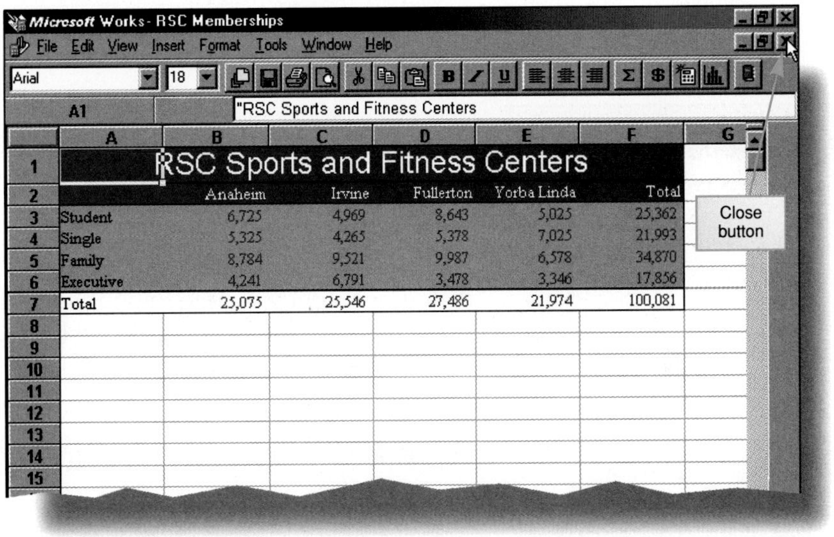

FIGURE 4-75

OtherWays
1. On File menu, click Close
2. Press CTRL+W
3. Press CTRL+F4

You can close a chart without closing the entire spreadsheet file by clicking the Close command from the File menu in the chart window.

If you have made any changes to a spreadsheet after it has been saved, a dialog box appears asking you if you want to save the changes before closing the spreadsheet. Click the Yes button in the dialog box to save changes.

Closing Works

After you have completed all your tasks, normally you will want to close Works and return to the Windows 95 desktop. To close Works, perform the steps on the next page.

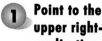 **To Close Works**

1 **Point to the Close button in the upper right-hand corner of the application window.**

The mouse pointer points to the Close button in the upper right-hand corner of the application window (Figure 4-76).

2 **Click the Close button.**

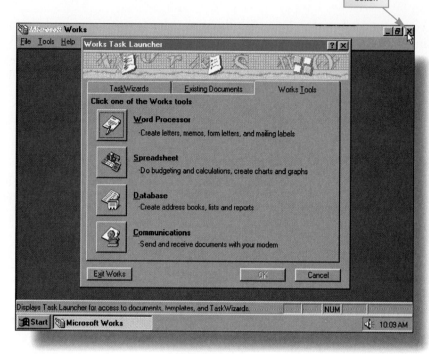

FIGURE 4-76

OtherWays

1. On File menu, click Exit Works
2. In Works Task Launcher dialog box, click Exit Works button
3. Press ALT+F4

Works is terminated, and the Microsoft Windows 95 desktop will again display. If you have made any changes to a spreadsheet after it has been saved, a dialog box appears asking you if you want to save the changes before exiting. Click the Yes button in the dialog box to save changes.

Opening an Existing Spreadsheet File

Once you have saved a spreadsheet on disk, you may need to retrieve the spreadsheet to make changes to it or otherwise process it. To retrieve the spreadsheet, you must open the spreadsheet. Opening a spreadsheet means the spreadsheet is retrieved from the disk into main memory. The easiest way to open an existing document is to use the **My Computer icon** located in the upper left corner of the desktop. Perform the following steps to open an existing spreadsheet.

Steps To Open An Existing Spreadsheet File

1 **Point to the My Computer icon in the upper left corner of the desktop.**

The mouse pointer points to the My Computer icon on the desktop (Figure 4-77).

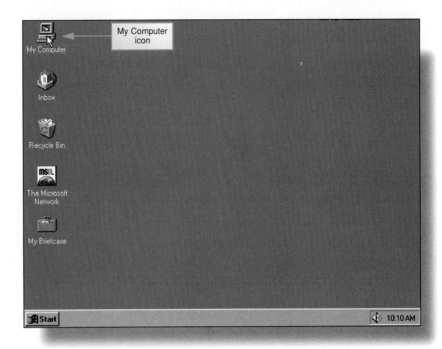

FIGURE 4-77

2 **Double-click the My Computer icon. When the My Computer window opens, point to the 3½ Floppy [A:] icon.**

When you double-click the My Computer icon, Windows 95 opens the My Computer window (Figure 4-78). The My Computer window contains icons representing the hard disk, floppy disk drive, CD-ROM drive, and two folder icons. Drive A in Figure 4-78 is a 3½ floppy disk drive. The icons that display on your screen may be different. The mouse pointer points to the 3½ Floppy [A:] icon.

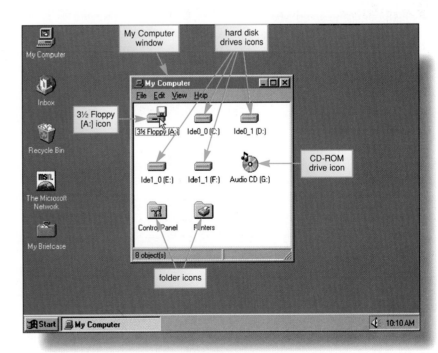

FIGURE 4-78

3 **Double-click the 3½ Floppy [A:] icon. When the 3½ Floppy [A:] window opens, point to the RSC Memberships icon.**

When you double-click the 3½ Floppy [A:] icon, Windows 95 opens the 3½ Floppy [A:] window (Figure 4-79) and displays the filenames on drive A. The mouse pointer points to the RSC Memberships icon. The charting icon identified with the file indicates the file is a spreadsheet.

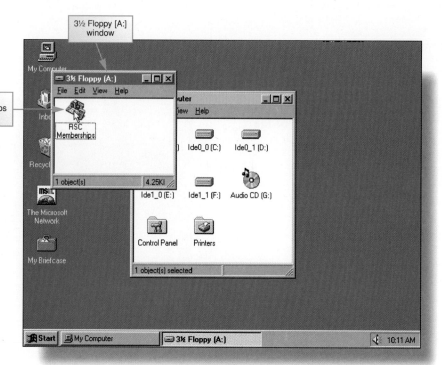

FIGURE 4-79

4 **Double-click RSC Memberships.**

Windows 95 first starts Works and then opens the spreadsheet, RSC Memberships, and displays it on the screen (Figure 4-80). You can revise or print the spreadsheet as required.

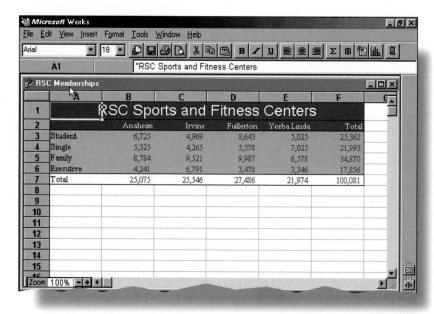

FIGURE 4-80

Other Ways

1. On toolbar click Task Launcher button, click Existing Documents tab, click desired document, click OK button
2. On File menu click Open, click desired document, click Open button
3. Press CTRL+O

You also can click one of the filenames at the bottom of the File menu to open that file.

Correcting Errors

When you create a spreadsheet, the possibility exists that you may make an error by entering the wrong text or data in a cell. In addition, it is possible that you must change a value in a cell even though it was correct when you entered it.

Works provides several methods for changing data in a spreadsheet and correcting errors. These methods are explained below.

Correcting Errors Prior to Entering Data into a Cell

If you notice an error in the entry bar prior to confirming the entry and entering the data into a cell, do one of the following:

1. Use the BACKSPACE key to erase back to the error and then type the correct characters. If the error is too severe, click the Cancel box in the entry bar or press the ESC key to erase the entire entry in the entry bar and reenter the data from the beginning.

Editing Data in a Cell

If you notice an error in the spreadsheet after confirming the entry and entering the data, highlight the cell with the error and use one of the following methods to correct the error.

1. If the entry is short, retype it and click the ENTER box or press the ENTER key. The new entry will replace the old entry. Remember that you must highlight the cell containing the error before you begin typing.
2. If the entry in the cell is long and the errors are minor, you may want to edit the entry rather than retype it. To edit an entry in a cell:
   a. Highlight the cell containing the error.
   b. Click the first character in error in the entry bar. Works places the insertion point at the location you clicked in the entry bar.
   c. Make your changes.

When you type characters in the entry bar, Works inserts the character and moves all characters one position to the right.

To delete a character in the entry bar, place the insertion point to the left of the character you want to delete and then press the DELETE key, or place the insertion point to the right of the character you want to delete and then press the BACKSPACE key.

While the insertion point is located in the entry bar, you may have occasion to move it to various points in the bar. Table 4-1 illustrates the means for moving the insertion point in the entry bar.

TABLE-4-1

TASK	MOUSE	KEYBOARD
Move the insertion point to the beginning of text	Click to left of first character	Press HOME
Move the insertion point to the end of text	Click to right of last character	Press END
Move the insertion point one character to the left	Click one character to left	Press LEFT ARROW
Move the insertion point one character to the right	Click one character to right	Press RIGHT ARROW
Move the insertion point anywhere in the entry bar	Click entry bar at appropriate position	Press LEFT ARROW or RIGHT ARROW
Highlight one or more characters	Drag mouse pointer over the characters	Press SHIFT+LEFT ARROW or SHIFT+RIGHT ARROW
Delete highlighted characters	None	Press DELETE

When you have finished editing an entry, click the Enter box or press the ENTER key.

Understanding how to correct errors or change entries in a spreadsheet is an important skill.

Clearing a Cell or Range of Cells

It is not unusual to enter data into the wrong cell or range of cells. In such a case, to correct the error you may want to delete, or clear, the data. Never highlight a cell and press the SPACEBAR to enter a blank character and assume you have cleared the cell. A blank character is text and is different from an empty cell even though the cell may appear empty.

Works provides a variety of methods to clear the contents of a cell or a range of cells. The various methods are explained in the following paragraphs.

TO CLEAR CELL CONTENTS — DELETE KEY

Step 1: Highlight the cell or range of cells.
Step 2: Press the DELETE key.

TO CLEAR CELL CONTENTS — EDIT MENU AND CLEAR COMMAND

Step 1: Highlight the cell or range of cells.
Step 2: Click Edit on the menu bar and click Clear.

TO CLEAR CELL CONTENTS — EDIT MENU AND CUT COMMAND OR CUT BUTTON

Step 1: Highlight the cell or range of cells.
Step 2: Click Edit on the menu bar and click Cut; or click the Cut button on the toolbar.

Each of these methods has differences you should understand. In the first method, when you press the DELETE key, the data in the cell or cells is cleared but the formatting remains. Thus, even after you clear the cells using the DELETE key, formatting such as dollar formats, bold, italic, underlining, and so on remain. To clear the formatting, you must individually turn off each of the formatting features or use the Cut command for clearing the cells.

When you use the Edit menu and Clear command, the data in the cell or range of cells is cleared, but the formatting remains. This method has the same effect as using the DELETE key.

When you use the Cut command from the Edit menu or click the Cut button on the toolbar, Works clears both the data and the formatting from the cell or range of cells. Actually, the data and the associated formatting are placed on the Windows Clipboard for potential pasting elsewhere, but if you never paste the data into the same or another Works document, in effect, the data and formatting have been entirely cleared from the spreadsheet.

Clearing the Entire Spreadsheet

Sometimes so many major errors are made with a spreadsheet that it is easier to start over. To clear an entire spreadsheet, follow these steps.

TO CLEAR THE ENTIRE SPREADSHEET

Step 1: Highlight the entire spreadsheet by clicking the box located just above row 1 and immediately to the left of column A, or click Select All on the Edit menu.

Step 2: Follow any of the three methods specified previously to clear the cell contents. The method used should be based on whether you want the formatting to remain.

An alternative to the previous steps is to click Close on the File menu and not save the spreadsheet. Works closes the spreadsheet. You can then click the Spreadsheet button in the Works Task Launcher dialog box to begin working on your new spreadsheet.

Project Summary

In this project, you have learned to start the Microsoft Works Spreadsheet tool, enter both text and numeric data into the spreadsheet, calculate the sum of numeric values in both rows and columns, and copy formulas to adjacent cells in both rows and columns. In addition, you have seen how to display the title centered across columns, display the title with color, and you learned how to use the AutoFormat feature to format a spreadsheet. Using the steps and techniques presented, you changed column widths and formatted numeric data in the Comma format.

Next, you learned to save a spreadsheet, print a spreadsheet, create a chart from spreadsheet data, print the chart, and open a spreadsheet. Finally, after completing the project, you know how to correct errors on the spreadsheet.

What You Should Know

Having completed this project, you should now be able to perform the following tasks:

- ◗ Change Column Widths *(W 4.33)*
- ◗ Clear Cell Contents *(W 4.50)*
- ◗ Clear the Entire Spreadsheet *(W 4.51)*
- ◗ Close the Spreadsheet *(W 4.45)*
- ◗ Close Works *(W 4.45)*
- ◗ Copy One Cell to Adjacent Cells in a Column *(W 4.23)*
- ◗ Copy One Cell to Adjacent Cells in a Row *(W 4.20)*
- ◗ Create a 3-D Bar Chart *(W 4.39)*
- ◗ Display Numbers with the Comma Format *(W 4.32)*
- ◗ Enter Column Titles *(W 4.14)*
- ◗ Enter Numeric Data *(W 4.16)*
- ◗ Enter Row Titles *(W 4.15)*
- ◗ Enter the Spreadsheet Title *(W 4.12)*
- ◗ Format Text and Change the Color of Cells *(W 4.24)*
- ◗ Open an Existing Spreadsheet File *(W 4.46)*
- ◗ Print a Chart *(W 4.41)*
- ◗ Print a Spreadsheet *(W 4.37)*
- ◗ Save a Spreadsheet *(W 4.35)*
- ◗ Start the Works Spreadsheet *(W 4.6)*
- ◗ Sum a Column of Numbers Using the AutoSum Button *(W 4.18)*
- ◗ Sum a Row of Numbers Using the AutoSum button *(W 4.22)*
- ◗ Use the AutoFormat command *(W 4.30)*
- ◗ View the Spreadsheet *(W 4.43)*

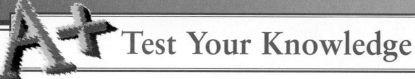 Test Your Knowledge

1 True/False

Instructions: Circle T if the statement is true or F if the statement is false.

T F 1. You can start the Works Spreadsheet by clicking the Spreadsheet button in the Works Task Launcher dialog box.

T F 2. The intersection of each column and each row is a cell.

T F 3. A Works spreadsheet contains a total of 256 columns and 8,192 rows.

T F 4. If text you enter in a cell contains more characters than can be displayed in the width of the cell, the overflow characters will always display in adjacent cells to the right.

T F 5. Works enters numbers right-aligned in cells.

T F 6. When using the AutoSum button to sum a column or row of values, Works always highlights the correct range to sum.

T F 7. You can use the fill handle to copy the contents of one cell to adjacent cells in a column or row.

T F 8. To quickly adjust the column width for best fit, double-click the cell displaying the largest entry in the column.

T F 9. To print a spreadsheet, click the Print button on the Charting toolbar.

T F 10. Clicking Close on the File menu in the chart window closes the spreadsheet file and displays the Works Task Launcher.

2 Multiple Choice

Instructions: Circle the correct response.

1. A _____ is a block of adjacent cells in a spreadsheet.
   a. group   b. highlight   c. chart   d. range

2. To enter numbers into a cell, the cell must be _____.
   a. empty   c. defined as a number
   b highlighted   d. formatted with the Comma format

3. To change a cell's background color, click _____.
   a. Format on the context-sensitive menu
   b. Color on the Format menu
   c. Format cells on the Format menu
   d. the Format button on the toolbar

4. Works enters numbers _____-aligned in a cell.
   a. left   b. center   c. right   d. decimal

5. After highlighting a range to chart, clicking the New Chart button on the toolbar will display _____.
   a. a 2-D Bar chart   c. the New Chart dialog box
   b. a 3-D Bar chart   d. a blank chart window with a Charting toolbar

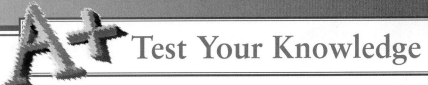

Test Your Knowledge

6. A chart title may contain up to _____ characters including spaces.

   a. 20   b. 30   c. 39   d. 40

7. You can save up to _____ charts for each spreadsheet.

   a. two   b. six   c. eight   d. ten

8. To print a chart, _____.

   a. click Print on the File menu in the charting window

   b. click the Print button in the spreadsheet window

   c. click Print on the File menu in the spreadsheet window

   d. press CTRL+P in the spreadsheet window

9. To delete a character in the entry bar, _____.

   a. place the insertion point at the right of the character to delete and then click the Cancel button

   b. place the insertion point to the left of the character to delete and then press the BACKSPACE key

   c. place the insertion point to the left of the character to delete and then press the SPACEBAR

   d. place the insertion point to the right of the character to delete and then press the BACKSPACE key

10. To clear both the data and the formatting from a cell, click _____.

   a. the DELETE key

   b. the Cut button on the toolbar

   c. Clear on the Edit menu

   d. the BACKSPACE key

3 Fill In

Instructions: In Figure 4-81, a series of arrows point to the major components of the Microsoft Works Spreadsheet window. Identify the parts of the window in the space provided.

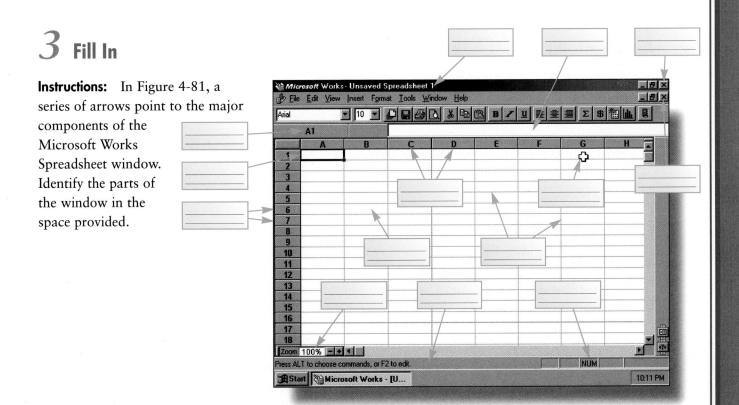

FIGURE 4-81

Test Your Knowledge

4 Fill In

Instructions: Write the appropriate command or button name to accomplish each task.

TASK	COMMAND OR BUTTON NAME
Display a chart	_____
Change a cell's background color	_____
Save a new spreadsheet	_____
Create a chart	_____
Add a column of numbers	_____
Apply the Comma format to a cell	_____
Change text color	_____
Center text across columns	_____
Print a spreadsheet	_____
Print a chart	_____
Close a spreadsheet	_____

Use Help

1 Reviewing Project Activities

Instructions: Use your computer to perform the following tasks to obtain experience using online Help.

1. Start the Microsoft Works Spreadsheet tool.
2. Click the Shrink Help button if necessary to display the Spreadsheet and Charting Menu in the Help window.
3. Click Create a chart on the Spreadsheet and Charting Menu. When the Creating a chart topic displays in the Help window, click To create a chart. Read and print To create a chart on the Step-by-step sheet.
4. Click the More Info tab. Click Quick tour. View the Quick tour on charting. Click the Done button.
5. Click the Menu button located below the Help window to return to the Spreadsheet and Charting Menu. Scroll the list to view the topic, Preview and print your spreadsheet or chart. Click the Preview and print your spreadsheet or chart icon.
6. When the Previewing and printing your spreadsheet or chart topic displays in the Help window, scroll the list to view the topic To print a chart. Click the To print a chart icon. Read and print the To print a chart topic.
7. Press the Back button located below the Help window to view the Previewing and printing your spreadsheet or chart topic. Scroll the list to view the topic To print your spreadsheet. Click the To print your spreadsheet icon. Read and print To print your spreadsheet.
8. Click the Close button in the application window to close Works.

Use Help

2 Expanding on the Basics

Instructions: Use Works online Help to better understand the topics listed below. Print the topic or topics that substantiate your answer. If no Print this topic icon is available, then answer the question on a separate piece of paper.

1. Using the key term, shortcut keys: spreadsheet highlighting, and the Index sheet in the Help topics: Microsoft Works dialog box, display and print the shortcut keys to highlight spreadsheet entries. Then answer the following questions.
   a. Which key or combination of keys highlights an entire column?
   b. Which key or combination of keys highlights an entire row?
   c. Which key or combination of keys highlights an entire spreadsheet?
2. Using the key term, changing number formats on spreadsheets, and the Index sheet in the Help topics: Microsoft Works dialog box, display the topic, To change the number format on spreadsheets. Read the Step-by-Step sheet and More Info sheet and then answer the following questions.
   a. How do you quickly format numbers as currency?
   b. What is General format?
   c. When will Works automatically format a cell as currency or percentage?
   d. How do you enter the fraction 1/16 into a spreadsheet cell?
   e. What should be done if you see #### instead of your entry in a cell?

Apply Your Knowledge

1 Charting Spreadsheet Data

Instructions: Start the Microsoft Works Spreadsheet Tool. Open the spreadsheet, Underwater Aquarium Sales, on the Student Floppy Disk that accompanies this book (Figure 4-82). Chart the range A2:E5 as a 3-D chart. Add the title, Underwater Aquarium Sales - Projections. Add a border and gridlines to the 3-D Bar chart. Print the 3-D chart.

	A	B	C	D	E	F
1	UNDERWATER AQUARIUM SALES					
2		1997	1998	1999	2000	TOTAL
3	FISH	$26,789	$29,520	$35,214	$38,950	$130,473
4	TANKS	15,640	17,820	21,500	25,840	80,800
5	ACCESSORIES	9,850	10,260	11,250	13,780	45,140
6	TOTAL	$54,276	$59,598	$69,963	$80,570	$264,407

A1   "UNDERWATER AQUARIUM SALES

FIGURE 4-82

In the Lab

1 Building a Regional Guitars Sold Spreadsheet

Problem: As the regional sales manager for Goodtime Music Company, you have been asked to analyze the yearly guitar sales for the region. The regional guitar sales are shown in Table 4-2. The spreadsheet and chart are shown in Figure 4-83.

TABLE 4-2				
	WEST	**NORTH**	**SOUTH**	**EAST**
Classical	5456	6782	5460	6000
Steel String	8457	7321	10540	9303
Electric	10250	9561	9652	11275
Bass	6541	4556	7485	7126

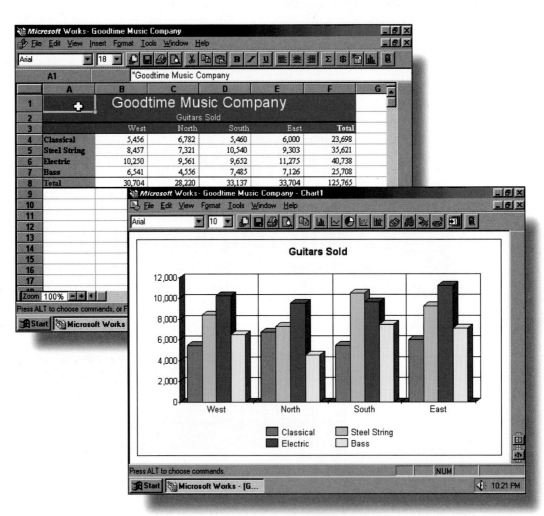

FIGURE 4-83

In the Lab

Instructions: Perform the following tasks:

1. Create the spreadsheet shown in Figure 4-83 using the numbers in Table 4-2.
2. Calculate the totals for the four regions, the guitar categories, and the company.
3. Format the spreadsheet title, Goodtime Music Company, as white 18-point Arial font and centered over columns A through F. Format the spreadsheet subtitle, Guitars Sold, as white 10-point Arial font and centered over columns A through F. Add a dark magenta solid pattern to the foreground of cells A1:F2.
4. Use AutoFormat and the Classic Columns table format for the remaining portion of the spreadsheet. The numbers display using the Comma format.
5. The column width should be 12 for columns A through F.
6. Print the spreadsheet you create.
7. Create the 3-D Bar chart from the spreadsheet data.
8. Print the 3-D Bar chart.
9. Save the spreadsheet with the chart using the filename, Goodtime Music Company.
10. Follow directions from your instructor for turning in this assignment.

2 Building a Current Employees Spreadsheet

Problem: As the director of human resources for the West Coast Fire Department, you have been asked to prepare a report of all employees by department. The current employees are shown in Table 4-3. The spreadsheet and chart are shown in Figure 4-84 on the next page.

TABLE 4-3				
	NORTH DIVISION	HILLS DIVISION	PARK DIVISION	OCEAN DIVISION
Firefighters	725	969	643	525
Engineers	325	265	378	425
Inspectors	784	521	687	578
Mechanics	241	791	478	346

In the Lab

Building a Current Employees Spreadsheet (continued)

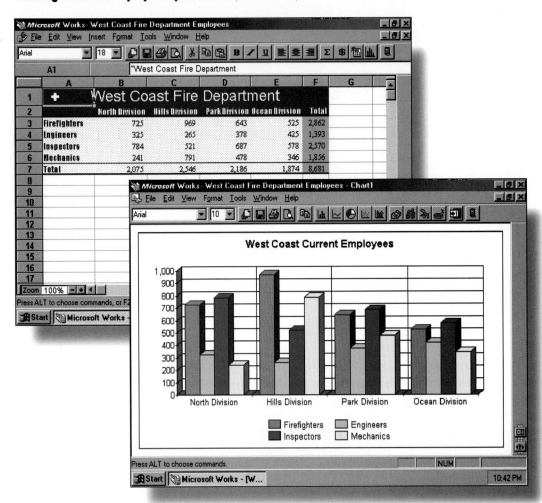

FIGURE 4-84

Instructions: Perform the following tasks:

1. Create the spreadsheet shown in Figure 4-84 using the numbers in Table 4-3 on the previous page.
2. Calculate the totals for the four divisions, the employee categories, and the department.
3. Format the spreadsheet title, West Coast Fire Department, as white 18-point Arial font and centered over columns A through F. Add a dark magenta solid pattern to the foreground of cells A1:F1.
4. Use AutoFormat and the Colorful Columns table format for the remaining portion of the spreadsheet. The numbers display using the Comma format.
5. The column width should be 12 for columns A through E. Column F width should be 6.
6. Print the spreadsheet you create.
7. Create the 3-D Bar chart from the spreadsheet data. Add the title, West Coast Current Employees, to the chart. Also include a border and gridlines for the chart. Print the 3-D Bar chart.

In the Lab

8. Save the spreadsheet with the chart using the filename, West Coast Fire Department Employees.
9. Follow directions from your instructor for turning in this assignment.

3 Building a Computer Software Sales Spreadsheet

Problem: As the director of marketing for Computer Software, Inc., you have been asked to prepare a report of software sales for the past four quarters. The sales are shown in Table 4-4. The spreadsheet and chart are shown in Figure 4-85.

TABLE 4-4

	QTR1	QTR2	QTR3	QTR4
Business	22990	33250	11987	22789
Database	42230	22564	11257	22461
Education	11196	21495	31856	11797
Graphics	21950	31023	21256	31789
Games	22520	33154	33937	44330

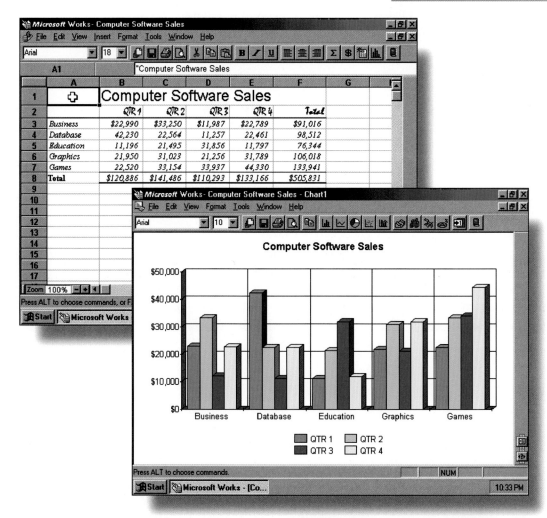

FIGURE 4-85

In the Lab

Building a Computer Software Sales Spreadsheet *(continued)*

Instructions: Perform the following tasks:

1. Create the spreadsheet shown in Figure 4-85 using the numbers in Table 4-4 on the previous page.
2. Calculate the totals for the four quarters, the software categories, and the company.
3. Format the spreadsheet title, Computer Software Sales, as 18-point Arial font and centered over columns A through F.
4. Use AutoFormat and the Financial Blue table format for the remaining portion of the spreadsheet.
5. The column width should be 12 for columns A and F.
6. Print the spreadsheet you create.
7. Create the 3-D Bar chart from the spreadsheet data. Add the title, Computer Software Sales, to the chart. Also include gridlines for the chart.
8. Print the 3-D Bar chart.
9. Save the spreadsheet with the chart using the filename, Computer Software Sales.
10. Follow directions from your instructor for turning in this assignment.

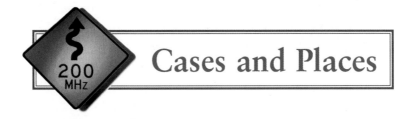

Cases and Places

The difficulty of these case studies varies:

▶ Case studies preceded by a single half moon are the least difficult. You can complete these case studies using your own computer or a computer in the lab.
▶▶ Case studies preceded by two half moons are more difficult. You must research the topic presented using the Internet, a library, or another resource, and then prepare a brief written report.
▶▶▶ Case studies preceded by three half moons are the most difficult. You must visit a store or business to obtain the necessary information, and then use it to create a brief written report.

Cases and Places

1 ▶ To save money, you are considering changing your car's oil, oil filter, and air filter yourself instead of going to the dealer or a local garage. You examine newspaper ads and make a few telephone calls to determine the prices of these items (Figure 4-86) to decide where to shop for these supplies.

TYPE OF RETAILER	QUARTS OIL	OIL FILTER	AIR FILTER	TOTAL COST
Discount	$5.95	$2.50	$4.25	
Auto parts	$4.95	$2.88	$3.55	
Auto dealer	$7.50	$5.50	$6.95	
Mini-mart	$9.00	$7.00	$9.10	

FIGURE 4-86

With this data, you want to produce a spreadsheet to analyze the total costs for five quarts of oil, an oil filter, and an air filter. Use the concepts and techniques presented in the project to create the spreadsheet.

2 ▶ You frequently fly to various cities to visit family and for business. In an attempt to earn a free ticket based on your mileage, you keep a record of the distance flown on four airlines during the past four years (Figure 4-87). Use the concepts and techniques presented in this project to prepare a spreadsheet to accumulate your distance flown on each airline and during each year.

AIRLINE	1992	1993	1994	1995
American	156	532	248	832
United	432	1043	341	963
Northwest	1865	621	832	2779
Continental	439	311	1521	379

FIGURE 4-87

3 ▶ The number of new cars and trucks sold has increased each year from 1991 to 1995, as indicated in Figure 4-88.

MODEL YEAR	DOMESTIC CARS (THOUSANDS)	IMPORT CARS SOLD (THOUSANDS)	DOMESTIC TRUCKS SOLD (THOUSANDS)	IMPORT TRUCKS SOLD (THOUSANDS)
1991	6,276	2,313	3,582	333
1992	6,195	2,140	4,026	247
1993	6,595	2,011	4,789	199
1994	7,173	1,977	5,499	155
1995	7,167	1,803	5,666	170

FIGURE 4-88

With this data, you want to create a spreadsheet to examine these increases. Use the concepts and techniques presented in this project to create the spreadsheet. Calculate the total domestic cars, import cars, domestic trucks, and import trucks sold each year and the total vehicles sold in each of the four categories for the past five years. Also, include bar graphs showing the number of domestic and import cars and the domestic and import trucks sold each year.

Cases and Places

4 ▶▶ Medical and fitness experts recommend aerobic exercise for at least 30 minutes three times weekly. You have decided to visit your campus' fitness center between classes and on weekend mornings in an attempt to improve your health. You speak with a fitness trainer who develops an aerobic training schedule for you. In addition, she recommends 30 minutes of spot toning on alternate days. You decide to exercise by using the treadmill for 24 minutes on Monday, Wednesday, and Friday, the stepper for 18 minutes on Tuesday, Thursday, and Saturday, and the rower for 18 minutes on Sunday, Wednesday, and Saturday. Also, you plan to use free weights for 30 minutes every other day beginning on Monday. Use the concepts and techniques presented in this project to prepare a spreadsheet to record the total minutes spent exercising on each piece of equipment and with the free weights each week. Chart your progress for four weeks. Then create a bar graph illustrating your exercise efforts.

5 ▶▶ The director of your school's fitness center has asked you to help her arrange more efficient scheduling of the facilities. She has asked you to determine which activities appeal to various age groups during the day. You administer a survey to all students and staff using the fitness center during the week and collect data on their ages and preferred activities. You discover that among students ages 17 – 21, 1143 participate in aerobics, 643 in swimming, 2,534 in toning, 423 in volleyball, 943 in running or walking, and 210 in tennis. Among students ages 22 – 29, 2338 participate in aerobics, 893 in swimming, 3021 in toning, 354 in volleyball, 1,932 in running or walking, and 521 in tennis. Among students ages 30 – 39, 964 participate in aerobics, 421 in swimming, 1950 in toning, 301 in volleyball, 1021 in running or walking, and 402 in tennis. Among students ages 40 – 49, 643 participate in aerobics, 398 in swimming, 978 in toning, 97 in volleyball, 793 in running or walking, and 389 in tennis. Among students ages 50 and older, 297 participate in aerobics, 318 in swimming, 419 in toning, 76 in volleyball, 521 in running or walking, and 320 in tennis. Using this information, create a spreadsheet showing the age groups that participate in each of these activities. Include a bar graph to illustrate your data.

6 ▶▶▶ The United States Post Office has started new services and has introduced new products in recent years. Visit your local post office, and ask the postmaster how the facility derives some of its revenues. In particular, find out how many first class commemorative and regular postage stamps (self-adhesive and regular), post cards (single and double), certificates of mailing, certified mail, money orders, and return receipts are sold each week for a two-month period. Using this information, together with the techniques presented in this project, create a spreadsheet showing the total for each category. Include a bar graph to illustrate your data.

7 ▶▶▶ Health experts recommend individuals obtain 10-20 percent of their total daily calories from fat, which for most people would be approximately 20 – 40 grams per day. Keep track of the total fat grams you consume daily during breakfast, lunch, dinner, and snacks for one week. You can determine the number of fat grams by examining the labels on the products, tables in nutrition books, or pamphlets at local fast food restaurants. Use the concepts and techniques presented in this project to prepare a spreadsheet. Include totals for each day of the week and each meal of the week to determine which days and meals are the healthiest for you. Include a bar graph to illustrate your data.

Microsoft *Works* 4

Windows 95

Creating Formulas, Sorting and Charting Data

Objectives

You will have mastered the material in this project when you can:

▶ Enter row titles
▶ Display row titles using wrap text
▶ Write and enter formulas
▶ Use arithmetic operators in formulas
▶ Use parentheses in formulas
▶ Use the Point mode to enter cell references in formulas
▶ Copy formulas in single and multiple columns
▶ Alter the range of the SUM function
▶ Use Easy Calc to create a formula
▶ Format a spreadsheet
▶ Change column widths
▶ Add color to a spreadsheet
▶ Sort rows in the spreadsheet
▶ Use Print Preview
▶ Zoom in and out on a print preview page
▶ Print in landscape orientation
▶ Create a 3-D pie chart
▶ Add data labels to a chart from nonadjacent columns
▶ Format a chart title and data labels
▶ Save and print a chart

Project 5

Order of the Day

Sort Your Priorities

Does it ever seem that life is a continuous collection of formulas? We have formulas for success, feeding babies, time management, winning at blackjack, sales and marketing management, and fitness. Formulas exist for fund-raising, playing the piano, and writing romance novels. In cooking and beverage making, formulas are known as recipes – probably the most famous of all is the closely guarded secret recipe for Coca-Cola. Some race cars are even known as Formula racers because of the set of specifications that manufacturers must follow in building them.

If it seems that people sometimes live by the numbers, there's a good reason: the desire for order is a natural human trait because order leads to simplification. Consider the words of Thomas Mann: "Order and simplification are the first steps toward the mastery of a subject –

the actual enemy is the unknown." This quest for order is evident in the burgeoning fields of self-help and corporate individual improvement programs. In the area of time management alone, many millions of dollars are spent every year on seminars, tapes, CDs, books, and time-management systems.

It should come as no surprise that the Microsoft Works Spreadsheet, as in so many sectors of human endeavor, is based on the proper application of formulas that are capable of being arranged in various *orders*, via sorting, to convey useful information. Besides the usual basic arithmetic operations, Works provides an extensive set of scientific and logical operators that furnish powerful ways to combine and compare entities, such as the investment attributes of IBM's stock versus that of Federal Express or one particular stock versus an entire portfolio. By using the sorting capabilities within Works, information can be classified or categorized according to the author's needs, such as price, earnings, purchase date, and so on.

Spreadsheets also can be used to organize your time. In his classic book, *How to Get Control of Your Time and Your Life*, Alan Lakein stresses the value of planning activities by order of importance relative to life objectives. By helping to sort out priorities and plan for A-goals, spreadsheets can be a powerful tool in that direction.

As a bonus, Works also provides several ways of evaluating data visually. Whereas numbers on a spreadsheet are precise in their meaning, it often is difficult to establish a direct spatial relationship between various types of data, such as which stock has grown the fastest or which represents the biggest share of a portfolio. Graphs, 3-D pie charts, and bar charts allow fast comparison of important relationships by translating tabular data to graphical images, making it easy to see the differences.

Whether you are using a spreadsheet to tabulate your latest winnings at the blackjack table or to figure out who is the leading driver on the Formula One circuit, you can be sure that formulas and ordering data on your spreadsheet will play important roles.

Project 5

Microsoft
Works 4
Windows 95

Creating Formulas, Sorting, and Charting Data

Case Perspective

This semester you have been hired as an intern with a financial consulting group. You have been asked to create a spreadsheet that contains the stock investment portfolio of the president. In particular, he wants to know the initial value of the stocks purchased, the current value of the stocks purchased, and the gain or loss of the stocks purchased. You also have been asked to analyze the portfolio summary of the stock investment portfolio.

Your task is to develop a spreadsheet to illustrate the stock investment portfolio. In addition, the president of the financial consulting group has asked to see a graphical representation of the current value of his stock investment portfolio.

Introduction

In Project 4, you learned that a spreadsheet is useful for presenting data and performing calculations. In addition to performing calculations using the SUM function, Works allows you to perform calculations based upon formulas you enter in selected cells.

The data in the spreadsheet in Project 4 was graphically illustrated using a 3-D Bar chart. Works allows you to graphically display data using many different types of charts. In addition, you can identify a specific order in which the rows in your spreadsheet appear.

Project Five

Project 5 produces the spreadsheet and chart shown in Figure 5-1. The spreadsheet contains the stock portfolio of an individual investor. The name of the stock, the purchase date, the number of shares purchased, and the purchase price per share occupy the first four columns. In the fifth column, titled Initial Value, Works calculates the initial value for the shares from a formula that multiplies the number of shares purchased (column C) times the purchase price per share (column D). For example, the investor bought five hundred shares of AST stock at a price of 4.75 per share. The initial value (500 * 4.75) is 2,375.00.

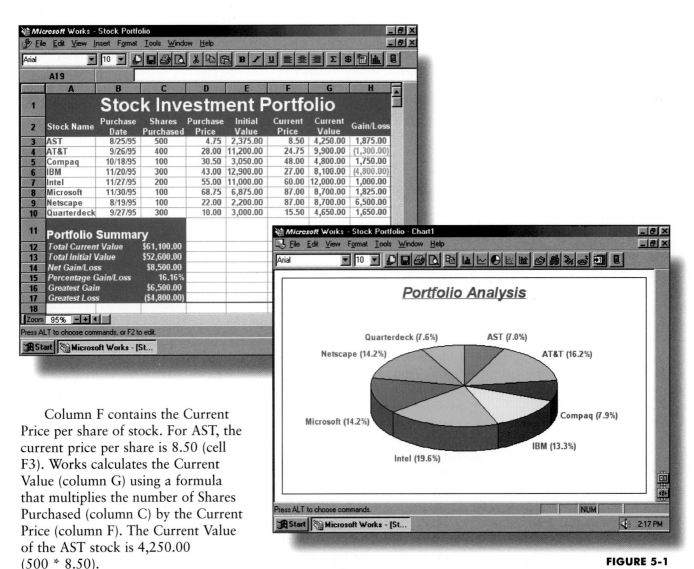

FIGURE 5-1

Column F contains the Current Price per share of stock. For AST, the current price per share is 8.50 (cell F3). Works calculates the Current Value (column G) using a formula that multiplies the number of Shares Purchased (column C) by the Current Price (column F). The Current Value of the AST stock is 4,250.00 (500 * 8.50).

In the spreadsheet in Figure 5-1, both the Purchase Price column and the Current Price column contain fictitious numbers. These values may not be the actual values of the stocks on the dates shown.

When the investor purchases and holds stock, the Current Value of the stock can increase or decrease from the Initial Value. If the Current Value is greater than the Initial Value, the investor has realized a gain. If the Current Value goes down and is less than the Initial Value, the investor has suffered a loss. Works calculates the Gain/Loss of a stock (column H) using a formula that subtracts the Initial Value (column E) from the Current Value (column G). For example, AST shows a gain because the Current Value minus the Initial Value is a positive value (4,250.00 - 2,375.00 = 1,875.00). If a stock has a loss, such as AT&T in row 4, the loss displays in red within parentheses.

More *About*
Creating Formulas

It is important that you understand how to create formulas in Works. Creating formulas properly are among the most powerful features in spreadsheets. Works performs each calculation in a formula in a specific order, depending on the operator. Works uses the same order as in algebra. If you want Works to perform the calculations in a different order, use sets of parentheses to override the normal order of calculations.

The box at the bottom of the screen in Figure 5-1 on the previous page contains the Portfolio Summary. The Total Current Value is the sum of the values in column G. The Total Initial Value is the sum of the initial values in column E. Net Gain/Loss is equal to the Total Current Value minus the Total Initial Value. The Percentage Gain/Loss is calculated by a formula that divides the Net Gain/Loss by the Total Initial Value. In the spreadsheet, Works uses a formula to divide the gain (8,500.00) by the Total Initial Value (52,600.00), yielding a Percentage Gain/Loss of 16.16%. The Portfolio Summary also includes the Greatest Gain (6,500.00) and the Greatest Loss (4,800.00) for the Stock Investment Portfolio.

In Figure 5-1 on the previous page, the stocks are displayed in alphabetical order based on the name of the stock. That is, AST is first, AT&T is second, Compaq is third, and so on. When you enter the records, however, you enter them in the sequence of the date they were purchased (column B). Therefore, the first stock you enter is Netscape, followed by AST, AT&T, and so on. You will use the sorting feature of Works to order the rows alphabetically by stock name.

After you complete the spreadsheet, you will prepare a chart based on the current values of the stocks. This chart (see Figure 5-1) is a **3-D Pie chart** illustrating the percentage of the portfolio each stock represents. A pie chart is commonly used to show percentages of a whole.

Spreadsheet Preparation Steps

To provide an overview of this project, the general steps to prepare the spreadsheet, printed report, and chart in Figure 5-1 are listed below.

1. Start the Works Spreadsheet.
2. Enter the spreadsheet title (Stock Investment Portfolio) and the column titles (Stock Name, Purchase Date, Shares Purchased, Purchase Price, Initial Value, Current Price, Current Value, and Gain/Loss).
3. Enter the Stock Name for the first stock, the Purchase Date, the number of Shares Purchased, and the Purchase Price.
4. Enter the formula to calculate the Initial Value (Shares Purchased times the Purchase Price).
5. Enter the Current Price.
6. Enter the formula to calculate the Current Value (Shares Purchased times Current Price).
7. Enter the formula to calculate the Gain/Loss (Current Value minus Initial Value).
8. Enter the data for the remaining stocks in the report.
9. Copy the formulas for Initial Value, Current Value, and Gain/Loss for each stock.
10. Enter the titles for the Portfolio Summary section.
11. Enter the formulas to calculate the Total Current Value, Total Initial Value, Net Gain/Loss, Percentage Gain/Loss, Greatest Gain, and Greatest Loss.
12. Format the spreadsheet.
13. Save the spreadsheet.
14. Add color to the spreadsheet.
15. Print the spreadsheet.
16. Prepare the 3-D Pie chart.
17. Print the 3-D Pie chart.
18. Save the spreadsheet and the 3-D Pie chart.

The following sections contain a detailed explanation of each of these steps.

Starting the Works Spreadsheet

To start the Works Spreadsheet, follow the steps used in Project 4. These steps are summarized below.

TO START THE WORKS SPREADSHEET

Step 1: Click the Start button on the taskbar, point to Programs, point to the Microsoft Works 4.0 folder on the Programs submenu, and then click Microsoft Works 4.0 on the Microsoft Works 4.0 submenu.

Step 2: When the Works Task Launcher dialog box displays, click the Works Tools tab. When the Works Tools sheet displays, click the Spreadsheet button.

Step 3: If the Microsoft Works window is not maximized, maximize it.

Step 4: If the Unsaved Spreadsheet 1 window is not maximized, maximize it also.

Entering the Spreadsheet Title and Column Headings

Complete the following steps to enter the spreadsheet title and column headings in the spreadsheet.

 Steps To Enter the Spreadsheet Title and Column Headings

1 **Highlight the cell where you will enter the spreadsheet title – cell A1 (Figure 5-2).**

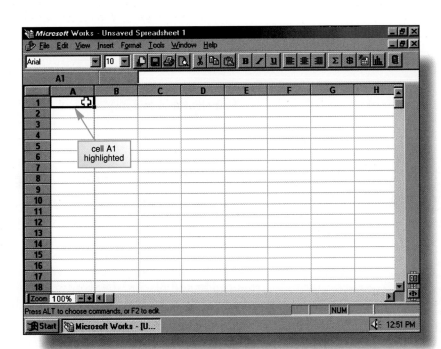

FIGURE 5-2

2 **Type the spreadsheet title,** `Stock Investment Portfolio`**, and press the ENTER key to confirm the entry.**

Works enters the spreadsheet title into cell A1 (Figure 5-3). The title overflows into cells B1 and C1 because cells B1and C1 are empty.

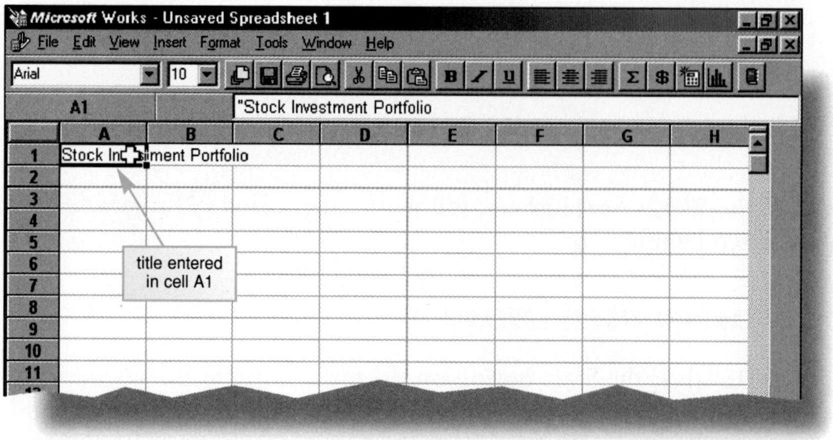

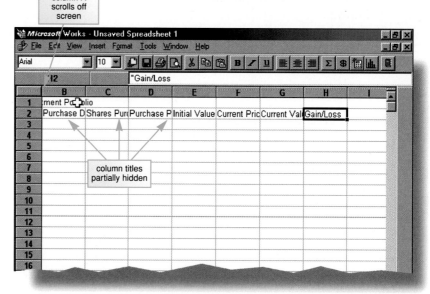

FIGURE 5-3

3 **Highlight the appropriate cells one at a time and enter each of the column headings (see Figure 5-1 on page W 5.5 for column titles).**

When you highlight cell H2, Works scrolls the screen one column to the right and column A scrolls off the screen. The column headings are entered in cells A2 through H2 (Figure 5-4). Column headings that are too long to display in a cell are partially hidden behind the adjacent cells to the right.

FIGURE 5-4

Some column headings do not display completely within the cells when they are entered (columns B, C, D, F, and G in Figure 5-4). Although these column titles do not completely display, the complete titles are contained within the cells.

Formatting Column Headings Using Wrap Text

Because some of the column headings cannot be read, it is recommended that you format the column titles at this point so the entire contents of the column headings display.

One method of formatting cells so all the words in the cell can be read is to **wrap text**. When you wrap text, Works fits the words in the cell by increasing the row height and placing the words on multiple lines within the cell. To format the column titles using wrap text, complete the following steps.

More *About* Wrapping text in a Cell

When entering lengthy text in a cell, you can press ALT+ENTER to end each line where you wish the line to end. When using the Wrap text check box in the Format Cells dialog box, Works determines how many words will fit on one line in the cell.

Steps **To Format Cells Using Wrap Text**

1 **Click the left scroll arrow to view column A. Highlight cells A2 through H2. Point to the highlighted range and right-click. When the context-sensitive menu displays, point to Format.**

Cells A2 through H2 are high-lighted (Figure 5-5). The context-sensitive menu displays and the mouse pointer points to the Format command.

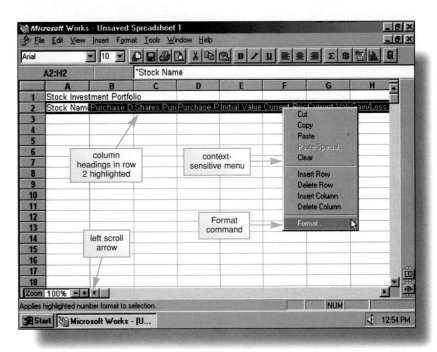

FIGURE 5-5

2 **Click Format. When the Format Cells dialog box displays, click the Alignment tab. When the Alignment sheet displays, click Center in the Horizontal box, click Center in the Vertical box, click the Wrap text below the Vertical box, and point to the OK button.**

The Center option button in the Horizontal box is selected, the Center option button in the Vertical box is selected, the Wrap text check box contains a check mark, and the mouse pointer points to the OK button (Figure 5-6). The Center option button in the Horizontal box directs Works to center the text horizontally within a cell; the Center option button in the Vertical box directs Works to center the text vertically within a cell.

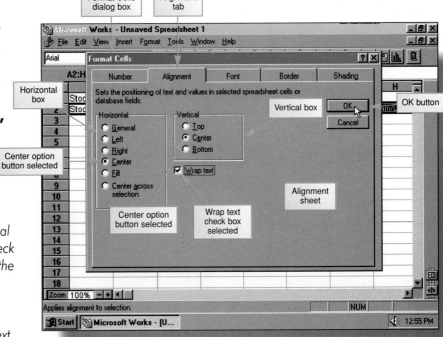

FIGURE 5-6

4 **Click the OK button in the Format Cells dialog box.**

Works displays the column headings centered both vertically and horizontally within the cells (Figure 5-7). Column headings that were too long to display in the cell now display on two lines. Works increases the row height to allow two lines to display.

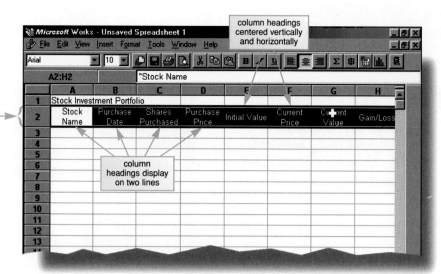

FIGURE 5-7

OtherWays

1. On Format menu click Alignment, click Wrap text

You now can clearly read each column title, which greatly simplifies entering the data that follows.

Entering Data

After entering the titles, the next step is to enter the data in the spreadsheet. The data consists of text (Stock Name), a date (Purchase Date), numeric data (Shares Purchased, Purchase Price, and Current Price), and formulas that calculate Initial Value, Current Value, and Gain/Loss. Enter data according to Purchase Date.

To enter the Stock Name, Purchase Date, Shares Purchased, and Purchase Price, perform the following steps.

Steps **To Enter Text, Date, and Numeric Data**

1 **Highlight the cell which is to contain the first stock name — cell A3 — and type** Netscape **as the stock name.**

Works displays the text in the entry bar and in the cell (Figure 5-8).

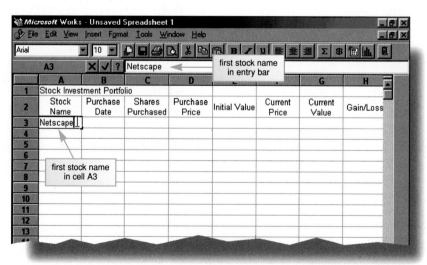

FIGURE 5-8

2 Press the RIGHT ARROW key, type the purchase date (8/19/95) in cell B3, press the RIGHT ARROW key, type the number of shares (100) in cell C3, press the RIGHT ARROW key, type the purchase price (22.00) in cell D3, and press the RIGHT ARROW key.

The values you typed are stored in the cells (Figure 5-9). The purchase price is not formatted in the Comma format. You will perform this formatting later. Cell E3 is highlighted.

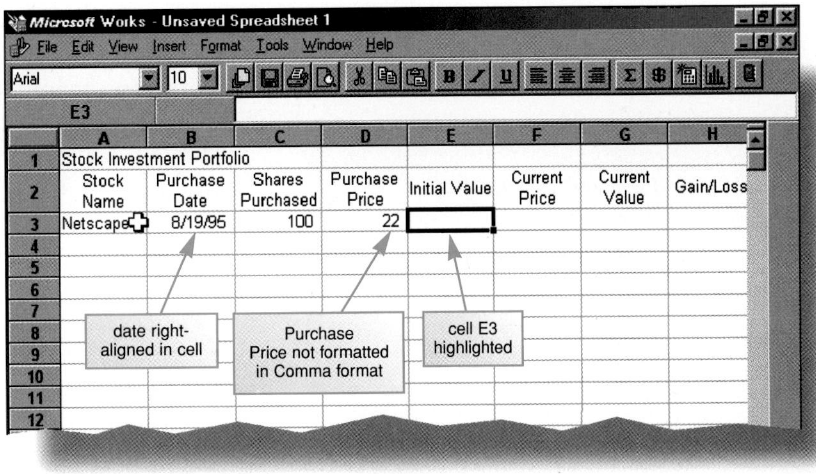

FIGURE 5-9

Works considers a date to be a numeric field and, therefore, stores it right-aligned in cell B3. Because cell D3 is not yet formatted, Works removes the decimal and trailing zeros in the value 22.00 and displays only 22.

Entering Formulas

The Initial Value, Current Value, and Gain/Loss fields in the spreadsheet are calculated based on formulas. Thus, to continue building the spreadsheet, you must enter the formulas in their respective cells.

In Works, a **formula** is an equation that calculates a new value from existing cell values within the spreadsheet. For example, the Initial Value is calculated based on the existing values in the Shares Purchased column and the Purchase Price column.

A formula always begins with an equal sign. It is followed by a combination of cell references, numbers, operators, and possibly functions, such as the SUM function used in Project 4.

In a formula, a **cell reference** identifies a cell that contains data to be used in the formula. For example, when you place the formula =C3*D3 in cell E3, Works will multiply the numeric value in cell C3 by the numeric value in cell D3 and place the product in cell E3. The asterisk (*) in the formula is called an **operator**. An operator specifies the arithmetic operation to be carried out in the formula. You can use five different operators in a formula. These operators are summarized in Table 5-1.

Formulas can contain more than two cell references or numeric values and also can contain multiple operators. For example, the formula =C4*(D4+H9)/F5 is a valid formula. To determine the results of this formula, Works performs the operations within the formula according to **standard algebraic rules**. First, any operation contained within parentheses is performed. Therefore, in the example formula in this paragraph, the first operation is to add the value in cell D4 to the value in cell H9.

Then exponentiation is performed, followed by any multiplication or division operations. Finally, addition and subtraction are performed. If two or more operators within the formula have the same order of evaluation, Works performs the operations from left to right. Thus, in the example formula above, Works would multiply the sum of the values in cell D4 and cell H9 by the value in cell C4 and then divide the result by the value in cell F5.

More *About*
Recalculation of Formulas

Every time you enter a value into a cell that is referenced by a formula in the spreadsheet, Works recalculates all formulas instantly. In large spreadsheets that include hundreds of calculations, this can be very time consuming. You can control when Works recalculates a spreadsheet by clicking Options on the Tools menu. On the Data Entry sheet, click Use manual calculation. Manual calculation tells Works not to update the spreadsheet each time you make a change that affects a formula. When you are ready to calculate the spreadsheet, press the F9 function key. This setting applies to the active spreadsheet only.

TABLE 5-1	
OPERATOR	FUNCTION
+	Addition
−	Subtraction
*	Multiplication
/	Division
^	Exponentiation

The examples in Table 5-2 further illustrate the way Works evaluates formulas. When writing formulas, you must take care to ensure the proper calculations are performed. One method to ensure the correct sequence is to use parentheses.

For example, if a formula in cell K12 were supposed to calculate the average of the values in cells L2, L4, and L6, the formula =L2+L4+L6/3 would not obtain the proper result because Works would first divide the value in cell L6 by 3 and then add the values in L2, L4, and the result of the division (L6/3).

The correct way to write the formula is =(L2+L4+L6)/3. In this formula, which uses parentheses, Works will first add the values in cells L2, L4, and L6. Then, it will divide the sum by 3, resulting in the average of the three numbers.

Whenever you enter a formula, review the formula carefully to ensure the correct calculation will occur.

In this project, the Initial Value is calculated by multiplying the number of Shares Purchased by the Purchase Price. From the spreadsheet in Figure 5-9 on the previous page, notice that for Netscape, the number of Shares Purchased is contained in cell C3 and the Purchase Price is located in cell D3. Therefore, the formula to calculate the Initial Value is =C3*D3.

To enter the formula that calculates the Initial Value, perform the following steps.

TABLE 5-2		
CELL VALUES	**FORMULA**	**RESULT**
C4=25	=F12+C4/D6	105
D6=5		
F12=100		
F2=4	=F2^3/H6+G8	20
H6=8		
G8=12		
E6=9	=(E6+G13)/D9+E8	4
G13=3		
D9=6		
E8=2		

Steps **To Enter a Formula**

1 **Highlight cell E3, the cell that will contain the formula, and type an equal sign.**

Works displays the equal sign in the entry bar and in cell E3 (Figure 5-10). The equal sign informs Works you are entering a formula. The Cancel box, Enter box, and Help box display in the entry bar.

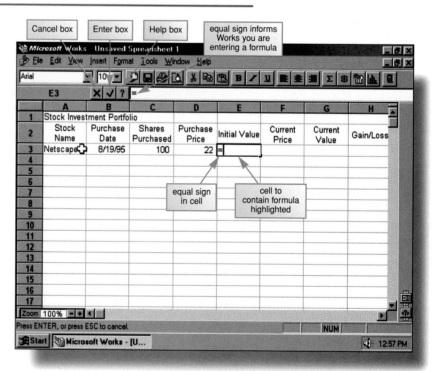

FIGURE 5-10

2 **Highlight the first cell in the formula – cell C3 – by clicking the cell or pressing an arrow key to move to the cell.**

*When you highlight the cell, Works places a black background in the cell and also places the cell reference in the formula (Figure 5-11). Works also indicates on the status bar that you are using the **Point mode**, which is the term used when you point to a cell that is to be included in a formula.*

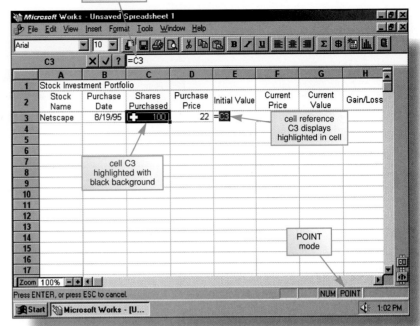

FIGURE 5-11

3 **Type the multiplication operator (*).**

Works displays the multiplication operator in both the entry bar and the cell where you are entering the formula (Figure 5-12). In addition, Works removes the temporary highlight from cell C3, which you pointed to in Step 2, and returns it to the cell containing the formula.

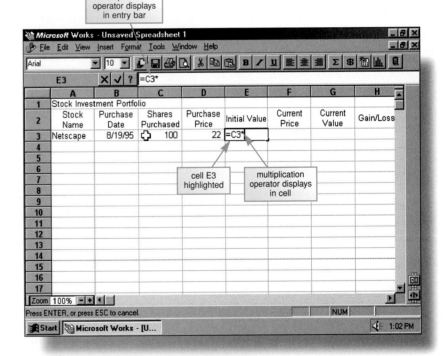

FIGURE 5-12

4 Highlight the second cell in the formula – cell D3 – by clicking the cell or using an arrow key to move to the cell.

Once again, Works places a black background in the highlighted cell and places the cell reference in the formula in both the entry bar and cell E3 (Figure 5-13). Point mode again displays on status bar.

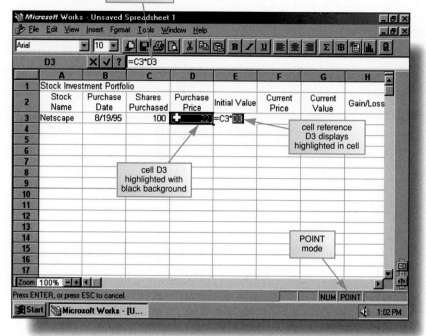

FIGURE 5-13

5 Enter the formula by clicking the Enter box or pressing the ENTER key.

Works enters the formula into cell E3 and performs the calculation (Figure 5-14). The result of the calculation is 2200, which is the product of 100 (the value in cell C3) multiplied by 22 (the value in cell D3).

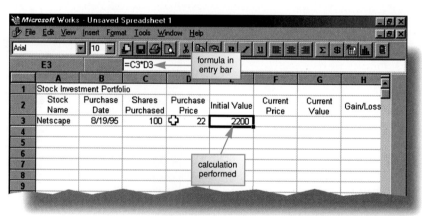

FIGURE 5-14

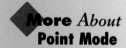

More *About* **Point Mode**

In Point mode you can use the mouse pointer or arrow keys to point to a cell to enter it in a formula. This saves you the trouble of having to enter the cell's contents with the keyboard. Using point mode also increases the accuracy of creating a formula.

In the previous steps, you selected the cells used in the formula by highlighting the cell with either the mouse or the arrow keys. Works also allows you to actually type the cell reference when you enter the formula. For example, to enter the formula in cell E3 in the previous illustration, you could type =C3*D3 and then press the RIGHT ARROW key; or click the Enter box; or press the ENTER key. This method, however, is prone to error because you may type an incorrect cell reference. It is recommended, therefore, that you use the pointing method of identifying cells to enter cell references into a formula because it leads to greater accuracy.

To continue to enter data for the Netscape stock, you must enter the Current Price into cell F3 and then enter the formula to calculate the Current Value in cell G3. To calculate the Current Value for Netscape, the number of Shares Purchased in cell C3 is multiplied by the Current Price in cell F3. Therefore, the formula is =C3*F3. The steps to enter the Current Price and the formula for the Current Value follow.

Steps: To Enter a Value and a Formula

1 **Highlight cell F3, type, 87, the current price for Netscape, press the RIGHT ARROW key, and then type an equal sign.**

Works enters the Current Price in cell F3, highlights cell G3, and displays the equal sign in both the entry bar and cell G3 (Figure 5-15).

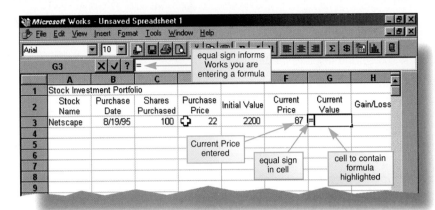

FIGURE 5-15

2 **Highlight the first cell in the formula – cell C3 – by clicking the cell or pressing an arrow key to move to the cell.**

Works highlights cell C3 with a black background and places the cell reference in the formula (Figure 5-16). Point mode displays on the Status bar.

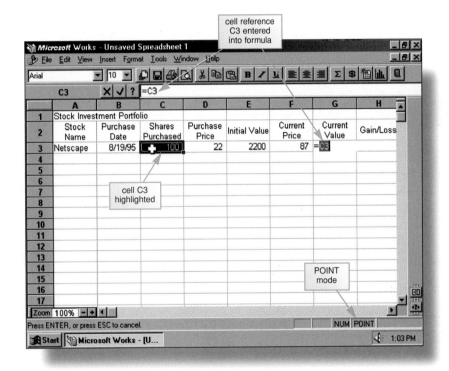

FIGURE 5-16

3 **Type the multiplication operator (*) and then highlight the second cell in the formula – cell F3.**

Once again, Works highlights cell F3 with a black background and places the cell reference in the formula (Figure 5-17).

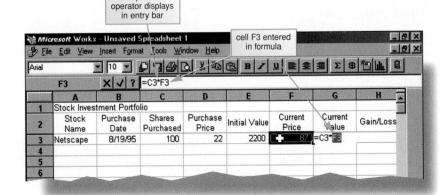

FIGURE 5-17

4 **Enter the formula by clicking the Enter box or pressing the ENTER key.**

*Works enters the formula into cell G3, calculates the result (100 * 87 = 8700) and displays the answer in cell G3 (Figure 5-18).*

FIGURE 5-18

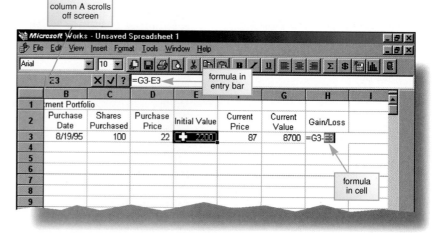

The last formula you must enter for the first row in the spreadsheet calculates the Gain/Loss of the stock by subtracting the Initial Value from the Current Value. You should enter this formula, =G3-E3, into cell H3 by performing the following steps.

Steps **To Enter a Formula**

1 **Highlight cell H3, type an equal sign, highlight cell G3, type a minus sign (-), and highlight cell E3.**

When you highlight cell H3, Works scrolls column A off the screen (Figure 5-19). The formula appears in the entry bar and in cell H3.

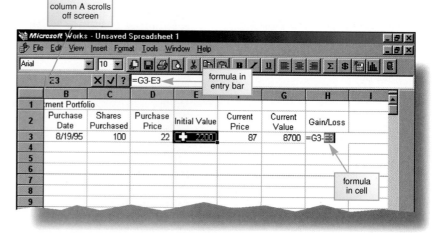

FIGURE 5-19

2 **Click the Enter box or press the ENTER key.**

Works enters the formula into cell H3 and calculates the result (8700 – 2200 = 6500) and displays the answer in cell H3 (Figure 5-20).

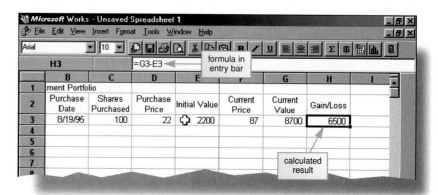

FIGURE 5-20

Entering the Spreadsheet Data

After you have entered the data for the first stock, Netscape, you must enter the data for the next stock into row 4 of the spreadsheet using the same method you used for row 3. After entering the data for row 4, you will enter the data for the remainder of the spreadsheet. To enter the data, complete the following steps (see Figure 5-21 and Figure 5-22).

TO ENTER SPREADSHEET DATA

Step 1: Highlight cell A4 and type the stock name, AST.

Step 2: Using the techniques described previously, enter the data in cells B4, C4, D4, and F4 (see Figure 5-21). Do not enter any formulas. You will copy the formulas from row 3 after you have entered all the other data in the spreadsheet. It is more efficient to copy the formulas all at one time instead of row by row.

Step 3: Enter the data for the subsequent rows (see Figure 5-22). Do not enter the formulas.

Copying a Formula

Once the data is entered in the spreadsheet, you must copy the formulas from cells E3, G3, and H3 down columns E, G, and H. You can use the **fill handle** to copy a formula down in a column. Recall from Project 3, the fill handle is the small rectangular dot located in the lower right corner of the heavy border around the highlighted cell.

To copy the formula that calculates the Initial Value in column E, perform the steps on the next page.

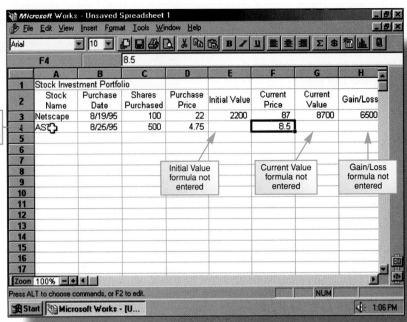

FIGURE 5-21

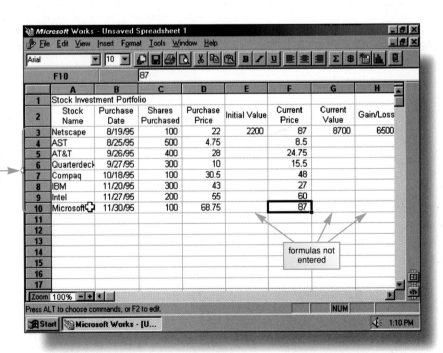

FIGURE 5-22

More *About*
Fill Handle

The fill handle is new to this release of Works. It is one of the most popular and impressive tools available with Works. Use the fill handle to copy a cell's contents down a column or across a row or both.

Steps To Copy a Formula

1 **Highlight the cell containing the formula to copy – cell E3. Position the mouse pointer on the fill handle. Drag the range you want to copy into (E4:E10).**

Cells E3 through E10 are highlighted (Figure 5-23).

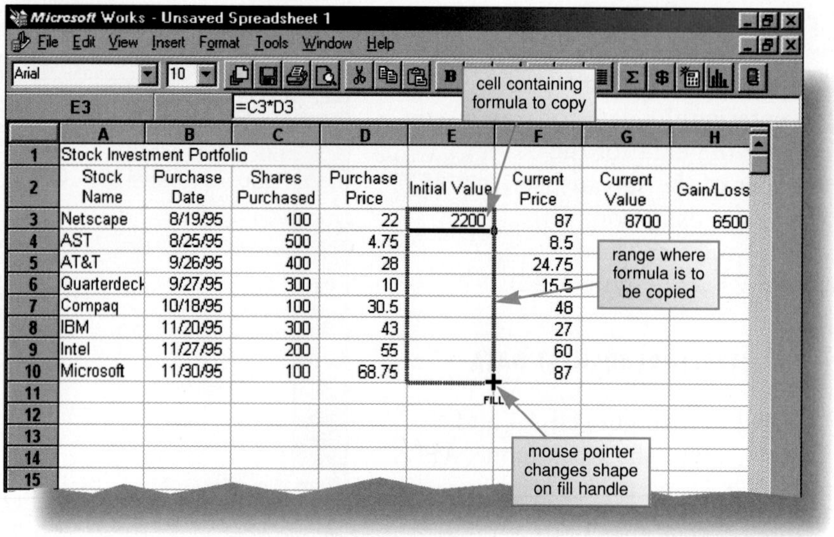

FIGURE 5-23

2 **Release the mouse button.**

Works copies the formula in cell E3 to the range E4:E10 and displays the calculated results in each of the cells (Figure 5-24). As with the SUM function in Project 3, the cell references for each row change to reflect the correct row. For example, the formula in cell E3 is =C3*D3 and the formula in cell E4 is =C4*D4.

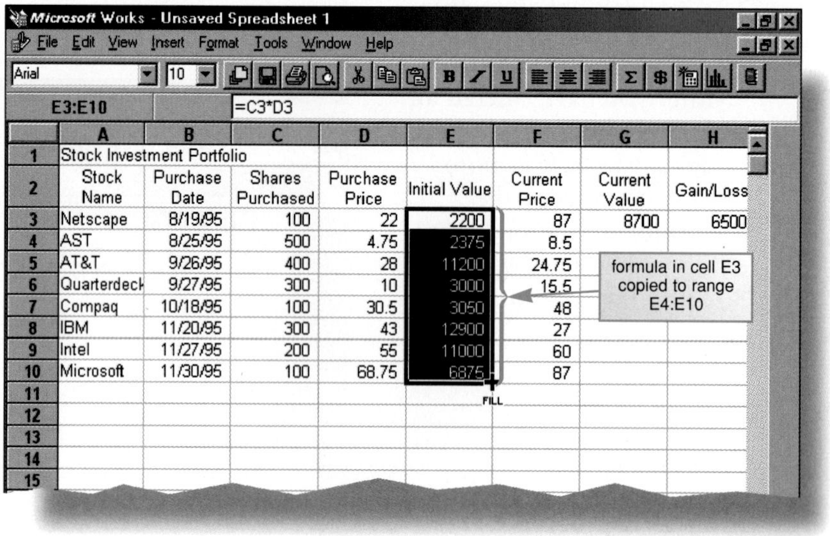

FIGURE 5-24

Copying Multiple Columns

The next step in building the spreadsheet is to copy the Current Value formula in cell G3 to cells G4:G10, and to copy the Gain/Loss formula in cell H3 to cells H4:H10. When you must copy cells in adjacent columns, you can copy the cells all at one time by highlighting multiple columns and using the fill handle. Perform the following step to copy cells in adjacent columns.

Steps To Copy Cells in Adjacent Columns

1 **Click the right scroll arrow to view cell H3. Highlight the adjacent cells containing the formulas to copy – cells G3 and H3. Position the mouse pointer on the fill handle located in the lower right corner of highlighted cell H3. Drag the range G4:H10. Release the mouse button.**

Cells G3 through G10 and cells H3 through H10 are highlighted (Figure 5-25). Works copies the formulas in cells G3 and H3 down their respective columns and displays the calculated results in each of the cells. The cell references within the cells are modified to reference the proper rows. Thus, cell G4 contains the formula =C4*F4, cell H4 contains the formula =G4-E4, and so on.

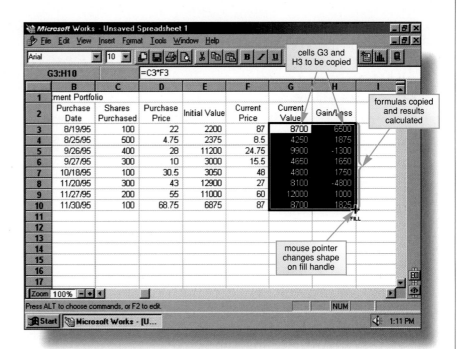

FIGURE 5-25

To remove the highlight, click any cell. Notice that when you copy the cells, Works performs the arithmetic in the formulas as part of the copying process and then displays the results in the cells.

Entering Portfolio Summary Data

The next step in building the spreadsheet for this project is to enter the Portfolio Summary data. This data includes the Total Current Value of all stocks, the Total Initial Value of all stocks, the Net Gain/Loss of the stocks, the Percentage Gain/Loss, the Greatest Gain, and the Greatest Loss.

To calculate the Total Current Value of all stocks, use the SUM function to sum the values in the range G3:G10 (see Figure 5-1 on page W 5.5). Similarly, use the SUM function to sum the values in the range E3:E10 to obtain the Total Initial Value. You obtain the Net Gain/Loss by calculating Total Current Value minus Total Initial Value (=C12-C13). Finally, determine the Percentage Gain/Loss by dividing the Net Gain/Loss by the Total Initial Value (=C14/C13).

Perform the steps on the next pages to enter the Portfolio Summary titles and the accompanying formulas.

Steps To Enter Titles and Formulas

1 **Highlight cell A11 and type** Portfolio Summary. **Then, type** Total Current Value **in cell A12, type** Total Initial Value **in cell A13, type** Net Gain/Loss **in cell A14, type** Percentage Gain/Loss **in cell A15, type** Greatest Gain **in cell A16, and type** Greatest Loss **in cell A17 (Figure 5-26).**

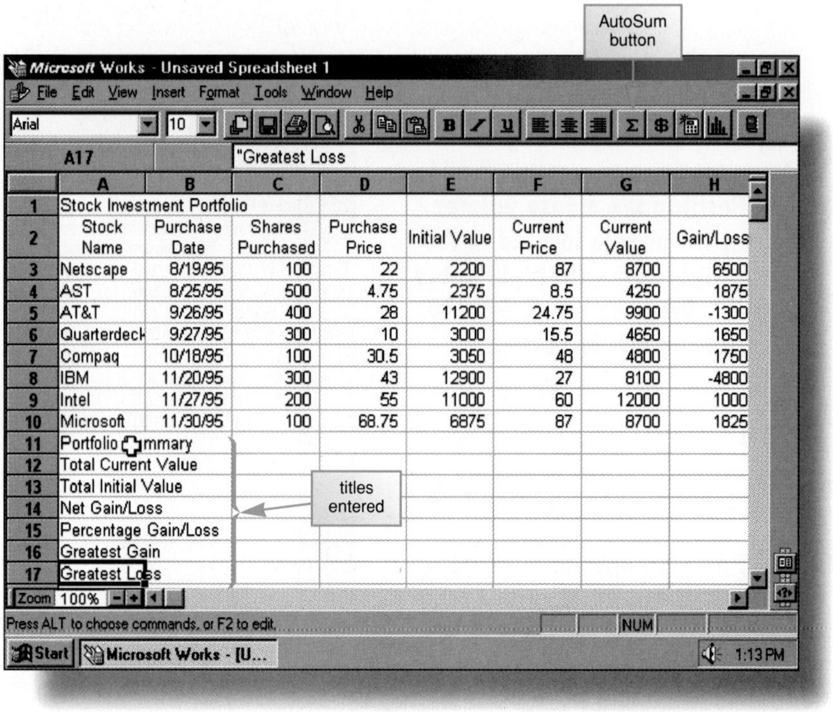

AutoSum button

FIGURE 5-26

2 **Highlight cell C12 where the Total Current Value will appear, and then click the AutoSum button on the toolbar.**

When you click the AutoSum button, Works chooses the most likely values to sum. In Figure 5-27, Works chose the range C3:C11 because those cells are immediately above cell C12. This is incorrect, however, because the chosen range contains Shares Purchased, not Current Values.

range C3:C11 placed in SUM function

AutoSum button

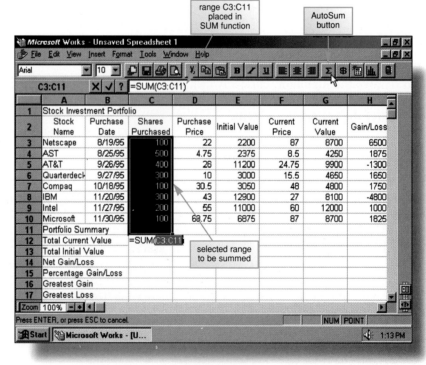

FIGURE 5-27

3 **Highlight the correct range by dragging cells G3:G10.**

When you highlight the range G3:G10, Works places the range in the SUM function (Figure 5-28).

FIGURE 5-28

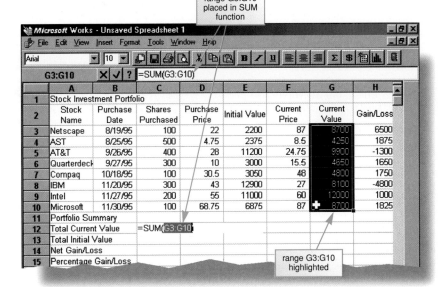

4 **Click the Enter box, press the ENTER key, or click the AutoSum button a second time.**

Works enters the SUM function in cell C12, calculates the sum, and displays the sum in the cell (Figure 5-29).

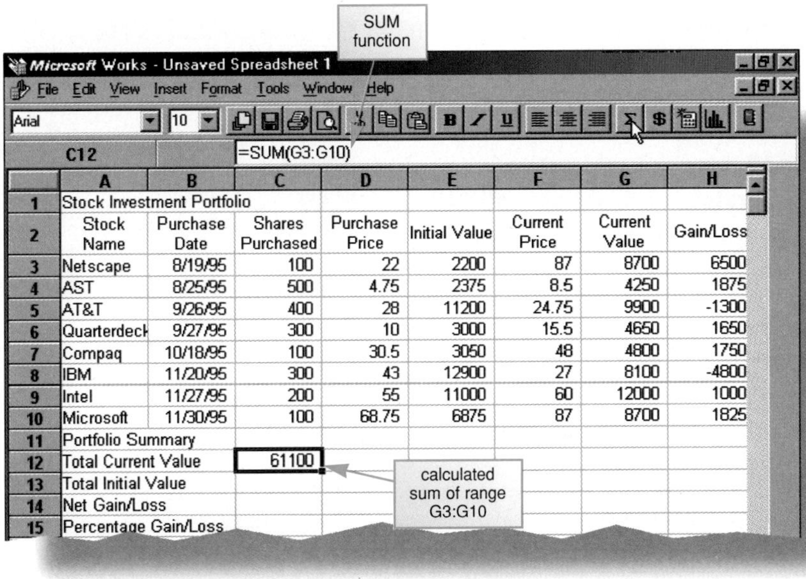

FIGURE 5-29

5 **Highlight cell C13, click the AutoSum button on the toolbar, and highlight the range E3:E10.**

The SUM function displays in cell C13 and in the entry bar (Figure 5-30). The range of cells highlighted (E3:E10) contains the values to add to obtain the Total Initial Value.

FIGURE 5-30

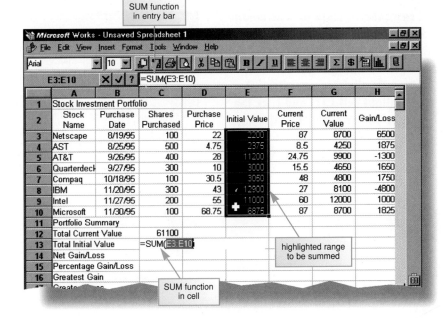

6 Click the Enter box, press the ENTER key, or click the AutoSum button a second time.

Works enters the SUM function into cell C13, calculates the sum of cells E3:E10, and displays the sum in the cell (Figure 5-31).

FIGURE 5-31

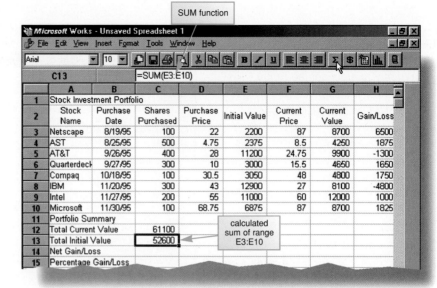

7 Enter the formula for Net Gain/Loss by first highlighting cell C14 and typing an equal sign (=). Then, highlight cell C12, type the subtraction operator (-), highlight cell C13, and click the Enter box or press the ENTER key.

Works enters the net gain/loss in cell C14 (Figure 5-32).

FIGURE 5-32

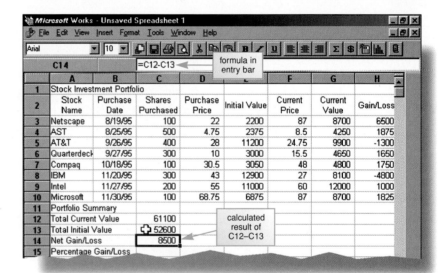

8 Enter the formula for Percentage Gain/Loss by first highlighting cell C15 and typing an equal sign. Then, highlight cell C14, type the division operator (/), highlight cell C13, and click the Enter box or press the ENTER key.

Works enters the percentage gain/loss in cell C15 (Figure 5-33).

FIGURE 5-33

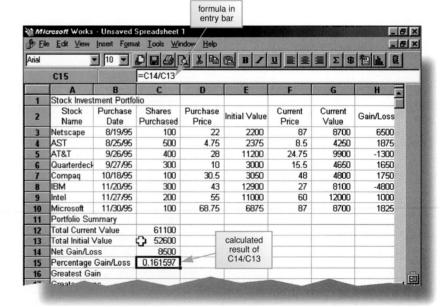

The final requirement for entering data in the spreadsheet is to calculate the greatest gain and the greatest loss found in column H of the stock investment portfolio. This is accomplished using the MAX and MIN functions. The **MAX function** is used to display the largest value in a range, and the **MIN function** is used to display the smallest value in a range.

A **function** is a built-in formula you can use in a Works spreadsheet. All functions begin with an equal sign and consist of the function name, a set of parentheses, and arguments. **Arguments** are the information you provide to a function to calculate a result. Arguments are enclosed in parentheses and separated by commas. For example, in the function =MAX(H3:H10), the function name is MAX and the argument is the range H3:H10.

To enter a function into a spreadsheet cell, you can type the entire function from the keyboard and press the ENTER key, or you can click the Easy Calc button on the toolbar. Clicking the **Easy Calc button** on the toolbar is the easier, more reliable method because Works enters the function in the correct format. To enter the MAX and MIN functions using the Easy Calc button on the toolbar, perform the following steps.

To Enter the MAX and MIN Functions Using Easy Calc

1 **Highlight cell C16 where the greatest gain will display. Point to the Easy Calc button on the toolbar.**

Cell C16 is highlighted and the mouse pointer points to the Easy Calc button on the toolbar (Figure 5-34).

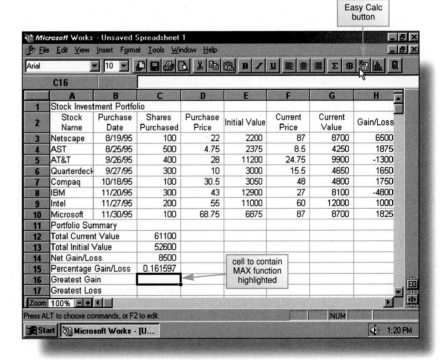

FIGURE 5-34

2 **Click the Easy Calc button on the toolbar. When the Easy Calc dialog box displays, point to the Other button in the Other calculations box.**

Works displays the Easy Calc dialog box (Figure 5-35). Cell C16 is highlighted and the mouse pointer points to the Other button in the Easy Calc dialog box. In the Common calculations box, five buttons (Sum, Multiply, Subtract, Divide, and Average) display that you can use to build formulas for adding, multiplying, subtracting, dividing and averaging numbers.

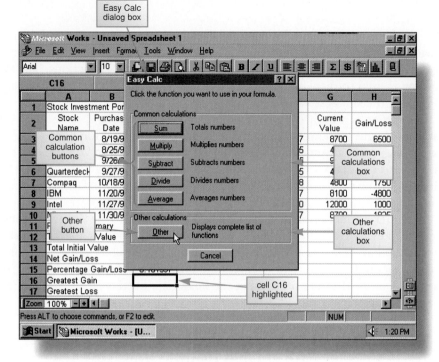

FIGURE 5-35

3 **Click the Other button in the Easy Calc dialog box. When the Insert Function dialog box displays, click Statistical in the Category box. Then click MAX(RangeRef0,RangeRef1,...) in the Choose a function list. Point to the Insert button.**

Works displays the Insert Function dialog box (Figure 5-36). The Statistical option button is selected in the Category box. The available statistical functions display in the Choose a function list. The MAX function is highlighted and a brief description of the MAX function displays in the Description box. Clicking the All option button in the Category box displays an alphabetical list of all the Works functions. The mouse pointer points to the Insert button.

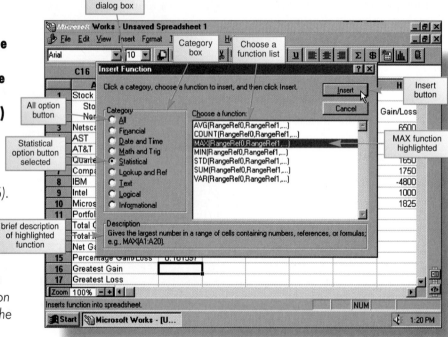

FIGURE 5-36

④ **Click the Insert button in the Insert Function dialog box. When the Easy Calc dialog box displays, highlight the range for which you want to find the largest value – H3:H10. Point to the Next button in the Easy Calc dialog box.**

Works displays the Easy Calc dialog box (Figure 5-37). A brief description of the MAX function displays in the MAX box. Information displays below the MAX function description indicating you are to highlight a range to be inserted in the MAX function. The range you highlighted displays in the Range text box. The completed MAX function displays in the What your formula will look like text box. Clicking the Back button returns you to the Easy Calc dialog box displayed in Figure 5-35. The mouse pointer points to the Next button.

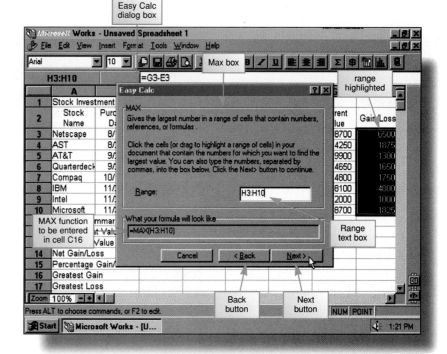

FIGURE 5-37

⑤ **Click the Next button in the Easy Calc dialog box. When the next Easy Calc dialog box displays, point to the Finish button.**

Works displays the next Easy Calc dialog box (Figure 5-38). The Final result box displays information instructing you to click the cell or type the cell reference into the Result at text box where you want the result of the MAX function to display. Cell C16 displays in the Result at text box because you highlighted the cell before clicking the Easy Calc button on the toolbar. The mouse pointer points to the Finish button.

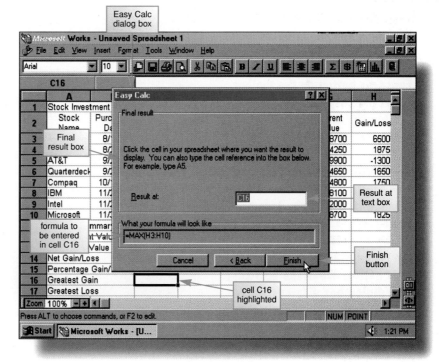

FIGURE 5-38

6 **Click the Finish button in the Easy Calc dialog box.**

Works enters the MAX function in cell C16 and determines the largest value in the range specified in the MAX function (Figure 5-39). The value 6500 displays in cell C16 because it is the largest value in the range H3:H10.

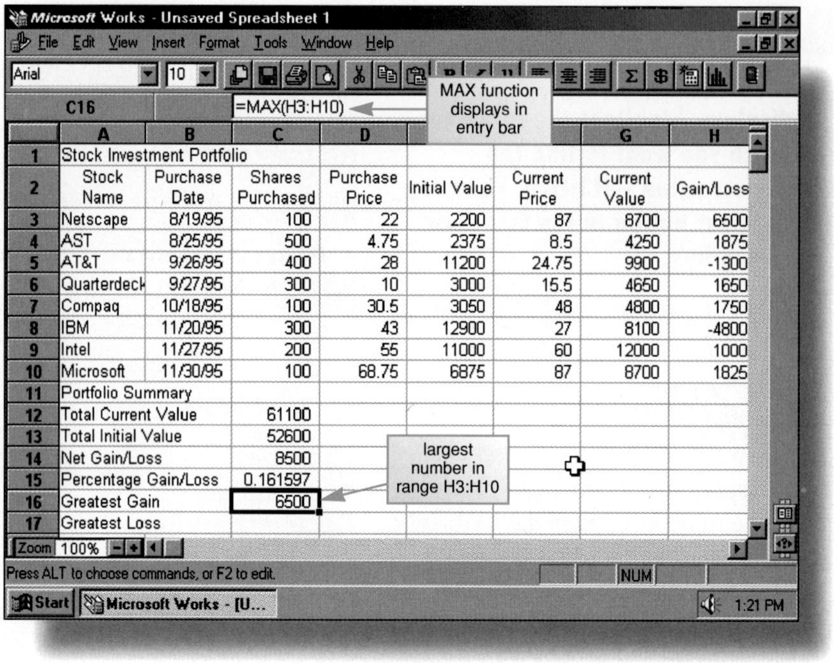

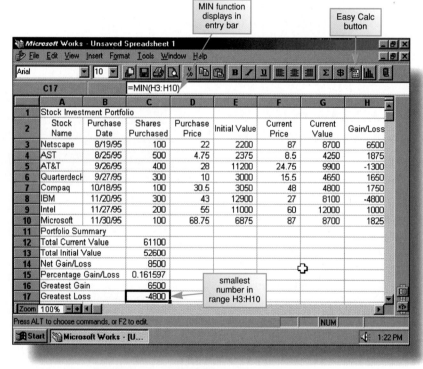

FIGURE 5-39

7 **Using the techniques for entering a function using the Easy Calc button as shown in Steps 1 through 6 above, enter the MIN function in cell C17. That is, highlight cell C17, and click the Easy Calc button on the toolbar. When the Easy Calc dialog box displays, click the Other button. When the Insert Function dialog box displays, click Statistical in the Category box. Highlight the MIN function in the Choose a function list. Click the Insert button. When the next Easy Calc dialog box displays, highlight the range, H3:H10, and click the Next button. When the next Easy Calc dialog box displays, ensure C17 displays in the Result at text box, and click the Finish button.**

Works enters the MIN function in cell C17 and determines the smallest value in the range specified in the MIN function (Figure 5-40). The value -4800 displays in cell C17 because it is the smallest value in the range H3:H10.

FIGURE 5-40

OtherWays

1. On Tools menu click Easy Calc, click desired function, click Insert button

2. On Insert menu click Insert Function, click desired function, click Insert button

Thus far, you have used the SUM, MAX, and MIN functions. These three functions are available in the **Statistical category**. Works has a total of 76 functions divided into eight categories. Figure 5-36 on page W 5.24 lists the eight categories in the Category box.

Works online Help provides detailed information about each of the functions. You can display detailed information about the specific function by displaying the Help menu to the right of the spreadsheet window, and typing an equal sign and the function name in a cell. Works will display an overview of the function in the Overview dialog box.

The spreadsheet data is now complete. All the data and formulas are contained within the spreadsheet.

Formatting the Spreadsheet

The next task is to format the spreadsheet. The formatted spreadsheet is shown in Figure 5-41. The requirements to complete the formatting are:

1. Make the entire spreadsheet bold.
2. Make the spreadsheet title 24-point Arial. Center the title across the columns.
3. Set the following column widths: A=12; B=11; C=11; D=9; E=10; F=10; G=10; and H=10.
4. Center the number of shares purchased in column C.
5. Set the Purchase Price, Initial Value, Current Price, Current Value, and Gain/Loss columns to the Comma format with two decimal positions. Negative amounts in the Gain/Loss column should display in red.
6. Make the title, Portfolio Summary, 14 point.
7. Make the titles in rows 12 through 17 in column A italic.
8. Set the Total Current Value, Total Initial Value and Net Gain/Loss values to the Currency format.
9. Set the Percentage Gain/Loss values to the Percent format.
10. Set the Greatest Gain and Greatest Loss values to the Currency format.
11. Place a border around the spreadsheet. Format the spreadsheet in color as illustrated.

More *About*
Formatting a Spreadsheet

Using colors and borders in a spreadsheet can change a boring spreadsheet into an interesting and professional-looking spreadsheet. Use colors and borders to draw a reader's attention to important information in the spreadsheet.

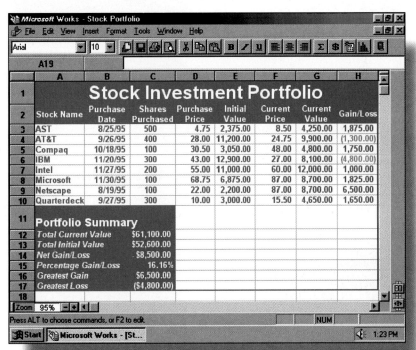

FIGURE 5-41

The steps required to accomplish this formatting are explained on the following pages.

Making the Entire Spreadsheet Bold

In Project 5, the entire spreadsheet will display in bold. Complete the following step to accomplish this task.

Steps To Make the Entire Spreadsheet Bold

1 Press CTRL+HOME to select cell A1. Hold down the SHIFT key. Move the mouse pointer to cell H17, and click. Click the Bold button on the toolbar.

Cells A1:H17 are highlighted. When you click the Bold button, Works changes the highlighted cells to the bold format (Figure 5-42). Notice the text in cell E2 now displays on two lines because the cell was formatted to wrap text earlier in the project. Using the SHIFT key to highlight information in the spreadsheet produces the same result as using SHIFT+click in the Word processor.

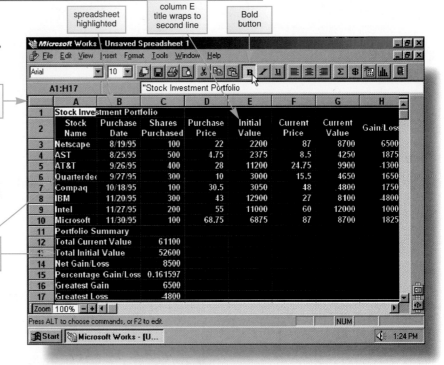

FIGURE 5-42

OtherWays

1. On Edit menu click Select All, on Format menu click Font and Style, click Bold, click OK
2. Click box above row 1 and to left of column A, on toolbar, click Bold

Formatting the Spreadsheet Title

The spreadsheet title is to display in 24-point Arial font. The title is to be centered across the columns. Complete the steps on the next pages to accomplish these tasks.

More About Selecting a Range

If dragging to select a range is a drag to you, consider using the F8 function key. To highlight a range, press the F8 function key to select one corner of the range and then the cell diagonally opposite it in the proposed range. When the range is highlighted, press the F8 function key to turn off the selection.

Steps **To Format the Spreadsheet Title**

1 **Highlight cell A1. Click the Font Size box arrow and point to 24 in the Font Size drop-down list.**

Cell A1 is highlighted and the mouse pointer points to 24 in the Font Size drop-down list box (Figure 5-43).

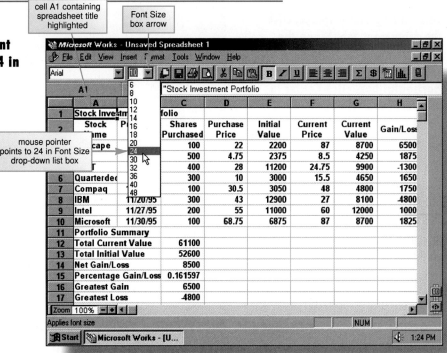

FIGURE 5-43

2 **Click 24. Highlight the range A1:H1. Then point to the highlighted range and right-click. When the context sensitive-menu displays, point to Format.**

Works displays the title in the 24-point Arial bold font (Figure 5-44). The context-sensitive menu displays and the mouse pointer points to the Format command.

FIGURE 5-44

3 Click Format on the context-sensitive menu. When the Format Cells dialog box displays, click the Alignment tab. When the Alignment sheet displays, click Center across selection in the Horizontal box, click Center in the Vertical box, and then point to the OK button.

The Alignment sheet displays in the Format Cells dialog box, the Center across selection option button is selected, the Center option button is selected, and the mouse pointer points to the OK button (Figure 5-45).

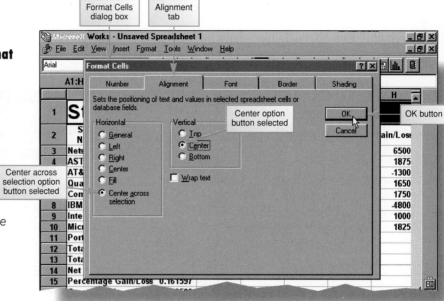

FIGURE 5-45

4 Click the OK button. Then click any cell to remove the highlight.

Works displays the spreadsheet title centered across the columns A through H of the spreadsheet (Figure 5-46). Notice that the vertical gridlines do not display in the area containing the title.

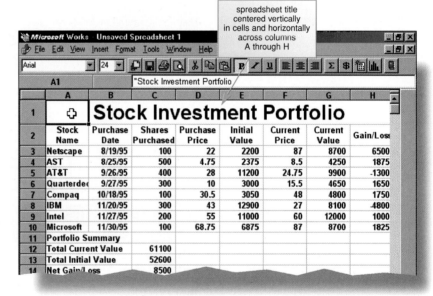

FIGURE 5-46

▶OtherWays

1. On Format menu click Font and Style, click 24 in the Size drop-down list, click Alignment tab, click Center across selection, click Center, click OK

◆ More About Column Widths

When a numeric entry in a cell is too long for the width of the column, Works will display ##### in the cell until you increase the column width. However, when a text entry is too long for the width of the column, Works displays the text in adjacent cells if the cells are empty.

The column titles were formatted when the titles were entered into the spreadsheet; therefore, the next step is to format the individual columns.

Changing Column Widths and Centering Data in a Column

You change the width of columns for a variety of reasons. You may wish to change the column width to improve the readability of the spreadsheet, to ensure that the columns are wide enough to properly display data after formatting, and sometimes so the entire spreadsheet will display on a single screen.

In this project, the width of columns A, B, and C must be increased. Other columns are to be changed according to the specifications on page W 5.27. Changing column widths is explained in the steps on the next pages. In addition, the steps explain how to center data in a selected column.

Steps **To Change Column Widths and Center Data in a Column**

1 **Highlight any cell in column A, click Format on the menu bar, and point to Column Width.**

Cell A1 is highlighted, the Format menu displays, and the mouse pointer points to the Column Width command (Figure 5-47).

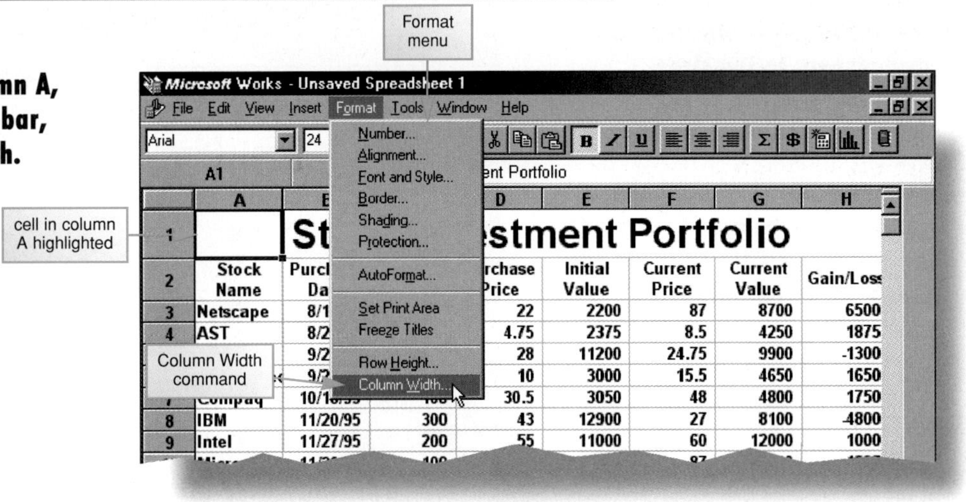

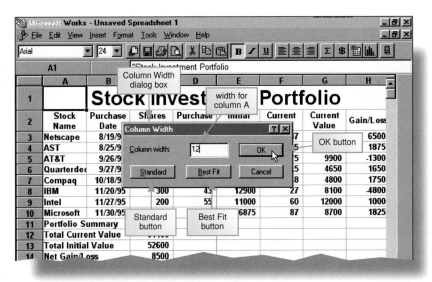

FIGURE 5-47

2 **Click Column Width. When the Column Width dialog box displays, type** 12 **in the Column width text box. Point to the OK button.**

Works displays the Column Width dialog box (Figure 5-48). The number 12 displays in the Column width text box and the mouse pointer points to the OK button. Clicking the Standard button applies the default column width to the highlighted column. Clicking the Best Fit button applies the column width to accommodate the largest entry in the highlighted column.

FIGURE 5-48

3 **Click the OK button in the Column Width dialog box.**

Works changes the width of column A to 12 and all the stock names fit in the column (Figure 5-49). When you increase the width of column A, part of column A scrolls off the screen.

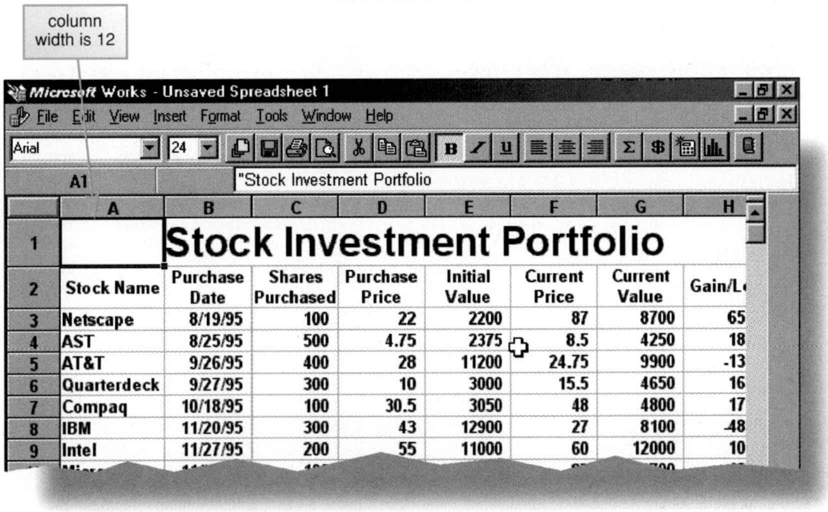

FIGURE 5-49

4 Using the techniques previously explained, change the widths of the remaining columns in the spreadsheet to the sizes specified on page W 5.27.

5 To center the number of shares purchased in column C, highlight the range, C3:C10, and click the Center Align button on the toolbar.

Works centers the number of shares purchased in column C (Figure 5-50).

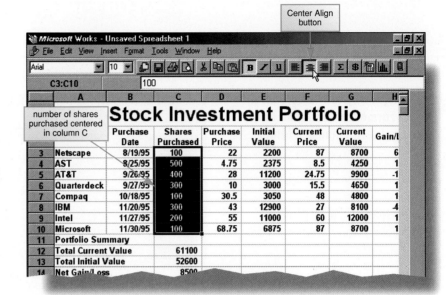

FIGURE 5-50

Formatting Data with the Comma Format

You now should format the numeric data containing dollar amounts in the Comma format. The Comma format will place a comma every third position to the left of the decimal point and will allow you to specify the number of positions to the right of the decimal point. In addition, any negative numbers will display in red. The following steps explain how to format selected cells using the Comma format.

 Steps To Use the Comma Format

1 Highlight the range of cells, D3:H10. These are the cells you want to format with the Comma format. Right-click the highlighted range. When the context-sensitive menu displays, point to Format.

Cells D3:H10 are highlighted, the context-sensitive menu displays, and the mouse pointer points to the Format command (Figure 5-51).

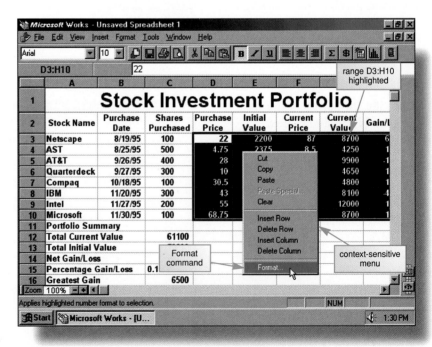

FIGURE 5-51

2 **Click Format. When the Format Cells dialog box displays, ensure the Number sheet displays and click Comma in the Format box. Click Negative numbers in red in the Comma box and then point to the OK button.**

The Format Cells dialog box displays (Figure 5-52). The Comma option button is selected, and a check mark displays in the Negative numbers in red check box. A sample of the format displays in the Sample box. The number 2 should display in the Decimal places text box because 2 is the default value. The mouse pointer points to the OK button.

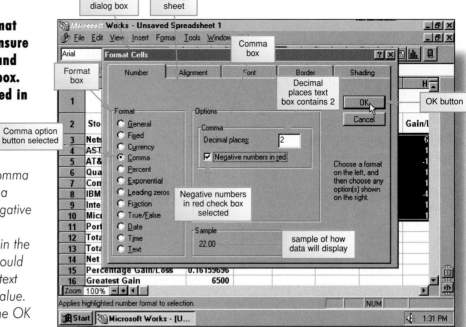

FIGURE 5-52

3 **Click the OK button in the Format Cells dialog box. Click any cell to remove the highlight.**

Works formats the highlighted range with the Comma format (Figure 5-53). The Comma format displays numeric values with two digits to the right of the decimal point. Notice that Works displays negative values in column H (Gain/Loss) in red with parentheses instead of minus signs.

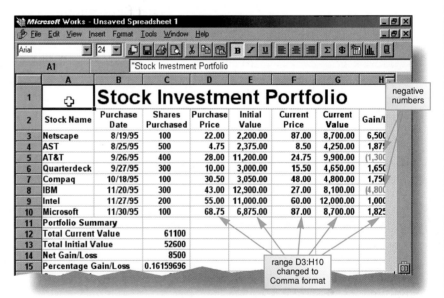

FIGURE 5-53

*Other***Ways**

1. On Format menu click Number, click Comma, click Negative numbers in red, click OK

The first portion of the spreadsheet is now formatted.

Changing Font Size and Row Height

The next step is to format the section of the spreadsheet labeled Portfolio Summary. In this section of the spreadsheet, the words, Portfolio Summary, will display in 14-point Arial bold and extra blank space appears above the words, Portfolio Summary. This requires changing the font size and the row height. To accomplish these tasks, complete the steps on the next page.

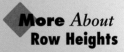

More *About*
Row Heights

Early spreadsheet users had to skip rows on the spreadsheet to improve the appearance of the it. With Works you can increase the row height to add space between information.

Steps To Change Font Size and Row Height

1 Highlight cell A11, click the Font Size box arrow. Click 14 in the Font Size drop-down list. Position the mouse pointer on the border line that separates row 11 and row 12 in the row headings on the left side of the spreadsheet.

The words, Portfolio Summary, display in 14-point Arial bold font (Figure 5-54). The mouse pointer becomes the shape of an equal sign with up- and down-pointing arrows. The word ADJUST displays below the mouse pointer.

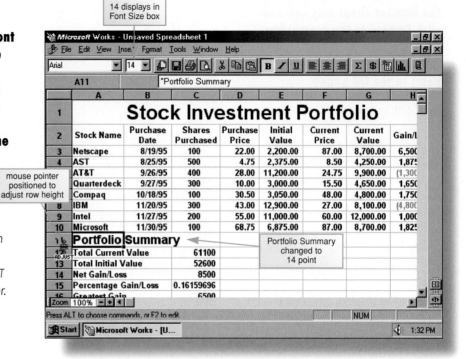

FIGURE 5-54

2 Drag the mouse pointer down the height of one row. Release the mouse button.

Works increases the height of row 11, causing a blank space to appear above the words, Portfolio Summary (Figure 5-55). Notice part of row 15 and all of rows 16 and 17 scrolled off the screen.

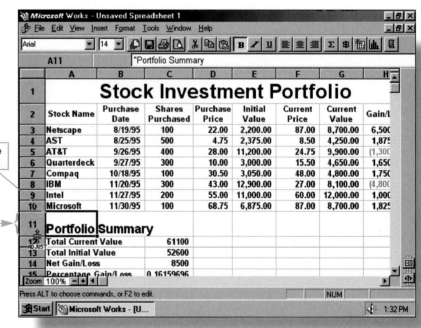

FIGURE 5-55

OtherWays

1. On Format menu click Row Height, type desired row height in Row height text box, click OK

The formatting of the title of this portion of the spreadsheet is now complete.

Font Style, Currency Format, and Percent Format

To complete the formatting of the spreadsheet, you must change the titles in rows 12 through 17 of column A to italic, and format the numbers in cells C12:C14 using the Currency format. **Currency format** displays values with a currency sign and commas every three places to the left of the decimal point. Also, change the number in cell C15 to Percent format, and format the numbers in cells C16:C17 to Currency format. To format numbers to Currency format, use the Currency button on the toolbar. Complete the following step to accomplish these tasks.

Steps **To Apply Italic Style, Currency Format, and Percent Format**

1 **Highlight the range A12:A17 and click the Italic button on the toolbar. Highlight the range C12:C14. Click the Currency button on the toolbar. Right-click cell C15. Click Format. In the Format Cells dialog box, ensure the Number sheet displays, click Percent, and then click the OK button. Highlight the range C16:C17 and click the Currency button on the toolbar.**

The Portfolio Summary section of the spread-sheet is now formatted (Figure 5-56). Notice in cell C15, when you select the Percent format, the number displays with two digits to the right of the decimal point and Works rounds the display of the number; that is, 0.16159696 displays as 16.16%.

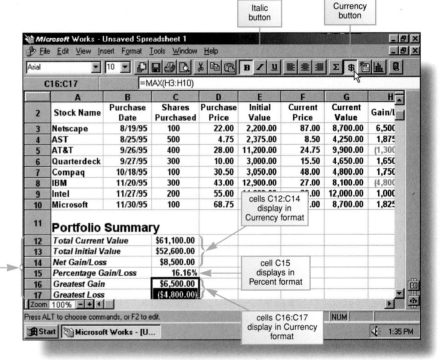

FIGURE 5-56

Saving the Spreadsheet

The data in the spreadsheet is complete. You should save the spreadsheet on disk. To save the spreadsheet on drive A using the filename, Stock Portfolio, perform the steps on the next page.

TO SAVE THE SPREADSHEET

Step 1: Click the CTRL+HOME keys. Click the Save button on the toolbar.

Step 2: When the Save As dialog box displays, type Stock Portfolio in the File name text box.

Step 3: Select drive A from the Save in drop-down list box.

Step 4: Click the Save button in the Save As dialog box.

Adding Color to the Spreadsheet

The final task in formatting the spreadsheet is to add color to selected portions of the spreadsheet. Color greatly enhances the impact a spreadsheet can have on those viewing it. In Figure 5-41 on page W 5.27, the report and column headings display in white inside cells that are dark magenta. The stock names and other values in the spreadsheet display in blue, and the Portfolio Summary section matches the spreadsheet title and column titles section. The entire spreadsheet is surrounded by a dark magenta border.

Adding Color to the Spreadsheet Title and Column Headings

In this project, the spreadsheet title and the column headings will display in white. The cells containing the spreadsheet title and the column headings will display dark magenta. Complete the following steps to color the spreadsheet title, column headings, and cells.

Steps **To Add Color to the Spreadsheet Title and Column Headings**

① **Highlight cells A1:H2. Right-click the highlighted range and point to Format on the context-sensitive menu.**

Cells A1:H2 are high-lighted, the context-sensitive menu displays, and the mouse pointer points to the Format command (Figure 5-57).

FIGURE 5-57

2 **Click Format. When the Format Cells dialog box displays, click the Font tab. Click the Color box arrow, scroll down if necessary to display White and click White. Point to the Shading tab.**

The Format Cells dialog box displays and the Font sheet displays in the front of the other sheets (Figure 5-58). The desired color (White) displays in the Color box.

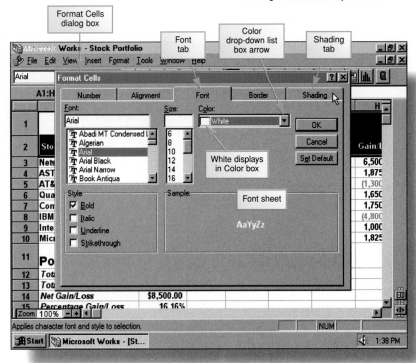

FIGURE 5-58

3 **Click the Shading tab. When the Shading sheet displays, click the solid pattern in the Pattern list box. In the Foreground list box, scroll down and click Dark Magenta. Point to the OK button in the Shading sheet.**

Works displays the Shading sheet (Figure 5-59). The solid pattern is selected in the Pattern list box. Dark Magenta is highlighted in the Foreground list box. The Pattern list box changes to dark magenta. The mouse pointer points to the OK button.

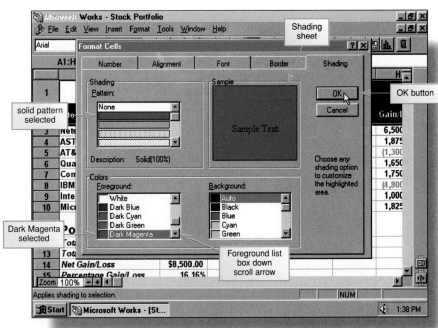

FIGURE 5-59

4 **Click the OK button in the Format Cells dialog box. Click any cell to remove the highlight.**

Works displays the title and headings in white and the cell color is solid dark magenta (Figure 5-60).

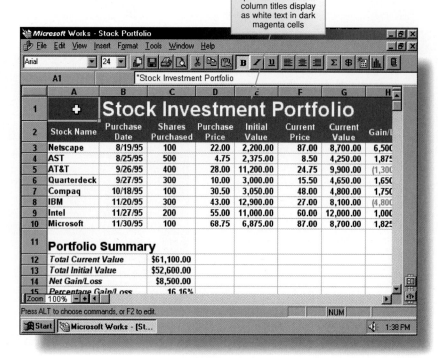

FIGURE 5-60

Displaying Spreadsheet Entries in Color

In this project, the text, date, and numbers in rows 3 through 10 will display in blue. Perform the following steps to display the entries in blue.

 Steps **To Display Spreadsheet Entries in Color**

1 **Highlight the range of cells A3:H10. Right-click the highlighted range and point to Format on the context-sensitive menu.**

Cells A3:H10 are highlighted, the context-sensitive menu displays, and the mouse pointer points to the Format command (Figure 5-61).

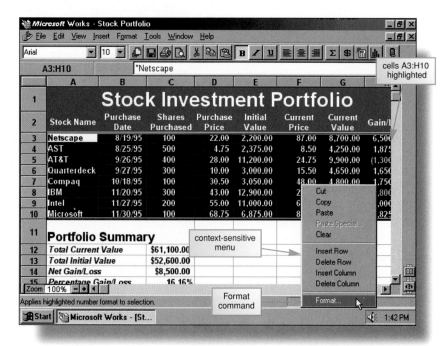

FIGURE 5-61

2 Click Format. When the Format Cells dialog box displays, click the Font tab. When the Font sheet displays, click the Color box. When the Color drop-down list displays, select Blue. Then point to the OK button.

The Font sheet displays in the Format Cells dialog box (Figure 5-62). Blue displays in the Color box and in the Sample box. The mouse pointer points to the OK button.

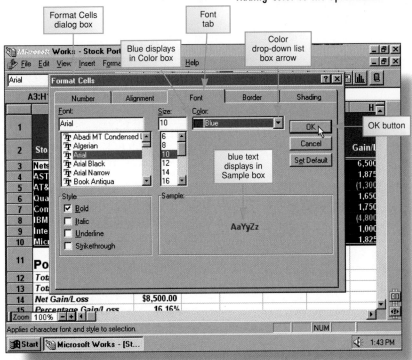

FIGURE 5-62

3 Click the OK button in the Format Cells dialog box. When the spreadsheet displays, click any cell to remove the highlight.

Works displays the text and numbers in the range, A3:H10, in blue (Figure 5-63). The negative numbers remain red.

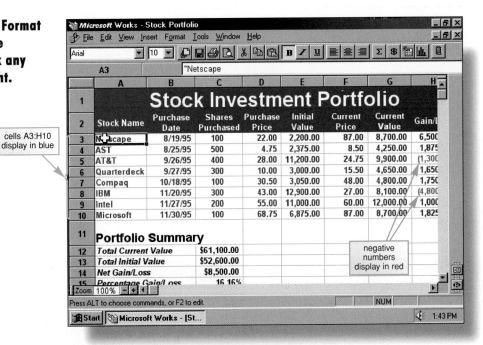

FIGURE 5-63

Adding Color to the Portfolio Summary Section of the Spreadsheet

The next step is to add color to the Portfolio Summary section of the spreadsheet. To add the color, perform the steps on the next page.

TO ADD COLOR TO THE SPREADSHEET

Step 1: Highlight cells A11:C17.
Step 2: Right-click the highlighted range.
Step 3: Click Format on the context-sensitive menu.
Step 4: In the Format Cells dialog box, click the Font sheet. On the Font sheet, click the Color box arrow.
Step 5: If necessary, scroll down until White displays. Click White.
Step 6: Click the Shading tab. On the Shading sheet, click the solid pattern in the Pattern list box. In the Foreground list box, scroll down and click Dark Magenta. Click the OK button in the Format Cells dialog box.
Step 7: Click any cell to remove the highlight.

The Portfolio Summary section of the spreadsheet displays with white characters in dark magenta cells (Figure 5-64).

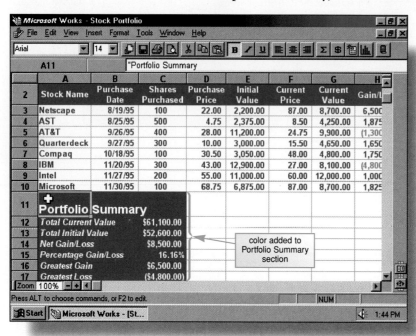

FIGURE 5-64

Adding a Border

The final step in formatting the spreadsheet is to outline the entire spreadsheet with a dark magenta border. Perform the following steps to complete this task.

 Steps To Add a Border to a Spreadsheet

1 **Highlight cells A1:H17, right-click the highlighted range, and point to Format.**

Cells A1:A17 are highlighted and the mouse pointer points to the Format command on the context-sensitive menu (Figure 5-65).

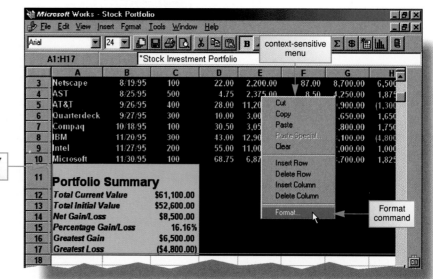

FIGURE 5-65

2 Click Format. When the Format Cells dialog box displays, click the Border tab. When the Border sheet displays, click Outline in the Border box and then select the medium solid line box in the Line style box. Scroll down in the Color list box to view Dark Magenta. Click Dark Magenta. Point to the OK button in the Format Cells dialog box.

Works displays the Border sheet in the Format Cells dialog box (Figure 5-66). The Outline selection contains a medium solid line. The medium solid line style is selected. These selections will cause Works to place a medium solid line outline (border) around the entire highlighted range. The border will be dark magenta.

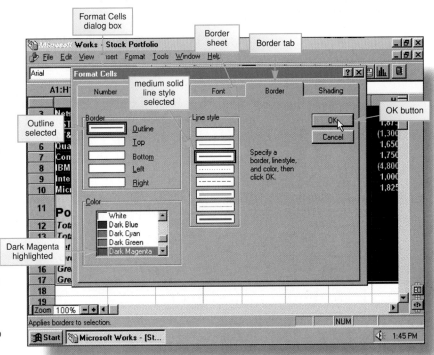

FIGURE 5-66

3 Click the OK button in the Format Cells dialog box. Click any cell to remove the highlight. Click the right scroll arrow to view column H.

Works places the dark magenta border around the highlighted range (Figure 5-67).

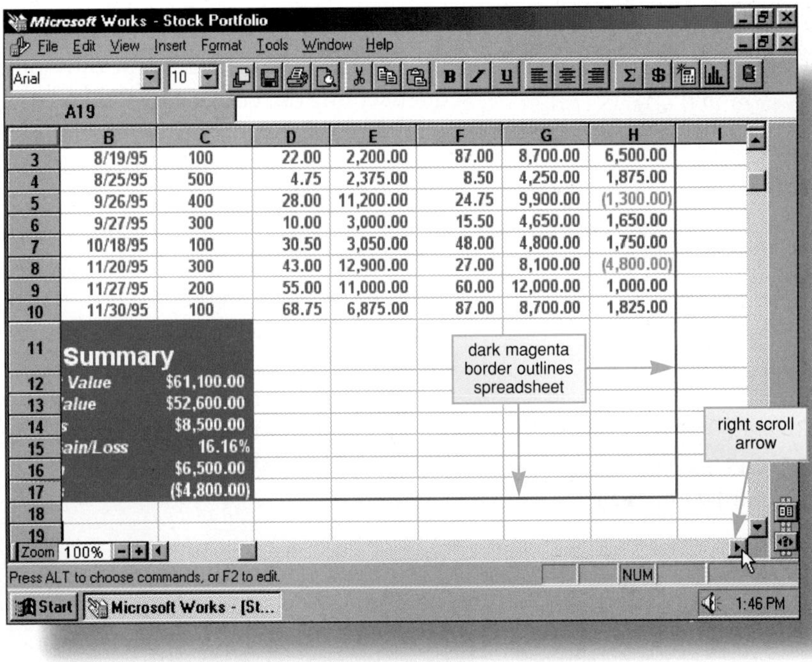

FIGURE 5-67

OtherWays

1. On Format menu click Border, click Outline, click medium solid line, click Dark Magenta, click OK

The formatting of the spreadsheet is now complete. When you are certain the spreadsheet appears in proper format and color, it is recommended that you again save the spreadsheet using the same filename. You now will have saved a spreadsheet that is formatted with color.

Sorting Rows

Initially, you entered the stocks in the spreadsheet in purchase date sequence; that is, you entered the stock purchased first (Netscape), then the stock purchased second (AST), and so on.

For the actual report, however, the stocks need to appear in alphabetical sequence. This change is illustrated in Figure 5-68.

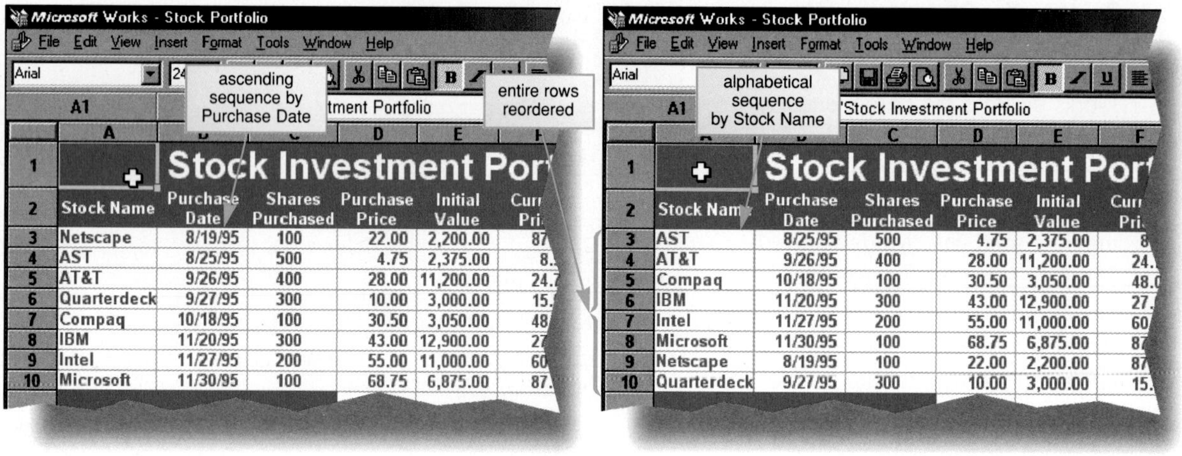

FIGURE 5-68

More *About* Sorting

Works can sort information and arrange selected rows of data in alphabetic or numeric order. Works sorts based on the information in a column. You can specify up to three columns in order of importance for Works to consider. Sorting is fast and useful for arranging any type of alphabetical or numerical information in a spreadsheet. If you want to save both the original and the sorted versions, save the original under one name and the sorted spreadsheet under a different name.

Notice that Works has not only placed the stock names in alphabetical sequence, but the entire rows have been reordered as well.

Sorting means placing rows of spreadsheet data in a prescribed sequence. The sequence can be either **ascending**, meaning the records appear from lowest to highest, or **descending**, meaning the records appear from highest to lowest. Table 5-3 illustrates this concept when sorting the stock names.

Notice that when the names are in ascending sequence, they move from the first letter of the alphabet toward the last letter of the alphabet. In descending sequence, they move from the last letter of the alphabet to the first letter of the alphabet.

When you sort numbers, ascending sequence moves from the lowest number to the highest number, while descending sequence moves from the highest number to the lowest number.

TABLE 5-3

UNORDERED	ASCENDING	DESCENDING
Netscape	AST	Quarterdeck
AST	AT&T	Netscape
AT&T	Compaq	Microsoft
Quarterdeck	IBM	Intel
Compaq	Intel	IBM
IBM	Microsoft	Compaq
Intel	Netscape	AT&T
Microsoft	Quarterdeck	AST

To sort the stocks in the Stock Investment Portfolio in ascending sequence by Stock Name, use the Sort command on the Tools menu, as shown in the following steps.

Steps **To Sort Rows**

① **Press CTRL+HOME. Highlight the range A3:H10, click Tools on the menu bar, and point to Sort.**

By highlighting the range A3:H10, you specify that Works should sort only those rows (Figure 5-69). Therefore, rows 11 through 17, for example, will not be included in the sorting process.

FIGURE 5-69

② **Click Sort. When the Sort dialog box displays, ensure Sort only the highlighted information is selected, and then point to the OK button.**

Works displays the Sort dialog box (Figure 5-70). In the What do you want to do? box, the Sort only the highlighted information option button is selected. This option instructs Works to sort only the highlighted information in the spreadsheet and ignore all other columns and rows. The mouse pointer points to the OK button.

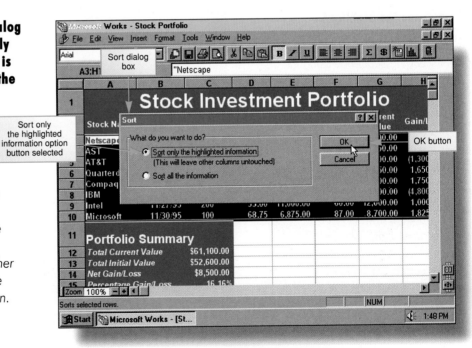

FIGURE 5-70

3 **Click the OK button in the Sort dialog box. When the second Sort dialog box displays, review the entries and then point to the Sort button.**

Column A displays in the Sort By box (Figure 5-71). This specifies column A is the column on which the sort will take place. This is determined by the range highlighted. You can determine the sort sequence by selecting either the Ascending or Descending option button. Ascend is the default selection. The No header row option button is selected in the My list has box. This selection indicates the column headings are not included in the highlighted range to be sorted. No further entries are required.

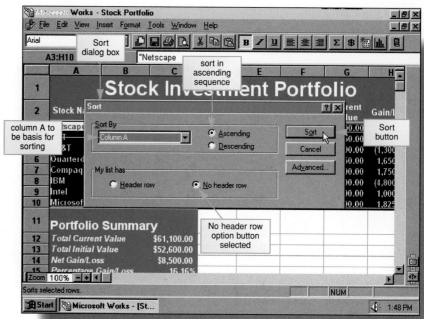

FIGURE 5-71

4 **Click the Sort button in the Sort dialog box. Click any cell to remove the highlight.**

Works sorts the highlighted rows in ascending sequence using the data in column A as the sequence order (Figure 5-72). During the sort, Works checks the contents of column A and arranges the rows in ascending order. Notice that the data in each of the rows has been resequenced as well so that the correct Purchase Date, Shares Purchased, and so on, remain with the sorted Stock Name.

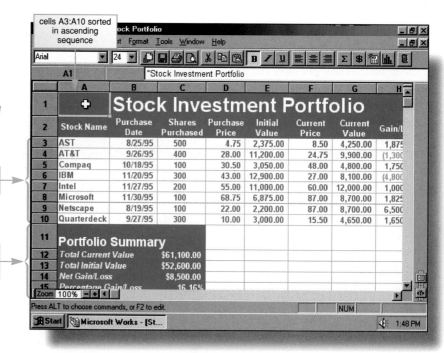

FIGURE 5-72

Exercise caution when sorting spreadsheet data. When selecting the range to sort, ensure the sort range includes all the rows and columns you want to sort. If you omit columns, the integrity of the data is destroyed. If you omit rows, the resulting sort order will be inaccurate. If you discover you have made a mistake while sorting, click Undo on the Edit menu immediately after the sort operation to reverse the sort.

After sorting, the spreadsheet is complete.

Saving the Spreadsheet

You should save the final version of the spreadsheet on disk. To save the spreadsheet, click the Save button on the toolbar.

Print Preview and Printing the Spreadsheet

The next task is to print the Stock Investment Portfolio. When a spreadsheet contains more than six columns or when you increase the width of the columns, the spreadsheet often will not fit across a piece of paper that is 8.5 inches wide and 11 inches long. To check whether it will fit, the best technique is to use Print Preview. Print Preview allows you to see the exact layout of your printed report prior to actually printing the report. In this project, because eight columns are required, Print Preview should be used to determine if the report will fit on a sheet of paper. To use Print Preview, perform the following steps.

 Steps To Use Print Preview

1 **Point to the Print Preview button on the toolbar (Figure 5-73).**

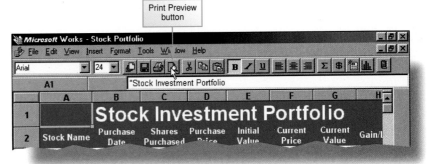

FIGURE 5-73

2 **Click the Print Preview button on the toolbar.**

Works displays a full page and the report as it will appear on the page (Figure 5-74). When you move the mouse pointer onto the page, it assumes the shape of a magnifying glass with the word ZOOM below it. The display in Figure 5-74 shows the entire page, but it can be difficult to read the actual report. Therefore, you should magnify the report.

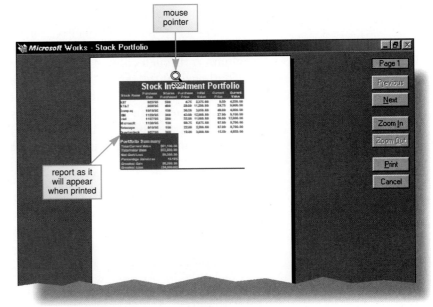

FIGURE 5-74

3 **Click two times within the document in Print Preview.**

When you click one time, Works magnifies the page to approximately one-half the size it will be when it prints. When you click a second time, the page displays full size (Figure 5-75). The displayed report does not contain the Gain/Loss column, which means the column will not appear on the printed report.

4 **To return to the spreadsheet from the Print Preview window, click the Cancel button.**

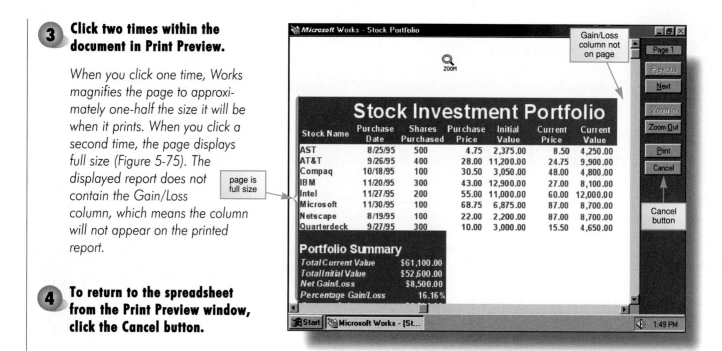

FIGURE 5-75

In the Print Preview window (see Figure 5-75), Works provides several buttons. If you click the Next button, you will see the next page in the report. Clicking the Previous button causes Works to display the previous page of the report. The Zoom In and Zoom Out buttons increase or decrease the size of the report in the Print Preview window in the same way as clicking the mouse when the mouse pointer is shaped as a magnifying glass on the report. The Print button allows you to print the report directly from the Print Preview window.

Printing Landscape Reports

Because the Gain/Loss column does not fit on a page with a width of 8.5 inches and a length of 11 inches, you have a number of options you can use to print the report. First, you can print the report anyway. Works will print column A through column G on the first page of the report and column H on the second page of the report. This is not normally a satisfactory technique, however.

The second option is to print the spreadsheet across the length of the paper instead of the width of the paper; that is, in effect turn the page ninety degrees so that the paper is 11 inches wide and 8.5 inches long. When you print a report in this manner, you are using the **landscape** page orientation as opposed to the **portrait** page orientation you use when the printed page is 8.5 inches wide by 11 inches long.

A third technique is to change the entire spreadsheet to a smaller font size. This technique, however, will substantially change the appearance of the report when you have designed the spreadsheet using multiple font sizes.

A fourth technique is to change the right and left margins. The default for the right and left margins is 1.25 inches. Reducing these margins to 1 inch or .5 inch may increase the width to properly display the spreadsheet.

A technique widely used to display spreadsheets that are wider than a standard sheet of paper is to use the landscape orientation. To print in landscape orientation, you must tell Works to use landscape orientation instead of portrait orientation. To accomplish this, perform the following steps.

Steps **To Print a Report in Landscape Orientation**

1 **Click File on the menu bar and point to Page Setup.**

The File menu displays and the mouse pointer points to the Page Setup command (Figure 5-76).

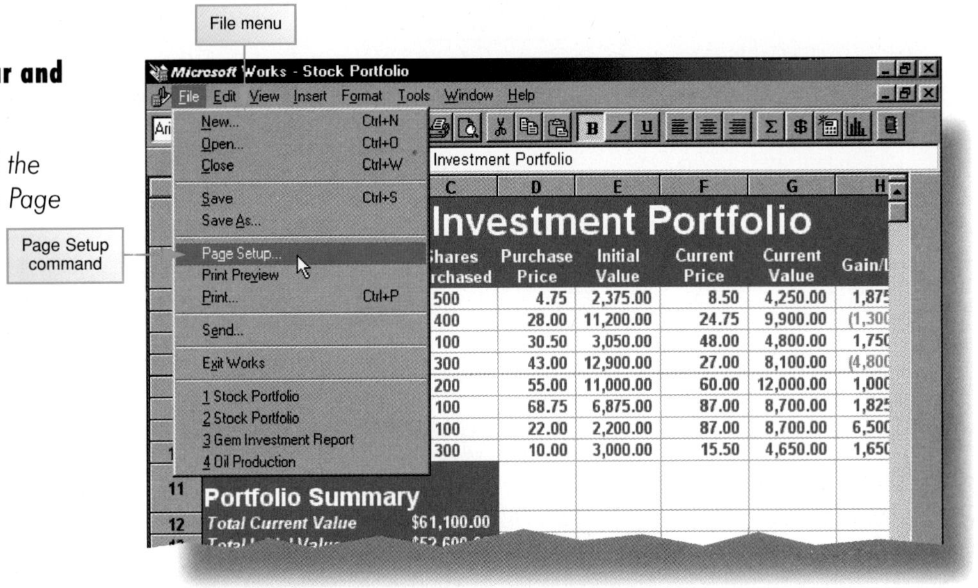

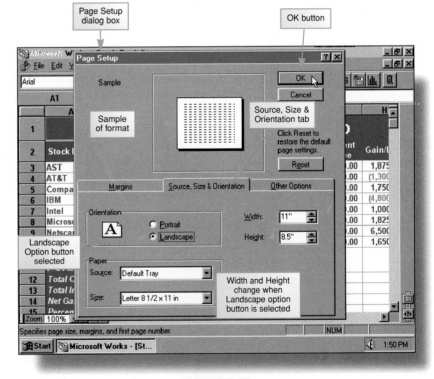

FIGURE 5-76

2 **Click Page Setup. When the Page Setup dialog box displays, click the Source, Size & Orientation tab. When the Source, Size & Orientation sheet displays, click Landscape in the Orientation box. Point to the OK button.**

The Page Setup dialog box displays (Figure 5-77). Within the Page Setup dialog box, the Source, Size & Orientation sheet displays. The Landscape option button is selected. When you select this option button, Works automatically changes the contents of the Width text box to 11" and the Height text box to 8.5". The Sample box changes to illustrate landscape orientation. The mouse pointer points to the OK button.

FIGURE 5-77

3 **Click the OK button in the Page Setup dialog box to return to the spreadsheet.**

Works is now set to print the spreadsheet in landscape orientation. To print the spreadsheet, perform the step on the next page.

TO PRINT THE SPREADSHEET IN LANDSCAPE ORIENTATION

Step 1: Click the Print button on the toolbar.

The landscape-oriented spreadsheet that is generated is shown in Figure 5-78. Notice that the entire spreadsheet appears on a single page.

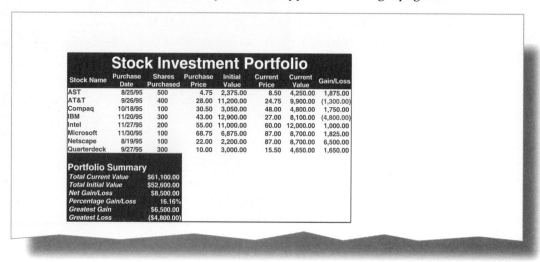

FIGURE 5-78

Once you have printed a spreadsheet in landscape orientation, landscape orientation remains the selection in the Page Setup dialog box for that spreadsheet. Therefore, if you are going to print the spreadsheet again, be aware that the spreadsheet will print in landscape orientation until you change back to portrait orientation.

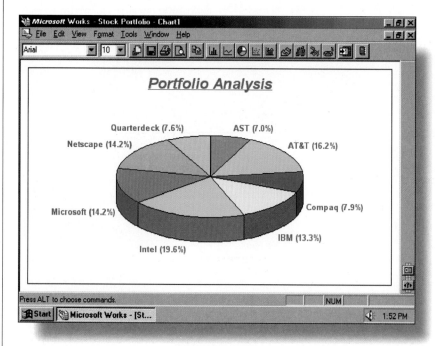

FIGURE 5-79

Charting the Spreadsheet

After you have printed the spreadsheet, your next task is to create a 3-D Pie chart. In Project 3, you created a 3-D Bar chart from data in adjacent columns. In this project, you will prepare a 3-D Pie chart based on the Current Value in column G and the Stock Names in column A (Figure 5-79). Notice that the 3-D Pie chart illustrates what proportion of the entire stock portfolio each stock's Current Value represents. The name of the stock and its percentage are included on the chart.

When you create a chart based on data from nonadjacent columns (column A and column G), you must use a slightly different procedure than you use to creat a chart from data in adjacent columns.

The procedure is: (1) highlight the range of data in column G to chart; (2) click the New Chart button on the toolbar; (3) select the 3-D pie chart; (4) add a chart title and a border; (5) add the labels from column A; and (6) format the chart title and data labels. To create the 3-D Pie chart, perform the following steps.

 Steps **To Create a Pie Chart from Nonadjacent Columns**

1 **Highlight the range to chart (cells G3:G10) and point to the New Chart button on the toolbar (Figure 5-80).**

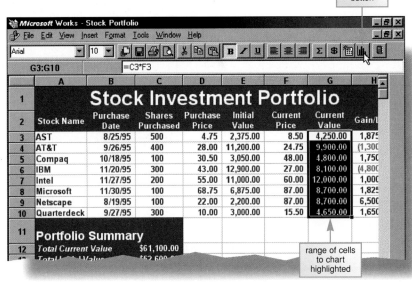

New Chart button

range of cells to chart highlighted

FIGURE 5-80

2 **Click the New Chart button on the toolbar. When the New Chart dialog box displays, click 3-D Pie in the What type of chart do you want? box. Press the TAB key and type** Portfolio Analysis **in the Title text box. Click Border in the Finishing touches box. Point to the OK button.**

Works displays the New Chart dialog box (Figure 5-81). The 3-D Pie chart is selected in the What type of chart do you want? box. The title for the chart displays in the Title text box. The check mark in the Border check box instructs Works to place a border around the chart. The Your Chart box contains a sample of the selected chart type. The mouse pointer points to the OK button.

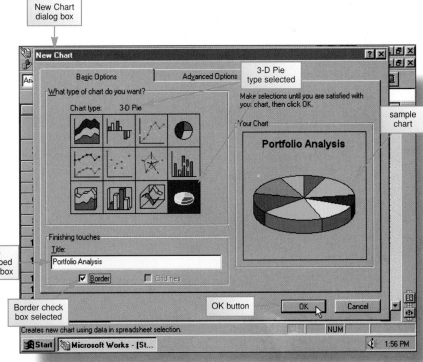

New Chart dialog box

3-D Pie type selected

sample chart

Portfolio Analysis typed in Title text box

Border check box selected

OK button

FIGURE 5-81

3 **Click the OK button in the New Chart dialog box.**

Works creates a 3-D Pie chart surrounded by a border (Figure 5-82).

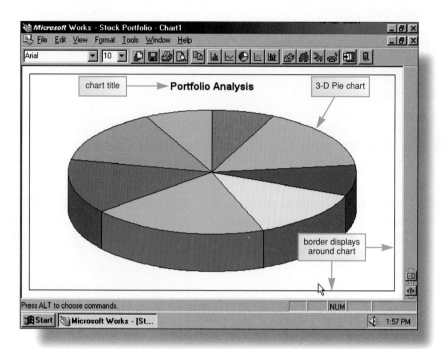

FIGURE 5-82

Adding Data Labels from Nonadjacent Columns

The 3-D Pie chart in Figure 5-82 charts the Current Value for each stock in the portfolio, but the chart labels, which include the name of the stock and the percentage that each slice in the pie chart represents, are not identified on the chart. The name of each corresponding stock is contained in the range A3:A10. To place the Stock Names on the chart, and display a label for the percentage that each slice represents, perform the following steps.

Steps **To Add Data Labels from Nonadjacent Columns**

1 **Click Edit on the Chart menu bar and point to Data Labels (Figure 5-83).**

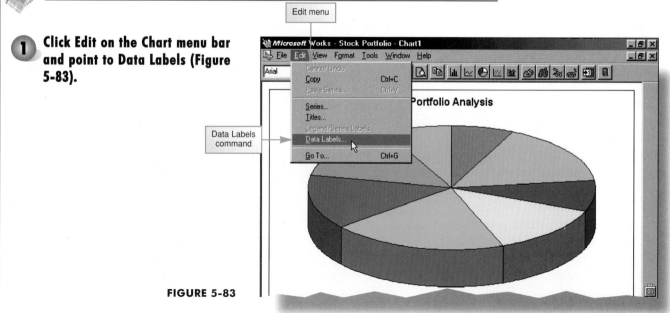

FIGURE 5-83

2 **Click Data Labels. When the Format Data Labels dialog box displays, click Cell Contents in the 1st Label box, click Percentages in the (2nd Label) box, press the TAB key and type** A3:A10 **as the range containing the Stock Names in the Cell Range text box. Point to the OK button.**

Works displays the Format Data Labels dialog box (Figure 5-84). Because Works allows two data labels for each entry in a pie chart, the dialog box contains option buttons for the 1st Label and the 2nd Label. In this project, the 1st Label uses the cell contents (the name of the stock) and the second label is for percentages. When you type the cell range A3:A10 in the Cell Range text box, you tell Works to use the contents of these cells for the first data label in the pie chart. The mouse pointer points to the OK button.

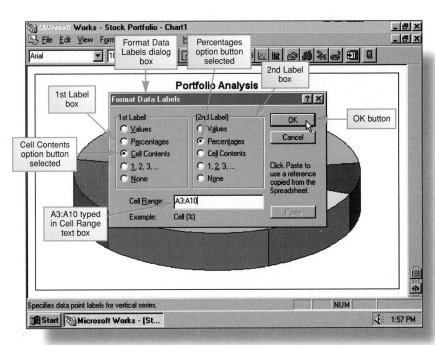

FIGURE 5-84

3 **Click the OK button in the Format Data Labels dialog box.**

Works uses the cell contents (Stock Names) from cells A3:A10 as data labels (Figure 5-85). Notice that Works uses the stock name AST from the first cell within the selected range, cell A3, for the number one slice of the pie chart (the number one slice is in the upper right corner), then the stock name AT&T for the second slice of the pie on the chart, and so on. The percentage of the whole each stock represents displays within parentheses as the second label.

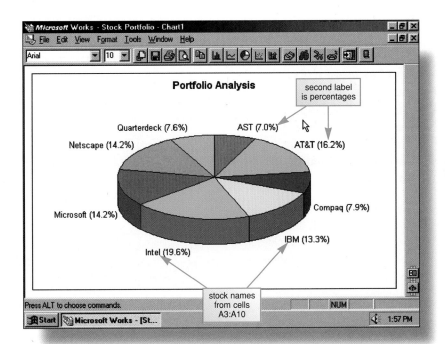

FIGURE 5-85

Formatting the Chart Title and Data Labels

The final task in preparing the chart is to format the title, Portfolio Analysis, and the data labels. Complete the following steps to accomplish this task.

Steps To Format Chart Titles and Data Labels

1 **Right-click the chart title, Portfolio Analysis. When the context-sensitive menu displays, point to Font and Style.**

Works selects the chart title and the context-sensitive menu displays (Figure 5-86). The mouse pointer points to the Font and Style command.

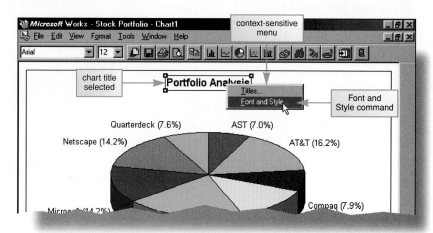

FIGURE 5-86

2 **Click Font and Style on the context-sensitive menu. When the Format Font and Style - Title dialog box displays, use the Size list box down scroll arrow to view 18, then click 18, click the Color box arrow and click Blue in the Color drop-down list. Click Bold (if it is not already selected), Italic, and Underline in the Style box. Point to the OK button.**

Works displays the Format Font and Style - Title dialog box (Figure 5-87). 18 displays in the Size box and Blue displays in the Color box. Bold, Italic, and Underline check boxes display check marks, indicating the title is to display in bold, italic and underlined. The Sample box displays the choices you have made. The mouse pointer points to the OK button.

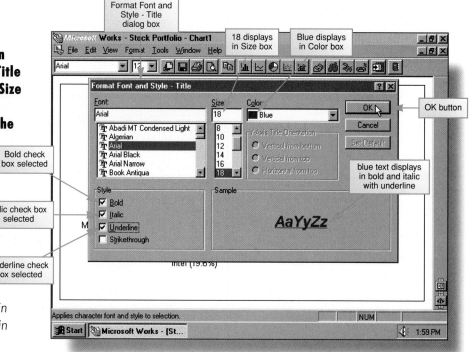

FIGURE 5-87

3 **Click the OK button in the Format Font and Style Title dialog box. Right-click any data label and point to Font and Style on the context-sensitive menu.**

Works makes the format changes and displays the chart title with the selections you made (Figure 5-88). The data labels are selected and a context-sensitive menu displays. The mouse pointer points to the Font and Style command.

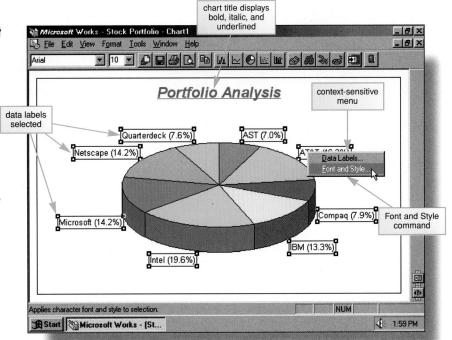

FIGURE 5-88

4 **Click Font and Style on the context-sensitive menu. When the Format Font and Style - Tick Labels, Data Labels, Etc. dialog box displays, click the Color box arrow and click Blue. Click Bold in the Style box. Point to the OK button.**

Works displays the Format Font and Style - Tick Labels, Data Labels, Etc. dialog box (Figure 5-89). Blue displays in the Color box and a check mark displays in the Bold check box. The mouse pointer points to the OK button.

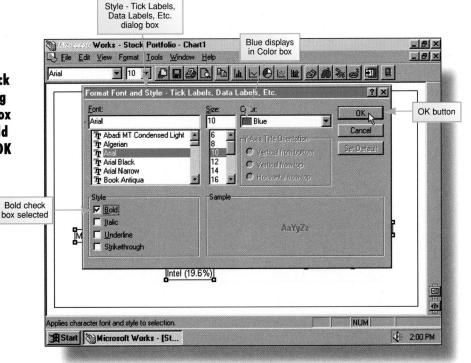

FIGURE 5-89

5 **Click OK.**

Works displays the data labels in 10-point Arial blue bold font (Figure 5-90).

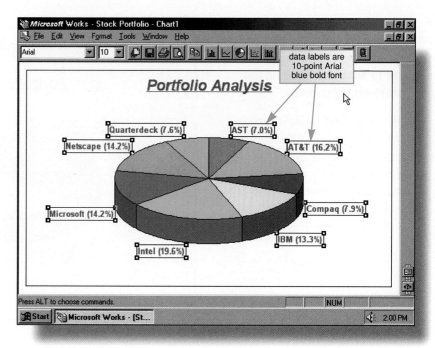

FIGURE 5-90

Printing a Chart

You can print a Works chart by using the following steps.

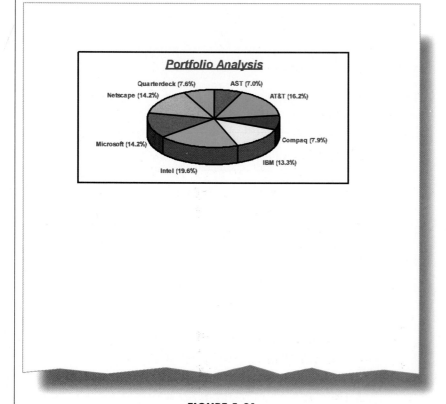

FIGURE 5-91

TO PRINT A WORKS SPREADSHEET CHART

Step 1: Click Page Setup on the File menu.

Step 2: Click the Source, Size & Orientation tab.

Step 3: Click Portrait in the Orientation box.

Step 4: Click the Other Options tab. Click Full page, keep proportions.

Step 5: Click the OK button in the Page Setup dialog box.

Step 6: Click the Print button on the Chart toolbar.

The printout in portrait orientation is shown in Figure 5-91.

Saving the Spreadsheet and the Chart

To save the spreadsheet and the chart, click the Save button on the toolbar. Both the spreadsheet and the chart will be saved on disk.

Closing Works

After you have completed working on the Project 5 spreadsheet and chart, you can close them to work on another Works project or you can close Works. To close Works, complete the following step.

TO CLOSE WORKS

Step 1: Click the Close button in the upper right corner of the application window.

Project Summary

In Project 5, you learned about Works formulas, operators, the sequence of operations in a formula, and how to enter a formula. You also learned how to format a spreadsheet and add color to it. The technique of sorting rows in the spreadsheet and printing the spreadsheet in landscape orientation was explained and illustrated.

Finally, you created a 3-D Pie chart that included labels in the chart from nonadjacent rows in the spreadsheet. You then learned how to format the chart title, format the data labels, and print the chart.

What You Should Know

Having completed this project, you should now be able to perform the following tasks:

- Add a Border to a Spreadsheet *(W 5.40)*
- Add Color to a Spreadsheet *(W 5.36, W 5.40)*
- Add Data Labels from Nonadjacent Columns *(W 5.50)*
- Change Column Widths and Center Data in a Column *(W 5.31)*
- Change Font Size and Row Height *(W 5.34)*
- Close Works *(W 5.55)*
- Copy a Formula *(W 5.18)*
- Copy Cells in Adjacent Columns *(W 5.19)*
- Create a Pie Chart from Nonadjacent Columns *(W 5.49)*
- Display Spreadsheet Entries in Color *(W 5.38)*
- Enter a Formula *(W 5.12, W 5.16)*
- Enter a Value and a Formula *(W 5.15)*
- Enter MAX and MIN Functions Using Easy Calc *(W 5.23)*
- Enter Spreadsheet Data *(W 5.17)*

- Enter Spreadsheet Title and Column Headings *(W 5.7)*
- Enter Text, Date, and Numeric Data *(W 5.10)*
- Enter Titles and Formulas *(W 5.20)*
- Format Cells Using Wrap Text *(W 5.9)*
- Format Chart Titles and Data Labels *(W 5.52)*
- Format a Spreadsheet Title *(W 5.29)*
- Make Entire Spreadsheet Bold *(W 5.28)*
- Print a Report in Landscape Orientation *(W 5.47)*
- Print a Works Spreadsheet Chart *(W 5.54)*
- Print the Spreadsheet in Landscape Orientation *(W 5.48)*
- Sort Rows *(W 5.43)*
- Start the Works Spreadsheet *(W 5.7)*
- Use Comma Format *(W 5.32)*
- Use Currency Format *(W 5.35)*
- Use Percent Format *(W 5.35)*
- Use Print Preview *(W 5.45)*

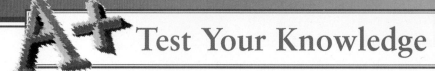 Test Your Knowledge

1 True/False

Instructions: Circle T if the statement is true or F if the statement is false.

T F 1. In Works, a formula is an equation that calculates a new value from existing values in cells within the spreadsheet.

T F 2. A formula always begins with an equal (=) sign.

T F 3. The order of calculation within a formula is multiplication and division first, followed by addition and subtraction, and finally, exponentiation.

T F 4. The five operators available for use within a formula are =, +, -, \, and %.

T F 5. If cell C9 contains the value 10, cell D9 contains the value 2, and cell E9 contains the value 6, then the formula =C9+D9+E9/3 produces the answer 6.

T F 6. When you want to copy formulas in adjacent columns, you can copy all the formulas at one time using the fill handle.

T F 7. Use the MAX function to determine the smallest value in a range.

T F 8. Works always displays negative numbers in a cell in red.

T F 9. If you sort last names in descending sequence, and the names Walter and Albert are on the list, the name Walter will be nearer the top than the name Albert.

T F 10. When printing a report using landscape orientation, you print on a page considered 8.5 inches long and 11 inches wide.

2 Multiple Choice

Instructions: Circle the correct response.

1. To confirm the entry of text data into a spreadsheet, you can _____.
   a. press the ENTER key
   b. press an arrow key
   c. click the Enter box
   d. all of the above

2. Always begin a formula with _____.
   a. a cell reference
   b. a plus sign
   c. a function name
   d. an equal sign

3. If cell C3 contains 21, cell C4 contains 3, and cell C5 contains 6, the formula =(C3+C4+C5)/C4 yields _____.
   a. 26
   b. 10
   c. 12
   d. 27

4. To copy the formulas in cells A3 and B3 to the range A4:B9, _____.
   a. highlight the range A4:B9, and then drag the fill handle
   b. highlight the range A3:B3, and then drag the fill handle
   c. highlight the range A3:B9, and then drag the fill handle
   d. click the Copy button on the toolbar

5. To place a border around the range, C12:D15, _____.
   a. highlight the range, C12:D15, and click the Border button on the toolbar
   b. right-click the highlighted range, C12:D15, click Format, click the Border tab, click Outline, and click the OK button
   c. highlight the range, C12:D15, and click the Outline button on the toolbar
   d. right-click the highlighted range, C12:D15, click Format, click the Font tab, click Outline, and click the OK button

6. To enter the MAX function in cell G12, highlight cell G12 and then _____.
   a. click Easy Calc in the toolbar
   b. click the MAX function button on the toolbar
   c. click Easy Calc on the Edit menu
   d. click Insert Function on the Edit menu

7. Which of the following is sorted in descending sequence?
   a. 91234, 623456, 4565, 321
   b. Waller, Jones, Barker, Aronson, Allred
   c. California, Texas, Utah, Washington
   d. 3123, 4123, 5123, 6123

8. When an entire spreadsheet will not print across an 8.5-inch wide page, the best option to fit the spreadsheet on a single page is to _____.
   a. print the report on two pages using portrait orientation
   b. print the report in landscape orientation
   c. delete two columns
   d. sort the columns into a different sequence

9. To add data labels to a chart, _____.
   a. click Data Labels on the Edit menu when the chart displays
   b. click Data Labels on the Edit menu when the spreadsheet displays
   c. click Data Labels on the context-sensitive menu when you right-click the chart
   d. right-click the chart and type the data labels

10. To print a chart, _____.
    a. click the Print button when the chart displays
    b. click the Print button when the spreadsheet displays
    c. click the Print Preview button when the chart displays
    d. click Page Setup when the chart displays

Test Your Knowledge

3 Fill In

Instructions: In the spaces provided, write the formulas required to accomplish the calculations specified.

1. Add the values in cells D20 and D25 and divide the result by the value in cell E30.

   _____

2. Multiply the value in cell S4 by the quotient of cell A1 divided by cell C1.

   _____

3. Multiply the value in cell A1 by the greatest value in the range A13:H20.

   _____

4. Subtract the value in cell F25 from the value in cell F24 and divide the result by the value in cell A10.

   _____

5. Divide the smallest value in the range A1:A14 by 3 times the product of cells D1 and D2.

   _____

4 Fill In

Instructions: Using the values shown in the spreadsheet in Figure 5-92, evaluate the formulas in the following problems below Figure 5-92.

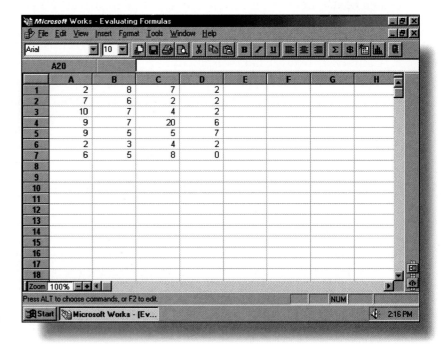

FIGURE 5-92

1. =A3+B1+C5   _____
2. =SUM(A1:A7)-SUM(B1:B7)   _____
3. =A7^D6/B6   _____
4. =MAX(A1:A7)-MIN(A1:A7)   _____
5. (C4-C7)/A1*A2   _____

Use Help

1 Reviewing Project Activities

Instructions: Use your computer to perform the following tasks to obtain experience using online Help.

1. Start the Microsoft Works Spreadsheet tool.
2. Display the Help window to the right of the document window. Click the Index button below the Help window to display the Help Topics: Microsoft Works dialog box.
3. Type `wrapping text: spreadsheets` in the Index text box. Read To wrap text within a cell on the Step-by-Step sheet. Print the document. Click the More Info tab. Print the document. Click Overview. Read and print the overview. Answer the following questions:
   a) When is wrapping text useful in a spreadsheet?

   _____

   b) List three types of data Works will not wrap in a spreadsheet.

   _____

2 Expanding on the Basics

Instructions: Use Works online Help to better understand the topics listed below. Print the topic or topics that substantiate your answer. If there is no Print this topic icon, answer the question on a separate piece of paper.

1. Using the key terms *showing formulas or results in cells* and the Index sheet in the Help topics: Microsoft Works dialog box, answer the following questions.
   a) Which menu contains the Formulas command?_____
   b) How do you turn on the Formulas command?_____
   c) How do you turn off the Formulas command?_____
   d) When the Formulas command is on, what do you see in the spreadsheet?

   _____

   e) When the Formulas command is off, what do you see in the spreadsheet?

   _____

   f) Explain how you would view a formula in a cell._____
2. Using the key terms *sorting spreadsheet entries* and the Index sheet in the Help topics: Microsoft Works dialog box, answer the following questions.
   a) How do you sort more than one column on a spreadsheet?

   _____

   b) Explain the steps necessary to sort more than three columns.

   _____

Apply Your Knowledge

1 Sorting Spreadsheet Data

Instructions: Start the Microsoft Works Spreadsheet tool. Open the A&M Yearly Sales document on the Student Floppy Disk that accompanies this book. The spreadsheet is illustrated in Figure 5-93. Perform the following sorts.

	A	B
1	**A & M Yearly Sales**	
2	Department	Sales
3	Toys	$63,498.00
4	Hardware	$1,045,671.00
5	Recreation	$985,231.00
6	Furniture	$1,155,642.00
7	Cosmetics	$78,945.00
8	Variety	$101,256.00
9	Shoes	$21,985.00
10	Housewares	$581,234.00
11	Clothing	$543,889.00

FIGURE 5-93

1. Sort the spreadsheet in ascending order by Department. Print this sorted version.
2. Sort the spreadsheet in descending order by Department. Print this sorted version.
3. Sort the spreadsheet in ascending order by Sales. Print this sorted version.
4. Sort the spreadsheet in descending order by Sales. Print this sorted version.

In the Lab

1 Building a Green Thumb Nursery April Sales Spreadsheet

Problem: As a new employee for the Green Thumb Nursery, you have been asked prepare a report of April sales. The sales for April are shown in Table 5-4. The spreadsheet and chart are shown in Figure 5-94.

TABLE 5-4			
PLANT	FLATS SOLD	FLAT PRICE	SALES RETURNS
Agapanthus	85	15.25	60.00
Azalea	135	12.50	62.50
Hibiscus	250	9.75	78.00
Impatiens	185	11.35	56.75
Nandina	236	7.50	75.00
Star Jasmine	100	11.75	105.75

In the Lab

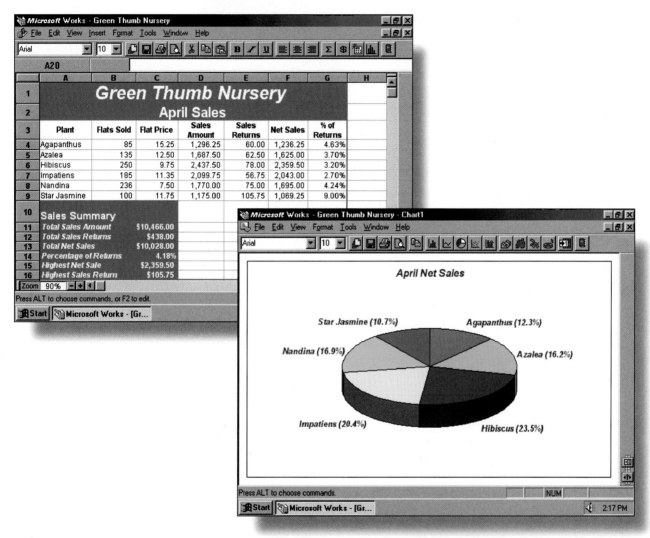

FIGURE 5-94

Instructions:

1. Create a spreadsheet in the format shown in Figure 5-94 using the text and numbers from the table.
2. On the spreadsheet, calculate the Sales Amount by multiplying the Flats Sold by the Flat Price.
3. On the spreadsheet, calculate the Net Sales by subtracting the Sales Returns from the Sales Amount.
4. Calculate the % of Returns by dividing the Sales Returns by the Sales Amount.
5. Calculate the Total Sales Amount and Total Sales Returns by summing the values in each of the respective columns.
6. Calculate the Total Net Sales by subtracting the Total Sales Returns from the Total Sales Amount.
7. Calculate the Percentage of Returns in row 14 by dividing the Total Sales Returns by the Total Sales Amount.

(continued)

In the Lab

Building a Green Thumb Nursery April Sales Spreadsheet *(continued)*

8. Determine the Highest Net Sale in row 15. Determine the Highest Sales Return in row 16.

9. Format the spreadsheet as shown in Figure 5-94 on the previous page. The title, Green Thumb Nursery, displays in 24-point Arial bold and italic and is centered across the range A1:G1. The title, April Sales, displays in 18-point Arial bold and is centered across the range A2:G2. The column widths are: A = 13; B = 11; C = 10; D = 11; E = 11; F = 10; and G = 10. Flat Price, Sales Amount, Sales Returns, and Net Sales are formatted in the Comma format. % of Returns is formatted in the Percent format. In the Sales Summary section, the title displays in 14-point Arial bold and the row titles display in 10-point Arial bold and italic. All numbers in the Sales Summary section are formatted with the Currency format except Percentage of Returns, which is formatted with the Percent format. Color the spreadsheet title and column titles white with dark cyan cells. Color the Sales Summary section text and numbers white with dark cyan cells. Place a dark cyan border around the spreadsheet.

10. Sort the spreadsheet into descending sequence by Plant name.

11. Save the spreadsheet you create on a floppy disk. Use the filename Green Thumb Nursery.

12. Print the spreadsheet you have created. Ensure all columns will print on one page.

13. Create the 3-D Pie chart illustrated in Figure 5-94 on the previous page from the Net Sales column contained on the spreadsheet. The title is dark red in 12-point Arial bold font. The data labels are dark red in 10-point Arial bold italic font.

14. Print the 3-D Pie chart in landscape orientation.

15. Sort the spreadsheet into ascending order by Net Sales.

16. Print the spreadsheet and chart in Net Sales sequence.

17. Save the spreadsheet and chart.

18. Follow directions from your instructor for turning in this assignment.

2 Building an Oil Production Report

Problem: As an intern for Jones Oil Exploration and Production Inc., you have been asked to prepare a report for the Chief Executive Officer. The data for the spreadsheet is shown in Table 5-5. The spreadsheet and chart are shown in Figure 5-95.

TABLE 5-5			
DATE	DRILLING LOCATION	BARRELS OF OIL PRODUCED	PRICE PER BARREL
05/25/97	Oklahoma	525	15.00
05/25/97	Texas	600	16.00
06/12/97	Louisiana	350	12.00
06/15/97	California	1000	12.00
06/25/97	Alaska	1200	13.00
07/19/97	Montana	320	13.00

In the Lab

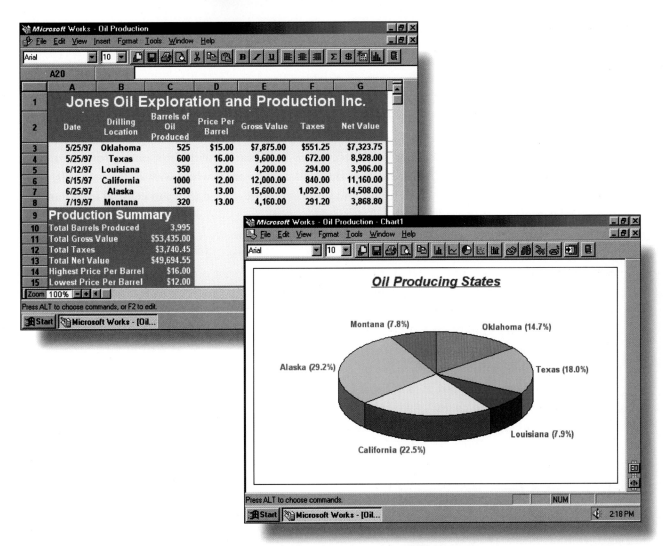

FIGURE 5-95

Instructions:

1. Create a spreadsheet in the format shown in Figure 5-95 using the text and numbers from the table.
2. On the spreadsheet, calculate the Gross Value by multiplying the Barrels of Oil Produced by the Price Per Barrel.
3. On the spreadsheet, calculate the Taxes by multiplying the Gross Value by 7%.
4. Calculate the Net Value by subtracting the Taxes from the Gross Value.
5. Calculate the Production Summary totals by summing the values in each of the respective columns.
6. Determine the Highest Price Per Barrel in row 14. Determine the Lowest Price Per Barrel in row 15.

(continued)

In the Lab

Building an Oil Production Report *(continued)*

7. Format the spreadsheet as shown in Figure 5-95 on the previous page. The entire spreadsheet displays in bold. The title displays in 18-point Arial bold and is centered across the range A1:G1. The column widths are: A = 11; B = 11; C = 11; D = 10; E = 12; F = 10; and G = 12. In the Production Summary section, the title displays in 14-point Arial bold and the row titles display in 10-point Arial bold. All numbers in the Production Summary section are formatted with the Currency format, except Total Barrels Produced, which is formatted with the Comma format and with no decimal places. Color the spreadsheet title and column titles white with dark cyan cells. Color the Production Summary section text and numbers white with dark cyan cells. Place a dark cyan border around the spreadsheet.

8. Sort the spreadsheet into ascending sequence by Drilling Location.

9. Save the spreadsheet you create on a floppy disk. Use the filename Oil Production.

10. Print the spreadsheet you have created. Ensure all columns will print on one page.

11. Create the 3-D Pie chart in Figure 5-95 on the previous page from the Net Value contained on the spreadsheet. The title is dark blue in 16-point Arial bold italic underlined font. The data labels are blue in 10-point Arial bold font.

12. Print the 3-D Pie chart in landscape orientation.

13. Sort the spreadsheet into ascending order by Barrels of Oil Produced.

14. Print the spreadsheet and chart in Barrels of Oil Produced sequence.

15. Save the spreadsheet and chart.

16. Follow directions from your instructor for turning in this assignment.

3 Building a Gem Investment Report

Problem: As an investment manager, you have been asked to analyze the gem investments held by a local client. The gem investments are shown in Table 5-6. The spreadsheet and chart are shown in Figure 5-96.

TABLE 5-6				
GEM	PURCHASE DATE	NUMBER OF GEMS PURCHASED	PURCHASE PRICE	CURRENT PRICE
Emerald	9/12/90	7	1,000.00	1,500.00
Ruby	10/23/91	5	2,000.00	4,900.00
Diamond	7/30/94	2	3,000.00	5,200.00
Onyx	11/15/95	4	4,800.00	4,200.00
Topaz	12/23/95	8	1,800.00	1,600.00

In the Lab

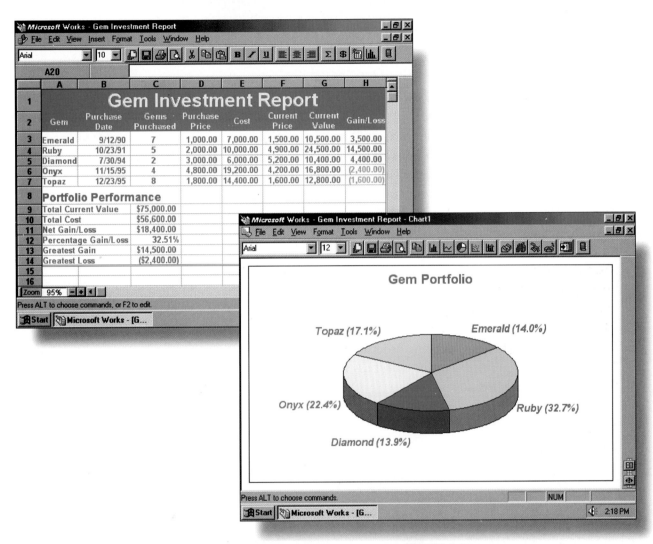

FIGURE 5-96

Instructions:

1. Create a spreadsheet in the format shown in Figure 5-96 using the numbers and text in Table 5-6.
2. On the spreadsheet, calculate the Cost by multiplying the Gems Purchased by the Purchase Price.
3. On the spreadsheet, calculate the Current Value by multiplying the Gems Purchased by the Current Price.
4. On the spreadsheet, calculate the Gain/Loss by subtracting the Cost from the Current Value.
5. On the spreadsheet, calculate the Total Current Value, Total Cost, Net Gain/Loss, and Percentage Gain/Loss.
6. On the spreadsheet, calculate the Greatest Gain and the Greatest Loss.

(continued)

In the Lab

Building a Gem Investment Report (continued)

7. Format the spreadsheet as shown in Figure 5-96. The entire spreadsheet is bold. The spreadsheet title displays in 24-point Arial. The Portfolio Performance title displays in 14-point Arial. The column widths are: A = 8; B = 12; C = 12; D = 10; E = 10; F = 10; G = 10; H = 10. Purchase Price, Cost, Current Price, Current Value, and Gain/Loss are formatted with the Comma format. Total Current Value, Total Cost, Net Gain/Loss, Greatest Gain, and Greatest Loss are formatted with the Currency format. Percentage Gain/Loss is formatted with the Percent format. Color the spreadsheet title and column titles yellow with blue cells. Color the spreadsheet row titles, numbers, and Portfolio Performance section blue. Place a blue double-line border around the spreadsheet.

8. Sort the spreadsheet into ascending sequence by Gem name.

9. Save the spreadsheet you create on a floppy disk. Use the filename, Gem Investment Report.

10. Print the spreadsheet you have created. Ensure all columns will print on one page.

11. Create the 3-D Pie chart illustrated in Figure 5-96 on the previous page from the Current Value column contained in the spreadsheet. The title is blue in 16-point Arial bold font. The data labels are blue in 12-point Arial bold italic font.

12. Print the 3-D Pie chart in landscape orientation.

13. Sort the spreadsheet into ascending order by Gain/Loss.

14. Print the spreadsheet and chart in Gain/Loss sequence.

15. Format the spreadsheet so that all formulas display. To do this, click Formulas on the View menu. Reduce the size of the spreadsheet and change the column widths so that all formulas display. For further information on this process, see Use Help 2, Expanding on the Basics, on page W 5.59. The screen should resemble the one shown in Figure 5-97. Print the spreadsheet on a single page.

16. Follow directions from your instructor for turning in this assignment.

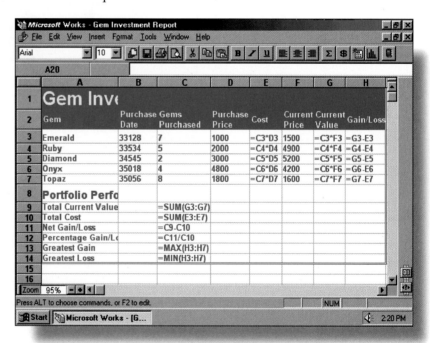

FIGURE 5-97

Cases and Places

The difficulty of these case studies varies:

▶ Case studies preceded by a single half moon are the least difficult. You can create the required spreadsheets based on information that already has been placed in an organized form.
▶▶ Case studies preceded by two half moons are more difficult. You must organize the information presented before using it to create the desired spreadsheets.
▶▶▶ Case studies preceded by three half moons are the most difficult. You must obtain and organize the necessary information before using it to create the required spreadsheets.

1 ▶ The Student Assistance Committee at your college offers short-term loans at simple interest. Loans are provided in five categories: tuition assistance, academic supplies, room and board, personal emergency, and travel expenses. Their duration and interest rates vary. At the end of the semester, the Student Assistance Committee summarized the loan activity (Figure 5-98).

LOAN TYPE	PRINCIPAL	RATE	TIME (YEARS)
Tuition Assistance	$48,000	10%	0.33
Academic Supplies	$16,000	12%	0.25
Room and Board	$26,500	15%	0.33
Personal Emergency	$5,500	8%	0.17
Travel Expenses	$4,000	17%	0.17

FIGURE 5-98

With this data, the Committee has asked you to develop a spreadsheet they can use at their next meeting. This spreadsheet should determine the interest accrued, amount due, and percentage of the total budget used for each loan type. The following formulas can be applied to obtain this information:

Interest = Principal x Rate x Time
Amount Due = Principal + Interest
Percentage of Budget = Principal / Total Principal

Include a total, maximum value, and minimum value for Principal, Interest, and Amount Due. Include a chart showing the portion of the total principal each loan type uses. Use the concepts and techniques presented in this project to create and format the spreadsheet and chart.

Cases and Places

2 ▸ The household electric bill has just arrived in the mail, and you have been accused of driving up the total by "burning the midnight oil." You are convinced your late-night studying has little effect on the total amount due. You obtain a brochure from the electric company that lists the typical operating costs of appliances based on average sizes and local electricity rates (Figure 5-99).

With this data, you produce a spreadsheet to share with your family. Use the concepts and techniques presented in these projects to create and format the spreadsheet.

APPLIANCE	COST PER HOUR	HOURS USED DAILY	TOTAL COST PER DAY	TOTAL COST PER MONTH (30 days)
Clothes dryer	$0.5331	2		
Iron	$0.1173	0.5		
Light bulb (150 watt)	$0.0160	5		
Personal computer	$0.0213	3		
Radio	$0.0075	2		
Refrigerator	$0.0113	24		
Stereo	$0.0053	4		
Television	$0.0128	6		
VCR	$0.0032	2		

FIGURE 5-99

3 ▸▸ Use the new car and truck spreadsheet created in Case Study 3 of Project 4 for this assignment. Execute each of these tasks: (a) Insert two columns at the right of the spreadsheet. (b) Add the headings and data for the Average Cost per Domestic Car and Average Cost per Import Car shown in Figure 5-100. (c) Calculate the percent of domestic cars sold as compared to import cars sold each year. (d) Calculate the percent of domestic trucks sold as compared to import trucks sold each year. (e) Calculate the additional cost of an import car as compared to a domestic car for each year. (f) Create bar graphs showing the average cost for domestic and import cars sold each year.

MODEL YEAR	DOMESTIC CARS SOLD (THOUSANDS)	IMPORT CARS SOLD (THOUSANDS)	DOMESTIC TRUCKS SOLD (THOUSANDS)	IMPORT TRUCKS SOLD (THOUSANDS)	AVG. COST PER DOMESTIC CAR	AVG. COST PER IMPORT CAR
1991	6,276	2,313	3,582	333	16,215	17,830
1992	6,195	2,140	4,026	247	17,152	19,792
1993	6,595	2,011	4,789	199	17,519	22,093
1994	7,173	1,977	5,499	155	18,198	24,078
1995	7,167	1,803	5,666	170	18,354	25,344

FIGURE 5-100

Cases and Places

4 ▶▶ Health experts recommend that individuals obtain 10 to 20 percent of their total daily calories from fat and 12 to 15 percent from protein. You decide to calculate how much fat and protein you need each day. For both amounts, begin by determining your realistic desirable weight. Then, take this ideal body weight and multiply by 11 if you are a woman or 12 if you are a man. This figure is the total calories you should eat per day to sustain that weight. To determine total grams of protein you should eat daily, find 12 percent of this daily calorie intake. Because four calories are in every gram of protein, divide the total protein calories by 4. To determine total grams of fat you should eat daily, divide the total calories you should eat per day by 9, and then divide this number by 10. This figure is the total grams of fat you should eat per day to maintain your fat intake at 10 percent of your total calories. Now multiply that number by 2 to determine the number of daily fat grams you are allowed to maintain your fat intake at 20 percent of total calories. These two numbers are your fat gram budget.

Use the concepts and techniques presented in these projects to prepare a spreadsheet for you and two of your family members or friends that contains the following information: desirable weight, total calories allowed per day, total protein grams, 10 percent fat gram allowance, and 20 percent fat gram allowance.

5 ▶▶ Occasionally, you buy several magazines at the newsstand so you can stay informed of current events, learn about your hobbies, and be entertained. In an effort to save money, you are considering subscribing to these magazines, even though you may not read every issue. To help you decide whether to subscribe, you make the list shown in Figure 5-101 showing the magazines you purchase frequently, the newsstand price, how many times you purchase the magazine each year, and the annual subscription cost. Use the concepts and techniques presented in these projects to prepare a spreadsheet to compare your yearly expenditure for each magazine to the cost of an annual subscription. Include annual newsstand and subscription costs for each magazine, along with the number of magazines you need to purchase to reach the break-even point. Then create a bar graph illustrating the annual costs.

MAGAZINE NAME	NEWSSTAND PRICE	ISSUES PURCHASED EACH YEAR	ANNUAL SUBSCRIPTION PRICE
Architectural Digest	$5.00	6	$39.95
Car and Driver	$2.95	10	$19.94
Fortune	$4.95	15	$56.94
Life	$4.95	3	$27.96
Money	$3.50	4	$29.95
Newsweek	$2.95	35	$35.55
PC Magazine	$3.95	15	$34.97
Psychology Today	$3.00	8	$15.97
U.S. News & World Report	$2.95	20	$39.00
Time	$2.95	35	$56.68

FIGURE 5-101

Cases and Places

6 ▶▶▶ Regular, moderate exercise lowers cholesterol and blood pressure, reduces stress, controls weight, and increases bone strength. Fitness experts recommend individuals who need to lose weight do so at the rate of 1 1/2 to 2 pounds per week. If an individual maintains a regular, sensible diet and burns 750 extra calories each day, he or she will lose about 1 1/2 pounds of fatty tissue a week. Visit a fitness center at your school or in your community to discuss various exercise options. Find out the types of activities offered (for example, aerobics, swimming, jogging, tennis, racquetball, basketball). Then, list how many calories are burned per hour when performing each of these activities. Using this information, create a spreadsheet showing the activities offered, the number of calories burned per hour performing these activities, and the number of calories burned and pounds lost if you exercise two hours, four hours, and seven hours a week while participating in each activity.

7 ▶▶▶ Banks often use a formula to determine how much money prospective buyers can afford to spend on a house. Visit a bank to learn how personnel analyze the financial status of their customers. With their formulas and estimates of your future income, create a spreadsheet showing how expensive a house you could manage to buy today and in five, ten, fifteen, twenty, and twenty-five years from now. Assuming you purchase a house for the amount indicated by the bank's formula and make a down payment of 10 percent, determine the amount of money you would need to put down for each house and the amount of money you would need to borrow.

Microsoft Works 4

Windows 95

What-If Analysis, Functions, and Absolute Cell References

Objectives

You will have mastered the material in this project when you can:

▶ Use the fill handle to enter a data sequence

▶ Use drag-and-drop to copy a range

▶ Round cell contents using the ROUND function

▶ Explain the difference between the ROUND function and the rounding obtained using the Comma format

▶ Enter a formula containing absolute cell references

▶ Copy a formula containing absolute and relative cell references

▶ Add borders to cells

▶ Insert a footer in a spreadsheet

▶ Freeze worksheet titles

▶ Perform what-if analysis on a spreadsheet with multiple variables

▶ Create a 3-D Stacked Bar chart

▶ Add category labels to a chart

▶ Change colors and patterns in a 3-D Stacked Bar chart

▶ Rename a chart

▶ Print a 3-D Stacked Bar chart in landscape orientation

Pattern for Success

What-if...

What if a woman sleeps with her husband's corpse for forty years? That question led to William Faulkner's celebrated short story, *A Rose for Emily*. Many successful writers use the technique of asking *what-if?* to hypothesize what would happen if a given set of circumstances were changed in some interesting way, thus evolving a new set of circumstances. The result can be a classic, such as Gustave Flaubert's *Madame Bovary*: What if the wife of a small-town doctor in France becomes bored with her life and seeks outside stimulation?

When applied to literature, this process is called *conjecture*, but when it is applied to the world of business, it is called *planning*. Ever since the introduction of VisiCalc in 1977, what-if analysis has become a mainstay of business forecasting and contingency planning, using various sets of circumstances — or scenarios — to determine the bottom-line fiscal impact of some action, such as increasing the sales force or cutting the price of a given product. In science, the word *paradigm* often is used to describe the archetype or model within which one or more variables is manipulated so the results can be observed.

Regardless of how the process is labled, what-if analysis has become a vital tool for managing businesses and conducting scientific research. The speed of modern computers has enhanced the capability to rapidly recalculate massive sets of numbers, but equally important is the sophisticated software that organizes the data and creates the user interface.

An excellent example of software capable of fast, versatile, what-if analysis is the Microsoft Works Spreadsheet tool. It not only facilitates efficient analysis, but it also is rich in well-designed human engineering features optimized for simplicity and ease-of-use.

What-if analysis can prove useful for a student. With the cost of attending some schools as high as $1,000 a week, it is prudent to ask whether career plans after college will be worth the money spent on schooling. To test this, a personal financial picture can be projected using the Works Spreadsheet tool to compare monetary needs, such as house and car payments, taxes, student loan repayment, living expenses, even vacations, versus various pay levels for different types of jobs. By manipulating the variables, *what-if analysis*, a user can answer such questions as, How much money will be needed? or How much is a large sum of money?

What-if analysis not only is about money, it also is about dreams, as so eloquently stated by William Butler Yeats:

But I, being poor, have only my dreams;
I have spread my dreams under your feet;
Tread softly because you tread on my dreams.

Microsoft
Works 4
Windows 95

What-If Analysis, Functions, and Absolute Cell References

Case Perspective

You have been asked by the Eastern Division management to prepare the projected budget for the following year using a Works spreadsheet. Management is concerned with the effect the projected expenses have on the net income for the year. Specifically, management wants to know how a one percent decrease in the projected expenses would affect net income. They also have requested that you chart the projected expenses for the year.

You are to use the Works Spreadsheet tool to prepare the projected budget and chart the projected expenses. Design the spreadsheet to answer what-if questions easily.

Introduction

In Project 4 and Project 5, you learned that a spreadsheet is useful for performing calculations and presenting data both as a spreadsheet and as a chart. You also can use spreadsheets to solve business, financial, and accounting problems that otherwise would be difficult to solve.

In particular, spreadsheets provide a means for asking **what-if questions** and obtaining immediate answers. For example, a business person might ask, *What if we decreased our projected expenses by 1 percent - how would the decrease affect our net income?* A Works Spreadsheet can easily provide the answer to this question.

Project Six

To illustrate the capability of Works to provide the answers to what-if questions, Project 6 produces the spreadsheet shown in Figure 6-1. The spreadsheet contains the quarterly projected revenue, expenses, and net income for the year. The spreadsheet also includes, in column F, the projected totals for the year for all revenues, expenses, and net income.

The revenue amounts in row 4 are estimates based on previous years' performances. The Returns for each month as shown in row 5 are determined by multiplying the Revenue in row 4 by the Returns percentage in cell B20. The Returns percentage shown in Figure 6-1 is 3%. Therefore, for Quarter 1, the Returns are 4,153.22 ($138,440.50*3%). The Net Revenue for each quarter, as shown in row 6, is determined by subtracting the Returns in row 5 from the Revenue in row 4. In Figure 6-1, the Net Revenue for Quarter 1 is $134,287.28 ($138,440.50 – 4,153.22).

Each of the quarterly projected expenses in the range B8:E11 – Product Liability, Manufacturing, Marketing, and Benefits – is determined by multiplying the Net Revenue in row 6 for each quarter by the appropriate expense percentage in the Assumptions section. As an example, the projected expenses for Quarter 1 are as follows:

1. Product Liability is $16,114.47 (134,287.28 * 12%).
2. Manufacturing is 47,000.55 (134,287.28 * 35%).
3. Marketing is 37,600.44 (134,287.28 * 28%).
4. Benefits is 20,143.09 (134,287.28 * 15%).

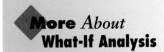

More About What-If Analysis

The single most important reason why millions of businesses use spreadsheet software is the ability to instantaneously answer what-if questions. It wasn't too long ago that what-if questions of any complexity could only be answered by large computers programmed by computer professionals. Microsoft Works gives the non-computer professional the capability of answering complex business-related questions quickly.

The Total Expenses for each quarter in row 12 of Figure 6-1 are the sum of the quarterly projected expenses in rows 8 through 11.

The Net Income for each quarter in row 13 is calculated by subtracting the quarterly Total Expenses in row 12 from the corresponding quarterly Net Revenue in row 6. Finally, the totals in column F are determined by summing the quarterly values in each row.

The Assumptions section of the spreadsheet in Figure 6-1 contains the values used in the formulas in the spreadsheet. Management can vary the values in the Assumptions section to ask what-if questions about their business. For example, they can ask, How much does our net income change

	A	B	C	D	E	F
1	Eastern Division Projected Budget Report					
2		Quarter 1	Quarter 2	Quarter 3	Quarter 4	Total
3	Revenue					
4	Revenue	$138,440.50	$198,534.85	$219,409.51	$153,753.25	$710,138.11
5	Returns	4,153.22	5,956.05	6,582.29	4,612.60	21,304.16
6	Net Revenue	$134,287.28	$192,578.80	$212,827.22	$149,140.65	$688,833.95
7	Expenses					
8	Product Liability	$16,114.47	$23,109.46	$25,539.27	$17,896.88	$82,660.08
9	Manufacturing	47,000.55	67,402.58	74,489.53	52,199.23	241,091.89
10	Marketing	37,600.44	53,922.06	59,591.62	41,759.38	192,873.50
11	Benefits	20,143.09	28,886.82	31,924.08	22,371.10	103,325.09
12	Total Expenses	$120,858.55	$173,320.92	$191,544.50	$134,226.59	$619,950.56
13	Net Income	$13,428.73	$19,257.88	$21,282.72	$14,914.06	$68,883.39
14						
15	Assumptions					
16	Product Liability	12%				
17	Manufacturing	35%				
18	Marketing	28%				
19	Benefits	15%				
20	Returns	3%				

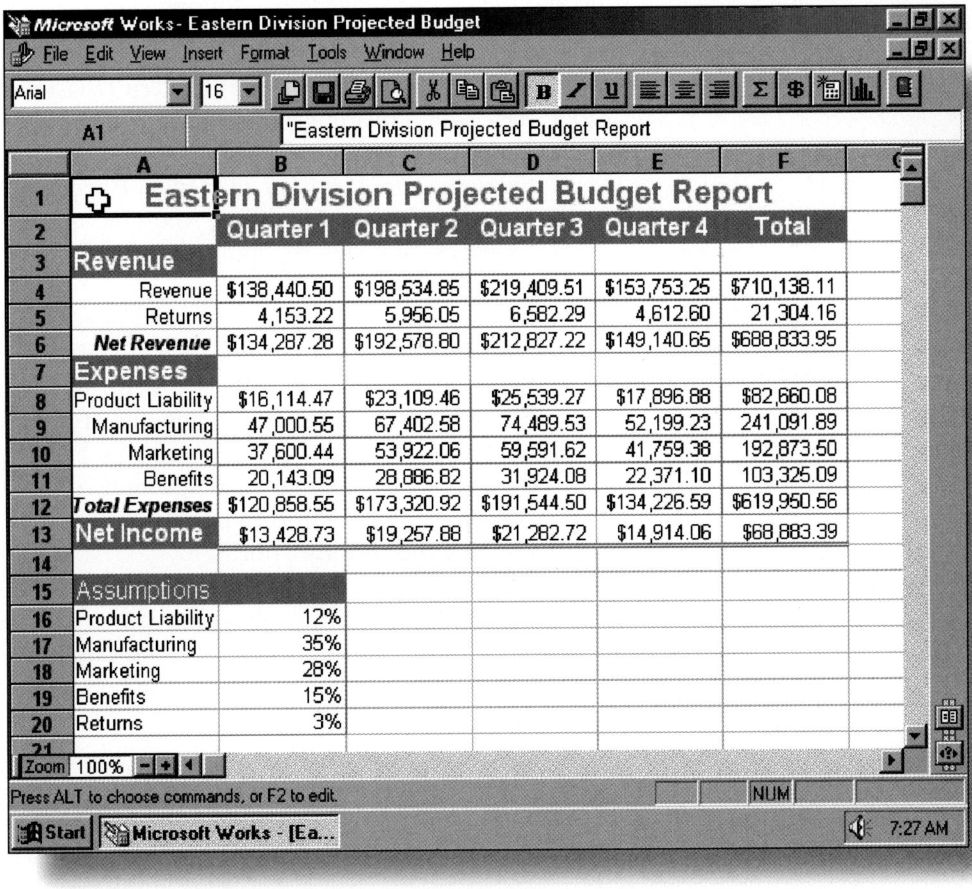

FIGURE 6-1

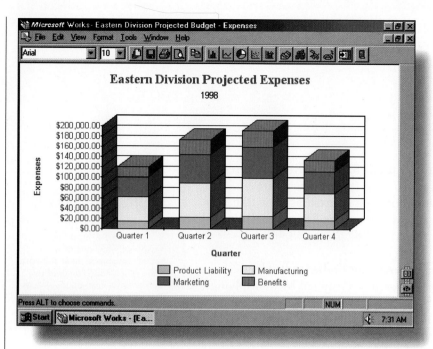

FIGURE 6-2

if we decrease our expenses by 1 percent? or What effect will a 2 percent increase in our returns have on our net income? This capability of quickly analyzing the effect of changing values in a spreadsheet is important in making business decisions.

From your work in Projects 4 and 5, you are aware of Works' capability for creating charts. In this project, you will create a 3-D Stacked Bar chart. The 3-D Stacked Bar chart in Figure 6-2 graphically illustrates the projected expenses for the four quarters. Each expense for the quarter is a different color, and they are stacked one on top of the other, so the stack represents the total expenses for a given quarter.

Spreadsheet Preparation Steps

The overall steps to prepare the spreadsheet in Figure 6-1 on the previous page and the chart in Figure 6-2 follow.

1. Start the Works Spreadsheet.
2. Enter the spreadsheet title (Eastern Division Projected Budget Report) and the column headings (Quarter 1, Quarter 2, Quarter 3, Quarter 4, and Total).
3. Enter the row headings (Revenue, Revenue, Returns, Net Revenues, Expenses, Product Liability, Manufacturing, Marketing, Benefits, Total Expenses, and Net Income).
4. Copy the expense labels to the Assumptions section.
5. Enter the projected percentages shown in Figure 6-1.
6. Enter the projected revenue.
7. Enter the formulas to calculate Returns, Net Revenue, Product Liability, Manufacturing, Marketing, Benefits, Total Expenses, and Net Income.
8. Format the title and column and row headings (bold the text and increase the font size, change the background color, and change the text color).
9. Format the values in the spreadsheet.
10. Increase the column widths.
11. Add borders to the spreadsheet.
12. Create a footer on the spreadsheet.
13. Format the Assumptions section (increase the font size, change the background color, and change the text color).
14. Print the spreadsheet.

15. Save the spreadsheet on a floppy disk.
16. Create the 3-D Stacked Bar chart based on data in the spreadsheet.
17. Add category labels to the chart.
18. Add titles to the 3-D Stacked Bar chart.
19. Change the chart segment colors and patterns.
20. Add y-axis gridlines to the chart.
21. Rename the chart.
22. Print the chart.

The following pages contain a detailed explanation of each of these steps.

Starting the Works Spreadsheet

To start the Works Spreadsheet, follow the steps you used in previous projects. These steps are summarized below.

TO START THE WORKS SPREADSHEET

Step 1: Click the Start button on the taskbar, point to Programs, point to Microsoft Works 4.0 on the Programs submenu, and then click Microsoft Works 4.0 on the Microsoft Works 4.0 submenu.

Step 2: When the Works Task Launcher dialog box displays, click the Works Tools tab.

Step 3: Click the Spreadsheet button on the Works Tools sheet.

Step 4: Maximize the application and document windows, if necessary.

Entering the Spreadsheet Title

To enter the spreadsheet title in cell A1, first highlight the cell in which the title belongs and then type the title as illustrated in the following step.

 Steps To Enter a Spreadsheet Title

1 **Highlight the cell where you will enter the title – cell A1. Type** Eastern Division Projected Budget Report **and then either press the ENTER key or click the Enter box to confirm the entry.**

Works enters the spreadsheet title into cell A1 (Figure 6-3).

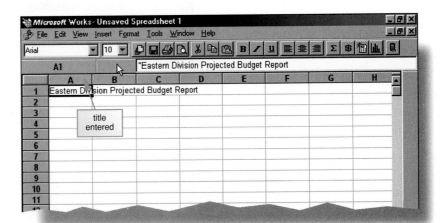

FIGURE 6-3

More *About*
Drag-and-Drop

If the mouse pointer does not change to a block arrow with the word DRAG below the arrow when you point to the border of a range to copy, the Enable drag-and-drop editing option is turned off. To turn it on, click Options on the Tools menu, click the General tab, and click Enable drag-and-drop editing.

Using the Fill Handle to Create a Data Series

In Projects 4 and 5, you used the fill handle to copy the contents of a cell or a range of cells to adjacent cells. You also can use the fill handle to automatically create a data series. A **data series** is a set of numbers, dates, or text that changes automatically by a specified amount. In Figure 6-1 on page W 6.5, Quarter 1, Quarter 2, Quarter 3, and Quarter 4 column headings display in row 2. To create this sequence, first select the cell or range that includes the data you want to use as the starting sequence. Then, drag the fill handle to select the range you want to fill. Perform the following steps to enter the first quarter, Quarter 1, in cell B2, create the data sequence, Quarter 2, Quarter 3, and Quarter 4, in the range C2:E2, and enter the column heading, Total, in cell F2.

Steps **To Enter a Data Sequence in a Range Using the Fill Handle**

1 **Highlight cell B2. Type** Quarter 1 **and then press the ENTER key or click the Enter box to confirm the entry. Click the Center Align button on the toolbar. Point to the fill handle on the lower right corner of cell B2.**

Quarter 1 displays centered in cell B2 (Figure 6-4). The mouse pointer changes to a cross and the word FILL, indicating the fill handle is selected.

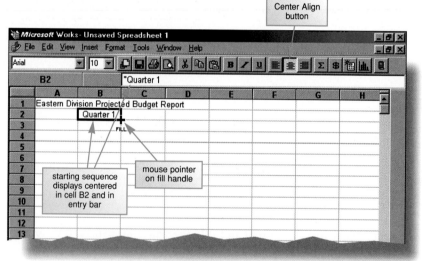

FIGURE 6-4

2 **Drag the range you want to fill — cells C2:E2.**

When you drag the fill handle through the cells, Works places a border around the cell you want to use as the beginning sequence (cell B2) and an outline around the range in which you want to extend the sequence (range C2:E2) (Figure 6-5).

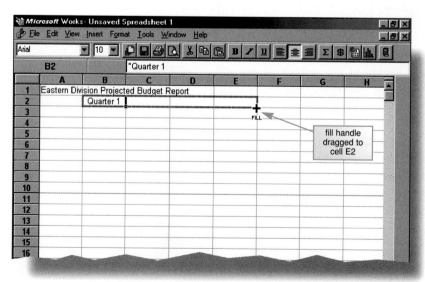

FIGURE 6-5

3 **Release the mouse button.**

Works places the sequence, Quarter 2, Quarter 3, and Quarter 4, in the range C2:E2 and centers each heading (Figure 6-6).

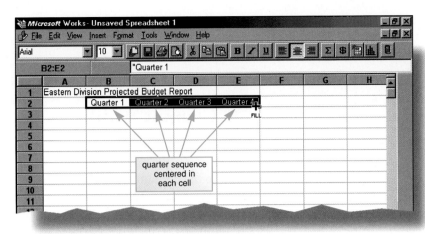

FIGURE 6-6

4 **Highlight cell F2 and then enter** Total **as the heading. Click the Center Align button on the toolbar.**

Works displays the column heading, Total, centered in cell F2 (Figure 6-7).

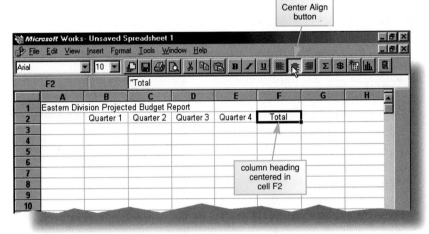

FIGURE 6-7

OtherWays

1. On Edit menu click Fill Series, click Autofill, click OK button

Besides creating the data series, the fill handle also copies the format of cell B2 (center aligned) to the range C2:E2. If you drag the fill handle past cell E2 in Step 2, Works continues to increment the quarters.

Works recognizes different types of data series. Table 6-1 illustrates several examples.

Notice in Examples 6 through 10 in Table 6-1 that you are required to enter the first data in the sequence in one cell and the second data in the sequence in an adjacent cell. If you create a sequence that increments each entry by a value other than one, Works uses the first two cells to establish the proper sequence. You then highlight both cells and drag the fill handle to extend a series that increments other than one.

Table 6-1

EXAMPLE	CONTENTS OF CELL COPIED USING FILL HANDLE	NEXT THREE VALUES IN EXTENDED SERIES
1	Qtr1	Qtr2, Qtr3, Qtr4
2	Monday	Tuesday, Wednesday, Thursday
3	January	February, March, April
4	Winter	Spring, Summer, Fall
5	Text 1.1	Text 1.2, Text 1.3, Text 1.4
6	July, September	November, January, March
7	1999, 2000	2001, 2002, 2003
8	1, 2	3, 4, 5
9	500, 450	400, 350, 300
10	-1, -3	-5, -7, -9

You can reduce the amount of numbers and text you have to type in a spreadsheet by using the fill handle to create a series for you.

Entering Row Headings and Increasing the Column Widths

In Project 5, you increased the column widths using the Column Width command after entering the values into the spreadsheet. Sometimes, you may want to increase the column widths before you enter the values and then, if necessary, adjust them later. The following steps illustrate how to enter the row headings in column A and increase the column width by dragging the column border. Perform the following steps to enter the row headings and increase the column width.

Steps To Enter Row Headings and Increase the Column Width by Dragging the Column Border

1 **Highlight cell A3. Enter** Revenue **in cell A3,** Revenue **in cell A4,** Returns **in cell A5, and** Net Revenue **in cell A6. Enter** Expenses **in cell A7,** Product Liability **in cell A8,** Manufacturing **in cell A9,** Marketing **in cell A10,** Benefits **in cell A11, and** Total Expenses **in cell A12. Enter** Net Income **in cell A13. Point to the border that separates column A and column B in the column heading.**

Works displays the row headings in column A (Figure 6-8). The mouse pointer changes to a symbol consisting of two vertical lines with arrows on the left and right sides and the word ADJUST. This indicates you can drag the column border left or right.

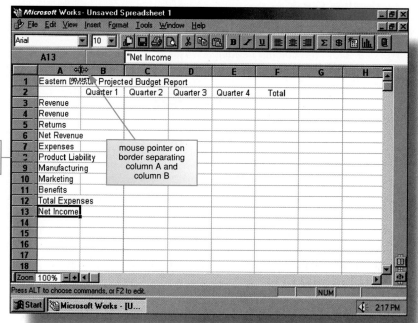

FIGURE 6-8

2 **Drag the column border slowly to the right until all the row headings in column A display to the left of the dotted line.**

As you drag, the proposed column border, represented by a dotted line, moves to the right (Figure 6-9). In some cases, when you drag a border, you will not get the border the exact width you want and you may have to experiment to achieve the correct width.

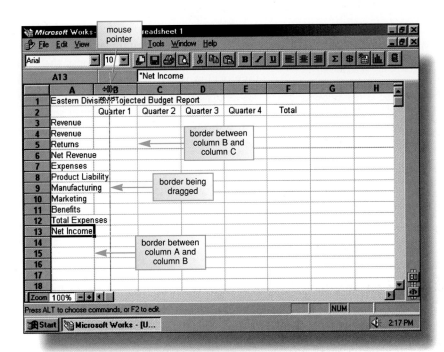

FIGURE 6-9

3 **Release the mouse button.**

Works changes the width of column A to the width you selected by dragging the border and displays the row headings in column A (Figure 6-10).

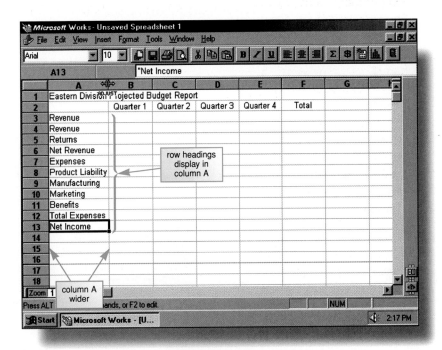

FIGURE 6-10

More *About*
the Fill Handle

The fill handle is new to Works 95 and is one of the most popular and impressive tools available with Works. Use it to copy to adjacent cells or to create a data series. However, to copy a potential series initiator, like the word January, to a past area, highlight the range you want to contain the text, type the text in the active cell in the highlighted range, and press the CTRL+ENTER keys instead of the ENTER key. Works immediately fills the selected range with the same data entered in the upper left cell of the highlighted range.

The advantage of dragging a column border to change the column width is that you can see the data on the screen and can visually fit the column width to the data without having to guess the correct column width. The major disadvantage occurs when you want to set the column width to an exact width, such as 20. Works does not display the actual column width as you drag the column border so the column width you set may not be the exact width you want and you will have to perform the process again.

Using Drag-and-Drop to Copy Cells

After you have entered the data once, you can copy it to other locations in the spreadsheet. The row headings in the Assumptions section in Figure 6-1 on page W 6.5 in the range A16:A19 are the same as the row headings in the range A8:A11 in Figure 6-9 on the previous page. Therefore, the range A8:A11 can be copied to the range A16:A19. In Projects 4 and 5, the fill handle worked well for copying a range of cells to an adjacent area, but you cannot use the fill handle to copy a range of cells to a nonadjacent area.

The easiest method of copying a cell or range of cells to a nonadjacent area is to use the **drag-and-drop** feature. Drag-and-drop copies selected cells by dragging the section to another area of the spreadsheet, and dropping the selected cells. Perform the following steps to copy the row headings in the range A8:A11 to the range A16:A19.

Steps **To Copy Cells Using Drag-and-Drop**

1 **Highlight the range A8:A11. Point to the border of the highlighted range so the mouse pointer changes to a block arrow with the word DRAG.**

The range A8:A11 is highlighted and the mouse pointer changes to a block arrow with the word DRAG (Figure 6-11).

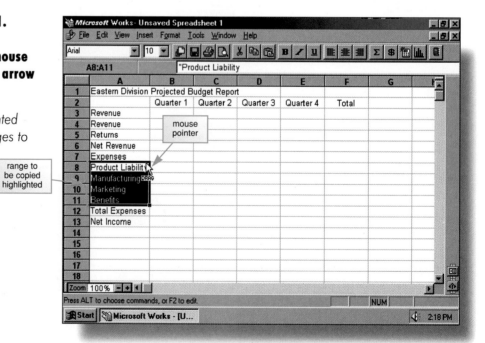

FIGURE 6-11

2 Hold down the CTRL key and drag the highlighted range down until the top line of the range you are dragging displays along the top of row 16.

Works displays the range being dragged as a outline and the mouse pointer displays with the word COPY below it (Figure 6-12).

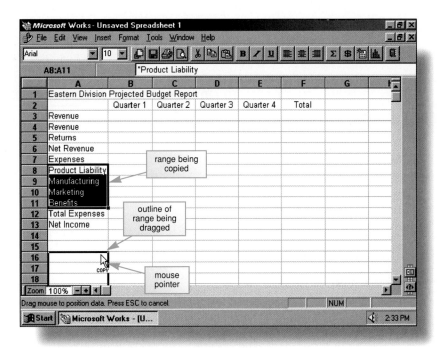

FIGURE 6-12

3 Release the mouse button.

Works places a copy of the data in the range A16:A19 and leaves the original data intact (Figure 6-13). The highlight is removed from the original data.

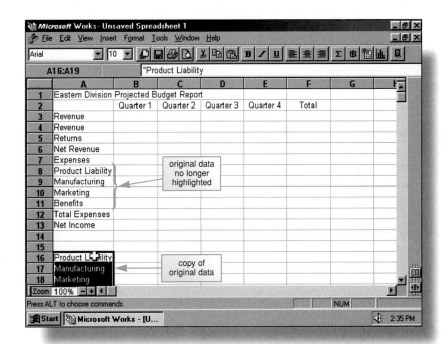

FIGURE 6-13

Other Ways

1. On Edit menu click Copy, highlight range to copy to, on Edit menu click Paste

2. On toolbar, click Copy button, highlight range to copy to, click Paste button

In the previous example, the drag-and-drop feature was used to copy a range of cells from one area of the spreadsheet to another area of the spreadsheet. If you want to move a range of cells, perform the following steps.

TO MOVE CELLS USING DRAG-AND-DROP

Step 1: Highlight the range to be moved.
Step 2: Point to the border of the selection until the mouse pointer changes to a block arrow and the word DRAG.
Step 3: Drag the selection to the desired location.

The data is removed from its original location and appears only in its new location. This is basically the same procedure that was used to copy data except the CTRL key is not used to move data.

More *About* Copying and Moving Cells

Use the fill handle to copy or move cells a short distance in a spreadsheet. Use the Copy and Paste commands on the Edit menu or Copy and Paste buttons on the toolbar to copy or move cells in a large spreadsheet. The fill handle does not use the Clipboard when copying or moving information.

Completing the Entries in the Assumptions Section

The Assumptions section in the range A15:A20 includes a title in cell A15, the row headings just copied, the row heading, Returns, in cell A20, and the percent values for all the expenses. Follow these steps to complete the entries in the Assumptions section.

Steps To Enter Percentages and Complete the Assumptions Section

1 **Highlight cell A15. Enter** Assumptions **as the row heading. Highlight cell A20. Enter** Returns **as the row heading.**

Works displays the row headings (Figure 6-14)

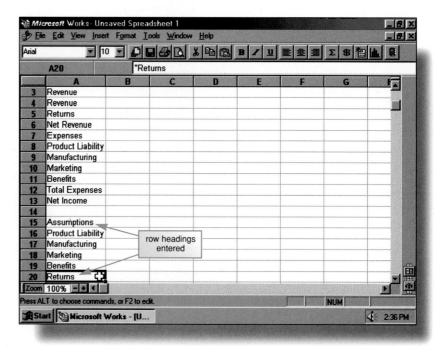

FIGURE 6-14

2 **Type** 12% **in cell B16 and** 35% **in cell B17. Type** 28% **in cell B18 and** 15% **in cell B19. Finally, type** 3% **in cell B20.**

Works displays the projected percentages (Figure 6-15).

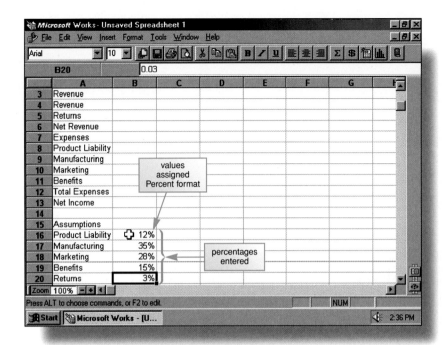

FIGURE 6-15

Notice in Figure 6-15 that entering the percent values in the Assumptions section with a percent sign (%) causes Works to recognize the entry as a percent and assign the Percent format to the cells.

Entering the Revenue Values

The next task in preparing the spreadsheet for Project 6 is to enter the revenue values in the range B4:E4. To enter the revenue values on the spreadsheet, complete the following steps.

TO ENTER THE REVENUE VALUES

Step 1: Press the CTRL+HOME keys. Highlight cell B4.

Step 2: Enter 138440.50 in cell B4, 198534.85 in cell C4, 219409.51 in cell D4, and 153753.25 in cell E4.

The revenue values for Quarter 1, Quarter 2, Quarter 3, and Quarter 4 display as shown in Figure 6-16.

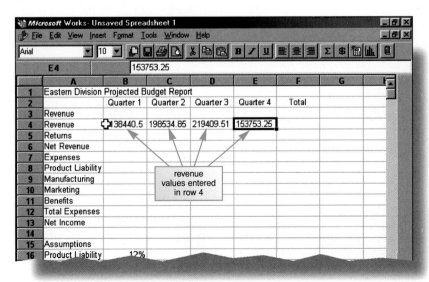

FIGURE 6-16

Rounding

Whenever you multiply numbers containing decimals by a decimal, the possibility exists that the answer will contain more than two digits to the right of the decimal point. This causes problems in applications representing dollars and cents. For example, to calculate the returns for Quarter 1, the value 138440.50 is multiplied by .03 (3%), resulting in the answer 4153.215. When 4153.215 is formatted to two decimal places, Works rounds the displayed value in the cell. Therefore, in the example, the answer to the calculation 138440.50 * .03 will display as 4153.22.

While this action takes care of the display issue, it does not solve the problem completely because even though the numbers are formatted correctly, the rounded values displayed in the cell are not the values Works uses in calculations. Thus, even though the value 4153.22 displays in the cell, the value 4153.215 will be used in calculations, resulting in answers in the spreadsheet that do not correspond to the values displayed in the cells. For example, continuing with the above example, subtracting 4153.215 from 138440.50 results in the answer 134287.285. After applying the comma format with two decimal places, 134,287.29 (138440.50 - 4153.22) displays as the answer. Clearly the subtraction displays the incorrect result. Such a calculation is illustrated in Table 6-2.

Table 6-2	
ACTUAL VALUES USED IN CALCULATIONS	VALUES DISPLAYED WITH COMMA FORMAT, TWO DECIMAL PLACES
138440.500	138440.50
-4153.215	-4153.22
134287.285	134287.29

To prevent these errors, you must use the **ROUND function** to round values used in calculations so the numbers used in calculations are the same as the numbers in the display. The ROUND function allows you to round any numeric value to the number of digits to the right or left of the decimal point that you specify. For the calculations in Project 6, the values should have two digits to the right of the decimal point.

The format of the ROUND function is ROUND(x,NumberOfPlaces), where x is the value to round and NumberOfPlaces is a value specifying the number of positions to the right or left of the decimal point. If the value in NumberOfPlaces is positive, Works rounds the value x to the number of decimal places to the right of the decimal point. If NumberOfPlaces is negative, Works rounds to the number of places to the left of the decimal point. If the number is zero, x is rounded to the nearest integer.

All values in Project 6 should contain two decimal places, so NumberOfPlaces should be 2.

More *About*
Absolute Cell References

Absolute cell referencing is one of the most difficult worksheet concepts to understand. An absolute cell reference instructs Works to keep the same cell reference as it copies a formula from one cell to another. The Copy feature, therefore, is the only command affected by an absolute cell reference.

Absolute Cell References

The next step in building the spreadsheet for Project 6 is to place the proper formula in cell B5 to calculate the projected returns for Quarter 1. The returns value is calculated by multiplying the projected revenue for Quarter 1 (cell B4) by the percent for returns in the Assumptions section of the spreadsheet (cell B20). Thus, the formula to determine the returns for Quarter 1 with the ROUND function is =ROUND(B4*B20,2).

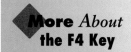

Before entering the calculation to determine the returns for Quarter 1, however, you need to become familiar with absolute cell references. Cell references used in a formula are one of two types – a relative cell reference or an absolute cell reference. When you use a **relative cell reference**, the cell reference in the formula will change when you copy the formula from one cell to the next. Relative cell reference is the type used in Project 4 and Project 5.

The returns percentage (cell B20) in the formula =B4*B20, however, always remains the same. That is, the formula to calculate the returns for Quarter 1 is B4*B20, the formula for Quarter 2 is C4*B20, the formula for Quarter 3 is D4*B20, and the formula for Quarter 4 is E4*B20. Notice that cell B20 is always used because it contains the percent for the returns value. When a cell's reference does not change as the formula is copied from one cell to the next, the cell reference is called an **absolute cell reference**.

When you enter cell references into a formula, Works assumes they are relative cell references. To specify that a cell reference is an absolute cell reference, you must enter the cell number in the absolute cell reference format, which is a dollar sign preceding the column letter and a dollar sign preceding the row number. Thus, in the formula, the absolute cell reference for cell B20 is B20.

Recall that Project 5 illustrated using the Easy Calc button on the toolbar to enter a function. You can also type the function in the cell as illustrated in Project 6.

The following steps illustrate entering the formula that contains the =ROUND function to calculate the returns for Quarter 1. The formula uses both relative and absolute cell references.

More *About* **the F4 Key**

Pressing the F4 key once to apply the absolute cell reference format to a cell reference places dollar signs preceding the column letter and the row number. Pressing the F4 key a second time applies a mixed cell reference because the dollar sign precedes only the row number. Clicking the F4 key a third time, applies a mixed cell reference again because the dollar sign precedes only the column number. Finally, pressing the F4 key a fourth time applies the relative cell reference.

 Steps **To Enter a Formula Containing Relative and Absolute Cell References**

1 **Highlight the cell to contain the formula – cell B5, and then type** =ROUND(**in the cell.**

The formula containing the beginning of the ROUND function displays in both the highlighted cell and the entry bar (Figure 6-17).

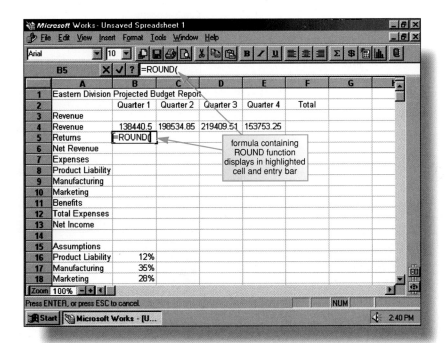

FIGURE 6-17

2 **Highlight the first cell to enter into the function – cell B4 – by clicking the cell or pressing the UP ARROW key to move the highlight to the cell.**

When you highlight cell B4, Works places a black background in the cell and also places the cell reference in the function (Figure 6-18).

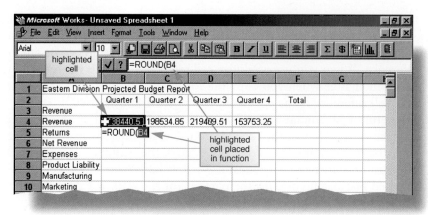

FIGURE 6-18

3 **Type the multiplication operator (*) and then click the down scroll arrow to view cell B20. Highlight the second cell in the function – cell B20.**

Works displays the multiplication operator in both the entry bar and the cell where you are entering the formula and places the cell reference in the function (Figure 6-19).

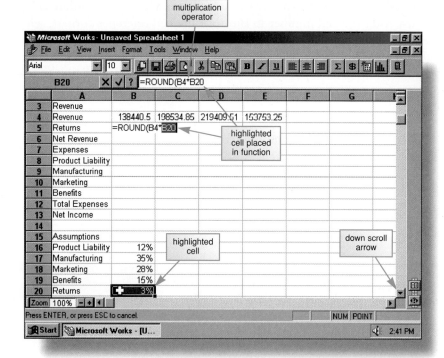

FIGURE 6-19

4 **Press the F4 key to change the B20 cell reference to an absolute cell reference.**

When you press the F4 key, Works places a dollar sign in front of the column letter and in front of the row number of the highlighted cell (Figure 6-20).

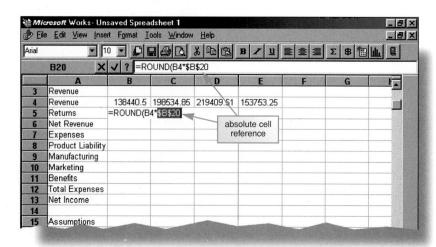

FIGURE 6-20

5 Type , 2) to complete the ROUND function (Figure 6-21).

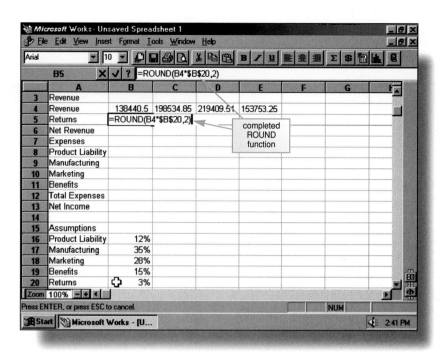

FIGURE 6-21

6 Click the Enter box or press the ENTER key.

Works enters the formula into the cell and performs the calculation (Figure 6-22).

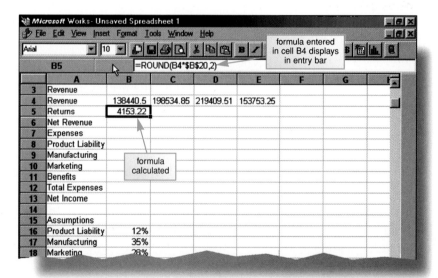

FIGURE 6-22

Copying Formulas with Relative and Absolute Cell References

The next step in building the Project 6 spreadsheet is to copy the formula in cell B5 containing the ROUND function to the range C5:E5. When you copy the formula, the reference to cell B4 will change to C4, D4, and E4, while the reference to cell B20 will remain the same. To copy a formula containing a function with both relative and absolute cell references, complete the steps on the next page.

Other Ways

1. On Insert menu click Function, click Math and Trig, click ROUND(x,NumberOf-Places), click Insert button, type desired data in function

2. Click Easy Calc button on toolbar, click Other button, click Math and Trig, click ROUND(x,NumberOf-Places), type desired data in Easy Calc dialog box

Steps To Copy a Formula with Relative and Absolute Cell References

1 **Highlight the cell containing the formula to copy – cell B5 – if necessary. Drag the fill handle across the range you want to copy into – cells C5, D5, and E5.**

The cell containing the formula to copy (cell B5) and the range where it is to be copied (C5:E5) are highlighted. Works copies the formula from cell B5 to the range C5:E5 (Figure 6-23). Works performs the calculations, which include rounding the result when required.

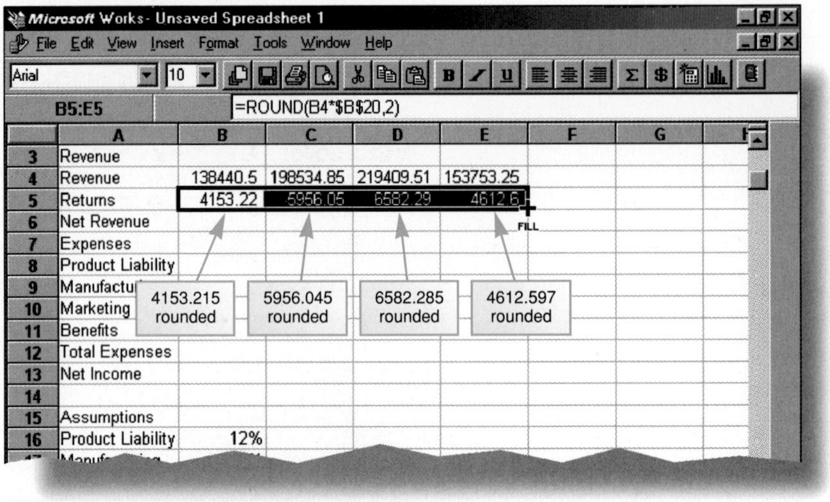

FIGURE 6-23

Entering and Copying a Formula

After you enter the returns formula into the Project 6 spreadsheet, the next step is to enter the net revenue formula into cell B6 and copy the formula to the range C6:E6. The net revenue is calculated by subtracting the returns from revenue. The returns value for Quarter 1 is contained in cell B5, while revenue is in cell B4. Therefore, the formula to calculate the net revenue for Quarter 1 is =B4-B5. The formulas for each of the ensuing quarters require both cell B4 and B5 to be changed when it is copied. Thus, this formula has no requirement for an absolute cell reference. To enter the formula in the range B6:E6 perform the following steps.

TO ENTER AND COPY A FORMULA

Step 1: Highlight cell B6, type = (equal sign), highlight cell B4 to place it in the formula, type - (subtraction operator), highlight cell B5 to place it in the formula, and click the Enter box or press the ENTER key.

Step 2: Highlight the cell containing the formula – cell B6. Drag the fill handle across the range to copy into – C6:E6.

The spreadsheet after you have completed these steps is shown in Figure 6-24.

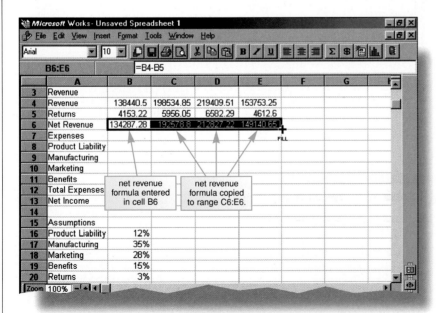

FIGURE 6-24

Entering Additional Functions and Formulas

The next step in this project is to determine the four projected expenses for Quarter 1 (see Figure 6-1 on page W 6.5). Each of the projected expenses for Quarter 1 is equal to the Quarter 1 Net Revenue in cell B6 multiplied by the corresponding projected percentage in the range B16:B19. Therefore, the formula to calculate the product liability expense for Quarter 1 is =B6*B16. Because the product liability percentage is contained in a single cell and should be used to calculate the expense for each of the quarters, cell B16 will be an absolute cell reference in the formula. In addition, the formulas to calculate the projected expenses for Quarter 1 contain the ROUND function. Therefore, the formula to calculate the product liability expense for Quarter 1 is =ROUND(B6*B16,2).

Perform the following steps to place the formulas that calculate the projected expenses for Quarter 1 into the spreadsheet.

Steps **To Enter Formulas**

1 **Highlight cell B8. Type** =ROUND(**in the cell. Highlight cell B6. Type** * **(multiplication operator). Highlight cell B16. Press the F4 key.**

Works displays the ROUND function in the entry bar and the cell (Figure 6-25). When you press the F4 key, Works places the cell reference in the formula as an absolute cell reference.

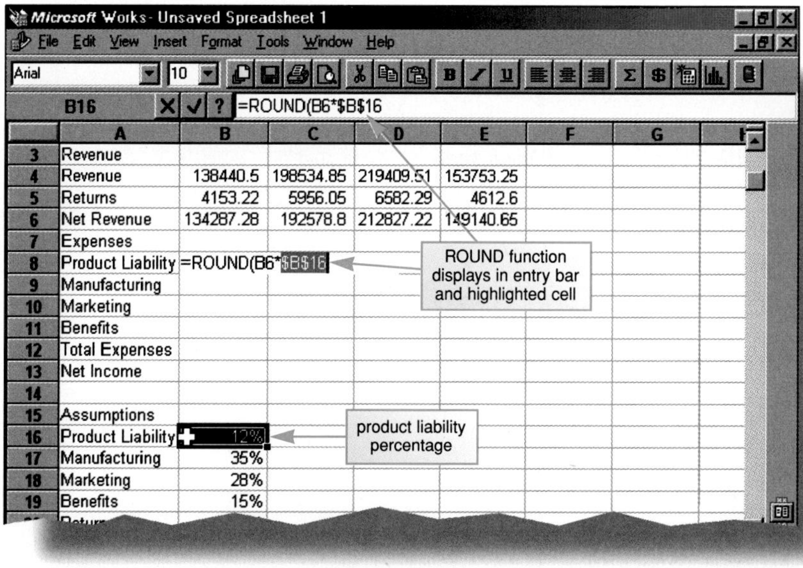

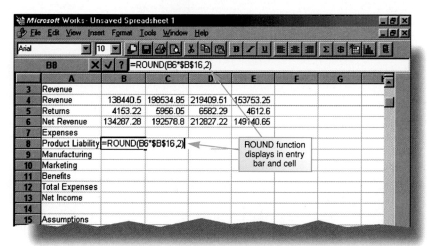

FIGURE 6-25

2 **Type** ,2) **to complete the ROUND function (Figure 6-26).**

FIGURE 6-26

3   Click the Enter box or press the ENTER key.

Works enters the ROUND function into the cell and performs the calculation (Figure 6-27). The result of the calculation is rounded to two places to the right of the decimal point.

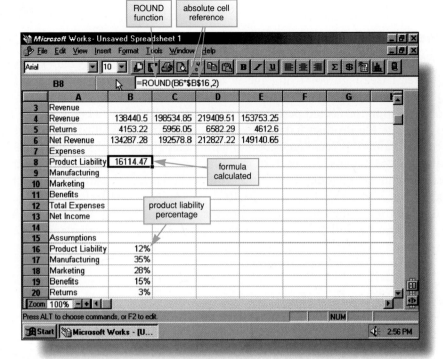

FIGURE 6-27

4   Highlight cell B9 and then type =ROUND(in the cell. Highlight cell B6. Type * (multiplication operator). Highlight cell B17. Press the F4 key. Type ,2) to complete the ROUND function. Click the Enter box or press the ENTER key.

Works confirms the entry into the cell and performs the calculation (Figure 6-28). The result of the calculation is rounded to two places to the right of the decimal point. The result of the calculation displays in the cell, and the ROUND function and formula display in the entry bar.

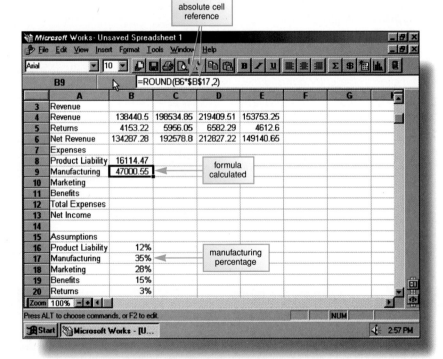

FIGURE 6-28

5 **Highlight cell B10 and then type =**ROUND(**in the cell. Highlight cell B6. Type** ∗ **(multiplication operator). Highlight cell B18. Press the** F4 **key. Type** ,2) **to complete the ROUND function. Click the Enter box or press the** ENTER **key.**

Works confirms the entry into the cell and performs the calculation (Figure 6-29). The result of the calculation is rounded to two places to the right of the decimal point. The result of the calculation displays in the cell, and the ROUND function and the formula display in the entry bar.

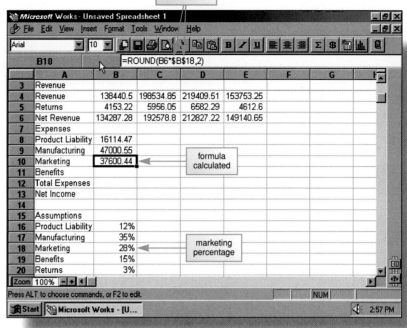

FIGURE 6-29

6 **Highlight cell B11 and type =**ROUND(**in the cell. Highlight cell B6. Type** ∗ **(multiplication operator). Highlight cell B19. Press the** F4 **key. Type** ,2) **to complete the ROUND function. Click the Enter box or press the** ENTER **key.**

The expenses for Quarter 1 display as shown in Figure 6-30.

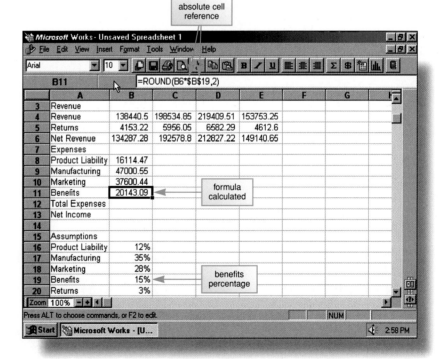

FIGURE 6-30

To calculate the Total Expenses in cell B12 for Quarter 1, use the AutoSum button on the toolbar to enter the SUM function to add the values in the range B8:B11. You obtain the net income in cell B13 for Quarter 1 by subtracting the total expenses (cell B12) from the net revenue (B6). The formulas for the Total Expenses and Net Income require the cells to be changed when copied. Thus, these formulas have no requirements for an absolute cell reference. To enter the formulas, perform the following steps.

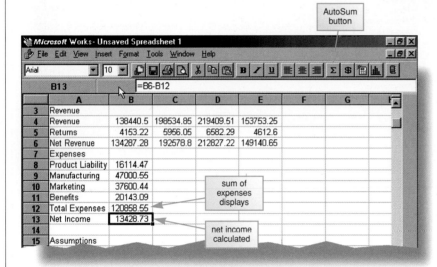

FIGURE 6-31

TO ENTER FORMULAS

Step 1: Highlight cell B12. Click the AutoSum button on the toolbar twice to enter the SUM function.

Step 2: Highlight cell B13 and then type = in the cell. Highlight cell B6 and then type − in the cell. Highlight cell B12 and then click the Enter box or press the ENTER key.

The spreadsheet after completing these steps is shown in Figure 6-31.

The formulas to calculate the four projected expenses for Quarter 1, the total expenses for Quarter 1, and the net income for Quarter 1 are entered on the spreadsheet. The next step is to copy the formulas in the range B8:B13 to the cells in the range C8:E13 so Works will calculate these formulas for Quarter 2 through Quarter 4. Copy the formula using the following steps.

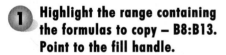
Steps **To Copy Formulas**

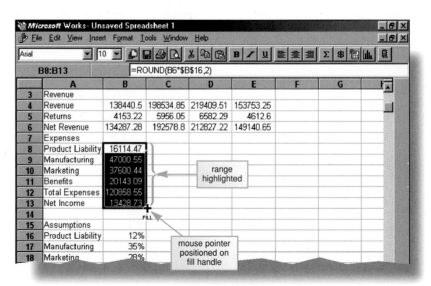

1 **Highlight the range containing the formulas to copy − B8:B13. Point to the fill handle.**

Works highlights the range and the mouse pointer is positioned on the fill handle (Figure 6-32).

FIGURE 6-32

2 Drag the range where the formulas are to be copied — C8:E13. Click any cell to remove the highlight.

Works copies the formulas from the range B8:B13 to the range C8:E13, calculates the copied formulas, and rounds the results when required (Figure 6-33).

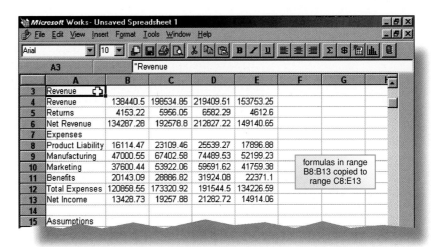

FIGURE 6-33

Completing the Entries

The final step in completing the entries in the spreadsheet is to determine the row totals in column F. Perform the following steps to obtain the required totals in column F using the AutoSum button on the toolbar.

TO SUM THE ROW TOTALS

Step 1: Press the CTRL+HOME keys. Highlight cell F4. Click the AutoSum button on the toolbar twice to enter the SUM function in cell F4.

Step 2: Point to the fill handle in cell F4. Drag the range F5:F6.

Step 3: Highlight cell F8. Click the AutoSum button on the toolbar twice to enter the SUM function in cell F8.

Step 4: Point to the fill handle in cell F8. Drag the range F9:F13.

Works places the SUM function in each cell of the highlighted range and calculates the sum of values across each row of the spreadsheet. The row totals display in column F as shown in Figure 6-34.

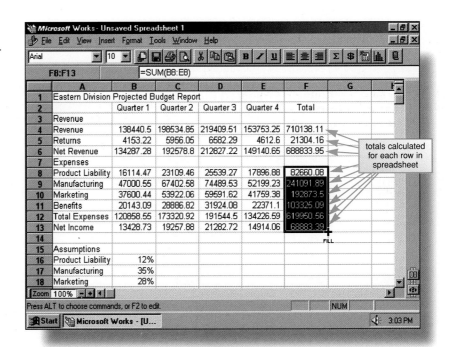

FIGURE 6-34

Saving the Spreadsheet

Now that the spreadsheet data is entered, you should save it on a floppy disk. To save the spreadsheet on drive A using the filename Eastern Division Projected Budget, complete the following steps.

TO SAVE THE SPREADSHEET

Step 1: Click the CTRL+HOME keys, if necessary. Click the Save button on the toolbar.

Step 2: When the Save As dialog box displays, type `Eastern Division Projected Budget` in the File name text box.

Step 3: Select 3 ½ Floppy [A:] in the Save in drop-down list box.

Step 4: Click the Save button.

Works saves the spreadsheet with the filename, Eastern Division Projected Budget, on the floppy disk in drive A.

Formatting the Spreadsheet

Formatting the spreadsheet in Project 6 includes changing font sizes and font styles and formatting the numeric data in the main section of the spreadsheet with dollar signs, commas, and decimal positions.

Formatting the Spreadsheet Titles, Column Headings, and Row Titles

The following formatting of the spreadsheet titles is required.

1. The spreadsheet title, Eastern Division Projected Budget Report, is to display in 16-point Arial bold font. The title is centered across the columns in the spreadsheet and aligned vertically at the top of the cells.

2. All column headings display in 12-point Arial bold font.

3. The row headings in cells A3, A7, and A13 display in 12-point Arial bold font. The row headings in the range A4:A6 and A8:A12 display right-aligned in the cells. The row headings in cells A6 and A12 display in bold and italics.

4. The column width in columns B, C, D, E, and F is 12.

To accomplish this formatting, complete the following steps (see Figure 6-35).

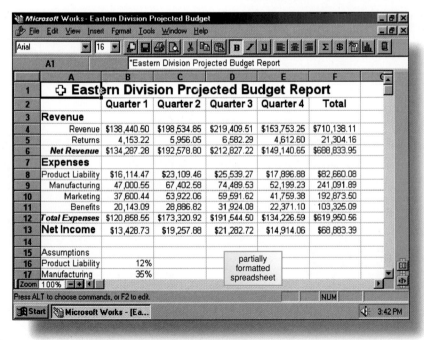

FIGURE 6-35

TO FORMAT TITLES

Step 1: Highlight the range A1:F1. Right-click the selection. Click Format on the context-sensitive menu. When the Format Cells dialog box displays, click the Alignment tab. On the Alignment sheet, click Center across selection in the Horizontal box. Click Top in the Vertical box. Click the Font tab. Click 16 in the Size list box. Click Bold in the Style box. Click the OK button in the Format Cells dialog box.

Step 2: Highlight the column headings in cells B2:F2. Click the Bold button on the toolbar.

Step 3: Highlight cell A3. Click the Font Size box arrow. Click 12. Click the Bold button on the toolbar. Highlight cell A7. Click the Font Size box arrow. Click 12. Click the Bold button on the toolbar. Highlight cell A13. Click the Font Size box arrow. Click 12. Click the Bold button on the toolbar.

Step 4: Highlight the range A4:A6. Click the Right Align button on the toolbar. Highlight cell A6. Click the Bold button on the toolbar. Click the Italic button on the toolbar.

Step 5: Highlight the range A8:A12. Click the Right Align button on the toolbar. Highlight cell A12. Click the Bold button on the toolbar. Click the Italic button on the toolbar.

Step 6: Highlight columns B, C, D, E, and F by dragging the column headings B, C, D, E, and F. Right-click the selection. Click Column Width on the context-sensitive menu. When the Column Width dialog box displays, type 12 in the Column width text box. Click the OK button. Click any cell.

Formatting the Numeric Values

The numeric values in the spreadsheet, even though they are generated by formulas, can still be formatted. The following formatting, as shown in Figure 6-35, is required.

1. The Revenue values in row 4, the Net Revenue values in row 6, the Product Liability values in row 8, the Total Expenses values in row 12, and the Net Income values in row 13 display in the Currency format with two decimal positions.
2. The Returns values in row 5, the Manufacturing values in row 9, the Marketing values in row 10, and the Benefits values in row 11 use the Comma format with two decimal positions.

To accomplish the formatting, complete the following steps.

TO FORMAT NUMERIC VALUES

Step 1: Highlight the range B4:F4. Click the Currency button on the toolbar. Highlight the range B6:F6. Click the Currency button on the toolbar. Highlight the range B8:F8. Click the Currency button on the toolbar. Highlight the range B12:F13. Click the Currency button on the toolbar.

Step 2: Highlight the range B5:F5. Right-click the selection. Click Format on the context-sensitive menu. When the Format Cells dialog box displays, click Comma in the Format box. Ensure 2 displays in the Decimal places text box. Click the OK button. Highlight the range B9:F11. Right-click the selection. Click Format on the context-sensitive menu. When the Format Cells dialog box displays, click Comma in the Format box. Ensure 2 displays in the Decimal places text box. Click the OK button.

The spreadsheet formatting is complete in its present form. The final step is to add color to the spreadsheet. Before adding color to the spreadsheet, however, it is recommended that you save the spreadsheet in its present form. Click the Save button on the toolbar to save the spreadsheet.

Adding Color to the Spreadsheet

Figure 6-1 on page W 6.5 illustrates the Eastern Division Projected Budget Report spreadsheet with color added to selected rows to enhance the appearance of the spreadsheet. The spreadsheet is formatted with the following colors:

1. The spreadsheet title displays in dark cyan.
2. The column headings in row 2 and the row headings in rows 3, 7, 13, and 15 display in white with a solid dark cyan pattern in the cells.
3. A dark cyan border displays around the values in the spreadsheet.
4. A dark cyan border displays around the Assumptions section of the spreadsheet.

The following steps explain how to add the required color to the spreadsheet.

 To Add Color to the Spreadsheet

1 **Right-click cell A1. Point to Format on the context-sensitive menu.**

Cell A1 is highlighted and the mouse pointer points to the Format command on the context-sensitive menu (Figure 6-36).

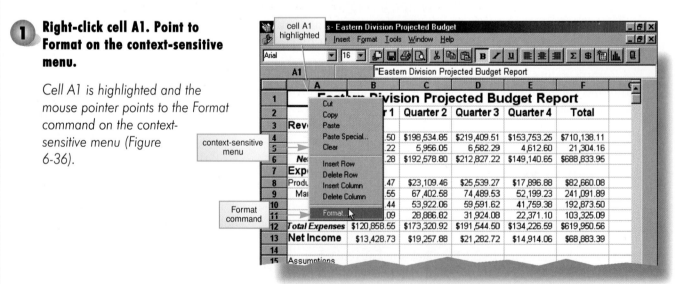

FIGURE 6-36

2 Click Format. When the Format Cells dialog box displays, click the Font tab. Click the Color box arrow. Scroll down and then click Dark Cyan. Point to the OK button.

Dark Cyan displays in the Color box and the mouse pointer points to the OK button (Figure 6-37). The Sample box displays the selections you have made.

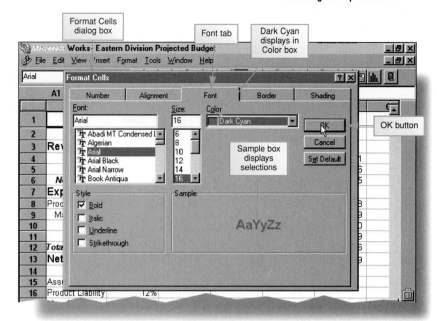

FIGURE 6-37

3 Click the OK button.

The spreadsheet title displays in dark cyan (Figure 6-38).

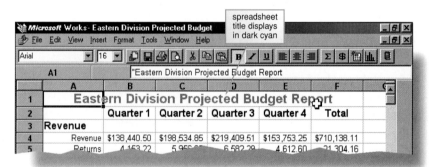

FIGURE 6-38

4 Highlight the range B2:F2. Right-click the selection and then point to Format on the context-sensitive menu.

The range B2:F2 is highlighted and the mouse pointer points to Format on the context-sensitive menu (Figure 6-39).

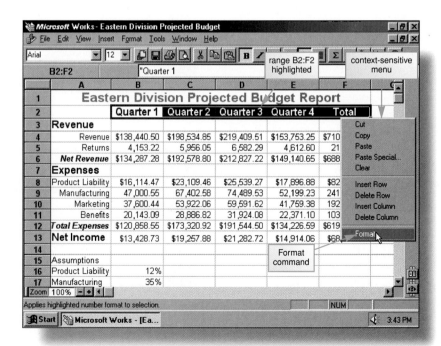

FIGURE 6-39

5 Click Format. When the Format Cells dialog box displays, click the Font tab. When the Font sheet displays, click the Color box arrow. Scroll down and then click White. Point to the Shading tab.

White displays in the Color box and the mouse pointer points to the Shading tab (Figure 6-40). The Sample box displays the selection you have made.

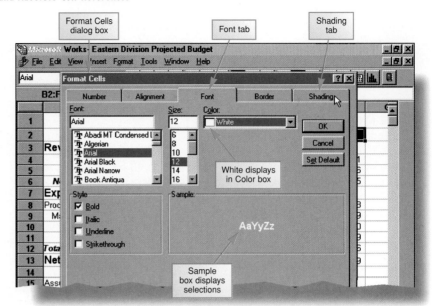

FIGURE 6-40

6 Click the Shading tab. On the Shading sheet, click the solid pattern in the Pattern list box. Scroll down the Foreground list box and then click Dark Cyan. Point to the OK button.

The Shading sheet displays (Figure 6-41). Dark Cyan displays in the Foreground list box and the mouse pointer points to the OK button. The Sample box displays the selections you have made.

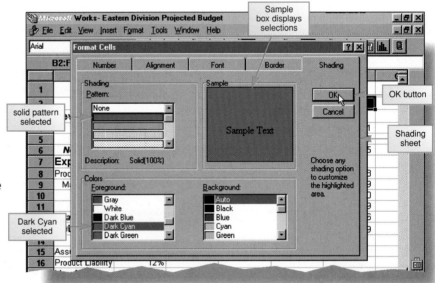

FIGURE 6-41

7 Click the OK button. Click any cell.

The column headings display in white with a cell color of dark cyan (Figure 6-42).

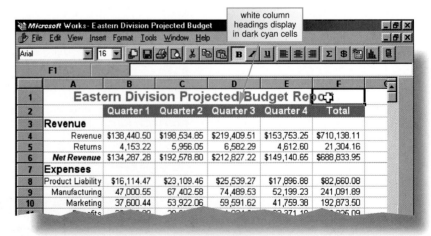

FIGURE 6-42

8 **Using the techniques illustrated in Steps 4 through 7, highlight cells A3, A7, and A13 and format the font white and the cell dark cyan.**

The row headings in cells A3, A7, and A13 display in white with a cell color of dark cyan (Figure 6-43).

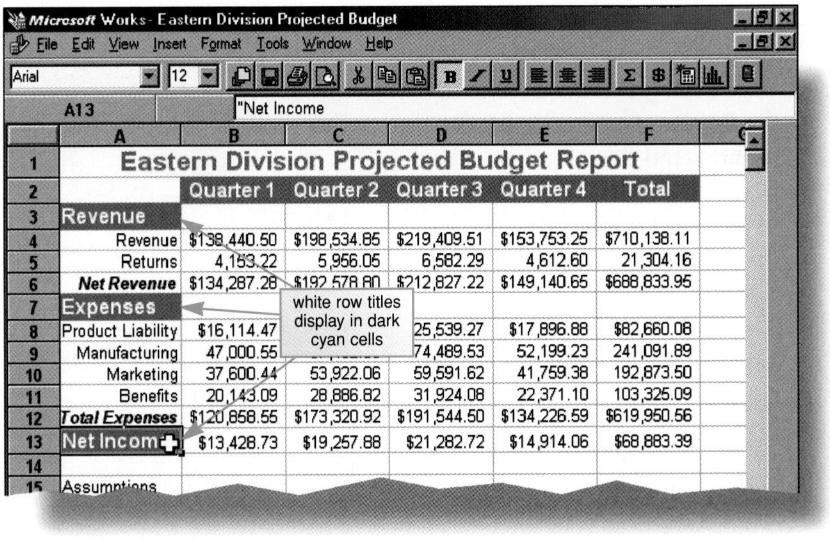

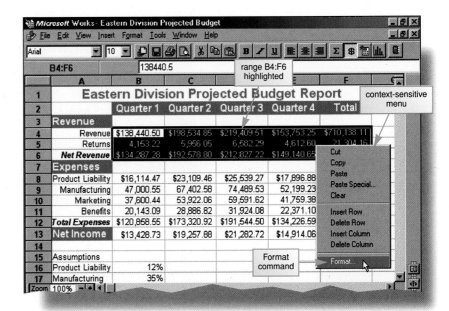

FIGURE 6-43

Adding Borders to Cells

In the spreadsheet in Figure 6-1 on page W 6.5, the ranges B4:F6 and B8:F12 contain a dark cyan border around each cell in the range. The range B13:F13 contains a double line below each cell in the range. To place a line, or border, around a cell or each cell in the range, first highlight the cell or range where the border is to be displayed. Then use Format on the context-sensitive menu, as shown in the following steps.

More About Underlines Versus Borders

An underline is not the same as applying borders to a cell. An underline only underlines the characters in a cell, which may or may not occupy the entire cell. A bottom border, on the other hand, encompasses the entire width of the cell, whether or not the cell contains characters.

Steps To Add a Border to a Range of Cells

1 **Highlight the range of cells B4:F6. Right-click the selected range to display the context-sensitive menu. Point to Format.**

The range B4:F6 is highlighted, the context-sensitive menu displays and the mouse pointer points to the Format command (Figure 6-44).

FIGURE 6-44

2 **Click Format on the context-sensitive menu. When the Format Cells dialog box displays, click the Border tab. On the Border sheet, scroll down and then click Dark Cyan in the Color list box. In the Border box, click the Outline box once to remove the thin line style. Click the Top, Bottom, Left, and Right boxes in the Border box. Point to the OK button.**

The Border sheet displays in the Format Cells dialog box (Figure 6-45). When you click the Outline box, Works removes the thin dark cyan line. A thin line displays in the Top, Bottom, Left, and Right boxes in the Border box because the thin line is the Line style default selection. Dark Cyan displays in the Color list box and the mouse pointer points to the OK button.

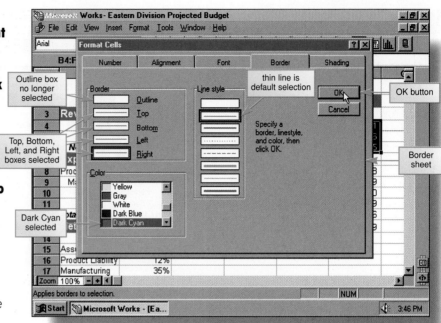

FIGURE 6-45

3 **Click the OK button. Click any cell to remove the highlight.**

The spreadsheet displays with dark cyan borders around all the cells in the range B4:F6 (Figure 6-46).

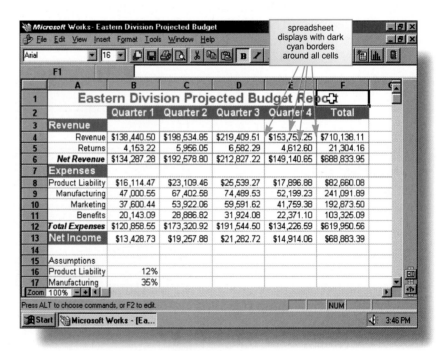

FIGURE 6-46

4 Highlight the range of cells B8:F12. Right-click the selected range to display the context-sensitive menu. Click Format on the context-sensitive menu. When the Format Cells dialog box displays, click the Border tab. On the Border sheet, click Dark Cyan in the Color list box. Click the Outline box once to remove the thin line style. Click the Top, Bottom, Left, and Right boxes in the Border box. Click the OK button. Click any cell to remove the highlight.

The spreadsheet displays with dark cyan borders around all the cells in the range B8:F12 (Figure 6-47).

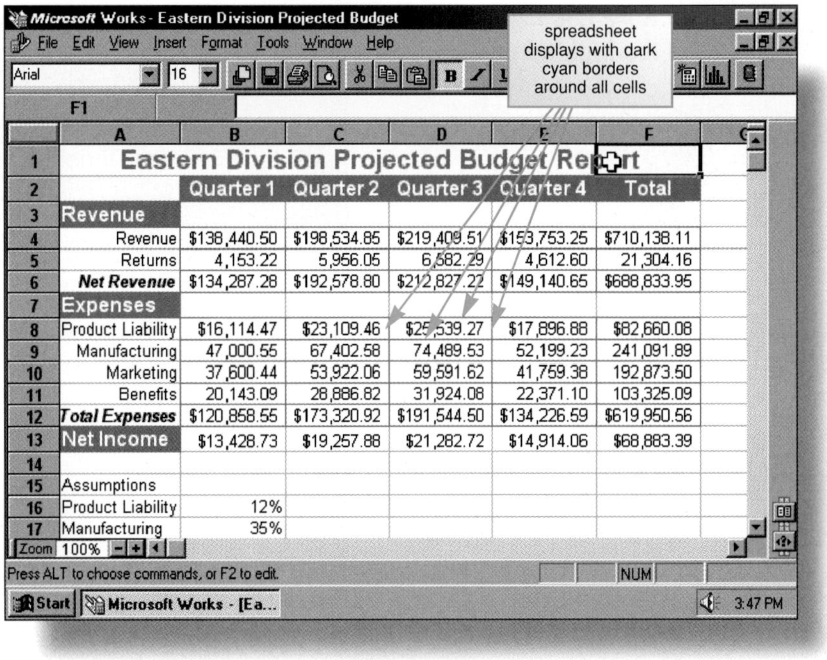

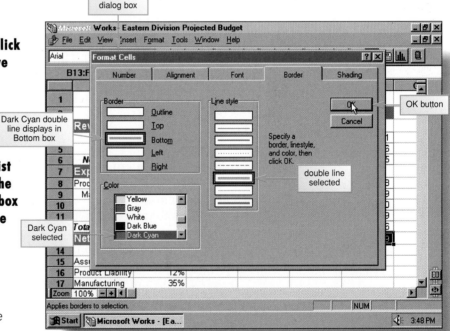

FIGURE 6-47

5 Highlight the range B13:F13. Right-click the selection and click Format on the context-sensitive menu. When the Format Cells dialog box displays, click the Border tab. On the Border sheet, click the double line box in the Line style box. Click Dark Cyan in the Color list box. Click the Bottom box in the Border box. Click the Outline box once to remove the double line style. Point to the OK button.

The Format Cells dialog box displays with the selections you have made (Figure 6-48). The double line box is selected in the Line style box. Dark Cyan is selected in the Color list box. A double line displays in the Bottom box. These selections inform Works to place a double line below the cells in the range B13:F13.

FIGURE 6-48

6 **Click the OK button. Click any cell to remove the highlight.**

The spreadsheet displays with a dark cyan double line border below the cells in the range B13:F13 (Figure 6-49).

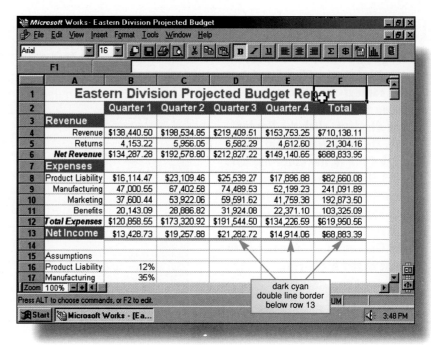

FIGURE 6-49

Formatting and Adding Color to the Assumptions Section

Cell A15 contains the title Assumptions. This title is to display in 12-point Arial white font in the cells with a dark cyan foreground (see Figure 6-1 on page W 6.5). The Assumptions section displays with a dark cyan border around the entire section. Complete the following steps to format and add color and a border to this section of the spreadsheet.

TO FORMAT AND ADD COLOR AND A BORDER TO THE ASSUMPTIONS SECTION

Step 1: Highlight the range A15:B15. Right-click the selection. Click Format on the context-sensitive menu. When the Format Cells dialog box displays, click the Font tab. Click 12 in the Size list box. Click the Color box arrow and then click White. Click the Shading tab. On the Shading sheet, click the solid pattern in the Pattern list box. Click Dark Cyan in the Foreground list box. Click the OK button.

Step 2: Highlight the range A15:B20. Right-click the selection. Click Format on the context-sensitive menu. When the Format Cells dialog box displays, click the Border tab. Click the solid thin line in the Line style box. Click Dark Cyan in the Color list box. Ensure the solid line style displays in the Outline box. Click the OK button. Press the CTRL+HOME keys.

Inserting Headers and Footers in Spreadsheets

Recall from Project 3, a **header** is special text that appears at the top of every printed page. A **footer** is special text that appears at the bottom of every printed page. Recall when using the Word Processor tool, you can create a header or footer in Normal view by clicking in the header (H) or footer (F) line and typing the desired text.

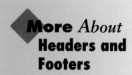

More *About*
Headers and Footers

In a spreadsheet, a header or footer cannot be longer than one line of text. You can insert special codes that automatically print the current date, current time, page number, filename, and so on but you cannot change the font or add effects such as bold, underline, or italics.

This project illustrates inserting a footer into the spreadsheet. To insert a footer into a spreadsheet, you will use Headers and Footers on the View menu to display the View Headers and Footers dialog box. In the dialog box, you will type the entry, &l Eastern Division Projected Budget Report&r&d. The entry, &l, is a code instructing Works to left-align the characters that follow. The report name (Eastern Division Projected Budget Report) is followed by the codes &r&d. The entry, &r, is a code instructing Works to right-align the characters that follow. The entry, &d, is a code instructing Works to print the current date in the form of month/day/year (for example, 10/15/97).

Follow these steps to insert a footer into the spreadsheet.

 Steps To Insert a Footer into the Spreadsheet

1 **Click View on the menu bar and point to Headers and Footers.**

Works displays the View menu and the mouse pointer points to the Headers and Footers command (Figure 6-50).

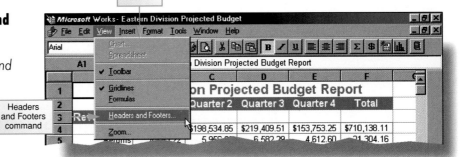

FIGURE 6-50

2 **Click Headers and Footers. When the View Headers and Footers dialog box displays, press the TAB key and then type** &lEastern Division Projected Budget Report&r&d **in the Footer text box. Point to the OK button.**

&lEastern Division Projected Budget Report&r&d displays in the Footer text box (Figure 6-51). If you click No header on first page, an X appears in the check box, and the header will not print on the first page. Clicking No footer on first page operates in a similar manner. The code,&l, in the Footer text box instructs Works to left-align the text, Eastern Division Projected Budget Report at the bottom of the page. The codes, &r&d, instruct Works to right-align the current date at the bottom of the page.

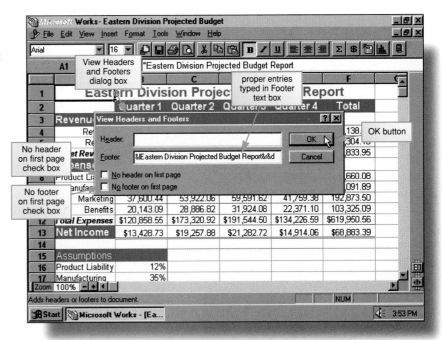

FIGURE 6-51

3 **Click the OK button.**

Works returns to the document window. The footer information entered into the dialog box will not display on the screen but will print .75 inch from the bottom of the page when you print the spreadsheet.

Header and Footer Codes

Works provides great flexibility in printing information on the header or footer line in a spreadsheet. Table 6-3 shows the list of codes you can use in the View Headers and Footers dialog box to control printing information.

The print date in long format code (&n) prints the date in the form of month, day, year (for example, October 15, 1997).

After inserting a footer, you can use print preview as explained in Project 1.

Saving the Spreadsheet

You should once again save the spreadsheet using the Save button on the toolbar. The spreadsheet will be saved with color.

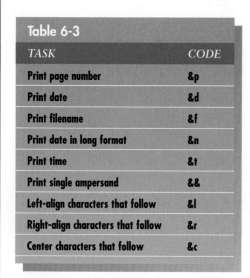

Table 6-3	
TASK	*CODE*
Print page number	&p
Print date	&d
Print filename	&f
Print date in long format	&n
Print time	&t
Print single ampersand	&&
Left-align characters that follow	&l
Right-align characters that follow	&r
Center characters that follow	&c

Printing a Portion of a Spreadsheet

Often, your next step will be to print the spreadsheet. To print the entire spreadsheet, follow the steps explained in previous projects. It also is possible to print a portion of a spreadsheet. For example, in Project 6, you may wish to print the spreadsheet but omit the Assumptions section on the printed output. To print a specific portion of a spreadsheet, perform the following steps:

TO PRINT A PORTION OF A SPREADSHEET

Step 1: Highlight the range A1:F13 as the portion of the spreadsheet to print.
Step 2: Click Format on the menu bar and then click Set Print Area.
Step 3: Click the OK button in the Microsoft Works dialog box to confirm the print area.
Step 4: Click the Print button on the toolbar.

Works prints the portion of the spreadsheet you designated as the print area (Figure 6-52). The current date displays right-aligned at the bottom of the page. The desired text displays left-aligned at the bottom of the page.

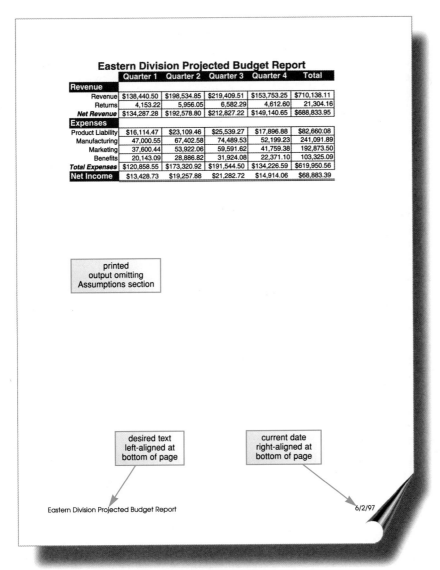

Eastern Division Projected Budget Report

	Quarter 1	Quarter 2	Quarter 3	Quarter 4	Total
Revenue					
Revenue	$138,440.50	$198,534.85	$219,409.51	$153,753.25	$710,138.11
Returns	4,153.22	5,956.05	6,582.29	4,612.60	21,304.16
Net Revenue	$134,287.28	$192,578.80	$212,827.22	$149,140.65	$688,833.95
Expenses					
Product Liability	$16,114.47	$23,109.46	$25,539.27	$17,896.88	$82,660.08
Manufacturing	47,000.55	67,402.58	74,489.53	52,199.23	241,091.89
Marketing	37,600.44	53,922.06	59,591.62	41,759.38	192,873.50
Benefits	20,143.09	28,886.82	31,924.08	22,371.10	103,325.09
Total Expenses	$120,858.55	$173,320.92	$191,544.50	$134,226.59	$619,950.56
Net Income	$13,428.73	$19,257.88	$21,282.72	$14,914.06	$68,883.39

printed
output omitting
Assumptions section

desired text
left-aligned at
bottom of page

current date
right-aligned at
bottom of page

Eastern Division Projected Budget Report

6/2/97

FIGURE 6-52

If you want to print the entire spreadsheet after setting the print area, you must reset the print area by performing the following steps.

TO SET THE ENTIRE SPREADSHEET AS THE PRINT AREA

Step 1: Click Edit on the menu bar and then click Select All.
Step 2: Click Format on the menu bar and then click Set Print Area.
Step 3: When the Microsoft Works dialog box displays, click the OK button.
Step 4: Click any cell to remove the highlight.

When you click the Print button on the toolbar or click Print on the File menu, the entire spreadsheet will print.

Creating a 3-D Stacked Bar Chart

A **3-D Stacked Bar chart** illustrates the relationship between two or more values and their totals by drawing 3-D stacked bars vertically across a chart. The 3-D Stacked Bar chart shown in Figure 6-53 shows the total expenses for each quarter, as well as the expense amount for each type of expense. The cyan segments represent the projected product liability expense for each quarter. For example, the product liability expense for Quarter 1 is approximately $15,000. The yellow segments represent the projected manufacturing expense for each quarter. The cyan segments and the yellow segments together represent the combined total of the projected product liability expenses and the projected manufacturing expenses for the quarter. For Quarter 1, the combined total for both projected expenses is approximately $60,000. Similarly, the turquoise segments on the chart illustrated in Figure 6-53 show the projected marketing expense for each quarter. The fuchsia segments represent the projected benefits expense for each month. From this chart, it is easy to see that the greatest projected expense for all quarters is for manufacturing.

A **set of segments** of the same color, such as the cyan segments representing the projected expenses for product liability, is called a **Y-series** or **value series**. Works allows up to six Y-series or value series in a chart.

The charted values are usually identified on the category axis by **category labels**. In the chart in Figure 6-53, the category labels Quarter 1, Quarter 2, Quarter 3, and Quarter 4 are displayed below the x-axis. A cluster of segments (representing the projected expenses for product liability, manufacturing, marketing, and benefits for one quarter) is called a **category**. All of the clusters of segments together (Quarter 1, Quarter 2, Quarter 3, and Quarter 4) are called the **category (X) series**.

All charts except pie charts have a horizontal axis called the **horizontal (X) axis** or **category axis** and a vertical axis called the **vertical (Y) axis** or **value axis**. The vertical (Y), or value, axis provides the measure against which values in the chart are plotted. In the example, the dollar amount of expenses is the value plotted. Works divides the y-axis into units based on the lowest and highest values in the spreadsheet automatically.

A **legend** on a chart identifies the information in a chart.

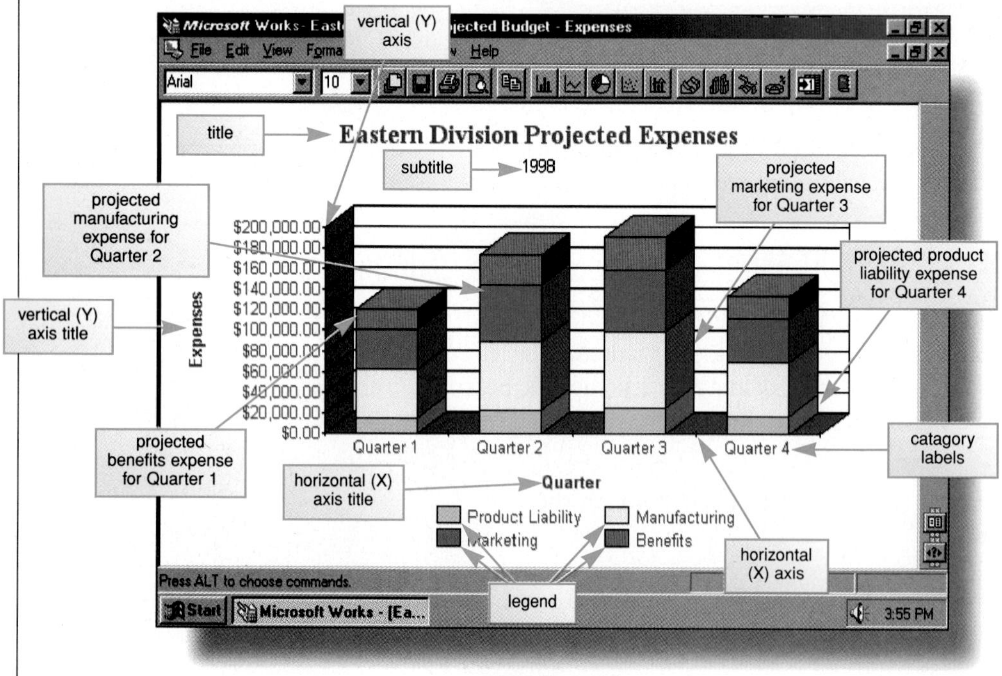

FIGURE 6-53

Creating the 3-D Stacked Bar Chart

The range of the spreadsheet to chart is A8:E11. Works will chart the row headings in the range A8:A11 as the legend. The range B8:E11 contains the data that will determine the height of the columns. To create the 3-D Stacked Bar chart, perform the following steps.

 Steps **To Create a 3-D Stacked Bar Chart**

1 **Highlight the range on the spreadsheet to chart – A8:E11. Point to the New Chart button on the toolbar.**

The row headings and cells containing the projected expenses for Quarter 1 through Quarter 4 are highlighted (Figure 6-54). The mouse pointer points to the New Chart button on the toolbar.

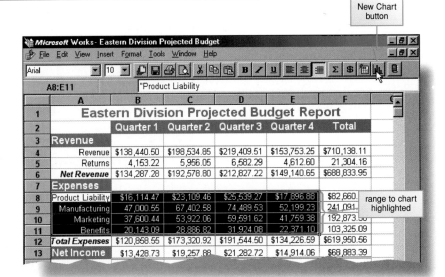

FIGURE 6-54

2 **Click the New Chart button on the toolbar. When the New Chart dialog box displays, click the 3-D Bar chart type in the What type of chart do you want? box. Press the TAB key and type** Eastern Division Projected Expenses **in the Title text box. Point to the OK button.**

Works displays the New Chart dialog box (Figure 6-55). The 3-D Bar chart type is selected in the What type of chart do you want? box. The title for the chart displays in the Title text box. The Your Chart box contains a sample of the selected chart type. The mouse pointer points to the OK button.

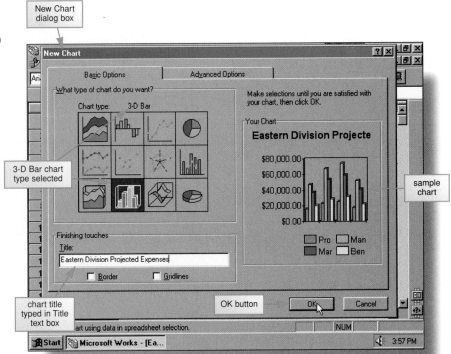

FIGURE 6-55

3 **Click the OK button. When the 3-D Bar chart displays in the chart window, point to the 3-D Bar Chart button on the Charting toolbar.**

Works displays the 3-D Bar chart (Figure 6-56). The chart title displays centered above the chart. The legend displays at the bottom of the chart. The mouse pointer points to the 3-D Bar Chart button on the Charting toolbar. Notice the category labels (Quarter 1, Quarter 2, Quarter 3, and Quarter 4) do not display on the x-axis because the labels were not selected in the range to chart.

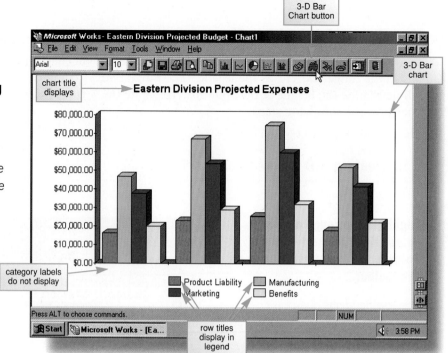

FIGURE 6-56

4 **Click the 3-D Bar Chart button on the Charting toolbar. When the Chart Type dialog box displays, point to the Variations tab.**

Works displays the Chart Type dialog box (Figure 6-57). The Basic Types sheet displays the twelve types of charts you can create. The 3-D Bar chart is selected. The mouse pointer points to the Variations tab.

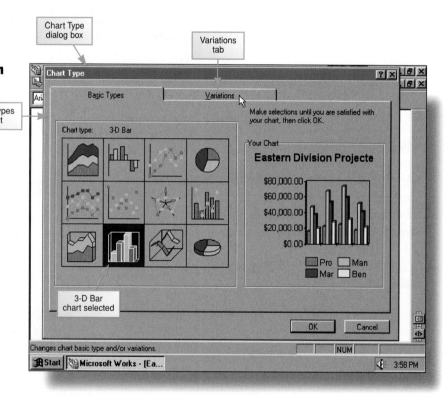

FIGURE 6-57

5 Click the Variations tab. When the Variations sheet displays, click the 3-D Stacked Bar chart type and then point to the OK button.

The Variations sheet displays (Figure 6-58). Six variations of a 3-D Bar chart display. The mouse pointer points to the OK button.

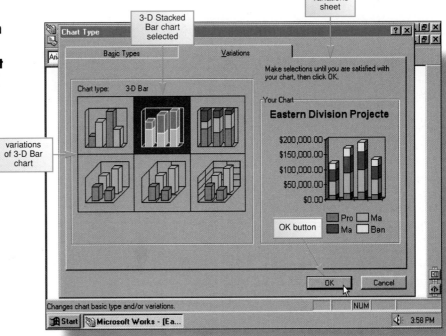

FIGURE 6-58

6 Click the OK button.

Works displays the 3-D Stacked Bar chart (Figure 6-59). Each vertical bar represents the total projected expenses for the quarter. Each segment in each bar represents the total projected expense for that category.

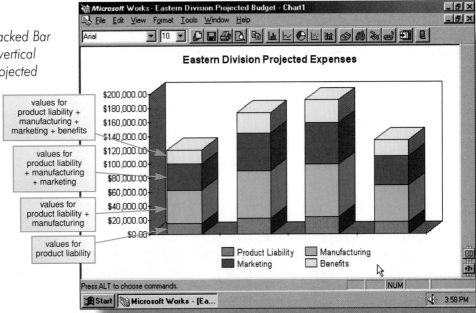

FIGURE 6-59

Adding Category Labels

Category labels are words that identify information along the horizontal (X) axis. In Figure 6-53 on page W 6.38, Quarter 1, Quarter 2, Quarter 3, and Quarter 4 are the category labels. These labels are found in the range B2:E2 on the spreadsheet. To add category labels to the chart, first display the spreadsheet and copy the range B2:E2. Then display the chart and use the Paste Series command on the Edit menu to paste the category labels below the horizontal (X) axis. Perform the following steps to add category labels to the chart.

Steps To Add Category Labels to a Chart

1 **Click Window on the menu bar and then point to Eastern Division Projected Budget.**

The Window menu displays and lists the open windows in the application (Figure 6-60). The chart is the active window, and Works indicates this by the check mark next to the chart name, Eastern Division Projected Budget - Chart 1.

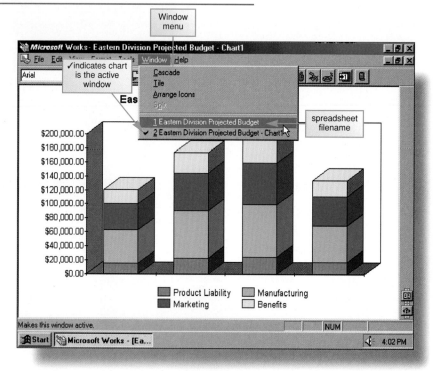

FIGURE 6-60

2 **Click Eastern Division Projected Budget. Highlight the range that contains the category labels – B2:E2. Click the Copy button on the toolbar.**

Works displays the spreadsheet and makes the spreadsheet window the active window (Figure 6-61). The range B2:E2 containing the category labels is highlighted. When you click the Copy button on the toolbar, Works places a copy of the highlighted range on the Clipboard.

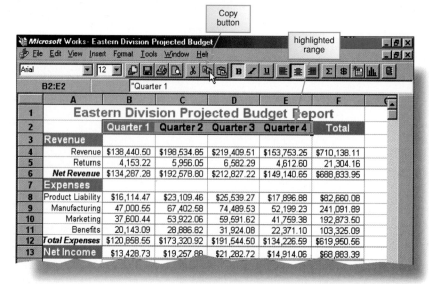

FIGURE 6-61

3 **Click Window on the menu bar and then point to Eastern Division Projected Budget - Chart 1.**

Works displays the Window menu and the mouse pointer points to the Eastern Division Projected Budget - Chart 1 filename (Figure 6-62).

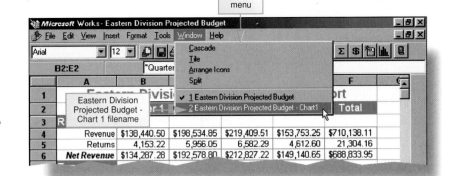

FIGURE 6-62

4 **Click Eastern Division Projected Budget - Chart 1. When the chart window displays, click Edit on the menu bar and then point to Paste Series.**

Works displays the chart window (Figure 6-63). The Edit menu displays and the mouse pointer points to the Paste Series command.

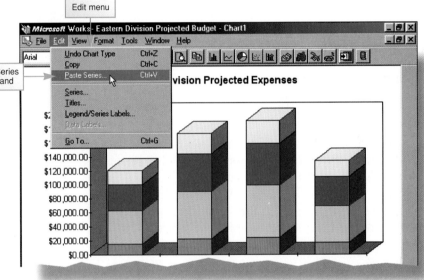

FIGURE 6-63

5 **Click Paste Series. When the Paste Series dialog box displays, click Category in the Use Selection For Series box. Point to the OK button.**

Works displays the Paste Series dialog box (Figure 6-64). The Category option button is selected. This option instructs Works to use the copied range (B2:E2) as category labels on the horizontal (X) axis.

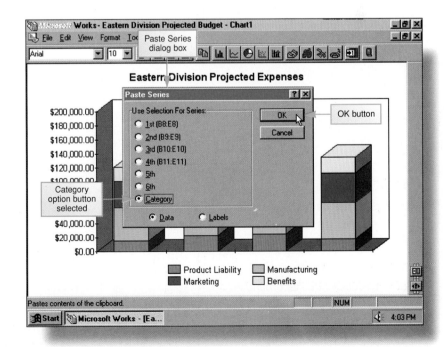

FIGURE 6-64

6 **Click the OK button.**

Works displays the 3-D Stacked Bar chart with the category labels, Quarter 1, Quarter 2, Quarter 3, and Quarter 4 at the bottom of the chart (Figure 6-65).

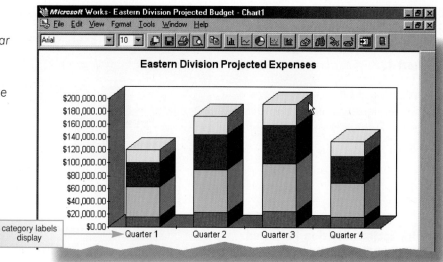

FIGURE 6-65

You can delete the category labels on a chart by clicking Series on the Edit menu, highlighting the Category (X) Series text box entry, and pressing the DELETE key.

When you create a chart, if the category labels are adjacent to the values in the spreadsheet to be charted and the category labels are highlighted, Works will display the labels on the chart automatically.

Adding Chart Titles to a 3-D Stacked Bar Chart

Chart titles can assist in making the chart easy to read and understand. Works allows you to add a title, subtitle, and titles on both the vertical and horizontal axes. In the 3-D Stacked Bar chart, the title is Eastern Division Projected Expenses and the subtitle is 1998. The vertical (Y) axis area contains the word, Expenses, and below the horizontal (X) axis is the word, Quarter. The title, Eastern Division Projected Expenses, was placed in the chart from the entry in the Title text box in the New Chart dialog box (see Figure 6-55 on page W 6.39). To add the remaining titles to the 3-D Stacked Bar chart, perform the following steps.

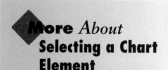

More *About*
Selecting a Chart Element

To quickly open the corresponding dialog box to edit any element on a chart, simply double-click the element. For example, to open the Edit Titles dialog box, double-click the title of the chart. Works places selection handles around the chart title and displays the Edit Titles dialog box.

Steps **To Add Titles to a 3-D Stacked Bar Chart**

1 **Right-click the chart title and point to Titles on the context-sensitive menu.**

When you right-click the title, Works places selection handles around the title and displays the context-sensitive menu (Figure 6-66). The mouse pointer points to the Titles command.

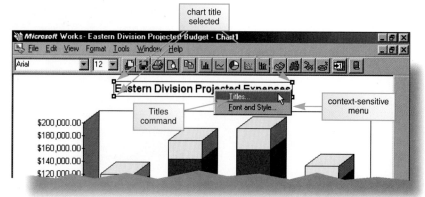

FIGURE 6-66

2 **Click Titles on the context-sensitive menu. When the Edit Titles dialog box displays, press the TAB key and then type** 1998 **in the Subtitle text box. Press the TAB key and then type** Quarter **in the Horizontal (X) Axis text box. Press the TAB key and then type** Expenses **in the Vertical (Y) Axis text box. Point to the OK button.**

Works displays the Edit Titles dialog box (Figure 6-67). The mouse pointer points to the OK button. The Chart title text box contains Eastern Division Projected Expenses because it was entered in the New Chart dialog box in Figure 6-55 on page W 6.39.

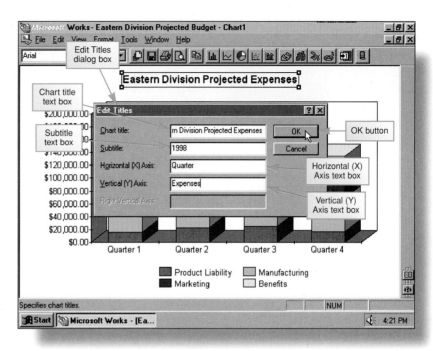

FIGURE 6-67

3 **Click the OK button.**

The 3-D Stacked Bar chart displays with the chart title, subtitle, vertical (Y) axis title, and horizontal (X) axis title (Figure 6-68).

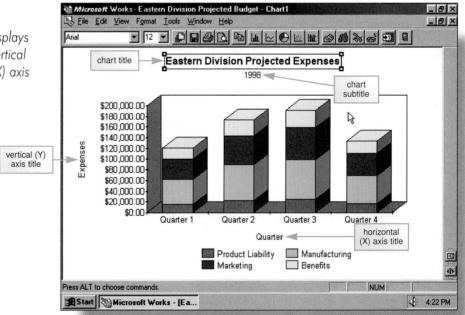

FIGURE 6-68

To delete a title, highlight the title to delete in the appropriate text box in the Edit Titles dialog box, press the DELETE key, and then click the OK button.

▶*Other***Ways**

1. On Edit menu click Titles, type desired title, click OK button

Table 6-4		
SERIES	*COLOR*	*PATTERN*
1st	Cyan	Solid
2nd	Yellow	Dense
3rd	Turquoise	Solid
4th	Fuchsia	Solid

Changing the Color and Pattern of Segments of a 3-D Stacked Bar Chart

When you create a 3-D Stacked Bar chart, Works assigns colors and patterns to the segments in the chart automatically. In the example 3-D Stacked Bar chart, the red bar represents product liability expenses, green represents manufacturing expenses, blue represents marketing expenses, and yellow represents benefits. You can change the colors of the segments of the 3-D Stacked Bar chart, patterns within the segments, or both. Table 6-4 illustrates the colors and patterns for each segment of the 3-D Stacked Bar chart for Project 6. To change the color and pattern of the 3-D Stacked Bar chart segments, perform the following steps.

Steps To Change Colors and Patterns in a 3-D Stacked Bar Chart

1 **Right-click the red segment for Quarter 1 in the 3-D Stacked Bar chart. When the context-sensitive menu displays, point to Shading and Color.**

Works displays selection handles around the red segments of Quarter 1, Quarter 2, Quarter 3, and Quarter 4 and displays the context-sensitive menu (Figure 6-69). The mouse pointer points to the Shading and Color command.

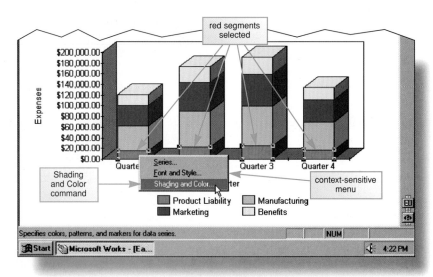

FIGURE 6-69

2 **Click Shading and Color on the context-sensitive menu.**

The Format Shading and Color dialog box displays (Figure 6-70). The 1st option button in the Series box is selected, indicating the entries in the Colors and Patterns list boxes describe the first series of values on the chart. Auto is highlighted in the Colors list box and in the Patterns list box. Auto means Works selects the color and pattern automatically. For the first series values, the auto color is red and the pattern is solid.

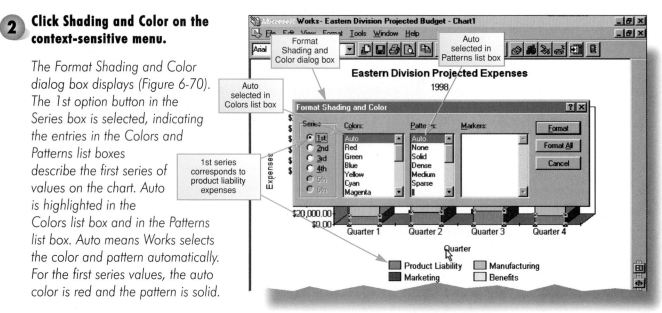

FIGURE 6-70

3 Point to the title bar of the Format Shading and Color dialog box and drag upwards so you can view the 3-D Stacked Bar chart. Click Cyan in the Colors list box. Click Solid in the Patterns list box. Click the Format button.

The color for product liability expenses, which corresponds to the 1st option button in the Series box, changes to cyan (Figure 6-71). Works applies the solid pattern to the product liability segment. The Cancel button changes to a Close button.

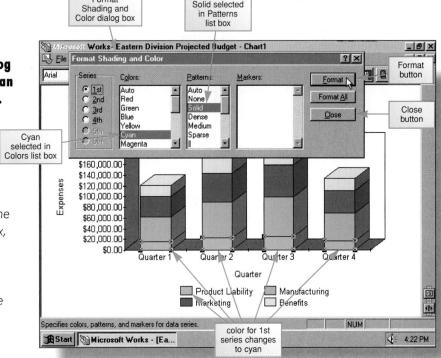

FIGURE 6-71

4 Following the techniques illustrated in Steps 1 through 3, change the color and pattern for the second, third, and fourth series. That is, for the second series, click 2nd in the Series box, click Yellow in the Colors list box, click Dense in the Patterns list box, and click the Format button. Refer to Table 6-4 for the series and the corresponding color and pattern. Point to the Close button.

The selections you made display in the Format Shading and Color dialog box and on the chart (Figure 6-72). The mouse pointer points to the Close button.

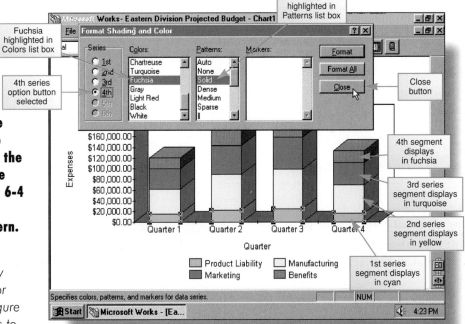

FIGURE 6-72

5 Click the Close button.

Works closes the Format Shading and Color dialog box (Figure 6-73). The 1st series segment displays in cyan, the 2nd series segment displays in yellow, the 3rd series segment displays in turquoise, and the 4th series segment displays in magenta. The legend also changes to reflect the changes in the segments.

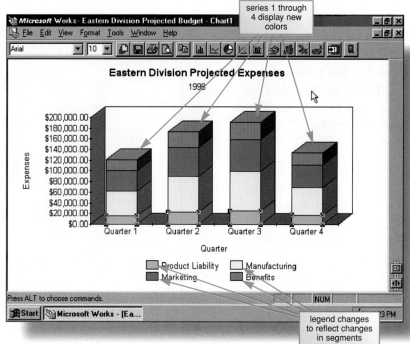

FIGURE 6-73

Adding Gridlines

When creating a 3-D Stacked Bar chart, gridlines often assist in making the chart easier to read. You can add gridlines extending horizontally from the y-axis or vertically from the x-axis. For Project 6, you are to display gridlines horizontally from the y-axis. To accomplish this, perform the following steps.

Steps **To Add Y-Axis Gridlines**

1 Right-click the y-axis. When the context-sensitive menu displays, point to Vertical (Y) Axis.

The y-axis is selected and the context-sensitive menu displays (Figure 6-74). The mouse pointer points to the Vertical (Y) Axis command.

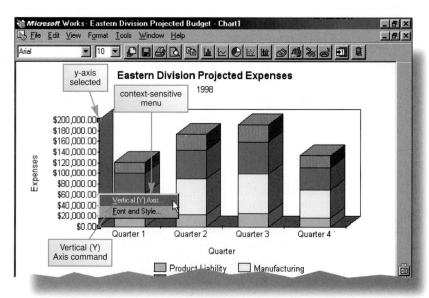

FIGURE 6-74

2 **Click Vertical (Y) Axis on the context-sensitive menu. When the Format Vertical Axis dialog box displays, click Show gridlines. Point to the OK button.**

Works displays the Format Vertical Axis dialog box (Figure 6-75). A check mark displays in the Show gridlines check box. The Show gridlines setting adds horizontal gridlines that originate from each number on the y-axis scale. The mouse pointer points to the OK button.

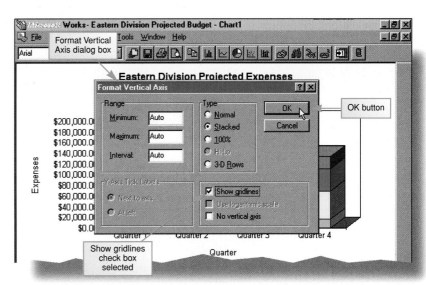

FIGURE 6-75

3 **Click the OK button.**

The 3-D Stacked Bar chart displays with y-axis gridlines (Figure 6-76). Notice the horizontal gridlines originate from each number on the y-axis scale.

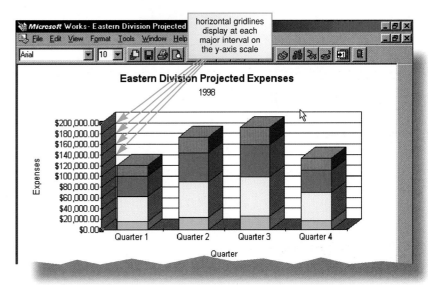

FIGURE 6-76

To remove the y-axis gridlines from the chart, display the Format Vertical Axis dialog box and remove the check mark from the Show gridlines check box.

You also can insert vertical gridlines by right-clicking the x-axis and clicking Horizontal (X) Axis. Then, click Show gridlines in the Format Horizontal Axis dialog box.

*Other***Ways**

1. On Format menu click Vertical (Y) Axis, click Show gridlines, click OK button

Changing Font, Font Size, and Font Style

To change the font, font size, and font style of text on a chart, first right-click the text, then click Font and Style on the context-sensitive menu and make the appropriate selections. In this project, the chart title displays in 16-point Times New Roman blue, bold font. The axes labels display in 10-point Arial blue bold font. The category labels and legend text display in 10-point Arial blue font. To change the font, font size, and font style in the chart, complete the steps on the next page (see Figure 6-77 on the next page).

TO CHANGE FONT, FONT SIZE, AND FONT STYLE

Step 1: Right-click the chart title. Click Font and Style.

Step 2: When the Format Font and Style - Title dialog box displays, click Times New Roman in the Font list box. Click 16 in the Size list box. Click Blue in the Color drop-down list box. Click the OK button.

Step 3: Right-click the x-axis label (Quarter). Click Font and Style.

Step 4: When the Format Font and Style - Axes Titles dialog box displays, click Blue in the Color drop-down list box. Click Bold in the Style box. Click the OK button.

Step 5: Right-click the legend text. Click Font and Style.

Step 6: When the Format Font and Style - Tick Labels, Data Labels, Etc. dialog box displays, click Blue in the Color drop-down list box. Click the OK button.

The formatted chart displays in Figure 6-77.

Renaming a Chart

Works allows you to give meaningful names to charts rather than the default names, Chart 1, Chart 2, and so on. To rename Chart 1 as Expenses, perform the following steps.

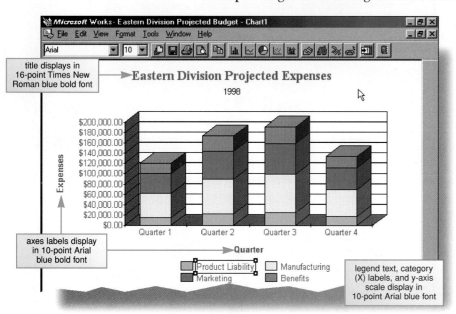

FIGURE 6-77

Steps **To Rename a Chart**

1 **Click Tools on the menu bar and point to Rename Chart.**

Works displays the Tools menu and the mouse pointer points to the Rename Chart command (Figure 6-78).

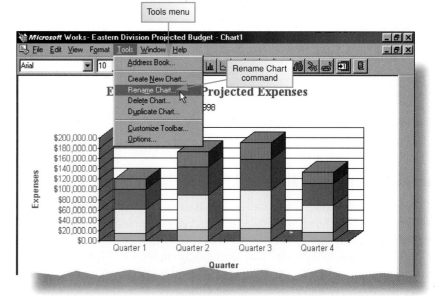

FIGURE 6-78

2 **Click Rename Chart. Type** Expenses **in the Type a name below text box. Point to the Rename button.**

Works displays the Rename Chart dialog box (Figure 6-79). The current chart name, Chart1, is highlighted in the Select a Chart list box. The name, Expenses, displays in the Type a name below text box and the mouse pointer points to the Rename button.

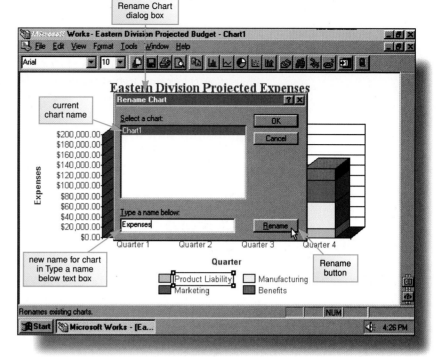

FIGURE 6-79

3 **Click the Rename button and then point to the OK button.**

Works changes the name of the chart in the title bar of the Works application window and in the Select a chart list box (Figure 6-80). The mouse pointer points to the OK button.

4 **Click the OK button to remove the Rename Chart dialog box from the screen.**

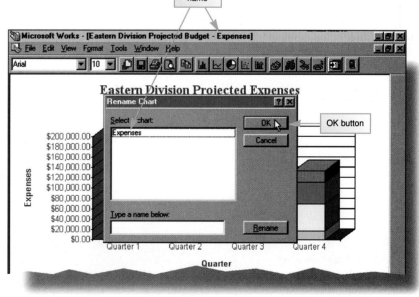

FIGURE 6-80

When renaming a chart, you can type a new name up to 15 characters for the selected chart. Renaming a chart can make it easier to identify on the View menu.

Two other commands are available on the Tools menu (see Figure 6-78). Delete Chart allows you to delete a chart from the spreadsheet file. To delete a chart, click Tools on the menu bar and then click Delete Chart, highlight the name of the chart to delete in the Select a chart list box of the Delete Chart dialog box, click the Delete button, and then click the OK button.

To duplicate a chart, click Duplicate Chart on the Tools menu. Click the chart to duplicate in the Select a chart list box of the Duplicate Chart dialog box, click the Duplicate button and then click the OK button. Works will duplicate the chart you select and name the new chart X, where X is the next number in sequence.

Previewing and Printing the 3-D Stacked Bar Chart

The chart for Project 6 is to print in landscape orientation. To preview and print the 3-D Stacked Bar chart, perform the following steps.

TO PREVIEW AND PRINT THE 3-D STACKED BAR CHART

Step 1: Click File on the Charting menu bar and then click Page Setup on the File menu.

Step 2: Click the Source, Size, & Orientation tab. In the Orientation box of the Source, Size, & Orientation sheet, click Landscape.

Step 3: Click the Other Options tab. In the Size box of the Other Options sheet, click Full page, keep proportions.

Step 4: Click the OK button.

Step 5: Click the Print Preview button on the toolbar.

Step 6: Review the print preview window to ensure the chart will print properly.

Step 7: Click the Print button in the print preview window to print the chart.

Works prints the chart in landscape orientation as shown in Figure 6-81.

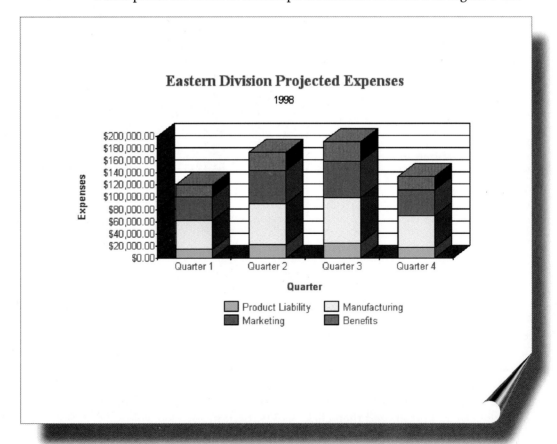

FIGURE 6-81

Works prints the chart. If you have a color printer, the chart prints in color. If not, the chart prints in varying shades of gray.

What-If Analysis

The automatic recalculation feature of Works is a powerful tool that can be used to analyze spreadsheet data. Using Works to examine the impact of changing values in cells that are referenced by a formula in another cell is called **what-if analysis**.

In Project 6, the projected quarterly expenses and net incomes in the range B8:F13 are dependent on the assumptions in the range B16:B20. Thus, if you change any of the percentages, Works immediately recalculates the quarterly expenses in rows 8 through 11, the quarterly total expenses in row 12 and the quarterly net incomes in row 13. As a result, these new values cause Works to recalculate a new, year net income in cell F13. Finally, because the projected quarterly net incomes in row 13 change, Works redraws the 3-D Stacked Bar chart, which is based on these numbers.

The what-if question posed at the beginning of Project 6, *What if the projected expense percentages decrease by 1 percent each - how would the decrease affect the net income?*, now can be answered.

Freezing Row Titles

To ensure that the column headings (range B2:F2), the projected percentages section (range A16:B20), and the net income in cell F13 display on the screen at the same time, you can **freeze** the column headings. You can freeze column headings to keep them on the screen while scrolling through other parts of a spreadsheet.

To freeze the headings in row 2 of the spreadsheet, highlight a cell below the row you want to freeze. Then on the Format menu, click Freeze Titles. Works freezes all the rows above the highlight. Using the following steps, freeze the headings in row 2 and perform a what-if analysis in the spreadsheet.

 Steps To Freeze Column Headings and Analyze Data by Changing Values

1 **Click Window on the menu bar and then click Eastern Division Projected Budget. Highlight cell A3. Click Format on the menu bar and then point to Freeze Titles.**

The spreadsheet displays in the document window and Works displays the Format menu (Figure 6-82). The mouse pointer points to the Freeze Titles command. Because a cell in row 3 is highlighted, Works will freeze all rows above row 3.

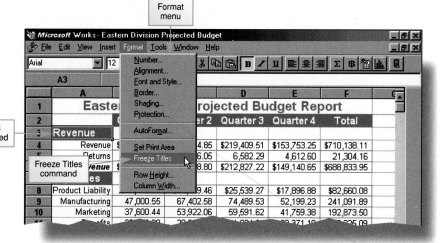

FIGURE 6-82

2 **Click Freeze Titles.**

Works displays a thin black line as a bottom border in row 2 (Figure 6-83).

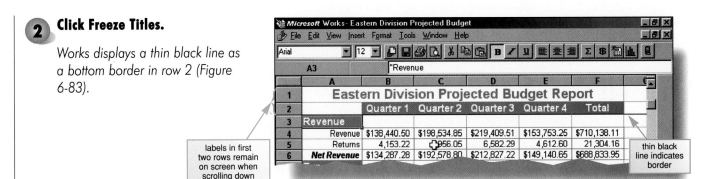

labels in first two rows remain on screen when scrolling down

thin black line indicates border

FIGURE 6-83

3 **Click the down scroll arrow four times to view the projected expenses, projected net income, and the Assumptions section of the spreadsheet.**

column headings and spreadsheet title frozen on screen

rows 3 through 6 do not display

The spreadsheet title in row 1 and the column headings in row 2 remain on the screen as you scroll down the window to view the Assumptions section (Figure 6-84). Rows 3 through 6 do not display on the screen.

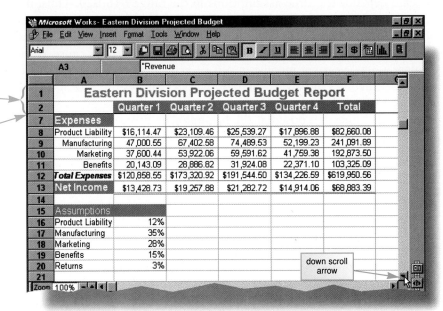

down scroll arrow

FIGURE 6-84

4 **Highlight cell B16. Enter** 11% **in cell B16 and** 34% **in cell B17. Enter** 27% **in cell B18 and** 14% **in cell B19.**

Works immediately recalculates all the formulas in the spreadsheet, including the projected net income total in cell F13 (Figure 6-85).

projected expenses recalculated

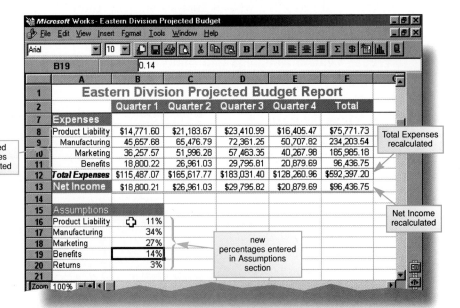

Total Expenses recalculated

Net Income recalculated

new percentages entered in Assumptions section

FIGURE 6-85

Notice that when you enter the new values, Works recalculates the spreadsheet. The recalculated values express the results that would be obtained if all the expenses were decreased by 1 percent.

Compare the total expenses and net incomes in Figure 6-84 and Figure 6-85. By reducing the projected product liability, manufacturing, marketing, and benefits percentages by 1 percent each, the total expenses in cell F12 decreases from $619,950.56 to $592,397.20, and the net income in cell F13 increases from $68,883.39 to $96,436.75 (see Figure 6-85). The 1 percent reduction in projected expenses translates into a net income gain of $27,553.36.

The titles are frozen until you unfreeze them. To unfreeze the titles, click Freeze Titles on the Format menu.

Project Summary

Project 6 introduced you to using Works to answer what-if questions. You learned how to use the fill handle to create a data series. You learned the difference between relative cell references and absolute cell references, how to enter both into a formula, and how to copy both to adjacent cells. The project presented steps showing you how to round values calculated by formulas. You learned to copy data to nonadjacent areas using drag-and-drop. Later, you learned to add a border to a range of cells. Creating footers on a spreadsheet also was illustrated.

Using Works charting capabilities, you learned to create a 3-D Stacked Bar chart from data in the spreadsheet. You learned how to add category labels to a chart and change colors and patterns to segments of a stacked bar chart. Finally, this project illustrated renaming a chart.

What You Should Know

Having completed this project, you should be able to perform the following tasks:

- Add a Border to a Range of Cells *(W 6.31)*
- Add Category Labels to a Chart *(W 6.42)*
- Add Color to the Spreadsheet *(W 6.28)*
- Add Titles to a 3-D Stacked Bar Chart *(W 6.44)*
- Add Y-Axis Gridlines *(W 6.48)*
- Change Colors and Patterns in a 3-D Stacked Bar Chart *(W 6.46)*
- Change Font, Font Size, and Font Style *(W 6.50)*
- Copy a Formula With Relative and Absolute Cell References *(W 6.20)*
- Copy Cells Using Drag-and-Drop *(W 6.12)*
- Copy Formulas *(W 6.24)*
- Create a 3-D Stacked Bar Chart *(W 6.39)*
- Enter a Data Sequence in a Range Using the Fill Handle *(W 6.8)*
- Enter a Formula Containing Relative and Absolute Cell References *(W 6.17)*
- Enter and Copy a Formula *(W 6.20)*
- Enter a Spreadsheet Title *(W 6.7)*
- Enter Formulas *(W 6.21, W 6.24)*
- Enter Percentages and Complete the Assumptions Section *(W 6.14)*

- Enter Row Headings and Increase the Column Width by Dragging the Column Border *(W 6.10)*
- Enter the Revenue Values *(W 6.15)*
- Format and Add Color and a Border to the Assumptions Section *(W 6.34)*
- Format Numeric Values *(W 6.27)*
- Format Titles *(W 6.27)*
- Freeze Column Headings and Analyze Data by Changing Values *(W 6.53)*
- Insert a Footer into a Spreadsheet *(W 6.35)*
- Move Cells Using Drag-and-Drop *(W 6.14)*
- Preview and Print a 3-D Stacked Bar Chart *(W 6.52)*
- Print a Portion of a Spreadsheet *(W 6.36)*
- Rename a Chart *(W 6.50)*
- Save the Spreadsheet *(W 6.26, W 6.36)*
- Set the Entire Spreadsheet as the Print Area *(W 6.37)*
- Start the Works Spreadsheet *(W 6.7)*
- Sum the Row Totals *(W 6.25)*

A+ Test Your Knowledge

1 True/False

Instructions: Circle T if the statement is true or F if the statement is false.

T F 1. If you enter 2000 in cell A1, 2100 in cell B1, highlight the range A1:B1, and then drag the fill handle across to cell E1, Works assigns cell E1 the value 2103.

T F 2. Use the fill handle to copy the data to a nonadjacent area.

T F 3. The format of the ROUND function is =ROUND(x,NumberOfPlaces) where x is the value to round and NumberOfPlaces is a value specifying the number of positions to round to the right or left of the decimal point.

T F 4. =ROUND(0,2.58) returns the value 0.

T F 5. An absolute cell reference means a cell's reference will change when a formula containing the cell reference is copied from one cell to another.

T F 6. To place a border around a cell, first highlight the cell where the border will appear, then click Border on the context-sensitive menu.

T F 7. A 3-D Stacked Bar chart shows the relationship between two or more values and their totals.

T F 8. The only way to display category labels on a chart is to include the labels when highlighting the range to chart.

T F 9. To freeze column headings in row 2 of a spreadsheet, highlight a cell in row 3, and then on the Format menu, click Freeze Titles.

T F 10. When performing what-if analysis, you normally change the value in one or more cells to answer the questions.

2 Multiple Choice

Instructions: Circle the correct response.

1. If you enter MONDAY in cell B4 and drag the fill handle through the range C4:E4, cell E4 will contain _____.
   a. Monday
   b. Thursday
   c. THURSDAY
   d. MONDAY

2. To ensure that whole numbers are used in calculations when the result of the calculation could result in decimals, use the _____ in the calculation.
   a. Comma format
   b. =ROUND function
   c. Currency format
   d. SUM function

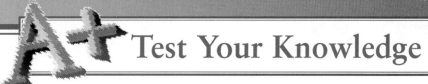

3. Cell G11 displays the value 125 in the cell due to the Comma format with zero decimals applied to the original entry of 124.736. The product of G11*10 equals _____.
   a. 1250
   b. 1247.40
   c. 1240.74
   d. 1247.36

4. When entering a formula, pressing the F4 key will _____.
   a. delete the formula
   b. change the selected cell to a relative cell reference
   c. confirm the formula into the cell
   d. change the selected cell to an absolute cell reference

5. To use the drag-and-drop method for copying a range of cells, the mouse pointer must point to the border of the range and change to the _____ shape with the word DRAG.
   a. block plus sign
   b. cross hair
   c. arrow
   d. split double arrow

6. To change the default 3-D Bar chart to a 3-D Stacked Bar chart, click _____.
   a. the 3-D Bar button on the Charting toolbar, click the Variations tab in the Chart Type dialog box, and then click the 3-D Stacked Bar chart style
   b. Format on the menu bar, click Chart Style, and then click the 3-D Stacked Bar chart style
   c. the 3-D Stacked Bar button on the toolbar
   d. the Chart Style button on the toolbar

7. You can add gridlines on the y-axis of a 3-D Stacked Bar chart by clicking _____.
   a. Gridlines on the context-sensitive menu
   b. Gridlines on the View menu
   c. Vertical Y-Axis on the context-sensitive menu
   d. Horizontal X-Axis on the context-sensitive menu

8. To change the default chart name, Chart1, to a new name, click Tools on the Charting menu bar, click _____, and then type the new name in the Type a name below text box.
   a. Rename Chart
   b. Duplicate Chart
   c. Delete Chart
   d. Create New Chart

9. To unfreeze titles previously frozen, click _____.
   a. Freeze Titles on the Format menu
   b. Unfreeze Titles on the Format menu
   c. the Freeze Titles button on the toolbar
   d. Freeze Titles on the context-sensitive menu

(continued)

Multiple Choice *(continued)*

10. When performing a what-if analysis, normally you change the _____ in order to answer your question.
    a. value in one or more cells
    b. formulas in one or more cells
    c. titles in one or more cells
    d. all of the above

3 Fill In

Instructions: In the spaces provided, describe the steps required to create a series in the following tasks.

Task 1: Copy the date in cell A4 (1/22/97) into the range A5:A12. Each date should be the next day in the week.

Steps: _____

Task 2: Copy the date in cell C2 (March 16, 1997) to the range D2:L2. Each date should be one week apart.

Steps: _____

Task 3: Copy the date in cell A12 (10/01/97) to the range A13:A40. The dates should be every other month, that is, October, December, February.

Steps: _____

Task 4: Copy the value in cell E1 (50,000) into the range E2:E10. The values should increment by 200. Display the values in the Currency format with two decimals.

Steps: _____

4 Fill In

Instructions: Identify the command that causes the dialog box to display and allows you to make the indicated changes.

CHANGES	COMMAND
1. Add a border to cells	_____
2. Create a footer in a spreadsheet	_____
3. Freeze worksheet titles	_____
4. Unfreeze worksheet titles	_____
5. Create a 3-D Stacked Bar chart	_____
6. Add category labels to a chart	_____
7. Change colors and patterns in a chart	_____
8. Rename a chart	_____

Use Help

1 Reviewing Project Activities

Instructions: Use your computer to perform the following tasks to obtain experience using online Help.

1. Start the Microsoft Works Spreadsheet tool.
2. Display the Help window to the right of the document window. Click the Index button below the Help window to display the Help Topics: Microsoft Works dialog box.
3. Type creating formulas in spreadsheets in the Index text box. Click To type your own formula SS topic. Read and print To type your own formula.
4. Click the More Info tab. Click Quick Tour: Formulas. When the Works Quick Tour: Formulas window displays, step through the tutorial by clicking the right arrow button at the bottom of the window. Click the Done button to return to the More Info sheet.
5. Click the Quick Tour: Functions. When the Works Quick Tour: Functions window displays, step through the tutorial by clicking the right pointing arrow at the bottom of the window. Click the Done button to return to the More Info sheet.
6. Click the Quick Tour: Cell and range references. When the Works Quick Tour: Cell and range references window displays, step through the tutorial by clicking the right arrow button at the bottom of the window. Click the Done button to return to the More Info sheet. Click the Close button in the Help Topics: Microsoft Works dialog box.
7. When the Unsaved Spreadsheet 1 document window displays, type =ROUND in cell A1. When the Overview, ROUND(x,NumberOfPlaces) dialog box displays, read and print the topic.

2 Expanding on the Basics

Instructions: Use Works online Help to better understand the topics listed below. Print the topic or topics that substantiate your answer. If a Print this topic icon is not available, then answer the question on a separate piece of paper.

1. Using the key terms, *charts: adding entries*, and the Index sheet in the Help topics: Microsoft Works dialog box, answer the following questions.
   a. How do you display a chart and spreadsheet side by side?

   _____

   b. Briefly explain how to add entries to a chart?

   _____

   c. How do you find the spreadsheet numbers used to plot a chart?

   _____

   d. Explain how to view a chart?

   _____

2. Using the key term, *freezing*, and the Index sheet in the Help topics: Microsoft Works dialog box, answer the following questions.
   a. How do you freeze row titles in a spreadsheet?

   _____

   b. How do you unfreeze row titles in a spreadsheet?

   _____

Apply Your Knowledge

1 Creating a Series

Instructions: Start the Microsoft Works Spreadsheet tool. Open the Create Series spreadsheet on the Student Floppy Disk that accompanies this book. The spreadsheet is illustrated in Figure 6-86. The spreadsheet contains the initial values for eight different series.

![Microsoft Works - Create Series spreadsheet showing row 3 with initial values: 6:00 AM, Sunday, January 01, 1997, Division 1, 0, Dept 1, January]

FIGURE 6-86

Use the fill handle on one column at a time to extend the seven different series as shown in Figure 6-87 through row 17. If Works does not recognize the pattern you wish to create, enter a second value in row 2. Save the spreadsheet using the filename, Create Series 2. Create a footer in the spreadsheet consisting of your last name and first name centered at the bottom of the page. Print the spreadsheet on one page.

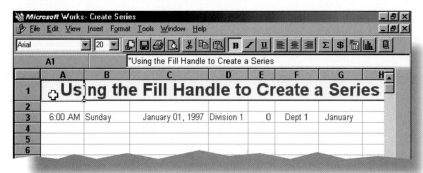

Microsoft Works - Create Series 2

	A	B	C	D	E	F	G	H
1	⇧Using the Fill Handle to Create a Series							
2								
3	6:00 AM	Sunday	January 01, 1997	Division 1	0	Dept 1	January	
4	7:00 AM	Monday	February 01, 1997	Division 2	100	Dept 2	February	
5	8:00 AM	Tuesday	March 01, 1997	Division 3	200	Dept 3	March	
6	9:00 AM	Wednesday	April 01, 1997	Division 4	300	Dept 4	April	
7	10:00 AM	Thursday	May 01, 1997	Division 5	400	Dept 5	May	
8	11:00 AM	Friday	June 01, 1997	Division 6	500	Dept 6	June	
9	12:00 PM	Saturday	July 01, 1997	Division 7	600	Dept 7	July	
10	1:00 PM	Sunday	August 01, 1997	Division 8	700	Dept 8	August	
11	2:00 PM	Monday	September 01, 1997	Division 9	800	Dept 9	September	
12	3:00 PM	Tuesday	October 01, 1997	Division 10	900	Dept 10	October	
13	4:00 PM	Wednesday	November 01, 1997	Division 11	1000	Dept 11	November	
14	5:00 PM	Thursday	December 01, 1997	Division 12	1100	Dept 12	December	
15	6:00 PM	Friday	January 01, 1998	Division 13	1200	Dept 13	January	
16	7:00 PM	Saturday	February 01, 1998	Division 14	1300	Dept 14	February	
17	8:00 PM	Sunday	March 01, 1998	Division 15	1400	Dept 15	March	

Press ALT to choose commands, or F2 to edit.　　NUM

Start　Microsoft Works - [Cr...　4:36 PM

FIGURE 6-87

In the Lab

1 Creating a Four-Month Budget Report and a 3-D Stacked Bar Chart

Problem: Create a four-month budget report where the expenses are calculated as percentages of the total income. Create a 3-D Stacked Bar chart from the expense data in the spreadsheet. The income is shown in the table below.

The spreadsheet is shown in Figure 6-88.

Instructions:

1. Create a spreadsheet in the format shown in Figure 6-88 using the numbers from the table.

2. In the spreadsheet, calculate the total for each item of income (Sales and Consultations) by adding the income for July, August, September, and October.

3. Calculate the total income by adding the sales and consultations values for July, August, September, October, and the total column.

4. Calculate the expenses for advertising, salaries, supplies, and truck by multiplying the total income for each month by the advertising, salaries, supplies, and truck percentages, respectively, found in the Budgeted Percentages section of the spreadsheet. Perform rounding as required.

INCOME	JULY	AUGUST	SEPTEMBER	OCTOBER
Sales	91875.50	125215.50	112075.50	110850.50
Consultations	4844.71	4350.00	3108.50	2750.00

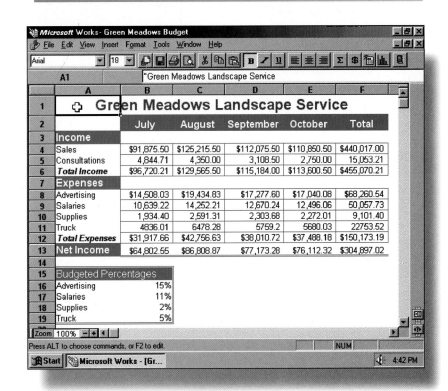

FIGURE 6-88

5. Calculate the total expenses for each month and the total for all expenses by adding the advertising, salaries, supplies, and truck expenses for each month and for the total column.

6. Calculate the net income by subtracting the total expenses for each month and for the total column from the total income for each month and for the total column.

7. Format the spreadsheet as shown. The widths for the columns are as follows: A = 15, B = 12, C = 12, 3-D Stacked Bar = 13, E = 12, and F = 12. The heights for the rows are as follows: row 2 = 18, row 3 = 15, row 7 = 15, row 13 = 15, row 15 = 15.

8. Save the spreadsheet you create on a floppy disk. Use the filename, Green Meadows Budget.

9. Print the spreadsheet you have created on a single page.

(continued)

In the Lab

Creating a Four-Month Budget Report and a 3-D Stacked Bar Chart *(continued)*

10. Create the 3-D Stacked Bar chart shown in Figure 6-89 from the expenses contained in the spreadsheet.

11. Format the 3-D Stacked Bar chart as shown in Figure 6-89. The chart title, Budgeted Expenses, displays in 32-point Times New Roman blue bold font. The chart subtitle, Green Meadows Landscape Service, displays in 12-point Times New Roman blue font. The axes labels display in 12-point Times New Roman blue font. Change the segment colors as follows: 1st = yellow, 2nd = blue, 3rd = light red, 4th = cyan.

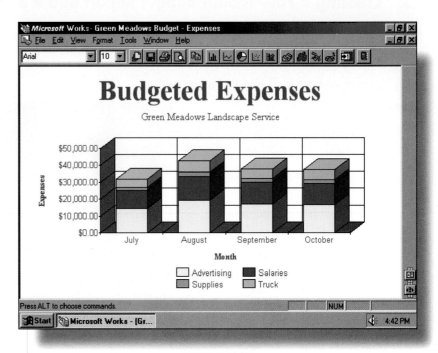

FIGURE 6-89

12. Save the spreadsheet and chart using the same filename as in step 8.

13. Print the chart in landscape orientation.

14. Analyze the effect on net income of decreasing the budgeted percentages by 1 percent.

15. Enter the following percentages in the spreadsheet for each of the budgeted expenses and answer the following questions:

    Advertising: 13%   Supplies: 5%

    Salaries: 10%   Truck: 4%

    a. What is the total net income for the four-month period as shown in the spreadsheet?

    _____

    b. What is the advertising expense for October? _____

16. Enter the following percentages in the spreadsheet for each of the budgeted expenses and answer the following questions.

    Advertising: 35%   Supplies: 15%

    Salaries: 25%   Truck: 14%

    a. What are the total expenses for the four-month period as shown in the spreadsheet?

    _____

    b. What is the total net income for the four-month period as shown in the spreadsheet?

    _____

17. Follow directions from your instructor for turning in this assignment.

In the Lab

2 Creating an International Manufacturing Projections Report and a 3-D Stacked Bar Chart

Problem: Create an International Manufacturing Projections report where the expenses are calculated as percentages of the total revenue. Create a 3-D Stacked Bar chart from the expense data in the spreadsheet. The revenue is shown in the table below.

REVENUE	JANUARY	FEBRUARY	MARCH	APRIL	MAY	JUNE
Sales	19378.85	17435.50	12075.50	10850.75	11850.25	15795.50
Other	2390.25	3015.50	2750.25	3458.25	4780.45	3945.50

The spreadsheet is shown in Figure 6-90.

	A	B	C	D	E	F	G	H	I
1	✛	**International Manufacturing**							
2				Half Yearly Report					
3			January	February	March	April	May	June	Total	
4	**Revenue**								
5	Sales	$19,378.85	$17,435.50	$12,075.50	$10,850.75	$11,850.25	$15,795.50	$87,386.35	
6	Other	2,390.25	3,015.50	2,750.25	3,458.25	4,780.45	3,945.50	20,340.20	
7	Total	$21,769.10	$20,451.00	$14,825.75	$14,309.00	$16,630.70	$19,741.00	$107,726.55	
8	**Expenses**								
9	Manufacturing	$8,707.64	$8,180.40	$5,930.30	$5,723.60	$6,652.28	$7,896.40	$43,090.62	
10	Research	2176.91	2045.1	1482.58	1430.9	1663.07	1974.1	10,772.66	
11	Marketing	3265.37	3067.65	2223.86	2146.35	2494.61	2961.15	16,158.99	
12	Administrative	4353.82	4090.2	2965.15	2861.8	3326.14	3948.2	21,545.31	
13	Commissions	653.07	613.53	444.77	429.27	498.92	592.23	3,231.79	
14	**Total Expenses**	$19,156.81	$17,996.88	$13,046.66	$12,591.92	$14,635.02	$17,372.08	$94,799.37	
15	**Net Income**	$2,612.29	$2,454.12	$1,779.09	$1,717.08	$1,995.68	$2,368.92	$12,927.18	
16									
17	**Assumptions**								
18	**Manufacturing**	40.00%							
19	**Research**	10.00%							
20	**Marketing**	15.00%							
21	**Administrative**	20.00%							
22	**Commissions**	3.00%							

FIGURE 6-90

Instructions:

1. Create a spreadsheet in the format shown in Figure 6-90 using the numbers from the table.
2. In the spreadsheet, calculate the total for each item of revenue (Sales and Other) by adding the revenue for January, February, March, April, May, and June.
3. Calculate the total revenue by adding the sales and other values for January, February, March, April, May, and June and the total column.
4. Calculate the expenses for manufacturing, research, marketing, administrative, and commissions by multiplying the total revenue for each month by the manufacturing, research, marketing, administrative, and commissions percentages, respectively, found in the Assumptions section of the spreadsheet. Perform rounding as required.

(continued)

In the Lab

Creating an International Manufacturing Projections Report and a 3-D Stacked Bar Chart *(continued)*

5. Calculate the total expenses for each month and the total for all expenses by adding the manufacturing, research, marketing, administrative, and commissions expenses for each month and for the total column.

6. Calculate the net income by subtracting the total expenses for each month and for the total column from the total income for each month and for the total column.

7. Format the spreadsheet as shown. The widths for the columns are as follows: A = 14, B through H = 12.

8. Save the spreadsheet you create on a floppy disk. Use the filename, International Manufacturing Budget.

9. Print the spreadsheet you have created on a single page. Use print preview to ensure the spreadsheet will print on one page.

10. Create the 3-D Stacked Bar chart shown in Figure 6-91 from the expenses contained in the spreadsheet.

11. Format the 3-D Stacked Bar chart as shown in Figure 6-91. The chart title, Budgeted Expenses, displays in 32-point Times New Roman red, bold font. The chart subtitle, International Manufacturing, displays in 14-point Book Antiqua black font. The axes labels display in red 10-point Arial bold italic font. Change the segment color for series 3 to purple.

12. Save the spreadsheet and chart using the same filename as in step 8.

13. Print the chart in landscape orientation.

14. Using the numbers in the table to the right, analyze the effect of changing the assumptions in rows 18 through 22 on the half-yearly net income in cell H15. Print both the spreadsheet and chart for each case.

15. Follow directions from your instructor for turning in this assignment.

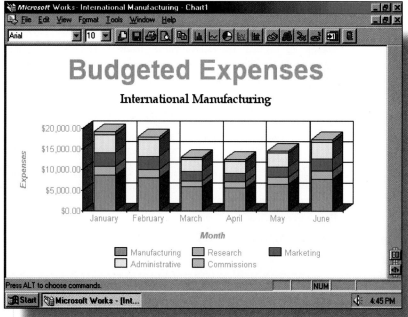

FIGURE 6-91

	CASE 1	CASE 2	CASE 3
Manufacturing	35%	37%	40%
Research	5%	7%	15%
Marketing	10%	12%	17
Administrative	15%	17%	20%
Commissions	3%	5%	5%

In the Lab

3 Creating a Six-Month Projections Report and a 3-D Stacked Bar Chart

Problem: Create a Six-Month Projections Report for On the Spot Printing. The calculations in the spreadsheet are dependent on the values contained in the Assumptions section of the spreadsheet. Create a 3-D Stacked Bar chart from the values in the spreadsheet. The spreadsheet is illustrated in Figure 6-92.

Instructions:

1. Create a spreadsheet in the format shown in Figure 6-92.
2. In the spreadsheet, calculate Copies Printed for January by entering Copies Printed in cell B16 in cell B5 (*Hint:* use =B16 as the formula in cell B5). Calculate the Copies Printed for February by multiplying Copies Printed in cell B5 by Increase in Copies Printed in cell B15. Copy cell B6 to the range B7:B10.
3. Calculate Copies Sold for January by multiplying the Copies Printed in cell B5 by the % Printed Sold in cell B17. Copy cell C5 to the range C6:C10.

FIGURE 6-92

	Microsoft Works - Projections Report				
A1		"On the Spot Printing			

	A	B	C	D	E	F
1	⊹	**On the Spot Printing**				
2		*Six-Month Projections Report*				
3						
4	**Date**	**Copies Printed**	**Copies Sold**	**Income**	**Expense**	**Net**
5	January	2,000	1,800	$1,800.00	$1,000.00	$800.00
6	February	2,200	1,980	$1,980.00	$1,100.00	$880.00
7	March	2,420	2,178	$2,178.00	$1,210.00	$968.00
8	April	2,662	2,396	$2,396.00	$1,331.00	$1,065.00
9	May	2,928	2,635	$2,635.00	$1,464.00	$1,171.00
10	June	3,221	2,899	$2,899.00	$1,610.50	$1,288.50
11	**Six Month Totals**	15,431	13,888	$13,888.00	$7,715.50	$6,172.50
12	**Assumptions**					
13	Price per Copy	$1.00				
14	Expense per Copy	$0.50				
15	Increase in Copies Printed	10.00%				
16	Copies Printed	2,000				
17	% Printed Sold	90.00%				
18						

4. Calculate Income for January by multiplying the Copies Sold in cell C5 by the Price per Copy in cell B13. Copy cell D5 to the range D6:D10.
5. Calculate Expense for January by multiplying the Copies Printed in cell B5 by the Expense per Copy in cell B14. Copy cell E5 to the range E6:E10.
6. Calculate Net for January by subtracting Expense in cell E5 from Income in cell D5. Copy cell F5 to the range F6:F10.
7. Calculate the six-month totals in row 11 by summing the values in the respective ranges.
8. Format the spreadsheet as shown. The widths for the columns are as follows: A = 23 and B through F = 11. Place a yellow border around the spreadsheet. Add a footer to the spreadsheet containing the current date centered on the report.
9. Save the spreadsheet you create on a floppy disk. Use the filename, Projections Report.
10. Print the spreadsheet you have created on a single page. Use print preview to ensure the spreadsheet will print on one page.

(continued)

In the Lab

Creating a Six Month Projections Report and a 3-D Stacked Bar Chart *(continued)*

11. Create the 3-D Stacked Bar chart shown in Figure 6-93 on the next page from the Income, Expenses, and Net values contained in the spreadsheet.

12. Format the 3-D Stacked Bar chart as shown in Figure 6-93. The chart title, Six-Month Projections Report, displays in 16-point Arial blue, bold font. The axes labels display in 12-point Times New Roman blue, bold font. Change the segment color for series 3 to purple.

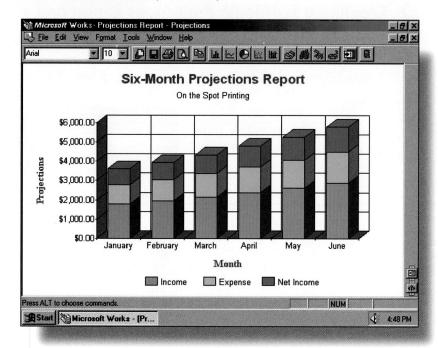

FIGURE 6-93

13. Save the spreadsheet and chart using the same file-name as in step 9.

14. Print the chart in landscape orientation.

15. Using the what-if capabilities of the spreadsheet, answer the following questions.

    a. If 2,000 copies are printed at $0.50 per copy and are sold at $1.00 each, what percentage of the copies printed must we sell to break even? (*Hint:* Break even occurs when the income is equal to the expenses; that is, the net is zero. In this question, you know three of the four variables (Price per Copy = $1.00; Expense per Copy = $0.50; Copies Printed = 2,000). To determine the % printed sold to break even, that is, to obtain a net of zero, you must enter different values in cell B17 until the net values in column F equal zero. Due to rounding discrepancies, June will not display a net of zero.

    b. If the expense per copy is $0.36, 2,000 copies are printed, and 45% of the copies are sold, at what price can the price per copy be and still break even?

    c. If the price per copy is $0.75, 2,000 copies are printed, and % printed sold is 40%, what can the maximum expense per copy be and still break even?

Cases and Places

The difficulty of the following case studies varies:

▶ Case studies preceded by a single half moon are the least difficult. You can create the required spreadsheet based on information that already has been placed in an organized form.

▶▶ Case studies preceded by two half moons are more difficult. You must organize the information presented before using it to create the desired spreadsheets.

▶▶▶ Case studies preceded by three half moons are the most difficult. You must obtain and organize the necessary information before using it to create the required spreadsheets.

1 ▶ Use the auto spreadsheet created in Case Study 1 of Project 4 for this assignment. Perform the following tasks using Figure 6-94 as a guide: (a) Change the heading of the second column from QUARTS OIL to 1 QUART OIL; (b) delete the data in this second column; (c) use the data in the 1 QUART OIL column in Figure 6-94 below to fill the second column; (d) insert a new column after this 1 QUART OIL column; (e) type the heading 5 QUARTS OIL in this new column; (f) calculate the cost of five quarts of oil in this new column by multiplying the 1 QUART OIL cost by 5; and (g) in the spreadsheet, compute the TOTAL COST by summing the 5 QUARTS OIL, OIL FILTER, and AIR FILTER columns.

TYPE OF RETAILER	1 QUART OIL	5 QUARTS OIL	OIL FILTER	AIR FILTER	TOTAL COST
Discount	$1.19		$2.50	$4.25	
Auto parts	$0.99		$2.88	$3.55	
Auto dealer	$1.50		$5.50	$6.95	
Mini-mart	$1.80		$7.00	$9.10	

FIGURE 6-94

2 ▶ Your college's student newspaper earns revenues from the sale of advertising space and from subscriptions. A fixed percentage of the proceeds is spent on marketing (20.75%), payroll (56.55%), commissions (2.25% of advertising sales), production costs (13.25%), and reporting expenses (3%). Your editor has summarized the paper's earnings during the past year on a bi-monthly basis (Figure 6-95).

With this data, prepare a spreadsheet for the editorial board's next meeting showing total revenues, total expenditures, and net incomes for each bi-monthly period. Include a chart that illustrates the net incomes. One board member wants to reduce marketing expenditures 3 percent and payroll costs 4 percent. Perform a what-if analysis reflecting the proposed changes in expenditure assumptions.

The Chronicle Bi-Monthly Earnings and Expenditures						
REVENUES:	FEBRUARY	APRIL	JUNE	AUGUST	OCTOBER	DECEMBER
Advertising	$2,500.78	$1,762.25	$2,134.56	$3,455.45	$2,987.95	$4,234.66
Subscriptions	$8,526.34	$8,526.34	$9,271.95	$12,082.14	$12,082.14	$9,721.63

FIGURE 6-95

Cases and Places

3 ▶▶ You want to send your daughter to a private school, but your income from doing freelance photography may not be sufficient to meet her tuition costs. You examine your job orders for the next six months — $5,000 in July, $5,850 in August, $3,760 in September, $6,240 in October, $6,430 in November, and $7,750 in December. Each month you spend 33.75% of the money for supplies, 2.5% for equipment, 6.25% for your retirement account, and 40% for food and clothing. The remaining profits (orders - expenses) are set aside for your child's education. You decide to create a spreadsheet that shows orders, expenses, and profits, for the next six months and totals for each category. Perform a what-if analysis to determine the effect of reducing the percent spent on supplies to 25%.

4 ▶▶ The owners of Candy Cane Lane, a local candy store, are revising their production figures. Business booms during six periods of the year: Valentine's Day (2,250 lbs. sold), Easter (1,950 lbs.), Mother's Day (1,150 lbs.), Father's Day (975 lbs.), Halloween (2,136 lbs.), and Christmas (1,750 lbs.). During these times, 28% of the store's output is fudge, 15% is taffy, 46% is boxed chocolate, and the remaining 11% is holiday-specific candy. The fudge sells for $6.25 per pound, the taffy for $1.15 per pound, the boxed chocolate for $5.75 per pound, and holiday-specific candy for $1.35 per pound. Create a spreadsheet the owners can use to determine optimum production levels. Show the amount of each candy produced on a holiday, potential sales for each type of candy, total potential sales for each holiday, total candy produced for the six holidays, and total potential sales for each type of candy.

5 ▶▶▶ In her will, your aunt left you stock in several computer companies. The stock is in three major categories: hardware (5,000 shares in Apple, 11,500 shares in Gateway 2000, 22,500 shares in IBM, and 7,000 shares in Intel), software (3,000 shares in Autodesk, 4,500 shares in Borland, 6,500 shares in Symantec, and 58,000 shares in Microsoft), and networking (2,500 shares in 3Com, 11,250 shares in Compaq, and 16,750 shares in Novell). Analysts expect these stocks to average a 5 percent return per year for a 10-year period. Using the latest stock prices, create a spreadsheet that organizes your computer stock portfolio and projects its annual value for the next 10 years. Group the companies by major categories, and include a total for each category.

6 ▶▶▶ Budgeting is a daunting task facing everyone from students to members of the U.S. Congress. Create and format a spreadsheet that reflects your monthly budget for the school year. Indicate the amount of money you have each month. Then hypothesize percentages for monthly expenditures (such as food, travel, and entertainment). Then, determine the expenditures for each month. Include a row for occasional expenses (such as books). Determine the amount of money remaining at the end of each month; this amount will become the money available for the subsequent month. Perform at least one what-if analysis to examine the effect of changing one or more of the spreadsheet values.

7 ▶▶▶ Freelance workers must monitor income and business expenses carefully to be profitable. Painters, landscapers, and consultants often work on a freelance basis. Interview someone who performs freelance work and create a spreadsheet reflecting on his or her profits during the past six months. Attempt to determine the percentage of the worker's income spent on business-related expenses. Ask the amount of occasional expenses incurred. With this information, determine the freelancer's expenses and profits for each of the six months. Include at least one chart that illustrates a significant aspect of the spreadsheet, such as the profits each month or the total amount applied to every business expense.

Microsoft Works 4

Windows 95

Using Form Design to Create a Database

You will have mastered the material in this project when you can:

▶ Define the elements of a database
▶ Start the Works Database tool
▶ Identify all elements on the Works Database screen
▶ Change a field size in form design view
▶ Correct errors when entering field names
▶ Save a database file
▶ Position fields in form design view
▶ Insert clip art into a form
▶ Enter a title in form design view using WordArt
▶ Format a title in form design view using WordArt
▶ Insert a rectangle into a form
▶ Add color to an object
▶ Format the field names in form design view
▶ Enter a text label in form design view
▶ Display the database in form view
▶ Enter text and numeric data into a database in form view
▶ Display the next record, previous record, first record, and last record in form view
▶ Display the database in list view
▶ Format the database in list view
▶ Change font size in list view
▶ Set field widths in list view
▶ Print the database in both list view and form view

A Thorough Search for the Right Mate

*Thoroughbred Database
Worth Millions to
Matchmaker*

What is the world coming to when Thoroughbred horses depend on computers for a date? Barry Weisbord of Lexington, Kentucky — known as the Matchmaker to the Horsey Set—parlayed an enthusiasm for the race track into a business that did $61 million in trading the first year. He pioneered the use of computer databases and sophisticated statistical software to virtually control the breeding of Thoroughbreds. At his company's black-tie auctions, bidders compete for the right to breed mares to top Thoroughbred studs. At stake are the rights to gene pools that go back twenty-four generations, to the mid-1600s.

This is just one example of the numerous business, scientific, and personal databases that help people organize and process the mountains of information modern society collects. A computer database, such as one developed using the Microsoft Works Database tool, is a catalog of information about a

THOROUGHBRED

particular subject: people, space programs, sales, books, movies, and so on. Using the computer's speed, data on a subject can be rapidly sorted according to different characteristics to find common denominators; say, all the movies directed by John Huston in which he also had an acting role. The more information about a given subject, the more useful a database becomes.

From keeping track of names, addresses, and phone numbers to creating a personal inventory of books, CDs, and videos, managing information is as important for students as for businesses. To make it easier to get started, Microsoft Works Database TaskWizards provide preprogrammed layouts, called templates. Among the many TaskWizards available are Address Book, Phone List, Loan Analysis, Schedule (classes and activities), and Student & Membership Information (club and team rosters). All you must do is simply add data.

Besides the many home and personal applications, databases are used for a multitude of business and scientific functions. Some databases keep track of genetic factors that aid in developing new disease-fighting drugs. Others organize satellite data for use in oil exploration or receive information from point-of-sale transactions that help refine retail merchandising. Still others track demographics and buying patterns to enhance consumer marketing.

As the world expands into the era of connectivity via the Internet and private networks, information sharing is now more flexible than ever. With the concept of distributed databases, individuals or groups can physically hold the storage medium where the information is kept, but anyone, anywhere, can access and use — even update — the data. Numerous data storage locations, often separated by thousands of miles, also can be linked electronically to form a single virtual database.

Behind the scenes, computer databases assume greater importance every day in the management of government, business, science, and personal activities. For those who know how to use them, databases can be the Thoroughbreds they ride to success on the information superhighway.

DEMOGRAPHICS

Project 7

Microsoft
Works 4
Windows 95

Case Perspective

The RSC Sports and Fitness Centers has grown rapidly as an expert in the field of exercise and health fitness providing state-of-the-art workout and health fitness facilities. The management has asked you to design and create a database of current members belonging to the facilities.

The information for the database can be found in the Membership department of the RSC Sports and Fitness Centers. Leanne Barchucci, assistant director of membership, maintains current information on all members. You have been asked to design and then create a database to hold information on each member of the centers. Leanne has requested an attractively designed database form that can be used to enter member information.

You are to analyze the data available on each member and create a database of all current members at the RSC Sports and Fitness Centers. Once the database is designed, you are to enter the information for each member in the database.

Using Form Design to Create a Database

Introduction

In Projects 1 and 2, you have used the Microsoft Works Word Processor and Spreadsheet tools. In this project, you will be learning about and using the Database tool.

The Works Database tool allows you to create, store, sort, and retrieve data. Many people record data such as the names, addresses, and telephone numbers of friends and business associates, records of investments, and records of expenses for income tax purposes. These records must be arranged so the data can be accessed easily when required.

The term **database** describes a collection of data organized in a manner that allows access, retrieval, and use of that data. The Works Database tool allows you to create a database; add, delete, and change data in the database; sort the data in the database; retrieve the data in the database; and create reports using the data in the database.

Project Seven

Project 7 shows you how to create a database using Microsoft Works. The database created in this project is shown in Figure 7-1. This database contains information about members belonging to the RSC Sports and Fitness Centers. The information for each member is stored in a record. A **record** contains all the information for a given person, product, or event. For example, the first record in the database contains information about Mr. Nimiira A. Sanji.

fields

DATE JOINED	TITLE	FIRST NAME	M.I.	LAST NAME	ADDRESS	CITY	STATE	ZIP	OCCUPATION	TYPE	CHARGE	DUES	KIDS CENTER
5/12/96	Mr.	Nimiira	A.	Sanji	79 Fuller	Orange	CA	92667	Teacher	Executive	Y	$120.00	$12.50
5/12/96	Dr.	Albert	G.	Sandler	26 Irning	Yuma	AZ	85364	Doctor	Family	Y	$89.00	$12.50
5/15/96	Ms.	Midge	W.	Maclone	94 Bourne	Placentia	CA	92670	Attorney	Single	N	$45.00	$12.50
5/15/96	Dr.	Edward	R.	Guen	170 Tremont	Irvine	CA	92715	Doctor	Family	N	$89.00	
5/17/96	Mr.	Rubin	E.	Gordon	1539 Centre	Yorba Linda	CA	92686	Teacher	Family	Y	$89.00	$12.50
5/25/96	Mr.	Ivan	I.	Fenton	228 Seaver	Irvine	CA	92715	Accountant	Single	Y	$45.00	$12.50
5/26/96	Mr.	David	L.	Dirsa	47 Concord	Orange	CA	92667	Salesrep	Student	Y	$35.00	
5/31/96	Mr.	Julian	P.	Coulon	216 Summer	Tustin	CA	92680	Teacher	Family	Y	$89.00	
6/1/96	Mr.	Jacob	W.	Chase	35 Chilton	Fullerton	CA	92635	Salesrep	Student	Y	$35.00	$12.50
6/1/96	Mrs.	Michele	Q.	Bovie	14 St. Lukes	Irvine	CA	92715	Accountant	Family	Y	$89.00	
6/3/96	Mr.	Stefano	U.	Branchi	58 Sullivan	Orange	CA	92667	Accountant	Family	Y	$89.00	
6/6/96	Mr.	Antonio	V.	Alonso	2468 Allston	Tustin	CA	92680	Teacher	Single	N	$45.00	$12.50
6/10/96	Mr.	Gabriel	A.	Vidal	40 Concord	Reno	NV	89503	Nurse	Executive	Y	$120.00	
6/12/96	Ms.	Olivia	D.	Brown	4 Hyde Park	Orange	CA	92667	Teacher	Student	Y	$35.00	
6/12/96	Ms.	Cathy	E.	Wain	520 Beacon	Santa Ana	CA	92705	Nurse	Single	Y	$45.00	$12.50
6/13/96	Dr.	Bei	F.	Wu	205 Kent	Santa Ana	CA	92705	Teacher	Executive	Y	$120.00	$12.50

records

FIGURE 7-1

A record consists of a series of fields. A **field** contains a specific piece of information within a record. For example, in the database shown in Figure 7-1, the first field is the Date Joined field, which contains the date on which the person joined. The Title field identifies the person as Mr., Mrs., Ms., or Dr. The First Name, M.I., and Last Name fields contain the first name, middle initital, and last name of each of the members.

The remaining fields in each of the records are:

1. Address: Street address of the member.
2. City: City in which the member lives.
3. State: State in which the member lives.
4. Zip: Zip code of the member's city.
5. Occupation: The occupation of the member.
6. Type: The type of membership held by the member. Four memberships are available – Student, Single, Family, and Executive.
7. Charge: Specifies whether the member has been approved to charge food and merchandise in the center on his account. If a member has charge privileges, this field will contain a Y, otherwise the field contains an N.
8. Dues: The monthly amount paid by each member for the use of the exercise and health facility.
9. Kids Center: The additional monthly amount paid by each member for the use of the Kids Center while at the center.

Each of these fields contains information for each member record. Thus, for record one, the member's first name is Nimiira, the middle initial is A., the last name is Sanji, he lives at 79 Fuller, Orange, CA. In record two, the First Name field contains Albert, the middle initial contains G., and the Last Name field contains Sandler. Dr. Sandler lives in Yuma, AZ, has a family membership on which he has charge privileges. He pays $89 a month for the use of the facility and $12.50 a month for the use of the Kids Center.

It is important you understand that a record consists of one or more fields. When you define the database, you will define each field within a record. After you define the fields, you can enter data for as many records as are required in your database.

Creating a Database

The following tasks will be completed in this project to create the database shown in Figure 7-1 on the previous page.

1. Start Microsoft Works and choose the Database tool.
2. Enter the field names and field formats required for the database. This step results in the database structure.
3. Change the size of fields in form design view, in which a single record displays on the screen.
4. Position the fields in form design view.
5. Save the database structure.
6. Insert clip art in the title area of the form. Enter the title, RSC Sports and Fitness Centers, and format the title with special effects. Place a thin rectangular bar beneath the clip art and title in the form.
7. Color the title and the thin rectangle beneath the title. Place a color border around the field entries.
8. Enter the text labels, MEMBER INFORMATION and ACCOUNT INFORMATION, as identifying labels to the sections of each member's record. Format the text labels.
9. Enter the data for the records in the database in form view.
10. Save the database with the data you have entered.
11. Switch to list view where the entire database displays on the screen.
12. Format the database in list view.
13. Print the database in form view.
14. Print the database in list view.

The following pages contain a detailed explanation of these tasks and terms.

Starting Microsoft Works

To start Microsoft Works, follow the steps you have used in the first two projects to open the Microsoft Works Task Launcher dialog box (Figure 7-2). This step is summarized on the next page.

More *About*
Creating a Database

To create a database quickly, the TaskWizards listed on the Works Task Launcher can be used. For example, the Address Book, Phone List, Employee Profile, and Business Inventory are wizard-generated databases that step the user through the creation of predesigned forms based on the Database tool. Database wizards are identified in the TaskWizards window by the Cards icon that displays to the left of the wizard name.

TO START MICROSOFT WORKS

Step 1: Click the Start button on the taskbar, click Programs, point to the Microsoft Works 4.0 folder on the Programs submenu, point to Microsoft Works 4.0 on the Microsoft Works 4.0 submenu, and then click Microsoft Works 4.0. When the Works Task Launcher dialog box displays, click the Works Tools tab and point to the Database button.

The Microsoft Works application program opens and the Works Task Launcher dialog box displays on the screen (Figure 7-2). The mouse pointer points to the Database button on the Works Tools sheet.

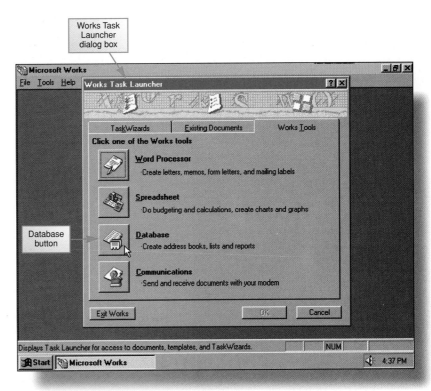

FIGURE 7-2

You have now started Works and are ready to use the Database tool.

Creating a Database

The next step is to start the Microsoft Works Database tool. When you start the Microsoft Works Database tool, Works opens the Create Database dialog box where you add fields to create your database. Each field has a format that indicates the type of data that can be stored in the field. The formats you will use in this project are:

1. **Text** – The field can contain any characters.

2. **Number** – The field can contain only numbers. Fields are assigned this type so they can be used in arithmetic operations. Fields that contain numbers but will not be used for arithmetic operations are usually assigned a format of Text. The Dues field and Kids Center field contain numbers and are assigned the Number format. The values in these fields display with dollar signs and decimal points.

3. **Date** – The field can contain text or numbers in a recognizable date format, such as 05/12/96 or May 12, 1996. The Date Joined field is assigned the Date format.

The field names and field formats are shown in Table 7-1.

**More *About*
Database Formats**

When assigning formats to fields that contain numbers but will not be used for arithmetic operations, use the Text format. For example, a zip code field should be assigned the Text format because zip codes will not be involved in any arithmetic. Also, zip codes that begin with zero must be assigned the Text format. Otherwise, the zip code 01075 will turn into 1075. Zip codes and phone numbers that include hyphens cannot use the Number format either.

TABLE-7-1			
FIELD NAME	*FIELD FORMAT*	*FIELD NAME*	*FIELD FORMAT*
Date Joined	Date	State	Text
Title	Text	Zip	Text
First Name	Text	Occupation	Text
M.I.	Text	Type	Text
Last Name	Text	Dues	Number
Address	Text	Charge	Text
City	Text	Kids Center	Number

To create the database, perform the following steps.

Steps: To Create a Database

1 **Click the Database button on the Works Tools sheet. If the First-time Help dialog box displays, click the To create a new database button.**

Works displays a blank database document containing the database name, Unsaved Database 1, within the Microsoft Works application window (Figure 7-3). Works displays the Create Database dialog box in front of the database window. The default name for the first field in the database, Field 1, displays highlighted in the Field name text box.

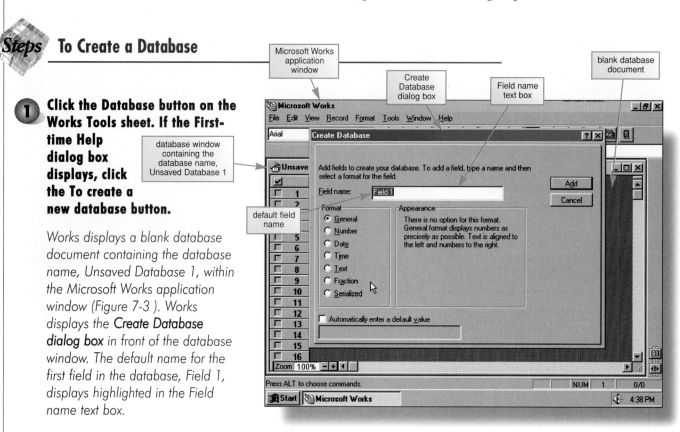

FIGURE 7-3

2 **Type** Date Joined **in the Field name text box. Click Date in the Format box. Verify the first date format is highlighted in the Appearance list. Then point to the Add button.**

Works displays the field name you typed in the Field name text box (Figure 7-4). When you click Date in the Format box, Works displays the Appearance box with a list of available formats for a date. The current date in the MM/DD/YY format is highlighted in the Appearance list. The mouse pointer points to the Add button.

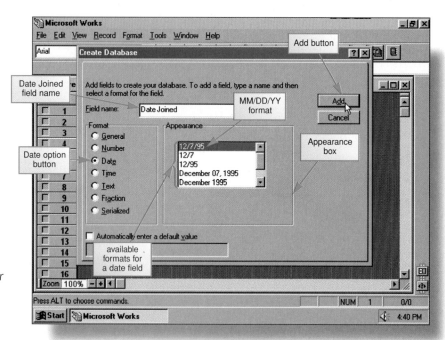

FIGURE 7-4

3 **Click the Add button in the Create Database dialog box. Type** Title **in the Field name text box. Click Text in the Format box. Then point to the Add button.**

When you click the Add button, Works adds the first field, Date Joined, to the database document located behind the Create Database dialog box (Figure 7-5). The Create Database dialog box remains on the screen, ready to accept another field definition. The second field name you typed, Title, displays in the Field name text box. The Text option button is selected, indicating any characters, symbols, or numbers can be entered in the field. Works displays information on the Text format in the Appearance box. The mouse pointer points to the Add button.

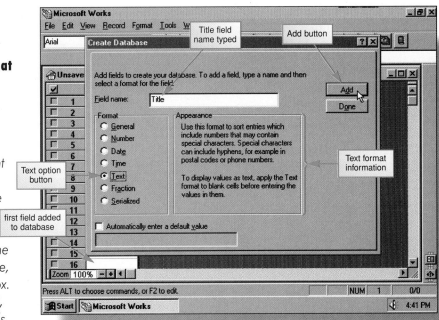

FIGURE 7-5

4 **Click the Add button to enter the Title field. Repeat Step 3 above to enter the field names for First Name, M.I., Last Name, Address, and City in the Create Database dialog box using the format specified previously in Table 7-1 on page W 7.7. Then, type** State **in the Field name text box. Click Text in the Format box. Click Automatically enter a default value located below the Format box. Type** CA **in the Automatically enter a default value text box. Then point to the Add button.**

Works adds the fields for Title, First Name, M.I., Last Name, Address, and City to the database document located behind the Create Database dialog box (Figure 7-6). The

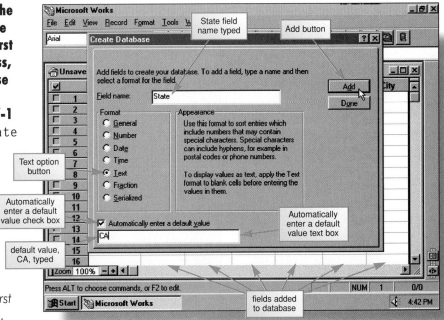

FIGURE 7-6

field name, State, displays in the Field name text box. The Text option button is selected. A check mark displays in the Automatically enter a default value check box. This instructs Works to automatically enter the value you typed in the Automatically enter a default value text box in this field for every record. The mouse pointer points to the Add button.

5 **Click the Add button in the Create Database dialog box. Enter the field names for Zip, Occupation, and Type in the Create Database dialog box using the format specified previously in Table 7-1 on page W 7.7. Then, type** Dues **in the Field name text box. Click Number in the Format box. Click $1,234.56 in the Appearance list. Verify the number 2 displays in the Decimal places list box. Point to the Add button.**

Works adds the State, Zip, Occupation, and Type fields to the database. The field name, Dues, displays in the Field name text box (Figure 7-7). When you click Number in the Format box, Works displays the Appearance box with

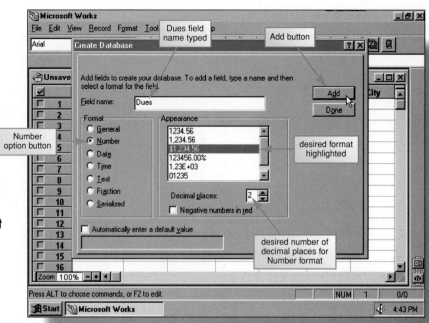

FIGURE 7-7

a list of available formats for a number. The $1,234.56 format is highlighted in the Appearance list. The value 2 displays in the Decimal places list box. This format instructs Works to add a dollar sign, a comma every three digits to the left of the decimal point, and two decimal places to a number. The mouse pointer points to the Add button.*

6 **Click the Add button in the Create Database dialog box. Type** Charge **in the Create Database dialog box, click Text in the Format box, click the Add button. Then, type** Kids Center **in the Field name text box. Click Number in the Format box. Verify $1,234.56 in the Appearance list is highlighted. Verify the number 2 displays in the Decimal places list box. Point to the Add button.**

Works adds the Charge field to the database. The field name, Kids Center, displays in the Field name text box (Figure 7-8). The $1,234.56 format is highlighted in the Appearance list. The mouse pointer points to the Add button.

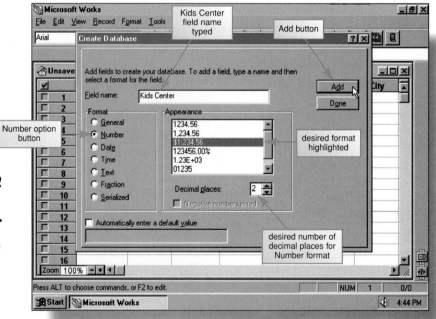

FIGURE 7-8

7 Click the Add button in the Create Database dialog box. When Works displays Field 15 in the Field name text box, point to the Done button.

Works adds the Kids Center field to the database. The default field name, Field 15, displays in the Field name text box (Figure 7-9). The mouse pointer points to the Done button.

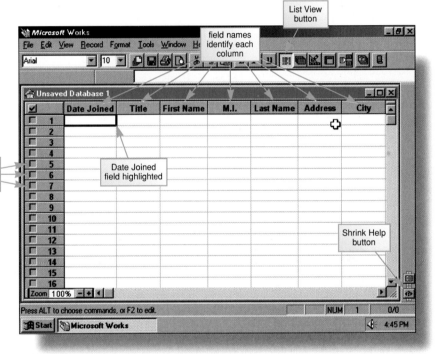

FIGURE 7-9

8 Click the Done button in the Create Database dialog box. If the Help window displays, click the Shrink Help button to minimize the window.

*Works closes the Create Database dialog box and displays the records in the database in a grid that resembles a spreadsheet (Figure 7-10). The screen in Figure 7-10 is presented in **list view**, which allows you to view multiple records at the same time. The field names identify each column and the record numbers identify each row. The Date Joined field for record 1 is highlighted by a dark border around the field. Only the first seven fields display on the screen. Use the scroll arrows, scroll*

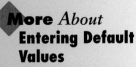

FIGURE 7-10

boxes, or scroll bars to view the additional fields. The toolbar contains six new buttons on the right side of the toolbar. These buttons are explained as they are used. The List View button is light gray and is recessed, indicating the screen is showing the database in list view.

You should note several points when entering the fields for a database. First, choose the field names with care so they reflect the contents of the field. In all subsequent uses of the database, you will refer to the data in the fields by these names, so it is important to be able to easily identify the contents of the fields. The maximum number of characters in a field name is fifteen characters, including spaces and punctuation. A field name can contain any character except a single quotation mark. You can enter up to 256 fields into your database.

More *About*
Entering Default Values

Using a default value in any field in a database that contains identical information saves time entering the data. However, the default value will not appear until you enter data in at least one other field in the record.

Second, if you make an error while typing a field name in the Create Database dialog box, you can correct the error by backspacing to remove the error and then type the correct characters. If you notice an error in a field name in list view, click any cell in the column that contains the incorrect field name. Then click Field on the Format menu and enter the correct field name in the Format dialog box. Click the OK button in the Format dialog box and Works will change the field name.

Saving the Database

Once you have defined the database by specifying all the field names, normally you should save your work so an accidental loss of power does not destroy it. To save your work on a floppy disk in drive A using the filename RSC Members, complete the following steps.

TO SAVE THE DATABASE

Step 1: Click the Save button on the toolbar.
Step 2: Type the filename, RSC Members, in the File name text box in the Save As dialog box.
Step 3: If necessary, click the 3½ Floppy [A:] icon in the Save in drop-down list box.
Step 4: Click the Save button in the Save As dialog box.

Works will save the file on the floppy disk in drive A and will place the name, RSC Members, in the title bar of the Works window.

Form Design View

After you have entered the field names into the database, the next step is to position the fields on a form so they are easy to read and use. You use the form design view to arrange fields on a form. **Form design view** is a database view in which you position fields on a form, insert graphics, or customize the form by adding color, labels, and borders. The final form design view of the database in this project is shown in Figure 7-11. Notice that each of the fields in the database is arranged on the page for ease of reading.

Four different elements are displayed in the form shown in Figure 7-11. The first is a clip art display of a tennis player in the upper left corner of the form. The second element contains the words, RSC Sports and Fitness Centers. RSC Sports and Fitness Centers is the name of the sports and fitness club. The words, RSC Sports and Fitness Centers, were created using a Works accessory called WordArt. **WordArt** allows you to display words on a database form in a variety of shapes and styles. You also may display a title on a database form using the standard fonts available as part of Works. In database terminology, when using standard font styles, the title would be called a **text label**. MEMBER INFORMATION and ACCOUNT INFORMATION shown in Figure 7-11 are text labels. A dark blue rectangle displays below the clip art and WordArt.

The third element on the form is the field name. A **field name** distinguishes a field from all other fields in the database. For example, in Figure 7-11, you can see that the field containing the date joined is called Date Joined, the field name for title is Title, the field for the first name is First Name, and so on. A field name always ends with a colon (:). In form design view, you can format each of the field names in a style that makes the form easy to read. In the database for Project 7, each of the field names displays in bold and italics.

The fourth element on the form is the field entry. A field entry is the actual data in the field. In Figure 7-11, the field entry for the Date Joined field is 5/12/96. The field entry for the Title field is Mr., the field entry for the First Name field is Nimiira, and so on. Field entries can contain any characters you wish and can be a maximum of 256 characters. By default, Works assigns a field width of 20 to each field. The default font is Times New Roman and the default point size is 12.

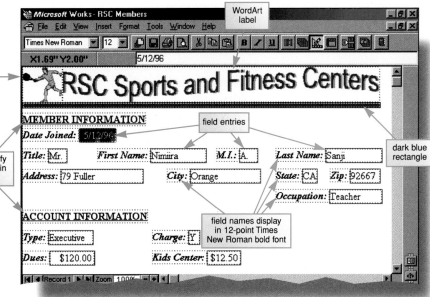

FIGURE 7-11

Notice that dotted lines display around all elements in form design view. This indicates you can select the elements for editing or change their locations on the form. In Figure 7-11, the field entry for Date Joined is highlighted, indicating it is selected. Three square handles display on the corners of the selected area. You can select the field name and the field entry area separately in form design view.

An important design decision is to determine the width of the field. You want the field to be large enough to contain the largest field entry but no larger. In most cases, you will be able to determine the proper width based on the maximum number of characters in the field entry, but the field width you specify when defining the field will not always correspond to the number of characters actually in the field because many fonts, such as Times New Roman, use variable-width characters. For example, when using 12-point Times New Roman, to place twenty letter i's in a field requires a width of 10, while placing twenty letter m's in a field requires a width of 37. If you use a font with a fixed width for each character, such as Courier New, then the width you choose will correspond exactly to the number of characters in the field. When you choose the width, estimate as closely as you can while remembering you can easily change the width of a field at a later time.

The field widths for the form design view of the database in Project 7 are shown in Table 7-2.

TABLE 7-2			
FIELD NAME	*FIELD WIDTH*	*FIELD NAME*	*FIELD WIDTH*
Date Joined	10	State	4
Title	5	Zip	8
First Name	15	Occupation	14
M.I.	5	Type	12
Last Name	15	Dues	12
Address	22	Charge	3
City	19	Kids Center	9

Formatting the Database Form in Form Design View

After you have entered the field names, the next step is to format the form so it is easy to read and use. You use the form design view of the database to format the form. Because someone may have to enter thousands of records into the database, the form should be easy to read and use.

Formatting the form consists of a number of separate tasks. The first is to change the margins of the form in form design view. The next task is to change the size of the fields. Then the fields are positioned on the form. Next you are to insert clip art in the title area; type, position, and format the title, RSC Sports and Fitness Centers, on the database form; place a border below the title; and add color in the title area. You then must change the style of the field names. The final step is to add a border around the field entries. Figure 7-11 on the previous page illustrates the form for Project 7 after formatting. The technique for formatting is explained on the following pages.

Displaying the Database in Form Design View

The first step in formatting the form is to display the database in form design view. Perform the following steps to display the database in form design view.

Steps To Display the Database in Form Design View

1 Point to the Form Design button on the toolbar.

The mouse pointer points to the Form Design button on the toolbar (Figure 7-12).

FIGURE 7-12

2 Click the Form Design button on the toolbar. Then, click the Maximize button in the database window.

Works displays the database in form design view (Figure 7-13). The field names you entered display on the form. Notice that the Charge field and Kids Center field do not display on the screen. You can use the scroll arrows, scroll buttons, and scroll bars to move around the database form.

FIGURE 7-13

Other Ways

1. On View menu, click Form Design
2. Press CTRL+F9

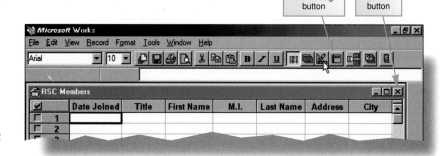

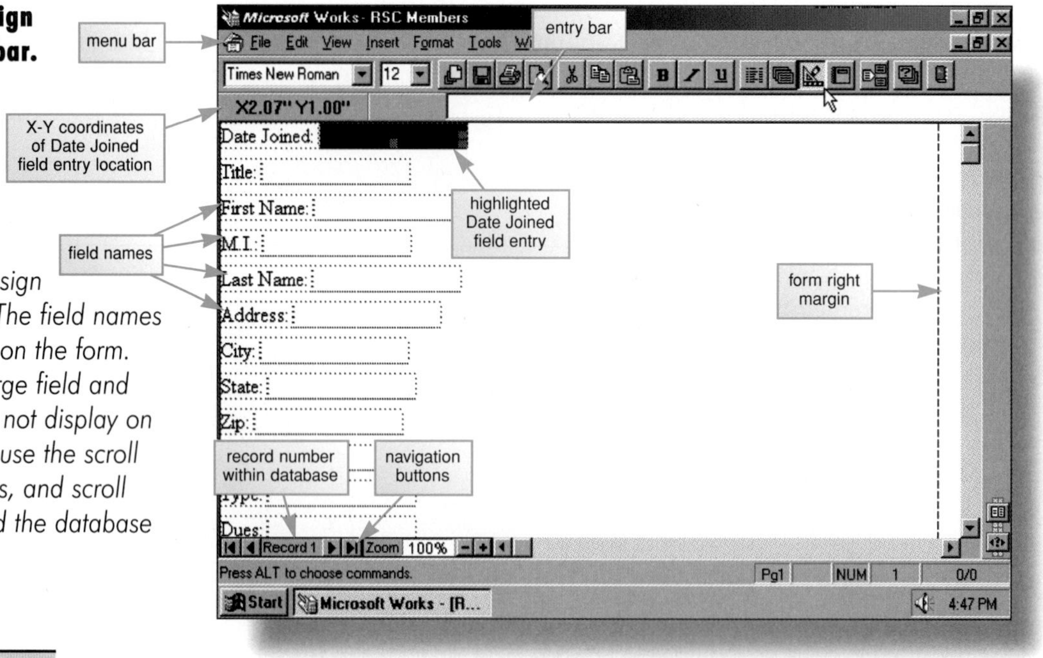

Although you can see in Figure 7-13 that the database window appears much the same as the word processing window and the spreadsheet window, some important differences are present. These differences are noted below.

MENU BAR The **menu bar** in the Works Database is the same as the menu bar in the Spreadsheet. The menu names are: File, Edit, View, Insert, Format, Tools, Window, and Help. Most of the Database menus, however, contain additional or different commands from the corresponding Works Spreadsheet menu. These commands are explained as they are used.

TOOLBAR The **toolbar** contains many of the same buttons as the Word Processor and Spreadsheet toolbars; however, the Database toolbar also contains a number of unique buttons on the right side of the toolbar. These buttons are explained as they are used. In Figure 7-13, the Form Design button is light gray and is recessed, indicating the screen is showing the database in form design view.

ENTRY BAR The Database **entry bar** functions in much the same manner as the Spreadsheet entry bar. When you type an entry into the database, the entry will display in the entry bar. The X and Y values shown in Figure 7-13 indicate the **X-Y coordinates** of the highlighted field on the screen. The X value specifies the number of inches from the left edge of the form. The Y value specifies the number of inches from the top of the form. In Figure 7-13, the X coordinate is 2.07" and the Y coordinate is 1.00". This means the field entry for Date Joined is located 2.07 inches from the left edge of the form and 1.00 inches from the top of the form.

RIGHT MARGIN MARKER The **right-margin marker** is the dashed vertical line down the right side of the screen in Figure 7-13. It marks the right margin on the form. The default margin setting is 1.25 inches on the right of the form.

SCROLL BAR The **scroll bar**, in addition to the normal scroll arrows, scroll box, and scroll bar, contains navigation buttons and a Zoom box. You use **navigation buttons** to move from record to record. The function of each of the buttons is described in Figure 7-14. The use of these buttons with a loaded database will be illustrated later.

The Zoom box is located to the right of the navigation buttons. The **Zoom box** controls how much of the record displays at one time in the database window. Clicking the Zoom box displays a list of available zoom percentages to magnify or reduce your database on the screen. You also can use the plus or minus buttons next to the Zoom box to control the display. To magnify your display, click the plus button. To reduce your display, click the minus button.

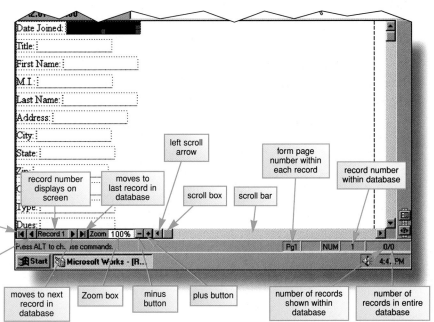

FIGURE 7-14

STATUS BAR   The **status bar** contains information regarding the database and the record currently displayed on the screen (see Figure 7-14 on the previous page). The entry Pg1 indicates that the screen shows page 1 of the record on the screen. In some instances, a record may consist of more than one form page. Works allows a maximum of eight pages to a record. The entry 1 following the NUM indicator indicates that record number 1 in the database is displayed on the screen. The next value, a number 0 (zero) separated from another number 0 (zero) by a slash (0/0), specifies the number of records currently available for display in the database and the total number of records stored in the database. Works allows a maximum of 32,000 records in a database.

Changing Form Margins

In this project, you must increase the area into which you will enter data to create the form shown in Figure 7-11 on page W 7.13. This requires setting the left and right margin to .75 inch each. To change the margins on the database form, perform the following steps.

Steps **To Change the Margins on the Database Form**

① **Click File on the menu bar and then point to Page Setup (Figure 7-15).**

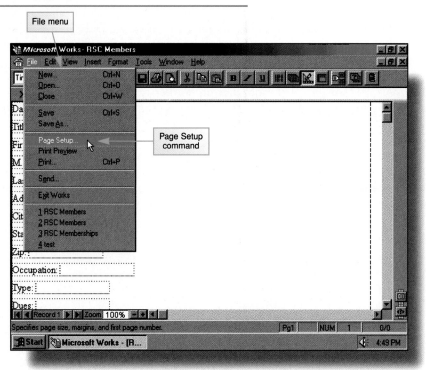

FIGURE 7-15

2 Click Page Setup. When the Page Setup dialog box displays, ensure the Margins sheet displays on screen. Change the Left margin to .75 and the Right margin to .75. Point to the OK button.

Works displays the Page Setup dialog box (Figure 7-16). The left and right margins have been changed to .75 and the mouse pointer points to the OK button.

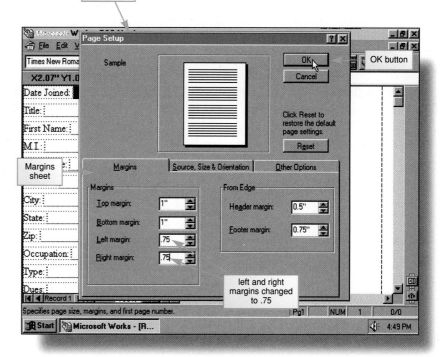

FIGURE 7-16

3 Click the OK button in the Page Setup dialog box.

The Works database form design view document screen displays (Figure 7-17). The dotted right margin line is not visible because of the change in margins. Works also has moved the default X–Y coordinates of the Date Joined field entry to the new location of X1.57" Y1.00".

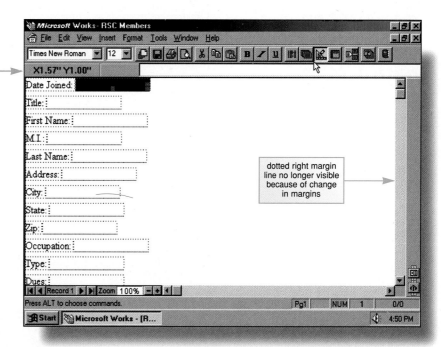

FIGURE 7-17

Setting Field Widths

The next step in formatting the form is to set the field widths for each of the fields in form design view. Table 7-2 on page W 7.13 shows the field widths for the form design view of the database. Perform the steps on the next two pages to set the field widths.

More *About*
Field Widths and Heights

In form view, the field width can be between 1 and 325 characters and the field height can be between 1 and 325 lines. When a field's height is more than one line, Works wraps the text to the next line when the text is longer than the field's width.

Steps   To Set Field Widths in Form Design View

1 **Click the Date Joined field entry. Click Format on the menu bar. When the Format menu displays, point to Field Size.**

The Date Joined field entry is highlighted (Figure 7-18). Works displays the Format menu and the mouse pointer points to the Field Size command.

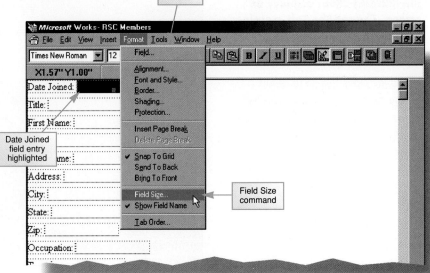

FIGURE 7-18

2 **Click Field Size. When the Format Field Size dialog box displays, type 10 in the Width text box. Point to the OK button.**

Works displays the Format Field Size dialog box (Figure 7-19). The value 10, which is the new field size, displays in the Width text box. The mouse pointer points to the OK button.

FIGURE 7-19

3 **Click the OK button in the Format Field Size dialog box.**

Works changes the width of the Date Joined field entry to 10 (Figure 7-20).

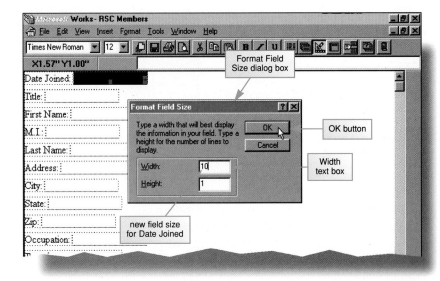

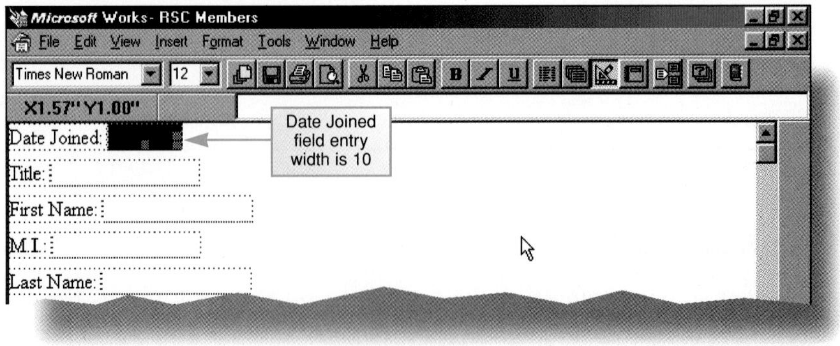

FIGURE 7-20

4 Using the techniques shown in Steps 1 through 3, set the remainder of the field entries to their proper widths as specified in Table 7-2 on page W 7.13.

The field entry widths are set to their new sizes (Figure 7-21). Notice that the Date Joined, Title, and First Name fields have scrolled off the screen.

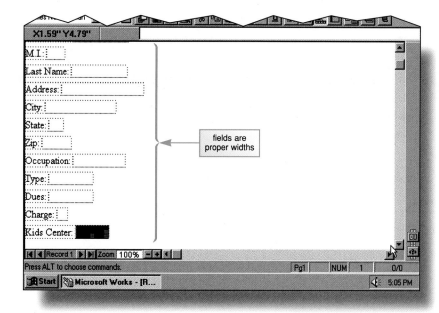

FIGURE 7-21

Positioning Fields on the Form

The first task of positioning the fields in the proper location requires that you determine **X-Y coordinates** for each of the fields. You can do this by dragging the field names and field entries to various locations until you are satisfied with their placement on the form. The coordinates in Table 7-3 are specified to assist in illustrating the technique of dragging fields in form design view. They were determined after moving the fields into various locations and then finally deciding on the best form layout. These locations can be modified at a later time, as will be seen when the clip art and form title are entered and formatted.

Perform the steps beginning on the next page to position the fields on the form.

More *About* Positioning Fields on a Form

When positioning fields on a form consider which fields are always filled and which fields are seldom filled. Entering data is faster and more efficient if the user doesn't need to press the TAB key to skip over seldom-used fields. Group the most-often-used fields together at the top of the form.

TABLE 7-3		
FIELD NAME	*X COORDINATE*	*Y COORDINATE*
Date Joined	X0.75″	Y1.00″
Title	X0.75″	Y1.33″
First Name	X2.00″	Y1.33″
M.I.	X4.00″	Y1.33″
Last Name	X5.00″	Y1.33″
Address	X0.75″	Y1.67″
City	X3.17″	Y1.67″
State	X 5.00″	Y1.67″
Zip	X 5.92″	Y1.67″
Occupation	X5.00″	Y2.00″
Type	X0.75″	Y2.67″
Dues	X0.75″	Y3.00″
Charge	X2.92″	Y2.67″
Kids Center	X2.92″	Y3.00″

Steps **To Position Fields on the Form**

1 **Scroll the screen up so the Date Joined field is visible. Highlight the Last Name field name by clicking the words Last Name.**

Works highlights the Last Name field name with a dark background and the block arrow mouse pointer displays with the word DRAG below it (Figure 7-22). You often will find it easier to move fields out of sequence. The Last Name field is moved in this step because it occupies the rightmost position on the second line of the form.

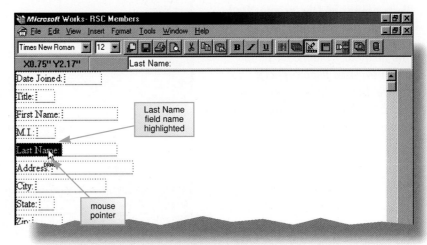

FIGURE 7-22

2 **Drag the Last Name field toward its location.**

As you drag the field, Works displays a dotted outline of both the field name and the field itself (Figure 7-23). The word MOVE displays under the mouse pointer. The coordinates of the outline are changed as you drag the outline. The field you drag remains highlighted and does not move while you drag.

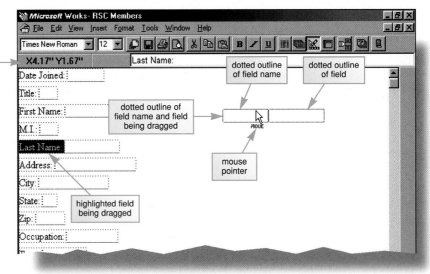

FIGURE 7-23

3 **When the dotted outline is at the desired location (X5.00″ Y1.33″), release the left mouse button.**

Works moves the highlighted field to the location of the dotted outline (Figure 7-24). After being moved, the field name remains highlighted.

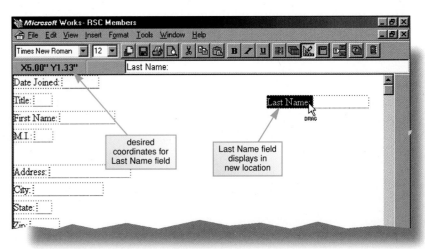

FIGURE 7-24

4 Using the same technique, move the M.I. field to coordinates X4.00" Y1.33", the First Name field to coordinates X2.00" Y1.33", and the Title field to coordinates X0.75" Y1.33".

The fields are moved to the prescribed locations (Figure 7-25). Each of the fields is on the same line (Y coordinate 1.33").

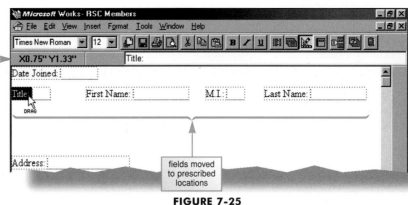

FIGURE 7-25

5 Drag the Zip, State, City, Address, and Occupation fields to their proper locations, as specified in Table 7-3 on page W 7.19.

Each of the fields is positioned in its proper location (Figure 7-26).

FIGURE 7-26

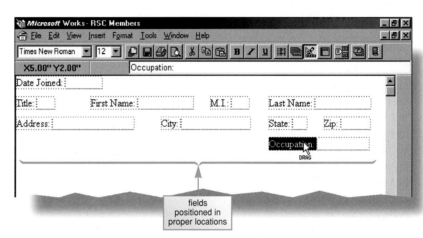

6 Use the down scroll arrow to view the remaining fields. Drag the remaining fields to their proper locations as specified in Table 7-3. Scroll up to view all fields in their proper locations.

All the fields are positioned in their proper locations (Figure 7-27).

FIGURE 7-27

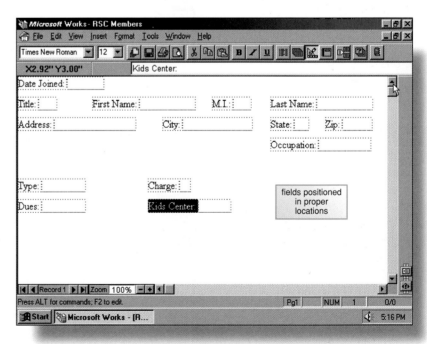

OtherWays

1. On Edit menu, click Position Selection

You should note that even after arranging the fields in the form, at any time you can move the fields to make the form more attractive and easier to read.

Moving the Field Names as a Unit

You must make room at the top of the form because the clip art will be inserted in the top left corner of the form and the title will be entered and increased in size and formatted using WordArt. The title will occupy an area approximately one inch at the top of the form. Below the title, you also will insert a bar and a text label to identify the information located after the label. To provide for this area at the top of the form, move the field names down approximately one inch. To move the field names down as a unit on the form, perform the following steps.

Steps **To Move Field Names as a Unit**

1 Scroll up and click the Date Joined field name. Hold down the CTRL key and click the Title field name. Continue this process until all fields on the database form are highlighted. Release the CTRL key.

All fields are highlighted on the form (Figure 7-28).

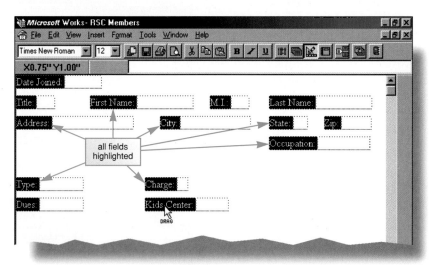

FIGURE 7-28

2 Click the Date Joined field name and drag all fields down by dragging the Date Joined field down.

After you highlight all field names, dragging a single field name will drag all field names as a unit (Figure 7-29).

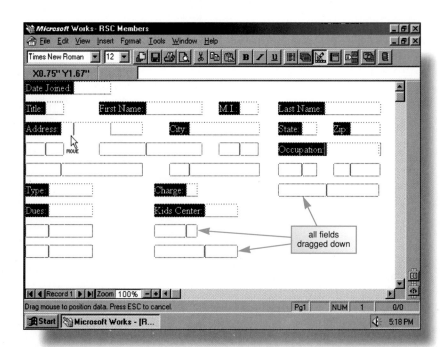

FIGURE 7-29

3 **When the coordinates are X0.75″ Y2.00″, release the left mouse button.**

The fields are repositioned on the database form (Figure 7-30). The Date Joined field is positioned at coordinates X0.75″ Y2.00″. The other fields retain their relative positions.

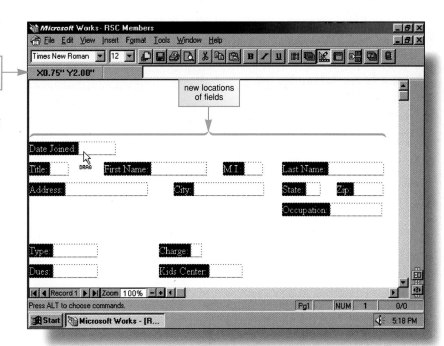

FIGURE 7-30

Formatting the Database Form Title Using Clip Art and WordArt

On the form in Figure 7-11 on page W 7.13, clip art is displayed in the upper left corner of the form and the title, RSC Sports and Fitness Centers, is formatted with special effects; that is, the title is displayed in a wave contour across the top of the form. Notice also that the letters display in dark blue and contain a shadow. A dark blue rectangular bar displays beneath the title. To insert the clip art, perform the following steps.

 To Insert Clip Art

1 **Position the mouse pointer in the upper left corner of the form at the coordinates X0.75″ Y1.00″ and click. Click Insert on the menu bar and point to ClipArt.**

The insertion point displays in the upper left corner on the form at the coordinates X0.75″ Y1.00″ (Figure 7-31). The Insert menu displays and the mouse pointer points to the ClipArt command.

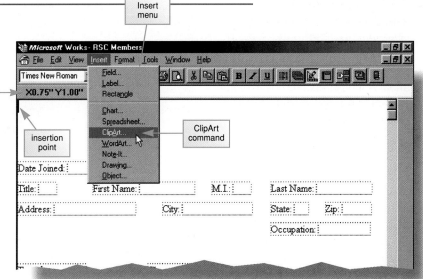

FIGURE 7-31

2 Click ClipArt. When the Microsoft ClipArt Gallery 2.0 dialog box displays, scroll to view Sports & Leisure in the Categories list. Click the clip art of the tennis player. Then point to the Insert button.

The Microsoft ClipArt Gallery 2.0 dialog box displays (Figure 7-32). When you click the clip art of the tennis player, Works places a blue border around the clip art. The mouse pointer points to the Insert button.

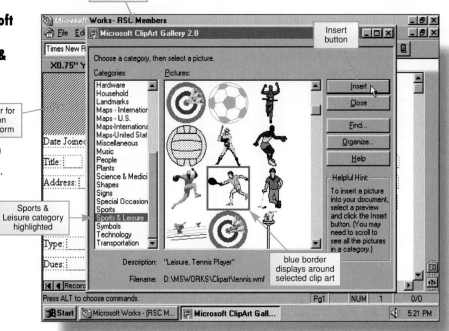

FIGURE 7-32

3 Click the Insert button in the Microsoft ClipArt Gallery 2.0 dialog box. Right-click the clip art and point to Format Picture.

Works inserts the clip art of the tennis player in the database form at the location of the insertion point (Figure 7-33). A rectangular box containing dotted lines and resize handles surrounds the clip art, indicating the clip art is an object and may be moved or resized. Because the clip art is too large for the title area, it must be resized. The context-sensitive menu displays and the mouse pointer points to the *Format Picture* command.

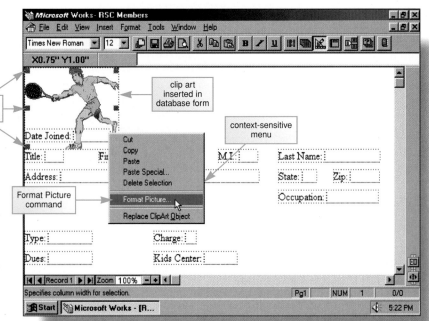

FIGURE 7-33

4 **Click Format Picture. When the Format Picture dialog box displays, type** 42 **in the Width text box in the Scaling box and then type** 43 **in the Height text box. Then, point to the OK button.**

Works displays the Format Picture dialog box (Figure 7-34). The Format Picture dialog box allows you to precisely control the size of an object. The values you entered for width and height, 42 and 43, display indicating you want the width to be 42% of the original width and the height to be 43% of the original height.

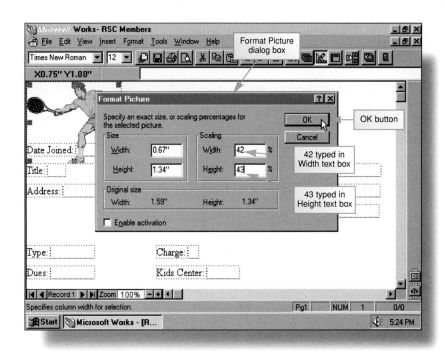

FIGURE 7-34

5 **Click the OK button in the Format Picture dialog box.**

Works displays the clip art of the tennis player at 42% of the original width and 43% of the original height when it is placed on the form (Figure 7-35).

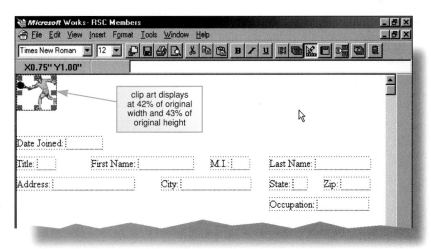

FIGURE 7-35

Using the Format Picture command allows more precise control over the sizing in applications where the exact size is important.

The next step is to enter and format the title, RSC Sports and Fitness Centers, on a database form using WordArt.

Entering and Formatting a Title on a Database Form

The title on the database form, RSC Sports and Fitness Centers, displays using special effects; that is, the characters in the title display in a wave-like contour from left to right. The characters in the title also display in navy with a silver shadow. To create a title with special effects, Works provides an accessory called **WordArt**. Complete the steps beginning on the next page to enter and format a title using WordArt.

Steps To Enter and Format a Title Using WordArt

1 **Position the insertion point at the coordinates X1.50" Y1.00". Click Insert on the menu bar and point to WordArt.**

The Insert menu displays and the mouse pointer points to the WordArt command (Figure 7-36). The insertion point is located at the coordinates X1.50" Y1.00". This is the position where Works will insert the title on the database form.

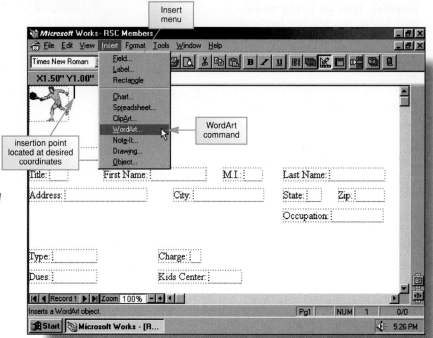

FIGURE 7-36

2 **Click WordArt.**

The Enter Your Text Here box displays (Figure 7-37). The default text, Your Text Here, is highlighted in the box. A shaded outline area containing the words, Your Text Here, displays above the window. After you type and display text, the text will display in the shaded outline area on the database form. A new menu bar and new toolbar also display. The toolbar contains a number of buttons unique to WordArt that assist in using WordArt. The buttons used in this project will be explained as needed. When you use WordArt, you are using the OLE 2.0 facilities of Works for Windows 95.

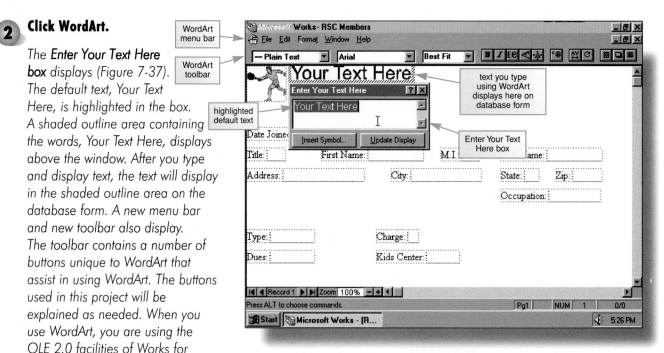

FIGURE 7-37

3 **Type** RSC Sports and Fitness Centers **in the Enter Your Text Here box and then click the Update Display button in the box.**

Works displays the words, RSC Sports and Fitness Centers, in the box as you type (Figure 7-38). When you click the Update Display button, the words, RSC Sports and Fitness Centers, display in the shaded outline area on the data-base form. The window remains displayed with the mouse pointer pointing to the Update Display button.

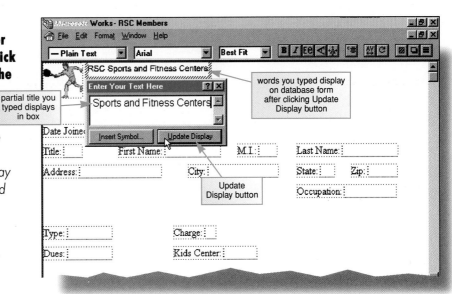

FIGURE 7-38

4 **Click the Shape box arrow on the toolbar. When the Shape drop-down list box displays, point to the first box on the right in the fourth row.**

*The Shape drop-down list box dis-plays and the mouse pointer points to the **Wave 2** shape (Figure 7-39).*

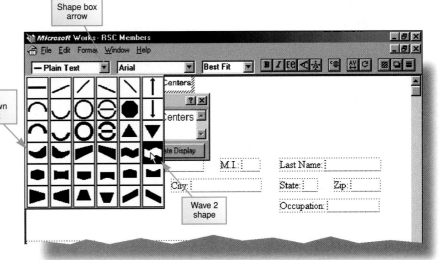

FIGURE 7-39

5 **Click Wave 2. Point to the Stretch button on the toolbar.**

*The words, RSC Sports and Fitness Centers, display in the object area on the form in compressed text (Figure 7-40). The shape you clicked, Wave 2, displays in the Shape box. The mouse pointer points to the **Stretch button** on the toolbar.*

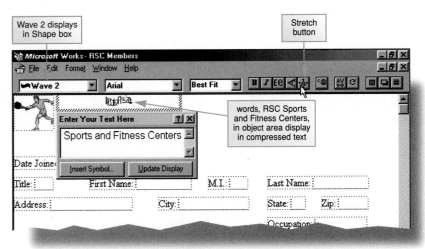

FIGURE 7-40

6 Click the Stretch button on the toolbar. Then click the Shadow button on the toolbar.

WordArt displays the words, RSC Sports and Fitness Centers, with a Wave 2 effect in the object area on the database form (Figure 7-41). The Shadow dialog box displays. The Choose a Shadow box displays eight special effects for shadows. The Shadow Color box displays Silver as the default color of the shadow.

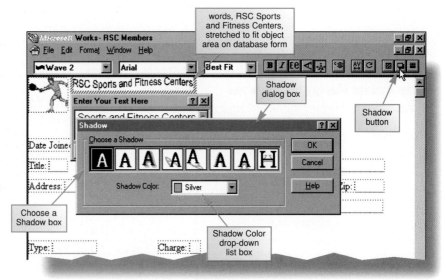

FIGURE 7-41

7 Click the second box on the left in the Choose a Shadow box. Then, point to the OK button in the Shadow dialog box.

WordArt displays the words, RSC Sports and Fitness Centers, with a silver shadow within the object area on the database form (Figure 7-42).

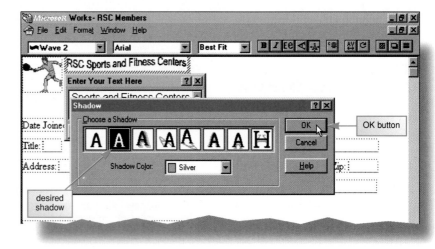

FIGURE 7-42

8 Click the OK button in the Shadow dialog box. Click the Shading button on the toolbar.

WordArt displays the words, RSC Sports and Fitness Centers, with a shadow within the object area on the database form (Figure 7-43). When you click the Shading button, WordArt displays the Shading dialog box. The Style box contains twenty-four fill patterns for the characters in the WordArt object. The Color box contains the foreground and background fill colors for the characters.

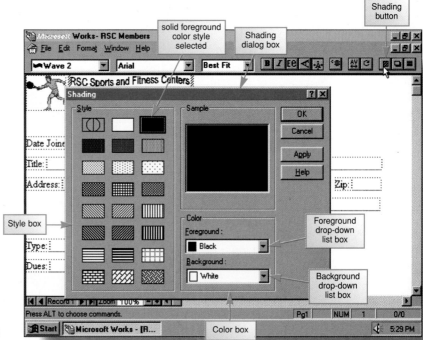

FIGURE 7-43

9 Click the solid foreground style box in the Style box. Click the Foreground box arrow, scroll the list to view Navy, and then click Navy. Point to the OK button.

The solid foreground style box is selected in the Style box (Figure 7-44). The Foreground drop-down list box displays Navy. The Sample box displays the solid navy fill pattern to be applied to the text on the database form. The mouse pointer points to the OK button.

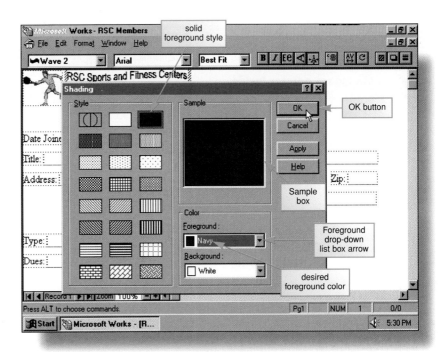

FIGURE 7-44

10 Click the OK button in the Shading dialog box. Click one time anywhere outside the Enter Your Text Here box. Then, point to the bottom center resize handle on the object border.

Works displays the formatted words, RSC Sports and Fitness Centers, on the database form in the object area (Figure 7-45). The X coordinate is 1.50" and the Y coordinate is 1.00". These coordinates refer to the leftmost and topmost position of the object containing the words, RSC Sports and Fitness Centers. The mouse pointer displays with a small square box and arrows pointing up and down. The word RESIZE displays beneath the arrows.

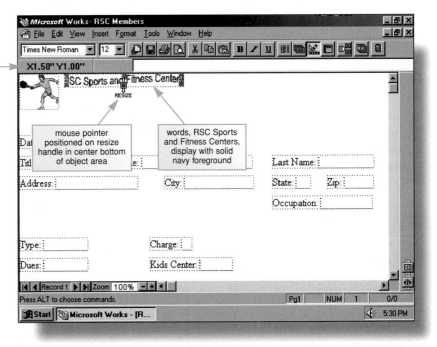

FIGURE 7-45

11 **Drag the resize handle down to approximately the bottom of the tennis player clip art. Then, place the mouse pointer inside the WordArt object. Drag the WordArt object to the left until the object is adjacent to right border of the clip art object. Place the mouse pointer on the right center resize handle.**

As you drag the resize handle down, the object expands vertically (Figure 7-46). The object area containing the words, RSC Sports and Fitness Centers, is moved to the left. It is possible to drag the resize handle in the lower right corner to expand the rectangular box both vertically and horizontally at one time. For some individuals, a two-step approach makes it easier to control the vertical and horizontal expansion. The mouse pointer is positioned on the right center resize handle.

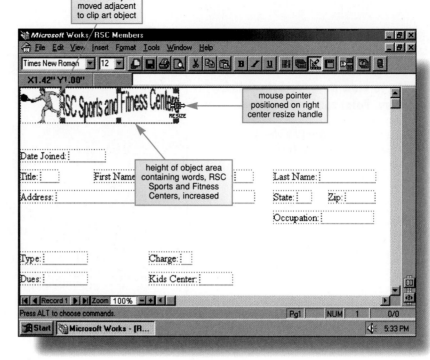

FIGURE 7-46

12 **Drag the right center resize handle to the right approximately one-quarter of an inch from the edge of the screen.**

The words, RSC Sports and Fitness Centers, expand horizontally to fill the object area (Figure 7-47).

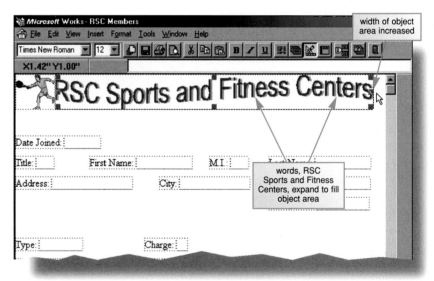

FIGURE 7-47

The words, RSC Sports and Fitness Centers, have now been formatted as required. WordArt provides many special effects for text when using Microsoft Works.

To edit the object, double-click the embedded object to open WordArt and make the desired changes to the object.

Inserting a Rectangular Bar Beneath the Title

To further enhance the title area, the area is to contain a rectangular bar beneath the clip art and the words, RSC Sports and Fitness Centers (see Figure 7-11 on page W 7.13). Complete the following steps to insert the bar.

 Steps **To Insert a Rectangular Bar in the Title Area**

1 **Position the insertion point below the clip art object at the coordinates X0.75" Y1.58" and then right-click. Point to Insert Rectangle.**

Works displays the insertion point below the clip art, and the coordinates X0.75" Y1.58" display (Figure 7-48). The context-sensitive menu displays and the mouse pointer points to the Insert Rectangle command.

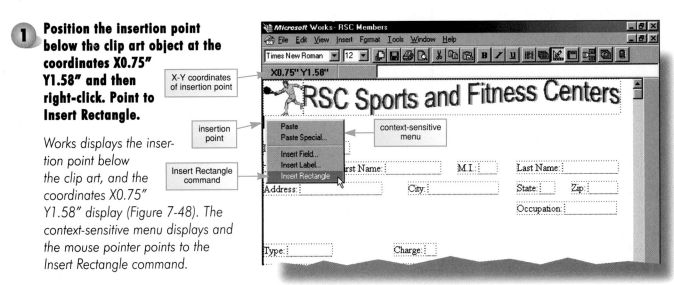

FIGURE 7-48

2 **Click Insert Rectangle. When the rectangle displays, position the mouse pointer on the resize handle in the lower right corner of the rectangle.**

Works displays a rectangle containing dotted lines and resize handles on the database form (Figure 7-49). The mouse points to the resize handle in the lower right corner.

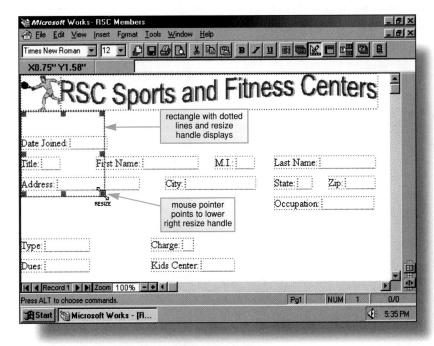

FIGURE 7-49

3 **Drag the resize handle up to the bottom of the ClipArt and to the right until the rectangle is the same width as the word art.**

Works displays the resized rectangle below the clip art and the words, RSC Sports and Fitness Centers, (Figure 7-50).

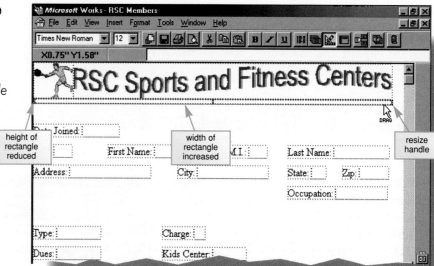

FIGURE 7-50

*Other*Ways

1. On Insert menu in form design view, click Rectangle

Adding Color to the Rectangle

The next step is to add color to the rectangle. Dark blue displays in the rectangular bar below the clip art and the words, RSC Sports and Fitness Centers. To add color, perform the following steps.

Steps **To Add Color to the Rectangular Bar**

1 **Right-click the rectangle and point to Shading.**

Resize handles display on the rectangle indicating it is selected (Figure 7-51). The context-sensitive menu displays and the mouse pointer points to the Shading command.

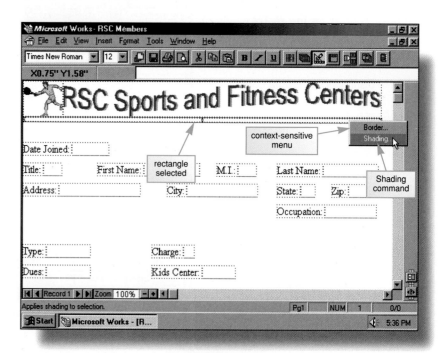

FIGURE 7-51

2 Click Shading. When the Format dialog box displays, click the solid pattern in the Pattern list box on the Shading sheet. Scroll down the Foreground list box in the Colors box to display Dark Blue. Then, click Dark Blue. Point to the OK button.

Works displays the Format dialog box (Figure 7-52). The solid pattern is selected in the Pattern list box and Dark Blue is highlighted in the Foreground list box. The Sample box displays a sample of the pattern and color you have selected. The mouse pointer points to the OK button.

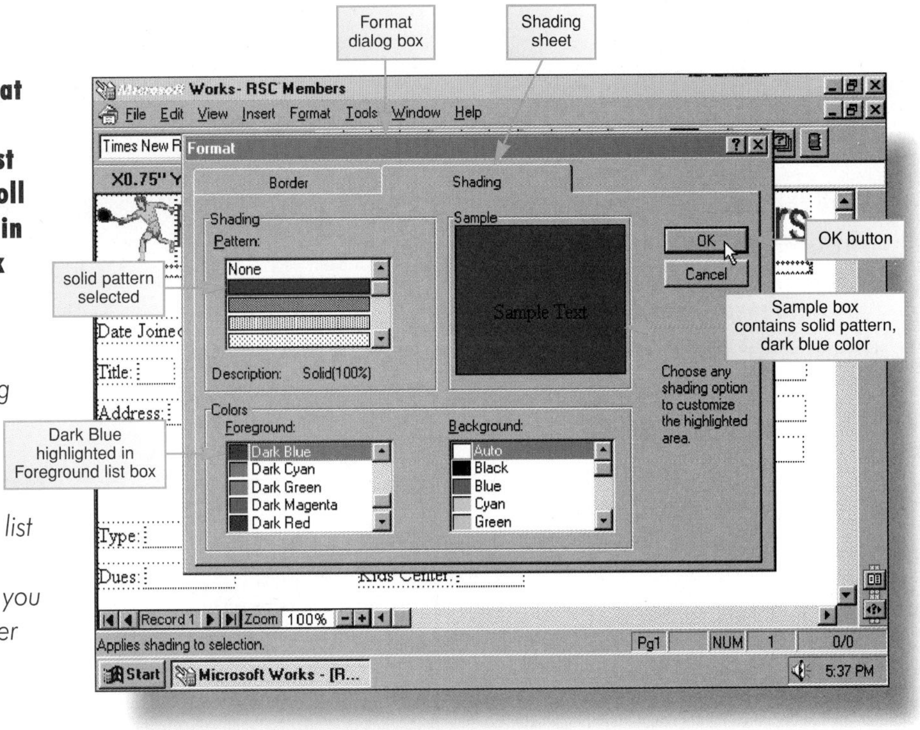

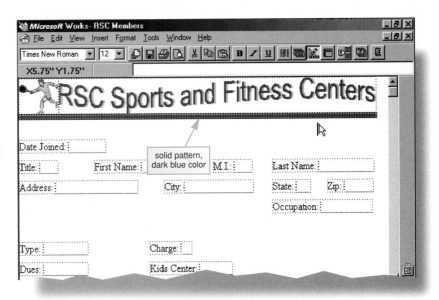

FIGURE 7-52

3 Click the OK button in the Format dialog box. Click anywhere on the form to remove the selection.

Works displays the rectangle with a solid pattern that is a dark blue color (Figure 7-53).

FIGURE 7-53

Most database forms in a modern computing environment use color to enhance the appearance of the form.

Formatting Field Names

To give further emphasis to the field names on the database form, each field name is to display in bold and italics. The steps on the next page explain how to display the field names in bold and italics.

Steps To Format the Field Names

1 **Click the Date Joined field name. Then, while holding down the CTRL key, click each field name on the database form to highlight them. Point to the Bold button on the toolbar.**

Each field name on the database form is now highlighted (Figure 7-54). The mouse pointer points to the Bold button on the toolbar.

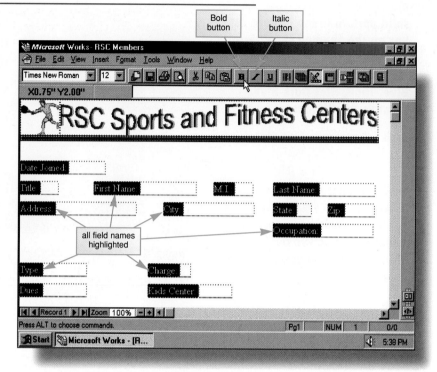

FIGURE 7-54

2 **Click the Bold button on the toolbar. Click the Italic button on the toolbar. Click anywhere on the database form to remove the highlighting.**

Each field name on the database form displays in bold and italics (Figure 7-55).

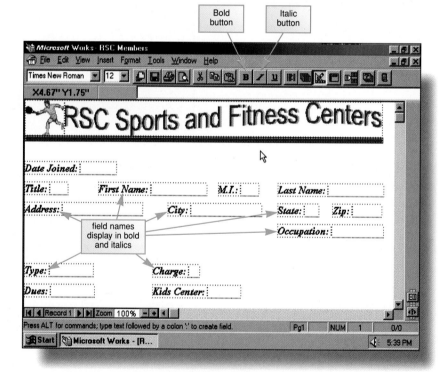

FIGURE 7-55

Adding a Border on Fields

The next step in developing the format of the database form is to add a color border to the fields. This technique precisely defines for the user where data is to appear. To accomplish this task, it is recommended that you first remove the field lines and then add the color borders. Perform the following steps to accomplish this task.

 Steps **To Remove Field Lines and Add a Border on Fields**

1 **Click the Date Joined field. Then highlight all the fields by holding down the CTRL key and clicking each of the fields. Click View on the menu bar and then point to Field Lines.**

All fields are highlighted, the View menu displays, and the mouse pointer points to the Field Lines command (Figure 7-56).

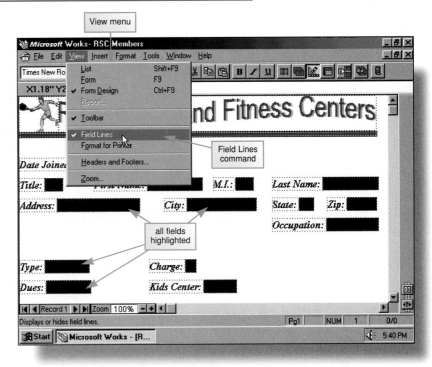

FIGURE 7-56

2 **Click Field Lines. Right-click the Date Joined field and then point to Border.**

Works no longer displays the field lines (Figure 7-57). The context-sensitive menu displays and the mouse pointer points to the Border command.

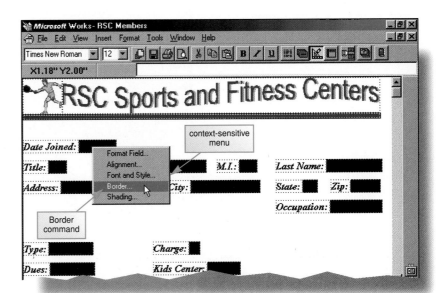

FIGURE 7-57

3 Click Border on the context-sensitive menu. When the Format dialog box displays, click the Outline box in the Border box and scroll down the Color drop-down list to view Dark Blue. Click Dark Blue. Then, point to the OK button.

The Format dialog box displays the selected entries and the mouse pointer points to the OK button (Figure 7-58).

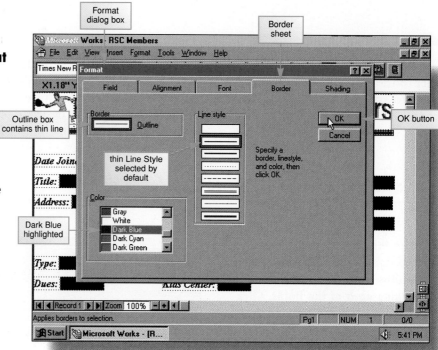

FIGURE 7-58

4 Click the OK button in the Format dialog box. Then, click the form to remove the highlights from the fields.

Works removes the highlight from the fields and applies the dark blue outline border to all fields (Figure 7-59).

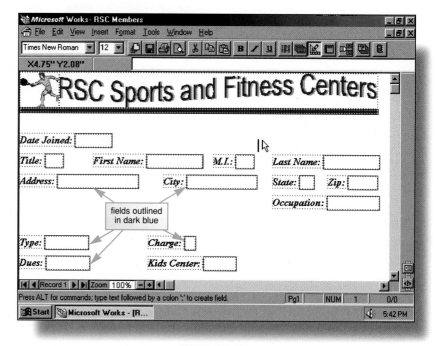

FIGURE 7-59

▶OtherWays

1. On Format menu in form design view, click Border

Adding Text Labels to the Database Form

The next step in formatting the form is to add two text labels to the database form. A **text label** is identifying information placed on a database form. Text labels can be any length and can contain any words or numbers that provide the description or instructions you need. The two text labels that display on the form are MEMBER INFORMATION and ACCOUNT INFORMATION as illustrated in Figure 7-13 on page W 7.14. To add the text labels, perform the following steps.

 Steps **To Add Text Labels to the Database Form**

1 **Position the insertion point at the coordinates X0.75" Y1.75" and then click.**

Works displays the insertion point at the coordinates X0.75" Y1.75" (Figure 7-60).

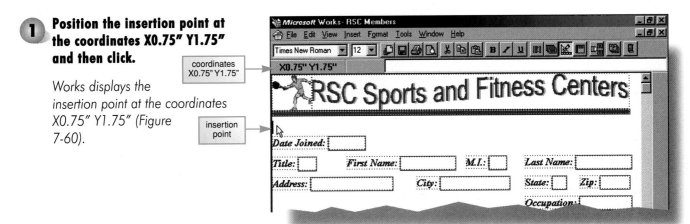

FIGURE 7-60

2 **Press the CAPS LOCK key and type** MEMBER INFORMATION **as the text label.**

Works displays the label in the entry bar and on the form (Figure 7-61).

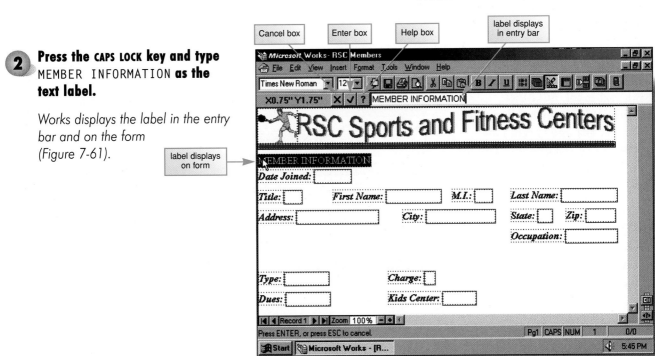

FIGURE 7-61

3 Click the Enter box or press the ENTER key. Position the mouse pointer at the coordinates X0.75" Y3.33" and then click. Type ACCOUNT INFORMATION and then click the Enter box or press the ENTER key. Then, press the CAPS LOCK key.

Works enters the first text label on the database form at the coordinates X0.75" Y1.75" (Figure 7-62). The second text label displays at the coordinates X0.75" Y3.33" on the database form.

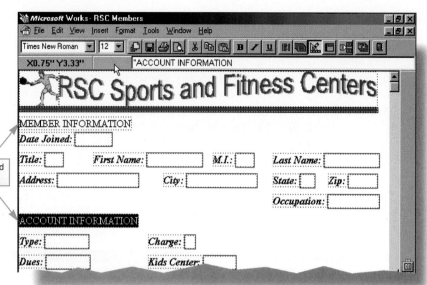

FIGURE 7-62

Adding an Underline and Bold to the Text Labels

The final task in developing the format of the database form is to add a single underline below the text labels and display the labels in bold. Perform the following step to accomplish this task.

Steps **To Underline and Apply Bold to Text Labels**

1 Click the text label, MEMBER INFORMATION. Then highlight the text label, ACCOUNT INFORMATION, by holding down the CTRL key and clicking the label. Click the Underline button on the toolbar. Click the Bold button on the toolbar.

Works highlights the text labels and displays a single line beneath the labels on the database form (Figure 7-63). The text labels also display in bold.

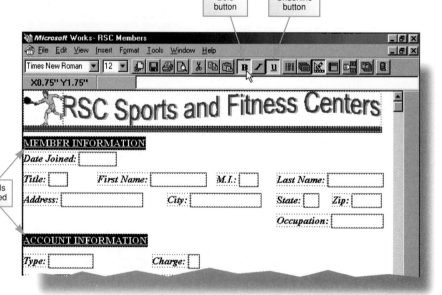

FIGURE 7-63

The format of the database form is now complete. In most cases, you should save the completed form on disk. To save the database, click the Save button on the toolbar.

Entering Data into the Database in Form View

The fields contained within each record of the database constitute the structure of the database. The **structure**, however, merely defines the fields within the database. The whole purpose of a database is to enter data so the data is available for printing, sorting, querying, and other uses. Therefore, the next step is to enter data into the database. The data can consist of text, numbers, formulas, and even functions.

More *About* **Form View**

Displaying one record at a time in form view is the easiest way to work with a database. Form view is similar to having a stack of paper forms inside your computer. You can also see titles, graphics, and other enhancements on the form.

Changing to Form View

Thus far, you have viewed the database in form design view. To type information into fields on a form, you use form view. **Form view** allows you to enter information into the database one record at a time. To change to form view perform the following steps.

 To Change to Form View

1 Point to the Form View button on the toolbar.

The mouse pointer points to the Form View button on the toolbar (Figure 7-64).

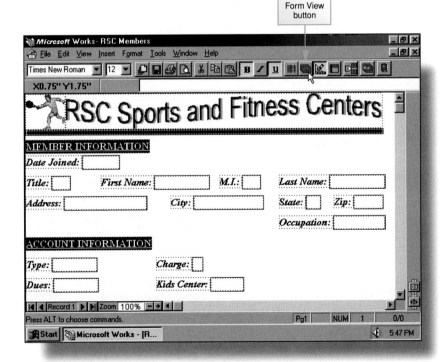

FIGURE 7-64

2 **Click the Form View button on the toolbar.**

Works displays the database in form view (Figure 7-65). Form view resembles form design view except no dotted lines surround the field names, field entries, or the objects on the database form. Works places a black background in the Date Joined field. The coordinates of the fields do not display in form view. Notice the Record menu name replaces the Insert and Format menu names on the toolbar.

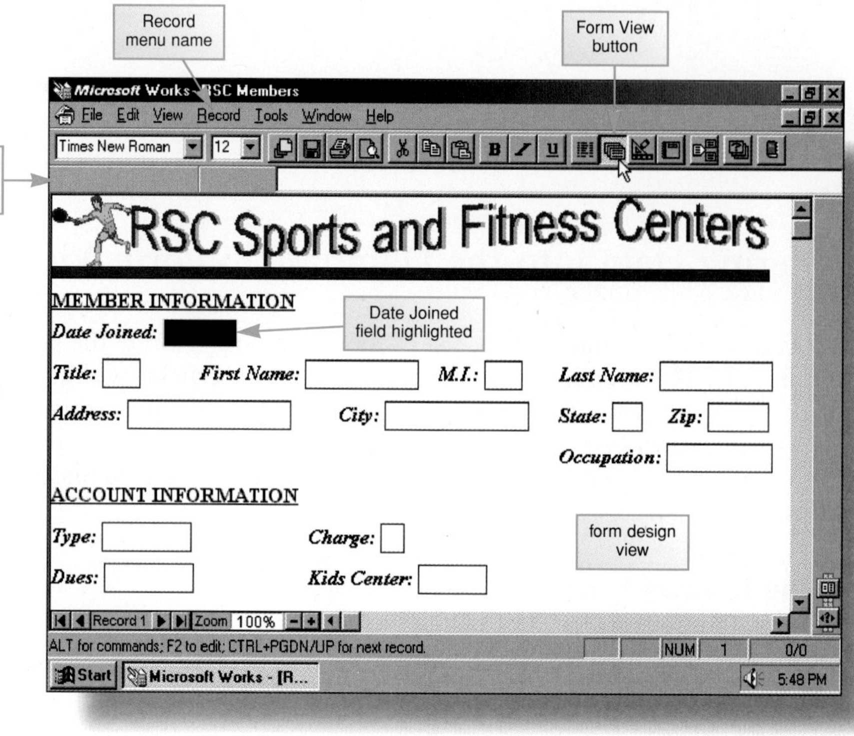

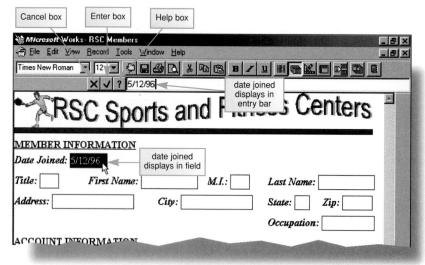

FIGURE 7-65

OtherWays
1. On View menu click Form
2. Press F9

Entering Data into the Database

To enter data, highlight the field where you want to enter the data and then type the data. To enter the data for the first record in the database, complete the following steps.

Steps **To Enter Data into the Database**

1 **Ensure the Date Joined field is highlighted. Type** 5/12/96 **into the field.**

Works places a black background in the Date Joined field (Figure 7-66). The date joined displays in the entry bar and in the field.

FIGURE 7-66

2 **Press the TAB key.**

Works enters the date into the Date Joined field and highlights the next field, Title, (Figure 7-67). When you press the TAB key, it causes both the data to be entered and the highlight to be moved from the previous field. If you press the ENTER key or click the Enter box, the data is entered but the highlight is not moved. Pressing the TAB key is the most efficient technique to enter data into a database. Notice when you enter information in the first field in the database, Works automaticallly enters CA in the State field because this field was formated with the default value of CA.

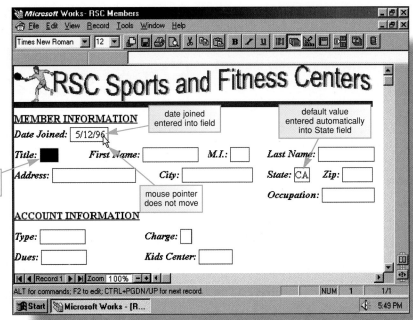

FIGURE 7-67

3 **Type Mr. in the Title field and then press the TAB key.**

Works enters the title, Mr., into the Title field and highlights the next field, First Name (Figure 7-68).

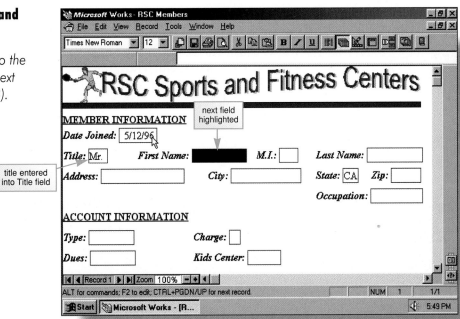

FIGURE 7-68

4 **Type and enter the remaining data for each of the fields in the first record. After entering the Kids Center value, press the ENTER key or click the Enter box.**

All the data for the first record is now entered (Figure 7-69). The Kids Center field is highlighted because you pressed the ENTER key or clicked the Enter box rather than pressing the TAB key. Pressing the TAB key would cause Works to highlight the Date Joined field in the second record.

FIGURE 7-69

Notice several important items in the record shown in Figure 7-69. First, Works considers the Date Joined field to be numeric because the field was formatted as a date field. Thus, the date entered is right-aligned in the field. Dues and Kids Center fields are also numeric fields and data is right-aligned in the fields. Second, text fields, such as Title and First Name, are left-aligned in their fields.

If you accidentally enter erroneous data, you can correct the entry by highlighting the field containing the error and entering the correct data. Works will replace the erroneous data with the correct data.

To continue entering data into the database, you must display the form for record number 2 on the screen as shown in the step on the next page.

Steps **To Display the Next Record in Form View**

1 **Ensure the Kids Center field is highlighted and press the TAB key.**

Works displays record number 2 (Figure 7-70). Notice that the Date Joined field is highlighted. When you press the TAB key, Works highlights the next field, even if the next field is in the next record in the database. The field names are formatted the same as in record number 1.

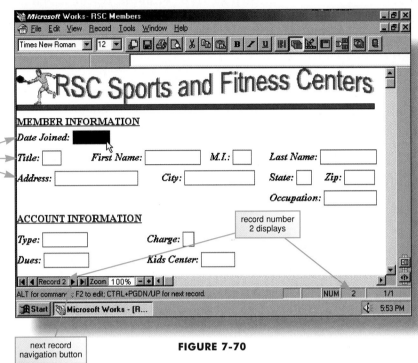

FIGURE 7-70

You also can move from one record to another using the navigation buttons on the scroll bar at the bottom of the screen (Figure 7-70). When record number 1 is displayed and you click the next record navigation button, Works will display record number 2. The field highlighted, however, is the same field as on record number 1. Therefore, in the sequence from Figure 7-69 to Figure 7-70, if you click the next record navigation button, record number 2 will display on the screen with the Kids Center field highlighted. When you are entering data into the database, normally you want the first field in the next record highlighted. Therefore, pressing the TAB key is the preferred way to move from the last field in one record to the first field in the next record.

With record number 2 displayed, complete the steps on the next page to enter the data for record number 2 (Figure 7-71).

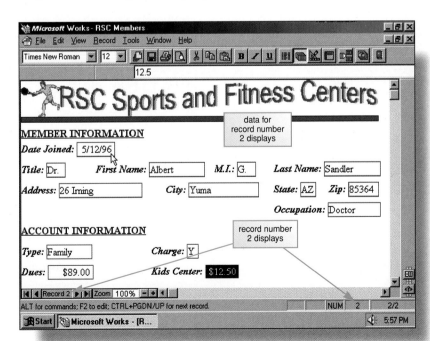

FIGURE 7-71

TO ENTER DATA FOR THE NEXT RECORD

Step 1: Type 5/12/96 in the Date Joined field and then press the TAB key.

Step 2: Type Dr. in the Title field and then press the TAB key.

Step 3: Complete the remainder of the record using the data shown in Figure 7-71 on the previous page. When you type 12.50 for the Kids Center, press the ENTER key or click the Enter box to enter the value in the field.

The screen after you enter this data is shown in Figure 7-71. Notice that even though the State field displayed CA after the date joined was entered, you can enter a different value in the field.

Continue entering the data for the remaining records in the database as specified in the following steps.

TO ENTER ALL DATA IN THE DATABASE

Step 1: With the Kids Center field in the second record highlighted, press the TAB key.

Step 2: Using the table in Figure 7-1 on page W 7.5 for data, enter the data for records 3 through 16. As you enter the data, you should periodically save the database so your work will not be lost in case of a power failure or other mishap. When you enter the data for the Kids Center field for record 16, press the ENTER key or click the Enter box.

Step 3: Click the Save button on the toolbar.

The database contains sixteen records. The sixteenth record is shown in Figure 7-72.

After you have entered all records, you may want to display the first record in the database. To accomplish this, perform the following steps.

Steps **To Display the First Record in the Database**

---

1 Point to the first record navigation button on the scroll bar (Figure 7-72).

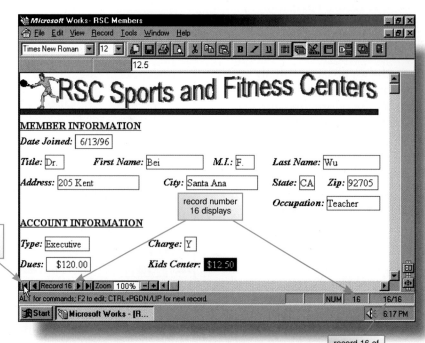

FIGURE 7-72

2 **Click the first record navigation button on the scroll bar.**

Works displays the first record in the database (Figure 7-73).

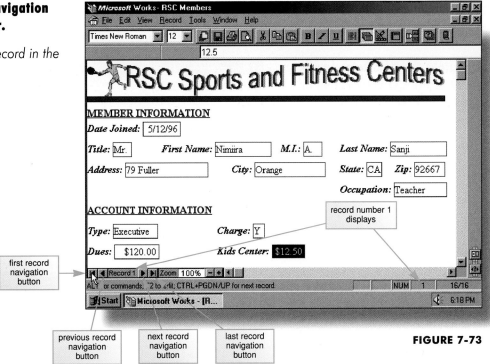

first record
navigation
button

previous record
navigation
button

next record
navigation
button

last record
navigation
button

FIGURE 7-73

To move from record to record in the database, you can use the next record navigation button or the previous record navigation button (Figure 7-73). To move to the last record in the database, click the last record navigation button. Works always displays the last record in the database as a blank record. For example, in the database for this project, sixteen records have been entered. If you click the last record navigation button, Works will display the seventeenth record, a blank record.

You also can move to a specific record in the database by selecting the Edit menu and clicking Go To. In the Go to text box in the Go To dialog box, enter the record number you want to display and click the OK button. In the Go To dialog box, you also can select a desired field.

List View

Thus far, you have created and formatted the database form in form design view and entered the data into the database one record at a time in form view. Works allows you to view multiple records at the same time using list view. To display the database in list view, perform the steps on the next two pages.

Other Ways

1. On Edit menu click Go To, type 1 in Go to text box, click OK button
2. Press CTRL+G, type 1 in Go to text box, click OK button
3. Press CTRL+HOME

More *About* **List View**

List view looks like a spreadsheet with records in rows and fields in vertical columns. In this view, you can enter data across one record at a time, or down one field at a time. Because you can see more than one record at a time, you can easily see whether you have duplicate records.

Steps To Display the Database in List View

1 Highlight the Date Joined field. Point to the List View button on the toolbar (Figure 7-74).

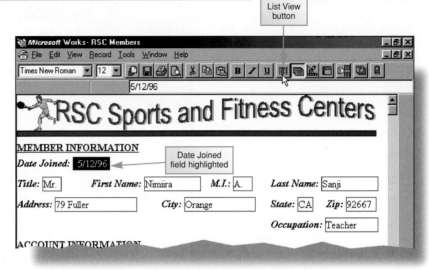

FIGURE 7-74

2 Click the List View button on the toolbar.

Works displays the records in the database in a grid that resembles a spreadsheet (Figure 7-75). Note that by default the type font changes to Arial and the point size to 10 in list view. The field names identify each column and the record numbers identify each row. All sixteen records in the database are displayed, but each record is not entirely displayed on the screen because the records are too long. Works adjusts the width of each column in the database to accommodate the field name entry. For example, the Date Joined column displays with a width of 12 to completely display the field name, Date Joined; the Title column displays with a width of 10. Field sizes can be different in list view from those that were in form view. The field sizes in Figure 7-75 must be adjusted because, for example, the entire Address field is not visible. The Date Joined field for record 1 is highlighted by a dark border around the field.

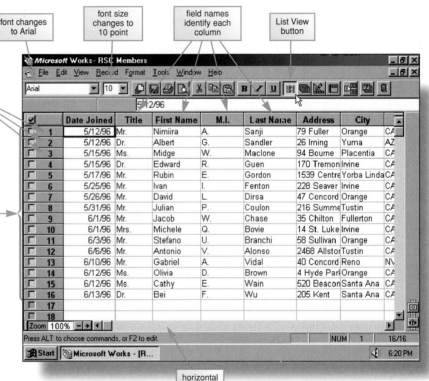

FIGURE 7-75

3 **Click the horizontal scroll bar one time to display the remainder of each record.**

Works displays the rightmost fields in the database records (Figure 7-76).

		State	Zip	Occupation	Type	Dues	Charge	Kids Center
	1	CA	92667	Teacher	Executive	$120.00	Y	$12.50
	2	AZ	85364	Doctor	Family	$89.00	Y	$12.50
	3	CA	92670	Attorney	Single	$45.00	N	$12.50
	4	CA	92715	Doctor	Family	$89.00	N	
	5	CA	92686	Teacher	Family	$89.00	Y	$12.50
	6	CA	92715	Accountant	Single	$45.00	Y	$12.50
	7	CA	92667	Salesrep	Student	$35.00	Y	
	8	CA	92680	Teacher	Family	$89.00	Y	
	9	CA	92635	Salesrep	Student	$35.00	Y	$12.50
	10	CA	92715	Accountant	Family	$89.00	Y	
	11	CA	92667	Accountant	Family	$89.00	Y	
	12	CA	92680	Teacher	Single	$45.00	N	$12.50
	13	NV	89503	Nurse	Executive	$120.00	Y	
	14	CA	92667	Teacher	Student	$35.00	Y	
	15	CA	92705	Nurse	Single	$45.00	Y	$12.50
	16	CA	92705	Teacher	Executive	$120.00	Y	$12.50
	17							
	18							

FIGURE 7-76

Other Ways
1. On View menu, click List
2. Press SHIFT+F9

Notice several important factors about the list view of the database. First, even though the field widths of the columns are not the same as the field widths in form view, the formatting of the data in each field is the same. For example, in Figure 7-76, the Dues and Kids Center field entries display the values with dollar signs and decimals.

Second, in Figure 7-76, when you clicked the scroll bar, the window display moved to the right one full window. If you click the scroll arrow, the window display moves one column at a time.

Third, when switching from form view to list view, the record and field highlighted in form view will be the record and field highlighted in list view. In Figure 7-74, the Date Joined field in record 1 is highlighted. When you change to list view (Figure 7-75), the Date Joined field in record 1 is still highlighted. This process works in the same manner when switching from list view to form view.

Formatting the Database in List View

When you format the database in list view, normally you will not change the field entry formats such as Text, Date, or Number. Instead, normally you change the field widths, font sizes, and other factors to accomplish two goals: (1) display all the data in the fields; and (2) if possible, size the list view so an entire record can print on a single page.

To accomplish these goals, you should proceed as follows: (1) change the font size from the default of 10 point to the smaller 8-point size; and (2) arrange the column widths to accomplish the goals. Complete the steps on the next page to format the database in list view.

Steps To Select the Entire Database and Change Font Size in List View

1 Click the horizontal scroll bar so the first fields in the database display. Click the selection box in the upper left corner of the grid above the row headings. Click the Font Size box arrow on the toolbar. Point to the number 8 in the Font Size drop-down list box (Figure 7-77).

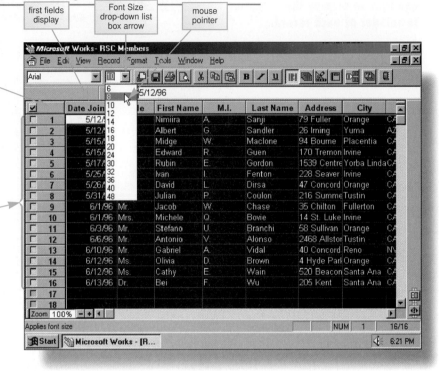

FIGURE 7-77

2 Click 8.

The entire database, including the field names, the record numbers, and the actual data in the database display in 8 point Arial font (Figure 7-78). A font size of 8 point is large enough to be readable but small enough to allow an entire record to print on one page in this project.

FIGURE 7-78

OtherWays

1. On Edit menu click Select All, on Format menu click Font and Style, click desired font size in Font Size drop-down list box, click OK button

2. Press CTRL+A, on Format menu click Font and Style, click desired font size in Font Size drop-down list box, click OK button

3. Press CTRL+SHIFT+F8

Setting Field Widths

The next step is to set the field widths for each of the fields in list view. Recall that the field widths set in list view will not necessarily be the same as those in form view, and changing the list view field widths will have no effect on the form view field widths.

Setting field widths in list view may involve some experimentation to determine the proper widths to show the field names, show all data in all records, and yet keep the field widths to a minimum. Table 7-4 shows the field widths for the list view of the database.

Perform the following steps to set the field widths of the fields in list view.

TABLE-7-4			
FIELD NAME	*FIELD WIDTH*	*FIELD NAME*	*FIELD WIDTH*
Date Joined	11	State	5
Title	5	Zip	6
First Name	10	Occupation	10
M.I.	3	Type	8
Last Name	10	Dues	8
Address	11	Charge	7
City	10	Kids Center	11

Steps **To Set Field Widths in List View**

1 Highlight the Date Joined field in any of the records by clicking the field. Then, click Format on the menu bar and point to Field Width (Figure 7-79).

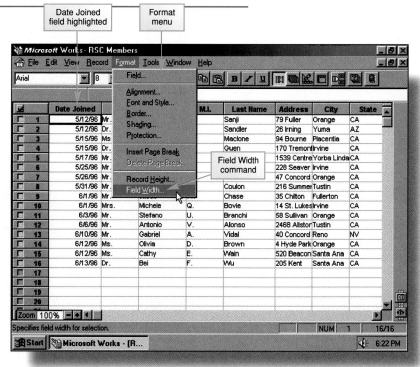

FIGURE 7-79

2 **Click Field Width. Type 11 in the Column width text box and then point to the OK button.**

Works displays the Field Width dialog box (Figure 7-80). The number 11 displays in the Column width text box and the mouse pointer points to the OK button.

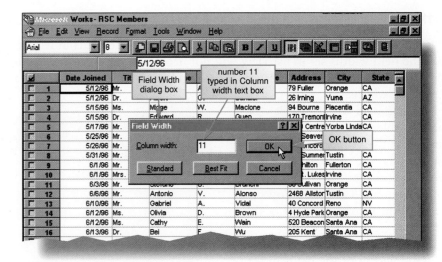

FIGURE 7-80

3 **Click the OK button in the Field Width dialog box.**

Works changes the width of the Date Joined field to 11 (Figure 7-81). All the values fit within the field.

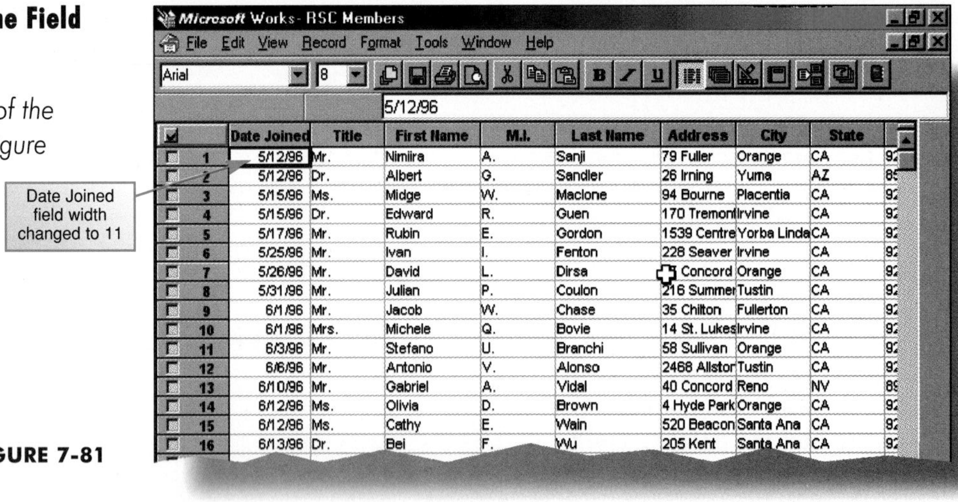

FIGURE 7-81

4 **Using the techniques shown in Steps 1 through 3, set the remainder of the field columns to their proper widths as specified in Table 7-4 on the previous page.**

After setting the field sizes, each of the fields is just wide enough to display both the field name and all the data in each field (Figure 7-82).

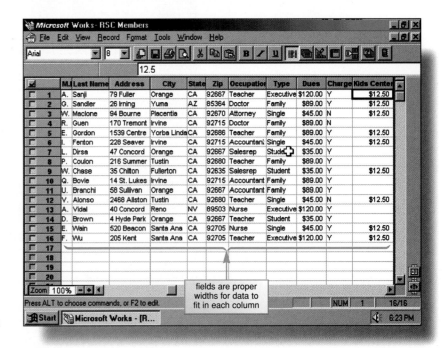

FIGURE 7-82

As previously stated, you also can drag the border to change the field width or use the Best Fit feature of Works. The method you choose when specifying the field width depends on your preference. Using the Field Width command from the Format menu is slower than dragging, but you can specify the exact field width. Dragging allows you to see the actual field width, but because Works does not display the field width on the screen, the only way to determine the exact width is by using the Field Width command from the Format menu.

Formatting the database in list view is now complete. Once the database is formatted, you should once again save the database. To save the database on drive A using the same filename (RSC Members), click the Save button on the toolbar.

Printing the Database

The next step is to print the database. You can print the database from either form view or list view. When you print from form view, normally you will see one record per page, with the record appearing in the same format as it displays on the screen. When you print from list view, you can view up to twenty entire records per page, assuming the record is not too long to fit on one page. The next section of this project describes the steps to print the database from both form view and list view.

Printing the Database in Form View

To print in form view, first you must display the database in form view on the screen. Then, after setting some options for how the database should print, click the Print button on the toolbar. The steps to perform these tasks follow.

Steps To Print the Database in Form View

1 If the database is displayed in list view, point to the Form View button on the toolbar (Figure 7-83).

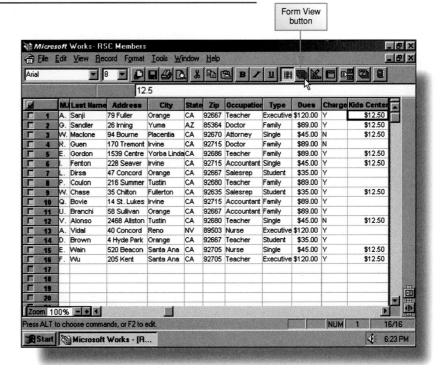

FIGURE 7-83

2 **Click the Form View button on the toolbar. Click File on the menu bar and then point to Print.**

Works displays the database in form view (Figure 7-84). The record number displayed and the field highlighted will be the same as when the database was displayed in list view unless another field is selected. The File menu displays and the mouse pointer points to the Print command.

FIGURE 7-84

3 **Click Print. Make the appropriate entries in the Print dialog box, and then point to the OK button.**

Works displays the Print dialog box (Figure 7-85). Make sure the All option button is selected. The mouse pointer points to the OK button.

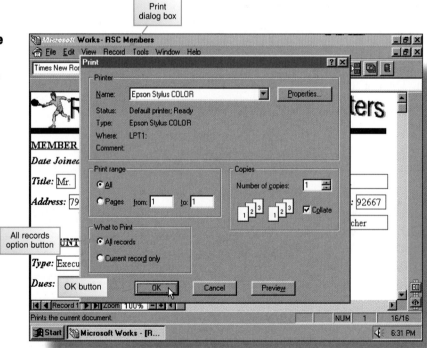

FIGURE 7-85

4 Click the OK button in the Print dialog box.

The form view records print (Figure 7-86).

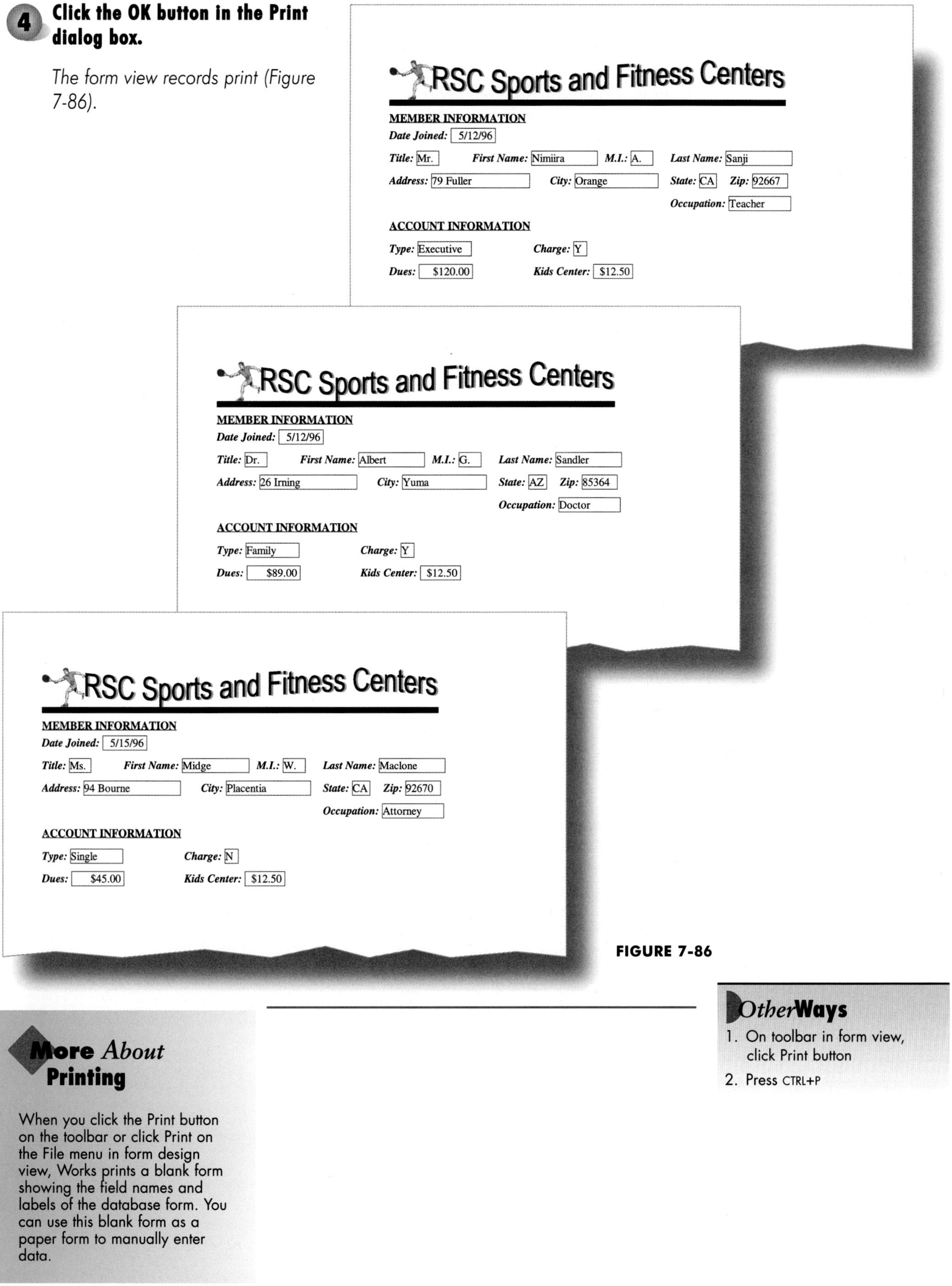

RSC Sports and Fitness Centers

MEMBER INFORMATION
Date Joined: 5/12/96

Title: Mr.   *First Name:* Nimiira   *M.I.:* A.   *Last Name:* Sanji
Address: 79 Fuller   *City:* Orange   *State:* CA   *Zip:* 92667
Occupation: Teacher

ACCOUNT INFORMATION

Type: Executive   *Charge:* Y
Dues: $120.00   *Kids Center:* $12.50

RSC Sports and Fitness Centers

MEMBER INFORMATION
Date Joined: 5/12/96

Title: Dr.   *First Name:* Albert   *M.I.:* G.   *Last Name:* Sandler
Address: 26 Irning   *City:* Yuma   *State:* AZ   *Zip:* 85364
Occupation: Doctor

ACCOUNT INFORMATION

Type: Family   *Charge:* Y
Dues: $89.00   *Kids Center:* $12.50

RSC Sports and Fitness Centers

MEMBER INFORMATION
Date Joined: 5/15/96

Title: Ms.   *First Name:* Midge   *M.I.:* W.   *Last Name:* Maclone
Address: 94 Bourne   *City:* Placentia   *State:* CA   *Zip:* 92670
Occupation: Attorney

ACCOUNT INFORMATION

Type: Single   *Charge:* N
Dues: $45.00   *Kids Center:* $12.50

FIGURE 7-86

Other Ways

1. On toolbar in form view, click Print button
2. Press CTRL+P

More *About* **Printing**

When you click the Print button on the toolbar or click Print on the File menu in form design view, Works prints a blank form showing the field names and labels of the database form. You can use this blank form as a paper form to manually enter data.

Printing a Single Record in Form View

When working in form view, you may want to print a single record. To print a single record, such as record 10, perform the following steps.

Steps To Print a Single Record in Form View

1 Click Edit on the menu bar and then point to Go To (Figure 7-87).

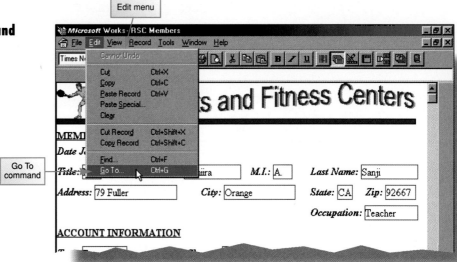

FIGURE 7-87

2 Click Go To. When the Go To dialog box displays, type 10 in the Go to text box. Then point to the OK button.

The Go To dialog box displays (Figure 7-88). The number 10 displays in the Go to text box, and the mouse pointer points to the OK button.

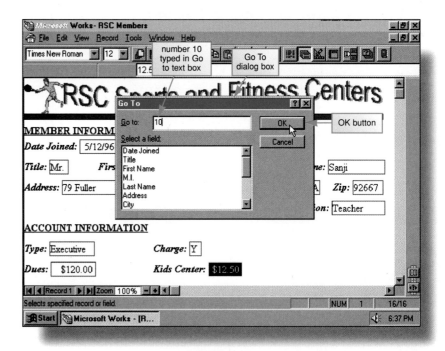

FIGURE 7-88

3 Click the OK button in the Go To dialog box. Click File on the menu bar and then point to Print.

Record 10 displays in form view (Figure 7-89). The File menu displays and the mouse pointer points to the Print command.

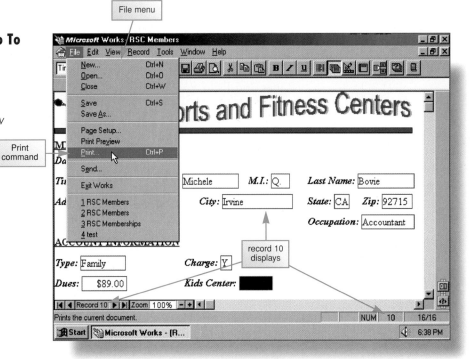

FIGURE 7-89

4 Click Print. When the Print dialog box displays, click Current record only in the What to Print box. Point to the OK button.

The Print dialog box displays (Figure 7-90). The Current record only option button is selected and the mouse pointer points to the OK button.

5 Click the OK button in the Print dialog box.

Record 10 in form view will print on the printer.

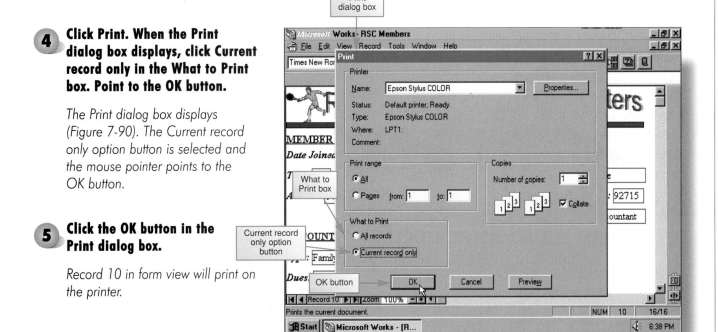

FIGURE 7-90

You have additional control over how form view records print by using the Page Setup command on the File menu. The dialog box that displays when using this command contains settings that allow you to control the printing of Field Lines and Field Entries. You also can control printing more than one record on a page.

It is also possible to print records in list view. The method to do this is explained in the following paragraphs.

Printing the Database in List View

Printing the database in list view allows you to print multiple records on one page. One of the concerns when printing in list view is to ensure the entire record fits on a single page. You can use the Print Preview feature of Works to determine if the record fits on one page. In this project, you must print the database using Landscape orientation in order to fit the entire record on a single page. To print using Landscape orientation, you must click Landscape in the Page Setup dialog box.

To use Print Preview and then print the list view of the database using Landscape orientation, perform the following steps.

Steps To Print the Database in List View

1 **If the database is not displayed in list view, display it in list view by clicking the List View button on the toolbar. Click File on the menu bar and point to Page Setup.**

Works displays the database in list view, the File menu displays, and the mouse pointer points to the Page Setup command (Figure 7-91).

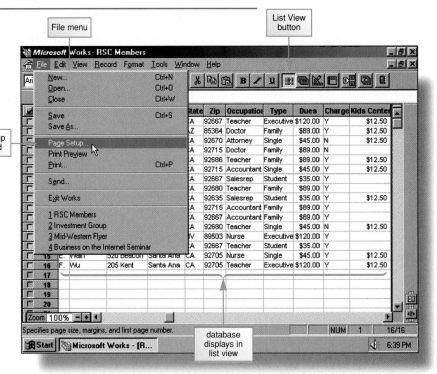

FIGURE 7-91

2 Click Page Setup. When the Page Setup dialog box displays, click the Source, Size & Orientation tab. Click the Landscape option button in the Orientation box and then point to the Other Options tab.

Works displays the Page Setup dialog box (Figure 7-92). Works automatically enters 11" in the Width text box and 8.5" in the Height text box when the Landscape option button is selected. The sample page illustrates Landscape orientation. The mouse pointer points to the Other Options tab.

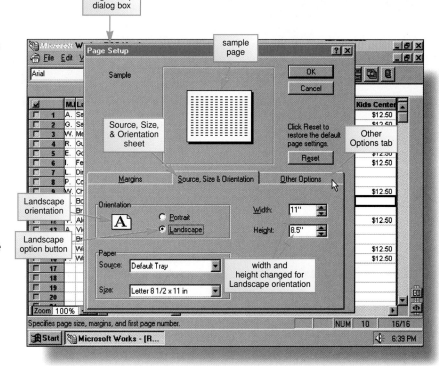

FIGURE 7-92

3 Click the Other Options tab. When the Other Options sheet displays, click Print record and field labels, and then point to the OK button.

The Other Options sheet displays (Figure 7-93). The Print record and field labels check box is selected, which means both the record numbers and the field labels will display on the report. If you leave this box unselected, only the field entries will appear on the report.

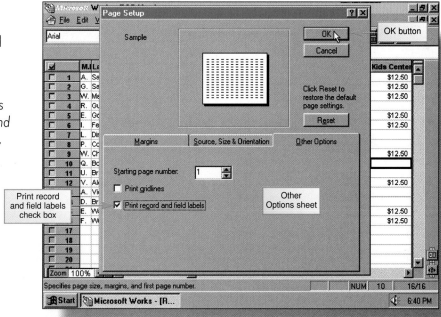

FIGURE 7-93

4 **Click the OK button in the Page Setup dialog box. Point to the Print Preview button on the toolbar.**

The list view of the database displays and the mouse pointer points to the Print Preview button (Figure 7-94).

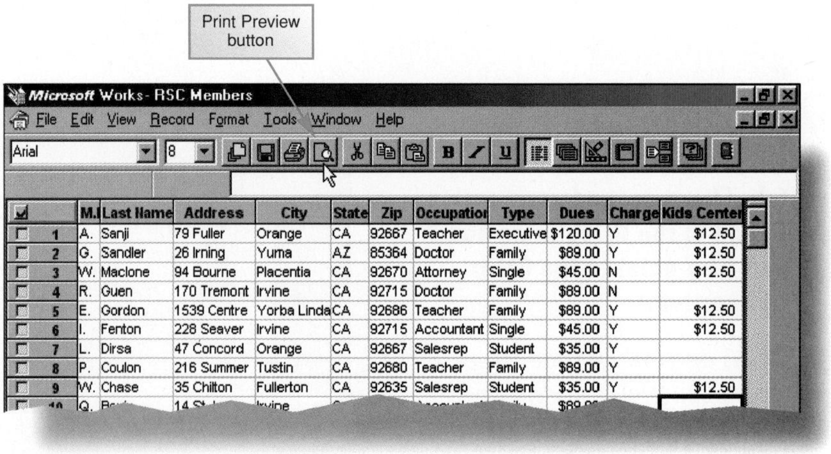

FIGURE 7-94

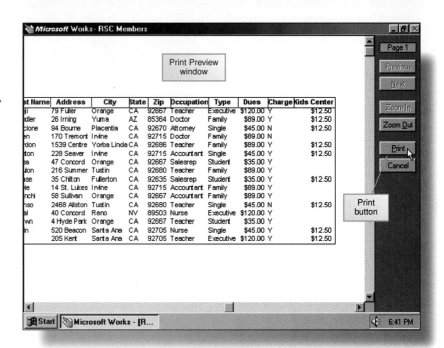

Print Preview button

5 **Click the Print Preview button. When the Print Preview window displays, place the mouse pointer on the report and click twice to magnify the view of the database. Scroll left and right to ensure the database displays properly. Point to the Print button.**

Works magnifies the report to approximately the same size as the list view display (Figure 7-95). You can see the Kids Center field fits on the page. Because the Kids Center field is the rightmost field in the list view of the database and all the other fields are to the left, the entire record fits on one page.

FIGURE 7-95

6 **Click the Print button.**

Works momentarily displays the Printing dialog box, and then prints the report (Figure 7-96). Notice the entire database fits on one page.

FIGURE 7-96

Exiting Works

After you have completed your work on the database, you can close the database file by clicking the Close button in the top right corner of the application window.

Project Summary

In this project, you learned to define the structure of a database using the Works Database tool. Using WordArt, you entered the database title. In form design view, you moved the fields to an appropriate location, formatted the field names, inserted clip art, inserted a title using WordArt, inserted a rectangle, and added color. Using the techniques you learned in an earlier project, you saved the database on disk. Then you entered data into the database in form view. Switching to the list view of the database, you specified the field widths for the fields. Finally, you printed the database using both form view and list view.

What You Should Know

Having completed this project, you should now be able to perform the following tasks:

- Add Color to the Rectangular Bar *(W 7.32)*
- Add Text Labels to the Database Form *(W 7.37)*
- Change Font Size *(W 7.48)*
- Change the Margins on the Database Form *(W 7.16)*
- Change to Form View *(W 7.39)*
- Create a Database *(W 7.7)*
- Display the Database in Form Design View *(W 7.14)*
- Display the Database in List View *(W 7.46)*
- Display the First Record in the Database *(W 7.44)*
- Display the Next Record in Form View *(W 7.43)*
- Enter All Data in the Database *(W 7.44)*
- Enter and Format a Title Using WordArt *(W 7.26)*
- Enter Data for the Next Record *(W 7.44)*
- Enter Data into the Database *(W 7.40)*
- Format the Field Names *(W 7.33)*

- Insert a Rectangular Bar in the Title Area *(W 7.31)*
- Insert Clip Art *(W 7.23)*
- Move Field Names as a Unit *(W 7.22)*
- Position Fields on the Form *(W 7.19)*
- Print a Single Record in Form View *(W 7.54)*
- Print the Database in Form View *(W 7.51)*
- Print the Database in List View *(W 7.56)*
- Remove Field Lines and Add a Border on Fields *(W 7.35)*
- Save the Database *(W 7.12)*
- Select the Entire Database and Change Font Size in List View *(W 7.48)*
- Set Field Widths in Form Design View *(W 7.17)*
- Set Field Widths in List View *(W 7.49)*
- Starting Microsoft Works *(W 7.6)*
- Underline and Apply Bold to Text Labels *(W 7.38)*

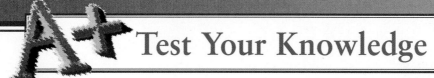

Test Your Knowledge

1 True/False

Instructions: Circle T if the statement is true or F if the statement is false.

T F 1. To create a new database, click the Database button in the Works Task Launcher dialog box.

T F 2. When you create a new database, you must enter a field name and a field format for each field in the database.

T F 3. Information in a database is divided into fields and characters.

T F 4. List view displays your database one record at a time on the screen.

T F 5. You use form view to position the fields and set field widths on the database form.

T F 6. You can specify a maximum of twenty-five fields in a database.

T F 7. In form view, dotted lines display around all elements, indicating you can select the elements for editing or changing their locations on the form.

T F 8. A text label is identifying information placed on a database form.

T F 9. You use form design view to enter data into a database.

T F 10. You can print a single record in form view.

2 Multiple Choice

Instructions: Circle the correct response.

1. Information in a database is divided into _____.
   a. form view and form design view
   b. characters and fields
   c. fields and records
   d. files and records

2. You can define up to _____ fields in a database.
   a. 25
   b. 256
   c. 32,000
   d. 1 million

3. To format the database form, use _____ view.
   a. form
   b. list
   c. form design
   d. print preview

4. To move from one field to the next in form view of the database, _____.
   a. click the first record navigation button
   b. press the TAB key
   c. click the List View button
   d. press the SHIFT+TAB keys

5. To move from the last record in the form view of the database to the first record in the form view of the database, _____.
   a. click the first record navigation button
   b. click the last record navigation button
   c. press the TAB key
   d. click the List View button

6. Works displays multiple records at a time in _____.
   a. form view
   b. list view
   c. form design view
   d. print preview

7. If a field is formatted to receive numeric data in a database, Works will enter the data _____.
   a. left-aligned in the field
   b. right-aligned in the field
   c. center-aligned in the field
   d. evenly across the field

8. To set the field widths for a field in list view, click _____ on the Format menu.
   a. Field
   b. Border
   c. Field Width
   d. Field Size

9. When you print a database in form view, _____.
   a. you can print all records in the database on one page
   b. you can print only the record in the screen window
   c. you must print all records
   d. you can print all records or any single record

10. When you print a database in list view, _____.
    a. you can choose to print gridlines and record and field labels
    b. you can choose to print the records in Landscape orientation
    c. you can use Print Preview to ensure all fields in the database will print
    d. all of the above

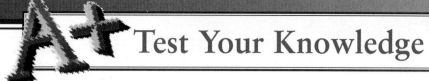

Test Your Knowledge

3 Understanding Form Design View

Instructions: In Figure 7-97, a series of arrows points to the major parts of a record displayed in form design view. Identify the parts of the database record in the space provided.

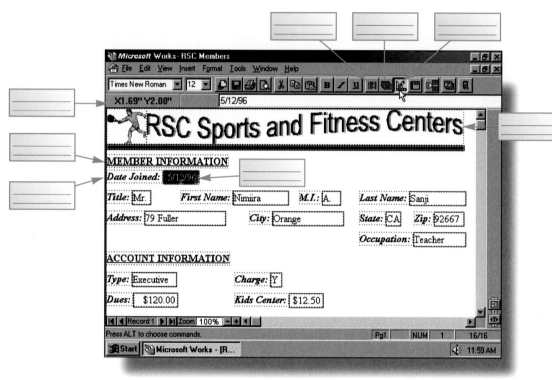

FIGURE 7-97

4 Working with Database Views

Instructions: Write the appropriate view in which to display a database to accomplish each task.

TASK	COMMAND OR BUTTON NAME
Position fields on a database form	
View the X-Y coordinates of a field	
Insert clip art	
Insert text labels	
Insert a rectangle on a database form	
Enter data in a database	
Change the field width	
Print a single record in a database	
Print multiple records on one page	

Use Help

1 Reviewing Project Activities

Instructions: Use your computer to perform the following tasks to obtain experience using online Help.

1. Start Microsoft Works.
2. When the Works Task Launcher dialog box displays, click the Cancel button. Click the Index button in the Help window to display the Help Topics: Microsoft Works window.
3. On the Index sheet, type `printing database forms` in the 1 Type a word for the action or item you want information about text box.
4. Click printing database forms in the 2 Click the Index entry you want list. Click To print a blank form DB. Read and print To print a blank form on the Step-by-Step sheet.
5. Click the More Info tab. Click Overview. Read and print Printing database information. Click the Done button.
6. Click the topic, To print more than one record on a page DB. Read and print To print more than one record on a page topic.
7. Click the Close button in the application window to close Works.

2 Expanding on the Basics

Instructions: Use Works online Help to better understand the topics listed below. Answer the questions on a separate piece of paper.

1. Start Microsoft Works.
2. When the Works Task Launcher dialog box displays, click the Database button. When the Create Database dialog box displays, use the question mark button in the upper right corner to answer the questions.
    a. What are the rules for typing a field name in the Field name text box in the Create Database dialog box?
    b. What button changes names depending upon the status of the Create Database dialog box?
    c. What is the purpose of the Serialized option in the Format box?
    d. Explain the difference between the 1234.56 format with zero decimal places and the 01235 format in the Appearance list.
3. Click the Close button in the application window to close Works.

Apply Your Knowledge

1 Understanding Form Design View and Form Formatting

Instructions: Start Microsoft Works. Open the document, Pet Supplies, on the Student Floppy Disk that accompanies this book. This file contains the form design view of the database before positioning and formatting the fields. Format the form as illustrated in Figure 7-98. Insert the clip art and use WordArt to insert the title, Pet Supplies, on the form. After formatting, print the form and turn in the form to your instructor.

FIGURE 7-98

In the Lab

1 Creating and Formatting an Alumni Database

Problem: Create a database that contains information regarding alumni donations given to the Alumni Scholarship Fund. The contents of the database are shown in the following table.

TABLE 7-5							
DONATION DATE	**TITLE**	**FIRST NAME**	**M.I.**	**LAST NAME**	**SCHOLARSHIP**	**CLASSIFICATION**	**DONATION**
10/16/97	Mr.	Wilson	B.	Haus	Business	Corporate	$1,500.00
10/17/97	Ms.	Anne	M.	Garcia	Music	Private	$100.00
10/22/97	Mr.	Donald	H.	Emerson	Science	Corporate	$700.00
10/31/97	Miss	Ealin	L.	Deras	Music	Private	$2,500.00
11/15/97	Mrs.	Melissa	R.	Deric	Science	Private	$500.00
11/22/97	Mr.	Donald	V.	Roy	Business	Corporate	$3,000.00
11/28/97	Mr.	Vincent	D.	Portofino	Business	Corporate	$5,000.00
12/3/97	Ms.	Lillian	J.	Henry	Fine Arts	Private	$850.00
12/15/97	Ms.	Ledy	R.	Mejia	Fine Arts	Private	$250.00
12/30/97	Mr.	Martin	V.	Lee	Business	Corporate	$400.00

In the Lab

Instructions: Perform the following tasks:

1. Create the database in the format shown in Figure 7-99. Experiment with the clip art size, title size, text label, and field positions to obtain the desired format.
2. Format the field names as shown in Figure 7-99.
3. Enter the data from the table into the database.
4. Determine the proper field widths so that in list view the entire record in the database prints on a single page.
5. Save the database on a floppy disk. Use the filename, Alumni Scholarship Donations.
6. Print the database in form view.
7. Print the database in list view.
8. Follow the directions from your instructor for turning in this assignment.

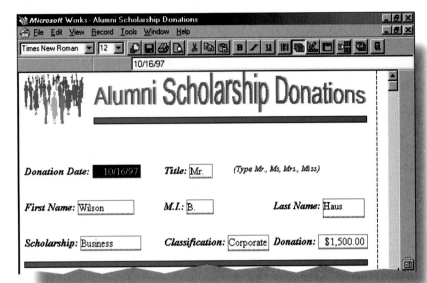

FIGURE 7-99

2 Creating and Formatting an Employee Database

Problem: Create a database that contains information regarding Custom Gifts, Intl employees. The contents of the database are shown in the following table.

TABLE 7-6

EMPLOYEE ID	DATE HIRED	FIRST NAME	LAST NAME	HOURLY RATE	WEEKLY HOURS	STATUS	DEPARTMENT
50123	4/13/93	Abraham	Ackerman	$16.50	40	F	Accounting
20157	5/26/93	Aaron	Sikora	$15.25	40	F	Purchasing
50105	6/14/93	Denzal	Simes	$15.75	35	F	Accounting
20158	7/15/93	Ben	Ryu	$14.75	40	F	Purchasing
30135	9/23/94	Sandra	Perez	$12.50	32	F	Customer Service
30235	12/1/94	Philip	Ortiz	$13.25	40	F	Customer Service
30698	8/3/95	Joni	Echsner	$10.50	20	P	Customer Service
30812	9/24/95	Mihai	Ochoa	$12.75	40	F	Customer Service
20587	10/15/95	Michelle	Quon	$11.35	40	F	Purchasing
50642	12/3/95	Duc	Dinh	$10.00	25	P	Accounting

(continued)

In the Lab

Creating and Formatting an Investor Database *(continued)*

Instructions: Perform the following tasks:

1. Create the database in the format shown in Figure 7-100. Experiment with the clip art size, title size, and field positions to obtain the desired format.

2. Format the field names as shown in Figure 7-100.

3. Enter the data from the table into the database.

4. Determine the proper field widths so that in list view the entire record in the database prints on a single page.

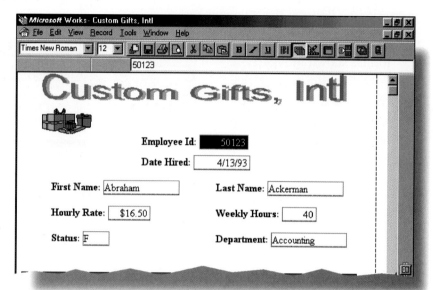

FIGURE 7-100

5. Save the database on a floppy disk. Use the filename Custom Gifts, Intl.

6. Print the database in form view.

7. Print the database in list view.

8. Follow the directions from your instructor for turning in this assignment.

3 Creating and Formatting an Investor Database

Problem: Create a database that contains information regarding investors in the Investment Group. The contents of the database are shown in the following table.

TABLE 7-7

DATE	TITLE	FIRST NAME	LAST NAME	ADDRESS	CITY	STATE	ZIP	OCCUPATION	FUND	SHARES	SHARE PRICE
9/12/97	Dr.	Thomas	Messer	13272 Grand	Yorba	CA	92686	Dentist	Technology	750	$10.00
9/15/97	Mr.	Robert	Kranitz	1300 Adams	Fullerton	CA	92633	Attorney	International	200	$18.00
9/25/97	Dr.	Elaine	Hince	10821 Capital	Bellevue	WA	98005	Teacher	Technology	1,200	$11.00
9/26/97	Miss	Janette	Lewis	1707 Kingman	Brea	CA	92621	Teacher	Growth	250	$17.00
9/27/97	Ms.	Ester	Guitron	530 Escanada	Anaheim	CA	93834	Salesperson	Aggressive	400	$16.00
9/28/97	Mr.	Joe	Gruden	2424 Holiday	Cerritos	CA	90701	Teacher	International	550	$9.00
9/28/97	Mrs.	Susan	Drussler	989 Grove	Irvine	CA	92754	Attorney	Technology	2,500	$7.00
10/6/97	Mr.	Essey	Meshi	555 Shafer	Yorba	CA	92686	Salesperson	Growth	800	$12.00
10/7/97	Dr.	Warren	Bacani	267 Portola	Tustin	CA	92670	Doctor	Aggressive	100	$23.00
10/9/97	Ms.	Rosey	Zamora	396 Barranca	Irvine	CA	92754	Attorney	Growth	750	$25.00

In the Lab

Creating and Formatting an Investor Database (*continued*)

Instructions: Perform the following tasks:

1. Create the database in the format shown in Figure 7-101. Experiment with the clip art size, title sizes, and field positions to obtain the desired format.
2. Format the field names as shown in Figure 7-101.
3. Enter the data from the table into the database.
4. Determine the proper field widths so that in list view the entire record in the database prints on a single page.
5. Save the database on a floppy disk. Use the filename, Investment Group.
6. Print the database in form view.
7. Print the database in list view.
8. Follow the directions from your instructor for turning in this assignment.

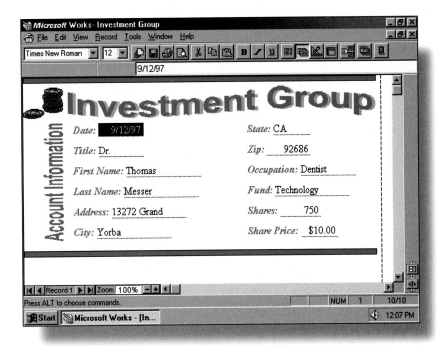

FIGURE 7-101

Cases and Places

The difficulty of these case studies varies:

▶ Case studies preceded by a single half moon are the least difficult. You are asked to create the required database based on information that has already been placed in an organized form.

▶▶ Case studies preceded by two half moons are more difficult. You must organize the information presented before using it to create the desired database.

▶▶▶ Case studies preceded by three half moons are the most difficult. You must choose a specific topic, then obtain and organize the necessary information before using it to create the required database.

Cases and Places

1 ▶ In the United States, 15 people out of 1,000 will suffer from pneumonia each year. In an effort to stay healthy, you investigate how these individuals get this disease. You learn that pneumonia is generally caused by various types of bacteria and viruses, as shown in Figure 7-102

CAUSE	WHEN SYMPTOMS APPEAR	BODY TEMPERATURE (FAHRENHEIT)	SYMPTOMS
Cytomegalovirus	Within several days	101	Tiredness
Influenza virus	Within hours of infection	104	Blue lips and nails
Legionnaire's disease bacterium	2-10 days	104	Chills
Mycoplasma	3-4 days	101	Headache
Pneumococcus bacterium	Within hours of infection	104	Chills
Other viruses	4-5 days	101	Tiredness

FIGURE 7-102

Create a database that contains this information, and enter the data from Figure 7-102. Design the form using clip art from the Microsoft ClipArt Gallery and WordArt.

2 ▶ Whale-watching expeditions have been growing in popularity. Now, you are considering planning such a trip to see the humpback or orca whales as a graduation present to yourself. After visiting several travel agencies and calling environmental organizations for details, you compile the information in Figure 7-103 to help you decide on a vacation destination.

DESTINATION	WHALE SPECIES	WATCHING SEASON	ACCESS
Antarctica	Humpback	Summer	Boat
Argentina	Orca	Summer/Fall	Boat
British Columbia	Orca	Summer	Boat/Shore
Dominican Republic	Humpback	Winter	Boat/Shore
Massachusetts	Humpback	Summer	Boat
Mexico	Humpback	All year	Boat/Shore
Norway	Orca	Summer	Boat
New Zealand	Orca	All year	Shore
South Africa	Orca	Fall	Shore

FIGURE 7-103

Create a database that contains these records, and enter the data from Figure 7-103. Design the form using Microsoft ClipArt, WordArt, and labels. Use rectangles to set off areas of the form.

Cases and Places

3 ▶ Every time you watch television or walk into a sporting goods store, you see the names of the top professional athletes as endorsements of particular products. You begin to contemplate how much these superstars earn on these endorsements and licensing royalties as compared to how much they earn competing in their sports. You also speculate about which sports are the most profitable. You research the subject and compile the data found in Figure 7-104 for 1996.

Create a database that contains these records, and enter the data from Figure 7-104. Determine each athlete's total earnings. For each sport (basketball, boxing, football, tennis, golf, auto racing, hockey, and baseball), list all the athletes and the total earnings from their salaries and endorsements.

PLAYER NAME	SPORT	SALARY (MILLIONS)	ENDORSEMENTS (MILLIONS)
Michael Jordan	Basketball	$3.9	$40.0
Mike Tyson	Boxing	$40.0	$0.0
Deion Sanders	Football	$16.5	$6.0
Riddick Bowe	Boxing	$22.0	$0.2
Shaquille O'Neal	Basketball	$4.9	$17.0
George Forman	Boxing	$10.0	$8.0
Andre Agassi	Tennis	$3.0	$13.0
Jack Nicklaus	Golf	$0.6	$14.5
Michael Schumacher	Auto racing	$10.0	$5.0
Wayne Gretzky	Hockey	$8.5	$6.0
Arnold Palmer	Golf	$0.1	$14.0
Drew Bledsoe	Football	$13.2	$0.7
Gerhard Berger	Auto racing	$12.0	$1.5
Evander Holyfield	Boxing	$11.0	$2.0
Pete Sampras	Tennis	$4.7	$6.5
Cal Ripkin Jr.	Baseball	$6.3	$4.0
Greg Norman	Golf	$1.7	$8.0
Dave Robinson	Basketball	$7.9	$1.7
Patrick Ewing	Basketball	$7.5	$2.0
Dale Earnhardt	Auto racing	$2.4	$6.0
Ki-Jana Carter	Football	$7.9	$0.5
Jean Alesi	Auto racing	$7.0	$1.0
Ken Griffey Jr.	Baseball	$6.2	$1.7
Grant Hill	Basketball	$2.8	$5.0
Frank Thomas	Baseball	$6.3	$1.5

FIGURE 7-104

Cases and Places

4 ▶▶ A potential employer has asked you to send him various materials, including a completed application, three letters of reference, your college transcripts, and several writing samples. You want him to receive this information the following day, so you call the post office and several overnight delivery companies for their rates. You learn that the post office offers Express Mail, which guarantees next day delivery by noon. The rates are $10.75 for up to eight ounces and $15 for up to two pounds. Airborne charges $14 for packages weighing up to eight ounces and $25 for packages weighing up to two pounds. Delivery on both is the following day before noon or before 5:00 p.m., depending on the package's destination. Federal Express separates its charges based on time of delivery. Packages weighing eight ounces or less cost $13 for priority delivery by 10:30 a.m. and $10 for standard delivery by 3:00 p.m. Packages weighing more than eight ounces and one pound or less cost $20 for priority delivery and $14 for standard delivery. Packages weighing more than one pound and two pounds or less cost $21.75 for priority delivery and $15 for standard delivery. Using this information, together with the techniques presented in this project, create a database showing the name of the delivery company, the rate for a package weighing eight ounces or less, the rate for a package weighing one pound or less, the rate for a package weighing two pounds or less, and delivery times.

5 ▶▶▶ You have managed to save $2,500 and want to invest this money in a six-month certificate of deposit (CD) to help save for next semester's tuition. Visit a local bank, credit union, and savings and loan association and make a list of the current interest rates, minimum investment amounts, total amounts earned in six months, penalties for early withdrawal, and other restrictions. Using this information, together with the techniques presented in this project, create a database showing the name of the financial institution, its address and telephone number, the interest rate, the total value of the CD in six months, the amount of interest earned, the amount you would be penalized if you withdrew the money in two months and in four months, and any other restrictions. Include a bar graph indicating the amount of interest you would earn and the total value of your investment.

6 ▶▶▶ You work for the classified ad section of your local newspaper. Your editors have decided to introduce a new service where readers can call the office and inquire if a particular car is being advertised. The editors have assigned this task to you. Begin by creating a database with fields for car manufacturer, model, year, price, transmission (automatic or manual), mileage, and engine size. Then enter data for 20 ads in today's newspaper. If any information is missing, enter the letters NA (not available). Test the project by performing queries to find records of cars from each of the past 10 years.

7 ▶▶▶ Food manufacturers claim that consumers can eat more nutritionally by purchasing specific items. For example, an ice cream manufacturer will label its products as low calorie (the product has 40 or fewer calories per serving), light calorie (1/3 fewer calories than the referenced product), or calorie free (fewer than 5 calories per serving). Visit a grocery store and examine the labels of five specific products claiming to be low, light, or calorie free. Then compare these five products to the referenced products. Using this information, together with the techniques presented in this project, create a database showing the name of the reduced-calorie product, the name of the referenced product, the serving size of each, and the number of calories per serving.

Project

8

Microsoft *Works 4*

Windows 95

Maintaining a Database

Objectives

You will have mastered the material in this project when you can:

▶ Explain adding new records to a database
▶ Explain deleting records from a database
▶ Explain changing and updating records in a database
▶ Explain changing and updating the record structure in a database
▶ Open an existing database file
▶ Add a record to a database in form view
▶ Add a record to a database in list view
▶ Delete a record from a database in form view
▶ Delete a record from a database in list view
▶ Change data in a database record
▶ Insert a new field in a database in list view
▶ Add a new field in a database in form design view
▶ Add data to a field using a formula
▶ Size and position an inserted field in form design view
▶ Delete a database field in form design view
▶ Delete a database field in list view
▶ Change a field name in form view
▶ Change a field size in form design view
▶ Reformat the database form in form design view
▶ Divide the list view of the database into panes
▶ Reformat a database
▶ Use the Slide to left option
▶ Add headers and footers to a form view report

Project
8

Maintaining
Rivers &
Databases

In the wee hours of April 13, 1992, the Chicago River crashed through the roof of an abandoned railroad tunnel built in the 1800s. Water from Lake Michigan roared into the basements of Chicago's downtown office buildings, ruining computers, irreplaceable paper files, and environmental equipment. Due to lack of maintenance, what started as a small crack grew into a hemorrhage that city workers desperately tried to shore up while officials sent out for competitive bids. Unfortunately, the river would not wait the several months required for the bid process. If the city had acted immediately, a repair job estimated at $75,000 could have saved the ultimate $1 billion loss. In another, more recent example, the quality of a $44 million seismic retrofit on the freeway overpasses in San Diego came into question because of faulty welds.

Individuals are seldom faced with problems that have such massive financial impact. Unlike the

Maytag repairman, however, people must contend with maintenance issues on a regular basis: cars, homes, dental work, even personal computers. All are issues important to health, safety, and well-being. How a person handles these can make the difference between a happy life and a trying one. Likewise, for many business people, scientific researchers, and self-employed individuals, professional survival depends on maintaining their computer databases.

Information flows in today's world like the waters of all the rivers combined. From telephone lines, customer service terminals, satellite feeds, the mail, and so on, literally billions of pieces of data enter daily into the databases of entities such as insurance companies, banks, mail-order firms, astronomical observatories, medical research labs, doctors' offices, automobile dealerships, home-based businesses, and multitudes of others. Based on the content of this information, decisions are made and actions taken, often triggering a corresponding flow of information to other interested users. The process of handling this data — the lifeblood of today's information-based society — is known as *database maintenance*.

Microsoft Works furnishes a powerful Database tool that facilitates designing the overall database, adding and deleting records, changing individual fields within records, and complete reformatting. A user can quickly arrange information in any order suitable to the required analysis or report.

Personal databases can organize information that is useful during college days, such as names, addresses, and telephone numbers of friends, family, and club members, or possessions such as CDs, tapes, videos, and books. Databases can also aid in mailing campaigns to employers or searches for the right graduate school. Works eases the job of maintaining those databases.

Though maintenance is a mundane subject, it does have its heroes. In Chicago, the maintenance supervisors might well have paraphrased Ralph Kramden of the Honeymooners, "When we need a *real* sewer expert, Ed Norton, where are you?"

Project

8

Microsoft

Works 4

Windows 95

Case Perspective

The RSC Sports and Fitness Centers are experiencing many changes regarding member information contained in the RSC Members database. They have asked you to maintain the database by making the necessary changes so that the most current information is reflected in the database.

You are to analyze the changes in data available on each member and update the database. The president would like a report listing the current members and their addresses. You are to prepare this report from information in the revised database.

Maintaining a Database

Introduction

The database developed in Project 7 for a sports club, called RSC Sports and Fitness Centers, can be used to provide a wide variety of information. Its use, however, is dependent upon current and correct data being stored in the database. For example, if the name of a member is misspelled, a member moves and has a new address, a new person decides to join, or a current member changes his or her membership type, the database must be updated to reflect these changes.

The process of ensuring that a database contains current and correct data is called database maintenance. **Database maintenance** involves four main activities. These activities are explained on the following pages.

1. **Adding new records to a database to reflect new activity**. If a new person joins the sports club, this person must be added to the database. In Figure 8-1 on the next page, the RSC Members database contains sixteen records. When a record for the new member, Mr. Cody L. Learner, is added to the database, the database contains seventeen records.

ADDING NEW RECORDS

BEFORE ADDING (LIST VIEW)

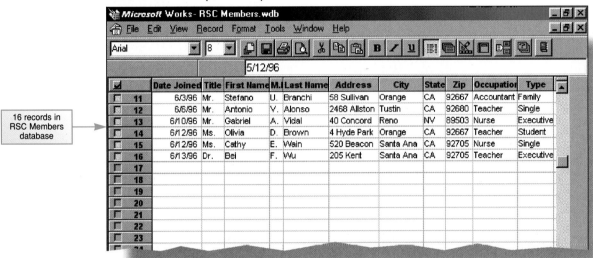

16 records in RSC Members database

FIGURE 8-1a

AFTER ADDING (LIST VIEW)

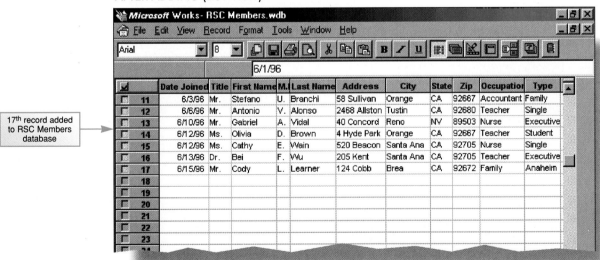

17th record added to RSC Members database

FIGURE 8-1b

2. **Deleting records from a database.** If a member decides to discontinue membership, his or her record must be removed from the database. In Figure 8-2, assume Michele Q. Bovie has decided to cancel her membership. The record for Michele Bovie, the tenth record in the database, must be deleted. When it is deleted, the RSC Members database will contain sixteen records instead of seventeen records, and each record moves up one row.

DELETING RECORDS

BEFORE DELETING (LIST VIEW)

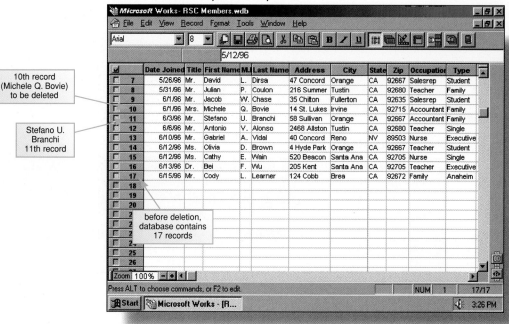

10th record (Michele Q. Bovie) to be deleted

Stefano U. Branchi 11th record

before deletion, database contains 17 records

FIGURE 8-2a

AFTER DELETING (LIST VIEW)

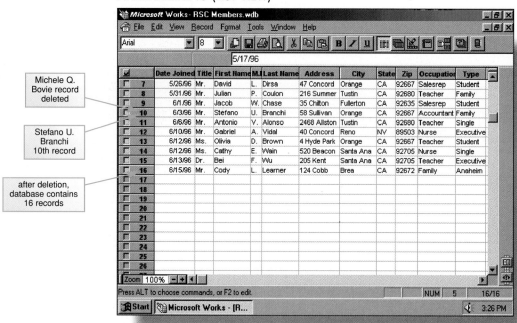

Michele Q. Bovie record deleted

Stefano U. Branchi 10th record

after deletion, database contains 16 records

FIGURE 8-2b

3. **Changing data in database records.** Whenever facts about records in a database change, the records in the database itself must be changed. For example, when a member moves, the member's record within the database must be changed to reflect the new address. In Figure 8-3, Antonio V. Alonso moved from Tustin, California to Yorba Linda, California. Three fields (Address, City, and Zip) are changed.

CHANGING RECORDS

BEFORE CHANGING (LIST VIEW)

FIGURE 8-3a

AFTER CHANGING (LIST VIEW)

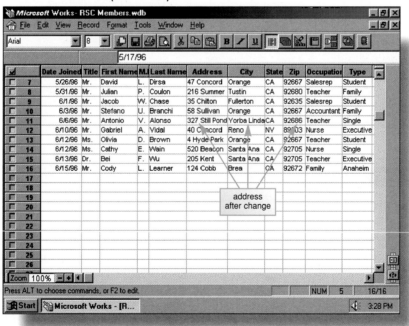

FIGURE 8-3b

4. **Changing the record structure.** Sometimes the initial design of a record in a database must be changed to include additional data. For example, in the membership database record, it may be determined that a Location field should be added to the database to more accurately identify where each member works out. This change is shown in Figure 8-4 on the next page. Notice that a Location field has been added to the database and that data

for each record has been placed in the field. Whenever a field is added to a database, data also must be placed in the field. You also may find a need to delete a field within the database, change a field name, alter the field size, or adjust the layout on the form.

CHANGING RECORD STRUCTURE

BEFORE ADDING LOCATION (LIST VIEW)

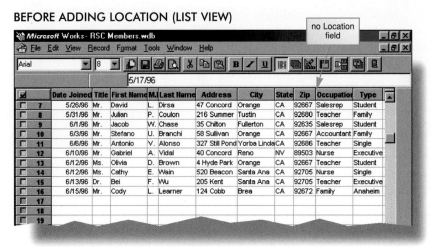

FIGURE 8-4a

BEFORE ADDING LOCATION (LIST VIEW)

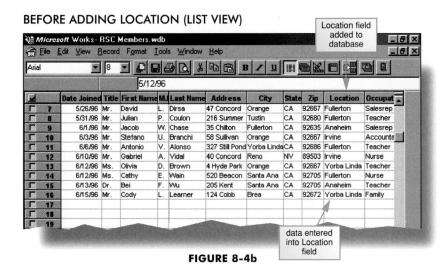

FIGURE 8-4b

Each of the four activities for maintaining a database can be performed in list view, form view, or form design view. Adding and deleting records or changing data in records can be performed in list view or form view. Changing the record structure can be performed in list view or form design view.

Project Eight

To illustrate the maintenance of a database, in Project 8 the following tasks are performed on the membership database created in Project 7:

1. A record for a new member, Cody L. Learner, is added to the database in form view.

2. A record for a new member, Lukas Conrad, is added to the database in list view.
3. The record for Michele Q. Bovie is deleted from the database in form view.
4. The record for Olivia D. Brown is deleted from the database in list view.
5. The address of Antonio V. Alonso is changed.
6. The Location field is inserted into the database in list view, and data is added to the Location field for all records.
7. The Total Dues field is inserted into the database in form design view.
8. Data is entered into the Total Dues field in form view using a formula.
9. The Occupation field is deleted from the database in form design view.
10. The Charge field is deleted from the database in list view.
11. The name of the Kids Center field is changed to Kids Club in form design view.
12. The fields are moved to a different location in form design view.

In addition, the techniques for viewing the database in panes is explained.

In some cases, a database can be changed to use the data for a different application. Figure 8-5 illustrates a database that contains only the names and addresses of the members from the RSC Members database. The technique for changing an existing database and creating a report from that changed database is shown in this project.

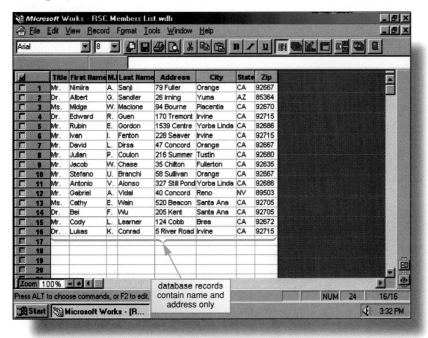

FIGURE 8-5

The following pages contain a detailed explanation of the tasks listed above.

Starting Works and Opening a Database File

To start Works and open the RSC Members database file on which you will perform maintenance, follow the steps used in previous projects. These steps are summarized on the next page.

More *About*
Database Filenames

Notice in Figure 8-5 on the previous page, the database filename displays with a filename extension (wdb). Works appends this extension automatically to a database filename when you save a file. By default, however, this extension does not display in the title bar of the Works application window. When this extension does display, an option has been turned on in the My Computer or Explorer window.

TO START WORKS AND OPEN A DATABASE FILE

Step 1: Double-click the My Computer icon on the desktop. When the My Computer window opens, double-click 3½ Floppy [A:].

Step 2: When the 3½ Floppy [A:] window opens, double-click the RSC Members file icon.

Step 3: Right-click the My Computer button on the taskbar and then click Close on the context-sensitive menu. Right-click the 3½ Floppy [A:] button on the taskbar and then click Close on the context-sensitive menu.

Step 4: After Works opens the RSC Members file, maximize the Works application window, if necessary, click the Form View button on the toolbar, and then maximize the RSC Members file document window.

The resulting Works window is shown in Figure 8-6.

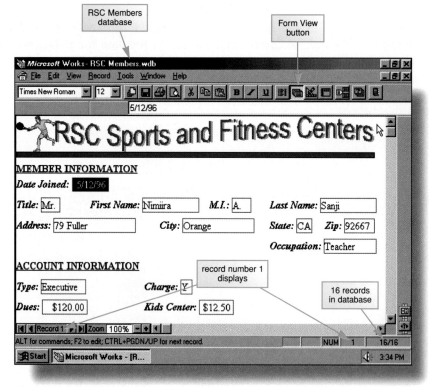

FIGURE 8-6

Adding Records to a Database

The first task in this project is to add two records to the membership database. The first record is for a member named Cody L. Learner, and the second record is for a member named Lukas Conrad. You will add the Learner record in form view and the Conrad record in list view.

Adding a Record in Form View

To add a record in form view, perform the following steps.

Steps To Add a Record to a Database in Form View

1 Click the Last Record navigation button.

Works displays an empty form for record number 17 (Figure 8-7). The Date Joined field is highlighted.

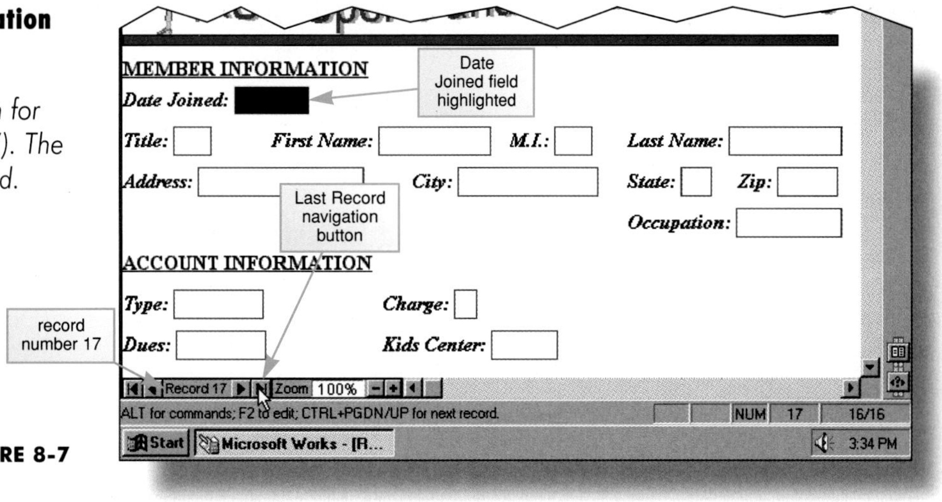

FIGURE 8-7

2 Type 6/15/96 **and press the TAB key. Type** Mr. **and press the TAB key. Type** Cody **and then enter the remainder of the data. After you type** 12.00 **as the Kids Center value, press the ENTER key.**

Works displays record 17 (Figure 8-8). When you press the TAB key after entering the date joined, Works automatically enters CA in the State field because this field was formatted with the default value of CA when the database was created in Project 7. The Dues value and the Kids Center value display with dollar signs and two decimal places. When you enter data in a new record and the fields already have been formatted, such as the Dues and Kids Center fields, Works automatically places the new data into the same format as the other records in the database.

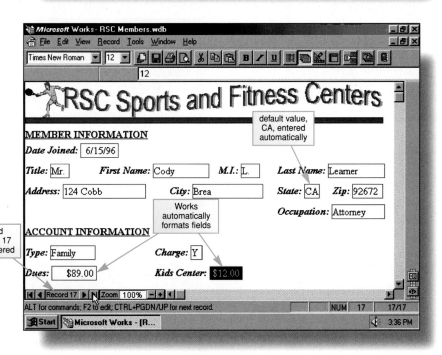

FIGURE 8-8

The record in Figure 8-8 is now added to the database. It is not, however, automatically saved on disk. Therefore, during the process of maintaining the database, you should periodically save the updated database on disk. To save the RSC Members database on the floppy disk in drive A, complete the following step.

More *About*
**Adding Records
in List View**

To add more than one record at
a time in list view, highlight the
same number of existing records
as the number of new records
you wish to add, and then right-
click the selection. Click Insert
Record.

TO SAVE AN UPDATED DATABASE USING THE SAME FILENAME

Step 1: Click the Save button on the toolbar.

Works saves the updated database on the floppy disk in drive A using the RSC Members filename.

If you wish to save the updated database using a different filename, use the Save As command from the File menu.

Adding a Record in List View

Works allows you to add a record to the database in list view as well as in form view. To add a record to the database in list view, perform the following steps.

Steps ## To Add a Record to a Database in List View

1 **Point to the List View button on the toolbar.**

The mouse pointer points to the List View button on the toolbar (Figure 8-9).

FIGURE 8-9

2 **Click the List View button. When the screen displays in list view, scroll to the left so the Date Joined field is visible and highlight the Date Joined field in the 18th record.**

Works displays the database in list view (Figure 8-10). When you switch the display from form view (Figure 8-9) to list view (Figure 8-10), the list view will have the Kids Center field highlighted because it was highlighted in form view. When you scroll to the left using the left scroll arrow, the rightmost fields scroll off the screen and the Date Joined field becomes visible.

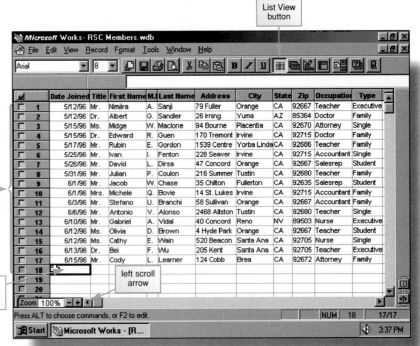

FIGURE 8-10

3 **Type** 7/2/96 **and press the** TAB **key.**

When you press the TAB *key, Works enters the date you typed into the Date Joined field and highlights the Title field (Figure 8-11). Notice when you press the* TAB *key after the date is typed, Works automatically enters the default value, CA, in the State field.*

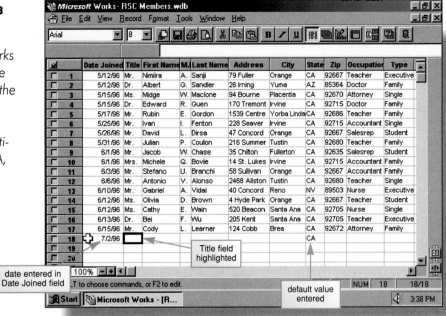

FIGURE 8-11

4 **Type** Dr. **and press the** TAB **key. Continue entering data until you reach the Type field. Type** Single **in the Type field, but do not press the** TAB **key.**

Works displays the data you type in each respective field (Figure 8-12). Notice that each entry follows the field formatting in the previous records.

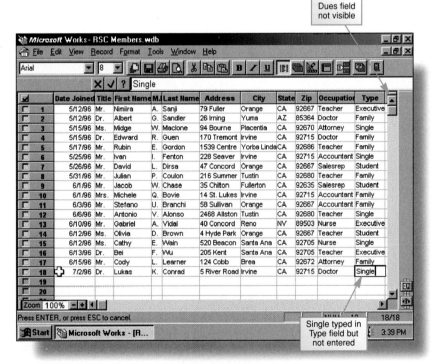

FIGURE 8-12

5 **Press the TAB key. Then type the remaining data for the record. After you type the value in the Kids Center field, press the Enter key.**

As you type the data and press the TAB key, Works scrolls the list view of the database to the left, one field at a time, until the Kids Center field is visible on the screen (Figure 8-13). The leftmost fields in the database scroll off the screen to the left. When you enter the data, the formatting is the same as for the data in the previous records.

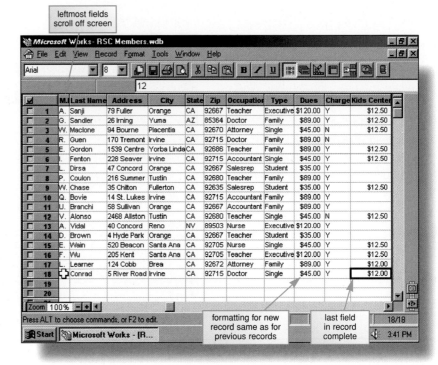

FIGURE 8-13

In the example just shown, the new record was entered at the end of the listing of database records. If you want to add the record at a particular place in the database (for example, as the 6th record), highlight the record number of the location where you want to insert the new record (for example, record 6), and click the **Insert Record button** on the toolbar. Works will move all records down one line (that is, record 6 will become record 7 and so on) and leave an open record above the highlighted record (for example, record 6). You then can enter the data for the record in same manner as shown in the previous example. You can also click Insert Record on the Record menu or context-sensitive menu to insert a record.

Adding new records is a fundamental operation when maintaining a database. Works allows you to add new records in form view or list view.

Deleting Records from a Database

Another fundamental operation when maintaining a database is deleting records from the database. You must delete a record from a database when the record contains data that no longer belongs in the database. In the sample project, records for members are deleted when the member decides to end his or her membership. You can delete records in form view or list view.

To illustrate the process of deleting records, assume Michele Q. Bovie (record 10) and Olivia D. Brown (record 13) decide to end their memberships.

Deleting a Record in Form View

To delete a record in form view, the record first must be displayed on the screen. The Go To command on the Edit menu allows you to display any record in the database when in form view. Then you click Delete Record on the Record menu to delete the record. This process is shown in the following steps.

Steps To Delete a Record in Form View

1 **Click the Form View button on the toolbar to return to form view. Then click Edit on the menu bar and point to Go To.**

The form view of the database displays on the screen (Figure 8-14). The Edit menu displays and the mouse pointer points to the Go To command.

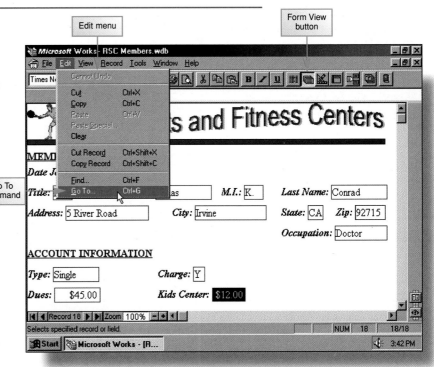

FIGURE 8-14

2 **Click Go To. When the Go To dialog box displays, type 10 in the Go to text box. Then point to the OK button.**

Works displays the Go To dialog box (Figure 8-15). Typing the number 10 in the Go to text box directs Works to display record number 10. The mouse pointer points to the OK button.

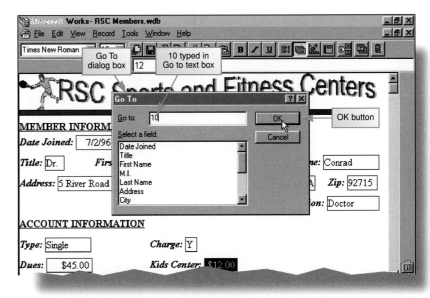

FIGURE 8-15

3 **Click the OK button in the Go To dialog box. When record number 10 displays, click Record on the menu bar and point to Delete Record.**

Record number 10, for Michele Q. Bovie, displays on the screen (Figure 8-16). This is the record you want to delete. The Record menu displays and the mouse pointer points to the Delete Record command.

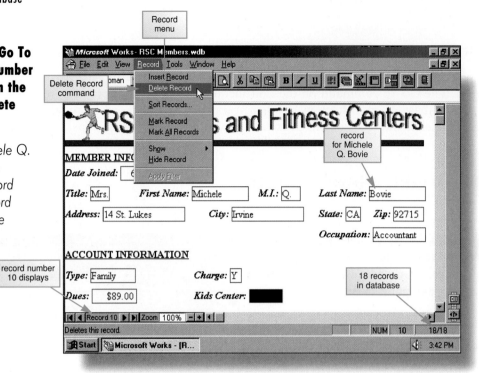

FIGURE 8-16

4 **Click Delete Record.**

The record for Michele Q. Bovie is deleted from the database and the record for Stefano U. Branchi is identified as record 10 (Figure 8-17). The Branchi record was record 11 before deleting the Bovie record. The database now contains 17 records instead of 18 records.

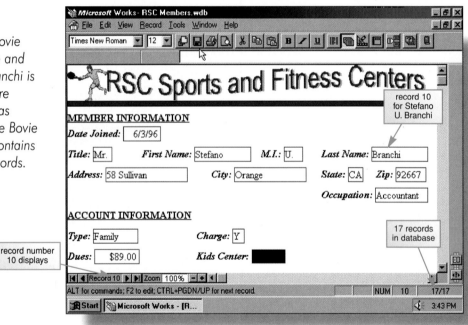

FIGURE 8-17

OtherWays

1. Press CTRL+G, type desired record number in Go to text box, click OK button

2. Press CTRL+SHIFT+X

You should be positive you have identified the proper record to delete. If you delete a record in error, however, you can click Undo Delete Record from the Edit menu to restore the deleted record to the database, provided you have not performed subsequent operations. Before deleting records, it is recommended that you save the database file so that if you make a mistake, a correct file is available for use.

Deleting a Record in List View

Works also allows a record to be deleted in list view. To delete a record in list view, the database must be displayed in list view and any one field in the record to be deleted must be highlighted. Perform the following steps to delete record 13, for Olivia D. Brown, in list view.

Steps **To Delete a Record in List View**

1 **Click the List View button on the toolbar to display the database in list view. If necessary, scroll to the left so the Date Joined field is visible. Then right-click any cell in record number 13. When the context-sensitive menu displays, point to Delete Record.**

The database displays in list view (Figure 8-18). The Date Joined field is highlighted, the context-sensitive menu displays, and the mouse pointer points to the Delete Record command.

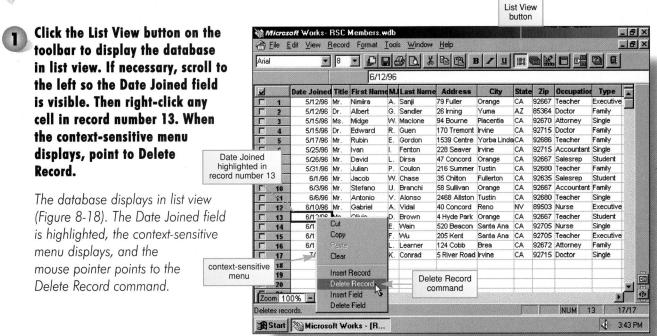

FIGURE 8-18

2 **Click Delete Record.**

Works deletes the record for Olivia D. Brown (Figure 8-19). Although the Date Joined field for record number 13 remains highlighted, the record is now for Cathy E. Wain, which was record number 14 before the deletion (see Figure 8-18). Notice that the database now contains 16 records instead of the 17 records it contained before deleting the record.

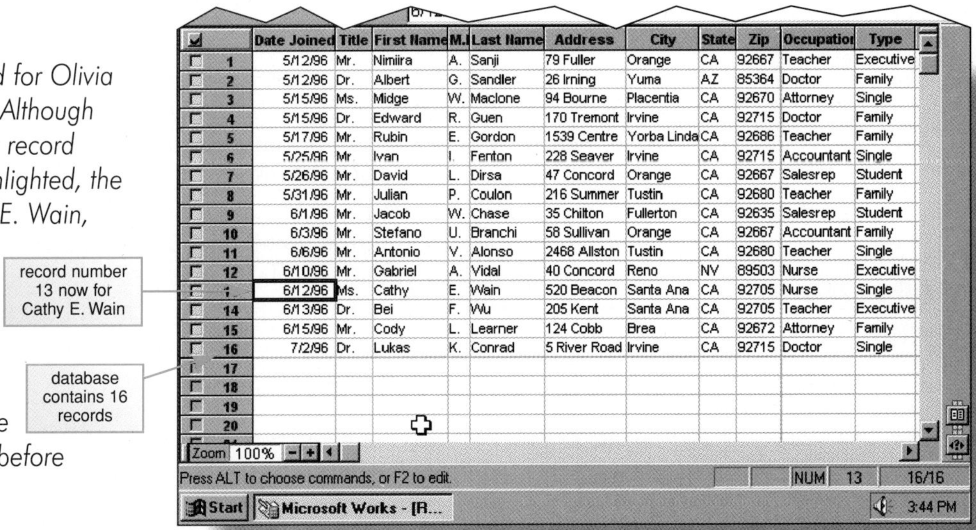

FIGURE 8-19

OtherWays

1. On Record menu click Delete Record

More *About*
**Deleting Records
in Form and
List View**

When deleting records in a
database in form or list view,
you can use the Undo Delete
Record command on the Edit
menu to restore the record.
Remember, however, this command must be used immediately
after deleting a record. It is also
an excellent idea to save the
database before deleting
records.

More *About*
Changing Data

In form or list view, highlight the
field to clear. Press the DELETE
key. Works clears the field entry.
If you previously applied formatting to the field (for example,
bold and center alignment),
Works retains the formatting.

More *About*
**Changing Data
in Form View**

The use of the context-sensitive
menu is limited in form view to
copying, cutting, or pasting
information in field entry positions only. When you right-click
a field name in form view, no
context-sensitive menu displays.

More *About*
**Changing the
Structure**

The ease with which the structure of a database can be
changed is a real advantage of
using a database like Works. The
structure you first defined
will not continue to be appropriate as you use the database. As
new situations arise, new fields
can be added or fields that no
longer are useful can be
deleted.

When you delete a record in either list view or form view, you can click Undo Delete Record on the Edit menu to restore the deleted record to the database, provided no subsequent operations have been performed. Be careful when deleting records to always save a copy of the file before beginning the deletion process.

Changing Data in a Database Field

Perhaps the most frequent change to a database is changing data. For example, in the members database, if a person moves, his or her address must be changed. To change data in form view, highlight the field in the record to be changed, type the new data, and press the ENTER key or click the Enter box. To change data in list view, highlight the field containing the data to be changed, type the new data, and press the ENTER key, click the Enter box, or press an arrow key. In this project, the address, city, and zip code of Antonio V. Alonso is changed from 2468 Allston, Tustin, 92680, to 327 Still Pond, Yorba Linda, 92686. To make these changes in list view, complete the following steps.

TO CHANGE DATA IN A LIST VIEW FIELD

Step 1: Highlight the Address field for record number 11 in the database.
Step 2: Type 327 Still Pond.
Step 3: Press the TAB key.
Step 4: Type Yorba Linda.
Step 5: Press the TAB key two times.
Step 6: Type 92686 and press the ENTER key or click the Enter box.

This change is reflected in the contents of the database in future steps in this project.

Inserting a New Field in a Database

A relatively common requirement is to modify the structure of the database after it has been created. For example, you may need to insert a new field in the database. A field can be inserted in the database using list view or form design view. A new field cannot be added in form view.

When you insert a field in the database, you must accomplish four tasks: (1) insert the new field in the database; (2) give a name to the new field; (3) size the new field properly; and (4) place data in the new field. The examples on the following pages illustrate these four tasks in both list view and form design view.

Inserting a New Field in List View

RSC Sports and Fitness Centers offer four different locations where members can use the facilities. To identify where each member attends, the records in the database must reflect this information. To insert a Location field before the Occupation field in the database in list view, size the field, and enter data into the field, perform the following steps.

Steps **To Insert a New Field in List View, Size the Field, and Enter Data**

1 **Right-click the field to the right of the location for the new field to be inserted (Occupation). Point to Insert Field on the context-sensitive menu. When the Insert Field cascading menu displays, point to Before.**

Works highlights the Occupation field (Figure 8-20). When you right-click the highlighted field, Works displays a context-sensitive menu. The right-pointing triangle to the right of the Insert Field command indicates a cascading menu is associated with the command. Works displays the Insert Field cascading menu and the mouse pointer points to Before. This command instructs Works to insert the new field to the left of the highlighted field (Occupation).

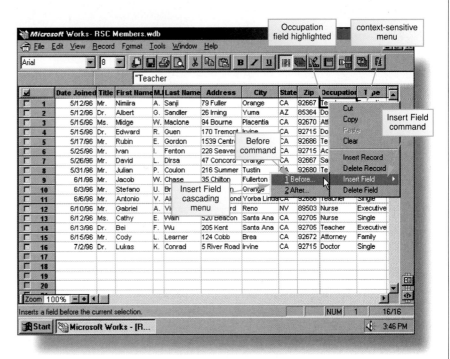

FIGURE 8-20

2 **Click Before. When the Insert Field dialog box displays, type Location in the Field name text box. Click Text in the Format box. Point to the Add button.**

Works displays the Insert Field dialog box (Figure 8-21). The field name, Location, displays in the Field name text box. The Text option button is selected. The mouse pointer points to the Add button. Notice the Type field in the document window displays to the right of the Insert Field dialog box.

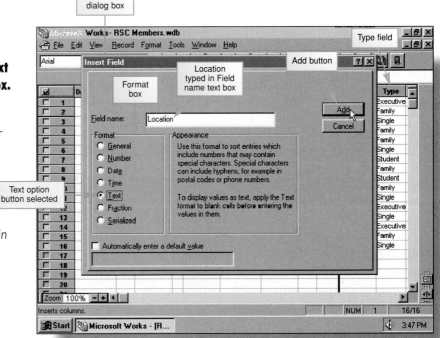

FIGURE 8-21

3 **Click the Add button in the Insert Field dialog box. Point to the Done button.**

When you click the Add button in the Insert Field dialog box, Works inserts the Location field to the left of the Occupation field. Field 11 displays as the default field name in the Field name text box. Notice the Occupation field now displays to the right of the Insert Field dialog box (Figure 8-22).

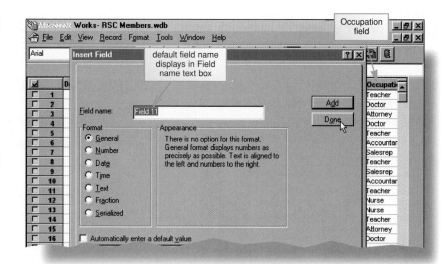

FIGURE 8-22

4 **Click the Done button in the Insert Field dialog box.**

Works closes the Insert Field dialog box and the new field, Location, displays to the left of the Occupation field (Figure 8-23).

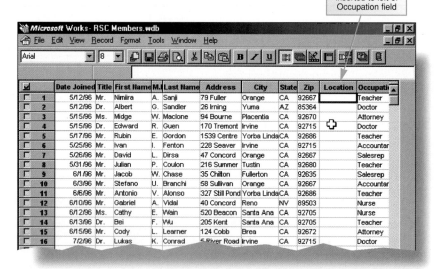

FIGURE 8-23

5 **Select the Location field for record number 1 (Nimiira A. Sanji) and type** Anaheim. **Then press the DOWN ARROW key, and type the location for Albert G. Sandler (** Irvine **). Press the DOWN ARROW key and continue this process until you have entered all locations.**

The locations for all members display in the Location field (Figure 8-24).

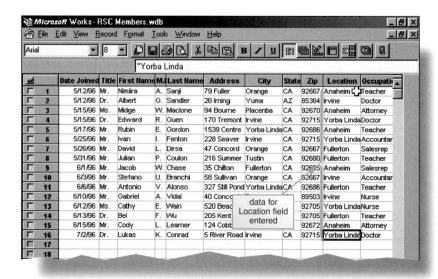

FIGURE 8-24

6 Position the mouse pointer on the border line between the Location field name and Occupation field name.

The mouse pointer changes to a vertical line with arrowheads on the left and right and the word ADJUST below, indicating you can drag the field border and resize the field (Figure 8-25).

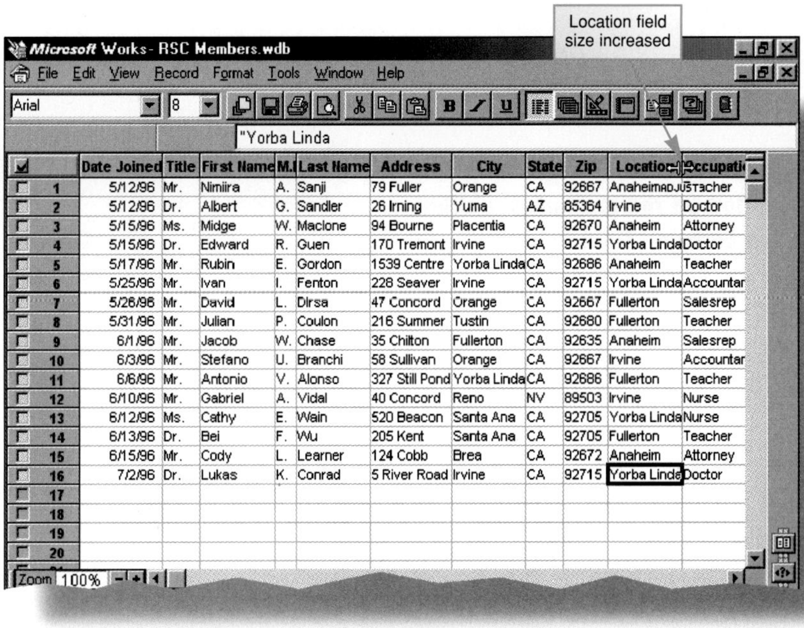

FIGURE 8-25

7 Drag the mouse pointer and column border to the right until there is an extra blank space to the right of Yorba Linda in the Location field. Release the mouse button.

The field size becomes larger as you drag to the right (Figure 8-26). The desired size is obtained when a blank space displays after the location entry, Yorba Linda. This is equal to a column width of 11.

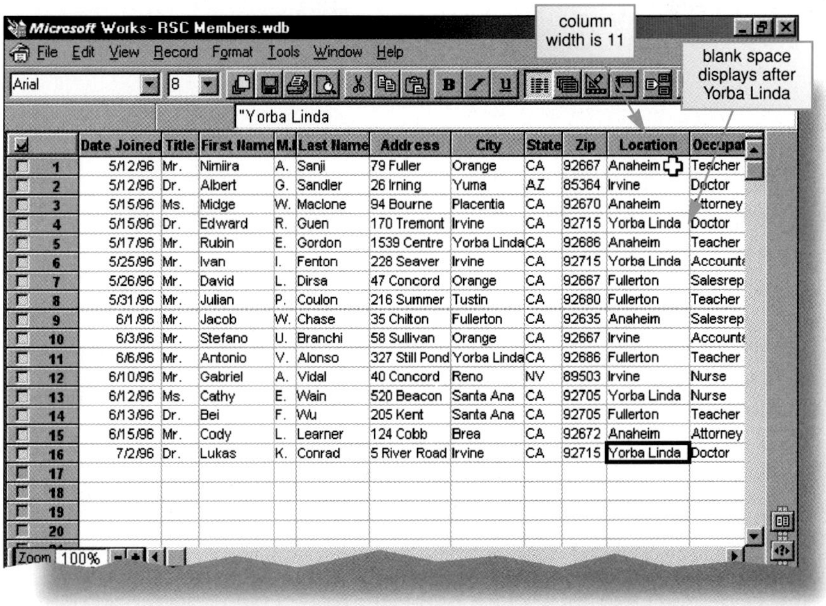

FIGURE 8-26

As you can see, when inserting a field in list view, you must name the field, insert the field, properly size the field, and enter the data for the field.

Notice in Step 1 on page W 8.19, you also can insert a field after (to the right of) the highlighted field. If you click After on the Insert Field cascading menu, the Location field would be inserted to the right of the Occupation field.

Sizing and Positioning an Inserted Field in Form Design View

When you insert a field in list view, the field is inserted into the database. As a result, it also will appear in form view. The new field, however, is neither positioned properly nor sized properly on the form. To position the field properly on the form and size the field, you must use form design view. Perform the steps on the next pages to size and position an Inserted filed in Form Design view.

*Other***Ways**

1. On Record menu click Insert Field, click Before, type desired name in Field name text box, click Add, click Done, on Format menu click Field Width, type desired column width, click OK button

Steps To Size and Position an Inserted Field in Form Design View

1 **Click the Form Design View button on the toolbar. Highlight the Location field name.**

Works displays the database in form design view (Figure 8-27). The record number and the highlighted field are the same as in list view (Figure 8-26 on the previous page). The inserted field name is highlighted and positioned in the upper left corner of the form. The field width is the Works form design view default value of 20. The mouse pointer displays with the word DRAG below the pointer.

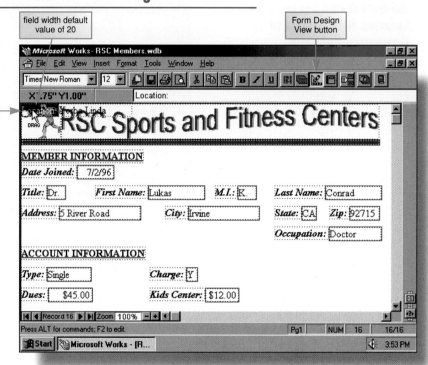

FIGURE 8-27

2 **Drag the Location field to coordinates X3.17″ Y3.00″.**

As you drag, an outline indicates where the field will be placed when you have completed the dragging operation, and the mouse pointer displays with the word MOVE below the pointer (Figure 8-28). Notice that part of the field overlaps the Occupation field. This will be corrected when the field width is reduced in size.

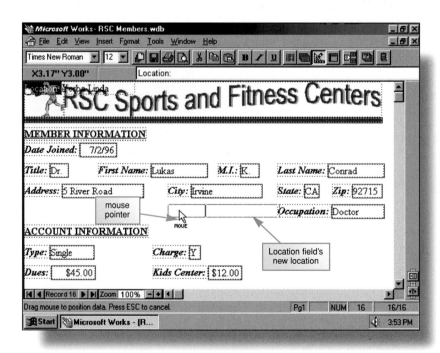

FIGURE 8-28

3 When the Location field is in the desired location, release the mouse button. Format the Field name so that it displays in bold and italic. Place a dark blue outline border around the field. Position the mouse pointer on the resize handle at the right side of the Location field entry box. Drag the resize handle to the left to reduce the field size for the Location field so that only the location, Yorba Linda, displays in the field entry.

The Location field is positioned on the form, formatted, and resized to a width of 14 (Figure 8-29). You may check the size of the resized field by clicking Field Size on the Format menu.

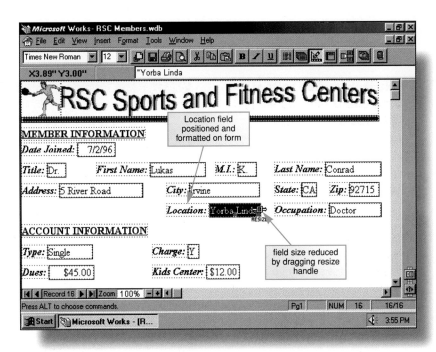

FIGURE 8-29

In virtually every case, when you insert a field using list view, you will need to resize and relocate the field in form design view.

After making changes to the database, it is suggested you save it by clicking the Save button on the toolbar.

Adding a Field in Form Design View

To add a field to a form you must use form design view. When you add a field in form design view, locate the position for the field on the form, enter the field, enter the format for the field, size the field, and format the field name.

In this project, a field called Total Dues is to be added to the database. Data for the Total Dues field will be entered using a formula that adds the Dues field value to the Kids Center field value. Therefore, you will format the Total Dues field as a number with a dollar sign, a comma, and 2 decimal places. The field width is 10. To add the Total Dues field to the database, perform the steps on the following pages.

Other Ways

1. On Edit menu click Position Selection, use arrow keys to position selection, on Format menu click Field Size, type desired width, click OK button

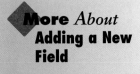

More *About* **Adding a New Field**

A variety of reasons exist why new fields are added to databases. Government regulations may change in such a way that an organization needs to maintain additional information.

Steps To Add and Format a Field in Form Design View

1 **Place the insertion point at the coordinates X5.00" Y4.00" by right-clicking the mouse pointer at that location on the form. When the context-sensitive menu displays, point to Insert Field.**

The insertion point displays at the coordinates X5.00" Y4.00" and the mouse pointer points to the Insert Field command on the context-sensitive menu (Figure 8-30).

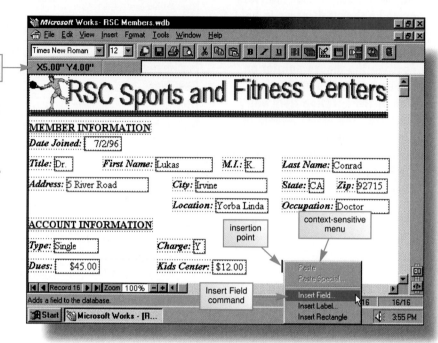

FIGURE 8-30

2 **Click Insert Field on the context-sensitive menu. When the Insert Field dialog box displays, type** Total Dues **in the Field name text box. Click Number in the Format box. Click the $1,234.56 format in the Appearance box. Ensure 2 displays in the Decimal places box and then point to the OK button.**

Works displays the Insert Field dialog box (Figure 8-31). The field name, Total Dues, is typed in the Field name text box. The $1,234.56 format is highlighted in the Appearance list box. The number 2 displays in the Decimal places box and the mouse pointer points to the OK button. These choices instruct Works to insert a field with the name, Total Dues, and apply a dollar sign, comma, and 2 decimal places as the format.

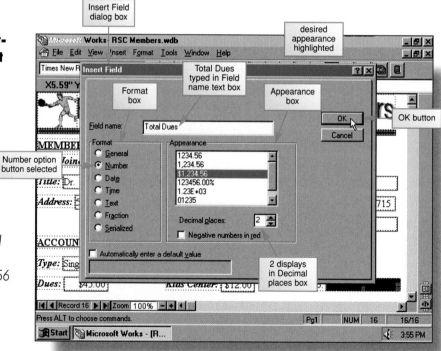

FIGURE 8-31

3 **Click the OK button in the Insert Field dialog box.**

When you click the OK button, Works places the Total Dues field with a width of 20 on the database form in form design view (Figure 8-32).

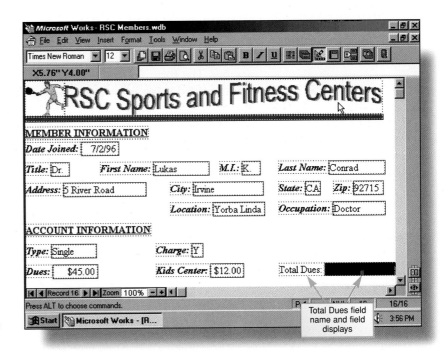

FIGURE 8-32

4 **Highlight the field name, Total Dues. Format the field name using 12-point Times New Roman bold and italic font. Add a dark blue border outline around the field entry. Size the field entry width to 10. Click anywhere on the form to remove the selection.**

The field name and field entry are formatted (Figure 8-33).

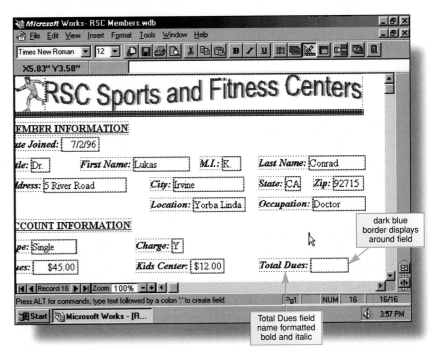

FIGURE 8-33

In Figure 8-33 you can see that the Total Dues field has been added to record 16. When you add a field to one record in form design view, Works adds the field to every other record in the database as well.

Using Formulas to Enter Data in Fields in Form View

Works allows you to enter not only actual data, but also **formulas** in a field. The formulas are similar to those you used when creating a spreadsheet. The formula begins with an equal sign and is followed by the names of the database fields that will be involved in the calculation.

*Other*Ways

1. In form design view, position insertion point at desired location on form, on Insert menu click Field, click Number, click $1,234.56, click OK button

2. Position insertion point at desired location on form, type desired field name followed by a colon, press the ENTER key, click Number, click $1,234.56, click OK button

In this project, the value in the Total Dues field is calculated by adding the value in the Dues field to the value in the Kids Center field. Thus, the formula is =Dues+Kids Center. The result of this calculation is the total dues owed by a member. The formula is entered in the Total Dues field in form view. To enter data in a field using a formula, perform the following steps.

Steps **To Enter Data in a Field Using a Formula**

1 Click the Form View button on the toolbar. Highlight the Total Dues field.

Works displays record number 16 and the Total Dues field is highlighted (Figure 8-34).

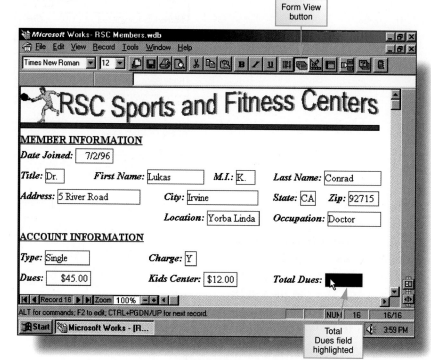

FIGURE 8-34

2 Type = (equal sign).

The equal sign you typed displays in the Total Dues field and the entry bar (Figure 8-35). The equal sign informs Works you are entering a formula.

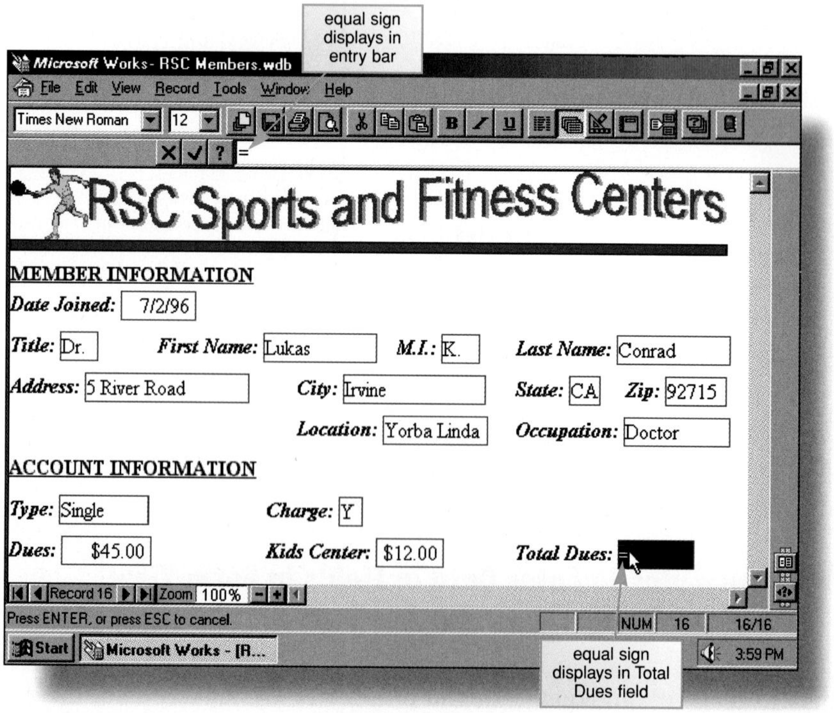

FIGURE 8-35

3 **Type** Dues+Kids Center **to complete the formula.**

As you type the formula, the characters display in the entry bar and partially display in the Total Dues field (Figure 8-36). The formula in the Total Dues field will add the value in the Dues field to the value in the Kid's Center field.

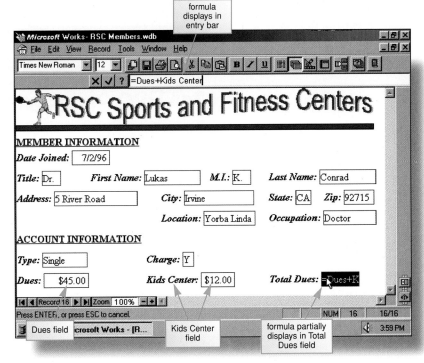

FIGURE 8-36

4 **Press the ENTER key or click the Enter box.**

Works calculates the results of the formula and places it in the Total Dues field (Figure 8-37). Because the Dues field contains the value $45.00 and the Kids Center field contains the value $12.00, the result in the Total Dues field is $57.00. The Total Dues field displays the value formatted with a dollar sign, a comma, and 2 decimal places because this format was specified when the field was inserted in form design view (see Figure 8-31 on page W 8.24).

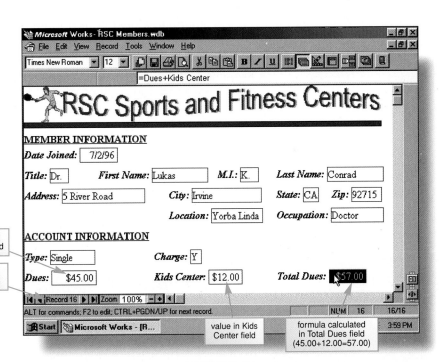

FIGURE 8-37

In Figure 8-37 you can see that the Total Dues field has been calculated for record number 16. When you enter a formula in a field for one record, Works applies the formula to the same field in all the records in the database. This is illustrated in Figure 8-38, where record number 1 in the database is displayed.

◆ **More** *About*
Adding Calculated Fields

Calculated fields play an important role in database management. When you enter a formula into a field, the formula is automatically copied to the same field in every other record. You can create a formula in form view or list view.

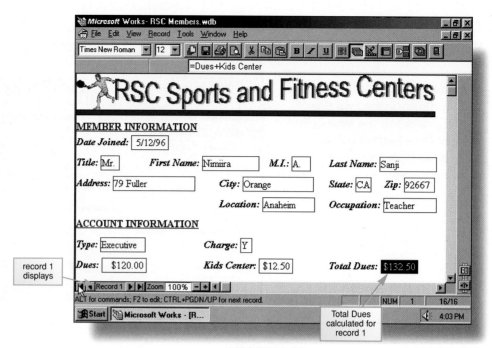

FIGURE 8-38

The Total Dues field in record number 1 is located in the same position as in record number 16 (see Figure 8-37 on the previous page). The number in the Total Dues field displays with a dollar sign and 2 decimal places; the value, $132.50, is obtained by adding the record number 1 Dues values ($120.00) to the record 1 number Kids Center values ($12.50). Similarly, each record in the database contains the Total Dues field, and in each record, the Total Dues value is calculated by adding the Dues value for that record to the Kids Center value for that record.

The Total Dues field, added in form design view, displays in list view with a font size of 10, which is the default size. No additional steps are necessary to format the Total Dues field in list view.

Adding or inserting fields in a database is an important procedure that occurs often when maintaining a database.

Deleting Database Fields

Just as it is important to be able to add fields to records in a database, it is necessary for you to be able to delete fields from a database. You should delete fields from a database when they are no longer needed so they do not use valuable disk and memory space.

In this project, both the Occupation and Charge fields are to be deleted from the database because they are no longer required for the members. The Occupation field will be deleted in form design view and the Charge field will be deleted in list view. You cannot delete fields in form view.

Deleting a Field in Form Design View

To delete the Occupation field when the database displays in form design view, complete the following steps.

Steps   **To Delete a Field in Form Design View**

1 **Click the Form Design View button on the toolbar. Highlight the field name of the field to be deleted (Occupation). Click Edit on the menu bar and point to Delete Selection.**

The Occupation field name is highlighted and the Edit menu displays (Figure 8-39). The mouse pointer points to the Delete Selection command.

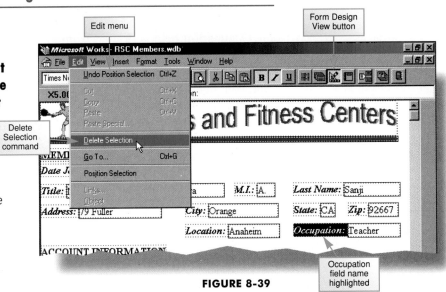

FIGURE 8-39

2 **Click Delete Selection. When the Microsoft Works dialog box displays, point to the OK button.**

Works displays the Microsoft Works dialog box with the message, Delete this field and all of its contents? (Figure 8-40). This dialog box is intended to act as a safeguard so you do not accidentally delete a field you want to retain. If you did not want to delete this field, you would choose the Cancel button.

FIGURE 8-40

3 **Click the OK button in the Microsoft Works dialog box.**

The Occupation field is deleted from the database (Figure 8-41).

FIGURE 8-41

▶ *Other***Ways**

1. In form design view, highlight the desired field name, press DELETE

Note these two important points when deleting a field in a Works database. First, even though you delete the field from a single record, such as record number 1 in Figure 8-41, the field is deleted from all records in the database. Thus, the Occupation field is deleted from all records in the database.

Second, when you are using form design view, once you have chosen the OK button in the Microsoft Works dialog box shown in Figure 8-40 on the previous page, the field is deleted and you cannot undo your action. Therefore, as a precaution, normally it is a good idea to save the database before deleting fields, so if you make a mistake you can recover the data.

Deleting a Field in List View

To delete the Charge field in list view, perform the following steps.

Steps **To Delete a Field in List View**

1 **Click the List View button on the toolbar. Use the right scroll arrow to view the Charge field. Right-click any cell in the Charge field. Point to Delete Field on the context-sensitive menu.**

In list view, the Charge field is high-lighted (Figure 8-42). This is the field to be deleted. The mouse pointer points to the Delete Field command on the context-sensitive menu.

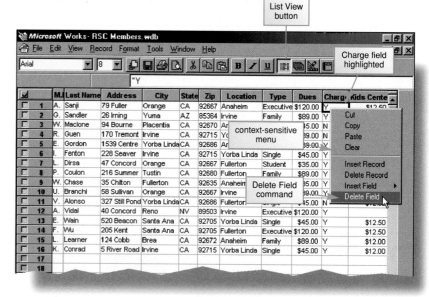

FIGURE 8-42

2 **Click Delete Field. When the Microsoft Works dialog box displays, point to the OK button.**

Works displays the Microsoft Works dialog box with the message, Permanently delete this information? (Figure 8-43). This dialog box is intended to act as a safeguard so you do not accidentally delete a field you want to retain.

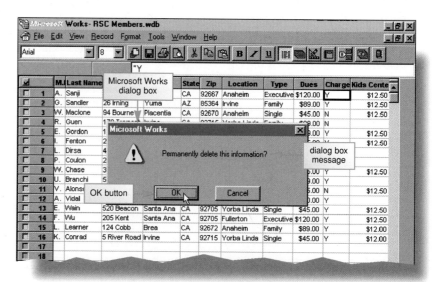

FIGURE 8-43

③ Click the OK button in the Microsoft Works dialog box.

Works deletes the highlighted field (Charge), moves the remaining fields left, and highlights the adjacent field to the right (Kids Center) (Figure 8-44).

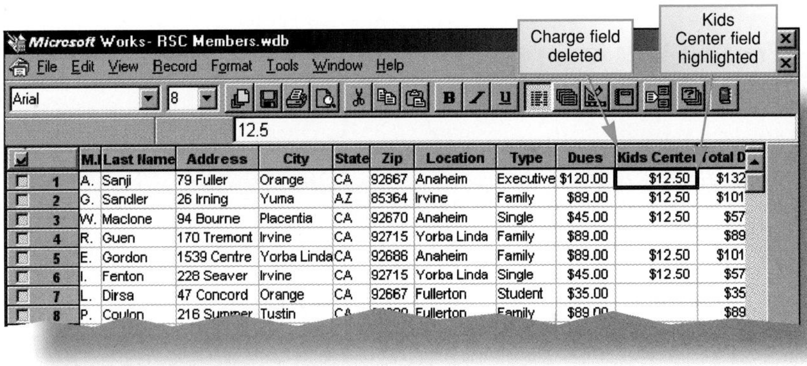

FIGURE 8-44

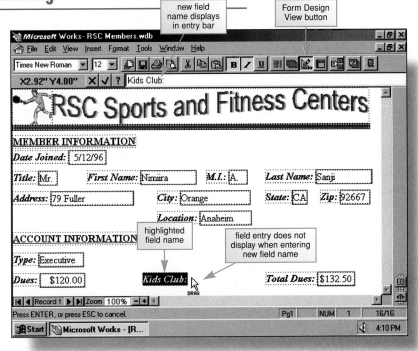

As in form design view, when you delete a field in list view, a dialog box displays as a safeguard to ensure you are deleting the correct field. Unlike form design view, however, once you have deleted a field in list view, you can use the Undo Delete Field command on the Edit menu to restore the deleted field if you have performed no subsequent operations. After the field has been restored, you may need to resize it to properly display the values.

Changing Field Names

On some occasions, a field name used in a database must be changed. This can occur when the name is not as descriptive as possible, when there is a possible conflict with another field name in the database, or for a variety of other reasons. In the membership database, change the Kids Center field name to Kids Club. To accomplish this task in form design view, complete the following steps.

Steps **To Change a Field Name in Form Design View**

① Click the Form Design View button on the toolbar to return to form design view. Then highlight the Kids Center field name and type `Kids Club:` **as the new name. Make sure you type the colon (:) after the new field name.**

The new field name, Kids Club, displays in the entry bar and in the field name position on the form (Figure 8-45). When you begin typing the words, Kids Club:, the field entry disappears. Typing a colon (:) after the field name identifies the words as a field name and not a label. Note that the Charge field, which was deleted in list view, no longer displays in form design view.

FIGURE 8-45

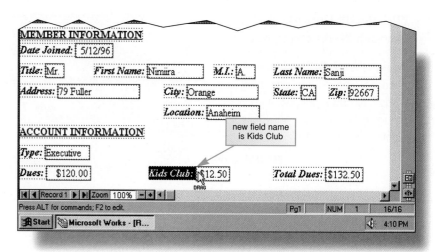

FIGURE 8-46

2 Press the ENTER key or click the Enter box.

Kids Club becomes the new field name (Figure 8-46).

When you view the database in list view, the name of the field will be Kids Club, as well.

An important consideration when changing a field name is that Works also will change any reference to the field name in formulas. To illustrate this, in Figure 8-47, the Total Dues field is highlighted. Notice in the formula displayed in the entry bar that the field name used is Kids Club, which is the new field name.

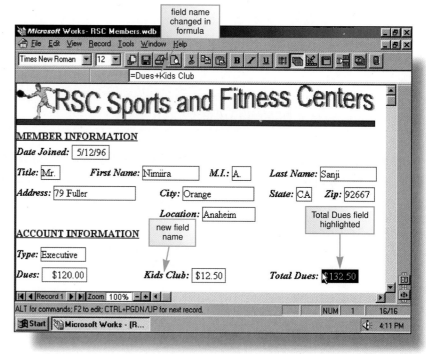

FIGURE 8-47

Rearranging Fields

When changes occur in a database record, you often will be required to modify the format of the record in form design view or list view. In this project, the fields are rearranged in both form design view and list view. Rearranging the fields in form design view has no effect on the position of the fields in list view, and rearranging the fields in list view has no effect on the position of the fields in form design view.

Rearranging Fields in Form Design View

Rearranging the fields in form design view may involve moving fields, adding labels, changing label styles or field styles, and other alterations. For the form design view of the members database, the changes are: (1) move the City, State, Zip, and Location fields to different locations on the form; (2) move the Account Information section down on the form.

To move the fields, perform the following steps (see Figure 8-48).

TO MOVE FIELDS IN FORM DESIGN VIEW

Step 1: Highlight the Location field name and drag it to the coordinates X2.92" Y3.67".

Step 2: Highlight the City field name and drag it to the coordinates X0.75" Y3.00".

Step 3: Highlight the State field name and drag it to the coordinates X2.92" Y3.00".

Step 4: Highlight the Zip field name and drag it to the coordinates X4.00" Y3.00".

Step 5: Highlight the **ACCOUNT INFORMATION** label, hold down the CTRL key and click Type, click Location, click Dues, click Kids Club, and click Total Dues. Drag the selection to the coordinates X0.75" Y3.50".

The form design view of the database after moving the fields to new positions is shown in Figure 8-48.

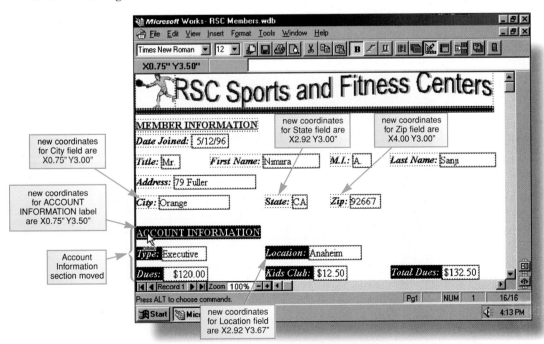

FIGURE 8-48

Rearranging Fields in List View

Initially, the order of fields in list view corresponds to the order in which you created them. However, you can arrange the fields in list view in any order you wish. In the list view of the members database, the Type field is to be moved to the left of the Location field. Perform the following steps to move a field in list view.

Steps To Move Fields in List View

1 **Click the List View button on the toolbar. If necessary scroll to view the Type field. Click the field name (Type) to highlight the field you want to move.**

The database displays in list view (Figure 8-49). When you click the field name, Type, Works highlights the entire column in the database. The mouse pointer changes to a left pointing arrow displaying the word DRAG under it, which indicates you can move the field to another location.

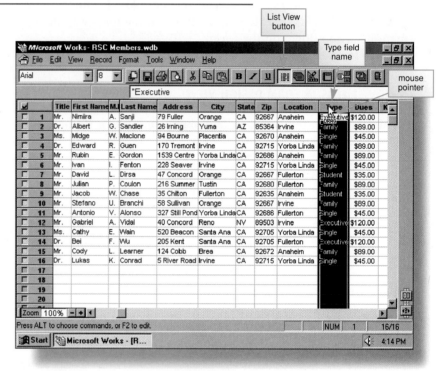

FIGURE 8-49

2 **Drag the field to the left of the Location field.**

As you drag the field, Works displays a vertical bar indicating the proposed location of the field (Figure 8-50). The word MOVE displays under the mouse pointer. The field you drag remains highlighted and does not move while you drag.

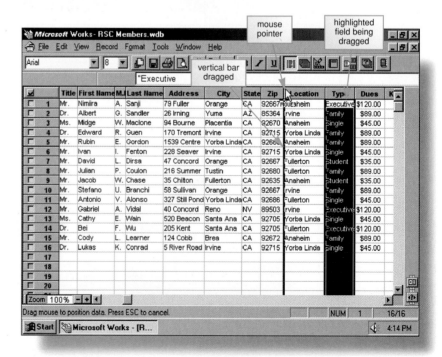

FIGURE 8-50

3 **When the vertical bar is in the desired location, release the mouse button.**

Works moves the highlighted field to the location of the vertical bar (Figure 8-51). After being moved, the field remains highlighted. Select any field to remove the selection.

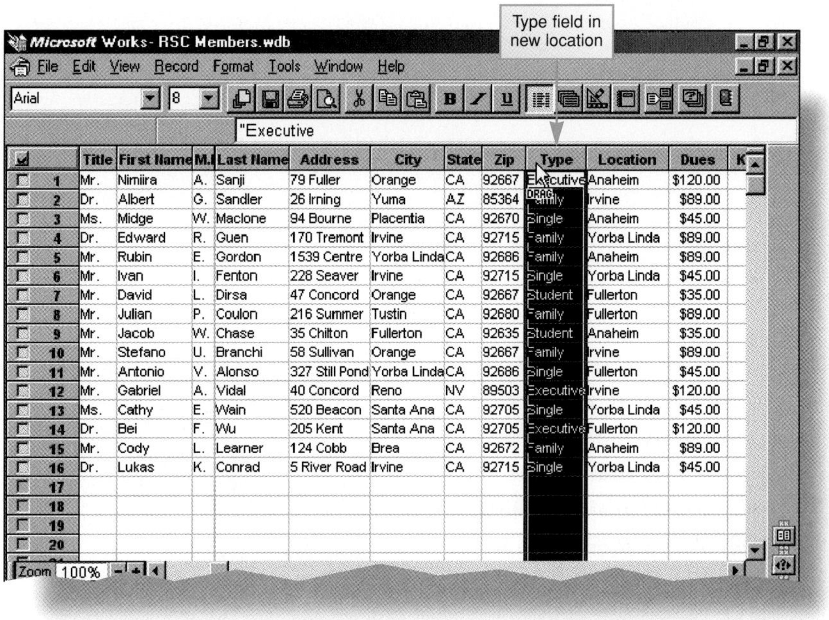

Type field in new location

FIGURE 8-51

After moving the Type field in list view, the maintenance of the database is complete. You should now save the revised database.

Saving a Revised Database

As you revise the database, it is normally a good practice to save the database periodically so your work is not lost in case of electrical or computer failure. If you are revising a database and want to keep the same filename, then you should save the database by clicking the Save button on the toolbar or by clicking Save on the File menu.

If you want to save the database using a different filename, such as RSC Members Revised, then use the Save As command as shown in earlier projects. Perform the following steps to save the database with a new name.

TO SAVE A DATABASE FILE WITH A NEW NAME

Step 1: Click Save As on the File menu.
Step 2: When the Save As dialog box displays, type RSC Members Revised in the File name text box.
Step 3: Select drive A: from the Save in drop-down list box.
Step 4: Click the Save button in the Save As dialog box.

Viewing the Database in List View

When you work with a database in list view, often the records contain more fields than can display on the screen at one time. In some cases, it is advantageous to view records with the leftmost and rightmost fields visible, but with some fields between them not visible. Works allows you to do this by dividing the database work area into two or more panes. A **pane** is a part of the window through which you can view a portion of the database. The panes are separated by a **vertical split**

> **O***ther***Ways**
> 1. Highlight field to move, on Edit menu click Cut, highlight location to paste field, on Edit menu click Paste.
> 2. Highlight field to move, on toolbar click Cut button, highlight location to paste field, click Paste button.
> 3. Highlight field to move, press CTRL+X, highlight location to paste field, press CTRL+V

bar, a **horizontal split bar**, or both. Suppose, for example, you want to view the name of the members in the database together with the Type, Location, Dues, Kids Club, and Total Dues fields. To split the window into a left pane and a right pane and view these fields together on the screen, perform the following steps.

Steps To View a Database in Panes

1 **If the database is not displayed in list view, click the List View button on the toolbar. Position the mouse pointer on the vertical split box, which is a thin bar to the left of the Zoom box at the bottom of the screen.**

The database displays in list view (Figure 8-52). The mouse pointer, when positioned on the vertical split box, changes shape to two vertical bars and two horizontal arrows with the word ADJUST beneath it. This mouse pointer shape indicates you can split the screen into two panes.

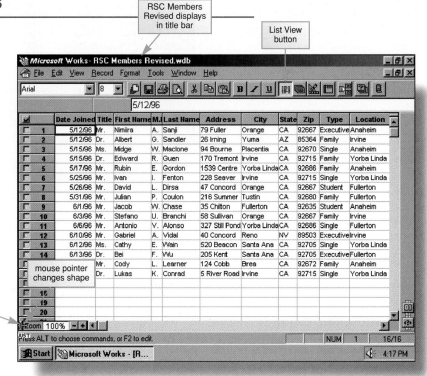

FIGURE 8-52

2 **Drag the vertical split bar to the right until the split bar rests in the first position of the Address field.**

When you drag the mouse pointer positioned on the vertical split box, a wide vertical line called the vertical split bar accompanies the mouse pointer (Figure 8-53). The split bar indicates where the window will be separated into panes. In Figure 8-53, the split bar is located at the beginning of the Address field. This location informs Works to make the Address field part of the right pane and the Last Name field part of the left pane.

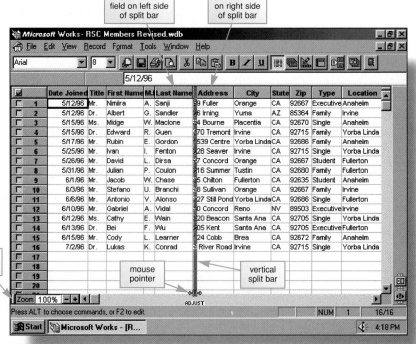

FIGURE 8-53

3 **Release the left mouse button and move the mouse pointer off the split bar.**

Works divides the window into two panes (Figure 8-54). Each pane has its own scroll bar, scroll box, and scroll arrows. This means you can scroll data in either pane left or right, and the data in the other pane will not move.

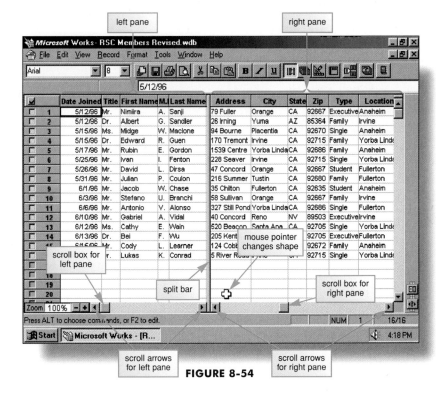

FIGURE 8-54

4 **Point to the right scroll arrow in the right pane and click the scroll arrow four times.**

The mouse pointer points to the right scroll arrow in the right pane (Figure 8-55). Each time you click the right scroll arrow, the data in the right pane moves one field to the left, but the data in the left pane does not move. As a result, the left pane displays the Date Joined, Title, First Name, M. I., and Last Name fields, while the right pane displays the Type, Location, Dues, Kids Club, and Total Dues fields. The fields between the Last Name and Type are hidden from view.

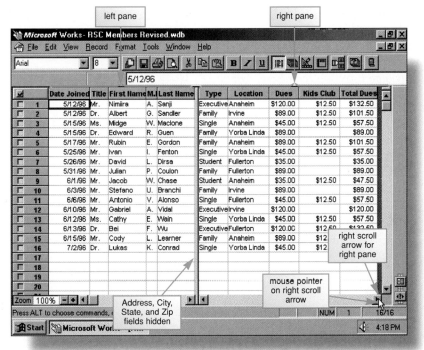

FIGURE 8-55

5 **Using the scroll arrows for the left and right panes, you can view any combination of fields you wish. To remove the panes and return to a single window, position the mouse pointer on the split bar.**

The mouse pointer changes shape and rests on the split bar (Figure 8-56).

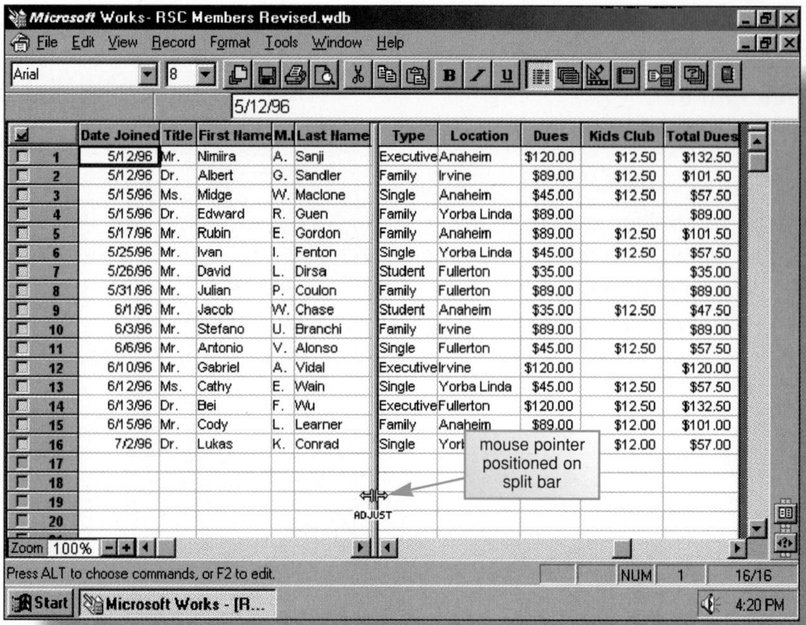

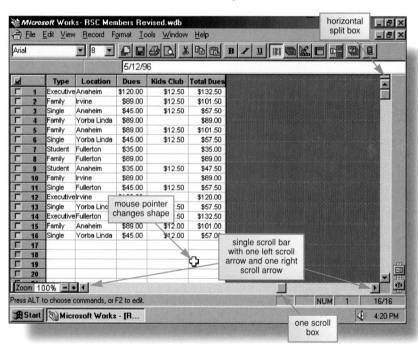

FIGURE 8-56

6 **Double-click the split bar.**

The split bar disappears and the separate panes no longer display (Figure 8-57). A single scroll bar, a single scroll box and one set of scroll arrows display at the bottom of the screen. The leftmost field (Type) in the right pane (Figure 8-56) becomes the leftmost field in the window.

FIGURE 8-57

Other Ways

1. On Window menu click Split

You can divide the list view window into an upper and lower pane by pointing to the horizontal split box (Figure 8-57) and dragging the split bar down to the desired location. This configuration is useful when your database consists of many records and you want to view records at the beginning of the database and other records in the middle or at the end of the database. For example, if the database contains 1,000 records, you could view records 1 through 10 in the upper pane, and records 990 through 1,000 in the lower pane. When you split the window into upper and lower panes, each pane has a separate vertical scroll bar.

You also can split the window into four panes, each with its own scroll bar, using one of two methods: (1) drag the vertical split bar to the desired location, and then drag the horizontal split bar to the desired location; or (2) click Split on the Window menu.

When you click Split on the Window menu, Works displays a horizontal and vertical split bar with a split pointer positioned at the intersection of the bars (Figure 8-58). You can drag the intersection around the window until you have selected the desired location, and then click to set the vertical and horizontal split bars in a permanent position.

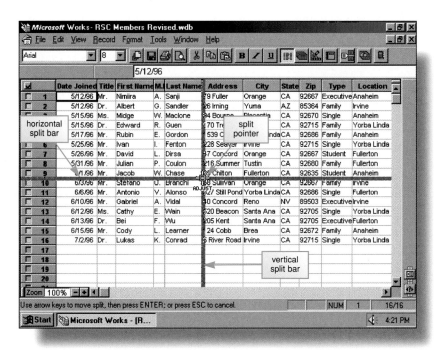

To return to a single window, place the mouse pointer at the intersection of the split bars, where it will once again change to the split pointer, and double-click.

Reformatting a Database

In some applications a database may contain data which, when used in a different format, can produce a report or provide useful information. The RSC Members Revised database is such an application. To create the report shown in Figure 8-59 on the next page, data in the RSC Members Revised database must be reformatted.

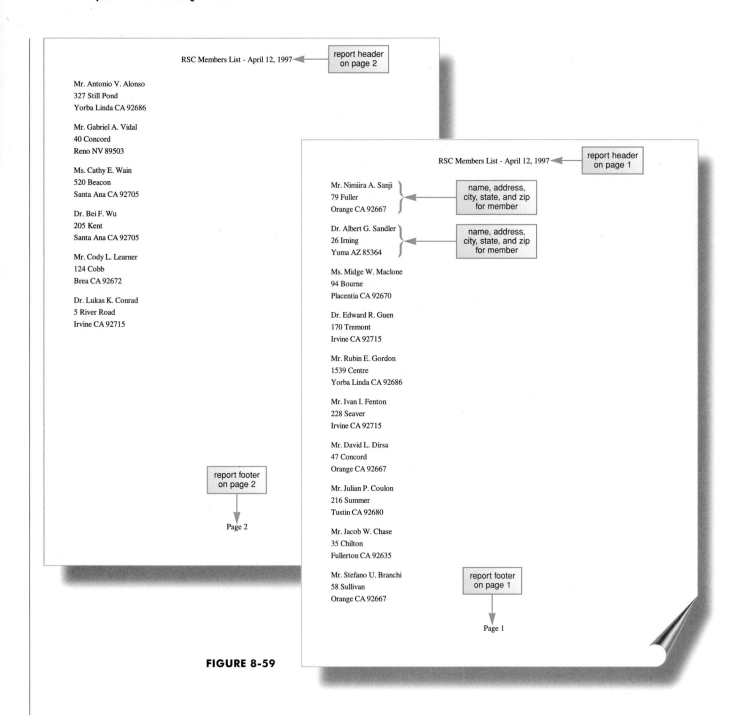

FIGURE 8-59

The reformatting process includes the following steps: (1) delete the fields in the RSC Members Revised database that are not needed for the report; (2) delete the clip art, WordArt title, and labels from the form design view of the database; (3) reformat the form design view of the database, including moving fields, removing field names, invoking the Slide to left option of the database, and changing settings in the Page Setup dialog box; (4) print the reformatted database in the new report format; and (5) save the reformatted database with a new name.

Each of these steps is explained in detail on the following pages.

Deleting Fields in a Database

The first task is to delete the fields not being used in the report. Complete the following steps to perform this task.

Steps **To Delete Fields in List View**

1 **With the RSC Members Revised database displayed in list view, scroll the window so the Type, Location, Dues, Kids Club, and Total Dues fields are visible. Drag the mouse pointer across these fields for record number 1. Right-click the selection and point to Delete Field.**

Works highlights the fields over which you dragged the mouse pointer (Figure 8-60). The context-sensitive menu displays and the mouse pointer points to the Delete Field command.

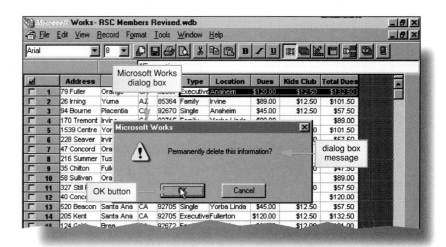

FIGURE 8-60

2 **Click Delete Field on the context-sensitive menu. When the Microsoft Works dialog box displays, point to the OK button.**

When you click Delete Field on the context-sensitive menu, Works displays the Microsoft Works dialog box with the message, Permanently delete this information? (Figure 8-61). The mouse pointer points to the OK button.

FIGURE 8-61

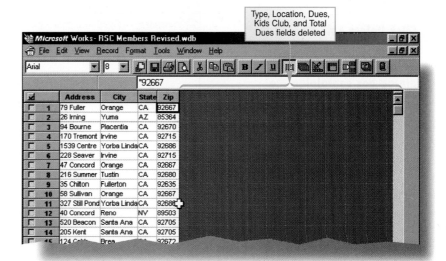

3 **Click the OK button in the Microsoft Works dialog box.**

Works deletes all the highlighted fields (Type, Location, Dues, Kids Club, and Total Dues fields) (Figure 8-62).

FIGURE 8-62

After deleting the fields in the list view, you must delete selected information in form design view.

Deleting Clip Art, WordArt, Fields, and Labels in Form Design View

The next task is to delete the clip art, the WordArt title, fields, and labels from form design view because this information is not used when producing the report. Complete the following steps to accomplish this task.

Steps To Delete Clip Art, WordArt, Fields, and Labels in Form Design View

1 **Click the Form Design View button on the toolbar to display the database in form design view. Click the clip art object. Then, while holding down the CTRL key, click the object containing the words RSC Sports and Fitness Centers, the rectangle, the MEMBER INFORMATION label, the Date Joined field name, and the ACCOUNT INFORMATION label. Right-click the selection and point to Delete Selection.**

The database displays in form design view (Figure 8-63). The selected fields, objects, and labels are highlighted. The mouse pointer points to the Delete Selection command on the context-sensitive menu.

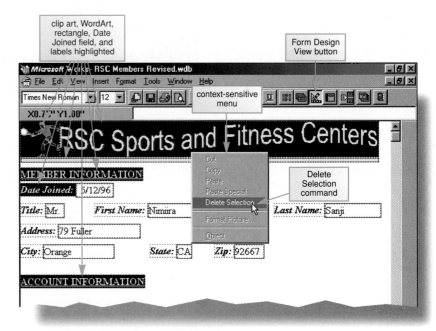

FIGURE 8-63

2 **Click Delete Selection on the context-sensitive menu. Click the OK button in the Microsoft Works dialog box containing the message, Delete this field and all its contents?**

The clip art, the words RSC Sports and Fitness Centers, the rectangle, the Date Joined field, the MEMBER INFORMATION label, and the ACCOUNT INFORMATION label are deleted (Figure 8-64).

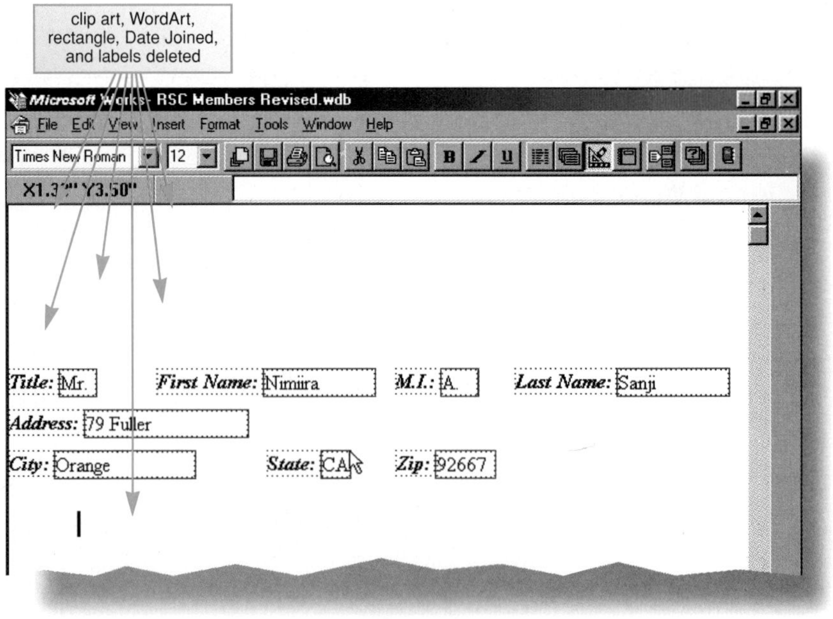

FIGURE 8-64

All the fields that are not needed to produce the output shown in Figure 8-59 on page W 8.40 are now deleted from the database. The remaining fields, Title, First Name, M.I., Last Name, Address, City, State, and Zip, are used to prepare the report.

Reformatting the Form Design View of the Database

The next task requires reformatting the form design view of the database. The first step is to rearrange the fields on the form, as shown in the following steps.

 Steps **To Rearrange Fields in Form Design View**

1 **Click the Title field name. Then, while holding down the CTRL key, click the First Name, M.I., and Last Name field names. Point to the Title field.**

The Title, First Name, M.I., and Last Name field names are highlighted (Figure 8-65).

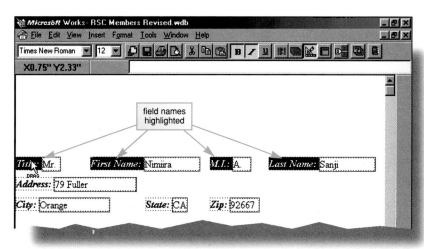

FIGURE 8-65

2 **Drag the highlighted fields upward as a unit to the coordinates X0.75" Y1.00" and release the mouse button.**

The Title, First Name, M. I., and Last Name fields move upward as a unit and are positioned at the top left section of the form (Figure 8-66).

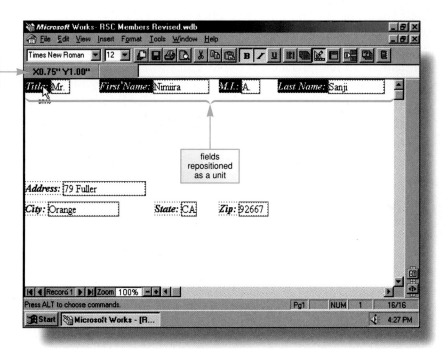

FIGURE 8-66

3 Highlight the Address field name and drag it to the coordinates X0.75" Y1.25". Highlight the City, State, and Zip fields and drag the City, State, and Zip fields as a unit to X0.75" Y1.50".

The fields are positioned in three rows near the top of the form (Figure 8-67).

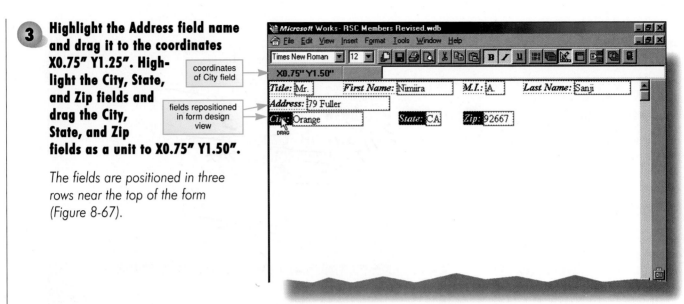

FIGURE 8-67

Removing the Border

After the fields are rearranged as shown in Figure 8-67, you must remove the border surrounding the field entries and then inform Works that when the fields print, they are to print next to each other. In addition, you must indicate to Works that the field names are not to print (see Figure 8-59 on page W 8.40). Perform the following steps to remove the border.

Steps **To Remove a Border around the Field Entries**

1 Highlight all the field entries, right-click the selection, and point to Border (Figure 8-68).

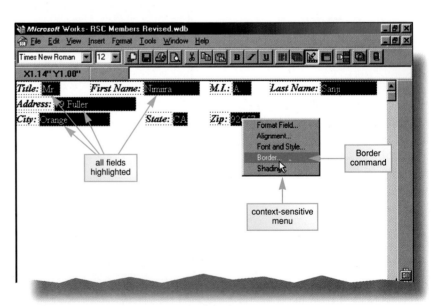

FIGURE 8-68

2 **Click Border. When the Format dialog box displays, click the empty box in the Line style box on the Border sheet and then point to the OK button.**

The Format dialog box displays (Figure 8-69). The Outline box in the Border box displays no line because the empty box in the Line style box is selected.

3 **Click the OK button in the Format dialog box.**

Works removes the borders around the fields.

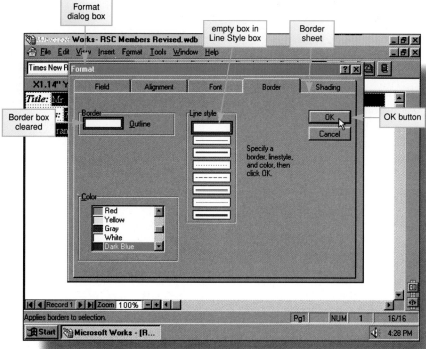

FIGURE 8-69

Sliding Fields to the Left and Hiding Field Names

The next step is to slide the fields to the left and hide the field names prior to printing. To accomplish this task, perform the following steps.

 To Select Slide to Left and Hide Field Names

1 **Highlight all the field entries in form design view, right-click the selection, and point to Alignment.**

Works highlights all the fields on the form and the mouse pointer points to the Alignment command on the context-sensitive menu (Figure 8-70).

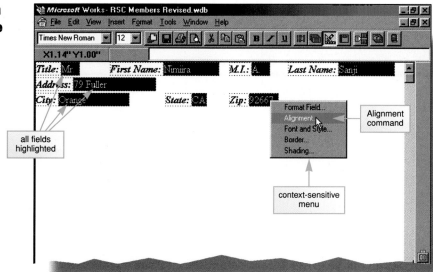

FIGURE 8-70

2 **Click Alignment. When the Format dialog box displays, click the Slide to left check box on the Alignment sheet and point to the OK button.**

Works displays the Format dialog box (Figure 8-71). The Slide to left check box is selected and the mouse pointer points to the OK button. The Slide to left option means that when the form view of the database is printed, the highlighted fields will be moved to the left with only a single space separating them from the fields to their left, regardless of the amount of space separating them on the form itself. If a field is the leftmost field on a line, such as the Title field, it prints at the left margin. The Slide to left option has no effect when the database displays in form design view on the screen.

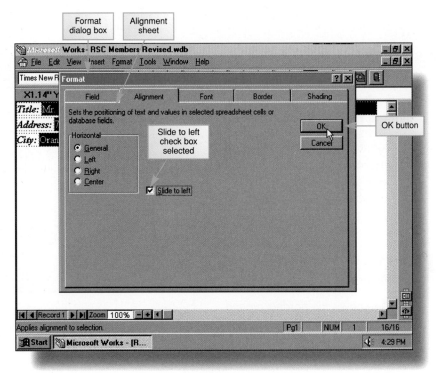

FIGURE 8-71

3 **Click the OK button in the Format dialog box. Then, with all the fields still highlighted, click Format on the menu bar and point to Show Field Name.**

Works displays the Format menu and the mouse pointer points to the Show Field Name command (Figure 8-72). The check mark beside the Show Field Name command indicates the command is selected, which means the field names display in form design view and will print when the database is printed.

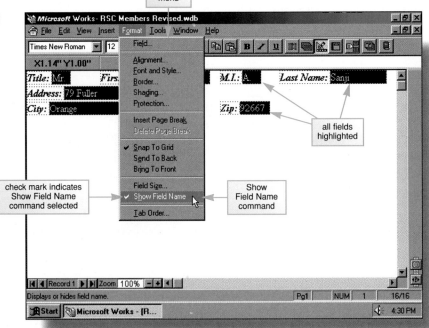

FIGURE 8-72

4 **Click Show Field Name.**

The field names no longer display in form design view (Figure 8-73). Notice that clicking the Show Field Name command when a check mark appears next to it turns off the option. If you were to click Format on the menu bar again and click Show Field Name, the field names of the highlighted fields once again would display in form design view.

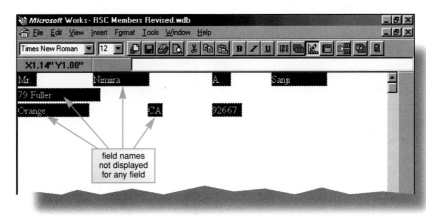

field names not displayed for any field

FIGURE 8-73

Notice two important aspects of the steps illustrated in Figure 8-72 and Figure 8-73. First, even though the field names do not display in form design view, the names are still associated with each field and the names do display in list view.

Second, although the fields on a single line are separated by multiple spaces in the form design view display, they will print with only one space between them because the Slide to left option in the Format dialog box has been selected for each field.

The use of the Slide to left feature allows you to produce different styles of reports from the same database.

Controlling Spacing between Records

To complete the preparation required to print the Members List shown in Figure 8-59 on page W 8.40, you must inform Works that multiple records are to print on the same page separated by a blank line. This requires the use of the Page Setup command on the File menu, as illustrated in the following steps.

  To Specify Space between Records and Not Print Field Lines

1 **Click File on the menu bar and point to Page Setup.**

Works displays the File menu and the mouse pointer points to the Page Setup command (Figure 8-74).

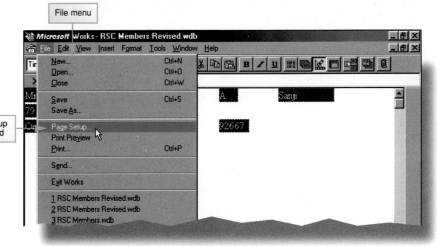

File menu

Page Setup command

FIGURE 8-74

2 Click Page Setup. When the Page Setup dialog box displays, click the Other Options tab. Then ensure that the Print field lines and the Page breaks between records check boxes are *not* selected. Type .2" in the Space between records text box. Point to the OK button.

Works displays the Page Setup dialog box (Figure 8-75). The Print field lines check box is not selected. The Page breaks between records check box is not selected, which informs Works not to place each record on a separate page. When multiple records print on the same page, you must indicate the space between each record. In Figure 8-75, the distance is specified as .2" in the Space between records text box. The mouse pointer points to the OK button.

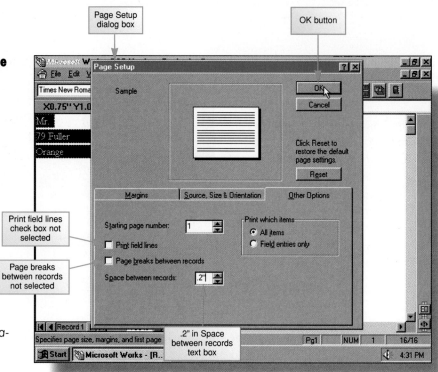

FIGURE 8-75

3 Click the OK button in the Page Setup dialog box.

Works returns to the form design view display of the database. Notice in Figure 8-75, in the Print which items box of the Page Setup dialog box, you can select either the All items option button or the Field entries only option button. It may appear that if you select the Field entries only option, you do not have to turn off the Show Field Names command on the Format menu. This is true if you are *not* using the Slide to left option. If you use the Slide to left option, however, Works prints only the field entry but leaves room on the report for the field name. Therefore, the only way to print the field entries next to each other is to turn off the Show Field Name command on the Format menu.

Headers and Footers

The last step before printing the database is to add a header and a footer to the report. The header contains the title, RSC Members List, together with the current date. The footer contains the page number. Headers and footers are displayed on form view database reports in much the same way as shown for the Spreadsheet tool in Project 6.

Recall that you can place certain codes in headers and footers to cause Works to display the corresponding information. In this project, use &n to place the current date in the header and &p to place the page number in the footer. A complete listing of the available codes is shown in Table 8-1 on page W 8.56.

To place a header and a footer on a form view database report, complete the following steps.

Steps To Place a Header and a Footer on a Form View Database Report

1 **Click View on the menu bar and point to Headers and Footers.**

Works displays the View menu and the mouse pointer points to the Headers and Footers command (Figure 8-76).

FIGURE 8-76

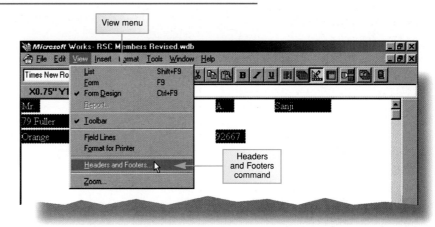

2 **Click Headers and Footers. When the View Headers and Footers dialog box displays, type** RSC Members List - &n **in the Header text box and** Page &p **in the Footer text box. Then point to the OK button.**

Works displays the View Headers and Footers dialog box (Figure 8-77). The Header and Footer text boxes contain the typed information. The mouse pointer points to the OK button.

3 **Click the OK button in the View Headers and Footers dialog box.**

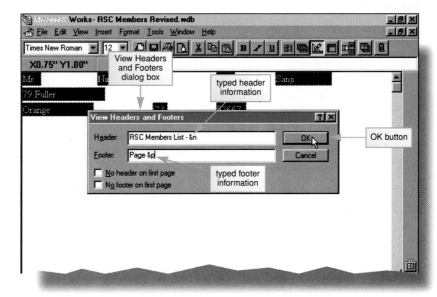

FIGURE 8-77

Works returns to the form design view display. No visible change takes place in the display, but the headers and footers will print when the report is printed.

Printing the Revised Database

The preparation of the report is now complete. To ensure the document will print properly, you may have to make some alterations to the database settings. To ensure the database will print properly and then to print the database, complete the following steps.

TO ENSURE PROPER PRINTING AND PRINT THE REVISED DATABASE

Step 1: Click the Form View button on the toolbar.
Step 2: Click File on the menu bar and click Page Setup.
Step 3: Click the Source, Size & Orientation tab in the Page Setup dialog box. Ensure the Portrait option button in the Orientation box on the Source, Size & Orientation sheet is selected.

> ◆ **M**ore *About*
> **Page Numbers in Headers and Footers**
>
> When you print database records, you may wish to number the pages starting with a number other than one. Click Page Setup on the File menu. Click the Other Option tab. In the Starting Page Number box, type a page number for the first page. Works numbers the pages beginning with this number.

More *About*
Printing in Form Design View

You can print a blank record form to use to manually copy data. Press CTRL+END in form design view to display a blank record, and then click the Print button on the toolbar.

Step 4: Click the OK button in the Page Setup dialog box.
Step 5: Click Print on the File menu.
Step 6: Ensure the All records option button in the What to Print box is selected.
Step 7: Choose the OK button in the Print dialog box.

Works prints the report (see Figure 8-59 on page W 8.40).

Saving the New Database

Once you have created the new database, save it using another name. To save the database using a different name, complete the following steps.

TO SAVE THE NEW DATABASE USING A DIFFERENT NAME

Step 1: Click Save As on the File menu.
Step 2: When Works displays the Save As dialog box, type the new filename in the File name text box.
Step 3: If necessary, select drive A from the Save in drop-down list box.
Step 4: Click the Save button in the Save As dialog box.

Project Summary

In this project you have learned about database maintenance. You added records to and deleted records from a database, learned how to make changes to records in a database, added fields to and deleted fields from the database, and changed the size of fields. You also changed the layout of the database in form design view and inserted a field containing a formula into the database. Finally, you derived a new database from an existing database and formatted a report.

What You Should Know

Having completed the project, you should now be able to complete the following tasks:

▶ Add a Record to a Database in Form View *(W 8.11)*

▶ Add a Record to a Database in List View *(W8.12)*

▶ Add and Format a Field in Form Design View *(W8.24)*

▶ Change a Field Name in Form Design View *(W8.31)*

▶ Change Data in a List View Field *(W8.18)*

▶ Delete a Field in Form Design View *(W8.29)*

▶ Delete a Field in List View *(W8.30)*

▶ Delete a Record in Form View *(W8.15)*

▶ Delete a Record in List View *(W8.17)*

▶ Delete Clip Art, WordArt, Fields, and Labels in Form Design View *(W8.42)*

▶ Delete Fields in List View *(W8.41)*

▶ Enter Data in a Field Using a Formula *(W8.26)*

▶ Insert a New Field in List View, Size the Field, and Enter Data *(W8.19)*

▶ Move Fields in Form Design View *(W8.33)*

▶ Move Fields in List View *(W8.34)*

▶ Place a Header and Footer on a Form View Database Report *(W8.49)*

▶ Rearrange Fields in Form Design View *(W8.43)*

▶ Remove a Border around the Field Entries *(W8.44)*

▶ Select Slide to Left and Hide Field Names *(W8.45)*

▶ Size and Position an Inserted Field in Form Design View *(W8.22)*

▶ Specify Space between Records and Not Print Field Lines *(W8.47)*

▶ View a Database in Panes *(W8.36)*

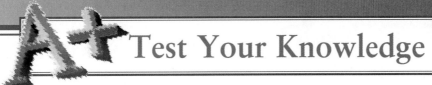

Test Your Knowledge

1 True/False

Instructions: Circle T if the statement is true or F if the statement is false.

T F 1. You can add a record to a database in form design view or list view.

T F 2. To delete a record in form view, display the record to delete on the screen, and then click Delete Record on the Record menu.

T F 3. To delete a record in list view, highlight any field in the record, and then click Delete Record on the toolbar.

T F 4. A good practice is to save a database before deleting records because once you delete a record and perform subsequent operations, there is no way to undo the delete operations.

T F 5. A field can be inserted in a database using either list view or form view.

T F 6. When you enter data in a field using a formula, the field name must begin with an equal sign.

T F 7. When you insert a field in list view, the field displays in the proper location in form design view.

T F 8. To separate the list view of a database into a left pane and a right pane, click Split on the Window menu.

T F 9. To eliminate panes from the list view of a database, double-click the split bar.

T F 10. To delete a label in form design view, highlight the label and click Delete Selection on the Edit menu.

2 Multiple Choice

Instructions: Circle the correct response.

1. To delete a record, _____.
   a. in form view, display the record to be deleted and click Delete Record on the toolbar
   b. in form design view, display the record to be deleted and click Delete Record on the Edit menu
   c. in list view, highlight the record to be deleted and click Delete Record on the toolbar
   d. in form view, display the record to be deleted and click Delete Record on the Record menu

2. Clicking Insert Field Before on the Insert menu inserts a new field to the _____.
   a. right of the highlighted field in list view
   b. left of the highlighted field in list view
   c. right of the highlighted field in form view
   d. left of the highlighted field in form design view

3. To save a database under a different name, click _____.
   a. Save on the toolbar
   b. Save As on the File menu
   c. Save As on the toolbar
   d. New File on the File menu

(continued)

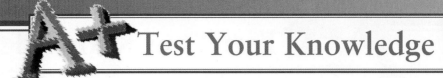

Test Your Knowledge

Multiple Choice *(continued)*

4. To specify the size of a field in form design view, _____.
   a. drag the field size box to the proper size
   b. click Field Size from the Edit menu, enter the width in the Width text box, and click the OK button in the Field Width dialog box
   c. click the Field Width button on the toolbar, enter the width in the Width text box, and click the OK button in the Field Width dialog box
   d. double-click the field name on the form

5. To delete a field, _____.
   a. in form view, highlight the field name to be deleted and click Delete Selection on the Edit menu
   b. in form design view, highlight the field name to be deleted and click Delete Selection on the Edit menu
   c. in list view, highlight the field to be deleted and click Delete Field on the toolbar
   d. in list view, highlight the field to be deleted and click Delete Record on the Record menu

6. To divide the list view of the database into four panes, _____.
   a. click Split on the Window menu
   b. click Pane on the Window menu
   c. double-click the vertical split bar
   d. drag the horizontal split bar to the desired location

7. To add a header to a printed report of a database displayed in form view, click _____.
   a. Headers & Footers on the Edit menu, type the header in the Header text box, and click the OK button
   b. Headers & Footers on the toolbar, type the header in the Header text box, and click the OK button
   c. Headers & Footers on the View menu, type the header in the Header text box, and click the OK button
   d. Headers & Footers on the Format menu, type the header in the Header text box, and click the OK button

8. The value &p appearing in the Header or Footer text box in the View Headers & Footers dialog box will cause the _____ to print on the report.
   a. report title
   b. current date
   c. filename
   d. page number

9. The value &n appearing in the Header or Footer text box in the View Headers & Footers dialog box will cause the _____ to print on the report.
   a. report title
   b. current date
   c. filename
   d. page number

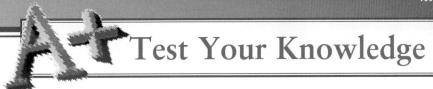

10. To print more than one record from form view on the same page of a report, _____.
    a. click No Page Break on the Format menu
    b. click Multiple Record in the Page Setup & Margins dialog box
    c. remove the X from the Page breaks between records check box and type a value in the Space between records text box in the Page Setup & Margins dialog box.
    d. type a number in the Space between records text box in the Page Setup & Margins dialog box

3 Fill In

Instructions: In the spaces provided, list the four primary activities used to maintain a database and give an example of each.

Activity 1: _____

_____

Activity 2: _____

_____

Activity 3: _____

_____

Activity 4: _____

_____

4 Fill In

Instructions: In each of the following maintenance activities, identify the appropriate view in which to display a database to accomplish each activity.

TASK	VIEW
Insert a record	_____
Insert a field	_____
Change a field name	_____
Change data	_____
Delete a field	_____
Delete a record	_____
Enter data	_____
Rearrange fields	_____
Size a field	_____
Print a database	_____
Enter data using a formula	_____
Delete clip art	_____

Use Help

1 Reviewing Project Activities

Instructions: Use your computer to perform the following tasks to obtain experience using online Help.

1. Start Microsoft Works.
2. When the Works Task Launcher dialog box displays, click the Cancel button. Click the Index button in the Help window to display the Help Topics: Microsoft Works window.
3. On the Index sheet, type deleting fields from databases in the 1 Type a word for the action or item you want information about text box.
4. Click deleting fields from databases in the 2 Click the Index entry you want list box. Click the To delete a field topic. Read and print To delete a field on the Step-by-Step sheet.
5. Click the More Info tab. Click Overview. Read and print Deleting database fields. Click the Done button.
6. Click To delete information from a form in the 2 Click the Index entry you want list. Read and print To delete information from a form on the Step-by-step sheet.
7. Click the Close button in the application window to close Works.

2 Expanding on the Basics

Instructions: Use Works online Help to better understand the topics listed below. Print the topic or topics that substantiate your answer. If there is no Print this topic icon, answer the question on a separate piece of paper.

1. Using the key terms, typing formulas in databases, and the Index sheet in the Help topics: Microsoft Works dialog box, answer the following questions.
   a. Explain how to calculate a field's contents using a formula in list view.

   _____

   _____

   b. What if the result of your formula is zero?

   _____

   _____

   c. What if Works displays the formula as text?

   _____

   _____

2. Click the Close button in the application window to close Works.

Apply Your Knowledge

1 Maintaining a Database

Instructions: Start Microsoft Works. Open the file, Suppliers, on the Student Floppy Disk that accompanies this book. The database is illustrated in form view in Figure 8-78. Perform the following maintenance:

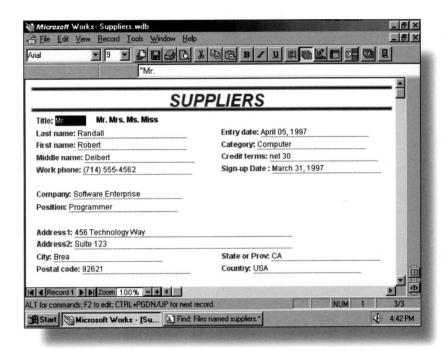

FIGURE 8-78

1. Delete the Country field.
2. Delete the Address 2 field.
3. Change the Middle name field to M.I.
4. Change the middle name in all the records to a middle initial.
5. Change the Position field name to Job Title.
6. Reformat the form view of the database to produce a report consisting of the name, address, city, state, and zip for each supplier.
7. Add a header and a footer to the report.
8. Print the form view of the database on one page.
9. Close Works. Do not save the reformatted database.

In the Lab

1 Maintaining an Alumni Database

Problem: Perform maintenance on the Alumni database created in the In the Lab 1 in Project 7. The contents of the database are shown in Table 8-1.

Table 8-1							
DONATION DATE	TITLE	FIRST NAME	M.I.	LAST NAME	SCHOLARSHIP	CLASSIFICATION	DONATION
10/16/97	Mr.	Wilson	B.	Haus	Business	Corporate	$1,500.00
10/17/97	Ms.	Anne	M.	Garcia	Music	Private	$100.00
10/22/97	Mr.	Donald	H.	Emerson	Science	Corporate	$700.00
10/31/97	Miss	Ealin	L.	Deras	Music	Private	$2,500.00
11/15/97	Mrs.	Melissa	R.	Deric	Science	Private	$500.00
11/22/97	Mr.	Donald	V.	Roy	Business	Corporate	$3,000.00
11/28/97	Mr.	Vincent	D.	Portofino	Business	Corporate	$5,000.00
12/3/97	Ms.	Lillian	J.	Henry	Fine Arts	Private	$850.00
12/15/97	Ms.	Ledy	R.	Mejia	Fine Arts	Private	$250.00
12/30/97	Mr.	Martin	V.	Lee	Business	Corporate	$400.00

Instructions:

1. Open the database you created in the In the Lab 1 in Project 7. If you did not create this database in Project 5, your instructor will provide you with the database file.
2. Add the two records shown in Table 8-2 to the database.

Table 8-2							
DONATION DATE	TITLE	FIRST NAME	M.I.	LAST NAME	SCHOLARSHIP	CLASSIFICATION	DONATION
12/31/97	Mr.	Brian	V.	Jarman	Science	Corporate	$3,500.00
12/31/97	Ms.	Anne	M.	Farmington	Fine Arts	Private	$1,100.00

3. When you add the Anne M. Famington record, you discover the Last Name field in form view is not large enough to display the entire name. Therefore, you must change the size of the field to a width of 13.
4. Delete the record for Lillian J. Henry.
5. Mr. Donald V. Roy donated an additional $1,000.00 to the Business scholarship fund. Modify his record to reflect the additional donation and change his classification from Corporate to Private.

In the Lab

6. The director of alumni relations has requested the database reflect the year of the last donation for each of the donors to the scholarship fund. If the donors have never contributed to the scholarship fund, place the entry NG in the field. Add the Last Donation field to the Alumni database. The field should be a width of 7 in form design view and a width of 13 in list view. Format the field name and field entry.

7. In form design view, move the bottom rectangle to the coordinates X1.33" Y4.42". Place the Last Donation field at the coordinates X1.33" Y4.08".

8. Table 8-3 contains the last names of the donors and their last donation date.

9. The public relations director did not like the field name Classification. He suggested changing it to Type. Make this change to the Classification field name.

10. Save the revised database on a floppy disk using the filename Revised Alumni Scholarship Donations.

11. Print the revised database in form view.

Table 8-3	
LAST NAME	LAST DONATION
Haus	1996
Garcia	1993
Emerson	NG
Deras	1996
Deric	1990
Roy	1997
Portofino	1996
Mejia	1992
Lee	1990
Jarman	NG
Farmington	NG

2 Maintaining an Employee Database

Problem: Perform maintenance on the Custom Gifts, Intl Employee database created in the In the Lab 2 in Project 7. The contents of the database are shown in Table 8-4.

Instructions:

1. Open the database you created in the In the Lab 2 in Project 7. If you did not create this database in Project 7, your instructor will provide you with the database file.

Table 8-4							
EMPLOYEE ID	DATE HIRED	FIRST NAME	LAST NAME	HOURLY RATE	WEEKLY HOURS	STATUS	DEPARTMENT
50123	4/13/93	Abraham	Ackerman	$16.50	40	F	Accounting
20157	5/26/93	Aaron	Sikora	$15.25	40	F	Purchasing
50105	6/14/93	Denzal	Simes	$15.75	35	F	Accounting
20158	7/15/93	Ben	Ryu	$14.75	40	F	Purchasing
30135	9/23/94	Sandra	Perez	$12.50	32	F	Customer Service
30235	12/1/94	Philip	Ortiz	$13.25	40	F	Customer Service
30698	8/3/95	Joni	Echsner	$10.50	20	P	Customer Service
30812	9/24/95	Mihai	Ochoa	$12.75	40	F	Customer Service
20587	10/15/95	Michelle	Quon	$11.35	40	F	Purchasing
50642	12/3/95	Duc	Dinh	$10.00	25	P	Accounting

(continued)

In the Lab

Maintaining an Employee Database (*continued*)

2. Two new employees have been hired. The data for the employees is shown in Table 8-5.

Table 8-5

EMPLOYEE ID	DATE HIRED	FIRST NAME	LAST NAME	HOURLY RATE	WEEKLY HOURS	STATUS	DEPARTMENT
50712	1/13/97	Olivia	Barker	$17.50	30	P	Accounting
20163	1/26/97	Charles	Senora	$13.25	40	F	Purchasing

3. Employee Philip Ortiz has resigned and is no longer with the company. Update the database to reflect this change.
4. Employee Duc Dinh's status has been changed from part-time (P) to full-time (F). Update the database to reflect this change.
5. The president of Custom Gifts, Intl has decided he would like to know the weekly pay that is paid to each employee and have this data stored in the database. To accomplish this task, add a new field named Weekly Pay to the database. The data in the field is generated from the formula, Hourly Rate multiplied by Weekly Hours. Format the field with a dollar sign and two digits to the right of the decimal point.
6. Save the revised database on a floppy disk using the filename, Revised Custom Gifts, Intl.
7. Print the revised database in form view.
8. Print the revised database in list view. The entire record should print on a single page.
9. A report that contains the name of each employee, the hourly rate, the weekly hours, the weekly pay, and department, is required (see Figure 8-79). Print the report so as many employees as possible appear on each page. Do not print the First Name field name and Last Name field name. Place a header containing the report title, Employee Listing, together with the current date, on each page. Print the page number as a footer on each page. Reformat the form design view of the database so you can prepare the report.
10. Save the reformatted database generated in Step 9 using the filename, Employee Listing.
11. Print the Employee Listing report.
12. Follow the directions from your instructor for turning in this assignment.

3 Maintaining an Investment Group Database

Problem: Perform maintenance on the Investment Group database created in the In the Lab 3 in Project 7. The contents of the database are shown in Table 8-6.

In the Lab

Custom Gifts, Intl Employee Listing - April 12, 1997

Michelle Quon   Departme:
Hourly Rate: $11.35
Weekly Hours: 40
Weekly Pay: $454.00

Duc Dinh   Departme:
Hourly Rate: $10.00
Weekly Hours: 25
Weekly Pay: $250.00

Olivia Barker   Departme:
Hourly Rate: $17.50
Weekly Hours: 30
Weekly Pay: $525.00

Charles Senora   Departme:
Hourly Rate: $13.25
Weekly Hours: 40
Weekly Pay: $530.00

Custom Gifts, Intl Employee Listing - April 12, 1997

Abraham Ackerman   Department: Accounting
Hourly Rate: $16.50
Weekly Hours: 40
Weekly Pay: $660.00

Aaron Sikora   Department: Purchasing
Hourly Rate: $15.25
Weekly Hours: 40
Weekly Pay: $610.00

Denzal Simes   Department: Accounting
Hourly Rate: $15.75
Weekly Hours: 35
Weekly Pay: $551.25

Ben Ryu   Department: Purchasing
Hourly Rate: $14.75
Weekly Hours: 40
Weekly Pay: $590.00

Sandra Perez   Department: Customer Service
Hourly Rate: $12.50
Weekly Hours: 32
Weekly Pay: $400.00

Joni Ochsner   Department: Customer Service
Hourly Rate. $10.50
Weekly Hours: 20
Weekly Pay: $210.00

FIGURE 8-79

Table 8-6

DATE	TITLE	FIRST NAME	LAST NAME	ADDRESS	CITY	STATE	ZIP	OCCUPATION	FUND	SHARES	SHARE PRICE
9/12/97	Dr.	Thomas	Messer	13272 Grand	Yorba	CA	92686	Dentist	Technology	750	$10.00
9/15/97	Mr.	Robert	Kranitz	1300 Adams	Fullerton	CA	92633	Attorney	International	200	$18.00
9/25/97	Dr.	Elaine	Hince	10821 Capital	Believue	WA	98005	Teacher	Technology	1,200	$11.00
9/26/97	Miss	Janette	Lewis	1707 Kingman	Brea	CA	92621	Teacher	Growth	250	$17.00
9/27/97	Ms.	Ester	Guitron	530 Escanada	Anaheim	CA	93834	Salesperson	Aggressive	400	$16.00
9/28/97	Mr.	Joe	Gruden	2424 Holiday	Cerritos	CA	90701	Teacher	International	550	$9.00
9/28/97	Mrs.	Susan	Drussler	989 Grove	Irvine	CA	92754	Attorney	Technology	2,500	$7.00
10/6/97	Mr.	Essey	Meshi	555 Shafer	Yorba	CA	92686	Salesperson	Growth	800	$12.00
10/7/97	Dr.	Warren	Bacani	267 Portola	Tustin	CA	92670	Doctor	Aggressive	100	$23.00
10/7/97	Ms.	Rosey	Zamora	396 Barranca	Irvine	CA	92754	Attorney	Growth	750	$25.00

(continued)

In the Lab

Maintaining an Investment Group Database *(continued)*

Instructions:

1. Open the database you created in the In the Lab 3 in Project 7. If you did not create this database in Project 7, your instructor will provide you with the database file.
2. Two investors, Kranitz and Bacani, have left the investment group. Remove their records from the database.
3. Four new investors have joined the investment group. Their information is contained in Table 8-7 below.

Table 8-7

DATE	TITLE	NAME	FIRST NAME	LAST ADDRESS	CITY	STATE	ZIP	OCCUPATION	FUND	SHARES	SHARE PRICE
10/12/97	Ms.	Maria	Runner	325 Spice Lane	Cerritos	CA	90701	Accountant	Technology	350	$10.00
10/15/97	Mr.	Albert	Learner	300 Still Pond	Fullerton	CA	92633	Retired	International	500	$18.00
11/05/97	Dr.	Joseph	Brunnel	2 Indian Way	Anaheim	CA	92822	Doctor	Technology	1,200	$11.00
11/06/97	Miss	Janette	Shelly	1974 Thomas Circle	Brea	CA	92621	Teacher	Growth	250	$17.00

4. When you enter the address for Janette Shelly, you find the entire address cannot display in the Address field in form view. Change the field size in form design view so the entire address will display.
5. If the Address field does not display entirely in list view, modify the width of the field so it will.
6. Investor Joe Gruden has moved to a new address. His new address is 1268 Gliden Way, Anaheim, CA 92823.
7. The president of the Investment Group has requested the database reflect the investment each investor has in the group. Add a new field, named Investment, to the database. The data in the field is generated from the formula, Shares multiplied by Share Price. Format the field with a dollar sign, a comma, and two decimal places. If necessary, redesign the form by moving other fields so the form is easy to read.
8. Save the modified database on a floppy disk using the filename, Revised Investment Group.
9. Print the revised database in form view.
10. Print the revised database in list view.
11. The president has requested a Name and Address list of all investors in the group. She wants as many names as possible on a single page. The member's first name, last name, address, city, state, and zip, should be included on the report. The report should also have a heading consisting of the title, Investment Group Roster, and the current date. The page number should appear at the bottom of the page. Place the heading and page number appropriately on the page.
12. Save the form generated in Step 11 using the filename, Investment Group Roster.
13. Print the Investment Group Roster.
14. Follow the directions from your instructor for turning in this assignment.

Cases and Places

The difficulty of these case studies varies:

▶ Case studies preceded by a single half moon are the least difficult. You are asked to create the required database based on information that already has been placed in an organized form.

▶▶ Case studies preceded by two half moons are more difficult. You must organize the information presented before using it to create the desired database.

▶▶▶ Case studies preceded by three half moons are the most difficult. You must choose a specific topic and then organize the necessary information before using it to create the required database.

1 ▶ Use the pneumonia database created in Case Study 1 of Project 7 for this assignment. Perform the following: (a) Insert a new field called Body Temperature (Celsius) to the right of the Body Temperature (Fahrenheit) field. (b) Size and position this new field on the form. (c) Calculate the values in the Celsius temperature field using this formula: 5/9 * (Fahrenheit - 32). (d) Print the revised database in form view. (e) Print the revised database in list view.

2 ▶ Use the athlete database in Case Study 3 of Project 7 for this assignment. Perform the following: (a) Add a new field called 1995 Rank to the right of the Sport field. (b) Add the athletes' ranks to this field. The athletes are listed in rank order in Figure 7-104 based on their total earnings in salary and endorsements for the year; for example, Michael Jordan is ranked Number 1 with his total earnings of $43.9 million, Mike Tyson is ranked 2, and Frank Thomas is ranked 25. (c) Add a new field called 1994 Rank to the right of the 1995 Rank. (d) Add the following data to the 1994 Rank field: Jordan – 1; Tyson – NR (not ranked); Sanders – 38; Bowe – NR; O'Neal – 2; Foreman – 15; Agassi – 9; Nicklaus – 3; Schumacher – 30; Gretzky – 6; Palmer – 4; Bledsoe – NR; Berger – 5; Holyfield – 8; Sampras – 11; Ripken – NR; Norman – 14; Robinson – 17; Ewing – 29; Earnhardt – 34; Carter – NR; Alesi – 20; Griffey – NR; Hill – NR; Thomas – NR. (e) Add the five records from Figure 8-80 to the database. (f) Print the revised database in form view. (g) Print the revised database in list view.

PLAYER NAME	SPORT	1995 RANK	1994 RANK	SALARY (MILLIONS)	ENDORSEMENTS (MILLIONS)
Boris Becker	Tennis	26	22	$3.3	$4.5
Hakeem Olajuwon	Basketball	27	NR	$5.8	$2.0
Michael Chang	Tennis	28	31	$2.6	$5.0
Barry Bonds	Baseball	29	NR	$6.8	$0.7
Steffi Graf	Tennis	30	19	$2.5	$5.0

FIGURE 8-80

Cases and Places

3 ▶ Use the whale-watching expedition database in Case Study 2 of Project 7 for this assignment. Perform the following: (a) You have learned that watching Bryde's whales from a boat is popular all year in Japan. Add a new record reflecting this new discovery. (b) Insert a new field called Location to the left of the Destination field. (c) Size and position this new field on the form. (d) Add the following data to the Location field: Patagonia (Argentina); Southern Ocean Whale Sanctuary (Antarctica); Campbell River (British Columbia); Bay of Samaná (Dominican Republic); Cape Cod (Massachusetts); Baja California (Mexico); Lofoten Islands (Norway); Kaikoura (New Zealand); and Cape Town to Cape Agulhas (South Africa). (e) Change the name of the Destination field to Country. (f) Print the revised database in form view. (f) Print the revised database in list view.

4 ▶▶ You need to send more application materials to the potential employer you contacted in Case Study 4 of Project 7. You verify the rates for sending the information and learn that the U.S. Postal System has changed the name of Express Mail to Expedient Mail. Also, Federal Express has changed its rates. Packages weighing eight ounces or less now cost $15.50 for priority delivery and $13.50 for standard delivery; packages more than eight ounces and one pound or less cost $22.50 for priority and $16.50 for standard; packages weighing more than one pound and two pounds or less cost $24.25 for priority and $17.50 for standard. Also, Federal Express has added a new category of delivery service called FedEx First Overnight, which guarantees delivery to addresses in select zip codes by 8:00 a.m. The rates for this new service are $40.50 for eight ounces or less, $47.50 for more than eight ounces and one pound or less, and $49.25 for more than one pound and two pounds or less. Make these changes and additions to the database. Print the revised database in form and list views.

5 ▶▶▶ Because interest rates fluctuate so rapidly, you want to update the certificate of deposit database you created in Case Study 5 of Project 7. Call or visit the same financial institutions and determine the current rates. Make the appropriate changes in the database, and print these revised rates in form and list views. In addition, determine the value of the CDs, amount of interest earned, and penalties for early withdrawal if you invested $1,000 and $5,000.

6 ▶▶▶ The used car service database you created in Case Study 6 of Project 7 has become very popular among readers. They have asked for more details to be included in the service, including category (automobile, truck, van, recreational, antique/classic, four-wheel drive), options (air conditioning, cruise control, power windows, power locks, sunroof); rims (aluminum, steel), and phone number. Add these fields to the database, enter data from ads in today's newspaper, and print the revised ads in form and list views.

7 ▶▶▶ As part of your efforts to eat more nutritious foods, you are watching your intake of cholesterol, sodium, carbohydrates, and protein. Add these fields to the food database you created in Case Study 7 of Project 7. Then examine the labels on the products you already entered in the database, and input the grams or milligrams of cholesterol, sodium, carbohydrates, and protein in the new fields. Print the revised database in form and list views.

Microsoft Works 4

Windows 95

Database Filters and Reports

Objectives

You will have mastered the material in this project when you can:

▶ Define filter
▶ Filter a database to display records containing values equal to those you specify
▶ Show all records in the database
▶ Filter a database to display records that are above a value
▶ Reverse a filter
▶ Filter a database to display records that match in more than one field
▶ Filter a database to display records that meet one of several conditions
▶ Apply a filter to a database
▶ Rename a filter
▶ Define a report listing the database records
▶ Add field names to a report definition
▶ Add field entries to a report definition
▶ Modify a Works report definition
▶ Sort, group, and filter records for a report
▶ Print a report
▶ Define a report with summary totals
▶ Define a report with intermediate totals
▶ Insert rows and field entries into a report definition
▶ Select records for printing
▶ Duplicate a report definition

Questions, Filters, & DATABASES

Shakespeare was a master at asking intriguing questions. He knew the value of a good *hook* and the fascination people have always had for questions. The city of Delphi, in ancient Greece, became famous for the Oracle who responded to questions posed by anxious petitioners. During the 1950s, American TV audiences sat spellbound watching the weekly spectacle of perspiring quiz show contestants in glass-enclosed booths groping for the answer to the latest mind-twister.

Questions. As in so many other areas of life, questions, such as, What information currently resides in a client's record? or What are the demographic profiles of all our clients? are the key to retrieving information from a database. In the special language of computers, requests for information often are called *filters*, and they provide the means of retrieving previously stored data.

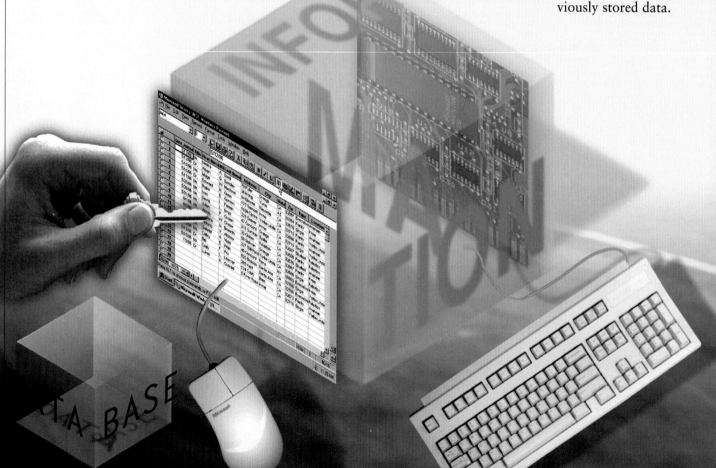

A database would be of little value if a user could not access the information it holds. That would be like trying to withdraw savings from the empty vault of one of the many Savings and Loan institutions that failed in the 1980s. The capability to *withdraw* saved data and present it in many different formats and styles is a strong suit for Works. Conditional filters are especially useful, allowing a user to fine-tune the search criteria.

The result of filtering a database is a set of data that may be displayed on a PC screen, sent to an output device, such as a printer, transmitted via FAX-modem to a client or associate, or simply modified and stored. One familiar example is that of sports announcers who routinely query massive data-bases containing player statistics maintained by professional sports organizations in order to use that information in play-by-play descriptions.

Students attending a college or university often need reports resulting from filtering personal databases kept on their own PCs or on a shared computer. Research for a particular course may require searching databases made available by, say, the School of Business or the Internet, and then blending the information into a paper.

Questions and filters are the keys to databases — and life. President John F. Kennedy might have been talking about that very subject when he said, "I can evade questions without help; what I need is answers."

Microsoft
Works
Windows 95

Database Filters and Reports

Case Perspective

Now that RSC Sports and Fitness Centers has created a database with current member data, the management wishes to ask questions concerning the data in the database and obtain answers. For example, they would like to know what members are located at the Anaheim club, the members who live in the city of Irvine, all members who joined the club after 5-31-96, and the members with a single or student membership.

In addition to answering the above questions, the management has asked you to prepare professionally designed reports listing all members in the RSC Sports and Fitness Centers. They would like a report showing the total members, the dues, the total Kids Club dues, and the Total dues for the club. Prepare these reports using the reporting capabilities of Microsoft Works.

Introduction

A database is designed to provide information. In addition to creating the database as shown in Project 7 and maintaining the database as shown in Project 8, you also must be able to obtain useful information from the database. Information is obtained from a database in two primary ways: (1) filters; (2) reports.

A **filter** is a request for information from a database. For example, a filter of the memberships database created in Project 7 and updated in Project 8 is, Display all the members at the Anaheim location (Figure 9-1). Notice in Figure 9-1 the only records that display are those for members at the Anaheim location. Works does not display the records for members at other locations. When you filter a database, Works shows the records that match the filter and hides the records that do not match the filter. Most often, filters are performed by an individual using the computer and requesting specific information from the database.

The Works Database tool also provides the means for creating a variety of reports. For example, the report shown in Figure 9-2 was created from the RSC Members Revised database. The report lists all the members in the club together with dues, Kids Club, and total dues owed by each member. At the bottom of the report, totals appear for all the records in the database. As you can see, 16 members owe Total Dues of $1,189.00, $136.50 for Kids Club, and $1,325.50 for Total Dues for Club.

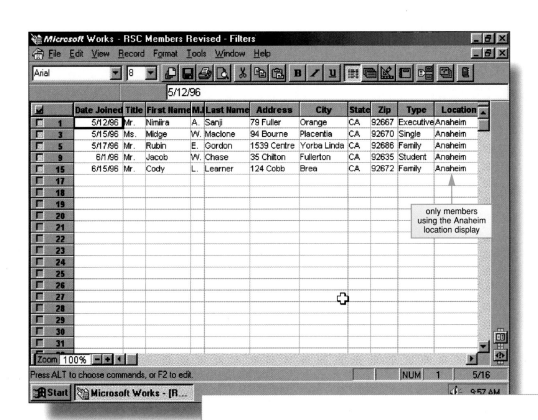

FIGURE 9-2

Filters and reports can be performed in combination with one another. For example, a filter can be performed to isolate specific data in the database and then a report can be printed using only that data. In Figure 9-3, the filter requesting those individuals living in California was performed. Then, a report was printed of all California members. The report groups the members by location listing each member's name, and dues, kids club and total dues. The report in Figure 9-3 lists the members from the Anaheim location. The totals at the end of each location show each location total members, total dues, total kids club, and total dues owed.

Obtaining information from a database is the reason for the existence of the database. Filters and reports provide the two primary means of obtaining information from a database.

Membership Totals

Title	First Name	M.I.	Last Name	Dues	Kids Club	Total Dues
Anaheim						
Mr.	Jacob	W.	Chase	$35.00	$12.50	$47.50
Mr.	Rubin	E.	Gordon	$89.00	$12.50	$101.50
Mr.	Cody	L.	Learner	$89.00	$12.00	$101.00
Ms.	Midge	W.	Maclone	$45.00	$12.50	$57.50
Mr.	Nimiira	A.	Sanji	$120.00	$12.50	$132.50
Total Members			5			
Total Dues			$378.00			
Total Kids Club			$62.00			
Total Dues for Club			$440.00			

FIGURE 9-3

Project Nine

To learn how to obtain information from a database through the use of both filters and reports, you will accomplish the following tasks in Project 9:

1. Using a filter, display all members who live in the city of Irvine.
2. Using a filter, display all members who joined the club after 5/31/96.
3. By reversing a filter, display all members who joined the club on or before 5/31/96.
4. Using a filter, display all family memberships at the Anaheim location.
5. Using a filter, display all members with a single or student membership.
6. Using a filter, display members who joined with a family membership at the Anaheim location during the two-week period of 5/15/96 through 5/29/96.
7. Create a report listing all members in the RSC Members Revised database.
8. Create a report listing all members in the RSC Members Revised database, the total members, the dues, total Kids Club, and total dues owed by the members.
9. For each location (Anaheim, Fullerton, Irvine, and Yorba Linda), create a report listing the members in alphabetical sequence in each location, the dues, the kids club, and the total dues owed. At the end of the report, list the number of members in each location, the dues, the total Kids Club, and the total dues owed.
10. Modify the report created in step 9 above to print on one page.

The steps to accomplish these tasks are explained on subsequent pages.

Starting Works and Opening a Works Database File

To accomplish the tasks just listed, first you must open the database that contains the data for the filters and reports. For Project 9, the database is the RSC Members Revised database. To open the RSC Members Revised database, follow the steps used in previous projects. These steps are summarized below.

TO START WORKS AND OPEN A DATABASE FILE

Step 1: Double-click the My Computer icon on the desktop. When the My Computer window opens, double-click 3½ Floppy [A:].

Step 2: When the 3½ Floppy [A:] window opens, double-click the RSC Members Revised file icon.

Step 3: Right-click the My Computer button on the taskbar and then click Close on the context-sensitive menu. Right-click the 3½ Floppy [A:] button on the taskbar and then click Close on the context-sensitive menu.

Step 4: After Works opens the RSC Members Revised file, maximize the Works application window, if necessary, click the List View button on the toolbar, and then maximize the RSC Members Revised file document window.

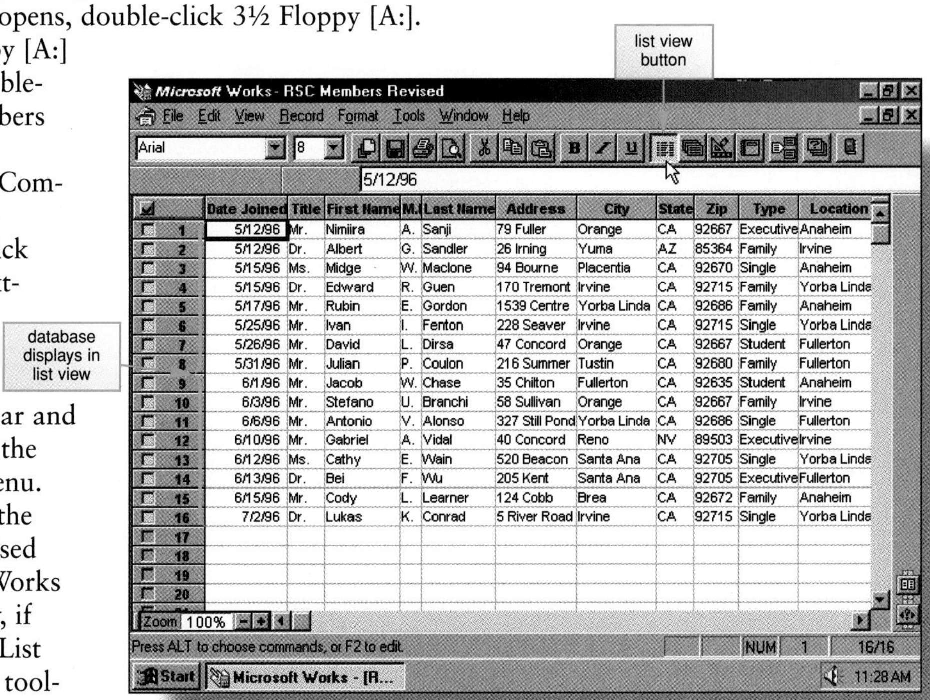

FIGURE 9-4

The resulting Works window is shown in Figure 9-4.

Working with Filters

A Works database **filter** is a request to the database to find records whose fields satisfy a certain criteria. The criteria used in a filter can vary depending on individual requirements. The following examples illustrate a variety of requests for information from the memberships database using filters.

More *About* **Filters**

Commonly, records in a database number in the hundreds or even thousands. When this is the case, you need the ability to select only certain records that meet one or more conditions. Filters allow you to display certain information you wish from a database. Filters are conditional statements that specify the criteria a record must match in order to be displayed. When you apply a filter, Works searches all records in the database and displays only the records that match the conditions specified by the filter.

Filtering for Records that Match Exactly

Quite often in a filter you will seek records that have a value in a certain field or fields equal to a value you specify. For example, the first filter in this project is to display all the members who live in the city of Irvine. Therefore, the criteria is that the value in the City field in the database must be equal to Irvine. To use a Works database filter to find all members who live in Irvine, you use the Filters button on the toolbar. Perform the following steps to create the filter.

Steps **To Filter for Records That Match Exactly**

1 **Point to the Filters button on the toolbar.**

The mouse pointer points to the Filters button on the toolbar (Figure 9-5).

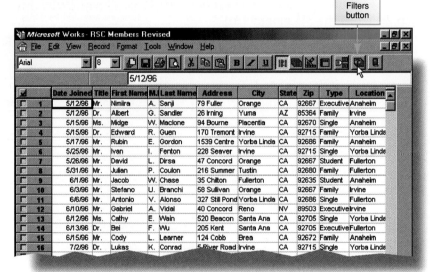

FIGURE 9-5

2 **Click the Filters button on the toolbar.**

Works displays the Filter dialog box (Figure 9-6). Works also displays the Filter Name dialog box over the Filter dialog box. The name, Filter 1, displays highlighted in the Type a name for the filter below text box. The words, Create, delete, modify, and apply filters, display in the status bar.

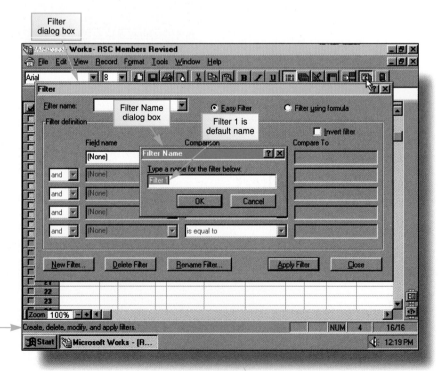

FIGURE 9-6

3 **Type** `City = Irvine` **in the text box. Point to the OK button in the Filter Name dialog box.**

The name of the filter displays in the Type a name for the filter below text box and the mouse pointer points to the OK button (Figure 9-7). The name of the filter you type in the Type a name for the filter below text box can be a maximum 15 characters.

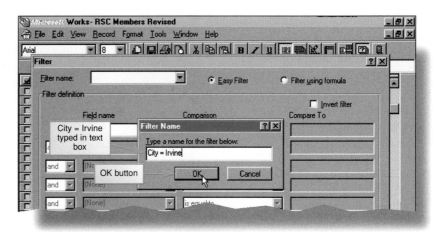

FIGURE 9-7

4 **Click the OK button in the Filter Name dialog box.**

Works removes the Filter Name dialog box and makes the Filter dialog box active (Figure 9-8). The name you typed in the Filter Name dialog box displays in the Filter name text box. The Filter definition box displays three columns (Field name, Comparison, and Compare To) with five boxes per column. The Field name box displays the highlighted word None.

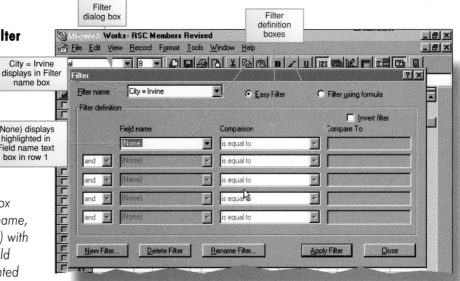

FIGURE 9-8

5 **Click the Field name box arrow. Scroll down and then point to the City field name.**

The Field name drop-down list box contains the name of every field in the database (Figure 9-9). The mouse pointer points to the City field name.

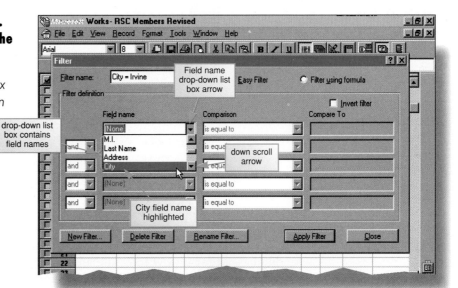

FIGURE 9-9

6 **Click City. Press the TAB key and ensure the words, is equal to, display in the Comparison text box. Press the TAB key and type** `Irvine` **in the Compare to box. Point to the Apply Filter button.**

The filter to display the records in the database for those members who live in the city of Irvine displays in the Filter dialog box (Figure 9-10). The mouse pointer points to the Apply Filter button.

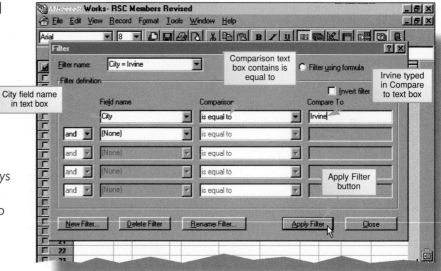

FIGURE 9-10

7 **Click the Apply Filter button in the Filter dialog box.**

Works displays in list view the records of those members in the database whose City field contains Irvine (Figure 9-11). In the status bar, 3/16 displays indicating that three records currently display out of a possible sixteen records.

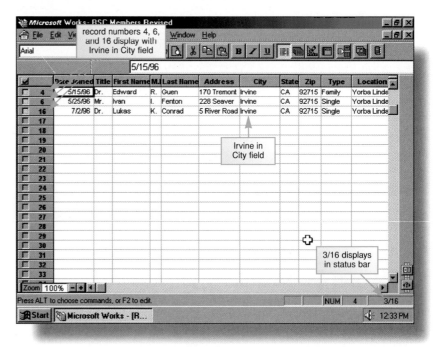

FIGURE 9-11

The filter method shown in Figure 8 through Figure 11 can be used whenever you want to display only records that exactly match a specific value in a field.

Other filters you might apply include displaying all records for a given location such as Anaheim or displaying all the records for members who live in a certain zip code.

In Figure 9-11, the database displays in list view. You also can display the database in form view to create and apply a filter. In form view, the selected records display one at a time on the screen. Thus, to see the three records in Figure 9-11 in form view, you would display each of the three records one at a time. To move to the next record, you can click the next record navigation button.

Showing All Records in the Database

After applying a filter, you may want to again display the entire database. To display all the records in the memberships database, perform the following steps.

Steps **To Show All Records in a Database**

1 **Click Record on the menu bar and then point to Show. When the Show cascading menu display point to 1 All Records.**

Works displays the Record menu (Figure 9-12). When you point to Show, Works displays the Show cascading menu with four additional commands. The mouse pointer points to the 1 All Records command.

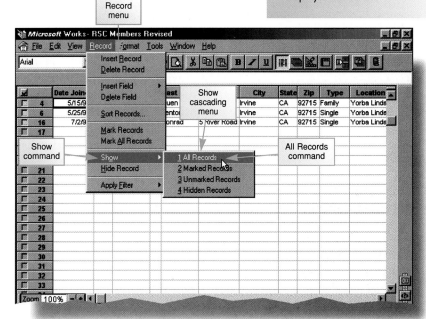

2 **Click 1 All Records. Click CTRL+HOME keys to view record number 1.**

Works displays the entire database in list view (Figure 9-13). Notice 16 records now display. Whenever you want to display all records in the database, you can use the 1 All Records command on the Show cascading menu.

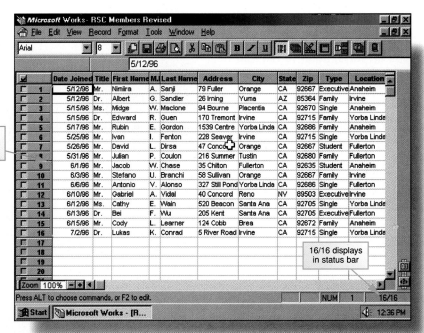

You do not have to display the entire database by clicking 1 All Records on the Show cascading menu in order to create additional new filters; although some individuals prefer to view all records before applying the same or a new filter.

If you want to apply the same filter again after you have displayed the entire database, you do not have to use the Filters button on the toolbar. Instead, you can click Record on the menu bar, and then click Apply Filter. When the Apply Filter cascading menu displays, click the name of the filter you want to view (for example, City = Irvine). You can use the Apply Filter command on the Record menu in either list view or form view.

Filtering for Records That Are Above or Below a Specific Value Based on Conditional Criteria

In the previous example of creating a new filter, the words, is equal to, appeared in the Comparison text box within the Filter dialog box. These words were the basis of the comparing operation. You also can specify other types of conditions that must be met in order for a record to display. You specify conditions using the words in the Comparison drop-down list box within the Filter dialog box.

To illustrate the use of conditional criteria other than is equal to when creating filters using the Filter dialog box, the second task in this project is to display the records of all members who joined RSC Sports and Fitness Centers after the date 5/31/96. To filter for records that are above a certain value using conditional criteria, complete the following steps.

Steps ## To Filter for Records That Are Above a Value Using Conditional Criteria

1 **Click the Filters button on the toolbar. When the Filter dialog box displays, point to the New Filter button.**

Works displays the Filter dialog box containing the criteria for the filter name City = Irvine (Figure 9-14). The mouse pointer points to the New Filter button.

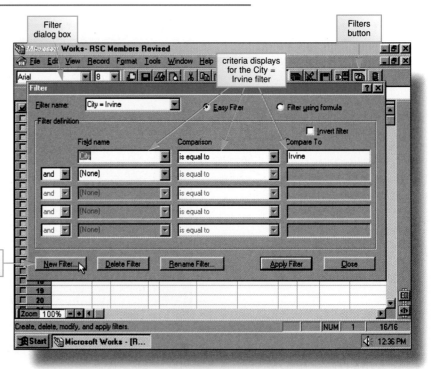

FIGURE 9-14

2 **Click the New Filter button. When the Filter Name dialog box displays, type** Date>5/31/96 **in the Type a name for the filter below text box. Point to the OK button.**

When you click the New Filter button in the Filter dialog box, Works displays the Filter Name dialog box (Figure 9-15). The filter name you typed displays in the Type a name for the filter below text box. The mouse pointer points to the OK button.

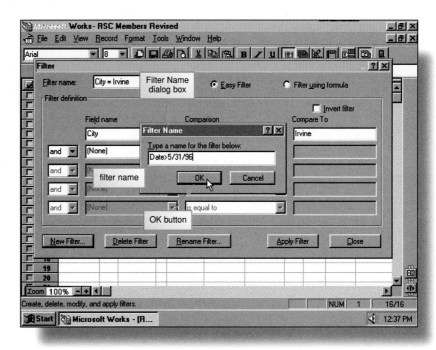

FIGURE 9-15

3 **Click the OK button in the Filter Name dialog box. Click the Field name box arrow and then click Date Joined. Click the Comparison box arrow and then point to is greater than in the drop-down list box.**

When you click the OK button in the Filter Name dialog box, Works removes the dialog box and makes the Filter dialog box active (Figure 9-16). The filter name you typed in the Filter Name dialog box in Step 2 above displays in the Filter name text box. Date Joined displays in the Field name text box. The field to be used as the basis of comparing is the Date Joined field. The mouse pointer points to the words, is greater than.

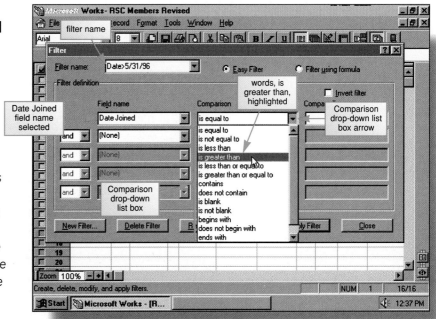

FIGURE 9-16

4 **Click is greater than. Type** 5/31/96 **in the Compare To text box. Point to the Apply Filter button.**

The words, is greater than, display in the Comparison text box and 5/31/96 displays in the Compare To text box (Figure 9-17). This value is to be compared to the value in the Date Joined field in the database. The mouse pointer points to the Apply Filter button. This filter instructs Works to display all records whose value in the Date Joined field is greater than 5/31/96.

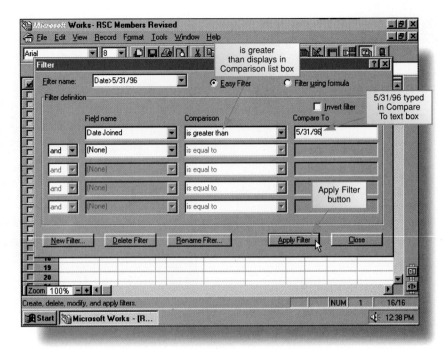

FIGURE 9-17

5 **Click the Apply Filter button.**

Works displays those records in list view that contain a value greater than 5/31/96 in the Date Joined field (Figure 9-18).

FIGURE 9-18

Inverting Filters

When Works applies a filter, it searches for the records in the database that satisfy the conditions in the filter and displays those records. You can view the records the filter did not select. When you reverse, or **invert**, a filter, Works hides the current records. That is, Works hides the records selected by the applied filter, and displays the hidden records instead.

The third task specified on page W 9.6 for this project is to display all members who joined the club on 5/31/96 or earlier. To accomplish this task, you can create a filter that tests for a value less than or equal to 5/31/96 in the Date Joined field. The screen in Figure 9-18 displays all records for members who joined after 5/31/96, with the hidden records of members who joined on 5/31/96 or earlier. Therefore, a simpler method to display these members is to reverse the results of a filter, as shown in the following steps.

Steps **To Reverse the Results of a Filter**

1 **Click the Filters button on the toolbar. When the Filter dialog box displays, ensure Date > 5/31/96 displays in Filter name text box. Click Invert filter. Point to the Apply Filter button.**

When you click the Filters button on the toolbar, Works displays the Filter dialog box (Figure 9-19). The filter name, Date > 5/31/96, displays in the Filter name text box. This is the filter you want to reverse. A ✓ displays in the Invert filter check box. This option specifies that the filter will display only those records that do not match the filter criteria in the Filter dialog box. The mouse pointer points to the Apply Filter button.

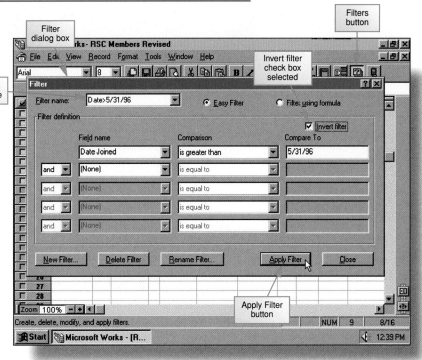

FIGURE 9-19

2 **Click the Apply Filter button in the Filter dialog box.**

Works switches the hidden records by reversing the records whose date joined is greater than 5/31/96 and displaying those records whose date joined is less than or equal to 5/31/96 (Figure 9-20).

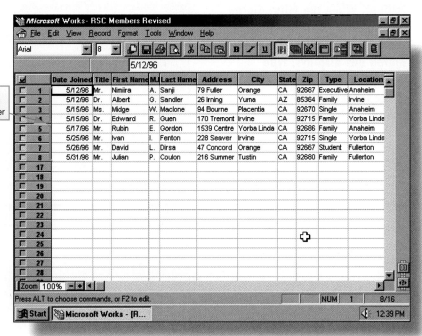

FIGURE 9-20

Other Ways

1. On Record menu click Show, click 4 Hidden Records on Show cascading menu

The Invert filter option is useful when performing filters because in effect it allows you to perform two filters by switching back and forth between the hidden records. In Figure 9-20 on the previous page, if you again click Invert filter in the Filter dialog box, the records hidden in Figure 9-20 will display and the screen will be the same as in Figure 9-18 on the page W 9.14.

Filtering for Records that Match in More than One Field

Works allows filters in which more than one field is involved in determining the records to display. In the fourth task listed for Project 9 on page W 9.6, you are to use a filter to display all family memberships at the Anaheim location. To accomplish this task, Works must examine the Type field to find all records containing Family AND must search all Family records to find the word Anaheim in the Location field. In the filter, the word AND is used. The word AND is called a logical operator in the filter because it logically joins two different fields. When the **AND logical operator** is used in a filter, both conditions must be true; that is, for a record to satisfy the filter criteria, both the value Family must be in the Type field AND the value Anaheim must be in the Location field. To perform this filter, complete the following steps.

Steps **To Filter for Records That Match in More than One Field**

1 **Click the Filters button on the toolbar. When the Filter dialog box displays, click the New Filter button. When the Filter Name dialog box displays, type** Family/Anaheim **in the Type a name for the filter below text box. Point to the OK button.**

Works displays the Filter dialog box. When you click the New Filter button, Works displays the Filter Name dialog box (Figure 9-21). The new filter name displays in the Type a name for the filter below text box. The mouse pointer points to the OK button.

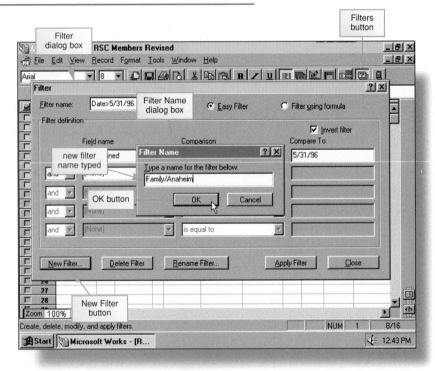

FIGURE 9-21

2 Click the OK button in the Filter Name dialog box. Click the Field name box arrow. Scroll down and then click Type. Press the TAB key. The Comparison text box should contain the words, is equal to. Press the TAB key and then type `Family` in the Compare To text box. Click the Field name box arrow in the second row, scroll down and then point to Location.

The first part of the filter is entered in the Filter dialog box (Figure 9-22). The mouse pointer points to the field name Location.

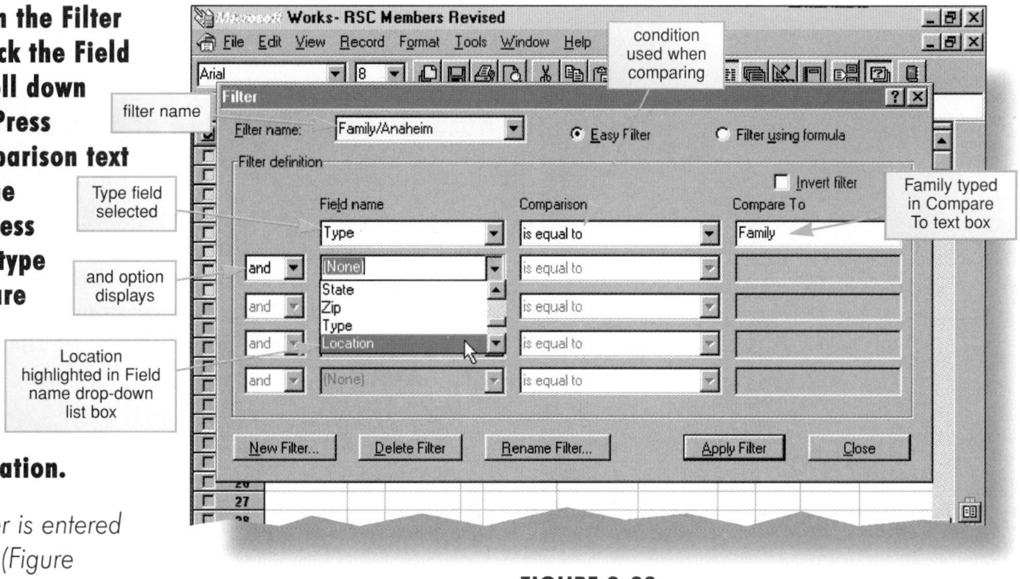

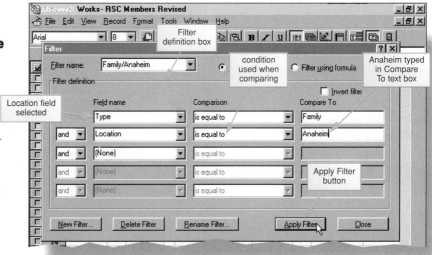

FIGURE 9-22

3 Click Location. Press the TAB key twice. Type `Anaheim` in the Compare To text box. Point to the Apply Filter button.

The next set of entries is made in the Filter dialog box and the mouse pointer points to the Apply Filter button (Figure 9-23). The filter to find records in the database with the Type field equal to Family AND the Location field equal to Anaheim is entered into the Filter definition box.

FIGURE 9-23

4 Click the Apply Filter button in the Filter dialog box.

Works displays the records of members who have a Family membership at the Anaheim location (Figure 9-24).

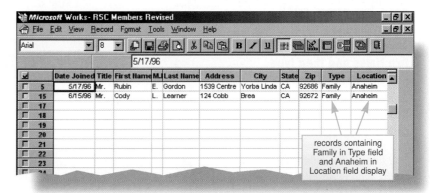

FIGURE 9-24

If necessary for your filter, you can specify up to five criteria using the AND logical operator.

Filtering for Records That Meet One of Several Conditions

A second logical operator that can be used in filters is called the **OR logical operator**. When the OR logical operator is used, if either or both of the conditions stated are true, then the criteria is satisfied. For example, the fifth task in this project is to use a filter to display all members with a Single or Student type membership. When you analyze this filter, the condition can be stated as display those records with the Type field equal to Single OR the Type field equal to Student. The logical operator OR means either or both. To perform this filter, complete the following steps.

Steps To Filter for Records That Meet One of Several Conditions

1 **Click the Filters button on the toolbar. When the Filter dialog box displays, click the New Filter button. When the Filter Name dialog box displays, type** Single/Student **in the Type a name for the filter below text box. Point to the OK button.**

Works displays the Filter dialog box and the Filter Name dialog box (Figure 9-25). The name you typed displays in the Filter Name dialog box. The mouse pointer points to the OK button.

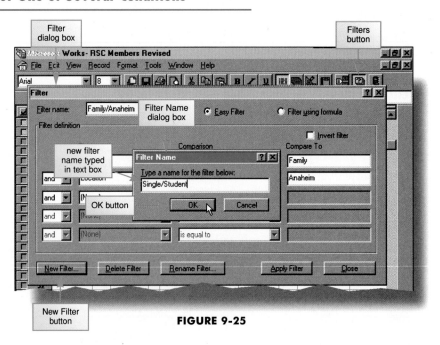

FIGURE 9-25

2 **Click the OK button in the Filter Name dialog box. Click the Field name box arrow, scroll down and then click Type. Press the TAB key two times and then type** Single **in the Compare To text box. Click the and box arrow and then point to the word or.**

The filter in the Filter dialog box states Type is equal to Single (Figure 9-26).

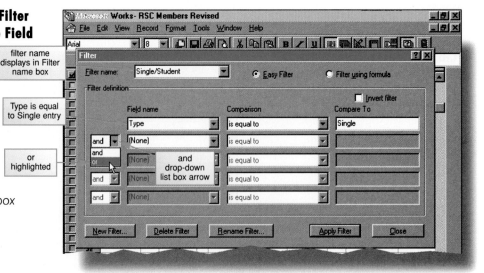

FIGURE 9-26

3 Click or in the drop-down list. Click the Field name box arrow, scroll down and then click Type. Press the TAB key twice and then Type Student in the Compare To text box. Point to the Apply Filter button.

The completed filter in the Filter dialog box states Type is equal to Single or Type is equal to Student (Figure 9-27). The mouse pointer points to the Apply Filter button.

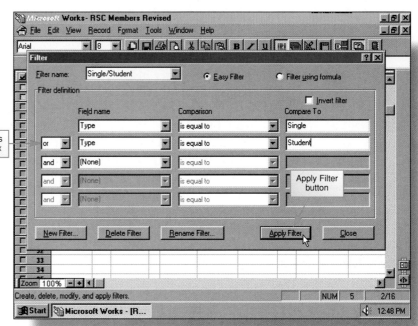

FIGURE 9-27

4 Click the Apply Filter button in the Filter dialog box.

The list view of the database displays records of individuals having a single or student type of membership (Figure 9-28).

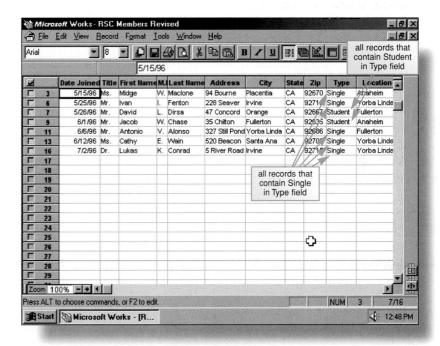

FIGURE 9-28

Works allows you to include up to five criteria per filter. This provides great flexibility in retrieving information from the database using its filter capabilities and the AND and OR logical operators.

More *About*
**Creating a Filter
Using a Formula**

When creating a filter using a
formula, Works enables you to
use math calculations in a criteria. This is useful when you
need to create a comparison by
adding, subtracting, multiplying,
or dividing one or more fields.
For example, the formula,
=(Dues+Kids Club)>VALUE
("100") filters records whose
Dues added to Kids Club is
greater than $100.00.

Creating a Filter Using a Formula

It is also possible to create a filter using a formula. When using a formula
to create a filter, you define the records you want to display by entering the
appropriate filter instruction. This technique can be used at any time, but must
be used when more than five conditions are stated in a filter.

The following example illustrates a filter that is created to display members
who joined during a two-week special the club offered 5/15/96 through 5/29/96.
In addition to the above criteria, the filter is to include those members who joined
with a Family type membership at the Anaheim location. To create a filter of this
type using a formula, you can write a **filter instruction** that is placed in the Enter a
filter formula in the box below text box in the Filter dialog box. The filter
instruction must begin with an equal sign, and equal signs also are used in the
instruction to describe the filter. Logical operators AND and OR are enclosed in
pound signs (#). The filter instruction to display members having a Family membership at the Anaheim location and who joined during the two-week period of
5/15/96 through 5/29/96 is:

='Date Joined'>=VALUE("5/15/96")#AND#'Date Joined'<=VALUE("5/29/96")
#AND#"Type'="Family"#AND#'Location'="Anaheim"

The following steps explain how to use a formula to create a filter to display
records of members who joined the Anaheim location with a Family membership
during the two-week period of 5/15/96 to 5/29/96.

Steps ## To Create a Filter Using a Formula

① **Click the Filters button on the
toolbar. When the Filter dialog
box displays, click the New
Filter button. When the Filter
Name dialog box displays,
type** 2 Week Special **in the
Type a name for the filter below
text box. Click the OK button.
Point to Filter using formula in
the Filter dialog box.**

*When you click the New
Filter button in the Filter
dialog box, Works displays
the Filter Name dialog box,
which allows you to type a new
filter name in the Type a name.
When you click the OK button in
the Filter Name dialog box, Works
displays the new filter name in the
Filter name box in the Filter dialog
box (Figure 9-29). The mouse
pointer points to the Filter using
formula option button.*

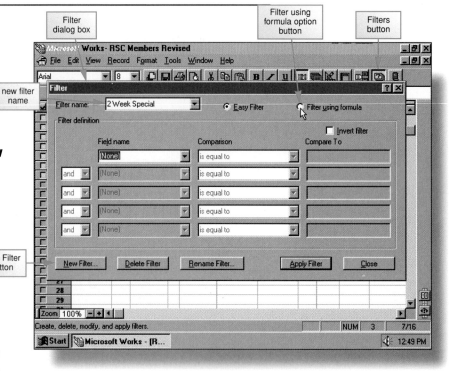

FIGURE 9-29

2 **Click Filter using formula.**

Works displays the Filter dialog box with the Filter definition box (Figure 9-30). The insertion point is located in the Enter a filter formula in the box below text box.

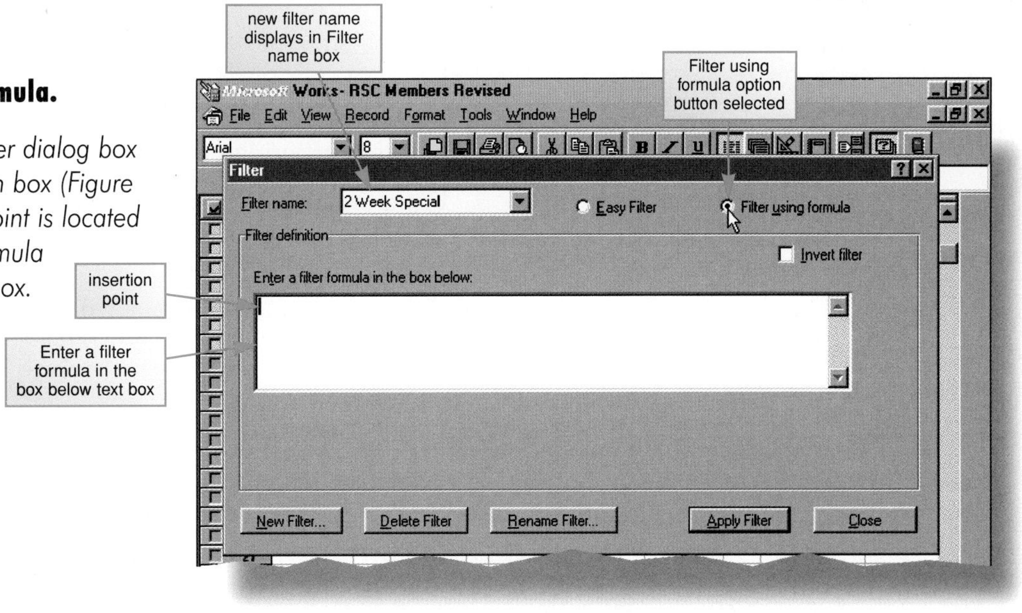

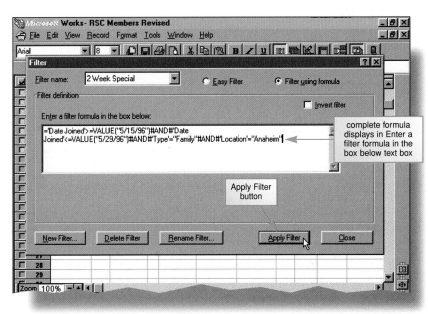

FIGURE 9-30

3 **Type** =`'Date Joined'>=VALUE("5/15/96")#AND#'Date Joined'<=VALUE("5/29/96")#AND#'Type'="Family"#AND#'Location'="Anaheim"` **in the Enter a filter formula in the box below text box. Point to the Apply Filter button.**

The complete formula displays in the Enter a filter formula in the box below text box (Figure 9-31). This filter instructs Works to display records of members whose date joined field contains a value between 5/15/96 and 5/29/96, type field contains Family, and location field contains Anaheim. The mouse pointer points to the Apply Filter button.

FIGURE 9-31

4 **Click the Apply Filter button.**

Works displays the record for the member who joined during the two-week period with a Family membership in Anaheim (Figure 9-32).

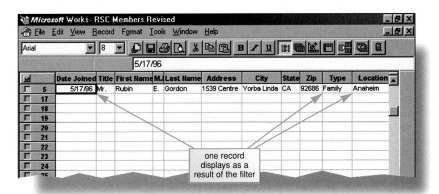

FIGURE 9-32

Table 9-1

OPERATOR	MEANING
=	Equal
<>	Not equal
>	Greater than
<	Less than
>=	Greater than or equal to
<=	Less than or equal to
"*text*"	Contains
<>"*text*"	Does not contain
""	Is blank
<>""	Is not blank
"text*"	Begins with
<>"text*"	Does not begin with
"*text"	Ends with

When developing filters that require multiple logical operators, you must use great care when you type the entries. Keep in mind the following rules for writing formulas:

1. Begin each formula with an equal sign.
2. When including a number to compare to, format using VALUE("number").
3. When including text to compare to, format using "text".
4. Separate each criterion with #AND# or #OR# operators.
5. Use conditional operator symbols to indicate what kind of comparison you want to perform.

A list of commonly used **conditional operators** and their meanings is shown in Table 9-1.

Applying an Existing Filter

Once you name a filter, you can apply the filter to the database at a later time by clicking the existing filter name in the Filter Name drop-down list box in the Filter dialog box. To apply the City = Irvine filter created earlier, complete the following steps.

Steps To Apply an Existing Filter

1 **Click the Filters button on the toolbar. When the Filter dialog box displays, click the Filter name box arrow and then point to City = Irvine.**

Works displays the Filter dialog box and the mouse pointer points to the filter name, City = Irvine, in the Filter name drop-down list box (Figure 9-33). The Filter name drop-down list box contains the names of all the filters that have been defined for the database. The criteria contained in the Filter dialog box is the most current filter applied to the database.

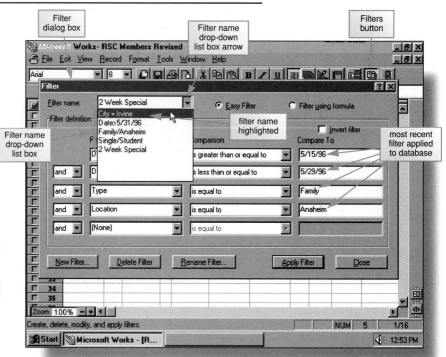

FIGURE 9-33

2 **Click City = Irvine in the Filter name drop-down list box. Point to the Apply Filter button.**

The existing filter name you wish to apply to the database displays in the Filter name box (Figure 9-34). The mouse pointer points to the Apply Filter button.

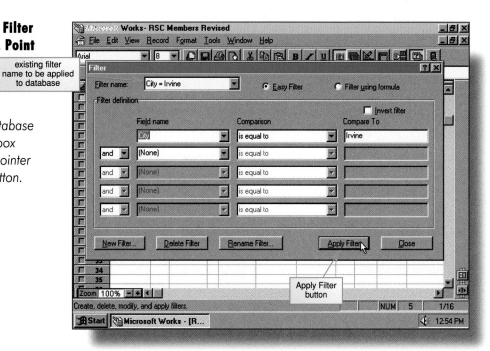

FIGURE 9-34

3 **Click the Apply Filter button.**

Works applies the City = Irvine filter to the database and displays all the records of members who live in the city of Irvine (Figure 9-35).

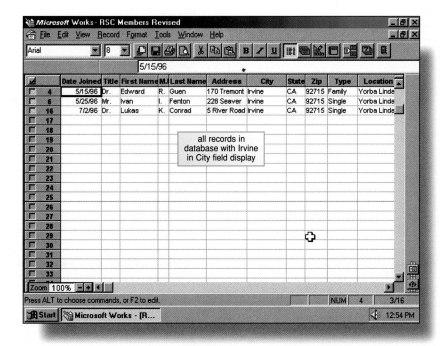

FIGURE 9-35

Applying an existing Filter is an important feature where the need arises to use a filter more than one time.

>Other**Ways**

1. On Record menu click Apply Filter, on Apply Filter cascading menu click desired filter name
2. Press F3

Deleting a Filter

Works allows you to assign a name to eight filters for any single database. You can delete previously named filters, however, to add another filter. To delete a filter, perform the following steps.

Steps **To Delete a Filter**

1 **Click the Filters button on the toolbar. When the Filter dialog box displays, click the Filter name box arrow and then point to Single/Student.**

Works displays the Filter dialog box (Figure 9-36). The existing filter name, Single/Student, is highlighted.

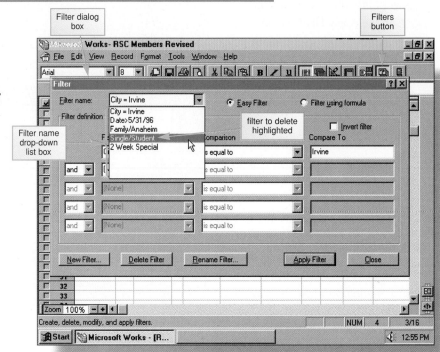

FIGURE 9-36

2 **Click Single/Student and point to the Delete Filter button.**

The filter to be deleted displays in the Filter name box and the mouse pointer points to the Delete Filter button (Figure 9-37).

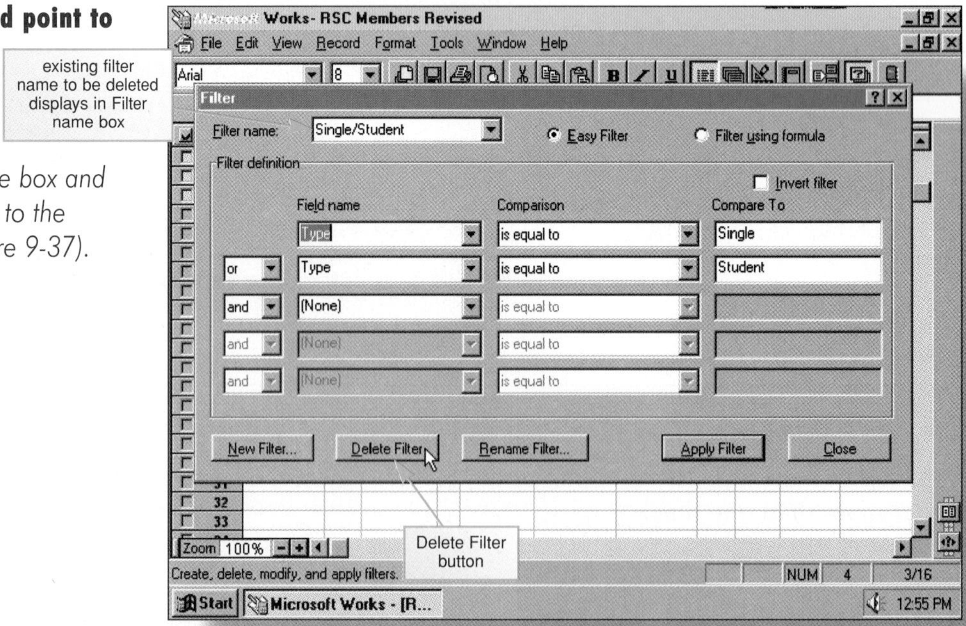

FIGURE 9-37

3 Click the Delete Filter button. When the Microsoft Works dialog box displays, point to the Yes button.

When you click the Delete Filter button, Works displays the Microsoft Works dialog box warning that the delete operation cannot be undone (Figure 9-38).

4 Click the Yes button in the Microsoft Works dialog box. Click the Close button in the Filter dialog box.

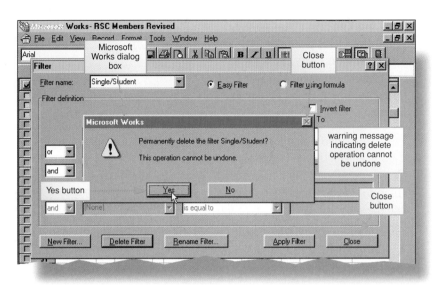

FIGURE 9-38

Other Ways

1. On Tools menu click Filters, click desired filter name in Filter name drop-down list box, click Delete Filter button, click Yes in Microsoft Works dialog box, click Close button

The filter name, Single/Student, is deleted and will no long display in Filter name drop-down list box.

Renaming a Filter

You can rename any filter you have previously named. To rename the City = Irvine filter to City/Irvine, perform the following steps.

Steps **To Rename a Filter**

1 Click the Filters button on the toolbar. When the Filter dialog box displays, click the Filter name box arrow and then click City = Irvine in the Filter name drop-down list box. Point to the Rename Filter button.

The City = Irvine filter displays in the Filter name box and the mouse pointer points to the Rename Filter button (Figure 9-39).

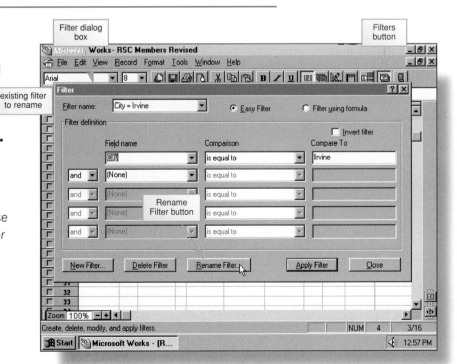

FIGURE 9-39

2 Click the Rename Filter button. When the Filter Name dialog box displays, type City/Irvine in the Type a name for the filter below text box. Point to the OK button.

The Filter Name dialog box displays (Figure 9-40). The new filter name, City/Irvine, displays in the Type a name for the filter below text box and the mouse pointer points to the Rename Filter button.

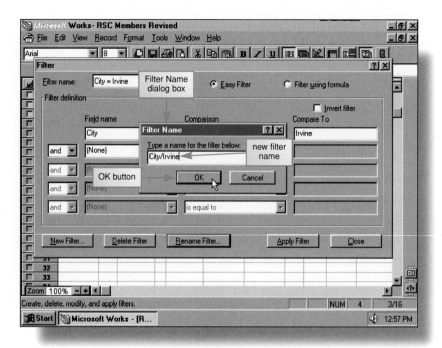

FIGURE 9-40

3 Click the OK button in the Filter Name dialog box. Point to the Close button.

Works changes the name of the filter name in the Filter name box from City = Irvine to City/Irvine (Figure 9-41).

4 Click the Close button in the Filter dialog box.

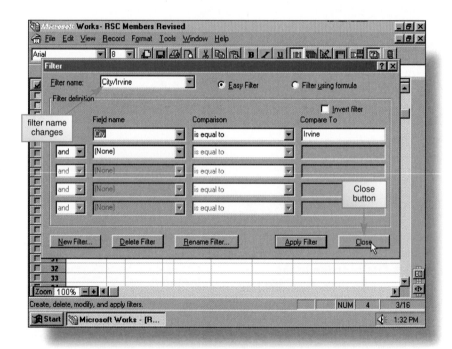

FIGURE 9-41

Works removes the Filter dialog box from the screen. The filter name City = Irvine is deleted and will no longer display in the Filter dialog box when referenced.

Saving a Database with Filters

You can save the database with the filters. Then, you can apply the filters at a later time. To save the database containing filters using a different filename, complete the following steps.

TO SAVE A DATABASE WITH FILTERS

Step 1: Click File on the menu bar and then click Save As.
Step 2: Type RSC Members Revised - Filters in the File name text box of the Save As dialog box.
Step 3: Click 3½ Floppy [A:] in the Save in drop-down list box, if necessary.
Step 4: Click the Save button.

Database Filter Summary

The Works Database filter capability allows you to view records in the database based on virtually any condition or combination of conditions you can specify, ranging from simply finding records with a given value in a field to complex conditions involving conditional and logical operators.

In addition to allowing you to view records in either list or form view on the screen, the filter capability allows you to select certain records for use in reports. The database reporting capabilities of Works are explained next.

Works Database Reports

Works provides the means to create a variety of printed reports from the data in a database. These reports can range from simple listings to involved reports with calculations and summaries. This section of Project 9 demonstrates a variety of reports you can obtain using the Works Database tool and the methods for creating these reports.

Using Works ReportCreator to Create Database Reports

When you print database records using the methods described in Project 7, you have little control over how Works formats the database. Works prints the records as they appear in form view or list view. Using **Works ReportCreator**, you can instruct Works to print only the fields you want, and you can direct Works to calculate and print report statistics. You can add titles, headers, and footers to a report. A maximum of eight reports can be defined for a single database. This section of Project 9 illustrates the capability of Works ReportCreator to create database reports.

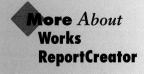

More *About* **Works ReportCreator**

Once you have stepped through the ReportCreator dialog box to create a report definition, you cannot go back to ReportCreator to make modifications. You must use report view and modify the report definition. Use the commands on the Tools menu to modify sorting, grouping, or filtering information on the report definition.

Figure 9-42 shows a simple report listing the members of RSC Sports and Fitness Centers. The title, first name, middle initial, last name, address, city, state, and zip code of each member are listed in the report. Three different categories of lines appear on the report: (1) the report title lines, which contain the words, RSC Members Listing, on one line and a solid pattern dark red bar on the next line; (2) the report Headings lines, which consist of the words, Title, First Name, and so forth, on one line and a solid pattern, light gray bar on the next line; and (3) the record lines (each individual record from the database). The record lines are followed by a border at the bottom of the last line. It is important you understand these three categories of lines because you will use these categories when defining the report.

To create the database listing shown in Figure 9-42, you must identify the report title and then select those fields that are to appear in the report. The headings are the field names of the fields you select. When you create a report, Works creates a **report definition** and displays it in report view. The report definition defines the general format of the report. This definition may be modified to meet particular needs. To define the report listing all members, complete the following steps.

RSC Members Listing

Title	First Name	M.I.	Last Name	Address	City	State	Zip
Mr.	Nimiira	A.	Sanji	79 Fuller	Orange	CA	92667
Dr.	Albert	G.	Sandler	26 Irning	Yuma	AZ	85364
Ms.	Midge	W.	Maclone	94 Bourne	Placentia	CA	92670
Dr.	Edward	R.	Guen	170 Tremont	Irvine	CA	92715
Mr.	Rubin	E.	Gordon	1539 Centre	Yorba Linda	CA	92686
Mr.	Ivan	I.	Fenton	228 Seaver	Irvine	CA	92715
Mr.	David	L.	Dirsa	47 Concord	Orange	CA	92667
Mr.	Julian	P.	Coulon	216 Summer	Tustin	CA	92680
Mr.	Jacob	W.	Chase	35 Chilton	Fullerton	CA	92635
Mr.	Stefano	U.	Branchi	58 Sullivan	Orange	CA	92667
Mr.	Antonio	V.	Alonso	327 Still Pond	Yorba Linda	CA	92686
Mr.	Gabriel	A.	Vidal	40 Concord	Reno	NV	89503
Ms.	Cathy	E.	Wain	520 Beacon	Santa Ana	CA	92705
Dr.	Bei	F.	Wu	205 Kent	Santa Ana	CA	92705
Mr.	Cody	L.	Learner	124 Cobb	Brea	CA	92672
Dr.	Lukas	K.	Conrad	5 River Road	Irvine	CA	92715

FIGURE 9-42

 Steps **To Define a Listing Report**

① **In list view, click Record on the menu bar, point to Show, and click 1 All Records on the Show cascading menu. Click CTRL+HOME to view record number 1. Click the Report View button on the toolbar. When the Report Name dialog box displays, type** Members **in the Type a name for the report below text box. Point to the OK button.**

Works displays the Report Name dialog box (Figure 9-43). If no report is defined for the database, clicking the Report View button always results in Works displaying the Report Name dialog box. The word, Members, displays in the Type a name for the report below text box. The mouse pointer points to the OK button.

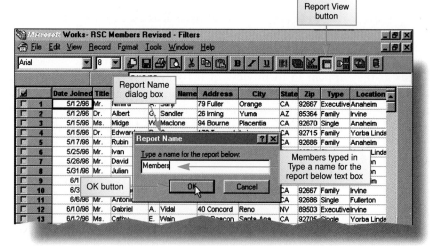

FIGURE 9-43

2 **Click the OK button. When the ReportCreator - Members dialog box displays, type** RSC Members Listing **in the Report title text box. Point to the Next button.**

Works displays the ReportCreator - Members dialog box (Figure 9-44). The Title sheet displays on top of five other tabbed sheets (Fields, Sorting, Grouping, Filter, and Summary). The title, RSC Members Listing, displays in the Report title text box. In the Report orientation box, Portrait is selected. In the Report font box, Arial displays in the Font text box and 8 displays in the Size text box. The Sample box displays the selections. The mouse pointer points to the Next button. These selections instruct Works to print the report title, RSC Members Listing, at the top of the report. The report will be printed in portrait orientation. The report font is 8-point Arial.

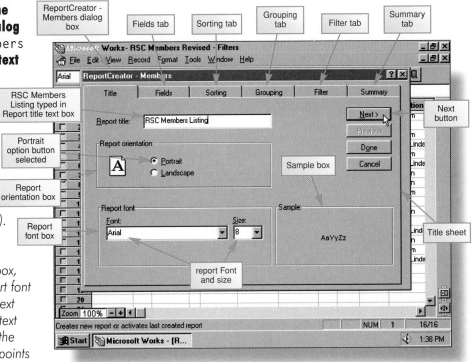

FIGURE 9-44

3 **Click the Next button. When the Fields sheet displays, highlight the field name, Title, in the Fields available list box by clicking the word, Title. Point to the Add button.**

When you click the Next button in the ReportCreator - Members dialog box, the Title sheet moves behind the Fields sheet (Figure 9-45). The field name, Title, is highlighted and the mouse pointer points to the Add button. The Fields available list box contains the names of the fields in the database. The Field order list box on the right shows all fields that have been selected to appear in the report. In Figure 9-45, no fields have been added. The Show field names at top of each page check box is selected. This option specifies that the database field names are displayed and printed as titles across the top of each page.

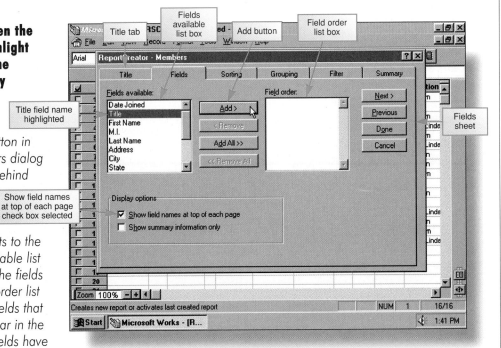

FIGURE 9-45

4 **Click the Add button to add the Title field to the Field order list box. The highlight in the Fields available box on the left moves to the next field name (First Name) automatically when you click the Add button. Click the Add button for each of the following fields: First Name, M.I., Last Name, Address, City, State, and Zip. Point to the Done button after all fields have been added to the Field order list box.**

Works places the field names you select in the Field order list box (Figure 9-46). The Type field name is highlighted, but because it is not in the report, you should not click the Add button. If you mistakenly place a field name that is not

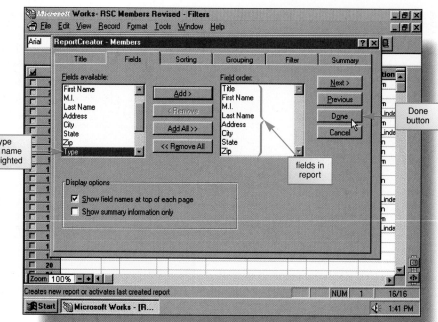

FIGURE 9-46

supposed to be in the report in the Field order list box, highlight the incorrect field name in the Field order list box and then click the Remove button. The field name will be removed from the Field order list box. The mouse pointer points to the Done button. The additional sheets in the ReportCreator - Members dialog box are not required for this report. Later reports will demonstrate the use of these sheets.

5 **Click the Done button in the ReportCreator - Members dialog box. When the ReportCreator dialog box displays informing you that the report definition has been created, point to the Modify button.**

After you have made the choices and entries in the ReportCreator - Members dialog box, Works displays the ReportCreator dialog box to inform you the report definition has been created. Works displays the report definition in report view behind the dialog box. The mouse pointer points to the Modify button.

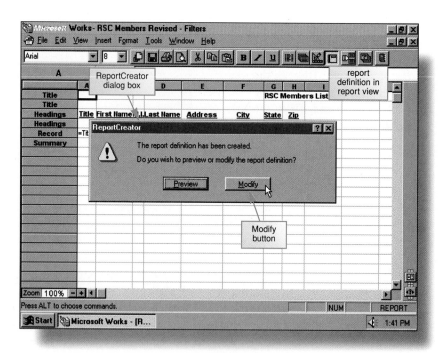

FIGURE 9-47

6 **Click the Modify button.**

Works display the report definition in report view (Figure 9-48).

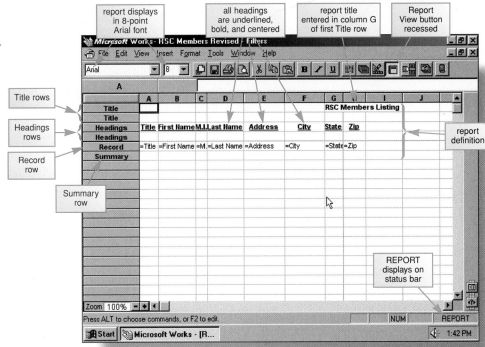

FIGURE 9-48

OtherWays

1. On Tools menu click ReportCreator, type desired report name, click OK button, make appropriate choices and entries in ReportCreator dialog box, click Done button

The **report definition** that displays in report view in Figure 9-48 contains columns and rows much like the list view of the database. Each column is identified by column letters. The rows are identified by row titles at the left of the window. The first two rows are **Title rows**. Works always displays the title (RSC Members Listing) you entered in the Report title text box in the Report Creator dialog box (see Step 2 on page W 9.29) in a column to the right in the first Title row. The title displays in 8-point Arial bold font. The second Title row is blank. The next two rows are **Headings rows**. The field names you selected in Step 3 and Step 4 display in the columns of the first Headings row. By default, Works displays the headings in bold underlined, and centered font in each column. The font and size used for the headings is the same as that used in the list view of the database (in this case, 8-point Arial font). The second Headings row is blank.

The **Record row** contains entries with an equal sign followed by the field names you selected for the report. This indicates Works will place the actual field entry in the report at the particular location. Although only one Record row appears in the report definition, one record line will print on the report for each record in the database. The **Summary row** defines the summary line of the report and is blank. Each field in the report definition and, therefore, the report itself displays in the same font and size as it was in the list view of the database. In this case, all fields display in 8-point Arial font. Fonts and font sizes can be changed for the fields on the report.

The Title row of a report definition will print a title only at the top of the first page of the report and not on subsequent pages. The heading lines print under the title line on the first page of the report and at the top of the page on each subsequent page because Show field names at top of each page was selected in Step 3 above. As previously stated, one record line will print for each record in the database. Summary lines, if specified in the Summary sheet of the ReportCreator dialog box, will print on the report after all the record lines have printed. In the listing report being created, no summary lines will print.

While the report definition developed by Works provides the structure of the desired report, often the report default format is not the precise format you want for the report. Prior to changing the report definition, however, you can view the report as it will print. To preview the report as it will print, perform the following steps (see Figure 9-42 on page W 9.28).

TO PREVIEW A REPORT

Step 1: Click the Print Preview button on the toolbar.
Step 2: Click the Zoom In button in the print preview window two times.

The report displays in the print preview window as shown in Figure 9-49.

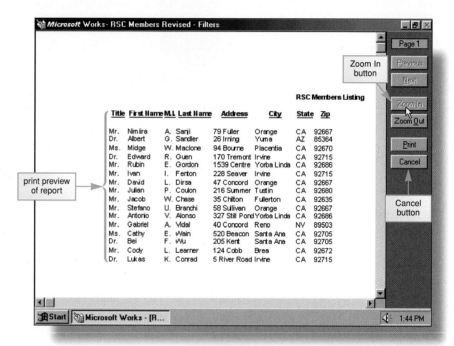

FIGURE 9-49

Modifying a Report Definition

In Figure 9-49, it is apparent that several areas of the report must be modified to achieve the report format shown in Figure 9-42 on page W 9.28. First, the title, RSC Members Listing, which will print to the right of the page in 8-point Arial bold font in its present format, must be changed to 14-point bold italic font and must be centered on the report. Second, the field headings, which will currently print in 8-point Arial bold underlined font, must be changed to 10 point with the underline removed. The record lines should display in 10-point Times New Roman font. In addition, the fields should be increased in width to improve the appearance of the report. In Figure 9-42, a solid pattern, dark red line separates the report title from the report headings, and a solid pattern, light gray bar appears after the column titles. To modify the current report definition to conform to the desired layout, perform the following steps.

Steps **To Modify a Report Definition**

1 **Click the Cancel button in the print preview window to return to the report definition in report view. Right click column G in the first Title row and then point to Cut.**

The cell containing the words, RSC Members Listing, is highlighted and the mouse pointer points to Cut on the context-sensitive menu (Figure 9-50).

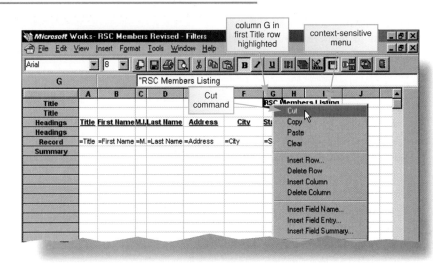

FIGURE 9-50

2 **Click Cut on the context-sensitive menu. Right-click column A in the first Title row, and then click Paste on the context-sensitive menu.**

Works cuts the words, RSC Members Listing, in column G of the first Title row and places it on the Clipboard. When you click Paste, Works pastes the words, RSC Members Listing, into column A of the first Title row (Figure 9-51).

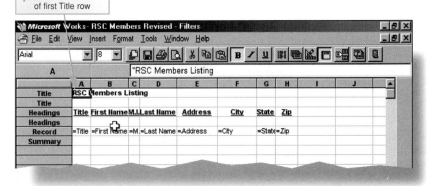

FIGURE 9-51

3 **Click the Font Size box arrow and then click 14 in the drop-down list box. Highlight columns A through H in the first Title row. Right-click the selection and then click Format on the context-sensitive menu. In the Format dialog box, click the Alignment tab, and then click Center across selection in the Horizontal box. Click the OK button. Click any cell to remove the highlight.**

The words, RSC Members Listing, display in 14-point Arial bold font, centered across columns A through H (Figure 9-52).

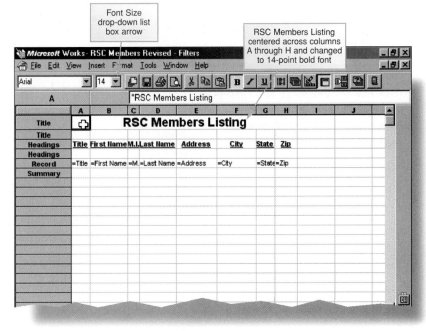

FIGURE 9-52

4 Highlight columns A through H in the first Headings row. Click the Underline button on the toolbar to remove the underline from the column headings. Increase the font size to 10. Right-click the selection and then click Format on the context-sensitive menu. In the Format dialog box, click the Alignment tab. Click Wrap text, click Center in the Horizontal box, click Center in the Vertical box and click the OK button. Using the Column Width command on the Format menu, change the column widths as follows: Title (6); First Name (11); M.I. (5); Last Name (14); Address (19); City (12); State (9); and Zip (7).

The Headings row is formatted as shown in Figure 9-53.

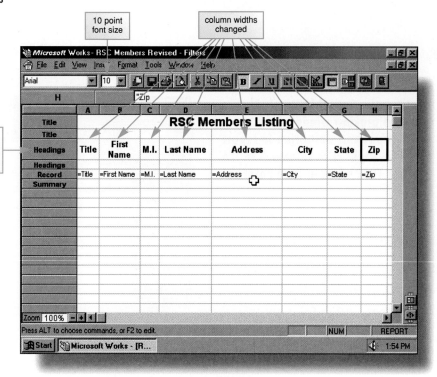

FIGURE 9-53

5 Highlight the Record row, columns A through H. Change the font to 10-point Times New Roman. Center the M.I. field and the State field by highlighting each field, and then on Format menu, click Alignment. Click Center in the Horizontal box of the Alignment sheet, and click the OK button in the Format dialog box. The centering will take place only on the printed report.

The Record row is changed to 10-point Times New Roman font (Figure 9-54).

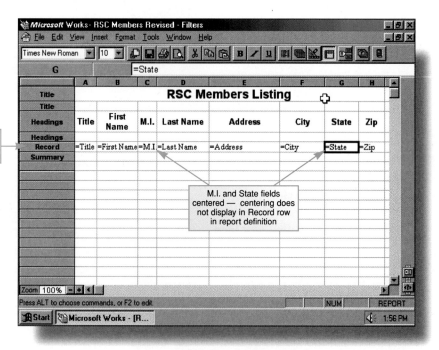

FIGURE 9-54

6 Highlight the second Title row, columns A through H. This row is currently blank. Right-click the selection. Click Format on the context-sensitive menu. When the Format dialog box displays, click the Shading tab. Click the solid pattern in the Pattern list box. Click Dark Red in the Foreground list box. Click the OK button. Highlight columns A through H in the second Headings row. Place a solid pattern, light gray color in this row using the Shadings sheet in the Format dialog box. Click any cell to remove the highlight.

The solid pattern, dark red line and the solid pattern, light gray line are added to the report definition (Figure 9-55).

color added in second Title row and second Headings row in columns A through H

FIGURE 9-55

The report definition is now complete.

Previewing and Printing the Report

Before printing the report, you should preview the report using the Print Preview button on the toolbar. To preview the report and print the report, perform the following steps.

 Steps To Preview and Print the Report

1 Point to the Print Preview button on the toolbar.

The mouse pointer points to the Print Preview button (Figure 9-56).

Print Preview button

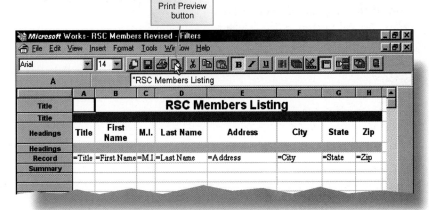

FIGURE 9-56

2 **Click the Print Preview button. Click the Zoom In button in the print preview window two times. Click the right scroll arrow in the print preview window two times. Click the down scroll arrow one time.**

The print preview window displays the report (Figure 9-57). When you click the Zoom In button, Works magnifies the report so it is easy to see. When using print preview, the screen will display in black and white unless you are using a color printer.

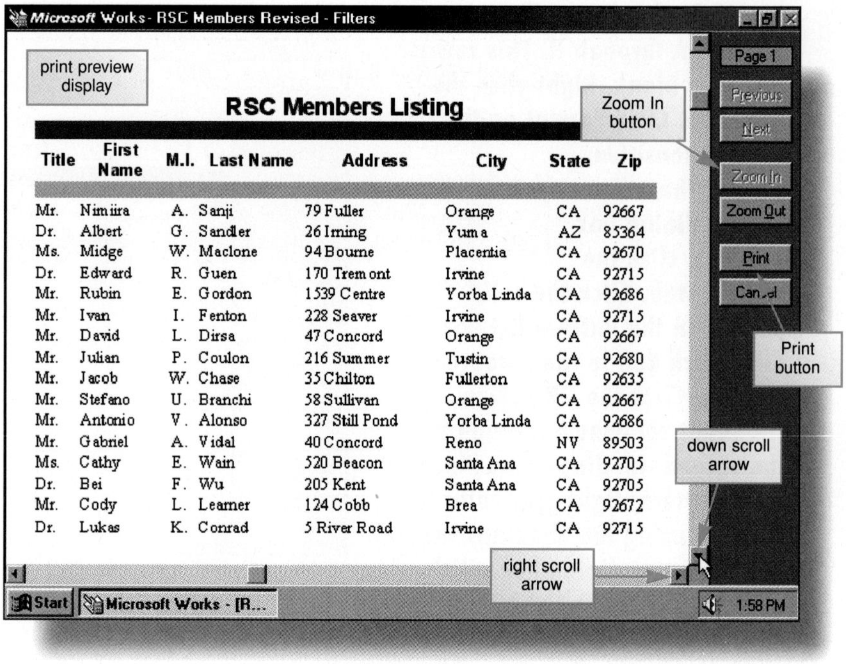

FIGURE 9-57

3 **The report displays in the correct format. Click the Print button in the print preview window to print the report.**

The report will print as shown in Figure 9-42 on page W 9.28.

With the report defined and printed, the tasks for creating the Members report are complete.

Saving the Database with a Report

You should now save the database. When you save the database, the report definition will be saved with the database file. To save the database using the same name, perform the following step.

TO SAVE THE DATABASE

Step 1: Click the Save button on the toolbar.

Viewing and Modifying a Report Definition

If you want to view, modify, or print the report at a later time, perform the following steps.

TO VIEW, MODIFY, OR PRINT A REPORT

Step 1: Display the database in list view or form view.
Step 2: Click View on the menu bar.
Step 3: Click Report.
Step 4: When the View Report dialog box displays, in the Select a report list box highlight the name of the report you want to see, and then click the Preview or Modify button in the View Report dialog box.
Step 5: Perform whatever tasks you require.
Step 6: Click the List View button on the toolbar to return to list view or click the Form View button on the toolbar to return to form view. You can always display a report definition through the use of the Report command on the View menu.

Sorting Records

When using the Database tool, Works provides sorting capabilities similar to those in the Spreadsheet tool. You can sort records alphabetically, numerically, or by date. The following steps explain how to sort the RSC Members Revised - Filters database so the records display in alphabetical order by the last name of the member.

Steps To Sort Records

◆ **More** *About*
Sorting Records

To sort records in a desired order for a report definition, you must use the Report Sorting command on the Tools menu or the Report Settings command on the Format menu. The Sort command on the Record menu in list view or form view sorts the records in the database only, not in the report definition.

① **Click the Report View button on the toolbar to display the report definition, if necessary. Click Tools on the menu bar and then point to Report Sorting.**

The Tools menu displays and the mouse pointer points to Report Sorting (Figure 9-58).

FIGURE 9-58

2 **Click Report Sorting. When the Report Settings dialog box displays, click the Sorting sheet, if necessary. Click the Sort by box arrow to display a list of field names. Click Last Name in the drop-down list box. Click Ascending in the Sort by box, if necessary. Point to the Done button.**

The Report Settings dialog box displays (Figure 9-59). The Report Settings dialog box contains three tabbed sheets, Sorting, Grouping, and Filter. The Sorting sheet displays on the screen. The Last Name field is selected and the Ascending option button is selected in the Sort by box. The mouse pointer points to the Done button.

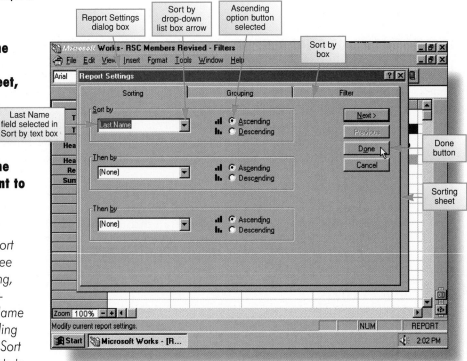

FIGURE 9-59

3 **Click the Done button. Point to the Print button on the toolbar.**

The report view of the only named report (RSC Members) displays (Figure 9-60).

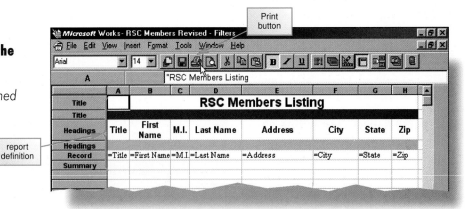

FIGURE 9-60

4 **Click the Print button on the toolbar.**

Works prints the report in alphabetical order by last name (Figure 9-61).

FIGURE 9-61

Other Ways

1. On Format menu click Report Settings, click Sorting tab, click desired options, click Done button

You cannot click Undo on the Edit menu to undo a sorting operation of records in a report definition. If you no longer desire the records sorted in alphabetical order, sort the records by date joined to arrange them in their original sequence. You can sort the database in any sequence you want using the Report Sorting command.

In some applications, the original records may be in a sequence that cannot be recreated by sorting. If so, either save the sorted database using a different filename or close the sorted database without saving it. In this way, the database in the original sequence remains on disk.

Reports with Summary Totals

Works provides the capability to define reports that contain summary totals calculated from data in the database. Two common summary totals are counting the number of records in a database and summing the values in fields within the database.

The next task in Project 9 is to create a report listing all members in the RSC Members database, the total members in the club, the dues owed by all members, the Kids Club dues owed by all members, and the total dues owed by all members. The report to be created is shown in Figure 9-62.

The report title is Membership Totals. This title should print at the top of every page of the report. As mentioned earlier, however, a value in the Title row of the report definition prints only on the first page of the report. Therefore, the title, Membership Totals, on the report shown in Figure 9-62 will be defined in a Headings row so it will print on each page of the report. The fields on the report include the Title, First Name, M.I., Last Name, Dues, Kids Club, and Total Dues. The field names display in the Heading lines of the report. Fields from each record in the database are printed as Record lines on the report. At the bottom of the report are four totals: Total Members, Total Dues, Total Kids Club, and Total Dues for Club. These totals, each of which prints on a line by itself, are Summary lines.

To create the report definition for the report shown in Figure 9-62, complete the steps on the next pages.

More *About*
Sorting Records for Report Definitions

In previous versions of Microsoft Works, you had to apply filters and sort the records before you created your reports. Works 4.0, however, has incorporated the filter and sort features so you do not need to do them beforehand.

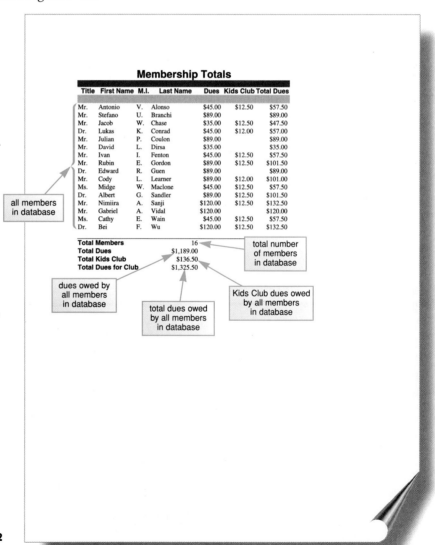

Membership Totals

Title	First Name	M.I.	Last Name	Dues	Kids Club	Total Dues
Mr.	Antonio	V.	Alonso	$45.00	$12.50	$57.50
Mr.	Stefano	U.	Branchi	$89.00		$89.00
Mr.	Jacob	W.	Chase	$35.00	$12.50	$47.50
Dr.	Lukas	K.	Conrad	$45.00	$12.00	$57.00
Mr.	Julian	P.	Coulon	$89.00		$89.00
Mr.	David	L.	Dirsa	$35.00		$35.00
Mr.	Ivan	I.	Fenton	$45.00	$12.50	$57.50
Mr.	Rubin	E.	Gordon	$89.00	$12.50	$101.50
Dr.	Edward	R.	Guen	$89.00		$89.00
Mr.	Cody	L.	Learner	$89.00	$12.00	$101.00
Ms.	Midge	W.	Maclone	$45.00	$12.50	$57.50
Dr.	Albert	G.	Sandler	$89.00	$12.50	$101.50
Mr.	Nimiira	A.	Sanji	$120.00	$12.50	$132.50
Mr.	Gabriel	A.	Vidal	$120.00		$120.00
Ms.	Cathy	E.	Wain	$45.00	$12.50	$57.50
Dr.	Bei	F.	Wu	$120.00	$12.50	$132.50

Total Members	16
Total Dues	$1,189.00
Total Kids Club	$136.50
Total Dues for Club	$1,325.50

all members in database

total number of members in database

dues owed by all members in database

total dues owed by all members in database

Kids Club dues owed by all members in database

FIGURE 9-62

Steps **To Define a Report with Summary Totals**

1 **Click Tools on the menu bar and then point to ReportCreator.**

Works displays the Tools menu and the mouse pointer points to the ReportCreator command (Figure 9-63).

FIGURE 9-63

2 **Click ReportCreator. When the Report Name dialog box displays, type** Member Totals **in the Type a name for the report below text box. Point to the OK button.**

Works displays the Report Name dialog box and the report name displays in the Type a name for the report below text box (Figure 9-64). The mouse pointer points to the OK button.

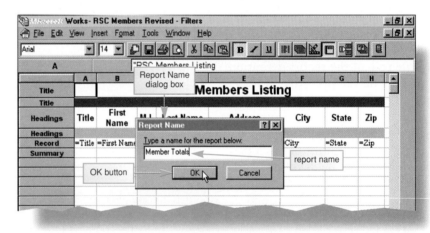

FIGURE 9-64

3 **Click the OK button. When the ReportCreator - Member Totals dialog box displays, press the DELETE key to erase the report title highlighted in the Report title text box. Point to the Next button.**

Works displays the ReportCreator - Member Totals dialog box (Figure 9-65). No report title is entered in the Report title text box. No report title is entered in the Report title text box because the report title will be part of the Headings rows in the report definition. The mouse pointer points to the Next button.

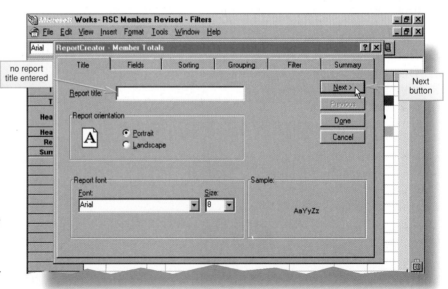

FIGURE 9-65

4 Click the Next button. Highlight Title in the Fields available list box and then click the Add button. The highlight moves down to the First Name field name. Click the Add button for the First Name field. The highlight moves down to the M.I. field name. Click the Add button for the M.I. field. The highlight moves down to the Last Name field name. Click the Add button for the Last Name field. Scroll down, highlight the Dues field name, and click the Add button. Click the Add button for the Kids Club field and the Total Dues field. Point to the Summary tab.

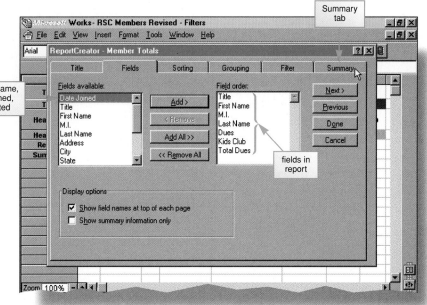

FIGURE 9-66

When you highlight the Title field name and then click the Add button, Works places the Title field name in the Field order list box and highlights the First Name field name in the Fields available list box on the left (Figure 9-66). Each of the highlighted and added field names displays in the Field order list box. When the last field name in the Fields available list box is added to the Field order list box, the highlight moves to the first field name in the Fields available list box (Date Joined). The mouse pointer points to the Summary tab.

5 Click the Summary tab in the ReportCreator - Member Totals dialog box. When the Summary sheet displays, click Count in the Summaries box.

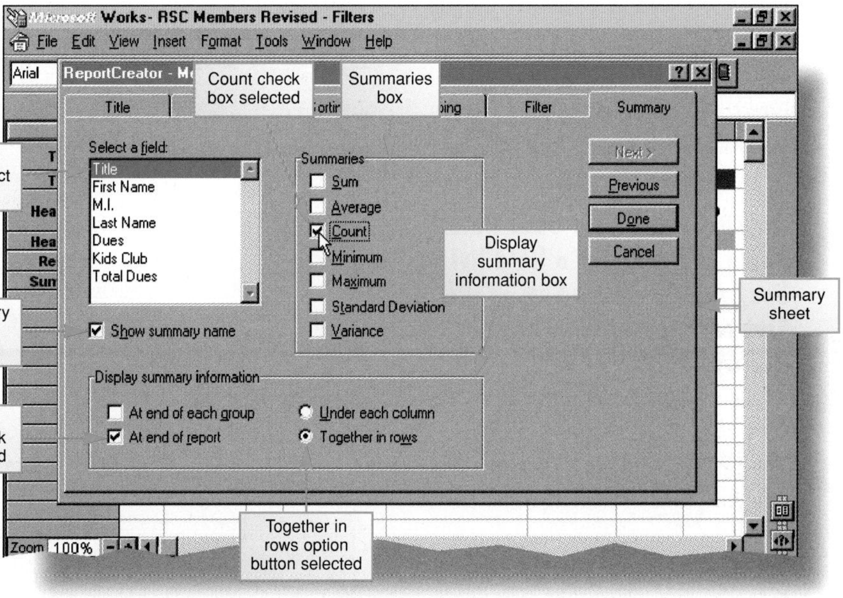

Works displays the Summary sheet (Figure 9-67). The Select a field list box on the left contains the field names of the fields in the report. The Title field name is highlighted. The Summaries box contains the types of summaries Works can generate for printing at the end of the report. By clicking Count, you indicate the number of records containing the Title field should be

FIGURE 9-67

counted. Because the database contains one record per member, a count of the number of records gives the number of members, which is the value to print. The Show summary name check box is selected below the Select a field list box by default. This specifies that a heading is included next to the calculated result. The At end of report check box is selected by default in the Display summary information box. This option specifies that the summary information is to print at the end of the report. The Together in rows option button is selected by default. This option specifies that the totals should be printed in rows at the end of the report instead of under each column of the fields being counted or summed.

6 **Highlight the Dues field name by clicking it in the Select a field list box, and then click Sum in the Summaries box.**

The Dues field name is highlighted and the Sum check box contains a ✓ (Figure 9-68). Clicking the Sum check box instructs Works to sum the value in the Dues field in each of the database records. At the end of the report, this sum will print.

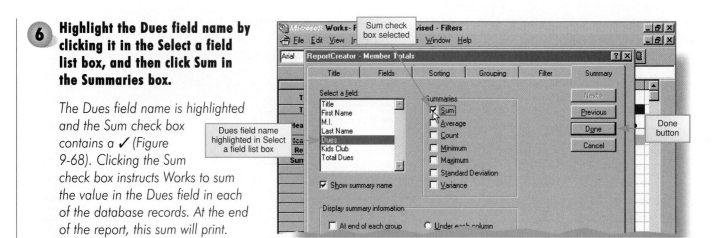

FIGURE 9-68

7 **Highlight the Kids Club field name in the Select a field list box, and then click Sum in the Summaries box.**

The Kids Club field name is highlighted and the Sum check box contains a ✓ (Figure 9-69). Selecting the Sum check box instructs Works to sum the value in the Kids Club field in each of the database records. At the end of the report, this sum will print.

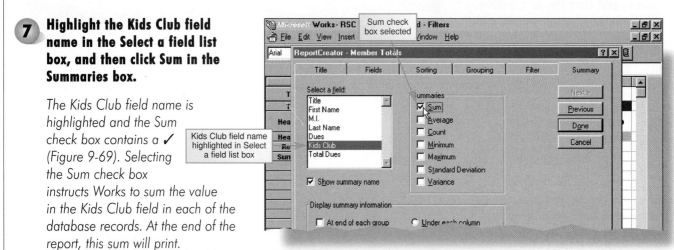

FIGURE 9-69

8 **Highlight the Total Dues field name in the Select a field list box, and then click Sum in the Summaries box. Point to the Done button.**

The Total Dues field name is highlighted and the Sum check box contains a ✓ (Figure 9-70). Selecting the Sum check box instructs Works to sum the value in the Total Dues field in each of the database records. At the end of the report, this sum will print. The mouse pointer points to the Done button.

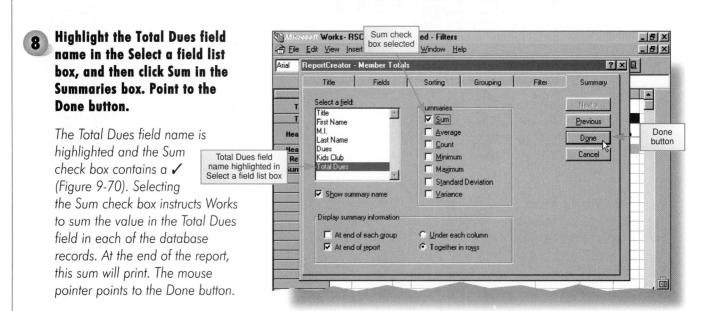

FIGURE 9-70

9 **Click the Done button. When the ReportCreator dialog box displays that tells you the report definition has been created, click the Modify button.**

Works displays the report definition (Figure 9-71). Nothing displays in the Title rows. The Headings row contains the field names of each field in the report in a bold, underlined format. The Record row contains each of the fields in the report. Five Summary rows are defined. The first Summary row contains a line at the bottom of the row. This border will print between the body of the report and the total lines. The next four Summary rows contain summary titles in column A of each row. In column D, formulas display the count of the Title field, the sum of the Dues field, the sum of the Kids Club, and the sum of the Total Dues field.

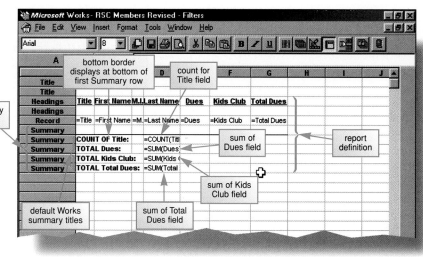

FIGURE 9-71

Modifying a Summary Report Definition

As with the previous report definitions, the definition of the summary report must be modified in order for it to produce the report shown in Figure 9-62 on page W 9.39. To display the report with the current report definition to determine the modifications, complete the following steps (see Figure 9-72).

TO DISPLAY PRINT PREVIEW

Step 1: Click the Print Preview button on the toolbar.

Step 2: Click the Zoom In button in the print preview window two times. Click the down arrow once.

Step 3: Review the screen to determine the modifications that must be made. Notice that no report title displays, the headings are in a different format, and the summary titles are not the same.

Step 4: Click the Cancel button in the print preview window.

FIGURE 9-72

To produce the report, the report definition must be modified using many of the techniques explained when you were creating the previous listing report. The two major tasks to accomplish are: (1) insert a report title; (2) format the summary report, including changing titles and adding color.

To insert the report title, Membership Totals, in a heading line, first you must insert two additional Headings rows in the report definition. To insert two blank rows in the report definition and add a report title, complete the following steps.

Steps To Insert Two Blank Headings Rows and Add a Title

1 **Highlight the two Headings rows by pointing to the row title in the first Headings row and dragging down through the second Headings row. Right-click the selection and then point to Insert Row.**

When you drag the Headings rows, the two Headings rows are highlighted (Figure 9-73). Works displays the context-sensitive menu and the mouse pointer points to the Insert Row command.

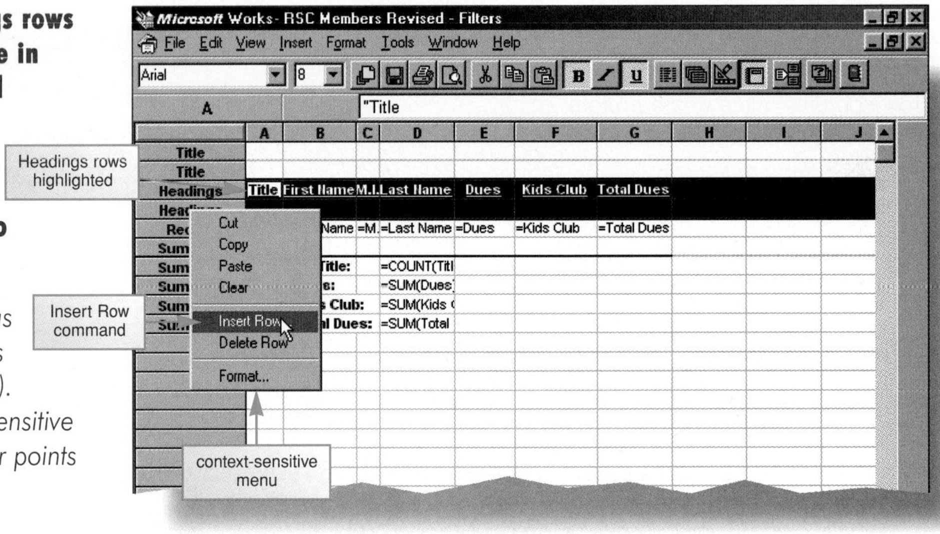

FIGURE 9-73

2 **Click Insert Row. When the Insert Row dialog box displays, point to the Insert button.**

Works displays the Insert Row dialog box (Figure 9-74). The word, Headings, is highlighted in the Select a row type list box because you dragged and highlighted the Headings rows in Step 1. The Select a row type list box indicates the type of row Works will insert. The mouse pointer points to the Insert button.

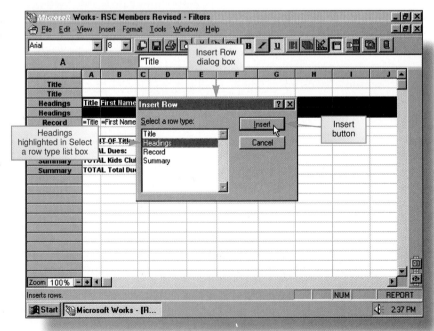

FIGURE 9-74

3 **Click the Insert button. When the two blank Headings rows display, highlight column A in the first Headings row, type** Membership Totals **and then press the ENTER key or click the Enter box.**

Works inserts two additional Headings rows above the two Headings rows you highlighted in Step 1 (Figure 9-75). Whenever you insert rows, the number of rows inserted always equals the number of rows highlighted, and the inserted rows always appear above the highlighted rows. The title, Membership Totals, is now included in the report definition in a heading line.

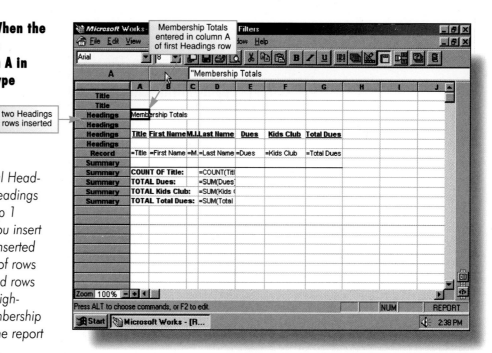

FIGURE 9-75

After entering the report title, you must format the report.

OtherWays

1. On Insert menu click Insert Row, click Insert button

Formatting the Summary Report

The techniques for formatting the report use techniques previously explained. Complete the following steps to format the report (see Figure 9-76 on the next page).

TO FORMAT THE SUMMARY REPORT

Step 1: Highlight the title, Membership Totals, in column A of the first Headings row. Change the font size to 16 point and bold.

Step 2: Highlight columns A through G in the first Headings row. Right-click the selection and then click Format on the context-sensitive menu. When the Format dialog box displays, click the Alignment tab. Click Center across selection in the Horizontal box. Click the OK button.

Step 3: Highlight the column titles in the third Headings row and change the font size to 10 point. Click the Underline button on the toolbar to remove the underline from the column titles.

Step 4: Highlight columns A through G beginning with the fourth Headings row through the last Summary row. Change the font size of the highlighted rows to 10 point.

Step 5: Highlight columns A through G of the Record row. Change the font to Times New Roman.

Step 6: Using the Column Width command from the Format menu, change only the following column widths: Title (7); First Name (13); M.I. (5); Last Name (17); Total Dues (12).

Step 7: Change the words, COUNT OF Title:, in the second Summary Row to the words, Total Members. Highlight the words, COUNT OF Title:, in column A of the second Summary row. Type Total Members and then press the DOWN ARROW key.

Step 8: Type Total Dues and then press the DOWN ARROW key.

Step 9: Type Total Kids Club and then press the DOWN ARROW key.

Step 10: Type Total Dues for Club and then press the ENTER key or click the Enter box

Step 11: Highlight the four Summary rows in column D that contain the formulas. Change the font to Times New Roman.

The report is now formatted as shown in Figure 9-76.

FIGURE 9-76

The next step is to add color to the report definition. To add color, perform following steps (see Figure 9-77).

TO ADD COLOR TO A REPORT DEFINITION

Step 1: Highlight columns A through G in the second Headings row, which is blank. Right-click the selection and then click Format on the context-sensitive menu. Click the Shading tab. Click the solid pattern in the Pattern list box, and then click Dark Red in the Foreground list box. Click the OK button.

Step 2: Highlight columns A through G in the fourth Headings row, which is blank. Right-click the selection and then click Format on the context-sensitive menu. Click the Shading tab. Click the solid pattern in the Pattern list box, and then click Light Gray in the Foreground list box. Click the OK button. Click any cell to remove the highlight.

Formatting the report is now complete. Figure 9-77 illustrates the new report definition. Notice in the previous steps that the report was modified from the top to the bottom of the report; that is, the Headings rows were inserted and completed first, and then the Summary rows were formatted and completed. While no set rules apply to the sequence in which a report definition should be modified, working from the top of the report definition to the bottom usually works well.

FIGURE 9-77

Again it should be pointed out that by placing the title in a Headings row, you ensure that the title will print at the top of each page of the report. Recall that if you place the title in the Title row of the report definition, it will print only on the first page of the report.

Printing the Modified Summary Report

To print the report after displaying the print preview window, complete the following steps.

TO PRINT THE REPORT

Step 1: Click the Print Preview button on the toolbar.
Step 2: Click the Zoom In button two times.
Step 3: Click the down scroll arrow two times.
Step 4: Click the right scroll arrow one time. Review the report to ensure it will print correctly.
Step 5: Click the Print button in the print preview window.

The report will print as shown in Figure 9-62 on page W 9.39.

Creating a database report with summary totals is a common requirement. Be sure you thoroughly understand the procedure for creating and printing a database report with summary totals.

Grouping and Filtering Records for Reports

The next task in this project is to create a report for each location listing the members at each location, the Dues owed, Kids Club owed, and Total Dues owed. At the end of the report for each location, list the Total Members, Total Dues, Total Kids Club, and Total Dues for Club (for that location). At the end of the report for all locations, list the totals for all locations. The report generated is shown in Figure 9-78.

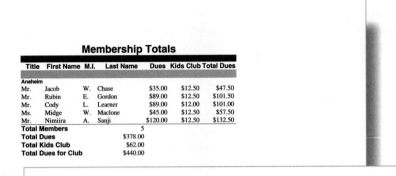

Membership Totals

Title	First Name	M.I.	Last Name	Dues	Kids Club	Total Dues
Anaheim						
Mr.	Jacob	W.	Chase	$35.00	$12.50	$47.50
Mr.	Rubin	E.	Gordon	$89.00	$12.50	$101.50
Mr.	Cody	L.	Learner	$89.00	$12.00	$101.00
Ms.	Midge	W.	Maclone	$45.00	$12.50	$57.50
Mr.	Nimiira	A.	Sanji	$120.00	$12.50	$132.50
Total Members			5			
Total Dues			$378.00			
Total Kids Club			$62.00			
Total Dues for Club			$440.00			

Membership Totals

Title	First Name	M.I.	Last Name	Dues	Kids Club	Total Dues
Fullerton						
Mr.	Antonio	V.	Alonso	$45.00	$12.50	$57.50
Mr.	Julian	P.	Coulon	$89.00		$89.00
Mr.	David	L.	Dirsa	$35.00		$35.00
Dr.	Bei	F.	Wu	$120.00	$12.50	$132.50
Total Members			4			
Total Dues			$289.00			
Total Kids Club			$25.00			
Total Dues for Club			$314.00			

Membership Totals

Title	First Name	M.I.	Last Name	Dues	Kids Club	Total Dues
Irvine						
Mr.	Stefano	U.	Branchi	$89.00		$89.00
Total Members			1			
Total Dues			$89.00			
Total Kids Club			$0.00			
Total Dues for Club			$89.00			

Membership Totals

Title	First Name	M.I.	Last Name	Dues	Kids Club	Total Dues
Yorba Linda						
Dr.	Lukas	K.	Conrad	$45.00	$12.00	$57.00
Mr.	Ivan	I.	Fenton	$45.00	$12.50	$57.50
Dr.	Edward	R.	Guen	$89.00		$89.00
Ms.	Cathy	E.	Wain	$45.00	$12.50	$57.50
Total Members			4			
Total Dues			$224.00			
Total Kids Club			$37.00			
Total Dues for Club			$261.00			

Membership Totals

Title	First Name	M.I.	Last Name	Dues	Kids Club	Total Dues
Total Members			14			
Total Dues			$980.00			
Total Kids Club			$124.00			
Total Dues for Club			$1,104.00			

FIGURE 9-78

Notice several important things about the report shown in Figure 9-78. First, the records for each location are grouped together. That is, all the records for members at the Anaheim location are together, followed by all the records for the Fullerton location, and so on. **Grouping** records allows you to separate the data into groups and print intermediate lines and summary lines based on the data in the group. In Figure 9-78, a page break occurs between each group of records in a given location. Thus, a page break occurs between the Anaheim and Fullerton locations, between the Fullerton and Irvine locations, and between the Irvine and Yorba Linda locations. By specifying that records are to be grouped in report view, you can print an Intermediate (INTR) row, such as the row that contains the location name before to the records at the particular location, and Summary (SUMM) row, such as the Total Members, Total Dues, Total Kids Club, and Total Dues for Club rows for each of the locations. For each location, the members are listed along with the dues, Kids Club, and total dues owed. Report totals for each location print after the individual record lines. Final totals for all locations print at the end of the report.

Second, the format of the reports in Figure 9-78 is virtually the same as the summary report in Figure 9-62 on page W 9.39, except the location name prints above the record entries and totals print at the end of each location.

Third, only members having CA in the State field print on the report. You can print only selected records by using the filter capability of Works to identify the records you want to print.

To create the reports shown in Figure 9-78, the records in the database must be sorted on the Location field in ascending sequence and then by the Last Name field in ascending sequence. The records are then grouped by the Location. Finally, you will create a filter to print only members in the state of California.

This section explains how to create the report shown in Figure 9-78.

Duplicating a Report Definition

To create the reports shown in Figure 9-78, you should duplicate the report called Member Totals and name the new report Location Totals. To duplicate a report definition, perform the following steps.

 Steps **To Duplicate a Report Definition**

1 **Click the List View button on the toolbar. Click Record on the menu bar. Point to Show and then click 1 All Records. Click Tools on the menu bar and then point to Duplicate Report.**

Works displays the Tools menu and the mouse pointer points to the Duplicate Report command (Figure 9-79).

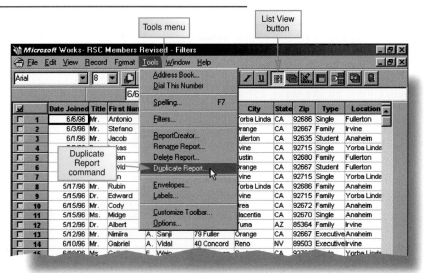

FIGURE 9-79

2 Click Duplicate Report. When the Duplicate Report dialog box displays, ensure that the words, Member Totals, are highlighted in the Select a report list box. Type Location Totals in the Type a name below text box. Point to the Duplicate button.

Works displays the Duplicate Report dialog box (Figure 9-80). Location Totals, which is typed in the Type a name below text box, will be the name of the new duplicated report definition. The report definition will be a duplicate of the report definition referenced by the name, Member Totals, that is highlighted in the Select a report list box. The mouse pointer points to the Duplicate button.

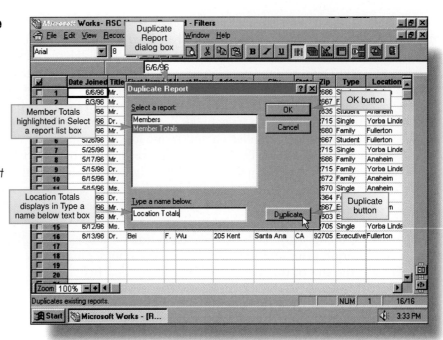

FIGURE 9-80

3 Click the Duplicate button and then click the OK button.

A duplicate of the report definition referenced by the name Member Totals is now available for use with the name Location Totals.

Displaying a Report Definition

To display the duplicate report definition given the name, Location Totals, perform the following steps.

Steps **To Display a Report Definition**

1 Click View on the menu bar and then point to Report.

The View menu displays and the mouse pointer points to the Report Command (Figure 9-81).

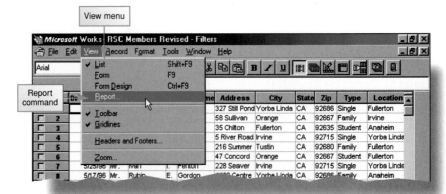

FIGURE 9-81

2 **Click Report. When the View Report dialog box displays, click Location Totals in the Select a report list box. Point to the Modify button.**

Works displays the View Reports dialog box (Figure 9-82). The report name, Location Totals, is highlighted. The mouse pointer points to the Modify button.

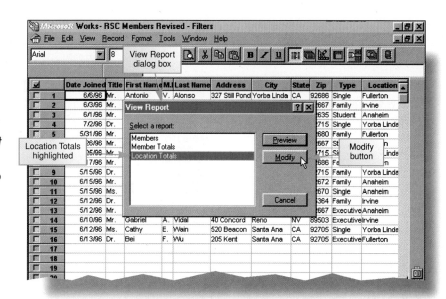

FIGURE 9-82

3 **Click the Modify button.**

The duplicate report definition named Location Totals displays (Figure 9-83).

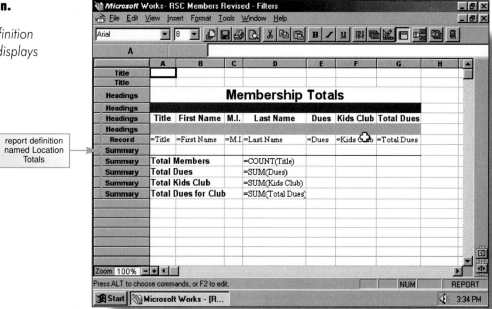

FIGURE 9-83

The duplicated report definition for the Location Totals report displays in report view. You are now ready to specify the sorting, grouping, and filtering necessary to create the report shown in Figure 9-78 on page W 9.48.

Sorting, Grouping, and Filtering Records

The report shown in Figure 9-78 on page W9.48 is sorted first by Location and then by Last Name. The report includes only members whose State field is CA.

To sort, group, and filter the records for the Location Totals report, perform the steps on the next pages.

More *About* **Grouping Records**

If you do not choose any fields to sort by, all the options on the Grouping sheet will be unavailable. The field you instruct Works to sort on is the field Works will use to group the records.

Steps To Sort, Group, and Filter Records

1 **Click Format on the menu bar and then point to Report Settings.**

Works displays the Format menu and the mouse pointer points to Report Settings (Figure 9-84).

FIGURE 9-84

2 **Click Report Settings. When the Report Settings dialog box displays, click the Sorting sheet, if necessary. Click the Sort by box arrow, scroll down to view Location. Click Location. Click the Then by box arrow and then click Last Name. Point to the Next button.**

Works displays the Report Settings dialog box (Figure 9-85). Location displays in the Sort by text box and the Ascending option button is selected by default. These settings instruct Works to sort the records by location in ascending order. Last Name displays highlighted in the Then by text box and the Ascending option button is selected by default. These settings instruct Works to sort the records by last name in ascending order. The mouse pointer points to the Next button.

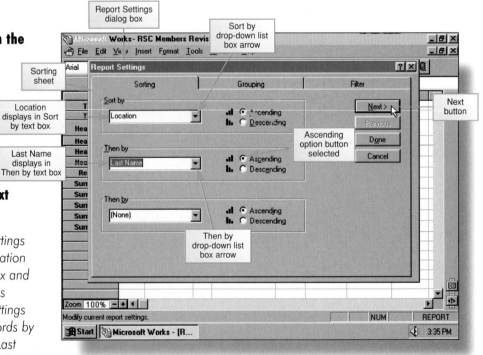

FIGURE 9-85

3 **Click the Next button. When the Grouping sheet displays, click When contents change in the Group by: Location box. Click Show group heading. Click Start each group on a new page. Point to the Next button.**

Works displays the Grouping sheet (Figure 9-86). In the Group by: Location box, the When contents change check box is selected, the Show group heading check box is selected, and the Start each group on a new page check box is selected. The When contents change option instructs Works to start a new group when the information in the location field changes. The Show group heading option instructs Works to use the field entry in the location field as the group heading. The Start each group on a new page option instructs Works to print each new group on a separate page.

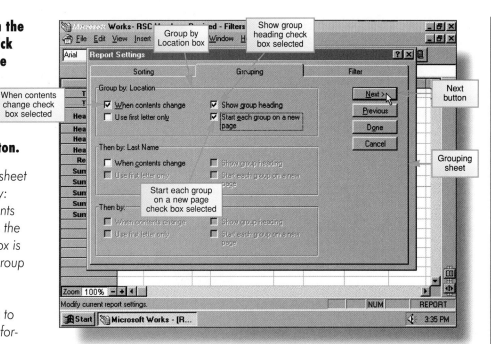

FIGURE 9-86

4 **Click the Next button. When the Filter sheet displays, click (All Records) in the Select a filter list box. Point to the Create New Filter button.**

Works displays the Filter sheet (Figure 9-87). (All Records) is highlighted in the Select a filter list box. The mouse pointer points to the Create New Filter button. The Filter Description box displays (All Records). Highlighting (All Records) in the Select a filter list box instructs Works to use all records when applying the filter. The Select a filter list box displays the available filter names in the current database.

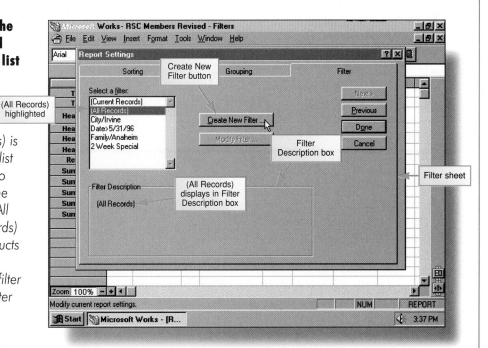

FIGURE 9-87

5 Click the Create New Filter button. When the Filter Name dialog box displays, type CA Members in the Type a name for the filter below text box. Point to the OK button.

Works displays the Filter Name dialog box (Figure 9-88). The filter name you typed displays in the Type a name for the filter below text box. The mouse pointer points to the OK button.

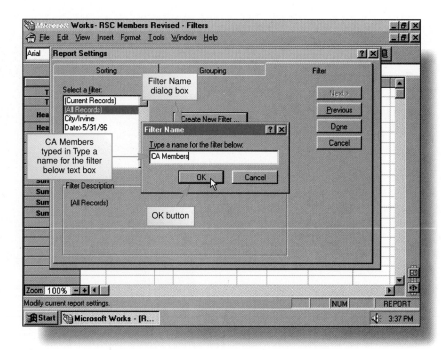

FIGURE 9-88

6 Click the OK button. When the Filter dialog box displays, click the Field name box arrow and scroll down to view State. Click State. Press the TAB key twice and type CA in the Compare To text box. Point to the OK button.

Works displays the Filter dialog box in front of the Report Settings dialog box (Figure 9-89). The filter name you typed displays in the Filter name list box. The criteria for the filter displays in the respective fields. The filter instructs Works to filter only records having CA in the State field. The mouse pointer points to the OK button.

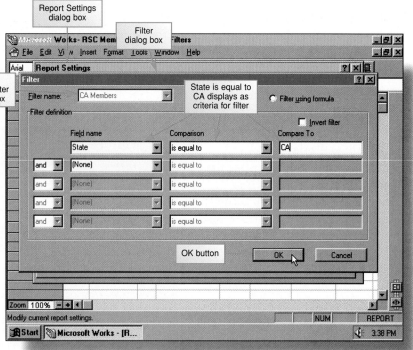

FIGURE 9-89

7 **Click the OK button. When the Filter sheet in the Report Settings dialog box displays, point to the Done button.**

Works displays the Report Settings dialog box and the mouse pointer points to the Done button (Figure 9-90). The new filter, CA Members, displays highlighted in the Select a filter list box. The filter criteria displays in the Filter Description box.

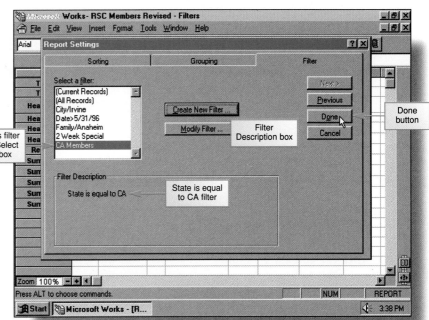

FIGURE 9-90

8 **Click the Done button.**

Works displays the report definition in report view (Figure 9-91). The Intr Location row displays below the third Headings row. This row will print each time the value in the Location field changes. It will print before the first record for the new location name. Two Summ Location rows display below the Record row. These rows are added because a group change will occur on the Location field. The Summ Location row contains the summary information for the sorted group. No information displays on the Summ Location rows. The dotted line that displays between the first and second Summ Location rows is a page break. Works inserts a page break because the Start each group on a new page check box was selected in Step 3 on page W 9.53.

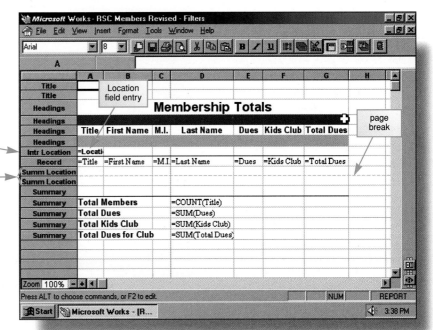

FIGURE 9-91

Modifying an Existing Report Definition

In Figure 9-91, you can see that several modifications must be made to the report definition so the report will print as shown in Figure 9-78 on page W 9.48. A new column must be inserted to the left of the Dues column. The Date Joined field name must be inserted in the Headings row and the Date Joined field entry must be inserted in the Record row. To insert a column, field name, and field entry into an existing report definition, complete the following steps.

Steps To Insert a Column, Field Name, and Field Entry into an Existing Report Definition

1 Right-click the column E heading and then point to Insert Column.

Column E is highlighted and the context-sensitive menu displays (Figure 9-92). The mouse pointer points to Insert Column.

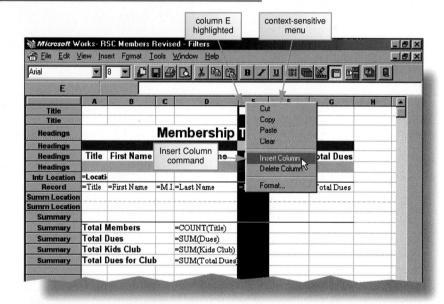

FIGURE 9-92

2 Click Insert Column on the context-sensitive menu. When the new column is inserted into the report definition, click column E in the third Headings row. Right-click the selection. When the context-sensitive menu displays, point to Insert Field Name.

The cell in the third Headings row of column E is highlighted and the mouse pointer points to Insert Field Name (Figure 9-93). The Insert Field Name command inserts a field name as a label into the report definition. The Insert Field Entry command inserts a field entry as data into the report definition. The Insert Field Summary command inserts a summary field into the report definition.

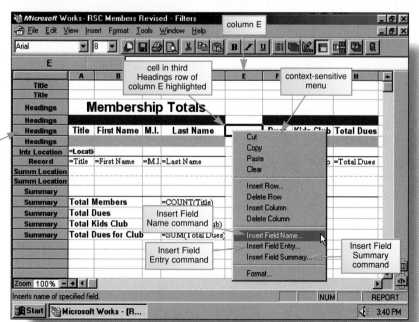

FIGURE 9-93

3 Click Insert Field Name. When the Insert Field Name dialog box displays, ensure Date Joined is highlighted in the Select a field list box, and then point to the Insert button.

Works displays the Insert Field Name dialog box (Figure 9-94). The Date Joined field is highlighted by default in the Select a field list box. The Select a field list contains the available field names for your report. The mouse pointer points to the Insert button.

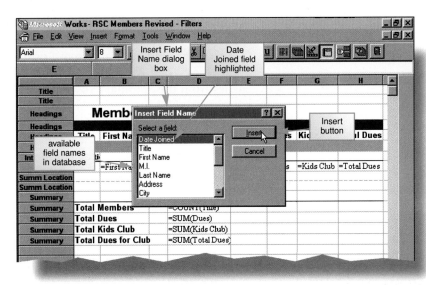

FIGURE 9-94

4 Click the Insert button. Click the Font Size box arrow on the toolbar and then click 10. Click the Bold button on the toolbar. Following the techniques illustrated in Steps 2 and 3 above, insert the Date Joined field entry in column E of the Record row; that is, right-click column E in the Record row, click Insert Field Entry on the context-sensitive menu. When the Insert Field Entry dialog box displays, ensure Date Joined is highlighted in the Select a field list box, and click the Insert button. Click the Font box arrow on the toolbar and then click Times New Roman. Click the Font Size box arrow on the toolbar and then click 10.

The field name, Date Joined, displays column E in the third Headings row in 10-point Arial bold font (Figure 9-95). The field entry, =Date Joined, displays in column E of the Record row in 10-point Times New Roman font.

FIGURE 9-95

Other Ways

1. On Insert menu click Insert Column, on Insert menu, click Insert Field Name or Insert Field Entry, highlight desired field, click Insert button

The additional modifications that must be made to the report definition so the report will print as shown in Figure 9-78 on page W 9.48 are as follows: (1) insert three additional Summ Location rows and copy the Total Members, Total Dues, Total Kids Club, and Total Dues for Club field names and field entries from the Summary rows to the SUMM Location rows; (2) add the proper color to the Headings rows above and below the field name, Date Joined; (3) wrap the field names in the Headings row; (4) format the Date Joined field entry as a Date format; and (5) remove the border that displays in the Intr Location row and insert the border in the first Summ Location row.

To modify the report so it will print as shown in Figure 9-78, complete the following steps.

TO MODIFY AN EXISTING REPORT DEFINITION

Step 1: Highlight columns A through H in the first Headings row. Right-click the selection. Click Format on the context-sensitive menu. When the Format dialog box displays, click the Alignment tab. Click Center across selection in the Horizontal box. Click the OK button.

Step 2: Right-click column D in the second Headings row and then click Copy on the context-sensitive menu. Right-click column E in the second Headings row in and then click Paste on the context-sensitive menu. Right-click column D in the fourth Headings row and then click Copy on the context-sensitive menu. Right-click column E in the fourth Headings row and then click Paste on the context-sensitive menu.

Step 3: Highlight columns A through H in the third Headings row. Right-click the selection and then click Format on the context-sensitive menu. When the Format dialog box displays, click the Alignment tab. Click Center in the Horizontal box, click Center in the Vertical box, click Wrap text, and then click the OK button.

Step 4: Highlight columns A through H in the Intr Location row. Right-click the selection and click Format on the context-sensitive menu. When the Format dialog box displays, click the Border tab. On the Border sheet, remove the Bottom line style in the Border box and then click the OK button.

Step 5: Right-click the Date Joined field entry in the Record row and then click Format on the context-sensitive menu. When the Format dialog box displays, click Date, highlight the DD/MM/YY format in the Date list box, and then click the OK button.

Step 6: Highlight the two Summ Location rows and the first Summary row. Right-click the selection and then click Insert Row on the context-sensitive menu. When the Insert Row dialog box displays, ensure Summ Location is highlighted in the Select a row type list box. Click the Insert button. Highlight columns A through D in the last four Summary rows. Right-click the selection and then click Copy on the context-sensitive menu. Right-click column A in the first Summ Location row and then click Paste on the context-sensitive menu.

Step 7: Highlight columns A through H in the first Summ Location row. Right-click the selection and click Format. When the Format dialog box displays, click Border. On the Border sheet, ensure the thin line style displays in the Line style box, and then click Top in the Border box. Click the OK button.

Step 8: Highlight columns A through H in the second Summary row. Right-click the selection and click Format. When the Format dialog box displays, click Border. On the Border sheet, ensure the thin line style displays in the Line style box, and then click Top in the Border box. Click the OK button.

Formatting the report definition is now complete. Figure 9-96 illustrates the new report definition. You should use print preview to preview the report to make sure the correct output is produced.

Again it should be pointed out that by placing the title in a Headings row, you ensure the title will print at the top of each page of the report. Recall that if you place the title in the Title row of the report definition, it will print only on the first page of the report.

Works allows a maximum of eight reports to a database. If you wish to create more than eight reports, you must delete one of the reports you created earlier. Use the Delete Report command on the Tools menu to delete a report.

Two incomplete tasks remain: (1) print the report; and (2) save the database.

To print the report, click the Print button on the toolbar. Works prints the report as shown in Figure 9-78 on page W 9.48.

To save the database with the same name, click the Save button on the toolbar.

Modifying a Grouped Report to Print on One Page

The previous report illustrated printing a grouped report on multiple pages. Figure 9-97 shows the previous report definition modified to print on one page. The Total Dues for Club prints on the Summ Location row when each location group changes and the Club Totals headings, Total Members, Total Dues, Total Kids Club, and Total Dues for Club print at the bottom of the page. To modify a grouped report to print on one page, complete the steps on the next page.

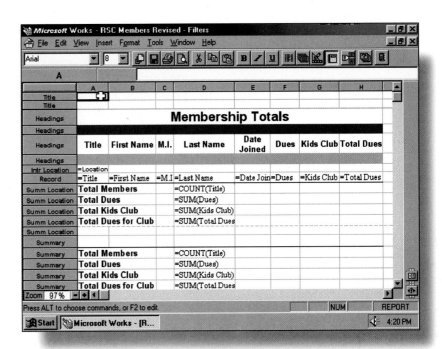

FIGURE 9-96

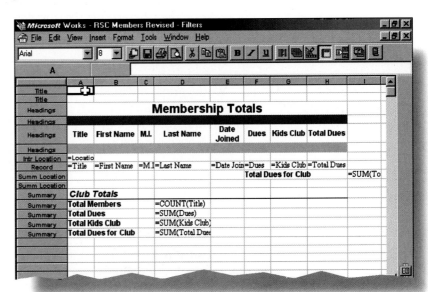

FIGURE 9-97

TO MODIFY A GROUPED REPORT TO PRINT ON ONE PAGE

Step 1: Click Tools on the menu bar and then click Duplicate Report. When the Duplicate Report dialog box displays, click Location Totals. Type Grouped 1 Page in the Type a name below text box. Click the Duplicate button. Click the OK button.

Step 2: Click View on the menu bar and then click Report. When the View Report dialog box displays, click Grouped 1 Page in the Select a report list. Click the Modify button.

Step 3: Highlight first three Summ Location rows. Right-click the selection and click Delete Row on the context-sensitive menu.

Step 4: Highlight columns A through D of the first Summ Location row. Click the Cut button on the toolbar. Highlight column F in the first Summ Location row and click the Paste button on the toolbar.

Step 5: Highlight column A in the second Summ Location row. Click Format on the menu bar and then click Delete Page Break.

Step 6: Right-click the Date Joined field entry in the Record row and then click Format on the context-sensitive menu. When the Format dialog box displays, click Date, highlight the DD/MM/YY format in the Date list box, and click the OK button.

Step 7: Click the Print Preview button on the toolbar to ensure the report will print correctly.

Step 8: Click the Print button on the toolbar.

Membership Totals

Title	First Name	M.I.	Last Name	Date Joined	Dues	Kids Club	Total Dues	
Anaheim								
Mr.	Jacob	W.	Chase		$35.00	$12.50	$47.50	
Mr.	Rubin	E.	Gordon	5/17/96	$89.00	$12.50	$101.50	
Mr.	Cody	L.	Learner	6/15/96	$89.00	$12.00	$101.00	
Ms.	Midge	W.	Maclone	5/15/96	$45.00	$12.50	$57.50	
Mr.	Nimiira	A.	Sanji	5/12/96	$120.00	$12.50	$132.50	
						Total Dues for Club		$440.00
Fullerton								
Mr.	Antonio	V.	Alonso	6/6/96	$45.00	$12.50	$57.50	
Mr.	Julian	P.	Coulon	5/31/96	$89.00		$89.00	
Mr.	David	L.	Dirsa	5/26/96	$35.00		$35.00	
Dr.	Bei	F.	Wu	6/13/96	$120.00	$12.50	$132.50	
						Total Dues for Club		$314.00
Irvine								
Mr.	Stefano	U.	Branchi	6/3/96	$89.00		$89.00	
						Total Dues for Club		$89.00
Yorba Linda								
Dr.	Lukas	K.	Conrad	7/2/96	$45.00	$12.00	$57.00	
Mr.	Ivan	I.	Fenton	5/25/96	$45.00	$12.50	$57.50	
Dr.	Edward	R.	Guen	5/15/96	$89.00		$89.00	
Ms.	Cathy	E.	Wain	6/12/96	$45.00	$12.50	$57.50	
						Total Dues for Club		$261.00

Club Totals

Total Members	14
Total Dues	$980.00
Total Kids Club	$124.00
Total Dues for Club	$1,104.00

FIGURE 9-98

Works prints the modified report on one page (see Figure 9-98). The Total Dues for Club prints for each group and the Club Totals heading, Total Members, Total Dues, Total Kids Club, and Total Dues for Club print at the end of the report. Notice the report lists only the California members. This is the filter that was applied to the Member Totals report. When you duplicated the Member Totals report to create the one page grouped report, this filter was also duplicated.

Multiple Grouping Reports

Works allows you to define reports with more than one grouped field. For example, you can define a report in which two fields, State and Location, are used for sort breaks. You can also define a report in which no Record row exists and the only rows that print are Summary rows. To prepare these types of reports, you must apply the concepts and techniques previously learned to create the new report formats.

Quitting Works

Now that all the reports have been defined and printed, you can quit Works. Click the Close button in the Works application window.

Project Summary

In this project, you learned how to obtain information from the records in a database through the use of filters and reports. You used a filter to find records with values in a field equal to values you specified, records with values greater than and less than values you specified, records with values in more than one field equal to values you specified, and you learned how to connect the criteria using the logical operators AND and OR.

In the report view of Works, you learned about defining a report to list records in a database and to list records and print summary totals. You used a filter to print only specific records in a database. Sorting and grouping records were presented showing you how to create a report with group totals and summary totals on both on a one page report and multiple page reports.

What You Should Know

Having completed this project, you should be able to perform the following tasks:

- Add Color to a Report Definition *(W 9.46)*
- Apply an Existing Filter *(W 9.22)*
- Create a Filter Using a Formula *(W 9.20)*
- Define a Listing Report *(W 9.28)*
- Define a Report with Summary Totals *(W 9.40)*
- Delete a Filter *(W 9.24)*
- Display Print Preview *(W 9.43)*
- Display a Report Definition *(W 9.50)*
- Duplicate a Report Definition *(W 9.49)*
- Filter for Records That Are Above a Value Using Conditional Criteria *(W 9.12)*
- Filter for Records That Match Exactly *(W 9.8)*
- Filter for Records That Match in More than One Field *(W 9.16)*
- Filter for Records That Meet One of Several Conditions *(W 9.18)*
- Format the Summary Report *(W 9.45)*
- Insert a Column, Field Name, and Field Entry into an Existing Report Definition *(W 9.56)*

- Insert Two Blank Headings Rows and Add a Title *(W 9.44)*
- Modify a Grouped Report to Print on One Page *(W 9.60)*
- Modify a Report Definition *(W 9.33)*
- Modify an existing Report Definition *(W 9.58)*
- Preview a Report *(W 9.32)*
- Preview and Print the Report *(W 9.35)*
- Print the Report *(W 9.47)*
- Rename a Filter *(W 9.25)*
- Reverse the Results of a Filter *(W 9.15)*
- Save a Database with Filters *(W 9.27)*
- Save the Database *(W 9.36)*
- Show All Records in a Database *(W 9.11)*
- Sort, Group, and Filter Records *(W 9.52)*
- Sort Records *(W 9.37)*
- Start Works and Open a Works Database File *(W 9.6)*
- View, Modify, or Print a Report *(W 9.37)*

A+ Test Your Knowledge

1 True/False

Instructions: Circle T if the statement is true or F if the statement is false.

T   F   1. A filter is a request for information from a database.

T   F   2. You can control the records that print on a report through the use of filters.

T   F   3. To create a filter, click the Create New Filter button on the toolbar.

T   F   4. The entry >=05/15/96 in the Filter dialog box instructs Works to find all records in which the value in the Date Joined field is less than or equal to 05/15/96.

T   F   5. If the entry State=CA displays in the Filter dialog box criteria boxes and the Invert Filter check box is selected, Works will display all records in which the value in the State field is equal to CA.

T   F   6. The and logical operator and the or logical operator cannot be used in a single filter.

T   F   7. To ensure a report title prints at the top of every page of the report, place the report title in the Title row in the report definition.

T   F   8. A row with the name, Summ Fund Location, on the report definition will print whenever the value in the Location field changes from one database record to the next.

T   F   9. A row with the name, Intr Location, on the report definition will print only if the value in the Location field in a record is the same as the value in the Location field in the previously printed record.

T   F   10. A maximum of eight filters and eight reports can be saved as a part of a database.

2 Multiple Choice

Instructions: Circle the correct response.

1. Which of the following is not a valid conditional operator for a field in a database filter?
   a. <15000
   b. <>15000
   c. =<>15000
   d. <=15000
2. To delete a filter, click _____.
   a. the Delete Filter button on the toolbar
   b. Delete Report on the Tools menu
   c. Duplicate Report on the Tools menu
   d. the Delete Filter button in the Filter dialog box
3. Works allows a maximum of _____ filters to be saved with a database.
   a. five
   b. eight
   c. ten
   d. twelve

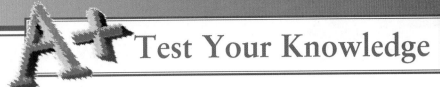 **Test Your Knowledge**

4. When you click the Report View button on the toolbar and no reports have been defined for the database, Works displays _____.
   a. a message in a Microsoft Works dialog box informing you no reports have been defined
   b. the Report Name dialog box
   c. the ReportCreator dialog box
   d. a sample report definition you can modify

5. The Title row of a report _____.
   a. prints only at the top of the first page in the report
   b. prints at the top of every page in the report
   c. must contain the name of the report
   d. cannot be left blank in the report definition

6. To count the number of records in a database and print the total at the end of the report, select a field in the report and then click _____ in the Summary sheet of the ReportCreator dialog box.
   a. Sum
   b. Count
   c. Maximum
   d. Add

7. The criteria, Date Joined <= 5/31/96, displays in the Filter definition box and the Invert Filter check box is selected. When the Apply Filter button is clicked, Works displays in list view _____.
   a. all members who joined on or before 5/31/96
   b. all members who joined after 5/31/96
   c. all members who joined on 5/31/96
   d. no records

8. Report view shows _____.
   a. your database records that will print
   b. your report definition
   c. your database records that will not print
   d. your current filter

9. In a report definition, a(n) _____ row appears at the beginning of each group if you sort and group records.
   a. Headings
   b. Intr
   c. Summ
   d. Summary

10. Works allows a maximum of _____ reports to be saved with a database.
    a. five
    b. eight
    c. ten
    d. twelve

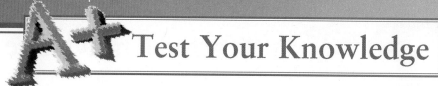

Test Your Knowledge

3 Fill In

Instructions: In the spaces provided in the COMMAND/BUTTON/OPTION column, write the name of the command, button, or option that accomplishes the task listed in the TASK column.

TASK	COMMAND/BUTTON/OPTION
Create a new filter	_____
Create a new report	_____
Sort a modified report	_____
Delete a filter	_____
Rename a filter	_____
Duplicate a report	_____
Invert a filter	_____
Show all records	_____

4 Fill In

Instructions: In the spaces provided, identify the appropriate row that is entered in a report definition.

WHAT IT DOES	TYPE OF ROW
Prints at the top of the first page	_____
Prints below the title on the first page and at the top of all other pages	_____
Appears at the beginning of each group if you sort and group records	_____
Prints fields from each record	_____
Appears at the end of each group if you sort and group records	_____
Prints at the end of the report	_____

Use Help

1 Reviewing Project Activities

Instructions: Use your computer to perform the following tasks to obtain experience using online Help.

1. Start Microsoft Works.
2. When the Works Task Launcher dialog box displays, click the Cancel button. Click Contents on the Help menu to display the Help Topics: Microsoft Works dialog box.
3. On the Contents sheet, click the Database icon. Click the Creating reports from your database information folder. Click the Create a Report folder. Read and print To create a report on the Step by Step sheet. Click the More Info tab. Click Overview on the More Info sheet and read and print the Overview. Click Quick Tour. Read the Quick Tour.
4. Click the Close button in the application window to close Works.

2 Expanding on the Basics

Instructions: Use Works online Help to better understand the topics listed below. Print the topic or topics that substantiate your answer. If no Print this topic icon is available, then answer the question on your own paper.

1. Using the key terms *calculating in database reports* and the Index sheet in the Help topics: Microsoft Works dialog box, answer the following questions.
a. Explain how to add summary information manually to an existing report.

   _____

b. Explain how to show each group and its summary on a separate page.

   _____

2. Click To add a formula to a report. On the Step-by-Step sheet, read and briefly explain the steps necessary to add a formula to a report.

   _____

3. Click the Close button in the application window to close Works.

Apply Your Knowledge

1 Defining a Report Definition

Instructions: Start the Works Database tool. Open the Suppliers Revised Report file on the Student Floppy Disk that accompanies this book. The screen in Figure 9-99 shows the report. The report to be printed should be grouped by Category and then by Last Name. The formatting of the report should be the same as shown in Figure 9-99. Perform the steps necessary to create the report and then print the report. Turn in a copy of the report to your instructor.

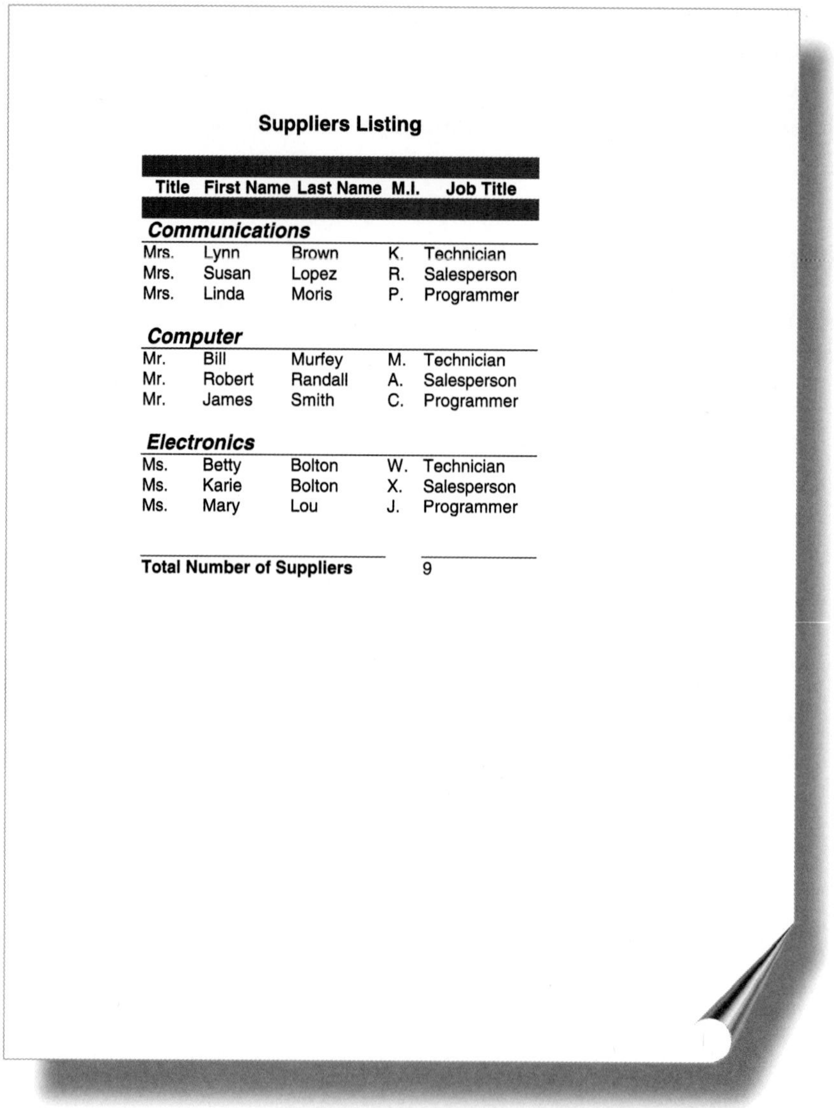

Suppliers Listing

Title	First Name	Last Name	M.I.	Job Title
Communications				
Mrs.	Lynn	Brown	K.	Technician
Mrs.	Susan	Lopez	R.	Salesperson
Mrs.	Linda	Moris	P.	Programmer
Computer				
Mr.	Bill	Murfey	M.	Technician
Mr.	Robert	Randall	A.	Salesperson
Mr.	James	Smith	C.	Programmer
Electronics				
Ms.	Betty	Bolton	W.	Technician
Ms.	Karie	Bolton	X.	Salesperson
Ms.	Mary	Lou	J.	Programmer

Total Number of Suppliers	9

FIGURE 9-99

In the Lab

1 Filters and Reports

Problem: Obtain information from the Alumni Scholarship Donations database created in In the Lab 1 in Project 7 and maintained and updated in In the Lab 1 in Project 8.

Instructions: Open the database you created in Project 7 In the Lab 1 and maintained and updated in In Project 8 In the Lab 1. If you do not have this updated database, your instructor will provide you with the database file.

1. Using a filter, display all the people in the Corporate type. Give the filter a name of your choice. Print the list view of the database after the filter.
2. Using a filter, display all people who donated more than $1,000.00. Give the filter a name of your choice. Print the list view of the database after the filter.
3. Display all people who donated $1,000.00 or less. Print the list view of the database after the filter.
4. Using a filter, display all people who donated more than $1,500.00 to the Business scholarships. Give the filter a name of your choice. Print the list view of the database after the filter.
5. Using a filter, display all people who donated to either the Science or Music scholarships. Give the filter a name of your choice. Print the list view of the database after the filter.
6. Using a filter with a name of your choice, answer the following questions:
   a. How many people in the database had never given before the current donation?
   b. How many people gave less than $2,000.00 to the Business or Music scholarship?
   c. How many people gave a donation in 1996?
7. Create a report listing all people in the Alumni Scholarship Donations database. The report should contain the title, first name, middle initial, last name, and donation amount. Format the report in a manner similar to the report shown in Figure 9-42 on page W 9.28. Name the report with a name of your choice.
8. Create a report listing all people in the Alumni Scholarship Donations database, the total number of people, and the total dollars donated. The report should contain the title, first name, middle initial, last name, scholarship, and donation. Format the report in a manner similar to the report shown in Figure 9-62 on page W 9.39. Name the report a name of your choice.
9. Create a report listing the donors in ascending sequence by scholarship. The fields on the report should be the same as the fields in the report created in number 8 above except the word, scholarship, should not print on each record line. For each scholarship, print the number of donors and the total dollars donated to the scholarship. At the end of the report, print the total number of donors and the total dollars donated. Format the report in a manner similar to the report shown in Figure 9-78 on page W 9.48. Name the report with a name of your choice.
10. Save the database with the reports and filters on a floppy disk using the filename, Revised Alumni Scholarship Donations Filters.
11. Follow the directions from your instructor for turning in this assignment.

In the Lab

2 Filters and Reports

Problem: Obtain information from the Custom Gifts, Intl Employee database created in In the Lab 2 in Project 7 and maintained and updated in In the Lab 2 in Project 8.

Instructions:

1. Open the database you created in Project 7 In the Lab 2 and maintained and updated in Project 8 In the Lab 2. If you do not have this updated database, your instructor will provide you with the database file.

2. Using a filter, display all full-time employees. Give the filter a name of your choice. Print the list view of the database after using the filter.

3. Using a filter, display all employees hired after 5/31/93. Give the filter a name of your choice. Print the list view of the database after using the filter.

4. Display all employees hired on 5/31/93 or earlier. Print the list view of the database after the filter.

5. Using a filter, display all employees who work full-time in the Customer Service department. Give the filter a name of your choice. Print the list view of the database after using the filter.

6. Using a filter, display all full-time employees in the Accounting or Purchasing department. Give the filter a name of your choice. Print the list view of the database after using the filter.

7. Using a filter, display all full-time employees in the Purchasing or Customer Service department. Give the filter a name of your choice. Print the list view of the database after using the filter.

8. Using a filter with the name of your choice, answer the following questions.
   a. How many employees were hired after 9/30/94?
   b. How many part-time employees are there?
   c. How many employees have an hourly rate of $12.00 or more?
   d. How many employees work more than 35 hours a week?

9. Create a report listing all employees in the Custom Gifts, Intl database. The report should contain the First Name, Last Name, Date Hired, and Weekly Pay. The listing should be in ascending sequence by Employee Name. Format the report in a manner similar to the report shown in Figure 9-42 on page W 9.28. Name the report with a name of your choice.

10. Create a report listing all employees in Custom Gifts, Intl, the total number of employees in Custom Gifts, Intl, and their total weekly pay. The report should contain the First Name, Last Name, Hourly Rate, Weekly Hours, and Weekly Pay. Format the report in a manner similar to the report shown in Figure 9-62 on page W 9.39. Name the report with a name of your choice.

11. Create a report listing the full-time employees in ascending sequence by department. The fields in this report should be the same as the fields in the report created in number 10 above except the word, department, should not print on each record line. For each department, print the total number of full-time employees and their total weekly pay. At the end of the report, print the total number of full-time employees and their total weekly pay. Format the report in a manner similar to the report shown in Figure 9-78 on page W 9.48. Name the report with a name of your choice.

12. Save the database with the reports on a floppy disk using the filename, Revised Custom Gifts, Intl Filters.

13. Follow the directions from your instructor for turning in this assignment.

In the Lab

3 Filters and Reports

Problem: Obtain information from the Investment Group database created In the Lab 3 in Project 7 and maintained and updated in In the Lab 3 in Project 8.

Instructions:

1. Open the database you created in Project 7 In the Lab 3 and maintained and updated in Project 8 In the Lab 3. If you do not have this updated database, your instructor will provide you with the database file.

2. Using a filter, display all the investors from the state of California. Give the filter a name of your choice. Print the list view of the database after the filter.

3. Using a filter, display all the investors who have invested more than $7,000.00. Give the filter a name of your choice. Print the list view of the database after the filter.

4. Display all the investors who have invested $7,000.00 or less. Print the list view of the database after the filter.

5. Using a filter, display all the investors who have invested more than 1000 shares in a Technology fund. Give the filter a name of your choice. Print the list view of the database after the filter.

6. Using a filter, display all investors who have invested in the Aggressive or International fund. Give the filter a name of your choice. Print the list view of the database after the filter.

7. Using a filter, display all the doctors in California who have invested in Technology funds. Give the filter a name of your choice. Print the list view of the database after the filter.

8. Using a filter with the name of your choice, answer the following questions.
    a. How many investors invested between 9/28/97 and 10/15/97?
    b. Which investors invested on 9/28/97?
    c. How many attorneys are in the Investment Group?

9. Create a report listing all investors of the Investment Group. The report should contain the title, first name, last name, address, city, state, and zip code. The report should be in alphabetic sequence by last name. Format the report in a manner similar to the report shown in Figure 9-42 on page W 9.28. Name the report with a name of your choice.

10. Create a report listing all investors of the Investment Group, the total number of investors in the group, and the dollars invested. The report should contain the first name, last name, shares, and investment. Format the report in a manner similar to the report shown in Figure 9-62 on page W 9.39. Name the report with a name of your choice.

11. Create a report listing the investors in alphabetic sequence within fund. The fields on this report should be the same as the fields in the report created in number 10. For each fund, print the number of investors in that fund, the total shares owned by the fund, and the total dollars invested in the fund. At the end of the report, print the total investors in all funds, the total shares in the group, and the total dollars invested by all investors. Format the report in a manner similar to the report shown in Figure 9-91 on page W 9.55. Name the report with a name of your choice.

(continued)

In the Lab

Filters and Reports *(continued)*

12. Modify the report created in Step 11 to print on one page. Print the total investment for each fund. Print the total investors, total shares, and total investment at the end of the report. Format the report in a manner you think is appropriate. Name the report with a name of your choice.

13. Save the database with the reports on a floppy disk using the filename, Revised Investment Group Filters and Reports.

Follow the directions from your instructor for turning in this assignment.

Cases and Places

The difficulty of the following case studies varies:

▶ Case studies preceded by a single half moon are the least difficult. You are asked to create the required database based on information that already has been placed in an organized form.

▶▶ Case studies preceded by two half moons are more difficult. You must organize the information presented before using it to create the desired database.

▶▶▶ Case studies preceded by three half moons are the most difficult. You must choose a specific topic and then organize the necessary information before using it to create the required database.

1 ▶ Your best friend tells you he has pneumonia. You decide to learn more about this illness. Using the pneumonia database modified in Case Study 1 of Project 8, use a query to list and then print the viruses and bacteria that could cause these conditions:

   (a) Yesterday his body temperature exceeded 39 degrees Celsius.
   (b) Today his temperature is under 102 degrees Fahrenheit.
   (c) You sat next to him at breakfast today, and at lunch you felt flu-like symptoms.
   (d) Now you are feeling tired and have the chills.

Create a report listing all bacteria and viruses in alphabetical order within Fahrenheit body temperature. Name the report.

Cases and Places

2 ▶ As the ultimate sports fan, you follow a variety of sporting events and read about the superstars in various publications. Use the database you modified in Case Study 2 of Project 8 to answer and print the following information:

(a) Which athletes earn at least $10 million in salary?
(b) Which athletes earn at least $10 million in salary and endorsements?
(c) In which sports do athletes earn less than $5 million in salary or endorsements?
(d) In which sports do athletes earn less than $5 in endorsements?

Create two reports listing 1995 and 1994 ranking stars in ascending order within sports. Name the reports.

3 ▶ You are ready to select a specific whale-watching expedition for your next vacation. Use the whale-watching database you modified in Case Study 3 of Project 8 to answer and print the following:

(a) Boat rides make you nauseated. Which excursions have access from the shore?
(b) The expedition cannot interfere with your school schedule. Which trips do not occur during the fall or winter?
(c) Which excursions are to destinations where orca or humpback whales are likely to be seen?
(d) Which boat excursions occur during the fall?

Create a report listing all whales in alphabetical order within season. Name the report.

4 ▶▶ The job application materials you have gathered need to arrive at a potential employer's office tomorrow. Use the database you modified in Case Study 4 of Project 8 to answer and print the following:

(a) Which delivery services guarantee delivery of a six-ounce package by noon at a cost of less than $15?
(b) Which services charge more than $15 to deliver any package?
(c) Which services charge $20 or less to deliver a 10-ounce package before noon?
(d) Which services charge more than $20 to deliver a 2-pound package?

Create two reports listing prices in descending order within delivery times by noon and after noon. Name the reports.

Cases and Places

200 MHz

5 ▶▶ Decide where you can get the best return on your money by using the certificate of deposit database you modified in Case Study 5 of Project 8 to determine:

    (a) Which financial institutions have interest rates above 6 percent?

    (b) Which banks and savings and loans will pay less than $200 interest on your $5,000 investment?

    (c) What are the penalties and restrictions for early withdrawal from credit unions and banks?

    (d) Which CDs of $1,000 or $2,500 will earn more than $25 in interest?

Create a report listing all total values of the CDs in ascending order within financial institutions. The report should contain interest rates, amounts of interest earned, and penalties for early withdrawal. Name the report.

6 ▶▶ The classified advertising manager asks you to demonstrate the used car service database you modified in Case Study 6 of Project 8. He wants to know:

    (a) Which automobiles manufactured after 1993 have automatic transmissions and mileage less than 75,000?

    (b) Which vehicles made by Chevrolet or Ford are selling for less than $10,000?

    (c) Which four-wheel drives or trucks have manual transmissions and at least a V-6 engine?

    (d) Which vehicles have aluminum rims and either air conditioning, cruise control, or a sunroof?

Create a report listing models in alphabetical order within manufacturer. Include the mileage, price, and seller's phone number. Name the report.

7 ▶▶ Your health-conscious friends want you to help them select nutritious foods. Use the food database you modified in Case Study 7 of Project 8 to answer their questions:

    (a) Which low-calorie foods have sodium levels that exceed 50 milligrams?

    (b) Which calorie-free products have fewer than 25 grams of carbohydrates?

    (c) Which products have no cholesterol or protein?

    (d) Which foods have serving sizes of more than 50 grams?

Create a report listing the names of the products in alphabetical order within calorie classifications (low, light, or calorie free). Include the number of calories and the amounts of cholesterol, sodium, carbohydrates, and protein in each. Name the report.

Microsoft *Works 4*

Windows 95

Integrating the Microsoft Works Tools

Objectives

You will have mastered the material in this project when you can:

▶ Create a letterhead using Microsoft Draw

▶ Open multiple document windows

▶ Insert the system date in a word processing document

▶ Use the Database Field command on the Insert menu

▶ Insert database placeholders in a document

▶ Set tab stops for a table

▶ Add an outline with a shadow to a table

▶ Insert a linked chart in a word processing document

▶ Change the size of a chart in a word processing document

▶ Tile open documents

▶ Use drag and drop to link a spreadsheet to a word processing document

▶ Print form letters using filtered names and addresses from a database

▶ Print envelopes

Just Add Text and Graphics,
Then Blend Well

"A vodka martini, Mr. Bond. Very dry. Mixed to your exacting specifications. Shaken, not stirred," said Doctor No, being careful not to crush the long-stemmed glass with his steel, mechanical fingers as he passed the drink to James Bond. This famous scene from the first movie about the fabled British secret Agent 007 serves up a perfect example of ingredients that have been mixed into a homogeneous blend. Many of life's most rewarding pleasures come from blending, or *integrating*, constituent parts, resulting in a mixture that is better than the individual components. Flour, shortening, eggs, and blueberries make blueberry pie. Combining paints of various colors on a canvas, Van Gogh produced his masterpieces. Verdi, Rossini, Wagner, and Mozart integrated music and stories to create operas.

Integration also can increase strength. Steel results from a blend of iron, carbon, and molybdenum. Cement, sand, gravel, and water form concrete. People of numerous ethnic groups have blended to constitute the United States populace.

Going one giant step further than merely providing individual word processor, spreadsheet, and database programs, Works also serves as the *blender*, allowing a user to integrate work results from those three components into a paper or presentation that is stronger and more attractive than stand-alone outputs. Through the technological marvel known as OLE (Object Linking and Embedding), charts, tables, graphs, clip art, and spreadsheets can be inserted to meld with text at exactly the right place, making a point while producing maximum visual appeal. The effect of this integrated package is greater than the sum of its parts because human beings process data faster and retain it better when given a visual "tag" to remember it by.

The student who has worked diligently through the Works projects to get to this point now has reached the culmination of a long journey. And from endings come new beginnings. The ability to use the tools in Works puts a student one-up on competitors, whether in pursuit of better grades or in launching a successful career.

Communicating forcefully and effectively in this ever-changing world is growing in importance, but many people have not kept pace in acquiring the necessary proficiency. Recent studies show that more jobs are available than qualified candidates, simply because modern-day careers demand a whole new skill-set whose major components are computer literacy and the ability to communicate.

In other words, the individual with a well-*integrated* education is better prepared for the long haul. Or, as Mr. Dickens might have said, such a person is entitled to have *Great Expectations*.

Microsoft

Works

Windows 95

Integrating the Microsoft Works Tools

Case Perspective

The RSC Sports and Fitness Centers are experiencing such growth in memberships that a new sports and fitness center is opening. The management desires to notify current members of this new facility. You have been asked to send a letter to selected members in the database illustrating the current memberships at each location and informing each member of the new management at the new facility. The management also has asked you to design a new logo for the club in celebration of the new facility opening and include this logo in the form letter.

You are to use the integrated features of Microsoft Works to create a form letter to be sent to selected members. Include a table listing the new management as well as a spreadsheet and chart showing the current memberships and the popularity of the Family memberships at each location. Prepare the form letter and print envelopes.

Introduction to Integrated Software Applications

In Projects 1 through 9, you used the Microsoft Works Word Processor, Spreadsheet, and Database tools. In addition, you inserted clip art into a document and graphically illustrated spreadsheet data using the charting capabilities of the Spreadsheet tool.

In business applications, you often will find it helpful to use information created by one of the Works tools in another Works application. For example, you may want to include a spreadsheet or a chart created by the Works Spreadsheet tool in a letter created by the Works Word Processor tool, or you may want to use the name and address fields in a database created using the Works Database tool to assist in creating form letters you are going to send to a number of individuals. These tasks can be accomplished using Microsoft Works because Works is an integrated software package that allows the various software tools to be used together to solve business problems.

Within any of the three Works tools, you can cut and paste or copy and paste data from one application to another. Between the Spreadsheet and the Word Processor you can use a special command that lets you create a link between a spreadsheet, its chart, and a word processing document so that when a change is made in the spreadsheet, information from the spreadsheet contained in the word processing document is updated. You also can drag a chart or spreadsheet to the word processing document and link them. This is called object linking and embedding (OLE). Project 10 illustrates these techniques.

Project Ten

In Project 10, you are to send a form letter to selected members of the RSC Sports and Fitness Centers. Figures 10-1a and 10-1b illustrate the form letters.

The letter is printed using the Works Word Processor tool. The name and address in the inside address of the letter are obtained from the database of members of the RSC Sports and Fitness Centers originally developed in Project 7 and later modified in Project 8. You also will use the names and addresses in the database to prepare envelopes.

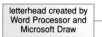

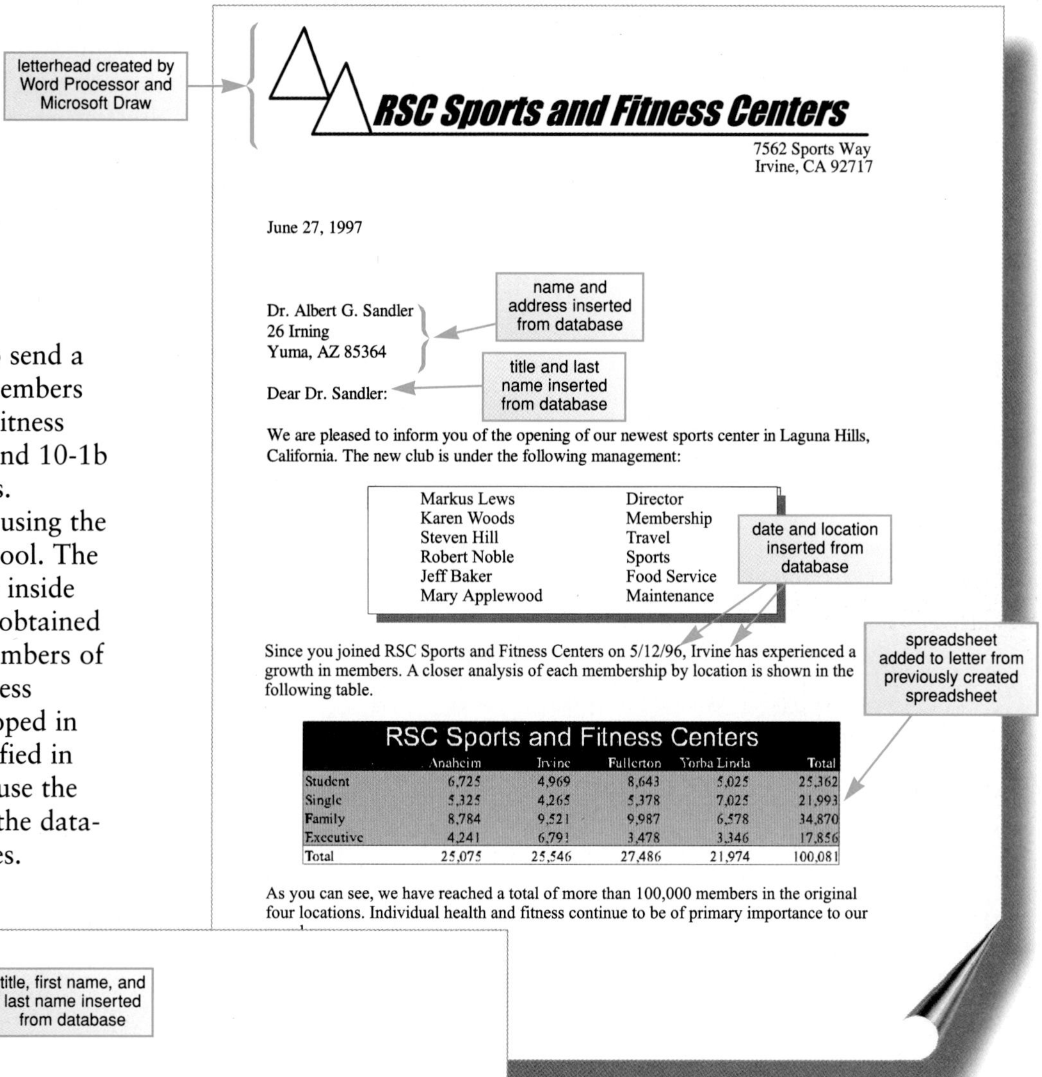

RSC Sports and Fitness Centers

7562 Sports Way
Irvine, CA 92717

June 27, 1997

Dr. Albert G. Sandler
26 Irning
Yuma, AZ 85364

name and address inserted from database

Dear Dr. Sandler:

title and last name inserted from database

We are pleased to inform you of the opening of our newest sports center in Laguna Hills, California. The new club is under the following management:

Markus Lews	Director
Karen Woods	Membership
Steven Hill	Travel
Robert Noble	Sports
Jeff Baker	Food Service
Mary Applewood	Maintenance

Since you joined RSC Sports and Fitness Centers on 5/12/96, Irvine has experienced a growth in members. A closer analysis of each membership by location is shown in the following table.

date and location inserted from database

spreadsheet added to letter from previously created spreadsheet

RSC Sports and Fitness Centers

	Anaheim	Irvine	Fullerton	Yorba Linda	Total
Student	6,725	4,969	8,643	5,025	25,362
Single	5,325	4,265	5,378	7,025	21,993
Family	8,784	9,521	9,987	6,578	34,870
Executive	4,241	6,791	3,478	3,346	17,856
Total	25,075	25,546	27,486	21,974	100,081

As you can see, we have reached a total of more than 100,000 members in the original four locations. Individual health and fitness continue to be of primary importance to our

FIGURE 10-1a

Page 2
Dr. Albert G. Sandler
June 27, 1997

title, first name, and last name inserted from database

The chart below shows the status of memberships at each location. As you can see from the chart, our Family memberships continue to be popular.

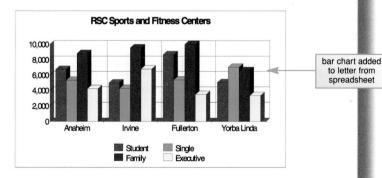

bar chart added to letter from spreadsheet

We are optimistic about the future and anticipate continued growth at RSC Sports and Fitness Centers.

Sincerely,

FIGURE 10-1b

The title, first name, middle initial, and last name in the salutation of the letter are from the database. The date and location an individual joined the RSC Sports and Fitness Centers contained in each record in the database, appear in the second paragraph of the letter. Each form letter contains a spreadsheet that presents detailed information about the memberships at each location. Each form letter also contains a 3-D Bar chart graphically illustrating the memberships by each location. The chart and spreadsheet are those explained in Project 4 of this book. The database, spreadsheet, and bar chart used to produce the form letter are illustrated in Figure 10-2.

Database - RSC Members Revised

DATE JOINED	TITLE	FIRST NAME	M.I.	LAST NAME	ADDRESS	CITY	STATE	ZIP	TYPE	LOCATION	DUES	KIDS CLUB	TOTAL DUES
5/12/96	Mr.	Nimiira	A.	Sanji	79 Fuller	Orange	CA	92667	Executive	Anaheim	$120.00	$12.50	$132.50
5/12/96	Dr.	Albert	G.	Sandler	26 Irning	Yuma	AZ	85364	Family	Irvine	$89.00	$12.50	$101.50
5/15/96	Ms.	Midge	W.	Maclone	94 Bourne	Placentia	CA	92670	Single	Anaheim	$45.00	$12.50	$57.50
5/15/96	Dr.	Edward	R.	Guen	170 Tremont	Irvine	CA	92715	Family	Yorba Linda	$89.00		$89.00
5/17/96	Mr.	Rubin	E.	Gordon	1539 Centre	Yorba Linda	CA	92686	Family	Anaheim	$89.00	$12.50	$101.50
5/25/96	Mr.	Ivan	I.	Fenton	228 Seaver	Irvine	CA	92715	Single	Yorba Linda	$45.00	$12.50	$57.50
5/26/96	Mr.	David	L.	Dirsa	47 Concord	Orange	CA	92667	Student	Fullerton	$35.00		$35.00
5/31/96	Mr.	Julian	P.	Coulon	216 Summer	Tustin	CA	92680	Family	Fullerton	$89.00		$89.00
6/1/96	Mr.	Jacob	W.	Chase	35 Chilton	Fullerton	CA	92635	Student	Anaheim	$35.00	$12.50	$47.50
6/3/96	Mr.	Stefano	U.	Branchi	58 Sullivan	Orange	CA	92667	Family	Irvine	$89.00		$89.00
6/6/96	Mr.	Antonio	V.	Alonso	327 Still Pond	Yorba Linda	CA	92686	Single	Fullerton	$45.00	$12.50	$57.50
6/10/96	Mr.	Gabriel	A.	Vidal	40 Concord	Reno	NV	89503	Executive	Irvine	$120.00		$120.00
6/12/96	Ms.	Cathy	E.	Wain	520 Beacon	Santa Ana	CA	92705	Single	Yorba Linda	$45.00	$12.50	$57.50
6/13/96	Dr.	Bei	F.	Wu	205 Kent	Santa Ana	CA	92705	Executive	Fullerton	$120.00	$12.50	$132.50
6/15/96	Mr.	Cody	L.	Learner	124 Cobb	Brea	CA	92672	Family	Anaheim	$89.00	$12.00	$101.00
7/2/96	Dr.	Lukas	K.	Conrad	5 River Road	Irvine	CA	92715	Single	Yorba Linda	$45.00	$12.00	$57.00

Spreadsheet - RSC Memberships

RSC Sports and Fitness Centers

	Anaheim	Irvine	Fullerton	Yorba Linda	Total
Student	6,725	4,969	8,643	5,025	25,362
Single	5,325	4,265	5,378	7,025	21,993
Family	8,784	9,521	9,987	6,578	34,870
Executive	4,241	6,791	3,478	3,346	17,856
Total	25,075	25,546			

Chart - RSC Memberships

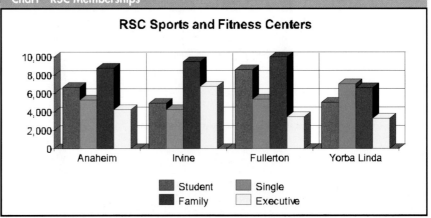

FIGURE 10-2

All members having a Family membership are to receive the letter. Works will generate one letter for each such person in the database, as shown in Figure 10-3.

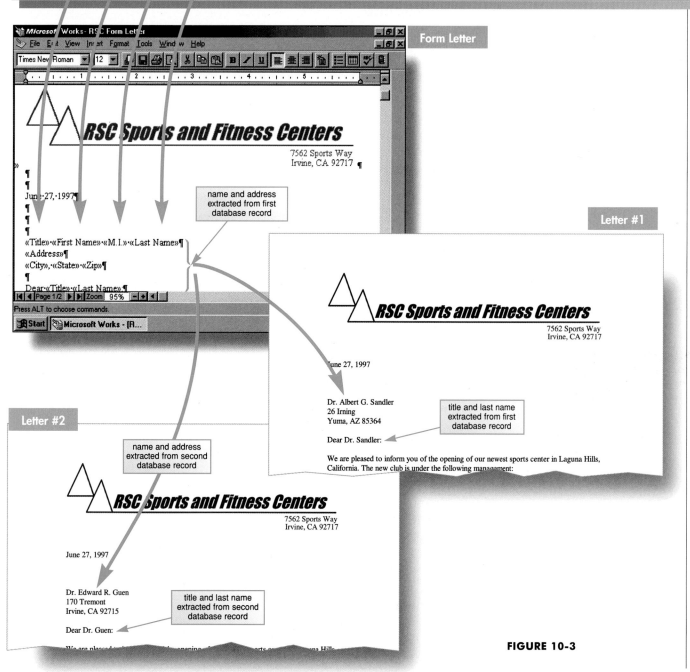

Database - RSC Members Revised

DATE JOINED	TITLE	FIRST NAME	M.I.	LAST NAME	ADDRESS	CITY	STATE	ZIP	TYPE	LOCATION	DUES	KIDS CLUB	TOTAL DUES
5/12/96	Dr.	Albert	G.	Sandler	26 Irning	Yuma	AZ	85364	Family	Irvine	$89.00	$12.50	$132.50
5/15/96	Dr.	Edward	R.	Guen	170 Tremont	Irvine	CA	92715	Family	Yorba Linda	$89.00		$89.00
5/17/96	Mr.	Rubin	E.	Gordon	1539 Centre	Yorba Linda	CA	92686	Family	Anaheim	$89.00	$12.50	$101.50
5/31/96	Mr.	Julian	P.	Coulon	216 Summer	Tustin	CA	92680	Family	Fullerton	$89.00		$89.00
6/3/96	Mr.	Stefano	U.	Branchi	58 Sullivan	Orange	CA	92667	Family	Irvine	$89.00		$89.00
6/15/96	Mr.	Cody	L.	Learner	124 Cobb	Brea	CA	92672	Family	Anaheim	$89.00	$12.00	$101.00

FIGURE 10-3

The form letter you will create contains a placeholder for the Title, First Name, Middle Initial, Last Name, and so forth. A **placeholder** is the name of a database field surrounded by chevron marks (<< >>). When you print a letter, placeholders in the letter are replaced by the actual data contained in the database.

When you print the form letter, Works creates a separate letter for each record in the database that contains the word, Family, in the Type field. Thus, the first letter printed is addressed to Dr. Albert G. Sandler because his record is the first record in the database that contains the word, Family, in the Type field (see Figure 10-3 on the previous page). The second letter printed is to be sent to Dr. Edward R. Guen because his record is the second record in the database that contains the word, Family, in the Type field.

After printing the form letters, you also will print an envelope for each of the people who will receive a letter. You create the envelope using a process similar to creating the form letter.

General Steps to Prepare the Form Letter

The general steps to prepare the form letter illustrated in Figure 10-1 on page W 10.5 are explained below.

1. Start Works.
2. Create the RSC Sports and Fitness Centers letterhead using Microsoft Draw.
3. Insert the current date in the letter.
4. Insert the placeholders of the fields from the database you will use for the inside address in the letter. When you print the letters, Works will replace these placeholders with the actual data from the database.
5. Type the salutation (Dear) and insert the Title field placeholder and Last Name field placeholder in the letter.
6. Type the body of the letter. Insert the Date Joined field placeholder and the Location field placeholder in the second paragraph.
7. Open the RSC Memberships spreadsheet file.
8. Insert the spreadsheet and 3-D Bar chart in the letter.
9. Save the letter on disk.
10. Print the form letters.
11. Create and print envelopes for the form letters.
12. Exit Works.

The following pages contain a detailed explanation of each of these steps.

Starting the Works Word Processor

To create the form letter you must first start the Works Word Processor. To start the Works Word Processor, follow the steps you used in the word processing projects to open the Microsoft Works Task Launcher dialog box (Figure 10-4), and then perform the following steps.

Steps To Start the Works Word Processor

1 **Click the Works Tools tab, and then point to the Word Processor button in the Works Task Launcher dialog box.**

The Works Tools sheet displays in the Works Task Launcher dialog box and the mouse pointer points to the Word Processor button (Figure 10-4).

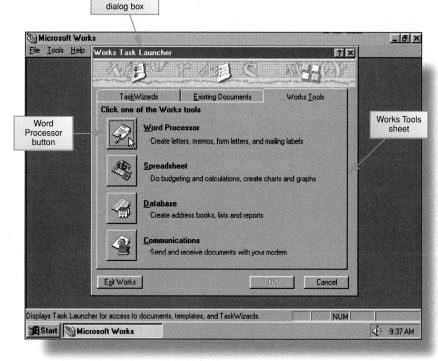

FIGURE 10-4

2 **Click the Word Processor button in the Works Task Launcher dialog box. When the Microsoft Works window displays, maximize the window, if necessary. Maximize the Unsaved Document 1 window, if necessary. If the Help window displays, click the Shrink Help button.**

Works maximizes the document window and places the document title, Unsaved Document 1, in the application window title bar (Figure 10-5). The word processing document displays in page layout view. The Header area displays at the top of the document. Any text typed in the Header area displays on the screen and prints at the top of every page. The vertical dotted lines indicate the left and right margins of the document. The insertion point displays in the leftmost position of the first line in the document.

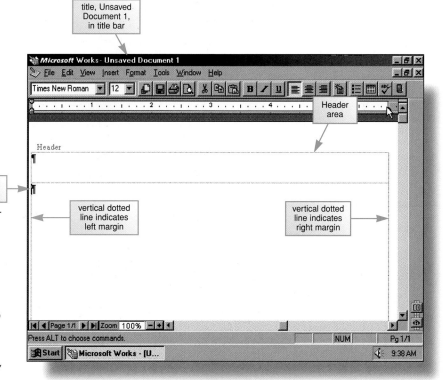

FIGURE 10-5

More *About*
MS Draw

Remember the saying: A picture
is worth a thousand words?
Although your writing may be
wonderful, how your document
looks may be as important. MS
Draw can help you if you need
illustrations to make a point or
to better communicate a message. MS Draw offers drawing
tools to create any shape. You
can create geometric forms,
design your own monograms
and letterheads and arrange
text in circles and squares.

Recall from Project 1, you can work with a Word Processor document in one of two view modes; page layout view or normal view. The first three projects illustrated creating documents in normal view. Project 10 illustrates creating a document in page layout view.

Using Microsoft Draw

The first task to prepare the form letter is to create a letterhead. In earlier projects, you used clip art and WordArt to create a title on a database form. In this project, you will use Microsoft Draw to import a company logo and text to be used as a letterhead.

Starting Microsoft Draw

To start Microsoft Draw, complete the following steps.

Steps **To Start Microsoft Draw**

1 **Click Insert on the menu bar and then point to Drawing.**

The Insert menu displays and the mouse pointer points to Drawing (Figure 10-6). The insertion point displays below the Header area in the document window. This is the location at which Works will insert the drawing created in Microsoft Draw.

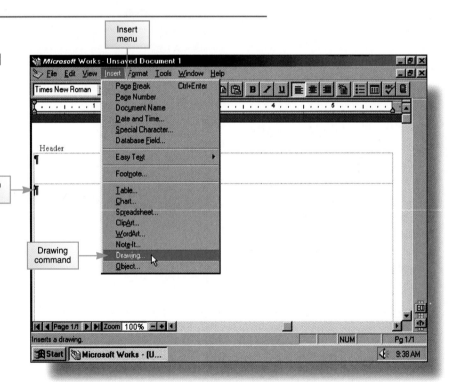

FIGURE 10-6

② **Click Drawing. When the Microsoft Draw window displays, maximize the window.**

*Works displays the maximized Microsoft Draw window (Figure 10-7). At the top of the window are the title bar and the menu bar. The blank workspace filling most of the MS Draw window is called the **drawing window**. The page inside the window is 22 inches square. You can use the scroll bars at the right side and bottom of the drawing window to scroll to the parts of the page that are hidden from view. Down the left side of the window is the **MS Draw Toolbox** containing nine drawing tools. Across the bottom of the screen are the **color palettes** that display the available colors for lines and filling shapes in the drawing window. Microsoft Draw gives you a color palette with two kinds of color: line color and fill color. Use line color for lines, frames, pattern foreground, and text. Use fill color for shape interiors and pattern background. You can have up to 100 line colors and 100 fill colors in a palette. By default the line color is black and the fill color is white.*

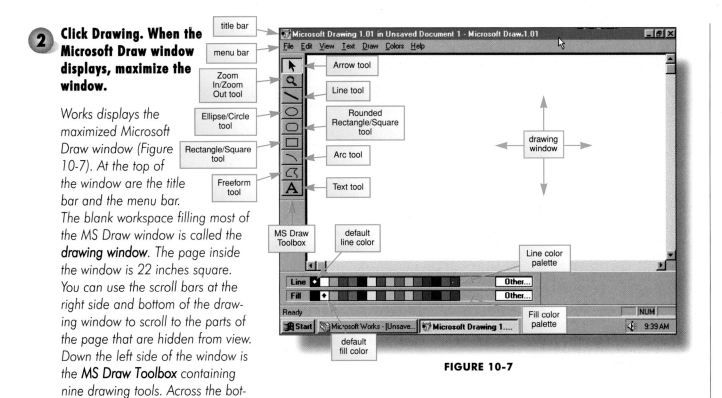

FIGURE 10-7

Using Microsoft Draw to Create a Logo

The logo for RSC Sports and Fitness Centers is two triangles offset from one another (see Figure 10-1a on page W 10.5). To create the logo for the letterhead, use the Freeform tool in the MS Draw Toolbox to create the first triangle. Then you can copy the first triangle to create the second triangle. To create the logo, perform the steps on the next pages.

◆ **More** *About* **Drawing Tools**

You can draw open objects or closed polygons using the Freeform tool. You can also draw open or closed freehand drawings. To draw polygons consisting of straight lines, you click at each vertex of the polygon. To draw freehand shapes, click the Freeform tool, then drag the cross hair mouse pointer, releasing where you want the line or shape to end. The Freeform tool remains in effect until you complete an object by double-clicking or pressing the ENTER key.

Steps To Create a Logo Using Microsoft Draw

1 Click Draw on the menu bar and point to Show Guides.

The Draw menu displays and the mouse pointer points to Show Guides (Figure 10-8). Notice a check mark does not display next to Show Guides, which indicates the Show Guides command is not active.

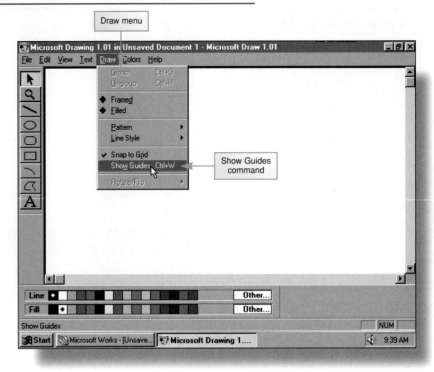

FIGURE 10-8

2 Click Show Guides.

*Works displays a vertical dotted line called a **vertical guide** and a horizontal dotted line called a **horizontal guide** (Figure 10-8). If you click one of the guides, Works displays the number of inches the guide is located down or to the right from the top left corner of the drawing window. When you drag the horizontal guide up or down or you drag the vertical guide left or right, the number displays and changes as you drag. When the guides initially display, as in Figure 10-9, the vertical guide is at the 3.000 position and the horizontal guide is at the 1.667 position. On the single screen initially displayed when you open Microsoft Draw, the top position for the horizontal guide is 0.000, the leftmost position for the vertical guide is 0.000, the bottom position for the horizontal guide is 3.333, and the rightmost position for the vertical guide is 6.000. Because the page inside the drawing window is 22 inches by 22 inches, by scrolling you can change the guides to a maximum of 21.917 each.*

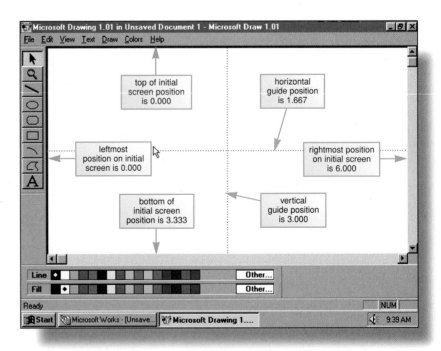

FIGURE 10-9

3 Drag the horizontal guide up to the 1.000 position. Drag the vertical guide left to the 1.000 position. Click the dark blue box on the Line color palette. Click the Freeform tool in the MS Draw Toolbox. Position the mouse pointer in the drawing window to the right of the Line tool.

The horizontal guide is positioned at 1.000 and the vertical guide is positioned at 1.000 (Figure 10-10). The diamond on the Line color palette indicates the color selection for a line. After selecting the Freeform tool and moving the mouse pointer into the drawing window, it changes shape. After you click the Freeform tool, Works recesses the tool. The mouse pointer is correctly positioned to the right of the Line tool in the drawing window.

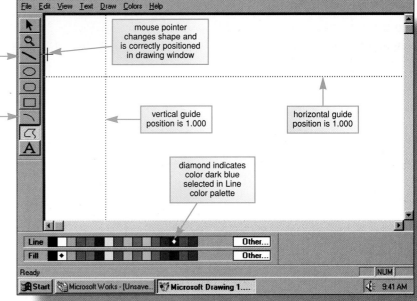

FIGURE 10-10

4 Click. Move the mouse pointer to the position where the first line segment is to end and then click (directly under the e in the View menu name in the drawing window).

The first line segment of the triangle displays (Figure 10-11). The line color displays dark blue.

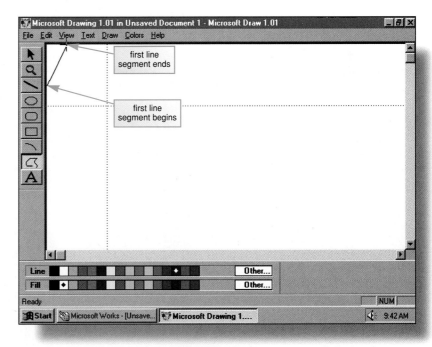

FIGURE 10-11

5 **Continue moving the mouse pointer and then clicking to draw the two additional connected line segments to form the triangle, ending the third line segment at the beginning of the first line segment. Click Draw on the menu bar and then point to Line Style. When the Line Style cascading menu displays, point to 2 Point.**

MS Draw draws a straight line from each point in the triangle (Figure 10-12). If your drawing does not resemble the illustration, you can press the DELETE key to delete the object. You then can draw it again. You also can click Undo on the Edit menu to delete the last object drawn. The Draw menu displays and Line Style is highlighted. The Line Style cascading menu displays

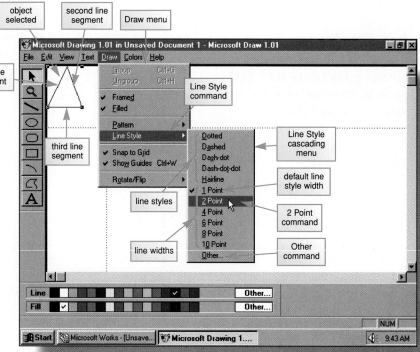

FIGURE 10-12

and the mouse pointer points to the 2 Point command. A check mark displays to the left of the 1 Point command, indicating the default line width. The Line Style cascading menu of the Draw menu gives you several line styles to apply to straight lines. You can draw dotted, dashed, dash-dot lines, hairlines, and other types of lines as well as lines in any of six standard widths. You also can customize the width of a line to any desired width not displayed on the Line Style cascading menu by clicking Other. A line may have only one style at a time. You may not mix styles. For example, you may not create a 4-point dashed line.

6 **Click 2 Point.**

The selected object displays dark blue lines with a width of 2 points (Figure 10-13). The first triangle is completed. You now can copy the first triangle to create the second triangle in the logo.

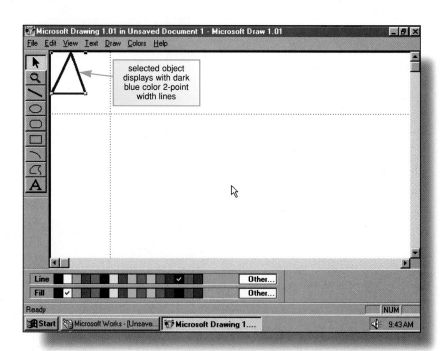

FIGURE 10-13

7 Ensure the object is selected. Click Edit on the menu bar and then click Copy. Click Edit on the menu bar and then click Paste. Point to the pasted object.

When you click Copy, Works places a copy of the object on the Clipboard. When you click Paste, Works pastes a copy of the selected object in the drawing window (Figure 10-14). The exact location of the pasted object in the drawing window will vary depending on the last copy and paste operation performed in Microsoft Draw. The mouse pointer points to the pasted object in the drawing window.

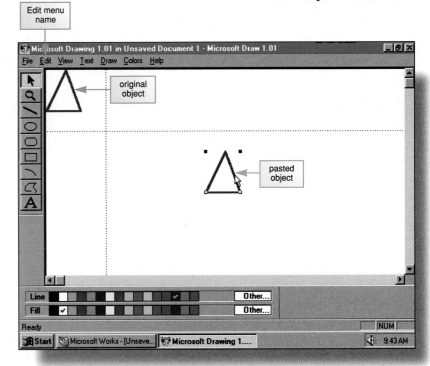

FIGURE 10-14

8 Drag the object to the upper left corner of the drawing window until the base of the triangle is positioned on the horizontal guide and to the left of the vertical guide.

The second triangle displays in the desired location in the upper left corner of the drawing window (Figure 10-15).

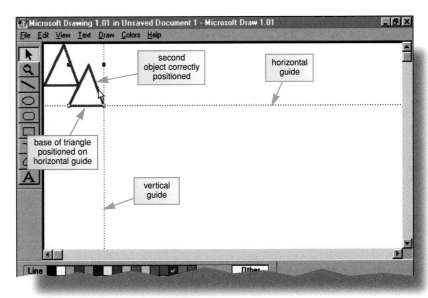

FIGURE 10-15

The logo for the letterhead is complete. The following section illustrates entering text and drawing a line in the MS Draw window.

Entering Text and Drawing a Line in the MS Draw Window

The text in the letterhead, RSC Sports and Fitness Centers, displays in 26-point Impact dark blue italic font. The line width and color below the text displays in 2-point dark blue. The address, city, state, and zip text display in 12-point Times New Roman dark blue font. To enter text and draw a line in the drawing window, perform the steps on the next four pages

Steps To Enter Text and Draw a Line in the Drawing Window

1 **Click the Text tool in the MS Draw Toolbox. Click Text on the menu bar and then point to Font.**

The Text tool is selected, the Text menu displays, and the mouse pointer points to Font (Figure 10-16). Dark blue is selected on the Line color palette.

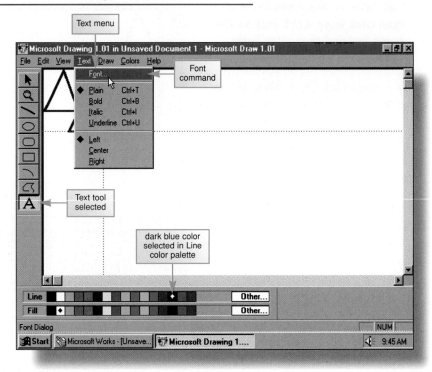

FIGURE 10-16

2 **Click Font. When the Font dialog box displays, use the down scroll arrow in the Font list box to view Impact. Click Impact. Click Italic in the Font style list box. Use the down scroll arrow in the Size list box to view 26. Click 26. Point to the OK button.**

Microsoft Draw displays the Font dialog box (Figure 10-17). Impact is highlighted in the Font list box and displays in the Font box. Italic is highlighted in the Font style list box and displays in the Font style box. Font size 26 is highlighted in the Size list box and displays in the Size box. The Sample box displays the selections you have made. The mouse pointer points to the OK button.

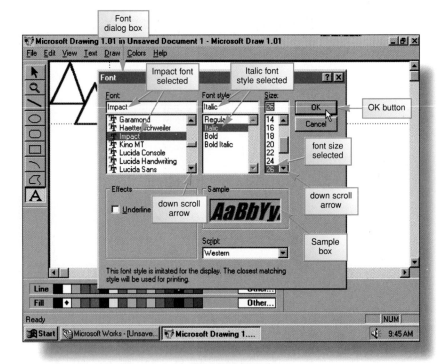

FIGURE 10-17

3 **Click the OK button. Position the text pointer on the vertical guide above the horizontal guide in the drawing window.**

The text pointer displays above the horizontal guide on the vertical guide (Figure 10-18).

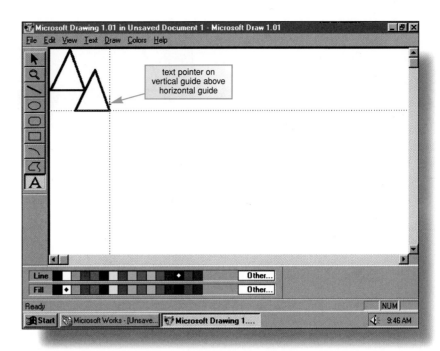

FIGURE 10-18

4 **Click in the drawing window. Type** RSC Sports and Fitness Centers **and then press the ENTER key or ESC key.**

When you click in the drawing window, an insertion point appears. After typing the text and pressing the ENTER key or the ESC key, the text displays and the text object is selected (Figure 10-19). The text displays in 26-point Impact dark blue, italic font.

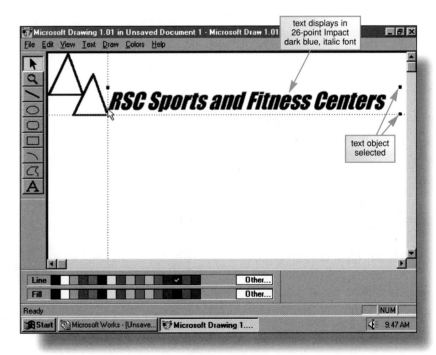

FIGURE 10-19

5 Drag the vertical guide to the 5.917 position. Click the Line tool in the MS Draw Toolbox. Click Draw on the menu bar, point to Line Style, and then click 2 Point on the Line Style Cascading menu. Position the mouse pointer to the right of the base of the second triangle. Press and hold down the SHIFT key and then drag to the vertical guide.

The vertical guide is positioned at the 5.917 position (Figure 10-20). The 2-point width dark blue line displays below the text. Holding down the SHIFT key as you drag constrains the line to the nearest 45° angle (0°, 45°, 90°, 135°, and so on).

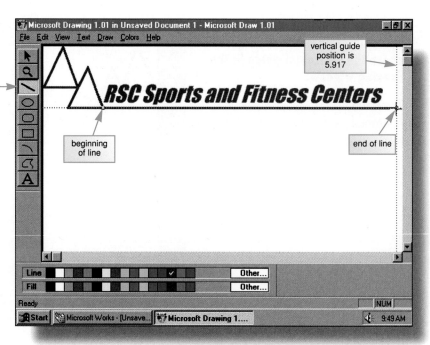

FIGURE 10-20

6 Click anywhere in the drawing window away from the object to remove the selection. Using the techniques illustrated in Steps 1 through 4 enter the address text and city, state, and zip text. That is, click the Text tool in the MS Draw Toolbox. Click Text on the menu bar and then click Font. When the Font dialog box displays, click Times New Roman in the Font list box. Click Regular in the Font style list box. Click 12 in the Size list box. Click the OK button. Click the text pointer below the e in Centers in the letterhead and then type 7562 Sports Way **for the address. Click anywhere in the drawing window away from the object to remove the selection. Click the Text tool in the MS Draw Toolbox. Click the text pointer below the address text and then type** Irvine, CA 92717 **for the City, State, and Zip. Click anywhere in the drawing window away from an object to remove the selection. You may have to experiment to achieve the correct position. You can select a text object and drag to the desired location.**

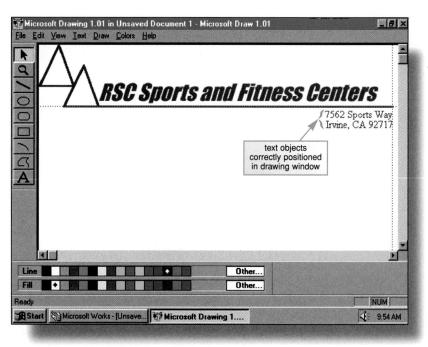

FIGURE 10-21

The text objects display in the drawing window (Figure 10-21).

7 Click File on the menu bar and then point to Exit and Return.

The File menu displays and the mouse pointer points to Exit and Return (Figure 10-22).

FIGURE 10-22

8 Click Exit and Return. When the Microsoft Draw dialog box displays asking, Save changes to Microsoft Drawing 1.01 in Unsaved Document 1?, click the Yes button. When the word processing document displays on screen, click the Zoom box on the status bar and then click Margin Width.

The logo and text are placed in the word processing document (Figure 10-23). A dotted outline with selection handles displays around the MS Draw object, indicating the object is selected. The entire width of the document displays between the margins because you clicked Margin Width on the Zoom list.

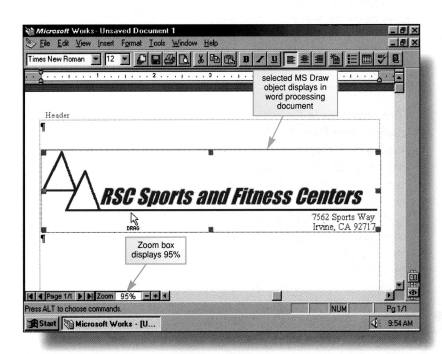

FIGURE 10-23

The letterhead for the form letter is now complete. Due to personal preferences or other reasons, you may find it necessary to edit and modify the object you created using MS Draw. To accomplish this task, perform the following steps.

TO EDIT A MICROSOFT DRAW OBJECT

Step 1: Double-click the MS Draw object.
Step 2: Maximize the MS Draw window.
Step 3: Click anywhere in the drawing window to remove the selections.
Step 4: Complete any required modifications.
Step 5: Click File on the menu bar and then click Exit and Return.

Saving the Document

To save the document, perform the following steps.

TO SAVE A DOCUMENT

Step 1: Click the Save button on the toolbar.
Step 2: Type RSC Form Letter in the File name text box of the Save As dialog box.
Step 3: Click 3½ Floppy [A:] in the Save in drop-down list box, if necessary.
Step 4: Click the Save button.

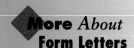

More *About* Form Letters

Form letters are much like ordinary letters with one major difference: they have placeholders for personal information. Placeholders are objects that mark the location on each form letter where you want to print the contents of a database field. Thus, the form letters are personalized to the addressee. An individual is likely to open and read a personalized letter.

Creating the Form Letter

The next step in creating the form letter is to insert the current date using the **Date and Time command** on the Insert menu.

Inserting the Current Date

In Project 2 you entered the date in a document using the Works Letter TaskWizard. You also can cause the current date to display or print in a document by using the Works Date and Time command on the Insert menu. When you insert the date in a document using the Date and Time command, you can control whether the inserted date will automatically update to today's date when you print the document. The current date is stored in the computer as part of the operating system. This technique is valuable if you are going to create form letters but are not certain of the exact date on which you will print the letters. No matter what day you print, the letter will contain the current date.

To insert the current date in the form letter, perform the following steps.

Steps To Insert the Date in the Form Letter

1 **Click to the right of the MS Draw object to remove the selection. Press the ENTER key three times. Click Insert on the menu bar and then point to Date and Time.**

Works displays the Insert menu and the mouse pointer points to the Date and Time command (Figure 10-24). The insertion point displays in the document where the date will be inserted.

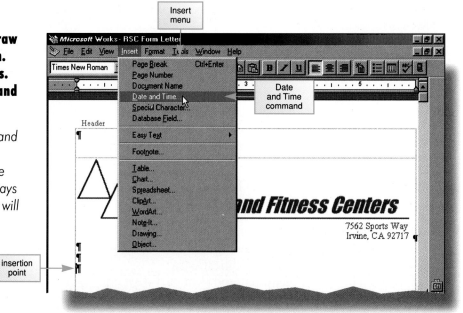

FIGURE 10-24

2 Click Date and Time. When the Insert Date and Time dialog box displays, click the long date format (Month, Day, Year) in the Select a format box. Ensure the Automatically update when printed check box is selected and then point to the Insert button.

Works displays the Insert Date and Time dialog box (Figure 10-25). The long date format is highlighted in the Select a format box. The Automatically update when printed check box is selected. This option instructs Works to automatically update the date in the document every time you open or print the document. The mouse pointer points to the Insert button. Works offers four other formats for inserting a date into a document, two formats for inserting the date and time into a document, and four formats for inserting a time into a document.

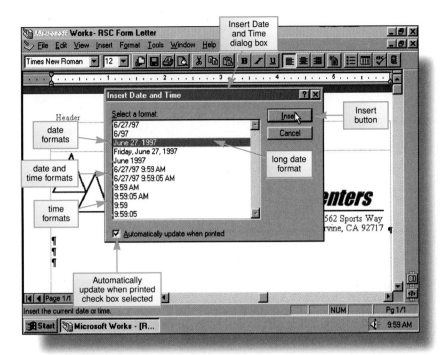

FIGURE 10-25

3 Click the Insert button.

Works inserts the current date into the form letter (Figure 10-26). The date that displays in your document will be different.

FIGURE 10-26

Entering the Inside Address

The next step is to enter the inside address of the letter, which contains the name and address of the individual to whom the letter will be sent. In this project, you are sending the same letter to many individuals. The names and addresses of the people who will receive the letter come from specific records in the RSC Members Revised database (see Figure 10-3 on page W 10.7).

To enter the inside address, you will use database placeholders, which are field names in the database surrounded by chevrons (<< >>). For example, <<Title>> is a placeholder for the Title field in the database. When Works prints a letter that contains the placeholder <<Title>>, it replaces the placeholder in the document with the data from the Title field in a record in the database.

You use the **Form Letters command** on the Tools menu to identify the database you want to use and the fields to insert. The Form Letter dialog box steps you through the process of creating a form letter by presenting you with a series of questions. Perform the following steps to insert database placeholders in the form letter.

Steps To Insert Database Placeholders in a Document

1 **Insert the floppy disk that contains the RSC Members Revised file from Project 8 in drive A. After inserting the current date, press the ENTER key four times to position the insertion point where you want to place the inside address. Click Tools on the menu bar and then point to Form Letters.**

Works displays the Tools menu and the mouse pointer points to Form Letters (Figure 10-27). The insertion point displays four lines below the current date.

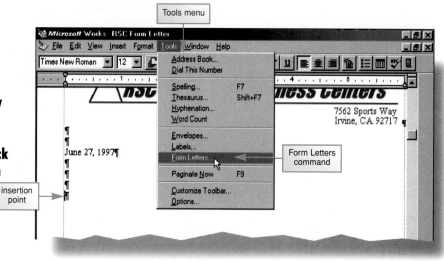

FIGURE 10-27

2 **Click Form Letters. When the Form Letters: RSC Form Letter dialog box displays, point to the Database tab.**

Works displays the Form Letters: RSC Form Letter dialog box (Figure 10-28). The Instructions sheet displays on top of five other tabbed sheets. The numbered list gives instructions to set up the form letters. The mouse pointer points to the Database tab. As you create the form letter, Works checks off each step in the instruction sheet.

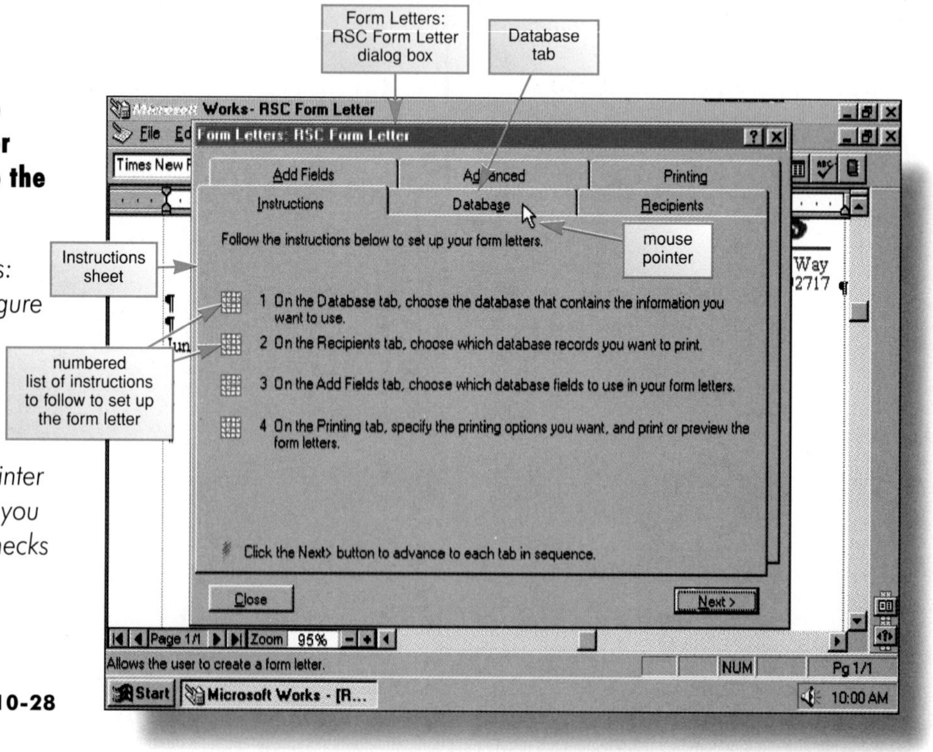

FIGURE 10-28

3 **Click the Database tab. When the Database sheet displays, point to the Open a database not listed here button.**

Works displays the Database sheet (Figure 10-29). The Choose a database list box displays database files that have been opened recently. The mouse pointer points to the Open a database not listed here button.

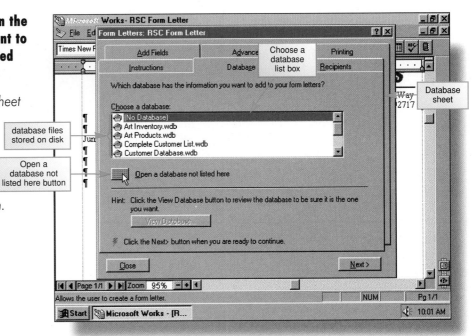

FIGURE 10-29

4 **Click the Open a database not listed here button. When the Use Another File dialog box displays, click the Look in box arrow and then click 3½ Floppy [A:], if necessary. Click RSC Members Revised. Point to the Open button.**

When you click the Open a database not listed here button, Works displays the Use Another File dialog box (Figure 10-30). The desired database file is highlighted.

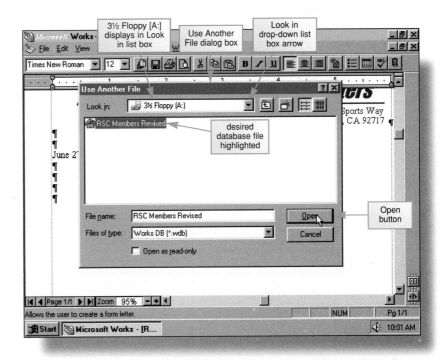

FIGURE 10-30

More *About* Inserting Database Placeholders in a Document

You can click the Next button in the Form Letters: RSC Form Letter dialog box to advance to each tab in sequence. You can also click any tab in any sequence to set up your form letters.

5 **Click the Open button. When the Form Letters: RSC Form Letter dialog box displays, click the Add Fields tab. When the Add Fields sheet displays, click Title in the Choose a field list box. Point to the Insert Field button.**

When you click the Open button in the Use Another File dialog box, Works displays the Form Letters: RSC Form Letter dialog box again. RSC Members Revised.wdb displays highlighted in the Choose a database list box. When you click the Add Fields tab the Add Fields sheet displays (Figure 10-31). The Title field name is highlighted. The mouse pointer points to the Insert Field button. The field names in the RSC Members Revised database display in the Choose a field list box.

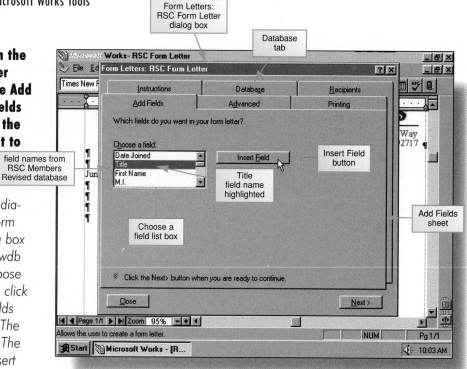

FIGURE 10-31

6 **Click the Insert Field button on the Add Fields sheet to place the placeholder for the Title field (<<Title>>) in the letter. The highlight moves down to the First Name field name. Point to the Insert Field button.**

Works places the Title field name enclosed in chevrons (<< >>) in the letter at the insertion point (Figure 10-32). The chevrons indicate the entry is a database placeholder and not regular text. The First Name field name in the Choose a field list box is highlighted. The mouse pointer points to the Insert Field button.

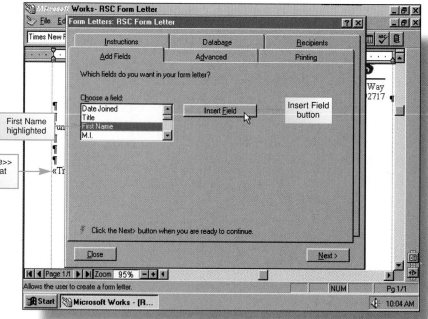

FIGURE 10-32

7 Click the Insert Field button on the Add Fields sheet. Click the Insert Field button to insert the M.I. field placeholder, the Last Name field placeholder, the Address field placeholder, the City field placeholder, the State field placeholder, and the Zip field placeholder using the steps previously explained. Point to the Close button.

The mouse pointer points to the Close button (Figure 10-33).

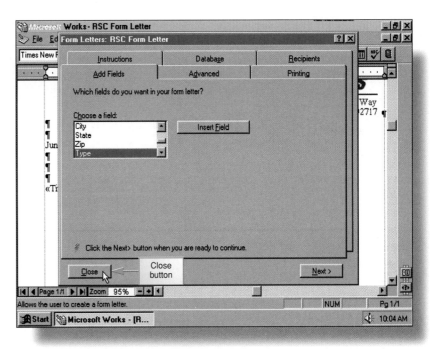

FIGURE 10-33

8 Click the Close button. When the letter displays, click to the right of the Last Name field placeholder.

Works displays the placeholders for the Title, First Name, M.I., Last Name, Address, City, State, and Zip in the letter on one line (Figure 10-34). Notice that Works automatically places a single blank space between placeholders. The insertion point displays to the right of the Last Name placeholder.

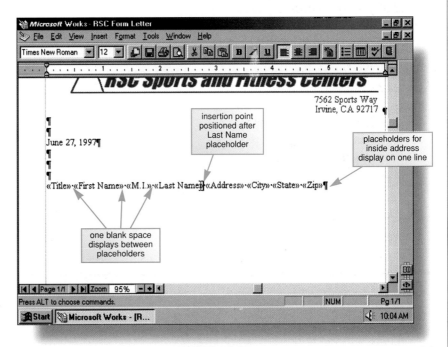

FIGURE 10-34

9 **Press the DELETE key to remove the blank space after the Last Name field placeholder. Press the ENTER key to move Address, City, State, and Zip field placeholders to the second line of the inside address. Click to the right of the Address field placeholder.**

Works removes the blank space after the Last Name field place-holder (Figure 10-35). When you press the ENTER key, the Address, City, State, and Zip field place-holders move to the second line of the inside address. The insertion point displays after the Address field placeholder.

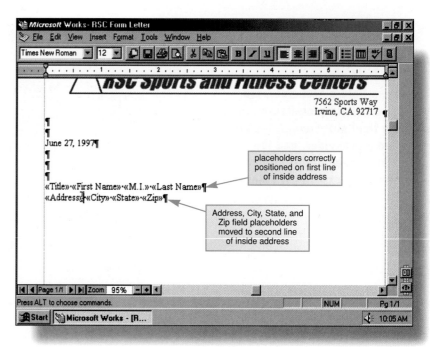

FIGURE 10-35

10 **Press the DELETE key to remove the blank space after the Address field placeholder. Press the ENTER key to move City, State, and Zip field placeholders to the third line of the inside address. Type a comma (,) after the City field placeholder. Click to the right of the Zip field placeholder and then press the ENTER key twice. Type** Dear **and then press the SPACEBAR one time.**

The field placeholders are correctly positioned in the inside address of the letter (Figure 10-36). A comma displays after the City field placeholder. The placeholders that are to display on the salutation line are <<Title>> and <<Last Name>>. Because these place-holders have already been inserted in the inside address using the Form Letters command, they can be copied to the salutation line.

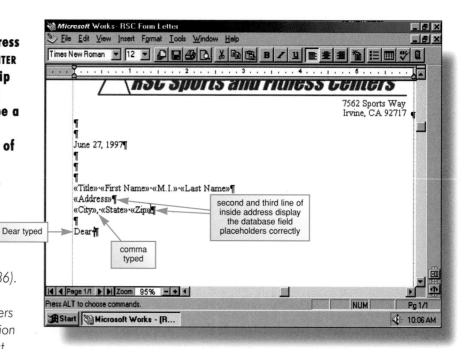

FIGURE 10-36

11 **Double-click <<Title>> in the first line of the inside address. Click the Copy button on the toolbar. Click where you wish the Title field placeholder to display in the salutation line and then click the Paste button. Double-click the <<Last Name>> placeholder in the first line of the inside address. Click the Copy button on the toolbar. Click where you wish the Last Name field placeholder to display in the salutation line and then click the Paste button. Type a colon (:) after the Last Name field placeholder. Press the ENTER key two times.**

Works copies the Title and Last Name placeholders in the first line of the inside address and pastes the Title and Last Name placeholders in the salutation line (Figure 10-37). A colon displays following the Last Name placeholder.

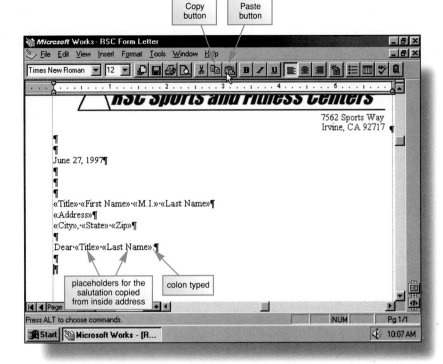

FIGURE 10-37

When using placeholders in a document, you can type any text, spaces, or punctuation before or after the placeholders to produce the required output.

You must use the Form Letters command on the Tools menu to insert placeholders in a letter. Once a placeholder is inserted into a letter, you can copy the placeholder to different locations in the letter. You cannot, however, type the field name and the chevrons yourself. If you type the field name and the chevrons yourself, Works will not insert the database field in the letter when the letter is printed.

Body of the Letter

The first paragraph of the body of the letter begins two lines below the salutation. To enter these lines, perform the following steps (see Figure 10-38 on the next page).

TO ENTER THE LETTER TEXT

Step 1: Type the first two lines of the letter.
Step 2: At the end of the second line, press the ENTER key two times.

Figure 10-38 illustrates the first paragraph of the letter. The first paragraph is followed by a table that lists the members of the new management for the RSC Sports and Fitness Centers.

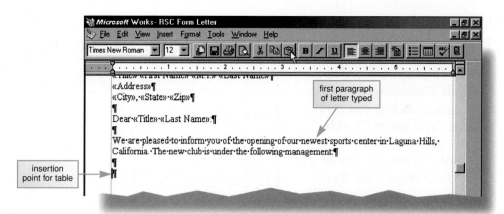

FIGURE 10-38

Creating the Table

A **table** is a group of related columns in a document. In Project 3, you created a table using the Table command on the Insert menu. Tables also may be created using the **tab stops** on the ruler. Tables created using tab stops should be relatively simple and not involve calculations within the table.

When you create a table, you must determine the general appearance of the table, how many columns you need, and the maximum width of each column in the table. The table structure of the table you are to create in the letter is illustrated in Figure 10-39.

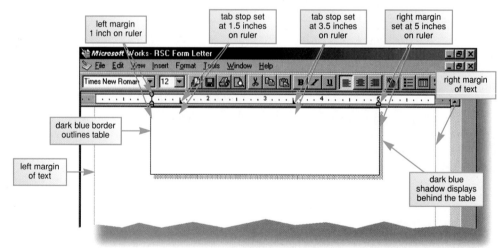

FIGURE 10-39

In the table in the form letter, a dark blue outline displays around the table. A dark blue shadow displays to the right and below the table. The area set aside for the table is four inches wide. The left border line is one inch from the left margin. The names are indented one-half inch from the left border. A corresponding border on the right is one inch to the left of the right margin. Because the table is smaller than the six-inch line used for text, you must change the left and right margins for the table area in the letter.

Setting Margins for the Table

To change the left and right margins in the table area of the letter, perform the following steps.

Steps **To Set Left and Right Margins for the Table**

① **Drag the left-margin indent marker to the one-inch position on the ruler.**

The first-line indent marker and the left-margin indent marker are set at the one-inch mark on the ruler (Figure 10-40). Works also indents the paragraph mark and insertion point one inch.

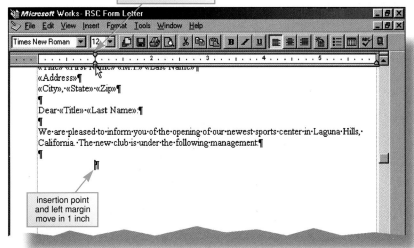

first-line indent marker and left-margin indent marker set at 1-inch position on ruler

insertion point and left margin move in 1 inch

FIGURE 10-40

② **Drag the right-margin indent marker to the five-inch position on the ruler.**

The margins for the table are now set (Figure 10-41).

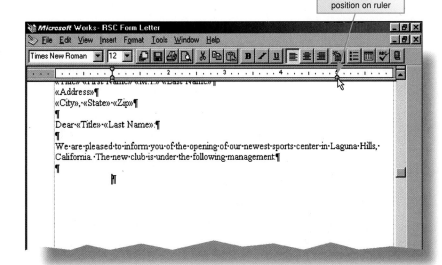

right-margin indent marker set at 5-inch position on ruler

FIGURE 10-41

Setting Tab Stops

The next step is to set the required tab stops for the table. You use **tab stops** when you create tables so the columns in the table will be vertically aligned. You must use two left-aligned tab stops in the table in the form letter. Set these tab stops at the 1.5-inch position and the 3.5-inch position on the ruler by performing the steps on the next page.

▶ Other Ways

1. On Format menu click Paragraph, click Indents and Alignment tab, type 1 in Left text box, type 1 in Right text box, click OK button

To Set Tab Stops

① **Click the 1.5-inch position on the ruler. Then, click the 3.5-inch position on the ruler.**

Works displays a left-aligned tab stop at the 1.5-inch position on the ruler and at the 3.5-inch position on the ruler (Figure 10-42).

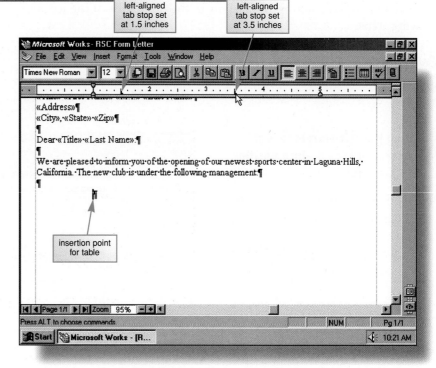

FIGURE 10-42

You can specify four types of tab stops when using the Works Word Processor. They are the left-aligned, right-aligned, center-aligned, and decimal-aligned tab stops. The **left-aligned tab stop** will cause text to print at the tab stop aligned to the left. This tab stop is commonly used when typing alphabetic information such as names. The **right-aligned tab stop** aligns data at the right margin set by the tab stop. The right-aligned tab stop is commonly used when typing numeric data. The **center-aligned tab stop** centers the typed characters beneath the tab stop position on the ruler. The **decimal-aligned tab stop** aligns numeric data on the decimal point in the number. Left-aligned tab stops are set by clicking the ruler. Other tab stops are set using the **Tabs command** on the Format menu and making appropriate entries in the Format Tabs dialog box.

Entering Text for the Table

The next step is to enter the names and titles of the new management into the table. End each line in the table except the last line by holding down the SHIFT key while pressing the ENTER key. This allows the entire table to be treated by Works as a single paragraph. The following steps illustrate how to enter text in the table.

Steps **To Enter Text in a Table**

1 **Ensure the insertion point is positioned at the beginning of the table. Press the TAB key. Type** Markus Lews **as the first entry.**

The first entry in the table displays (Figure 10-43).

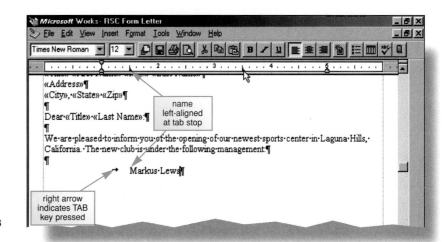

FIGURE 10-43

2 **Press the TAB key again. Type** Director **as the next entry. Press and hold down the SHIFT key and then press the ENTER key to end the first line in the table.**

The first line of text displays in the table (Figure 10-44). The insertion point appears on the next line indented one inch from the zero position on the ruler. The end-of-line mark indicates the end of the line but not the end of the paragraph.

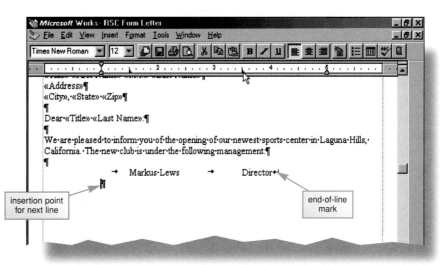

FIGURE 10-44

3 **Press the TAB key and type the remaining names and titles. Press the TAB key at the beginning of each line in the table. Press the ENTER key at the end of the last line in the table.**

The names and titles display left-aligned in the columns in the table (Figure 10-45).

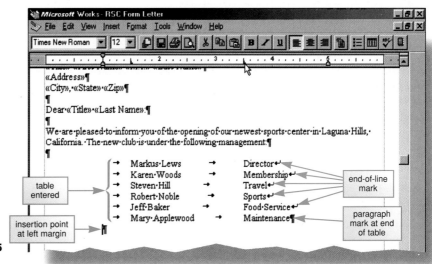

FIGURE 10-45

You use tables in applications that require data to be arranged in vertical columns. A table may consist of two, three, or more columns, and the columns in a table can use the left-, right-, center-, or decimal-aligned tab stops or any combination of tab stops.

Creating an Outline with a Shadow

Works allows you to add various types of borders to paragraphs. One or more paragraphs can be completely outlined with or without a shadow, or you can cause a border to display on only the top, bottom, left, or right of a paragraph by using options found in the Borders and Shading dialog box associated with the **Borders and Shading command** on the Format menu or context-sensitive menu.

You can use eleven types of border line styles. In the sample project, a dark blue outline border with a shadow displays around the table. Perform the following steps to create an outline with a shadow around the table.

Steps To Create an Outline Border with a Shadow

1 **Highlight the table by clicking to the left of the first TAB mark, pressing and holding down the SHIFT key, and then clicking to the left of the paragraph mark in the table.**

Works highlights the table (Figure 10-46). Notice the paragraph mark in the table is not highlighted. Recall from Project 1 that when you format the last paragraph in a document, the formatting remains in place for subsequent paragraphs. If you included the paragraph mark for the table in the highlight and applied an outline border, the outline format also would be applied to the paragraph mark located after the table.

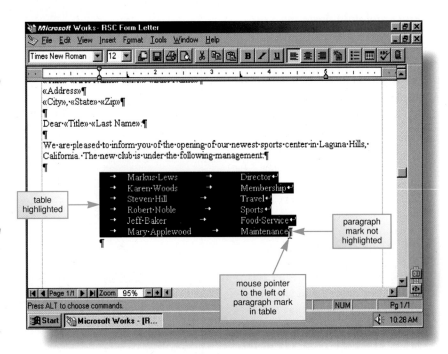

FIGURE 10-46

2 **Right-click the selection and then point to Borders and Shading.**

The context-sensitive menu displays and the mouse pointer points to Borders and Shading (Figure 10-47).

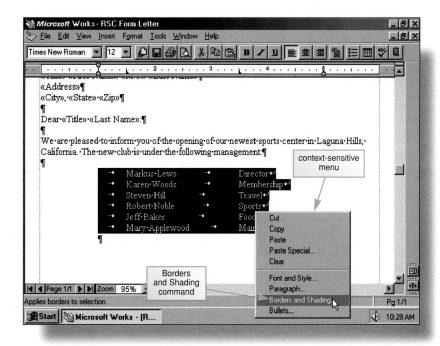

FIGURE 10-47

3 **Click Borders and Shading on the context-sensitive menu. When the Borders and Shading dialog box displays, click the Borders sheet, if necessary, and then click the thin line box in the Line style box. Scroll to view Dark Blue in the Color list box. Click Dark Blue. Click Outline with shadow in the Border box and then point to the OK button.**

Works displays the Borders and Shading dialog box (Figure 10-48). The Borders and Shading dialog box contains three tabbed sheets (Borders, Shading, and Page). The selections on the Borders sheet tell Works to place a dark blue thin out-line with a shadow around the high-lighted paragraph (Figure 10-48). The mouse pointer points to the OK button. The Sample box displays the selections you made.

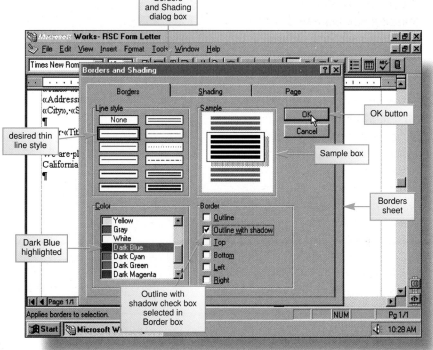

FIGURE 10-48

4 Click the OK button. Click in front of the paragraph mark outside the bottom left corner of the table.

Works places a dark blue outline with a shadow around the table (Figure 10-49). The insertion point is located at the one-inch left margin.

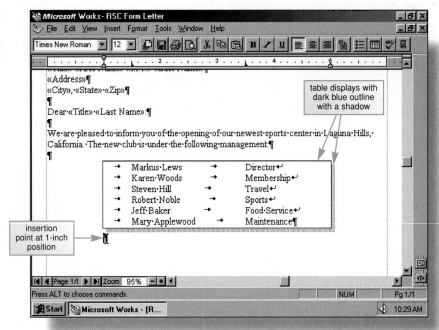

FIGURE 10-49

5 Press the CTRL+Q keys to remove the paragraph formatting (margin and tab stops) associated with the table.

Works removes the paragraph formatting. The margin markers move to the zero position and the 6-inch position on the ruler (Figure 10-50).

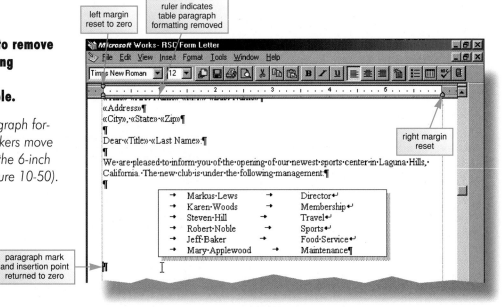

FIGURE 10-50

Typing a Paragraph Containing Additional Placeholders

In the next paragraph in the letter, the first sentence contains the words, Since you joined RSC Sports and Fitness Centers on (Figure 10-51). This text is followed by the database placeholders <<Date Joined>> and <<Location>>. This indicates the date joined and location from the database will be inserted in the text. Following the location placeholder is the remainder of the sentence contained in the paragraph.

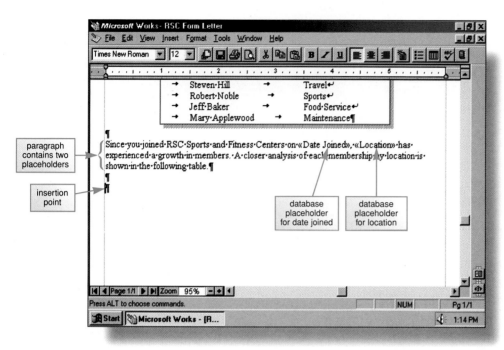

FIGURE 10-51

To type the sentence and insert additional database placeholders in the paragraph, complete the following steps.

Steps **To Insert Additional Database Placeholders in a Paragraph**

1 **Press the ENTER key to add a blank line after the table. Type** Since you joined RSC Sports and Fitness Centers on **and place a blank space following the last word, on. Click Insert on the menu bar and then point to Database Field.**

Works displays the Insert menu and the mouse pointer points to Database Field (Figure 10-52). The insertion point is located in the document where the database field Date Joined will be inserted.

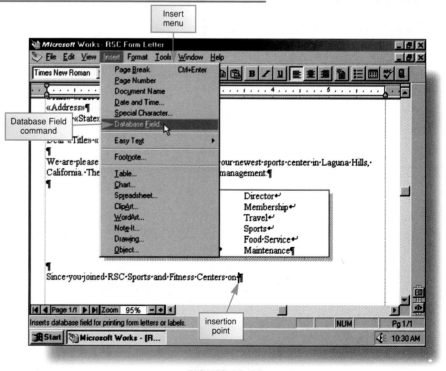

FIGURE 10-52

2 **Click Database Field. When the Insert Field dialog box displays, ensure Date Joined is highlighted in the Select a field list box and then point to the Insert button.**

Works displays the Insert Field dialog box (Figure 10-53). Works displays the database name, RSC Members Revised.wdb, in the Database box because the RSC Members Revised.wdb database was selected in Figure 10-30 on page W 10.23. The field names in the RSC Members Revised.wdb database display in the Select a field list box. The Date Joined field name is highlighted. The mouse pointer points to the Insert button.

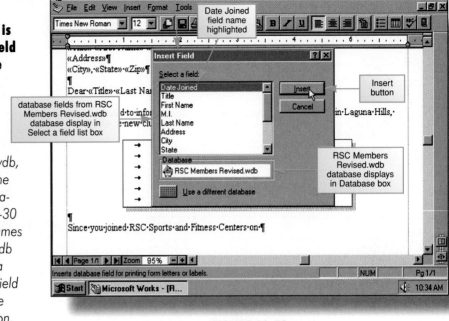

FIGURE 10-53

3 **Click the Insert button to insert the date joined placeholder (<<Date Joined>>) in the letter. Use the down scroll arrow in the Select a field list box to view the Location field. Click Location. Point to the Insert button.**

The Location database field name is highlighted and the mouse pointer points to the Insert button (Figure 10-54).

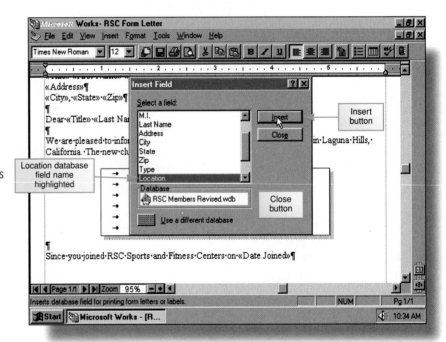

FIGURE 10-54

4 **Click the Insert button and then click the Close button. Type a comma (,) after the date joined placeholder and then type the rest of the paragraph. Press the ENTER key twice.**

The paragraph displays with the database place-holders <<Date Joined>> and <<Location>> in the letter (Figure 10-55). A comma displays after the date joined placeholder.

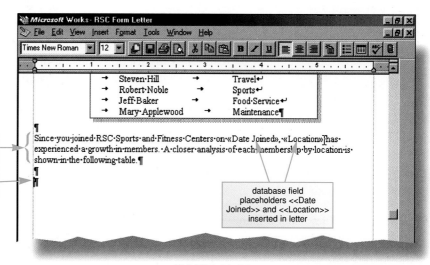

paragraph typed

insertion point

database field placeholders <<Date Joined>> and <<Location>> inserted in letter

FIGURE 10-55

Other Ways

1. On Tools menu click Form Letters, click Add Fields tab, highlight desired field, click Insert Field button, click Close button

Linking a Spreadsheet to a Word Processing Document

The next step is to add the spreadsheet to the letter. To link a spreadsheet to a word processing document, both the spreadsheet and the word processing files must be open. You then can link a spreadsheet to a document using drag-and-drop.

Opening the Spreadsheet File

To open the RSC Memberships spreadsheet file, perform the following steps (see Figure 10-56).

TO OPEN THE SPREADSHEET FILE

Step 1: Insert the floppy disk that contains the RSC Memberships file from Project 4 in drive A.
Step 2: Click File on the menu bar and then click Open.
Step 3: When the Open dialog box displays, click 3½ Floppy [A:] in the Look in drop-down list box, if necessary. Click RSC Memberships and then click the Open button.

The RSC Memberships spreadsheet file displays on the screen as shown in Figure 10-56.

More *About* **Linking Information**

Use linking to transfer informa-tion between Works documents when you expect the source of the information to change. With linking, you copy the informa-tion and Works automatically updates the information when the source changes. You can link information into a Works document from any Windows program that supports linking.

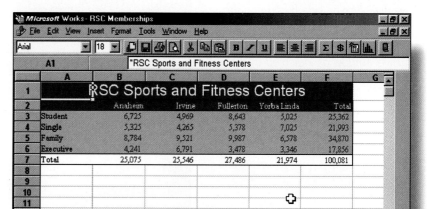

FIGURE 10-56

Linking a Spreadsheet File to a Word Processing Document

The RSC Memberships spreadsheet file is now open. To link a spreadsheet to a word processing document using drag-and-drop perform the following steps.

Steps To Link a Spreadsheet File to a Word Processing Document

1 **Click Window on the menu bar and then point to Tile.**

Works displays the Window menu and the mouse pointer points to Tile (Figure 10-57).

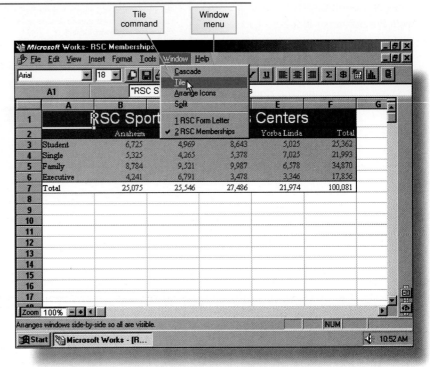

FIGURE 10-57

2 **Click Tile. Point to the RSC Form Letter title bar.**

The spreadsheet document window and the word processing document window display side by side on the screen (Figure 10-58). The spreadsheet (RSC Memberships) is still the active window as indicated by the dark blue title bar. The mouse pointer points to the RSC Form Letter title bar.

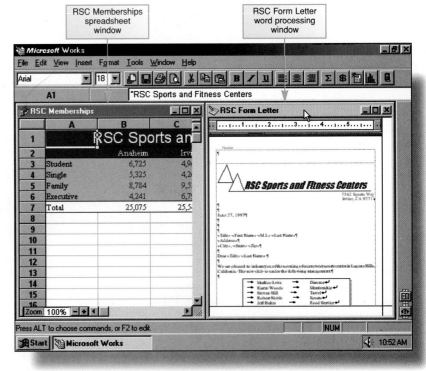

FIGURE 10-58

3 Click the RSC Form Letter title bar. Use the down scroll arrow to view the insertion point.

When you click the RSC Form Letter title bar, Works makes that the active window (Figure 10-59). The insertion point displays in the word processing document where the spreadsheet will be inserted.

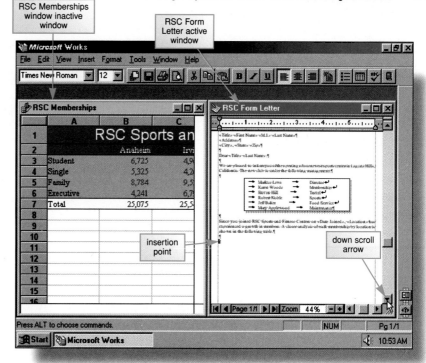

FIGURE 10-59

4 Highlight the range A1:F7 in the spreadsheet, which is the range to be inserted in the word processing document. Position the mouse pointer on the border of the selected range so the pointer shape changes to a block arrow with the word DRAG.

The range is highlighted (Figure 10-60). The mouse pointer changes to a block arrow with the word DRAG. The mouse pointer indicates you can drag the highlighted range of the spreadsheet.

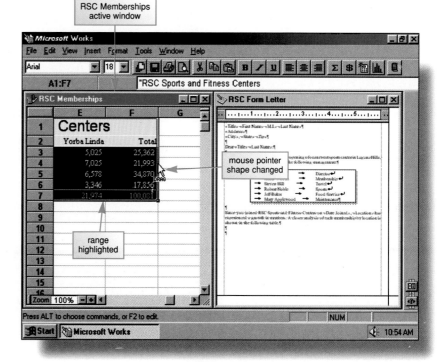

FIGURE 10-60

5 **Drag to the paragraph mark in the word processing document to where the spreadsheet is to appear.**

When you begin to drag the selected range, the word below the mouse pointer changes to MOVE. When you drag to the word processing document, the word changes to COPY, indicating you are going to copy the highlighted spreadsheet range into the word processing document (Figure 10-61).

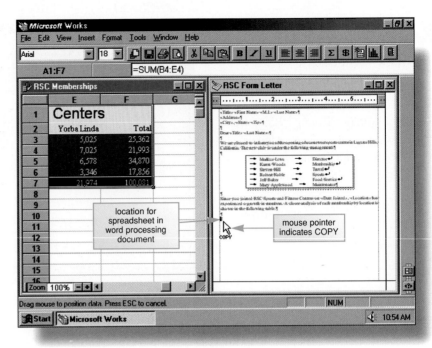

FIGURE 10-61

6 **Point to the Yes button in the Microsoft Works dialog box that asks if you want to link the copied data to the original data.**

Works displays the Microsoft Works dialog box asking if you want to link the copied data to the original data (Figure 10-62). If you click the Yes button, the spreadsheet will be linked with the word processing document. If you click No, the spreadsheet becomes an embedded object in the word processing document.

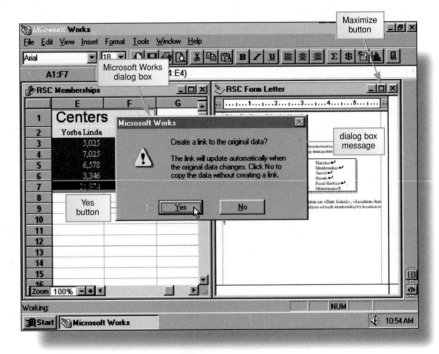

FIGURE 10-62

7 **Click the Yes button. Click the Maximize button in the word processing document window. Click the Center Align button on the toolbar.**

Works copies the highlighted range of the spreadsheet into the form letter and centers it between the margins (Figure 10-63). The spreadsheet in the form letter is linked to the RSC Memberships spreadsheet.

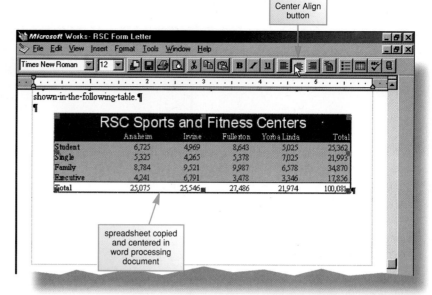

Center Align button

spreadsheet copied and centered in word processing document

FIGURE 10-63

The spreadsheet is now linked to the word processing document. When a change is made to the original spreadsheet, Works automatically updates the spreadsheet in the word processing document.

Continuing the Letter

After inserting the spreadsheet in the letter and positioning the insertion point to the right of the spreadsheet, perform the following steps to continue entering the letter (see Figure 10-64).

Steps **To Enter the Letter**

1 **Click to the right of the spreadsheet. Press the ENTER key one time. Click the Left Align button on the toolbar. Press the ENTER key one time. Type the next paragraph and then press the ENTER key.**

The typed paragraph displays (Figure 10-64). The Footer area displays at the bottom of the page in page layout view only. Any text typed in the Footer area will print at the bottom of every page.

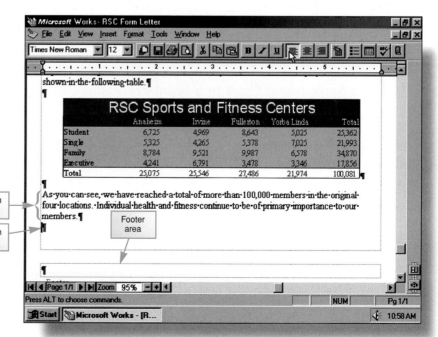

paragraph typed

insertion point

Footer area

FIGURE 10-64

2 Press the ENTER key one time. Type the next paragraph and then press the ENTER key two times.

When you press the ENTER key, Works advances to the top of the second page and places the entire paragraph on the second page (Figure 10-65). The Header area displays at the top of the second page. Page 2/2 displays to the left of the Zoom box at the bottom of the screen. The insertion point is properly positioned for the chart.

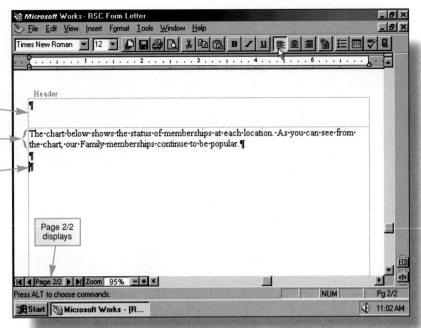

FIGURE 10-65

Adding a Spreadsheet Chart to the Letter

In Works, a chart created from a spreadsheet can be inserted into a word processing document. In the form letter for this project, the 3-D Bar chart displays the four types of memberships by location.

When you insert a chart in the word processing document, the chart remains linked to the spreadsheet. If you change a value in the spreadsheet, then the change also will be reflected in the chart inserted in the word processing document. You should link information in a document when you want to be sure that all associated documents have the latest version of the linked information. Perform the following steps to link this chart to the form letter using the **Chart command** on the Insert menu.

Steps **To Link a Spreadsheet Chart to a Word Processing Document**

1 Click the Center Align button on the toolbar to center the insertion point.

Works centers the insertion point (Figure 10-66).

FIGURE 10-66

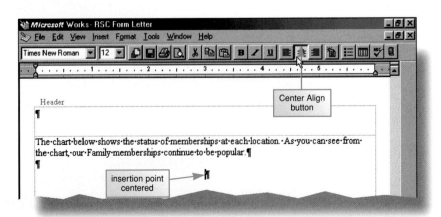

2 **Click Insert on the menu bar and then point to Chart.**

The Insert menu displays and the mouse pointer points to Chart (Figure 10-67).

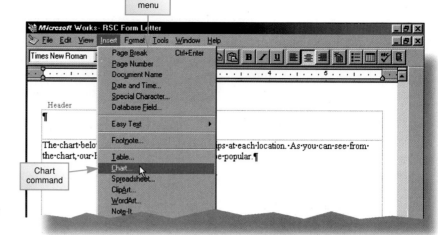

FIGURE 10-67

3 **Click Chart. When the Insert Chart dialog box displays, click Use an existing chart, if necessary, to select it. Click RSC Memberships.wks in the Select a spreadsheet list box and then click Chart1 in the Select a chart list box. Point to the OK button.**

The Insert Chart dialog box displays (Figure 10-68). The Select a spreadsheet list box displays the name of the only open spreadsheet file, the highlighted RSC Memberships.wks. Chart1 is selected in the Select a chart list box. The mouse pointer points to the OK button.

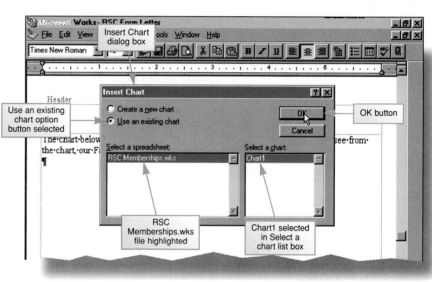

FIGURE 10-68

4 **Click the OK button.**

Works inserts the chart at the insertion point (Figure 10-69). Notice the chart width extends the entire margin width of the document.

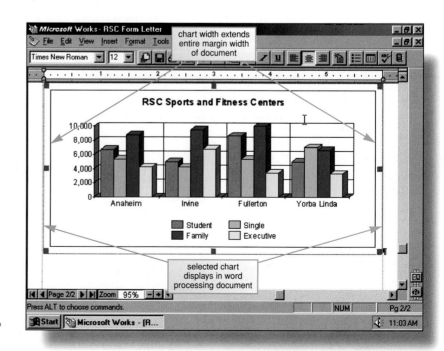

FIGURE 10-69

Because the spreadsheet chart is linked through the use of the Chart command, any change you make to the spreadsheet that changes the chart will cause Works to automatically update the chart in the word processing document. This process is illustrated later in the project.

A spreadsheet document must be named and saved before you can link information contained in it.

Notice that when you insert the chart in the word processing document, the spreadsheet document must be open. If you close all documents and want to print the letter at a later time, however, the spreadsheet file does not need to be open. When you open the word processing document, Works will inform you that linked information is contained within the document and ask if you want to update the linked information. If you do, click the Yes button in the dialog box; otherwise, click the No button.

Changing the Size of a Chart in a Word Processing Document

When inserting a chart into a document, the chart retains its size unless it is higher or wider than the margins. If the chart is too large, Works scales it to fit within the margins. At times it may be desirable to reduce or enlarge the size of the chart you have placed in a word processing document. To change the size of the chart in the form letter, complete the following steps.

Steps To Change the Size of a Chart

1 **If the chart is not selected, click inside the chart to select it. Click Format on the menu bar and then point to Picture.**

*Works selects the chart by placing a border around the chart with **handles** you can drag to resize the chart (Figure 10-70). The Format menu displays and the mouse pointer points to the Picture command.*

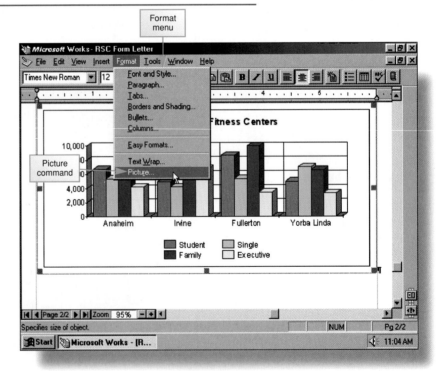

FIGURE 10-70

2 **Click Picture. When the Format Picture dialog box displays, type** `5.5"` **in the Width text box in the Size box and then type** `3.25"` **in the Height box. Point to the OK button.**

The Width box displays 5.5" and the Height box displays 3.25" in the Format Picture dialog box (Figure 10-71). This indicates the chart width is to be decreased approximately ½-inch from the original size of 6.06 inches and the height is to be increased approximately ¼-inch over the original size of 2.98 inches. The original size of the chart displays in the Original size box.

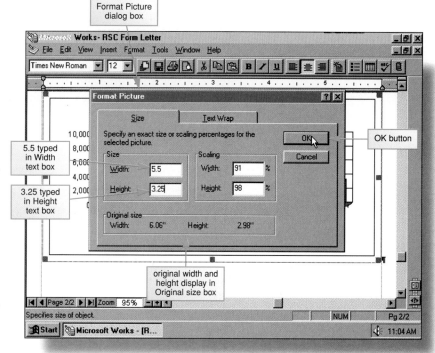

FIGURE 10-71

3 **Click the OK button. Click the paragraph mark to the right of the chart so the chart is no longer selected.**

Works increases the height and reduces the width of the chart in the letter (Figure 10-72). The insertion point displays to the right of the chart.

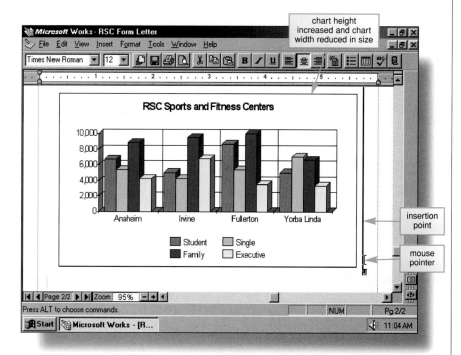

FIGURE 10-72

▶ *Other***Ways**

1. Drag handles that display when the chart is selected

Completing the Letter

After inserting the chart in the letter, changing its size, and positioning the insertion point at the right of the chart, continue typing the remaining portion of the letter. To do this, perform the steps on the next page (see Figure 10-73).

TO COMPLETE THE LETTER

Step 1: Press the ENTER key one time.
Step 2: Click the Left Align button on the toolbar.
Step 3: Press the ENTER key one time.
Step 4: Type the next paragraph, the complimentary closing, and the name and title of the person sending the letter.

The remaining portion of the letter is illustrated in Figure 10-73.

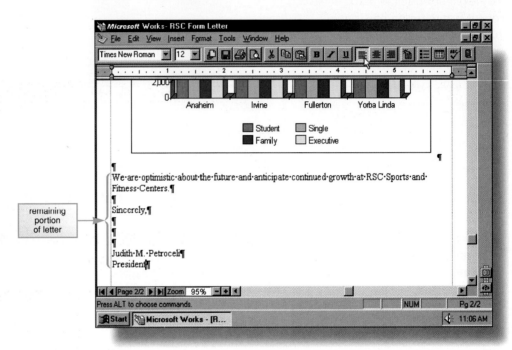

remaining portion of letter

FIGURE 10-73

More *About*
Page Layout View

Use page layout view to view headers and footers. This view presents all aspects of your document on the screen as they will appear when printed. Headers and footers appear at the top and bottom of every page.

Adding a Header in Page Layout View

When writing a two-page form letter, the second page of the letter should contain a header that identifies the page number, title, first name, middle initial, and last name of the person to whom the letter is addressed and the current date. You should enter each of these items in the Header area of the first page of the form letter. Each item should be on a separate line as shown in Figure 10-1 on page W 10.5 and display in 10-point font size. To create a header in page layout view, perform the following steps.

Steps **To Add a Header in Page Layout View**

1 **Press the CTRL+HOME keys. Position the insertion point to the left of the paragraph mark in the Header area. Click the Font Size box arrow and click 10. Type** Page **and then press the SPACEBAR. Click Insert on the menu bar and then click Page Number.**

When you press the CTRL+HOME keys, Works moves the insertion point to the beginning of the document. The text you typed, Page, displays in the first line in the Header area in 10-point font size (Figure 10-74). The placeholder, *page*, instructs Works to print the page number in the header when the document is printed.

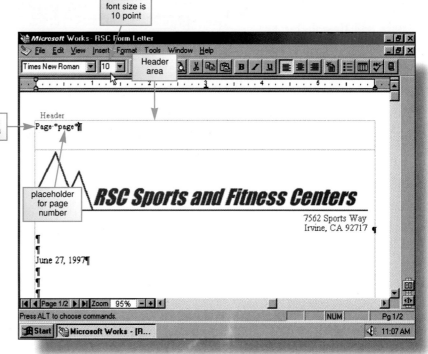

FIGURE 10-74

2 **Press the ENTER key. Click Insert on the menu bar and then click Database Field. When the Insert Field dialog box displays, highlight Title in the Select a field list box and then click the Insert button. Click the Insert button to insert each of the three database fields, First Name, M.I., and Last Name as placeholders in the Header area. Click the Close button.**

When you press the ENTER key, Works moves the insertion point to the first position in the second line of the Header area. The database placeholders for <<Title>>, <<first name>>, <<M.I.>>, and <<last name>> display in the second line of the Header area (Figure 10-75). When the letter is printed, Works will replace the placeholders with the actual database field names.

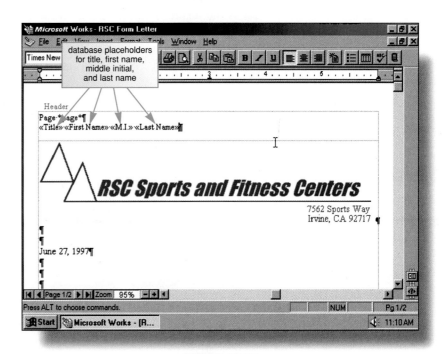

FIGURE 10-75

3 Press the ENTER key. Click Insert on the menu bar and then click **Date and Time**. When the Insert Date and Time dialog box displays, click the long date format. Click the Insert button.

Works inserts the date in the third line of the header (Figure 10-76). The actual date on your screen may be different.

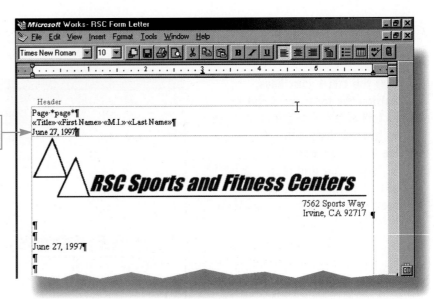

FIGURE 10-76

Removing a Header from the First Page

The header is to print on the second page of the form letter only. By default Works prints the header text at the top of each page in a document. You can suppress the header from printing on the first page but still include the first page in the overall page numbering by clicking No header on first page in the Page Setup dialog box. To remove a header from the first page, perform the following steps.

Steps **To Remove a Header from the First Page**

1 Click File on the menu bar and then point to Page Setup.

Works displays the File menu and the mouse pointer points to Page Setup (Figure 10-77).

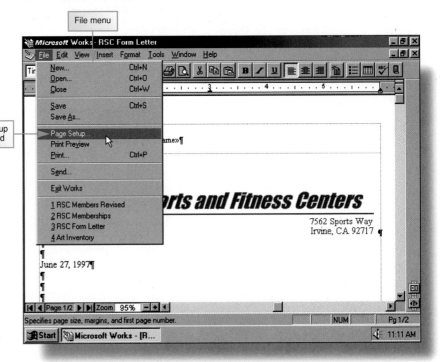

FIGURE 10-77

2 **Click Page Setup. When the Page Setup dialog box displays, click the Other Options tab. When the Other Options sheet displays, click No header on first page. Point to the OK button.**

Works displays the Page Setup dialog box (Figure 10-78). The No header on first page check box is selected on the Other Options sheet. The Starting page number text box displays the number 1. This instructs Works to start numbering the page number inserted in the Header area with the number 1. Because No header on first page is selected, the first page number that will print will be the number 2 on the second page.

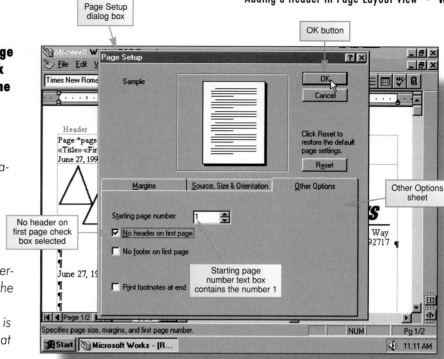

FIGURE 10-78

3 **Click the OK button.**

Works removes the text from the Header area on Page 1 of the document (Figure 10-79). The insertion point displays to the left of the letterhead on the first line of the document. Notice Works also removed the paragraph mark in the Header area. Compare Figure 10-79 to Figure 10-74 on page W 10.47 in which the paragraph mark remained. When you specify no header on the first page, you cannot type text in the Header area on the first page of the document.

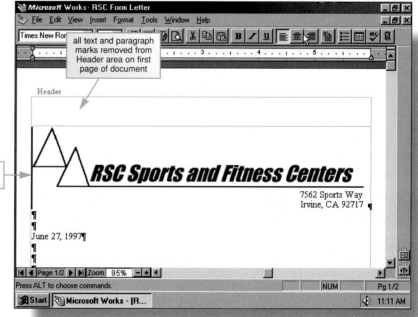

FIGURE 10-79

4 Click the move to next page button located to the right of the page number at the bottom of the screen. Press the **ENTER** key three times to insert three blank lines between the last line in the header and the first line in the document.

The header displays in the Header area on the second page of the document (Figure 10-80). Three blank lines display between the header text and the first line in the document.

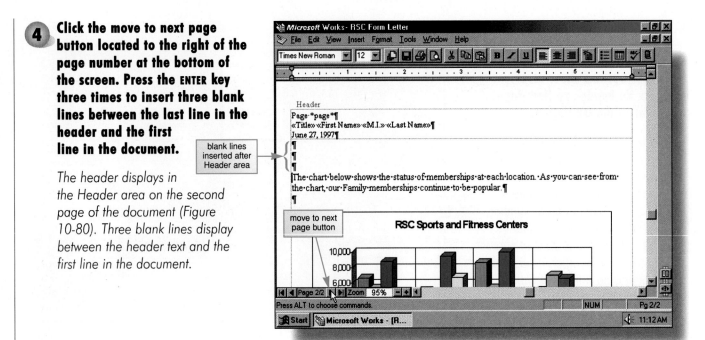

FIGURE 10-80

Checking the Spelling of a Letter

After you have completed the letter, you should check the letter for spelling errors. To check the spelling, perform the following steps.

TO CHECK THE FORM LETTER FOR SPELLING ERRORS

Step 1: Press the CTRL+HOME keys to move the insertion point to the beginning of the form letter.
Step 2: Click the Spelling Checker button on the toolbar.
Step 3: Correct any spelling errors in the form letter.

You have completed creating the form letter. Click the Save button on the toolbar to save the letter.

Selecting Individuals to Receive the Form Letter

After creating the form letter and saving the letter on a floppy disk, the next step is to print the letter. In this project, you are to send form letters to only those members having a family type membership. This is indicated by Family in the Type field in the database (see Figure 10-3 on page W 10.7).

To identify the records to be used for the printed form letter, you must filter the database. To filter the database for all members having a family type membership, perform the following steps.

To Filter a Database

1 **Click Tools on the menu bar and point to Form Letters.**

Works displays the Tools menu and the mouse pointer points to Form Letters (Figure 10-81).

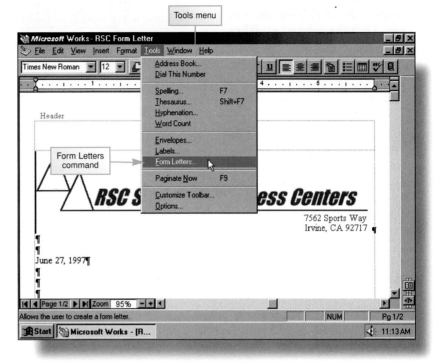

FIGURE 10-81

2 **Click Form Letters. When the Form Letters: RSC Form Letter dialog box displays, click the database tab, if necessary, and ensure RSC Members Revised.wdb displays highlighted in the Choose a database list box. Click the Recipients tab. When the Recipients sheet displays, click Filtered records in the database. Point to the Change Filter button.**

Works displays the Form Letters: RSC Form Letter dialog box (Figure 10-82). The Filtered records in the database option button is selected. (No Filters) displays in the Current Filter list box. This indicates no filters exist for the database. The mouse pointer points to the Change Filter button.

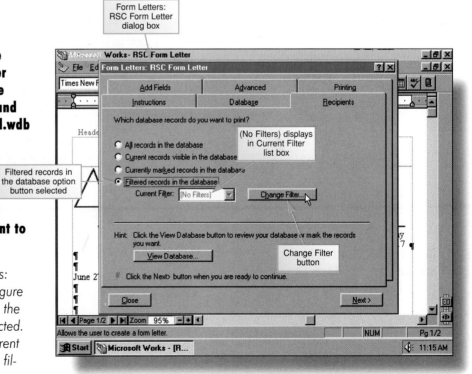

FIGURE 10-82

3 Click the Change Filter button. In the Filter Name dialog box type Family in the Filter name text box. Click the OK button. When the Filter dialog box displays, click the Field name box arrow. Scroll the list to view Type and then click Type. Ensure the Comparison list box displays the comparison words, is equal to. Press the TAB key twice and then type Family in the Compare To text box. Point to the OK button.

The Filter dialog box displays and the filter name you typed in the Filter Name dialog box displays in the Filter name list box (Figure 10-83). The Field name list box displays Type, the Comparison list box displays the words, is equal to, and the Compare To text box displays Family. These criteria instruct Works to filter records whose Type field is equal to Family. The mouse pointer points to the OK button.

4 Click the OK button. When the Form Letters: RSC Form Letter dialog box displays, point to the Close button.

Works displays the Form Letters: RSC Form Letter dialog box (Figure 10-84). Family displays in the Current Filter list box and the mouse pointer points to the Close button.

5 Click the Close button in the Form Letters: RSC Form Letter dialog box.

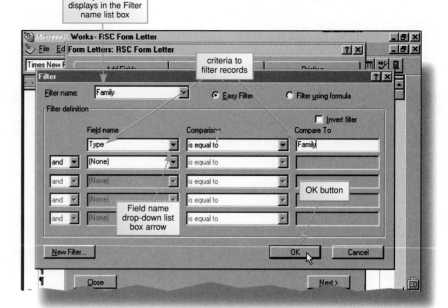

FIGURE 10-83

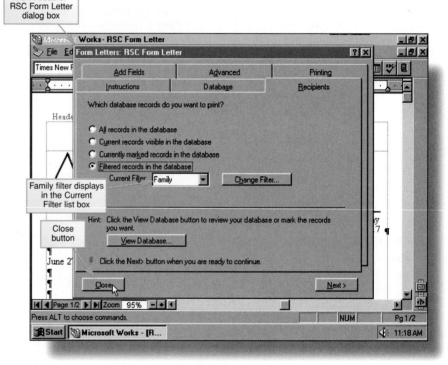

FIGURE 10-84

Works closes the Form Letters: RSC Form Letter dialog box and displays the form letter. The records you are to use in the form letter are now selected from the database.

Printing the Form Letters

Printing the form letters using database fields in the records found by the filter is the next step in this project. The following procedure illustrates printing form letters.

Steps To Print Form Letters

1 Click File on the menu bar and then point to Print (Figure 10-85).

File menu

Print command

FIGURE 10-85

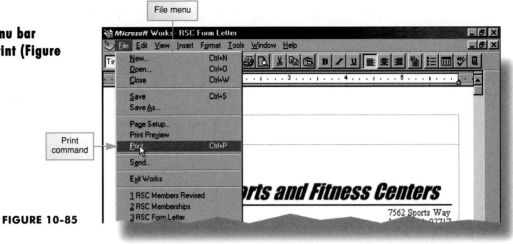

2 Click Print. When the Print dialog box displays, ensure Main Document is selected in the What to Print box and the Print Merge check box below the Copies box is selected. Point to the OK button.

The Print dialog box displays (Figure 10-86). The Main Document option button and the Print Merge check box are selected. These options instruct Works to print the form letters and replace each database placeholder with the actual data from the filtered records in the database. The mouse pointer points to the OK button.

Print dialog box

Print Merge check box selected

Main Document option button selected

OK button

FIGURE 10-86

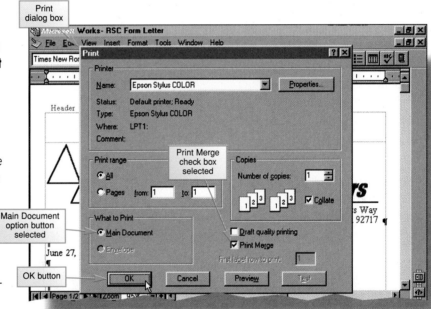

3 Click the OK button. When the message in the Microsoft Works dialog box displays asking if you want to print all records from the filter Family, point to the OK button.

Works displays the Microsoft Works dialog box asking whether to Print all records from filter Family (Figure 10-87).

Microsoft Works dialog box

OK button

FIGURE 10-87

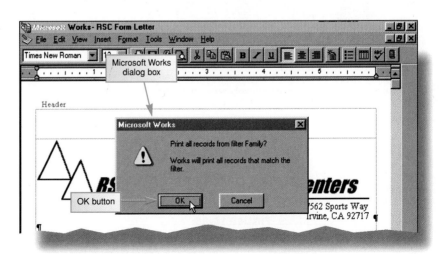

4 Click the OK button.

Works momentarily displays the Printing dialog box and then prints the form letters using fields from the database records. A total of six letters are printed because six database records contain the word Family in the Type field. The first letter is shown in Figure 10-88.

RSC Sports and Fitness Centers

7562 Sports Way
Irvine, CA 92717

June 27, 1997

Dr. Albert G. Sandler
26 Irning
Yuma, AZ 85364

Dear Dr. Sandler:

We are pleased to inform you of the opening of our newest sports center in Laguna Hills, California. The new club is under the following management:

Markus Lews	Director
Karen Woods	Membership
Steven Hill	Travel
Robert Noble	Sports
Jeff Baker	Food Service
Mary Applewood	Maintenance

Since you joined RSC Sports and Fitness Centers on 5/12/96, Irvine has experienced a growth in members. A closer analysis of each membership by location is shown in the following table.

RSC Sports and Fitness Centers

	Anaheim	Irvine	Fullerton	Yorba Linda	Total
Student	6,725	4,969	8,643	5,025	25,362
Single	5,325	4,265	5,378	7,025	21,993
Family	8,784	9,521	9,987	6,578	34,870
Executive	4,241	6,791	3,478	3,346	17,856
Total	25,075	25,546	27,486	21,974	100,081

As you can see, we have reached a total of more than 100,000 members in the original four locations. Individual health and fitness continue to be of primary importance to our

Page 2
Dr. Albert G. Sandler
June 27, 1997

The chart below shows the status of memberships at each location. As you can see from the chart, our Family memberships continue to be popular.

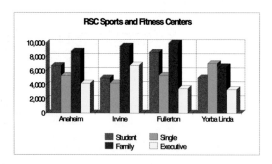

We are optimistic about the future and anticipate continued growth at RSC Sports and Fitness Centers.

Sincerely,

Judith M. Petroceli
President

FIGURE 10-88

The capability of inserting a chart and spreadsheet into a letter, using fields in a database in a letter, and sending form letters to individuals in a database based on certain criteria illustrates the power of Microsoft Works as an integrated software package.

Creating and Printing Envelopes

After you print the form letters, the final step is to create and print envelopes. To print envelopes, your printer must have the capability of printing directly onto envelopes. If you are unable to print envelopes on your printer, you can print names and addresses on mailing labels and then attach each label to an envelope or package. This project illustrates creating and printing envelopes.

To create envelopes, you will use the same information that is in the inside address of the letters; that is, the title, first name, middle initial, last name, address, city, state, and zip. Prior to creating the envelopes, however, you must know the type and size of the envelope you are using. Envelopes come in a variety of sizes. Works provides the dimensions of sixteen frequently used envelopes.

To create the envelopes, perform the following steps.

> **More** *About*
> **Creating and**
> **Printing Envelopes**
>
> A word processor document can include instructions for printing envelopes or labels, but not both. If you choose to create envelopes in a Word Processing document, you cannot use that same document for labels.

Steps **To Create Envelopes**

1 **Click Tools on the menu bar and then point to Envelopes.**

The Tools menu displays and the mouse pointer points to Envelopes (Figure 10-89).

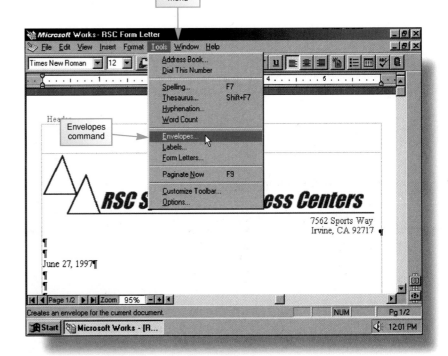

FIGURE 10-89

2 Click Envelopes. When the Envelopes: RSC Form Letter dialog box displays, read the numbered instructions for creating envelopes on the Instructions sheet. Point to the Envelope Size tab.

Works displays the Envelopes: RSC Form Letter dialog box (Figure 10-90). The Instructions sheet displays and the mouse pointer points to the Envelope Size tab. The Envelopes: RSC Form Letter dialog box contains eight tabbed sheets. The Instructions sheet lists the steps you follow to create envelopes. You can click the Next button to step through the process or click the tab of a specific task. As you create the envelopes, Works checks off each step in the Instructions sheet. The Instruction number 2 displays a check mark to the left of the instruction. The check mark displays because the RSC Members Revised.wdb database was selected in Figure 10-30 on page W 10.23.

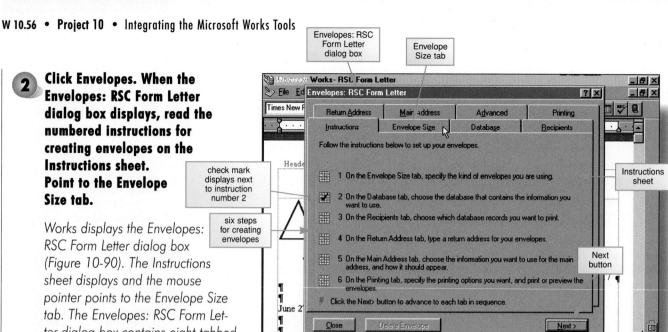

FIGURE 10-90

3 Click the Envelope Size tab. When the Envelope Size sheet displays, ensure Size 10 (4 1/8″ x 9 ½″) is selected in the Choose an envelope size list box. Point to the Database tab.

Works displays the Envelope Size sheet (Figure 10-91). The desired envelope size is highlighted in the Choose an envelope size list box and the mouse pointer points to the Database tab. You can click the Custom button to specify dimensions for envelopes that are not listed in the Choose an envelope size list box.

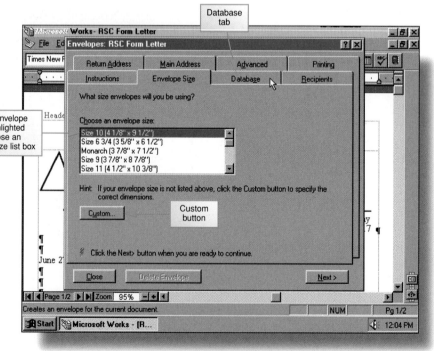

FIGURE 10-91

4 Click the Database tab. When the Database sheet displays, ensure RSC Members Revised.wdb is highlighted in the Choose a database list box. (If the RSC Members Revised.wdb filename does not display in the Choose a database list box, click the Open a database not listed here button (see Figure 10-30 on page W 10.23) to open the database file on drive A. Point to the Recipients tab.

Works displays the Database sheet (Figure 10-92). The desired database filename displays in the Choose a database list box because this database file was selected as the file to use in creating the form letters in Figure 10-30 on page W 10.23. The mouse pointer points to the Recipients tab.

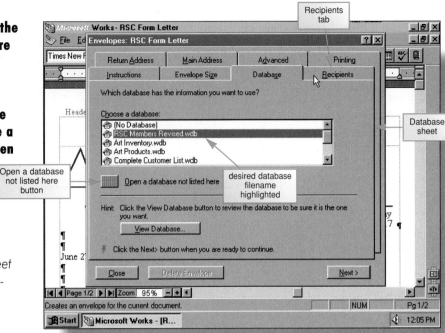

FIGURE 10-92

5 Click the Recipients tab. When the Recipients sheet displays, click Filtered records in the database. Ensure Family displays in the Current Filter box. Point to the Return Address tab.

Works displays the Recipients sheet (Figure 10-93). The Filtered records in the database option button is selected and Family displays in the Current Filter box. These selections instruct Works to print envelopes for records from the existing Family filter. The Family filter, created in Figure 10-84 on page W 10.52 filters records whose Type field contains the text, Family. The mouse pointer points to the Return Address tab.

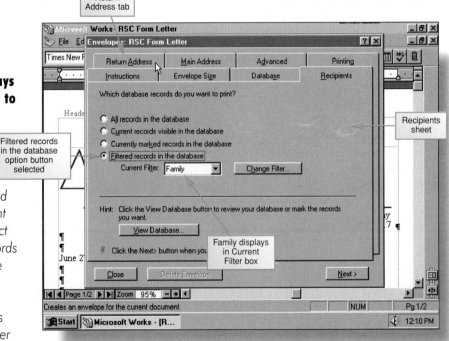

FIGURE 10-93

6 **Click the Return Address tab. When the Return Address sheet displays, type** RSC Sports and Fitness Centers **in the Return address list box. Press the ENTER key. Type** 7562 Sports Way **and press the ENTER key. Type** Irvine, CA 92717 **and then, point to the Main Address tab.**

Works displays the Return Address sheet (Figure 10-94). The return address that will print in the upper left corner of each envelope displays in the Return address text box. The mouse pointer points to the Main Address tab.

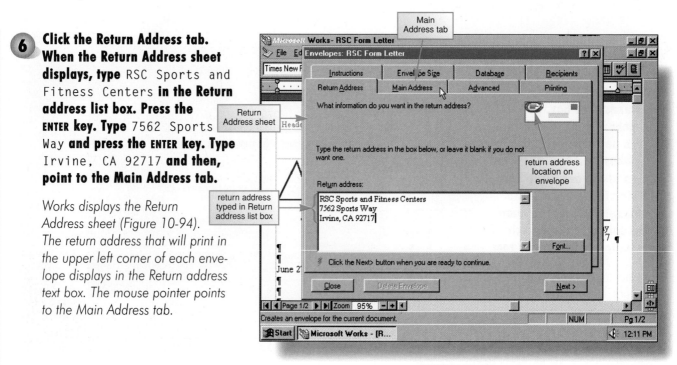

FIGURE 10-94

7 **Click the Main Address tab. When the Main Address sheet displays, highlight Title in the Choose a field list box and then point to the Add Field button.**

Works displays the Main Address sheet (Figure 10-95). The database field names from the RSC Members Revised database file display in the Choose a field list box. The Title field name is highlighted and the mouse pointer points to the Add Field button. Clicking the New Line button moves the insertion point to the next line in the Main address box. Clicking the Clear All button removes all database field name placeholders from the Main address box. The main address will print in the center of each envelope.

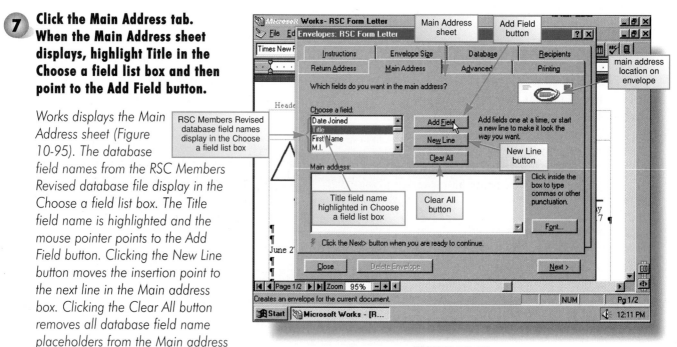

FIGURE 10-95

8 Click the Add Field button. The highlight moves down and the First Name field name is highlighted. Click the Add Field button. Click the Add Field button to insert the M.I. field name. Click the Add Field button to insert the Last Name field name. Press the ENTER key or click the New Line button to move the insertion point to the beginning of the second line. Insert the remaining fields (Address, City, State, and Zip) using the techniques just described. Type a comma (,) after the City placeholder is entered. End each line by pressing the ENTER key or pressing the New Line button. Point to the Printing tab.

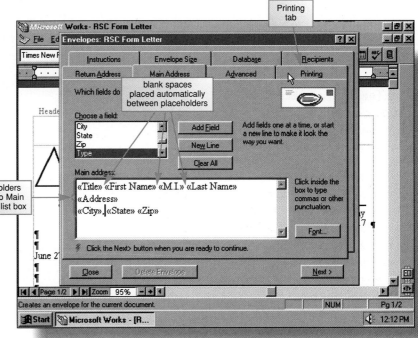

FIGURE 10-96

Works displays the placeholders in the Main address list box (Figure 10-96). You may type any text, spaces, or punctuation marks before or after the placeholders. The mouse pointer points to the Printing tab.

9 Click the Printing tab. When the Printing sheet displays, point to the Preview button.

Works displays the Printing sheet (Figure 10-97). The mouse pointer points to the Preview button.

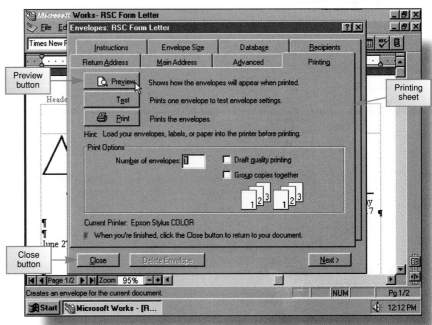

FIGURE 10-97

10 Click the Preview button. When the Microsoft Works dialog box displays a message asking if you wish to preview all records from the Family filter, click the OK button. When the preview window displays, point to the Cancel button.

Works displays the Microsoft Works dialog box asking if you wish to preview all records from the Family filter. When you click the OK button in the Microsoft Works dialog box, the first envelope to print displays in the print preview window (Figure 10-98). The return address displays in the upper left corner of the envelope and the main address displays in the center of the envelope. The mouse pointer points to the Cancel button.

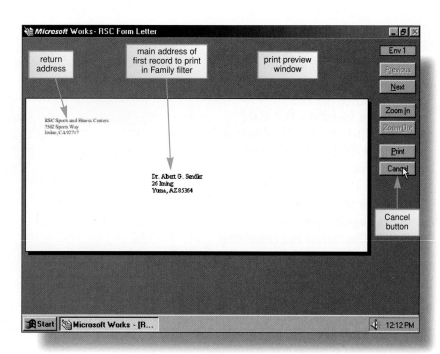

FIGURE 10-98

11 Click the Cancel button in the print preview window to return to the Envelopes: RSC Form Letter dialog box. Click the Close button in the Envelopes: RSC Form Letter dialog box to return to the document in page layout view.

Works displays the word processing document in page layout view and inserts the placeholders for the envelope at the beginning of the document (Figure 10-99). Works adds a manual page break to separate the envelope from the rest of the document. Works labels the beginning of the document as Envelope above the return address.

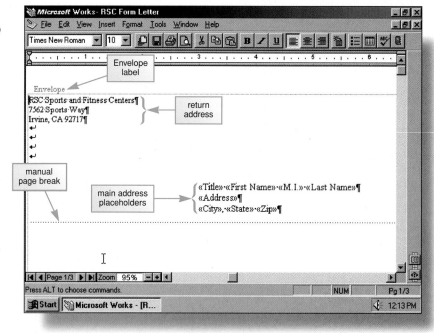

FIGURE 10-99

More *About*
Printing Envelopes

To print a test envelope, on the File menu, click Print. When the Print dialog box displays, ensure the Envelope option button is selected. Remove the check mark in the Print Merge check box. Click the OK button. Works prints the envelope with the placeholders instead of the merged database information.

Printing the Envelopes

After creating the envelopes, the next step is to print the envelopes. Works can print envelopes using your printer's manual feed or envelope bin, or using continuous form-feed envelopes. The method to print envelopes is presented in the following steps.

Steps **To Print Envelopes**

1 **Insert the envelopes in the printer. Click File on the menu bar and then click Print. When the Print dialog box displays, ensure Envelope is selected in the What to Print box. Point to the OK button.**

Works displays the Print dialog box (Figure 10-100). The Envelope option button is selected in the What to Print box. This option instructs Works to print the envelopes. The Main Document option instructs Works to print the form letters. The Print Merge check box is selected. This option instructs Works to replace the database placeholders with the contents from the database. The mouse pointer points to the OK button.

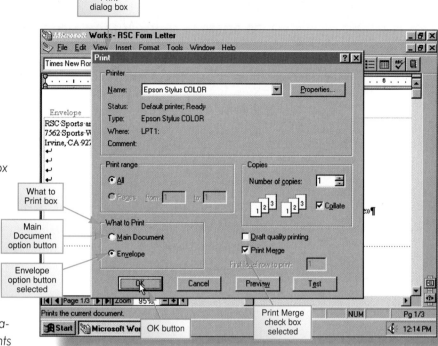

FIGURE 10-100

2 **Click the OK button. When the Microsoft Works dialog box displays confirming that you wish to print all records from the Family filter, click the OK button.**

Works displays the Microsoft Works dialog box confirming that you wish to print all records from the Family filter. When you click the OK button in the Microsoft Works dialog box, the envelopes print (Figure 10-101, which illustrates three of the six envelopes).

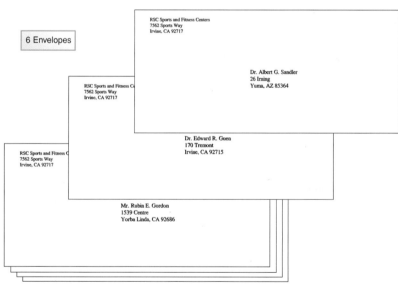

FIGURE 10-101

O*ther***Ways**

1. On Tools menu click Form Letters, click Printing tab, click Print button, click Close button

When you save the file, the format of the envelope also is saved. To delete an envelope from a word processing document, perform the following steps.

TO DELETE AN ENVELOPE FROM A WORD PROCESSING DOCUMENT

Step 1: Open the word processing document that contains the envelope.
Step 2: Click Tools on the menu bar and then click Envelopes.
Step 3: Click the Delete Envelope button in the Envelopes dialog box.
Step 4: Click the OK button in the Microsoft Works dialog box.

Works will remove the envelope from the word processing document.

Printing Mailing Labels

In addition to printing envelopes, you can print mailing labels. You can print names and addresses on mailing labels and then attach each label to an envelope or package. To do so, click Tools on the menu bar and then click Labels. You must know the type and size of the mailing labels you are using. Mailing labels are commonly placed one, two, or three across a page and come in a variety of sizes. You add information for the address in the same way as you do on the envelopes.

To print a mailing label, click File on the menu bar and then click Print. Click Mailing Labels in the What to Print box in the Print dialog box. Click the OK button in the Print dialog box.

Exiting Works

You have completed the form letter and the envelopes. You can exit Works as explained in previous examples. Be sure to save the latest version of the form letter.

Changing Entries in the Spreadsheet

At some later time you may want to send an updated letter to other members of RSC Sports and Fitness Centers notifying them of new developments. As previously discussed, the spreadsheet and chart are linked to the word processing document, meaning that any change in the original spreadsheet will cause the spreadsheet and chart in the letter to be updated. To be sure these changes are occurring correctly, perform the following steps.

Steps **To Change Entries in the Spreadsheet**

1 **If you have exited Works, start Works. Then open the RSC Memberships spreadsheet file. Open the RSC Form Letter file and click the Yes button in the Microsoft Works dialog box that asks if you want to update the links. Click Window on the menu bar and then click Tile. View the spreadsheet in both the RSC Form Letter file and the RSC Memberships by scrolling each document.**

The spreadsheet and chart display in their respective tiled windows (Figure 10-102).

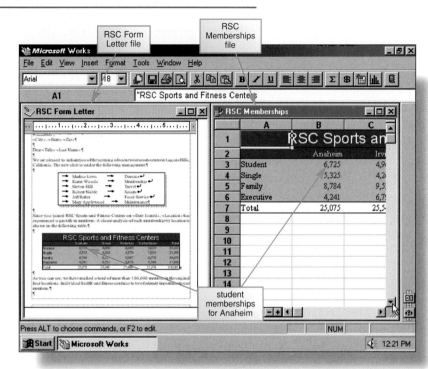

FIGURE 10-102

2 **Highlight cell B3 in the RSC Memberships window and enter** 6,000 **to change the student memberships for Anaheim.**

When you enter the new student membership for Anaheim in the RSC Memberships spreadsheet, the student membership for Anaheim in the RSC Form Letter spreadsheet is updated (Figure 10-103).

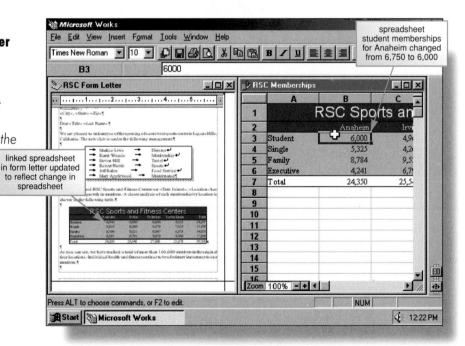

FIGURE 10-103

3 **To determine if the chart in the letter has been updated, click anywhere in the word processing window and scroll down in the RSC Form Letter window to display the chart.**

The bar illustrating the student memberships for Anaheim is reduced to 6,000 indicating the chart also has been updated (Figure 10-104).

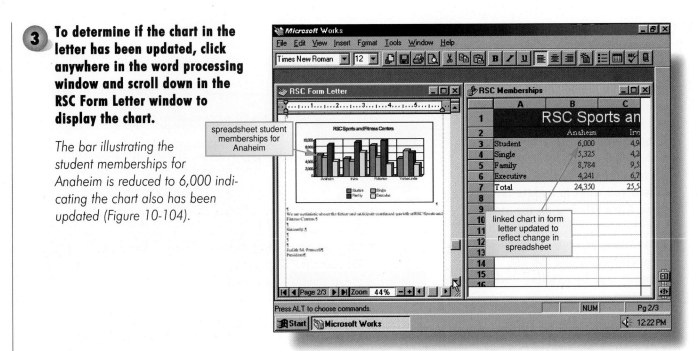

FIGURE 10-104

At this time, new updated form letters can be sent out or the updated spreadsheet saved for future use.

The capability of utilizing the integrated features of Microsoft Works provides great flexibility and power to users of personal computers.

Project Summary

In Project 10, you learned to use many of the integrated features of Microsoft Works. This project illustrated the use of these Works integrated features using names and addresses from a database in a form letter, inserting a chart and spreadsheet in a form letter, sending the form letters to selected individuals, and preparing and printing envelopes.

You are now able to use the drawing capabilities of Microsoft Draw to embed a drawn object in a word processing document. You learned to create tables in a document and place an outline border with a shadow around a table.

What You Should Know

Having completed this project, you should be able to perform the following tasks:

▶ Add a Header in Page Layout View *(W 10.47)*

▶ Change Entries in a Linked Spreadsheet *(W 10.63)*

▶ Change the Size of a Chart *(W 10.44)*

▶ Check the Form Letter for Spelling Errors *(W 10.50)*

▶ Complete the Letter *(W 10.46)*

▶ Create a Logo Using Microsoft Draw *(W 10.12)*

▶ Create an Outline Border with a Shadow *(W 10.32)*

▶ Create Envelopes *(W 10.55)*

▶ Delete an Envelope from a Word Processing Document *(W 10.62)*

▶ Edit a Microsoft Draw Object *(W 10.19)*

▶ Enter Text and Draw a Line in the Drawing Window *(W 10.16)*

▶ Enter Text in a Table *(W 10.31)*

▶ Enter the Letter Text *(W 10.26, W 10.41)*

▶ Filter a Database *(W 10.51)*

▶ Insert Additional Database Placeholders in a Paragraph *(W 10.35)*

▶ Insert Database Placeholders in a Document *(W 10.22)*

▶ Insert the Date in the Form Letter *(W 10.20)*

▶ Link a Spreadsheet Chart to a Word Processing Document *(W 10.42)*

▶ Link a Spreadsheet File to a Word Processing Document *(W 10.38)*

▶ Open the Spreadsheet File *(W 10.37)*

▶ Print Envelopes *(W 10.61)*

▶ Print Form Letters *(W 10.53)*

▶ Remove a Header from the First Page *(W 10.48)*

▶ Save a Document *(W 10.20)*

▶ Set Left and Right Margins for the Table *(W 10.29)*

▶ Set Tab Stops *(W 10.30)*

▶ Start Microsoft Draw *(W 10.10)*

▶ Start the Works Word Processor *(W 10.9)*

A+ Test Your Knowledge

1 True/False

Instructions: Circle T if the statement is true or F if the statement is false.

T F 1. To start Microsoft Draw, click MS Draw on the Insert menu in the Word Processor window.

T F 2. In Microsoft Draw, the MS Draw Toolbox contains the selection of colors you can use.

T F 3. The Show Guides command in Microsoft Draw displays a series of ten horizontal and ten vertical lines on the screen to assist in precisely positioning images.

T F 4. A database placeholder consists of a field name from a database with chevrons on each side of the field name.

T F 5. To enter a database placeholder in a document, you can type the placeholder with the chevrons on either side.

T F 6. Special characters such as a comma cannot be placed between placeholders.

T F 7. You cannot set special margins for a table.

T F 8. When creating a table that is more than one line long, press the SHIFT+ENTER keys at the end of each line except the last line.

T F 9. To outline a table with a shadow, use the Borders and Shading command on the Format or context-sensitive menu.

T F 10. To prevent a header from printing on the first page of a word processing document, click in the Header area, highlight the text, and press the DELETE key.

2 Multiple Choice

Instructions: Circle the correct response.

1. To start Microsoft Draw, _____.
   a. click the Drawing button on the toolbar
   b. click Drawing on the Insert menu
   c. click Picture on the Insert menu
   d. click Object on the Edit menu

2. Database placeholders in a word processing document are surrounded by _____.
   a. chevrons
   b. quotation marks
   c. brackets
   d. parentheses

3. In Microsoft Draw, click the _____ tool to enter text in the drawing window.
   a. Freeform
   b. Line
   c. Text
   d. Rectangle/Square

4. To return to the word processing document from Microsoft Draw, click _____ on the File menu in the Microsoft Draw window.
   a. Close
   b. Exit
   c. Exit and Return
   d. New

5. When using placeholders in a document, you can type any _____ before or after the placeholders to produce the required output.
   a. text
   b. spaces
   c. punctuation
   d. all of the above

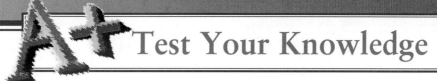

6. You can specify _____ types of tab stops when using the Works Word Processor.
   - a. one
   - b. two
   - c. three
   - d. four

7. To link a spreadsheet to a word processing document, use _____.
   - a. the Paste command on the Edit menu
   - b. drag and drop
   - c. the Insert command on the Edit menu
   - d. the Picture command on the Insert menu

8. To link a spreadsheet chart to a word processing document, use the _____.
   - a. Chart command on the Insert menu
   - b. Database field command on the Insert menu
   - c. drag and drop feature
   - d. Paste command on the Edit menu

9. A spreadsheet file must be _____ before you can link information contained in it.
   - a. named
   - b. opened
   - c. save
   - d. all the above

10. To display two open files on the screen at the same time, _____.
    - a. double-click in the open workspace area
    - b. click in the left margin area
    - c. click Tile on the Window menu
    - d. click Split on the Window menu

3 Fill In

Instructions: In the spaces provided, explain the steps necessary to link a spreadsheet to a word processing document.

1. _____
2. _____
3. _____
4. _____
5. _____

4 Fill In

Instructions: In the spaces provided, explain the steps necessary to link a chart to a word processing document.

1. _____
2. _____
3. _____
4. _____
5. _____

Use Help

1 Reviewing Project Activities

Instructions: Use your computer to perform the following tasks to obtain experience using online Help.
1. Start the Microsoft Works Word Processor tool.
2. Display the Help window to the right of the document window. Click the Index button below the Help window to display the Help Topics: Microsoft Works dialog box.
3. Click the Index tab in the Help Topics: Microsoft Works dialog box.
4. Type envelopes: creating by typing addresses in the 2 Click the Index entry you want list box.
5. Read the numbered procedure on the topic, To address a single envelope, on the Step-by-Step sheet. Print this topic by clicking the Print this topic icon at the bottom of the numbered procedure.
6. Click the Another way icon at the bottom of the Step-by-Step procedure on To address a single envelope. Read and print Another Way To address a single envelope.
7. Click the More Info tab. On the More Info sheet, click To mark records. Read and print To mark records.
8. Click the Close button in the application window to close Works.

2 Expanding on the Basics

Instructions: Use Works online Help to better understand the topics listed below. Print the topic or topics that substantiate your answer. If a Print this topic icon is unavailable, then answer the question on a separate piece of paper.
1. Using the key terms, *form letters: creating*, and the Index sheet in the Help topics: Microsoft Works dialog box, answer the following questions.
    a. Explain how to send form letters to only certain people in the database.
    b. Explain how to add addresses from a second database.
    c. Explain how to move the database placeholders to another location in your letter.
    d. Explain how to delete a placeholder.
2. Click the Close button in the application window to close Works.

Apply Your Knowledge

1 Using Microsoft Draw to Create a Letterhead

Instructions: Start Microsoft Works. Use the Word Processor tool and Microsoft Draw to create the letterhead shown in Figure 10-105. After creating the letterhead, save and print the document. Turn in a copy to your instructor.

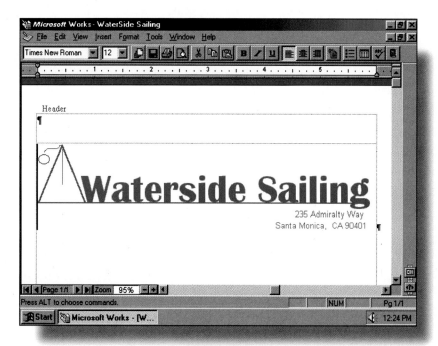

FIGURE 10-105

In the Lab

1 Creating and Printing the Collegiate Testing Center Form Letters and Envelopes and Inserting a Chart in a Word Processing Document

Problem: Collegiate Testing Center is a private educational group that tests students in English, mathematics, and verbal skills. After students are tested, a letter is sent advising them of the results of their tests. Six students recently completed the testing program. A database of the students and their test scores is illustrated in the table on the next page.

(continued)

In the Lab

Creating and Printing the Collegiate Testing Center Form Letters and Envelopes and Inserting a Chart in a Word Processing Document *(continued)*

TEST DATE	FIRST NAME	LAST NAME	ADDRESS	CITY	STATE	ZIP CODE	MATH	ENGLISH	VERBAL	TEST LOCATION
6/23/97	Larry	Dalisay	181 N. Avenida	Brea	CA	92621	701	554	510	Hills College
6/23/97	Ciro	El Guira	56 Murica Aisle	Irvine	CA	92715	450	500	525	Hills College
6/23/97	Molly	Garner	1513 N. Van Ness	Santa Ana	CA	92705	545	554	510	Hills College
6/23/97	Santa	Manzi	35 Chilton	Fullerton	CA	92635	653	700	710	Hills College
6/23/97	Laura	Sainz	2041 S. Sprague	Brea	CA	92621	600	610	620	Hills College
6/23/97	Jack	West	1333 Iris Lane	Irvine	CA	92715	475	425	435	Hills College

The spreadsheet in Figure 10-106 contains student test scores, and the average test scores in English, mathematics, and verbal skills for the six students taking the tests.

After determining the test results, a letter is sent to each individual tested informing him or her of the results of the test. An example of the letter is illustrated in Figure 10-107.

To establish the database, create the spreadsheet, and then send letters to each individual. The Collegiate Testing Center has decided to utilize a personal computer.

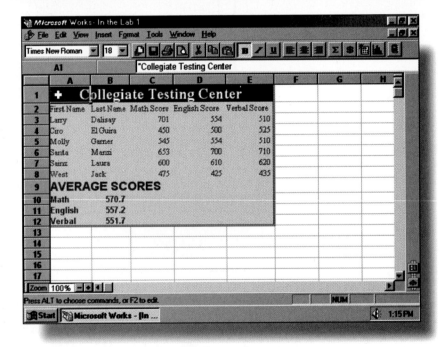

FIGURE 10-106

Instructions: To complete this assignment, perform the following tasks.

1. Create the database of the students in the table above. Save the database on a floppy disk using an appropriate filename.
2. Create a spreadsheet and the associated chart for the average scores from the information in Figure 10-106. Save the spreadsheet on a floppy disk using an appropriate filename.

In the Lab

3. Create and print form letters following the format in Figure 10-107 to be sent to each student taking the test. Insert the student's test scores in the letter from information in the database. The bar chart in the letter is from the chart for the average test scores associated with the spreadsheet. Save the form letter on a floppy disk using an appropriate filename.
4. Print an envelope for each student.

   Turn in printed copies of the letters, spreadsheet, database in list view, and envelopes to your instructor after completing the assignment.

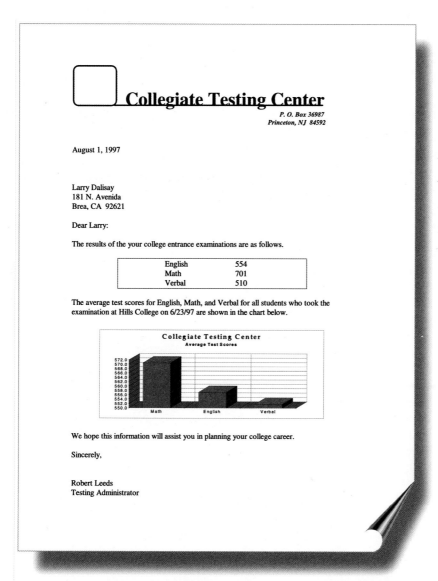

FIGURE 10-107

In the Lab

2 Creating and Printing the Alumni Association Form Letters and Envelopes and Inserting a Chart and Spreadsheet in a Word Processing Document

Problem: The Alumni Association consists of alumni of the college who solicit funds for scholarships. Funds donated may be designated for scholarships in Athletics, Business, Fine Arts, Humanities, or Math/Science. A database of alumni members is illustrated in the table below.

DONATION DATE	TITLE	FIRST NAME	LAST NAME	ADDRESS	CITY	STATE	ZIP CODE	MEMBER TYPE	DONATION AMOUNT
1/12/97	Mr.	Vincent	Johnson	32 Mono Lane	Long Beach	CA	90808	Corporate	$1,500.00
1/13/97	Mrs.	Patricia	Henderson	575 Brookdale St	Cerritos	CA	90701	Corporate	$2,500.00
1/19/97	Mr.	Lyle	Simmons	1707 Kingman	Dana Point	CA	92629	Private	$100.00
1/19/97	Ms.	Anne	Garcia	325 Escanada	Irvine	CA	92754	Corporate	$1,000.00
1/20/97	Ms.	Ealin	Henry	698 Portola Way	Long Beach	CA	90808	Private	$75.00
1/21/97	Dr.	Ledy	Lu	1 Harbor Drive	Dana Point	CA	92629	Private	$250.00
1/26/97	Mrs.	Melissa	White	632 Lanai Lane	Tustin	CA	92670	Corporate	$1,750.00
1/27/97	Mr.	Donald	Riley	45 Winsor Drive	Cerritos	CA	90701	Corporate	$3,500.00
1/28/97	Ms.	Karen	Ward	24 Holiday	Brea	CA	92621	Private	$15.00

At the end of each academic year, the Scholarship chairperson sends a letter to the members of the Alumni Association showing the percentage of funds donated to the various academic areas and the total amount donated to the Scholarship program. A spreadsheet showing the funds donated in each area and the total amount of funds donated is shown in Figure 10-108.

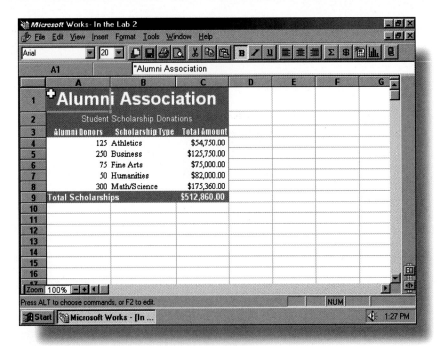

FIGURE 10-108

In the Lab

A letter is sent to only those individuals who are identified in the database as Private in the Member Type field. An example of the letter sent to each alumnus is illustrated in Figure 10-109. You have been directed to create the database, spreadsheet, chart, and letter using a personal computer.

Alumni Association
College by the Sea
1 Island Drive
Santa Monica, CA 92401

June 2, 1997

Mr. Lyle Simmons
1707 Kingman
Dana Point, CA 92629

Dear Mr. Simmons:

The new Alumni Association officers for 1997-1998 are:

Mike Brown	President
Cathy Smith	President-Elect
Karen Rowan	Alumni Services
Paul Harold	Fund-raising
Monica McCabe	Homecoming

We are pleased to announce that donations to the Student Scholarship Fund have increased for the third year. The chart below shows the percentage of funds donated to the various divisions of the college.

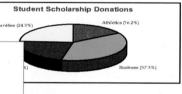

Student Scholarship Donations

Humanities (24.3%) Athletics (16.2%)

Business (57.3%)

...munity made a number of generous gifts to the Business

Page 2
Mr. Lyle Simmons
June 2, 1997

The report below details the donations to our student scholarship program.

Alumni Association
Student Scholarship Donations

125	Athletics	$54,750.00
250	Business	$125,750.00
75	Fine Arts	$75,000.00
50	Humanities	$82,000.00
300	Math/Science	$175,360.00
Total Scholarships		**$512,860.00**

Thank you for your gift of $100.00 on 1/19/97. Our alumni are making a difference!

Sincerely,

Karl Kugan
Scholarship Chairperson

FIGURE 10-109

(continued)

In the Lab

Creating and Printing the Alumni Association Form Letters and Envelopes and Inserting a Chart and Spreadsheet in a Word Processing Document *(continued)*

Instructions Part 1:   To complete this assignment, perform the following tasks.
1. Create the database. Save the database on a floppy disk using an appropriate filename.
2. Create the spreadsheet and chart. Save the spreadsheet on a floppy disk using an appropriate filename.
3. Create and print form letters following the format in Figure 10-109 for each individual in the database identified as Private in the Member Type field. Insert the chart and spreadsheet created in Step 2 above. Save the form letter on a floppy disk using an appropriate filename.
4. Print an envelope for each alumnus.

Instructions Part 2:
1. The Alumni Association just received a new $12,000.00 donation for Fine Arts scholarships. Update the spreadsheet to reflect this addition and print the updated letter and spreadsheet.

Turn in printed copies of the database, the spreadsheets, letters, and envelopes to your instructor.

3 Creating and Printing the Regional Real Estate Association Form Letters and Labels and Inserting a Chart and Spreadsheet in a Word Processing Document

Problem: At the end of each month, the Regional Real Estate Association sends out letters to its broker members listing the total sales in various categories of real estate. A database of the members of the real estate association is illustrated in the table to the right.

TITLE	LAST NAME	FIRST NAME	ADDRESS	CITY	STATE	ZIP	CLASS
Ms.	Page	Mary	17272 Walnut	Fullerton	CA	92633	Sales
Mr.	Rolla	James	1401 Avocado	Brea	CA	92621	Sales
Mr.	Anderson	Roberto	2011 Westcliff	La Habra	CA	90631	Broker
Mrs.	Parsons	Rose	1400 Quail	Fullerton	CA	92633	Sales
Ms.	Canaloni	Loraine	1550 Bayside	Santa Monica	CA	92401	Broker
Ms.	Crenshaw	Risa	11450 Lampson	Brea	CA	92621	Sales
Mr.	Welliver	Jo	9667 Ellis	Cerritos	CA	90701	Broker
Mr.	Revera	Vance	15641 Whiteoak	Cerritos	CA	90701	Sales

In the Lab

A spreadsheet showing real estate sales in each major classification is illustrated in Figure 10-110.

A letter is sent to only those individuals who are identified in the database as a broker in the Class field. An example of the letter sent to each broker is illustrated in Figure 10-111 on the next page. You have been directed to create the database, spreadsheet, chart, and letter using a personal computer.

Instructions Part 1: To complete this assignment, perform the following tasks.

1. Create the database. Save the database on a floppy disk using an appropriate filename.

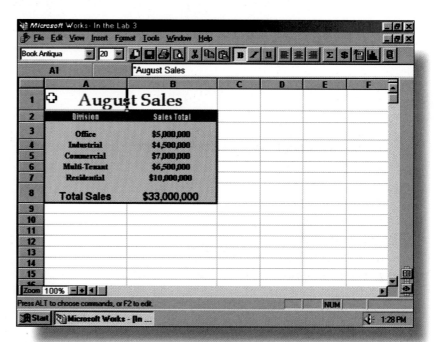

FIGURE 10-110

2. Create the spreadsheet and chart. Save the spreadsheet on a floppy disk using an appropriate filename.
3. Create and print form letters following the format in Figure 10-111 for each individual in the database identified as a broker in the Class field. Insert the chart and spreadsheet created in Step 2 in the letters. Save the form letter on a floppy disk using an appropriate filename.
4. Print an envelope for each member.

Instructions Part 2:
1. An additional $12 million for August sales of office properties should be added to the spreadsheet.
2. Print the updated letter and spreadsheet.
3. Turn in printed copies of the database in list view, the spreadsheet, letters, and the envelopes to your instructor after completing the assignment.

(continued)

In the Lab

Creating and Printing the Regional Real Estate Association Form Letters and Labels and Inserting a Chart and Spreadsheet in a Word Processing Document *(continued)*

Regional Real Estate Association

1150 South Canyon Road
Fullerton, CA 92633

September 1, 1997

Mr. Roberto Anderson
2011 Westcliff
La Harbra, CA 90631

Dear Mr. Anderson:

The following officers for the Regional Real Estate Association have been elected at our last meeting. They are as follows:

President	Daryl Bauman
Vice President	Susan Bayley
Secretary	Van Lupo
Treasurer	Mai Ho
Publications	Lee Howard
Tours	Ben Myers

Sales in all divisions of real estate increased for the first time in a year. The chart below shows the percentage of sales in each division for the month of August

August Sales

Residential (30.3%) Office (15.2%)
Industrial
Multi-Tenant (19.7%) Commercial

As you can see, residential sales have increased as ha
indicate these divisions will continue to grow.

Page 2
Mr. Roberto Anderson
September 1, 1997

A more detailed analysis is contained in the following table.

August Sales

Division	Sales Total
Office	$5,000,000
Industrial	$4,500,000
Commercial	$7,000,000
Multi-Tenant	$6,500,000
Residential	$10,000,000
Total Sales	$33,000,000

We are optimistic that the real estate market will continue to expand.

Sincerely,

Paulette Kissell
Executive Director

FIGURE 10-111

Cases and Places

The difficulty of these case studies varies:

▶ Case studies preceded by a single half moon are the least difficult. You are asked to create the required reports, charts, and form letters based on information already placed in an organized form.
▶▶ Case studies preceded by two half moons are more difficult. You are asked to create the required reports, charts, and form letters. You must organize the information presented to complete the task.
▶▶▶ Case studies preceded by three half moons are the most difficult. You are asked to create the required reports, charts, and form letters. Use conventional resources, such as the library, local businesses, the Internet, and your own experiences beyond the college environment.

1 ▶ Hospital supervisors schedule surgeries in each operating room suite. To eliminate downtime, they track each doctor who uses a room, the type of procedure, and the length of time in the suite. The operating room supervisor at your local hospital has asked you to help her computerize her records for implants involving hips, knees, and pacemakers. She gives you the following data showing procedures three surgeons have performed in the past week and length of time in minutes for each: Dr. Brown, hip – 140, knee – 95, knee – 105, knee – 110; Dr. Green, hip – 125, hip – 130, knee – 135, knee – 130; Dr. White, pacemaker – 45, pacemaker – 50, pacemaker – 55, pacemaker – 45. Prepare a report for her. Include charts showing the average time each doctor spends performing each surgery.

2 ▶ The local fitness center, Busy Bodies, has begun offering new programs and services geared toward total health consciousness for the 1990s. They include massages for $50 an hour or $30 per half hour, nutrition counseling for $20 per hour, and personal training for $25 a session or 5 sessions for $100. The fitness director has drafted a letter announcing these services and a list of current fitness center members. With this information, create a database containing the members' names, addresses, membership expiration dates, and type of memberships (premium or standard). Then, create and print form letters to send to each member. Print a mailing label for each member.

3 ▶▶ Your Busy Bodies membership letters in case study 2 were so successful that the fitness director now has difficulty meeting the demand for services. He has asked you to help him schedule times that are convenient for members in an effort to meet Busy Bodies' pledge of complete customer satisfaction. You want to start the process by determining the optimal schedule for members with premium memberships. Create a letter to send to these members stating Busy Bodies' concern about the problem and efforts to remedy it. Include a survey that asks which times are the most convenient for massages, nutrition counseling, and personal training sessions, using the ranges 6:00 a.m. – 10:00 a.m., 10:00 a.m. – 2:00 p.m., 2:00 p.m. – 6:00 p.m., and 6:00 p.m. – 10:00 p.m. Tell these members they will receive a 10 percent discount on next year's dues if they return the survey to you within one week. Then, create a spreadsheet to help analyze their responses. Finally, write a report for the fitness director, and include charts for each of the services.

Cases and Places

4 ▶▶ Your department chairperson wants to determine if recent graduates in the department are finding employment related to their major. Create a database containing each graduate's name, address, telephone number, month of graduation, year of graduation, and degree (certificate, associate's, bachelor's, master's). Then, create a form letter to send to students who have graduated within the past two semesters. Explain the purpose of the letter, and tell them the department chairperson will be calling them during the month to discuss their job placement efforts since graduation. Print form letters to send to each graduate and a mailing label for each one. Finally, print a list of the graduates' names and telephone numbers for your department chairperson.

5 ▶▶▶ Visit a local ice cream shop and observe the buying habits of 20 customers. Record the product type (ice cream, yogurt, sundae, soda), flavor, and size. Create a report for the ice cream shop manager that includes charts showing percentages of type, flavor, and size purchased.

6 ▶▶▶ Student organizations on campus often need help publicizing their fund-raising activities. Locate a club that has scheduled an event that will occur within the next month. Contact one of the organization's officers and volunteer to help with publicity. Create a database containing the name, address, major, and telephone number of ten of your classmates. Then, create a form letter publicizing the activity. Print a letter and mailing label for each of these students.

7 ▶▶▶ Each long-distance telephone company, including AT&T, MCI, and Sprint, claims it has the lowest rate. Research these claims using data from these three companies and at least three lesser-known long distance providers. Create a spreadsheet listing each company's name, telephone number, day hours, evening hours, late night hours, weekend hours, day rate, evening rate, late night rate, weekend rate, monthly fees, operator-completed charges, discounts, and any other features. Prepare a report contrasting each provider's services to those offered by AT&T, MCI, and Sprint. Create a bar chart to graphically compare the costs of the providers.

Works Functions

Works Functions

Introduction

A **Works function** is a built-in equation you can use in Works spreadsheets or databases. Works has 76 functions that allow you to perform a variety of calculations.

The general format of a function consists of the function name, a set of parentheses, and arguments, as illustrated in Figure A-1.

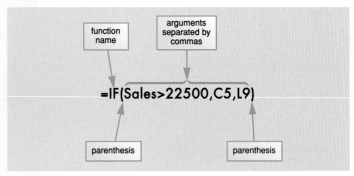

=IF(Sales>22500,C5,L9)

FIGURE A-1

Most Works functions use one or more **arguments**, which are values the function uses in its calculations. For instance, in the function SQRT(25), SQRT is the function and 25 is the argument. This function gives the result, 5, which is the square root of 25.

Functions and their arguments must be written in a specific way, called the **function syntax**. Some of the rules for function syntax are:

1. An argument can be a number or an expression that results in a number. This means an argument can be a number, a cell, a range reference, a range name, another function, a field name, or any allowable combination. Some arguments also can contain text, or string, data.

2. The arguments must be separated by a comma.
3. The arguments of a function must be inside parentheses.
4. Some functions can use only a range reference, range name, or field name as an argument. Some functions have no arguments.

A numeric function can be placed inside any mathematical formula that allows a numeric value in that place. For example, the following is a valid use of a function.

=45-SQRT(25)*200

The following pages contain a list of the names of all Works functions, their syntax, the result they produce, and an example of the function. In some cases, a special note about the function is included as well. To see the result of each function when using Works, enter each example that follows in a spreadsheet cell.

Works Functions

FUNCTION NAME:	ABS
Syntax:	ABS(x)
Result:	Gives the absolute (positive) value of x
Example:	=ABS(-8) equals 8

FUNCTION NAME:	ACOS
Syntax:	ACOS(x)
Result:	Gives the arccosine of x
Example:	=ACOS(-0.5) equals 2.094

FUNCTION NAME:	AND
Syntax:	AND(Logical0,Logical1,...)
Result:	Gives 1 (TRUE) if all of the arguments are TRUE (nonzero) and gives 0 (FALSE) if one or more arguments are false (zero)
Example:	=AND(2+2=4,2+3=5) equals 1 (TRUE)

FUNCTION NAME:	ASIN
Syntax:	ASIN(x)
Result:	Gives the arcsine of x
Example:	=ASIN(-0.5) equals -0.524

FUNCTION NAME:	ATAN
Syntax:	ATAN(x)
Result:	Gives the arctangent of x
Example:	=ATAN(1) equals 0.785

FUNCTION NAME:	ATAN2
Syntax:	ATAN2(x-coordinate,y-coordinate)
Result:	Gives the arctangent of an angle defined by the x- and y-coordinates
Example:	=ATAN2(1.1) equals 0.785

FUNCTION NAME:	AVG
Syntax:	AVG(RangeReference0,RangeReference1,...)
Result:	Gives the average of values in RangeReferences
Example:	=AVG(2,25,9,16,8) equals 12
Special Note:	RangeReferences can be numbers, cell references, range references, or formulas

FUNCTION NAME:	CHOOSE
Syntax:	CHOOSE(Choice,Option0,Option1,...)
Result:	If Choice is equal to 0, Option0 appears in the cell; if choice is equal to 1, option1 appears in the cell, and so on
Example:	=CHOOSE(A1,5,10,15,20) If cell A1 = 0, then the cell where the function was entered will contain a 5; if cell A1 = 1, then the cell where the function was entered will contain a 10, and so on
Special Note:	If Choice is less than zero or greater than the number of options in the list, CHOOSE gives the error value ERR

FUNCTION NAME:	COLS
Syntax:	COLS(RangeReference)
Result:	Gives the number of columns in RangeReference
Example:	=COLS(A5:F7) equals 6

FUNCTION NAME:	COS
Syntax:	COS(x)
Result:	Gives the cosine of x (an angle measured in radians)
Example:	=COS(1.047) equals 0.5

FUNCTION NAME:	COUNT
Syntax:	Count(RangeReference0,RangeReference1,...)
Result:	Gives the number of cells contained in RangeReferences
Example:	=COUNT(A5:A10,B1:B20) equals 26
Special Note:	Count adds 1 for every cell that contains a number, formula, text, ERR, and N/A

FUNCTION NAME:	CTERM
Syntax:	CTERM(Rate,FutureValue,PresentValue)
Result:	Gives the number of compounding periods needed for an investment, earning a fixed Rate per compounding period, to grow from a PresentValue to a FutureValue
Example:	=CTERM(.10,2000,1000) equals 7.273
Special Note:	Rate must be expressed as an interest rate either as a percentage or as a percentage in a decimal form

FUNCTION NAME:	DATE
Syntax:	DATE(Year,Month,Day)
Result:	Gives a date number ranging from 1 to 65534 for the date specified by Year, Month, and Day
Example:	=DATE(94,7,4) equals 34519
Special Note:	This function usually is used in calculations with values for other dates

FUNCTION NAME:	DAY; MONTH; YEAR
Syntax:	DAY(DateNumber); MONTH(DateNumber); YEAR(DateNumber)
Result:	Day, Month, and Year give the number of the day, month, or year specified by DateNumber
Example:	=DAY(34519) equals 4; =MONTH(34519) equals 7; YEAR(34519) equals 94

FUNCTION NAME:	DDB
Syntax:	DDB(Cost,Salvage,Life,Period)
Result:	Uses the double-declining balance method to find the amount of depreciation in a specific Period
Example:	=DDB(20000,1000,10,2) equals $3,200.00
Special Note:	Cost is the amount paid for the asset. Salvage is the value of the asset at the end of its life. Life is the number of years you expect the asset to be in use. Period is the time period for which you want to find the depreciation amount

FUNCTION NAME:	ERR
Syntax:	ERR()
Result:	ERR gives the error value ERR
Example:	=(IF(A1=0,ERR(),A1)) equals ERR when cell A1 contains 0
Special Note:	Use to force a cell to display ERR whenever a specified condition exists

FUNCTION NAME:	EXACT
Syntax:	EXACT(TextValue0,TextValue1)
Result:	Compares two strings of characters and gives 1 (TRUE) if they are exactly the same, 0 (FALSE) if they are not
Example:	=EXACT("Fred","Thomas") equals 0 (FALSE)

FUNCTION NAME:	EXP
Syntax:	EXP(x)
Result:	Gives e to the power of x, where e is 2.71828, which is the base number of natural logarithms
Example:	=EXP(1) equals 2.718
Special Note:	To compute powers of other bases, use the exponential operator (^)

FUNCTION NAME:	FALSE
Syntax:	FALSE()
Result:	FALSE gives the logical value 0 (FALSE)
Example:	=IF(A1>10,TRUE(),FALSE()) equals FALSE if A1 contains 5
Special Note:	You can use FALSE() instead of 0 to create more readable logical formulas

FUNCTION NAME:	FIND
Syntax:	FIND(FindText,SearchText,Offset)
Result:	Finds one string of text (FindText) within another string of text (SearchText) and returns the number of the character at which FindText occurs. The search begins at the offset number (0 is the first character, one is the second character, etc.)
Example:	=FIND("eat","The Beatles",0) equals 5

FUNCTION NAME:	FV
Syntax:	FV(Payment,Rate,Term)
Result:	Gives the future value of an ordinary annuity of equal Payments, earning a fixed Rate of interest per Term, compounded over several Terms
Example:	=FV(2000,5.75%,20) equals $71624.26

FUNCTION NAME:	HLOOKUP
Syntax:	HLOOKUP(LookupValue,RangeReference,RowNumber)
Result:	Searches the top row of RangeReference until it finds the number that matches LookupValue. Then it goes down the column the number of rows indicated by RowNumber to get the entry
Example:	=HLOOKUP(1997,C4:G7,2)
Special Note:	Arrange numbers in top row in ascending order

FUNCTION NAME:	HOUR; MINUTE; SECOND
Syntax:	HOUR(TimeSerialNumber); MINUTE(TimeSerialNumber); SECOND(TimeSerialNumber)
Result:	HOUR gives the number for the hour represented by TimeSerialNumber as an integer ranging from 0 through 23; MINUTE gives the number for the minute represented by TimeSerialNumber as an integer ranging from 0 through 59; SECOND gives the number for the second represented by TimeSerialNumber as an integer ranging from 0 through 59
Example:	=HOUR(0.70035) equals 16; =MINUTE(0.70035) equals 48; =SECOND(0.70035) equals 30

FUNCTION NAME:	IF
Syntax:	IF(Condition,ValueIfTrue,ValueIfFalse)
Result:	Determines whether Condition is true or false, then gives either ValueIfTrue or ValueIfFalse
Example:	IF(A1>100,D1,E1)

FUNCTION NAME:	INDEX
Syntax:	INDEX(RangeReference,Column,Row)
Result:	Gives the value in a cell in RangeReference at the intersection of the Column and Row
Example:	=INDEX(A2:C5,2,1)
Special Note:	Column and row numbering begins with zero

FUNCTION NAME:	INT
Syntax:	INT(x)
Result:	Gives the integer part of x
Example:	=INT(7.9) equals 7
Special Note:	INT deletes the digits to the right of the decimal point without rounding to the nearest integer

FUNCTION NAME:	IRR
Syntax:	IRR(Guess,RangeReference)
Result:	Gives the internal rate of return for the cash flow series in RangeReference
Example:	=IRR(10%,B1:H1)

FUNCTION NAME:	ISERR
Syntax:	ISERR(x)
Result:	Gives the logical value 1 (TRUE) if x is the error value ERR, otherwise, it gives the logical value 0 (FALSE)
Example:	=ISERR(3/0) equals 1

FUNCTION NAME:	ISNA
Syntax:	ISNA(x)
Result:	Gives the logical value 1 (TRUE) if x is the value N/A, otherwise, it gives the logical value 0 (FALSE)
Example:	=IF(ISNA(A1),2,1) equals 2 if A1 contains the value N/A

FUNCTION NAME:	LEFT
Syntax:	LEFT(TextValue,Length)
Result:	Gives the first (or leftmost) character (or characters) in a phrase
Example:	=LEFT("Works Word Processor",5) gives Works

FUNCTION NAME:	LENGTH
Syntax:	LENGTH(TextValue)
Result:	Gives the number of characters and spaces in a string of text
Example:	=LENGTH("Spreadsheet tool") gives 16

FUNCTION NAME:	LN
Syntax:	LN(x)
Result:	Gives the natural logarithm of x
Example:	=LN(EXP(3)) equals 3
Special Note:	x must be a positive number

FUNCTION NAME:	LOG
Syntax:	LOG(x)
Result:	Gives the base 10 logarithm of x
Example:	=LOG(10) equals 1
Special Note:	x must be a positive number

FUNCTION NAME:	LOWER
Syntax:	LOWER(TextValue)
Result:	Converts all uppercase letters of text to lowercase
Example:	=LOWER("ABCDEF") gives abcdef

FUNCTION NAME:	MAX
Syntax:	MAX(RangeReference0,RangeReference1,...)
Result:	Gives the largest number contained in RangeReferences
Example:	=MAX(B2:F2)

FUNCTION NAME:	MID
Syntax:	MID(TextValue,Offset,Length)
Result:	Gives a specific number of characters from a text string, starting at the position you specify
Example:	=MID("The Beatles",5,3) equals eat

FUNCTION NAME:	MIN
Syntax:	MIN(RangeReference0,RangeReference1,...)
Result:	Gives the smallest number contained in RangeReferences
Example:	=MIN(B2:F2)

FUNCTION NAME:	MINUTE
Syntax:	MINUTE(TimeSerialNumber)
Result:	Gives the number for the minute of the time represented by TimeSerialNumber
Example:	=MINUTE(.7253) equals 24

FUNCTION NAME:	MOD
Syntax:	MOD(Numerator,Denominator)
Result:	Gives the remainder (modulus) of a Denominator divided into a Numerator
Example:	=MOD(10,4) equals 2

FUNCTION NAME:	MONTH
Syntax:	MONTH(DateSerialNumber)
Result:	Gives the number for the month specified in DateSerialNumber
Example:	=MONTH(33706) equals 4

FUNCTION NAME:	N
Syntax:	N(RangeReference)
Result:	Gives the entry in the first cell in the range as a value; if the cell contains text, N returns zero
Example:	If cell A1 contains the text JANUARY and cell A2 contains 123.32, then =N(A1:A2) equals 0 (zero)

FUNCTION NAME:	NA
Syntax:	NA()
Result:	Gives the value N/A
Example:	=IF(A10,NA(),A1) equals NA if A1 contains 0
Special Note:	N/A is treated as numeric

FUNCTION NAME:	NOT
Syntax:	NOT(Logical)
Result:	Reverses the value of its argument
Example:	=NOT(1+1=3) equals 1 (TRUE)

FUNCTION NAME:	NOW
Syntax:	NOW()
Result:	Gives the date and time number for the current date and time
Example:	=NOW()
Special Note:	Time number is updated at every recalculation

FUNCTION NAME:	NPV
Syntax:	NPV(Rate,RangeReference)
Result:	Gives the net present value of a series of cash flow payments represented by numbers in RangeReference, discounted at a fixed Rate per period
Example:	=NPV(10%,B2:F2)-B1 equals $1,784.82

FUNCTION NAME:	OR
Syntax:	OR(Logical0,Logical1,...)
Result:	Gives 1 (TRUE) if one or more arguments are TRUE; gives 0 (FALSE) if all the arguments are false
Example:	=OR(1+1=3, 2+2=7) equals 0

FUNCTION NAME:	PI
Syntax:	PI()
Result:	Gives the number 3.14159...
Example:	=PI()

FUNCTION NAME:	PMT
Syntax:	PMT(Principal,Rate,Term)
Result:	Gives the periodic payment for a loan or an investment of Principal based on a fixed interest Rate per compounding period over a given Term
Example:	=PMT(15000,9%/12,24) equals $685.27

FUNCTION NAME:	PROPER
Syntax:	PROPER(TextValue)
Result:	Capitalizes the first letter of each word and any text that follows any character other than a letter
Example:	=PROPER("this is a string") equals This Is A String

FUNCTION NAME:	PV
Syntax:	PV(Payment,Rate,Term)
Result:	Gives the present value of an ordinary annuity of equal Payments, earning a fixed interest Rate per period, over several periods (Term)
Example:	=PV(5000,9%,10) equals $32,088.29

FUNCTION NAME:	RAND
Syntax:	RAND()
Result:	Gives a random number from 0 up to, but not including 1
Example:	=RAND()

FUNCTION NAME:	RATE
Syntax:	RATE(FutureValue,PresentValue,Term)
Result:	RATE gives the fixed interest rate per compounding period needed for an investment of PresentValue to grow to a FutureValue over several compounding periods (Terms)
Example:	=RATE(1500000,500000,6) equals 20.09%

FUNCTION NAME:	REPEAT
Syntax:	REPEAT(TextValue,Count)
Result:	Repeats text as many times as you specify
Example:	=REPEAT("book",5) equals bookbookbookbookbook

FUNCTION NAME:	REPLACE
Syntax:	REPLACE(OldText,Offset,Length,NewText) ·
Result:	Exchange one string of text for another
Example:	=REPLACE("abcdefffi",6,2,"gh") equals abcdefghi

FUNCTION NAME:	RIGHT
Syntax:	RIGHT(TextValue,Length)
Result:	Returns the last (or rightmost) characters or characters in a phrase
Example:	=RIGHT("uvwxyz",3) equals xyz

FUNCTION NAME:	ROUND
Syntax:	ROUND(x,NumberOfPlaces)
Result:	Rounds x to the specifed NumberOfPlaces to the left or right of the decimal point
Example:	=ROUND(9.15,1) equals 9.2
Special Note:	If NumberOfPlaces is positive, x is rounded to the number of decimal places to the right of the decimal point; if NumberOfPlaces is 0, x is rounded to the nearest integer

FUNCTION NAME:	ROWS
Syntax:	ROWS(RangeReference)
Result:	Gives the number of rows in RangeReference
Example:	=ROWS(C2:E5) equals 4

FUNCTION NAME:	S
Syntax:	S(RangeReference)
Result:	Gives the text in the first cell in a range
Example:	If cell A1 contains CA and cell A2 contains WY, =S(A1:A2) equals CA

FUNCTION NAME:	SECOND
Syntax:	SECOND(TimeSerialNumber)
Result:	Gives the number for the second of the time represented by TimeSerialNumber
Example:	=SECOND(0.7253) equals 26

FUNCTION NAME:	SIN
Syntax:	SIN(x)
Result:	Gives the sine of x
Example:	=SIN(1.047) equals 0.866
Special Note:	x is an angle measured in radians

FUNCTION NAME:	SLN
Syntax:	SLN(Cost,Salvage,Life)
Result:	Uses the straight-line depreciation method to find the amount of depreciation in one period
Example:	=SLN(10000,2000,4) equals $2,000

FUNCTION NAME:	SQRT
Syntax:	SQRT(x)
Result:	Gives the square root of x
Example:	=SQRT(25) equals 5
Special Note:	If x is negative, Works gives the value ERR

FUNCTION NAME:	STD
Syntax:	STD(RangeReference0,RangeReference1,...)
Result:	Gives the population standard deviation of RangeReferences
Example:	=STD(B2:G2)

FUNCTION NAME:	STRING
Syntax:	STRING(x,DecimalPlaces)
Result:	Gives the value converted to text, with the specified number of decimal places
Example:	=STRING(256,2) equals 250.00 as text

FUNCTION NAME:	SUM
Syntax:	SUM(RangeReference0,RangeReference1,...)
Result:	Gives the total in all values in RangeReferences
Example:	=SUM(B2:G2)

FUNCTION NAME:	SYD
Syntax:	SYD(Cost,Salvage,Life,Period)
Result:	Uses the sum-of-years'-digits method to find the amount of depreciation in a specific Period
Example:	=SYD(50000,8000,10,7) equals $3054.55
Special Note:	Cost is the amount paid for the asset; Salvage is the amount you expect to obtain when you sell the asset at the end of its life; Life is the number of periods you expect to use the asset; Period is the period for which you want to find the depreciation

FUNCTION NAME:	TAN
Syntax:	TAN(x)
Result:	Gives the tangent of x
Example:	=TAN(0.785) equals 0.9992

FUNCTION NAME:	TERM
Syntax:	TERM(Payment,Rate,FutureValue)
Result:	Gives the number of compounding periods necessary for a series of equal Payments, earning a fixed interest Rate per period, to grow to a FutureValue
Example:	=TERM(200,7.75%/12,5000) equals 23.25

FUNCTION NAME:	TIME
Syntax:	TIME(Hour,Minute,Second)
Result:	Gives a time number for the time specified by Hour, Minute, and Second
Example:	=Time(16,48,0) equals 0.7 (time number of 4:48:00 p.m.)
Special Note:	The time number is a fraction ranging from 0.0 through 0.999, representing times from 0:00:00 or 12:00:00 p.m. through 23.59.59 or 11:59:59 p.m; Hour is generally a number ranging from 0 through 23; Minute and Second are generally numbers ranging from 0 through 59

FUNCTION NAME:	TRIM
Syntax:	TRIM(TextValue)
Result:	Removes all spaces from TextValue except for single spaces between words
Example:	If cell A1 contains A Pretty Morning, then =TRIM(A1) equals A Pretty Morning

FUNCTION NAME:	TRUE
Syntax:	TRUE()
Result:	Gives the logical value 1 (TRUE). You can use TRUE() instead of 1 to create more readable logical formulas
Example:	=IF(A1>10,TRUE(),FALSE())

FUNCTION NAME:	UPPER
Syntax:	UPPER(TextValue)
Result:	Converts all text in TextValue to uppercase
Example:	=UPPER("appendix a") equals APPENDIX A

FUNCTION NAME:	VALUE
Syntax:	VALUE(TextValue)
Result:	Converts a number entered as text to its corresponding numeric value
Example:	=VALUE("$578.04") equals 578.04

FUNCTION NAME:	VAR
Syntax:	VAR(RangeReference0,RangeReference1,...)
Result:	Calculates the variance of the numbers in RangeReferences
Example:	=VAR(B2:F2)

FUNCTION NAME:	VLOOKUP
Syntax:	VLOOKUP(LookupValue,RangeReference,ColumnNumber)
Result:	Searches the leftmost column of RangeReference until it finds the number that matches the LookupValue; then it goes to the right by the number of columns indicated by ColumnNumber to get the entry
Example:	=VLOOKUP(1997,B10:E14,2)
Special Note:	Arrange numbers in column in ascending order

Index